THE
WELSH VOCABULARY
OF THE
BANGOR DISTRICT

VOL I

THE
WELSH VOCABULARY

OF THE

BANGOR DISTRICT

BY

O. H. FYNES-CLINTON, M.A.

PROFESSOR OF FRENCH AND ROMANCE PHILOLOGY AT THE
UNIVERSITY COLLEGE OF NORTH WALES, BANGOR

VOL I

FACSIMILE REPRINT by
LLANERCH PUBLISHERS
FELINFACH, (1995)

ISBN 1 897953 72 6

Also Published By Llanerch

THE CELTIC DRAGON MYTH
by J. F. Campbell & George Henderson

NAMES FROM THE DAWN OF BRITISH LEGEND
TALIESIN, ANEIRIN, MYRDDIN/MERLIN. ARTHUR
by Toby D Griffen

THE MYATICAL WAY AND THE ARTHURIAN QUEST
by Derek Bryce

A MEDIEVAL PRINCE OF WALES
THE LIFE OF GRUFFUDD AP CYNAN
translated by D. Simon Evans

MABINOGION
THE FOUR BRANCHES
translated by Charlotte Guest

FOLK-LORE OF MID & WEST WALES
by Jonothan Ceredig Davies

THE PHYSICIANS OF MYDDFAI
translated by John Pughe

PEREDUR
AN ARTHURIAN ROMANCE FROM THE MABINOGION
translated by Meirion Pennar

TALIESIN POEMS
translated by Meirion Pennar

THE BLACK BOOK OF CARMARTHEN
translated by Meirion Pennar

THE GODODDIN: OF ANEIRIN
translated by Steve Short

SYMBOLISM OF THE CELTIC CROSS
by Derek Bryce

For a complete list write to:
LLANERCH PUBLISHERS
FELINFACH, LAMPETER, DYFED
WALES, SA48 8PJ.

INTRODUCTION

The early decades of the present century were marked by a mature interest in Welsh linguistic studies on the part of both native and continental scholars. This renewed scholarly interest was undoubtedly triggered by the publication in Leipzig in 1853 of *Grammatica Celtica* by the Bavarian schoolmaster Johan Kaspar Zeuss (1806-56). His scholarship placed the Celtic languages firmly within the Indo-European fold for the first time. The work was applauded by John Peter (Ioan Pedr; 1833-77) the enlightened but neglected grammarian from Bala, who like John Rhŷs was very much aware of the need to introduce mainstream continental scholarship to Welsh linguistic studies. John Rhŷs (1840-1915) interpreted the theories of continental scholars - especially those of the Leipzig linguistic school in his *Lectures in Welsh Philology* published in 1877; *A Welsh Grammar: Historical and Comparative* by John Morris Jones (1842-1929) appeared in 1913. Although the main academic interest of these Welsh scholars and their continental mentors was historical, they were also responsible for encouraging and motivating the early work accomplished in dialectology. The study of the spoken language would, it was thought at least initially, help to confirm the theories of continental diachronic linguists like August Leskien (1840-1916), Herman Osthoff (1847-1909) and Karl Brugmann (1849-1919). It would also assist the unravelling of early historical and literary texts. That was sufficient justification for mainstream historical linguists to dabble in dialectology!

The Oxford phonetician Henry Sweet (1845-1912) published a study of the Welsh dialect of Nant Gwynant in 1882-84 and Thomas Darlington (1864-1908) had worked on a series of dialect projects in England before embarking on an investigation of dialect boundaries in mid Wales. The efforts of *Cymdeithas Llafar Gwlad* and of The Guild of Graduates of the University of Wales to initiate a comprehensive national dialect survey failed miserably; the Dialect Section of the Guild aimed 'to collect the fullest possible information as to the spoken language of Wales in all its varieties'. The project directors, John Rhŷs and Edward Anwyl (1866-1914) however, were unable to agree on a common strategy and although there is some scant evidence that Anwyl planned a comprehensive Welsh Dialect Dictionary, not everyone agreed with his policy of publishing lengthy word lists in *The Transactions of the Guild of Graduates*. In 1910 Professor O.H. Fynes-Clinton (1869-1941) wrote to Anwyl, 'I am not sure that a dialect can be well represented by a mere list of words'. *The Welsh Vocabulary of the Bangor District* by Fynes-Clinton was published by Oxford University Press in 1913 and was most ambitious work by far on the Welsh dialect of a particular locality to appear during that decade. John Jones (Myrddin Fardd; 1836-1921) published *Gwerin-Eiriau Sir Gaernarfon* in 1909 and *A Glossary of the Demetian Dialect of North Pembrokeshire* by William Meredith Morris (1967-1920) had appeared in 1910.

The interest of continental scholars in the dialects of Welsh had also been aroused. The best known work is Alf Sommerfelt's *Studies in Cyfeiliog Welsh*, published in 1925, but Rudolph Thurneysen (b. 1857), Hugo Schuchardt (1842-1927) and Rudolph Trebitsche (d. 1919) must also be counted among the pioneers in the field. Trebitsche conducted field work in Wales in 1909 and succeeded in recording on wax cylinders examples of the speech of informants from Aberdare, Llandysul, Llanwenog, Machynlleth, Llanfairpwll, Llanrhaeadr, Rhuddlan and Cwm (Flintshire). These early recordings by Trebitsche are conserved at *Osterreichissche Akademie der Wissenschaften Phonogrammarchiv.*

Osbert Henry Fynes-Clinton was born in 1869. His father Osbert Fynes-Clinton was rector of Barlow Moor, Didsbury, near Manchester. He graduated from St. John's College Cambridge and in 1822 was elected 'Taylorian Scholar' in Spanish by the University. He taught French at King Edward's School, Aston, Birmingham until 1904 when he was appointed professor of French at the University College of North Wales. On his retirement in 1937 he was elected professor emeritus; in 1939 he was awarded the degree of D.Litt *honouris causia.* He was buried at Llanfairpwll in 1941. An obituary by his great friend Sir Ifor Williams, professor of Welsh at Bangor, appeared in the North Wales Chronicle 22 August 1941.

Although very few publications in the field of Romance scholarship are attributed to Fynes-Clinton, *The Welsh Vocabulary of the Bangor District* has assured him an honourable place in Welsh linguistic studies. The work was complied between 1904 and 1912 and in marked contrast to contemporary studies of dialect classified every lexical item, noted the pronunciation of words, recorded the inflection of verbs and included copious examples of usage taken from oral and literary sources. Together with *An English and Welsh Dictionary*, D. Silvan Evans *A Welsh Vocabulary of the Bangor District* must have pride of place on the bookshelf of all who are even vaguely interested in Welsh lexicography. In May 1922 a valuable appendix to the *Welsh Vocabulary of the Bangor District* appeared in *The Bulletin of the Board of Celtic Studies*. That appendix is reproduced in the second volume of this facsimile edition.

Original copies of *The Welsh Vocabulary of the Bangor District* are rare and expensive and this new two volume edition sensibly priced from Llanerch Publishers is to be warmly welcomed.

David Thorne
Department of Welsh Language and Literature
University of Wales
Lampeter

LIST OF SUBSCRIBERS

PROFESSOR SIR EDWARD ANWYL, M.A., 62 Marine Terrace, Aberystwyth.

PROFESSOR E. V. ARNOLD, Litt.D., Bryn Seiriol, Bangor.

MR. CHARLES H. BARBER, Bookseller, 24 St. Ann Street, Manchester.

PROFESSOR OSBORN J. BERGIN, National University, Dublin.

MR. HENRY BLACKWELL, Bookbinder, University Place and Tenth Street, New York. Three copies.

THE HON. L. A. BRODRICK, 7 Cadogan Gardens, London, S.W.

REV. S. L. BROWN, M.A., The Church Hostel, Bangor.

MESSRS. CORNISH BROS., Booksellers, 37 New Street, Birmingham.

THE HON. SOCIETY OF THE CYMMRODORION, per Sir E. Vincent Evans, 64 Chancery Lane, London, W.C.

H. R. DAVIES, Esq., M.A., J.P., Treborth, Bangor.

J. H. DAVIES, Esq., M.A., 20 North Parade, Aberystwyth.

MRS. MARY DAVIES, 12a Eton Road, Hampstead, London, N.W.

PROFESSOR T. WITTON DAVIES, B.A., Ph.D., D.D., Bryn Haul, Bangor.

O. M. EDWARDS, Esq., M.A., Board of Education, Whitehall, London, S.W.

SIR E. VINCENT EVANS, 64 Chancery Lane, London.

GRIFFITH EVANS, Esq., M.D., Brynkynallt, Bangor.

J. GWENOGVRYN EVANS, Esq., M.A., D.Litt., Tremvan, Llanbedrog, Pwllheli.

W. H. GIBBON, Esq., M.A., 3 Mount Pleasant, Portmadoc.

PRINCIPAL D. R. HARRIS, M.A., Normal College, Bangor.

SIR IVOR HERBERT, Bart., M.P., Llanarlu Court, Raglan, Mon.

PROFESSOR T. HUDSON-WILLIAMS, M.A., D.Litt., Plas Tirion, Bangor.

REV. W. HUGHES, Llanuwchllyn Vicarage, Bala.

E. T. JOHN, Esq., M.P., Llanidan Hall, Llanfair P.G., Anglesey.

EDMUND J. JONES, Esq., Fforest Legionis, Pont Neath Vaughan, near Neath, S. Wales.

PROFESSOR J. MORRIS JONES, M.A., Llanfair P.G., Anglesey.

W. HOPKINS JONES, Esq., Norwood, Bangor.

PROFESSOR W. LEWIS JONES, M.A., Ceinwen, Bangor.

THE RIGHT HON. LORD KENYON, K.C.V.O., Gredington, Whitchurch, Salop.

J. O'NEILL LANE, Esq., Tournafulla, co. Limerick.

LIBRARIES :—

THE NATIONAL LIBRARY OF WALES, Aberystwyth, per John Ballinger, Esq., M.A.

THE UNIVERSITY COLLEGE OF WALES, Aberystwyth.

THE UNIVERSITY COLLEGE OF NORTH WALES, Bangor, per Rev. T. Shankland.

THE UNIVERSITY COLLEGE OF SOUTH WALES AND MONMOUTHSHIRE, Cardiff.

THE CENTRAL LIBRARY, Cardiff, per Henry Farr, Esq.

THE PUBLIC LIBRARY, Edinburgh, per Mr. James Thin, Bookseller, 54, 55 and 56 South Bridge, Edinburgh.

THE UNIVERSITY LIBRARY, Edinburgh, per F. C. Nicholson, Esq., M.A.

PREFACE

My aim in the present book has been to make an accurate record of the words in colloquial use in one clearly defined district in Wales. In a language like Welsh, which at present has no recognized spoken standard, no hard and fast line can be drawn in the spoken language between literary words and those which belong purely to the domain of dialect; and there are probably few words which in their form, use, or pronunciation could be said to be precisely identical in all parts of the country. Hence my design has been not to compile a glossary of a particular dialect but rather a vocabulary of spoken Welsh as represented by the usage in a particular district. It appeared to me that such a compilation, however imperfect and incomplete, could scarcely fail to be of service for comparative purposes to workers in other dialects as well as to those who desire to obtain a knowledge of colloquial Welsh, and at the same time might possibly be the means of preserving some words and expressions which are now rapidly becoming obsolete and are known only to the older inhabitants. I have spared no pains to make the work as accurate as possible, but it would be vain to pretend to any hope that I have always succeeded. The number of words still in use might probably be largely extended but I am unwilling to delay further the publication of a work which has already occupied me for nine years.

Like all compilers of dictionaries I have been frequently beset with difficulties as to which words to omit and which to include. On the one hand are literary or book words—such, for instance, as have obtained a kind of semi-colloquial standing through their frequent use in the Bible or by their

common occurrence in newspapers; and on the other hand
are English words with which some speakers, especially the
younger, plentifully interlard their conversation. The
general criterion I have employed in such matters is the
usage of older speakers. Among words which might be
described as literary, I have included all such as are in
frequent and indispensable use, especially those which offer
any point of interest with regard to meaning or pronunciation, but omitting, as a rule, long compounds. As to English
words, I have included those which differ in a marked way
as to pronunciation or meaning from present English
standard usage, such as *grât* 'grate', *stowt* 'plucky'; those
which have demonstrably formed part of the language for
several centuries and those of very common and indispensable use. If I appear sometimes to have acted arbitrarily
or inconsistently, I must plead as an excuse the extreme
difficulty of deciding in many such cases.

In marking out the boundaries of the district I have
chosen, I was chiefly guided by convenience, but they are
also, in the main, geographical. The district extends from
Bangor along the coast eastwards to the point where Penmaenmawr meets the sea, thence along the northern slopes of the
hills past Llanfairfechan, Aber, and Llanllechid to Bethesda,
Rhiwlas, and the village of Pentir. From Pentir to Bangor
an arbitrary line had to be drawn somewhere and I have
adopted roughly the road between the two places, which
runs almost due north.

The symbols I have employed are, with a few exceptions,
those of the Association Phonétique. In the alphabetical
arrangement I have placed *ē* with *e*, and *ö* and *ø* with *o* in
order to facilitate reference, since *ē*, *ö* and *ø* are, almost
without exception, merely the first elements of diphthongs.
In all matters connected with the sounds of the language
I have continually referred to Sweet's article on Spoken
North Welsh in the 'Philological Society's Transactions' for
1882-4 (reprinted in 'Collected Papers of Henry Sweet',
Oxford, 1913). In all cases in which I have arrived at

a different conclusion, it has only been after the most careful consideration. I regret that I was only able to make use of Professor Morris Jones's grammar at the latter end of the book.

I deemed it desirable, wherever possible, to give the orthography of each word according to some recorded instance previous to the nineteenth century. To obtain as much uniformity as possible I give the form employed in Davies's Welsh-Latin and Latin-Welsh Dictionary (1632). If the word does not occur here I have had recourse to the Bible (ed. 1620) or, failing this, to various other books especially of the sixteenth, seventeenth and eighteenth centuries, and to the unfinished dictionary of Silvan Evans. Failing these again I have used Richards's, and finally Owen Pughe's dictionary. It is beyond the scope of the work to give the forms occurring in older literature, except where any analogy occurs with modern colloquial usage. As regards words of English origin, which are usually omitted in dictionaries, I give a greater number of examples of their occurrence, particularly if they are words of long standing in the language. The nature of the subject has, I need hardly mention, necessitated references to books of very varying authority. The whole of this part of my work would require a much greater expenditure of time than I have had at my disposal to bring it to anything like completion.

I will now mention the names of my principal informants, to all of whom I am deeply indebted for their patient and ready help. The groundwork of the book represents the speech of the following, in the order in which I made their acquaintance. I refer to them under their initials in the course of the work, wherever this seemed desirable.

My late landlady, Miss Elizabeth Jones (E.J.), of Cooldaragh, Bangor, born at Pentir on Oct. 25, 1859, whose *obiter dicta* form a not inconsiderable part of the volume. She has also given me much valuable information as to the meaning of some of the more unusual words.

Mr. John William Jones (J.J.) of Tan 'r Allt, Aber, born at Aber on June 8, 1839. He had received no education and was unable to speak English, but was a self-taught man who had read a considerable amount of Welsh literature. He also had a very wide knowledge of the place-names of his district. During my frequent visits I obtained from him a large amount of information, particularly as regards terms used in farming and in slate-quarries, he having worked many years in the latter at Bethesda. He took the greatest pains in supplying all the details I sought until a short time before his death, which occurred on August 18, 1909.

Mr. Owen Hughes (O.H.), who lived in a small two-roomed cottage at Blaen Nant Isaf, Nant y Felin, Llanfairfechan, born at Llanfairfechan on January 6, 1835. I made his acquaintance late in 1909 at the recommendation of Mr. J. W. Jones. He was entirely ignorant of English. During my weekly visits of four hours extending over the greater part of three years he imparted to me an extraordinary amount of information of every kind and in particular terms connected with farming and the sea. His knowledge of place-names was also very extensive. I attach especial importance to the information obtained from him, as he was the oldest of my informants, was the least affected by literary influences, and I had had more than five years' experience with the dialect when I made his acquaintance. He died after a very short illness on November 3, 1912, in full possession of his mental and physical powers, only ten days after my last visit to him, and when the present work was already in the press. .

I must also add the name of Mr. Richard Jones, 48 Fountain Street, Bangor, who supplied me with most of the names of fish.

My sincerest thanks are also due to my father-in-law, the Rev. W. Hughes (W.H.), Vicar of Llanuwchllyn, who supplied me with many words and phrases and grammatical minutiæ; to Mr. and Mrs. H. O. Hughes of Bangor, who have always been most ready to clear up any doubtful point during the reading of the proofs and have given much further information ; it is to them that the word ' (Bangor) ' usually refers in the text ; to Professor T. Hudson-Williams, who has read all the proofs from page 193 onwards, and by his frequent references to Carnarvon usage enabled me to make some important additions, whenever this coincided with that of Bangor ; and especially to Mr. Ifor Williams (I.W.), Assistant Lecturer in Welsh at the University College of North Wales—a native of Tregarth near Bangor—for his indispensable aid in supplying me at the beginning with a large number of words which formed the nucleus of the rest, for clearing up many difficulties during the course of the work, for reading the greater part of my MS. and the whole of the proofs also. I have also received much valuable aid and advice from Professor J. Morris Jones. Lastly, I have pleasure in expressing my debt in various ways to Miss Grace Ellis, Mr. J. E. Griffith, Mr. W. Hopkins Jones, Mr. W. J. Parry of Bethesda, the Rev. T. Shankland, Professor P. J. White, and Dr. J. Lloyd Williams.

O. H. FYNES-CLINTON.

Sept. 22, 1913.

LIST OF ABBREVIATIONS AND BOOKS CONSULTED

A. A collection of ballads, songs, etc., of the eighteenth century by various writers, at the Library of the University College, Bangor, bound together in one volume, in a somewhat imperfect state. It is impossible to give exact references.

Anwyl. A Welsh Grammar for Schools by E. Anwyl, M.A. . . . Third Edition. London. 1907.

B. A collection of ballads, songs, etc., of the eighteenth century at the Library of the University College, Bangor, of the same character as A, but in a more imperfect state.

B.B.C. The Black Book of Carmarthen, reproduced and edited by J. Gwenogvryn Evans. Pwllheli. 1906.

B.C. Gweledigaetheu y Bardd Cwsc (by Ellis Wynne). Llundain. 1703. Reprint ed. by J. Morris Jones, Bangor. 1898.

B.H. Bown o Hamtwn, edited from the Hengwrt MSS. by the Rev. Robert Williams, M.A. London. 1878.

Bible. References in all cases are to the edition of 1620.

C. A collection of ballads, songs, etc., of the eighteenth century at the Library of the University College, Bangor, of the same character as A and B.

C.C. (Canwyll y Cymry) Y Pedwarydd Ran o waith Mr. Rees Prichard Gynt Ficcer Llanddyfri yn Shîr Gaerfyrddyn. Y nawr gynta yn Brintiedig . . . Llundain . . . 1672.

C.Ch. Campeu Charlymaen, edited from the Hengwrt MSS. in the Peniarth Library by the Rev. Robert Williams, M.A. London. 1878. (Date of MS. 1336.)

C.C.M. The Cefn Coch MSS. Two MSS. of Welsh Poetry, written principally during the eighteenth century. Edited by the Rev. J. Fisher, B.D. Liverpool. 1899.

C.F. Cymru Fydd (Periodical printed and published by E. W. Evans, Dolgelley): Llafar Gwlad Llanfair Pwll Gwyngyll by J. M. Jones, B.A., 1889, pp. 438–440; Llafar Gwlad Bethesda by J. Owen Jones, Bala, 1889, pp. 676–679; Llafar Gwlad Niwbwrch, Mon., by the Rev. Robert Hughes, 1890, pp. 331–334.

C.L.C. Cymdeithas Llen Cymru. I. Carolau: gan Richard Hughes. Caerdydd. 1900 [c. 1590–1638]. II. Hen Gerddi Gwleidyddol. Caerdydd. 1901 [1588–1660]. III. Casgliad o Hen Ganiadau Serch. Caerdydd. 1902 [MSS. date from 1599 to 1638]. IV.

Casgliad o Hanes-gerddi Cymraeg. Caerdydd. 1903 [seventeenth and eighteenth century]. V, VI. Caniadau yn y Mesurau Rhyddion. Caerdydd. 1905 [1450–1700].

D. Antiquæ Linguæ Britannicæ, Nunc vulgò dictæ Cambro-Britannicæ ... et Lingvæ Latinæ Dictionarium Duplex ... Londini, Impensis Joan. Davies SS. Th. D. An. Dom. 1632. [References to the Botanology are indicated by (Bot.), to the List of Proverbs by (Prov.).]

D.F. Deffyniad Ffydd Eglwys Loegr (Jewel's Apology) ... Wedi ei gyfieuthu o Ladin, yn Gymraeg, drwy waith M. Kyffin ... Llunden. 1595. Reprint ed. by Wm. Prichard Williams. Bangor. 1908.

D.G. Barddoniaeth Dafydd ab Gwilym o grynhoad Owen Jones a William Owen. Llundain. 1789.

D.P.O. Drych y Prif Oesoedd gan Theophilus Evans. [2nd ed. Shrewsbury. 1740.] Reprint ed. by Samuel J. Evans, M.A. Bangor and London. 1902.

F.N. Y Flodeugerdd Newydd. Casgliad o gywyddau'r bedwaredd ganrif ar ddeg, y bymthegfed a'r unfed ar bymtheg. We'di eu golygu gyda nodiadau gan W. J. Gruffydd, M.A. Caerdydd. 1909.

Forrest. The Vertebrate Fauna of North Wales by H. E. Forrest. London. 1907.

G.C. The History of Gruffydd ap Cynan. The Welsh Text with Translation, Introduction and Notes, by Arthur Jones, M.A. Manchester. 1910. [Date, middle thirteenth century.]

G.I. Detholiad o waith Gruffydd ab Ieuan ab Llewelyn Fychan, edited by the Rev. J. C. Morrice, M.A. Bangor Welsh MSS. Society. 1910. (fl. 1500–1525.)

G.O. The Poetical Works of the Rev. Goronwy Owen ... edited ... by the Rev. Robert Jones, B.A. ... in two volumes. London. 1876. (Vol. I contains the Poems; vol. II contains Life and Correspondence.)—b. 1723, d. 1769.

G.R. A Welsh Grammar and other Tracts by Griffith Roberts. A Fac-simile Reprint Published as a Supplement to the Revue Celtique, 1870–1883. Paris.—Contains among other matter: Dosparth Byrr ar y rhann gyntaf i ramadeg cymraeg ... [Milan.] 1567. (Griffith Roberts employs 'd', 'l', and 'u' with a diacritical mark under them for the usual 'dd', 'll', and 'w'. For purposes of convenience I have employed the usual orthography in these cases. The numbers in brackets refer to the pages of the introduction.)

Griffith. The Flora of Anglesey and Carnarvonshire by John E. Griffith, F.L.S., F.R.A.S. Bangor. (No date.)

H.D. Welsh Botanology ; ... a Systematic Catalogue of the Native Plants of the Isle of Anglesey, in Latin, Welsh, and English ... by Hugh Davies, F.L.S. London. 1813.

H.S. Gwaith Barddonol Howel Swrdwal a'i fab Ieuan—edited by the Rev. J. C. Morrice, M.A. Bangor Welsh MSS. Society. 1908. (fl. 1430–1460.)

I.D. Casgliad o waith Ieuan Deulwyn—edited by Ifor Williams, M.A. Bangor Welsh MSS. Society. 1909.

I.G. Gweithiau Iolo Goch gyda nodiadau hanesyddol a beirniadol gan Charles Ashton. Croesoswallt. 1896.

Iolo MSS.: Iolo Manuscripts. A Selection of Ancient Welsh Manuscripts, in prose and verse, from the collection made by the late Edward Williams ... Llandovery. 1848.

J.M.J. A Welsh Grammar ... by J. Morris Jones, M.A. Oxford. 1913.

K.H. (Kyfreithau Howel Da). The Laws of Howel Dda, edited by Timothy Lewis, M.A. London. 1912.

L.A. The Elucidarium and other tracts in Welsh from Llyvyr Agkyr Llanddewivrevi, A.D. 1346, ed. by J. Morris Jones, M.A., and John Rhŷs, M.A. Oxford. 1894.

L.G.C. The poetical works of Lewis Glyn Cothi, edited by the Rev. Walter Davies ... and the Rev. John Jones, M.A. ... Oxford. 1837.

M.A. The Myvyrian Archaiology of Wales ... 3 vols. London. 1801–1807.

Medd. An. Y Meddyg Anifeiliaid : yn cynnwys achosion, arwyddion a thriniaeth afiechyd sydd ar wartheg, ceffylau a defaid. Wrexham. No date.

M.F. Myrddin Fardd (J. Jones). Gwerin-eiriau Sir Gaernarfon : eu hystyr a'u hanes. Pwllheli. 1907.

M.Ll. Gweithiau Morgan Llwyd o Wynedd. Vol. I, ed. by Thomas E. Ellis. Bangor and London. 1899 ; vol. II, ed. by John H. Davies. Bangor and London. 1908.—b. 1619, d. 1659.

N.E.D. A New English Dictionary on Historical Principles, edited by James A. H. Murray, LL.D. Oxford. 1888–

O.P. A Dictionary of the Welsh Language by W. Owen Pughe, D.C.L., F.A.S. 2nd ed. Denbigh. 1832.

Pedersen. Vergleichende Grammatik der Keltischen Sprachen von Holger Pedersen. Göttingen. 1908–

P.G.G. Pattrwm y Gwir-Gristion neu Ddilyniad Iesu Grist ... Wedi ei droi yn Gymraeg Gan W.M. A.B. Argraffwyd yn' Ghaerlleon ... 1723. Reprint ed. by H. Elvet Lewis. Bangor. 1908.

P.P. Promptorium Parvulorum [1440]. Early English Text Society. 1908.

R. Antiquæ Linguæ Britannicæ Thesaurus being a British, or Welsh-English Dictionary ... by Thomas Richards, Curate of Coychurch. Bristol. 1753.

R.B. (Red Book). Y Llyvyr Coch o Hergest. Vol. I (The

Mabinogion). Edited by John Rhŷs, M.A., and J. Gwenogvryn Evans. Oxford. 1887.

R.B. II. Do., Vol. II. The Text of the Bruts from the Red Book of Hergest. Edited by John Rhŷs, M.A., and J. Gwenogvryn Evans. Oxford. 1890.

Rhŷs. Celtic Folklore Welsh and Manx, by John Rhŷs, M.A., D.Litt. Oxford. 1901. (In two volumes.)

Rowland: A Grammar of the Welsh Language . . . by Thomas Rowland . . . Fourth edition. Wrexham (1876).

S. Strachan: An Introduction to Early Welsh. By the late John Strachan. Manchester. 1909.

S.E. A Dictionary of the Welsh Language by D. Silvan Evans, Carmarthen. 1893–1896. A to Ennyd. [An asterisk denotes that a quotation is given indicating the use of the word at least as early as the seventeenth century.]—Also An English-Welsh Dictionary by D. Silvan Evans. Denbigh. 1852.

S.G. Y Seint Greal . . . Edited . . . from the copy preserved among the Hengwrt MSS. . . . by the Rev. Robert Williams, M.A. . . . London. 1874.

S.J.E. Studies in Welsh Phonology by Samuel J. Evans. London and Newport. 1909.

Sweet. Spoken North Welsh in the Transactions of the Philological Society, 1882–4. (Pt. III.) pp. 409–484.

T.G.G. Transactions of the Guild of Graduates (of the University of Wales). Cardiff.

T.N. Gwaith Thomas Edwards (Twm o'r Nant). Liverpool. 1874.—b. 1735, d. 1810.

Welsh Orthography. The Report of the Orthographical Committee of the Society for utilizing the Welsh Language. [Reprint.] Carnarvon. 1905.

W.LL. Barddoniaeth William Llŷn a'i Eirlyfr, ed. by the Rev. J. C. Morrice, M.A. Bangor. 1908.—b. 1535, d. 1580.

W.M.M. A Glossary of the Demetian Dialect of North Pembroke-shire (with Special Reference to the Gwaun Valley) by the Rev. W. Meredith Morris, B.A. Tonypandy. 1910.

W.S. A Dictionary in Englyshe and Welshe by Wyllyam Salesbury [1547.] (Reprint by the Cymmrodorion Society, 1877.)

Yny lhyvyr hwnn. Yny lhyvyr hwnn a Ban o gyfreith HoweL Dan olygiaeth John H. Davies, M.A. Bangor and London. 1903. (The original title-page of the first tract reads: Yny lhyvyr hwnn y traethir. Gwyddor kymraeg. Kalandyr. Y gredo, ney bynkeu yr ffydd gatholig . . . 1546.)

All words from English dialects have been taken from Wright's English Dialect Dictionary, except when otherwise stated, and, needless to say, I have also constantly referred to Murray's Dictionary.

INTRODUCTION

The signs I have employed are the following :—

Sign	Usually written	As in	Sign	Usually written	As in
a	a	rhan	*ŋ*	ng	sang
b	b	bara	*ŋ́*	ng	ngenau
d	d	da	*ŋ̊*	ng(h)	nghof
ð	dd	lladd	*ŋ̊́*	ng(h)	nghefn
e	e	pen	*o*	o	llon
ĕ	e	gwneud	*ö*	o	coeden
f	ff	ffa	*ø*	a, y	mawnen, cywarch
g	g	gardd			
ǵ	g	genau	*p*	p	pen
h	h	haf	*r*	r	garw
i	i	dim	*r̥*	r(h)	rhaw
i̯	i	iawn	*s*	s	saith
ç	i	hiaith	*ʃ*	si	siarad
k	c	coll	*ʃⁱ*	si	trwsio
ḱ	c	ci	*t*	t	tad
χ	ch	llwch	*θ*	th	nyth
l	l	malu	*u*	w	pwll
ḷ	l	clo	*v*	f	barf
l̥	ll	lle	*w*	w	gwyn
m	m	mam	*w̥*	w(h)	*whatch*
m̥	m(h)	mhen	*y̠*	u, y	dull, llyn
n	n	nyth	*ə*	y	dynion
n̥	n(h)	nhad	*ʒ*	z, s	Eng. azure, pleasure

: indicates that the preceding vowel is long, e. g. *ta:d*, tad.

· before a syllable indicates that that syllable is stressed, e. g. *kəm·ra:ig*, Cymraeg. This sign is not used when the stress is regular, i. e. on the penultimate.

_ below a consonant, i. e. *l̲*, *r̲*, indicates that that consonant is long, e. g. *kal̲on*, calon ; *tor̲i*, torri.

GENERAL REMARKS.

Welsh in this district is spoken on a higher key than English. The syllable following the stress often has a tendency to rise, and is pronounced with much greater force than in English. The organs of speech are slightly tenser than in English, but not nearly so much so as in French. The soft palate is pressed back so that nasalization is extremely slight. It is in fact possible to close the passage of the nostrils without causing any appreciable effect on the sounds, except, of course, those of the nasal consonants.

THE VOWELS.

Vowels in monosyllables may be long or short. In stressed penultimates, vowels are appreciably longer before a single voiced consonant than before voiceless or double consonants.

We take the vowels in the following order :—

Back vowels : *a, o, u.*
Mixed vowels : *y, ĕ, ŏ, ə, ɐ.*
Front vowels : *i, e.*

Back Vowels.

a. Sweet's mid-back-wide-outer. Slightly more forward than English 'a' in 'father', but not so much as French 'a' in 'rage'. In unstressed syllables *a* often tends towards the obscure sound of *ə* as in *gavə̄ylŏð*, gafaelodd, 'he took hold'.

a· is the same sound lengthened. This sound often represents 'ae' in monosyllables, as *ļa·θ* beside *ļa·yθ*, llaeth, 'milk'. This, however, is not the case when 'ae' form the last letters in the word, except in *ma·*, sometimes for *ma·y*, mae, 'is'.

o is the rounded form of *a*, nearly the same as Eng. 'o' in 'boy', or French 'o' in 'note'.

o· is the same sound lengthened, but somewhat closer. The difference, however, is only slight, and not nearly so appreciable as I have heard it from some speakers from South Wales. Intermediate between *o* and *o·*, both as regards length and closeness, is *o* before a single voiced consonant in a stressed penultimate, e. g. *bona*, bonau, 'stumps'. I have used only one sign to represent these 'o' sounds, because the difference between them is slight, and is always governed by fixed rules. *o:* often represents ' oe ' (= *o.y*) in monosyllables, as *o:ð* beside *o:yð*, oedd, ' was '. This, however, is not the case when the letters ' oe ' are final, as in *no:y*, noe, ' a dish used in making butter '.

u. Sweet's high-back-narrow-round, like French ' ou ' in ' tout ', but less rounded. This sound often represents ' wy ' in final syllables, as *eglus* beside *egluys*, eglwys, ' church '; *annul* beside *annuyl*, anwyl, ' dear '. This is sometimes the case even when ' wy ' is final, e. g. *ëyru*, aerwy, ' a cow-house yoke '; ·*dëydsonu*, ' dywedasant hwy, ' they said '.

u: is the same sound lengthened. This sound occasionally represents ' wy ' in monosyllables, e. g. *du:n* beside *du:yn*, dwyn, ' to steal '. This is never the case when ' wy ' is final except in *ꞗnhu:*, hwynthwy, ' they '.

Mixed Vowels.

y. Sweet's high-mixed-narrow, i. e. the middle of the tongue comes into close contact with the palate. The lips are in the *i* position.

y: is the same sound lengthened. A slightly lowered and rounded form of this sound is sometimes heard in the exclamation *dy:l*, a euphemism for *dyu*, Duw, ' God '.

ë. Sweet's mid-mixed-narrow. The middle of the tongue is lowered from the *y* position. This sound only occurs in the diphthongs *ëi* and *ëy*. [See diphthongs.]

ö. Sweet's mid-mixed-narrow-round. This is a rounded form of *ë*. It occurs, properly speaking, only in the diphthongs *öi*, *öy*, but sometimes it represents *o* in stressed penultimates, especially before syllables containing *o* or *u*, as *döduy*, dodwy, ' to lay (eggs) '. It also sometimes represents ' oe ' in the stressed penultimates of compound words, as *trödvað*, troedfedd, ' foot ' (measure); *kösnoθ*, coesnoeth, ' bare-legged '.

ꙇ. Sweet's low-mixed-narrow. This is the short form of the vowel sound in Eng. ' sir ', and quite distinct from Eng. ' u ' in ' but '. For the sake of convenience I have used the same sign to express the so-called irrational vowel which occurs so frequently in unstressed antepenultimates, e. g. *kꙇfꙇla*, ceffylau, ' horses ', as it is difficult to analyse these very short unstressed vowel sounds. The sound in such cases seems often to be nearer that of ' er ' in Eng.

'better', but slightly more advanced. Sweet ('Spoken North Welsh') often omits the vowel in these cases, but, though such pronunciations do no doubt sometimes occur in quick speech, they are not, in my opinion, characteristic of this district, except in certain combinations of letters, e. g. *ḻgada*, 'eyes'.

ɒ. I use this sign to express two very similar 'o' sounds. The first is a rounded form of *ə* (Sweet's low-mixed-narrow-round), which represents 'y' before a consonantal 'w' in stressed pen-ultimates, e. g. *bɒwyd*, bywyd, 'life'. Otherwise it only occurs in diphthongs. The other sound may be described as a rounded form of the first element in the diphthong 'ow' in Eng. 'how' (Sweet's low-mixed-wide-round). This sound represents 'ɑw' in stressed penultimates. [See diphthongs.]

Front Vowels.

i. Sweet's high-front-narrow, like French 'i' in 'dit', but slightly lower (more open).

i· is the same sound lengthened.

e. Sweet's mid-front-wide, very slightly lower (more open) than Eng. 'e' in 'pen', as *het*, 'hat', *meθy*, methu, 'to fail'. Before a single voiced consonant in stressed penultimates the sound is slightly higher (more closed) than English 'e' in 'pen', as *gweny*, gwenu, 'to smile', *meðul*, meddwl, 'to think'. As in the case of *o* I have used only one sign to represent the sounds, because the difference is very slight and is always governed by fixed rules.

e· is the lengthened form of the second of the above-mentioned sounds, but perhaps slightly more closed.

THE DIPHTHONGS.

The diphthongs are *ai, a·i, au, a·u, ay, a·y, eu, e·u, ēi, ēy, iu, i·u, oi, oy, o·y, ōi, ōy, ɒu, ui, u·i, uy, u·y, yu, y·u*.

ai represents 'ai' in monosyllables, e. g. *taid*, 'grandfather'. It occurs also in a few final syllables, as in *arwain*, 'to lead'. Final 'ai' usually becomes *a*.

a·i represents 'ae' before 'g', as in *kəm·ra·ig*, Cymraeg, 'Welsh'.

au represents 'aw' in monosyllables ending in a consonant, e. g. *maur*, mawr, 'great'. It also occurs in a few final syllables, as *darḻau*, darllaw, 'to brew'; *distau*, distaw, 'silent'. It some-times represents 'ow', as in *taur*, töwr, 'thatcher'; *ţraur*, tröwr,

' ploughman '. It does not generally occur in stressed penultimates except before *j*, e. g. *kaujo*, bancawio, ' to fasten (a fish-hook) to the gut '. It is heard, however, in *tauson.* and some other forms from *tewi*, ' to be silent'.

a:u represents ' aw ', when final, in monosyllables, e. g. *ḷa:u,* llaw, ' hand '. It occurs also in *nosta:uχ,* nosdawch, ' good night'.

ay represents ' au ' in monosyllables, e. g. *hayl,* haul, ' sun ' ; and in final stressed syllables as *ka·say,* cashau, ' to hate'. It represents ' ai ' in *bayχ,* baich, ' burden ', and *brayχ,* braich, ' arm '.

a:y represents ' ae ' in monosyllables, e. g. *ha:yl,* hael, ' generous ' ; ' au ' in a few cases as *pa:yn,* paun, ' peacock ' ; and sometimes Eng. ' a, ai ', as *pa:yn,* ' pane ' ; *pla:yn,* ' plain ' ; *pa:ynt,* ' paint'.

eu represents ' ew ' in monosyllables, except when final, and in stressed penultimates followed by a consonant, as *teuχ,* tewch, ' be silent ' ; *teudur,* tewdwr, ' thickness '. It occurs in a final syllable in *kɔłteu,* ' stiff ' (of liquids); *pendeu,* pendew, ' thick-headed, dull '.

e:u represents ' ew' when final in monosyllables, as *te:u,* tew, ' fat '.

ẽï represents ' ei ' in stressed penultimates, as *k̃ẽinjog,* ceiniog, ' penny'; ' ae, eu ' in stressed penultimates when followed by a consonant + *i* or *j*, as *gwẽïδi,* gwaeddi, ' to cry out' ; *dẽigjan,* deugain, ' forty ', ' ai ' in a few monosyllables, as *r̥hẽï,* rhai, ' some ' ; *nẽid,* naid, ' leap'; and Eng. ' i ' as *pr̥ẽïvat,* ' private '. In monosyllables the *ẽ* element is very distinct, but in stressed penultimates the *i* is generally predominant. Thus *gwẽïθjo, pẽïdjo* often sound to an unaccustomed ear like *gwi:θjo, pi:djo.* Sometimes the *ẽ* undoubtedly disappears, as in *ista,* eistedd, ' to sit'; *i∫o,* eisieu, ' want '; *tr̥i:o,* treio, ' to ebb', ' to try '.

ÿ represents ' ae ', ' eu ' and ' ey ' in stressed penultimates (but see under *ẽï*), as *ÿlod,* aelod, ' member '; *bẽÿdy,* beudy, ' cow-shed'; *dẽÿd,* dweyd, dywedyd, ' to say '. It occurs also in a few monosyllables, as *gwẽÿ,* gweu, ' to weave '; *hẽÿ* beside *hay,* hau, ' to sow '. In monosyllables the *ẽ* element is very distinct, but in stressed penultimates the *y* is predominant. Sometimes the *ẽ* disappears, as in *fry:o,* ' to quarrel ' (Eng. ' fray ', ' affray ').

iu represents ' iw ' and ' yw ' and Eng. ' u ' and ' ew '. The existence of the sound *iu* in Welsh (though contrary to the opinion of Sweet, ' Spoken North Welsh,' p. 417) is sufficiently proved by the literary word ' gwiw ', which is undoubtedly pronounced *gwiu*, and could scarcely be pronounced otherwise. This sound may be distinctly heard when it occurs initially as in *ius*, 'use'; *iuſo*, 'to use' (but *jurχ*, iwrch, 'roebuck'). Other examples are *niul* (which Sweet writes *njuul*, i. e. *nju:l*), niwl, 'mist'; *ļiu*, lliw, 'colour'. This diphthong has replaced *yu* in a great number of words, as *ļiu*, llyw, 'helm'·; *ŗhiu*, rhyw, 'some'. *iu* also occurs in *diujol*, duwiol, 'godly'. Cf. also *ədi,̣* ydyw, 'is'. The literary 'yw', 'is', is always pronounced *iu*.—On the other hand we have *saiθ njurnod*, saith niwrnod, 'seven days'.

i:u occurs in *ţŗi:uχ*, triwch, 'try'; *gwni:uχ*, 'sew', etc.

oi̯ represents 'oi' in monosyllables, as *ţŗoi,* troi, 'to turn'; and in stressed final syllables as *para·toi,̣* paratoi, 'to prepare'.

oy occurs very rarely as representing 'oe' in final syllables in compound words, e. g. in *kŗaχgoyd,* crachgoed, 'the shoots which grow out of the stump of a tree which has been sawn off'. Even in such cases *oy* more often tends to become *o* or *öy*.

o:y represents 'oe' in monosyllables, as *ko:yd,* coed, 'wood'. The consciousness of incorrectness in substituting *o:* for *o:y* (see under *o:*), e. g. *kŗo:n* for *kŗo:yn*, croen, 'skin', sometimes leads to the opposite process of substituting *o:y* for *o:*. Thus *fo:ys* is a very common pronunciation of *fo:s*. I have also heard *bo:yn* for *bo:n*, bon, 'stump, stem' (J.J.).

öi̯ represents 'oi' in stressed penultimates, as *ļöia*, lloi, 'calves', and 'oe' in stressed penultimates followed by a consonant or consonants + *i* or *j* as *köidjo*, coedio, 'to timber'.

öy represents 'oe (oy)' in stressed penultimates (but cf. *öi̯*), as *köydan*, coeden, 'tree'; *köysa*, coesau, 'legs'. This is the prevailing pronunciation of the district, but *uy* is sometimes heard instead, thus *kuydan, kuysa* (O.H. had *uy* very frequently). The forms *möyθa* and *muyθa* appear also in literature, viz. 'moethau' and 'mwythau'. On the other hand *öy* is occasionally heard for *uy*, as *höylys* for *huylys*, 'convenient'. Before 'u', *öy* tends to become *ëy*, as *glëyu* beside *glöyu*, gloyw, 'bright'; *kŗëyu* beside *kŗöyu*, croyw, 'clear'.

ɐu. For the two varieties of this diphthong cf. under *ɐ*. The first variety where *ɐ* is a rounded form of *ə* (Sweet's low-mixed-narrow-round) represents 'yw' in a stressed penultimate before a consonant, as *bɐujog*, bywiog, 'lively'; *ŗhɐujog*, rhywiog, 'kindly'. The second variety where *ɐ* is approximately a rounded form of the first element of the Eng. diphthong ' ow ' in ' how ' (Sweet's low-mixed-wide-round) represents (1) ' ow ' in monosyllables, as *dɒuχ*, dowch for deuwch, ' come '; *ṛhɒud*, rhowyd for rhoddwyd, pret. pass. of rhoddi, ' to give '. (2) ' aw ' followed by more than one consonant in *mɒurθ*, Mawrth, ' March ', and *dy:ð mɒurθ*, dydd Mawrth, ' Tuesday '. (3) It is heard also in *kɒuk*, ' one of the turned down ends of a horse-shoe ', and *ṛhɒuk*, ' a rut '. (4) It generally represents ' aw ' in stressed penultimates, as *mɒunan*, mawnen, ' a piece of peat '. (5) Eng. ' ou ', as *slɒut*, ' plucky '.

ui represents vocal ' w ' + ' y ' before a consonant + *i* or *j*, as *ṛhuidi*, rhwydi, ' nets '; *ḷuidjon*, pl. of *ḷu:yd*, llwyd, ' brown '.

u:i represents ' ywi ' in *klu:is*, clywais, ' I heard '.

uy represents vocal ' w ' + ' y ' in all positions except in monosyllables and the cases mentioned above under *ui*. Final ' wy ' followed by a 'consonant, however, often becomes *u* (see under *u*). ' Ydwyf' always becomes (ə)*du*. The change from *uy* into *u* sometimes, by a contrary process, produces a change from *u* into *uy* (cf. under *o:y*), e. g. *manuyl*, manwl, ' careful, detailed '.

u:y represents vocal ' w ' + ' y ' in monosyllables, as *du:y*, dwy, ' two '. *u:y* occasionally becomes *u:* (except when final) or *u:* followed by a glide. An instance of the contrary process is *hu:ynt*, hwnt, ' beyond '.

yu represents ' uw ' and ' yw '. Cf., however, under *iu* the large number of cases in which ' yw ' is represented by *iu*. A slightly lowered form of *y* is often heard in *dyu*, Duw, ' God '. Cases of *yu* representing ' yw ' are *byu*, byw, ' to live '; *klyu*, *klyuχ*, clyw, clywch, ' hear '.

y:u occurs in *dy:uχ*, duwch, ' blackness '.

THE CONSONANTS.

Preliminary remarks. The voiced consonants are more complete in their vocality, especially when initial, than their English equivalents, and approach very nearly the corresponding French sounds. (Cf., as regards *d*, Rousselot, ' Principes de Phonétique expérimentale ', vol. i, pp. 500–1.) For exceptions to this general rule see below, especially as regards *sḅ*, *sg*, and final *ḅ*, *d*, *g* in monosyllables after a short vowel. Final consonants in monosyllables after a short vowel are long.

We deal with the consonants in the following order :—

(a) *h, j, ç, w, w̥.*

(b) the liquids and nasals, *l, ļ, ļ̣,*[1] *n, ṇ, r, ṛ, m, ṃ, ŋ, ŋ́, ŋ, ŋ́.*

(c) the spirants, *ð, θ, f, v, χ, s, ʃ, ʃ́, ȝ.*

(d) the labial, dental, and guttural stops, *p, b, t, d, k, ḱ, g, ǵ.*

h does not differ materially from the Eng. ' h ', but is pronounced rather more forcibly in monosyllables, whether initially or after *ṃ, ṇ, ŋ, ŋ́,* and *ṛ.* When enclitic, as in *hi* after a noun, the *h* is very slight, and often disappears. ' H ' following *b, d, g,* and sometimes *v,* causes these letters to become voiceless, and the ' h ' itself, when not stressed, disappears. Thus we have *i ṃha:p i,* ' her son ' ; *i θa:t i,* ' her father ' ; *i χe:k i,* ' her mouth ' (or, more correctly, *i ṃha: pi,* etc.) ; *gnëyt hyn,* ' to do this ' ; *drəkḱin,* from ' drwg ' and ' hin ', ' bad weather ' ; *f hy:n,* fy hun, ' myself ' ; *krəf·hay,* cryfhau, ' to strengthen '. When *i* follows *h* the tongue is so close to the palate that friction is set up.

j is the consonant corresponding to *i,* and differs from Eng. ' y ' only in the greater tenseness of the tongue ('narrow' instead of ' wide ').

ç is the voiceless sound corresponding to *j.* It undoubtedly occurs sometimes, as in *i hçaiθ,* ei hiaith, ' her language ', but it appears to be rather an individual peculiarity than the general rule, and the ear is satisfied whether *j* or *ç* is used. Instances where the sound may occur are, moreover, very rare.

w is the consonant corresponding to *u.* It differs from English ' w ' only in the tongue being tenser and the lips more rounded. For the pronunciation of *gw* before a consonant see *g.*

w̥ is the voiceless form of *w,* like the sound sometimes heard in Eng. ' what ', but it is always followed by a distinct *h* sound. This sound is very rare, and only occurs in the mutation of words beginning with *w* derived from English, as *i w̥atʃ,* ' her watch '.

The liquids and nasals, *l, ļ, ļ̣,*[1] *n, ṇ, r, ṛ, m, ṃ, ŋ, ŋ́, ŋ, ŋ́.*

It should be stated that when a voiced consonant stands after a stressed syllable between two vowels the preceding vowel is slightly lengthened, and the consonant, which opens the next syllable, is naturally short (except in the case of *m,* which is always doubled

---

[1] *ļ* is really a spirant, but it will be more convenient to treat it with the other *l* sounds.

in this position and the preceding vowel short). But among voiced consonants *l* and *r* have the peculiarity that they may be either long, preceded by a short vowel, or short, preceded by a slightly lengthened vowel. Hence, in the case of these two consonants it is necessary to mark the length when it occurs (*l̯*, *r̯*). *n*, on the other hand, may be either single, preceded by a slightly lengthened vowel, or double, preceded by a short vowel.

l differs little from Eng. ' l '. The back of the tongue is raised, producing (but in a lesser degree) the " dull " sound of the letter as heard in English, but the tip of the tongue is nearer the upper teeth than in the English sound, and is more spread out. Long *l* occurs in only a few words, as *kal̯on*, calon, 'heart'; *kal̯yn*, canlyn, ' to follow'; *kol̯yn*, colyn, 'sting'; *kul̯a*, cwla, 'poorly'; *lol̯yn*, fem. *lol̯an*, 'a foolish talker'; *tal̯aχ*, comp. of *tal*, 'tall'; *dal̯iθ*, 3. s. fut. of *dal*, 'to hold'. It is also distinctly heard after a short vowel at the end of monosyllables before the enclitic pronouns *i* and *o*, as *i nal̯i*, *i ðal̯o*, 'to hold me, hold him'. A variety of *l* occurs after *ð* and *θ*, the point of contact being the surface of the tongue a short distance from the tip instead of the actual tip, e.g. *fɔðlon*, ffyddlon, 'faithful'; *mɛ̄yθlon*, maethlon, 'nutritious'.

l̥ is the voiceless sound corresponding to *l*, resembling the sound used by some French speakers in such words as 'peuple', 'cycle'. This sound occurs after *k*, *p*, *t*, *m̥h*, *n̥h*, *ŋh*, as *kl̥y:st*, clust, 'ear'; *pl̥y:*, plu, 'feathers'; *tl̥aud*, tlawd, 'poor'; *ə m̥l̥hi:θ*, ymhlith, 'among'; *ə n̥l̥hodi*, fy nhlodi, 'my poverty'; *ə ŋl̥hy:st*, 'my ear'. The *h* in these latter instances, it will be observed, follows the *l̥*.

l̥ is a voiceless 'l' sound with no corresponding voiced sound. The tip of the tongue is in the same position as for *l*, but the back of the tongue is not raised. The lips are in the *i* position. The sides of the tongue come into contact with the upper teeth, and the air is emitted through the teeth on one side, generally on the right, but in the case of some speakers, on the left.

n is the same as English ' n ' except that the tip of the tongue is nearer the teeth. *n* is completely voiced after *k* and *p*, as in *knaud*, cnawd, 'flesh'; *pnaun*, prydnawn, 'afternoon'. The use of *nn* corresponds very closely with older literary usage, except that the doubled letter only occurs after a stressed syllable. *nn* is also distinctly heard when *n* occurs at the end of a monosyllable after a short vowel, and is followed by one of the enclitic pronouns *i* or *o*, as *ə m̥henni*, fy mhen i, 'my head'; *i benno*, ei ben o, 'his head'. As in most languages *n* normally becomes *m* before *p* and *b* and *ŋ* before *k* and *g*, especially in very common connections, as *əm braːv*, yn braf, 'fine'; *kiŋ glettad*, cyn caleted, 'as hard'. Even *hem bobol*, hen bobl, 'old people'; *hogam baːχ*, hogen bach, 'little girl' (with a very short *m*) are occasionally heard. Before *ð* and *θ* the point of contact is the surface instead of the tip of the tongue, as in *hogan ðaː*, hogen dda, 'good girl'.

n̥ is the voiceless sound corresponding to *n*. It is always followed by a full, distinctly enunciated *h*, as (*ə*) *n̥haːd*, fy nhad, 'my father'. *n̥h* however does not always correspond to Welsh 'nh', e.g. *brenhinoð*, brenhinoedd, 'kings'. *n* is not affected when it precedes the verbal termination -*ˈhay*, as *tənˈhay*, tynnhau, D., 'to tighten'; nor by the stressed prefix *an*-, as *ˈanˈhuylys*, anhwylus, 'inconvenient'. Even when *an*- is followed by an etymological 'nh' no *n̥* is heard (except possibly in the case of unusual emphasis), as *ˈanˈhëilum*, annheilwng, 'unworthy'—unless the second element consists of a monosyllable, as *ˈanˈn̥heːg*, annheg, 'unfair'. Nor does *n̥h* occur in an unstressed syllable in the body of a word, e.g. *manoḷḷ*, manhollt, in *kyːn manoḷḷ*, 'a fine-splitting chisel'. Cf. also *anoð*, 'difficult', from 'an-' and 'hawdd'. 'Nhr' is pronounced *n̥r̥h*, as *ə n̥r̥hoːyd*, fy nhroed, 'my foot'. Occasionally the *n̥* is not heard in such cases, and we have *ə r̥hoːyd*.

r is the sound of Eng. 'r' in 'parallel', but the point of contact with the tongue is slightly further back. *r̥* represents a long or trilled *r*. Its use corresponds very closely to the 'rr' of older literary usage.

r̥ is the voiceless sound corresponding to *r*. It occurs after *k*, *p*, and *t*, as *kr̥oːyn*, croen, 'skin'; *pr̥in*, prin, 'scarce'; *tr̥oːyd*, troed, 'foot'. Otherwise *r̥* only occurs at the beginning of a word or stressed syllable (or after initial *m̥* or *n̥*), where it is always followed by a full, distinctly enunciated *h*. The verbal termination -*ˈhay* does not affect *r*, e.g. *bərˈhay*, byrhau, 'to shorten'.

m resembles very closely Eng. 'm'. After a stressed syllable between two vowels *m* is always doubled, except after a diphthong. A variety of *m* sometimes occurs in which the lower lip comes into contact with the upper teeth (instead of with the upper lip) as frequently in German in such words as Kampf, fünf, etc. (cf. Jespersen, 'Lehrbuch der Phonetik', p. 19). This sound may be not unfrequently heard when *n* precedes *v*, as in *di:olχ ən vaur*, diolch yn fawr, 'thank you very much'.

m̥ is the voiceless sound corresponding to *m*, and is always followed by a full, distinctly enunciated *h*. It occurs only initially as the mutated form of *p*, and in a few aphetic forms such as *m̥hary*, amharu, 'to injure'; *m̥hëyθyn*, amheuthun, 'dainty'; and sometimes in *m̥haran*, maharen, 'ram'. When followed by *n* or *r* the *h* follows these sounds, as *ə m̥nhelin*, fy mhenelin, 'my elbow'; *ə m̥rhe:s*, fy mhres, 'my money'. When unstressed *m* sometimes takes the place of *m̥h*. O.H. had *əm muḷheli*, ym Mhwllheli, 'in Pwllheli'.

ŋ is the sound corresponding to 'ng' in Eng. 'rang', but the point of contact between the back of the tongue and the palate is somewhat further back.

ŋ́ is formed in the same way as the above but much further forward, the middle of the tongue coming into contact with the middle of the hard palate. It is followed by a slight *j*-like sound. *ŋ́* occurs only before the vowels *e*, *ĕ*, and *i*, and before *a* in the mutation of words derived from English beginning with *ǵ*, as *ŋ́amjo* from *ǵamjo*, 'to make fun' = Eng. 'game'.

ŋ̥ is the voiceless sound corresponding to *ŋ*, and represents 'ngh', but only occurs initially as the mutated form of *k*, as *ə ŋ̥halon*, fy nghalon, 'my heart'; but ·*aŋ̥·hovjo*, anghofio, 'to forget'; ·*aŋ̥·fredin*, anghyffredin, 'uncommon'. *ŋ̥* is always followed by a full, distinctly enunciated *h*, but when followed by *n* or *r*, the *h* follows these sounds, as *ə ŋ̥nhaud*, fy nghnawd, ·my flesh'; *ə ŋ̥rhy:s*, fy nghrys, 'my shirt'.

ŋ̥́ is the voiceless sound corresponding to *ŋ́*, and occurs only before *e*, *ĕ*, and *i*, and sometimes before *a* in certain words derived from English, as the mutated form of *k*. Like *ŋ́*, *ŋ̥́* is always followed by *h*.

The spirants, ð, θ, *f*, *v*, χ, *s*, *ʃ*, *ʃ'*, *ʒ*.

ð is a sound resembling the Eng. 'th' in 'the', but the tip of the tongue touches the back of the lower teeth while the surface of the tongue comes in contact with the points of the upper teeth. The contact, however, is slight, hence its tendency when final to disappear, as in *ista*, eistedd, 'to sit'; *gar* beside *garð*, gardd, 'garden'; *for* beside *forð*, ffordd, 'road'. Final *ðv*, which occurs in the semi-literary words *deðv*, deddf, 'law, ordinance', and *l̨eðv*, lleddf, 'flat' (in music), is pronounced with gradually falling breath, and does not in the remotest degree suggest two syllables.

θ is the voiceless sound corresponding to *ð*, but is pronounced with more force. It resembles the sound of Eng. 'th' in 'thin'.

f is the same sound as Eng. 'f', but pronounced with slightly greater force.

v is the same sound voiced, but the contact between the upper teeth and lower lip is very slight. When final and not preceded by a consonant it generally disappears. It remains, however, as a rule in the first pers. pres. sing. fut. when standing alone or following *na:(g)* in answering a question, as *neuχi brɔnny hun?* *gna:v*, 'will you buy this? Yes'. It remains also in a few other words, as *bra:v*, braf, 'fine'; *do:v*, dof, 'tame'; *gwi:v*, gwif, 'lever'; *r̥hu:yv*, rhwyf, 'oar'. In final *vn, vr*, as in *k̃evn, l̨yvr*, the sound gradually dies away, and the two letters do not in the slightest degree produce the impression of forming two syllables. This is, however, not the case with *vl*, as in *gwevl*. Here the *v* and *l* have practically equal stress, as in the Eng. 'level'.

χ is the voiceless guttural spirant like the German 'ch', formed with the back of the tongue against the soft palate. The friction is very strong. In the combination *χw* the *w* is pronounced quite separately.

s. In this sound the tip of the tongue is close behind the upper teeth, and the breath passes along the centre of the blade of the tongue and between the upper teeth. It has a much "softer" or less hissing sound than Eng. 's', and is slightly aspirated. In the treatment of *s* followed by a labial, guttural, or dental stop I have followed the recommendation of Professor J. Morris Jones, 'Welsh Orthography', pp. 26, 27, and write *sb, sg*, but *st*. In *sb* and *sg* the *b* and *g*, instead of having the usual full vocality, have a voiceless on-glide like that heard in English 'b' and 'g', especially when initial. In *st* the *t* is entirely voiceless, but it loses its strong aspiration and resembles French 't'. When the order is inverted I write *bs, ks*, and *ds*. In these cases *b* and *d* have a voiceless off-glide, while *k* retains its voiceless character like *t* as stated above, but without its usual strong aspiration.

ʃ, ʃ. These sounds are in a state of transition. They are of late introduction, and individuals are still occasionally to be met with who are unable to pronounce them, and substitute *s* or *sj.* The prevailing pronunciation of *ſ* resembles very closely that of Eng. ‘sh’, but the point of contact is slightly further forward, i.e. on the arched rim instead of behind it. Before *a*, *o*, and *u* in final syllables the tongue is slightly more arched, producing the palatalized sound *ſ'*. Other speakers seem to pronounce *ſ* exactly like Eng. ‘sh’, and these make no distinction between *ſ* and *ſ'*. After the borrowed sound *tſ, ſ* appears never to be palatalized.

g is the voiced sound corresponding to *ſ*, but it is never palatalized. This sound occurs only in the combination *dg*, as in *dgug*, ‘jug’.

The labial, guttural, and dental stops, *p, b, t, d, k, ᴋ, g, ǵ.*

Note. When Old and Middle Welsh ‘p’, ‘t’, ‘c’ form combinations with one another in the body of a word, the first letter remains voiceless (losing, however, its strong aspiration); but the second becomes voiced with a voiceless on-glide. But when ‘t’ forms the second element, though it remains voiceless, it loses its strong aspiration and resembles French ‘t’. I write, therefore, *pt, pg, tb, tg, kb, kt.*

When the tenues follow voiceless spirants (including *ɫ*) the same phenomenon takes place, except that after *θ* we have *d* preceded by a voiceless on-glide instead of *t*. Thus we have *ɫb, ɫg, ɫt*; *θb, θg, θd*; *ſb, ſg, ſt*; *χb, χg, χt*; *sb, sg, st* (cf. Morris Jones, ‘Welsh Orthography’, pp. 25, 26). See also under *s*.

When final *b, d, g* come before a word beginning with the same letter respectively, both letters frequently become voiceless, especially among old speakers (cf. the well-known rule in cynghanedd), e.g. *po:p pluyðyn* (O.H.); *ne:p pyθ* (O.H.); *gubot tim* (J.J.); *n to:?*, onid do? (J.J.); *dim ɔnt tu:r*, dim ond dwr (O.H.); *ɔvat tu:r* (O.H.); *ɔsbryt tɣu:g* (O.H.); *klu:at tim* (O.H.); *nɔuvat ty:ð* (O.H.); *dëyt tɔwinjaθ* (O.H.); *tebik ᴋin i*, tebyg genyf, ‘I suppose’. *g* also becomes *k* in *ɣhak kwilɪð !*, rhag cywilydd !, ‘for shame!’

p is like Eng. ‘p’, but the lips are more tightly compressed and the emission of breath is much greater, and the consequent breath-glide (except in the cases mentioned above) is much more marked, and renders completely voiceless a succeeding *l* or *r*. This

strong emission of breath does not, however, produce the impression
of 'h', as in Irish.   At the end of a stressed syllable, between
two vowels (except after a diphthong), p is always doubled.

b is the same sound voiced, but the strong aspiration is, of course,
absent.   When final after a short vowel, *b* is very short, and has
a voiceless off-glide, e.g. *heb*, 'without'.   In final *bl* the two letters
are sounded with practically equal stress, e.g. *nobl*, Eng. 'noble'.
The same is the case with the semi-literary *gwobr*, 'reward, prize'.

t is pronounced by contact of the tip of the tongue with the
upper teeth.   As regards breath, all that has been said with regard
to *p* applies equally to *t*.   Even when final, a strong breath-glide
is heard after it.   This is one of the most noticeable points to an
English ear in Welsh speakers of English.

d is the same sound voiced, but the strong aspiration is, of course,
absent.   According to Rousselot, 'Principes de Phonétique expérimentale', p. 596, *d* is pronounced with greater lingual energy than
t.   When final after a short vowel *d* is very short and has a voiceless
off-glide, e.g. *sad*, 'firm'.   In final *dl* the two letters are sounded
with practically equal stress, e.g. *anadl*, 'breath', *banadl*, 'broom'.

k.   In this sound the contact of the back of the tongue with the
palate is slightly further back than in English, but not so far back
as in Irish.   As regards breath all that has been said about *p* and *t*
applies equally to *k*, and like them it is doubled at the end of a
stressed syllable, between two vowels, except after a diphthong.

ꝁ is the same sound as *k*, but the contact of the tongue and the
palate is much further forward than in English, and is followed by
a *j*-like glide (not to be confused with *kj*).   *ꝁ* occurs only before
the vowels *e*, *ē*, and *i*, and before *a* in certain words derived from
English.   The glide above mentioned is always noticeable before
e, *ē*, and *i*, but before *a* it varies considerably in different speakers.
In *kj* the *k* seems to occupy an intermediate position as to the
palate between the ordinary *k* and *ꝁ*; and the same may be said
when *k* is preceded by *e* or *i* and is followed by *ꝁe* or *ꝁi* as in
pikꝁin.

g is the same sound as *k*, but voiced, and without its strong
aspiration.   When *g* is final, in a monosyllable, after a short vowel,
it is very short, and has a voiceless off-glide.   Final *g* after *s* is
whispered (cf. Sweet, 'Spoken North Welsh', p. 420).   In *gw*
before a consonant the *g* is pronounced with the lips in the *w*

position. After *i* a very slight glide may be heard before *g* in deliberate pronunciation, as e.g. in *ki:g*.

ǵ is the same sound as *k*, but voiced, and it occurs in the same positions.

NOTE AS TO DOUBLE LETTERS.

There can be no reasonable doubt that *k, p, t,* and *m* are doubled at the end of a stressed syllable before a vowel, and that the doubling of these letters in general written usage until recently represents an actual fact. The use of *nn* also coincides very closely with the older spelling. The difference between *n* and *nn* is marked by a difference in the preceding vowel also. Before *nn*, as already stated, the vowel is very short; before *n* the vowel is half-long, and in the case of *e* and *o*, closer than before the doubled letter. Any native with an ear for sound can distinguish between *n* and *nn* without hesitation. At the same time the distinctness of these double letters is not nearly so great as e.g. in Italian, because the first element is shorter. It is certainly not the case, as Sweet implies ('A Primer of Phonetics', § 159), that the doubling of the *t* sound, e.g. in *etto*, is merely apparent—the effect produced upon the ear by a fresh stress or a new impulse beginning on the consonant. The stress on the *e* and the second *t* is, it is quite true, nearly equal, but the other *t* before the latter is as distinctly heard as e.g. in Eng. 'a right to'. Thus the Welsh pronunciation of the Eng. 'pretty' is certainly *pṛitti*. In 'cadw' (*kadu*), the instance of "open stress" mentioned by Sweet, the case is quite different. The *k* and *d* here also have almost equal stress, but the *a* is half long, and there is nothing which suggests doubling of the consonant, whereas in *etto* the first vowel is extremely short.

In the case of *l, r* (after short consonants), and the voiceless spirants, the matter is not so easy to decide, as length and doubling in these sounds are more difficult to distinguish. In old usage 's' was generally doubled, but there were obvious reasons against doubling such digraphs as 'ch', 'ff', 'll', and 'th'. My own conclusion is that these letters are long (not doubled) in the stressed position, but that owing to the relatively strong stress with which final syllables are pronounced, they are occasionally doubled in cases of unusual emphasis; and the same may be said of *k, p, t, f,* when preceding a liquid or *j*, as *byttṛa, kikkjo,* for *bytṛa* and *kikjo*.

THE VERB.

gweld, gwelad, 'to see'.

Present and Future.

Sing.	1.	*gwela(v)*
	2.	*gweli*
	3.	*gweliθ, gwelif, gwe:l*
Pl.	1.	*gwelan, gwelun*
	2.	*gweluχ*
	3.	*gwelan*

Imperfect.

Sing.	1.	*gwelun*
	2.	*gwelat*
	3.	*gwela*
Pl.	1.	*gwelan*
	2.	*gwelaχ*
	3.	*gwelan*

Preterite.

Sing.	1.	*gwelis* [1]
	2.	*gwelist*
	3.	*gweloð*
Pl.	1.	*gwelson*
	2.	*gwelsoχ*
	3.	*gwelson*

Pluperfect. [2]

Sing.	1.	*gwelsun*
	2.	*gwelsat*
	3.	*gwelsa*
Pl.	1.	*gwelsan*
	2.	*gwelsaχ*
	3.	*gwelsan*

---

[1] Very rare instances of -*as* occur as *kədjas, kəməutas.*

[2] I retain this name for purposes of convenience, but the tense is used only in a conditional or past conditional sense.

Pres. Subjunctive.

Sing. 1.   [*gnelo(v)*] from *gnĕyd*
     2.   —
     3.   [*gnelo*]
Pl.   1.   [*gnelon*]
     2.   [*gnelox*]
     3.   [*gnelon*]

Imperative.

Sing. 1.   —
     2.   *gwe:l, gwela*
     3.   *gwelad*
Pl.   1.   *gwelun*
     2.   *gwelux*
     3.   *gwelan*

Passive.

Present   *gwelir*
Imperfect   [*klu:id* from *klu:ad* with pret. meaning]
Preterite   *gweluyd*
Pluperfect [1]   [*l̯esid* from *gal̯y*]

---

[1] I retain this name for purposes of convenience, but the tense is used only in a conditional or past conditional sense.

a, conj. and prep., *ag* before vowels, the letter *j*, *ma:y*, *mi* (particle), *nid*, *r* (particle=yr), *vel*, *veḷy*, and sometimes *wedi* and *wedyn*. [*a χwedi*, *a χwedyn* are also still often heard among old people. Cf. also *a χǝno vo* by the side of *a gǝno vo* = a ganddo fo.] The radical is often heard after *a* instead of the spirant mutation.

I. 'and', written 'a' and generally 'ac' at all periods, but sometimes 'ag': *gwi:r a χeluyð*, 'truth and falsehood'; *kḷo: a χlikjaa*, 'lock and latch'; *ṭrol a χefyl*, 'cart and horse'; *day a θair*, 'two (shillings) and three(pence)'; *bara kaus* (*χaus*), 'bread and cheese'; *a fe:θ araḷ*, 'and what is more'. Occasionally *a:*, *a:g* when emphatic: *i vjaun a:g aḷan*, 'inside *and* outside'. (2) in a verbless clause, the whole having a relative or adjectival force, 'and, with': *dy:n a θavod de:u* (*te:u*) *gǝno vo*, 'a thick-tongued man' (i. e. a man who speaks thickly); *het a θolk ǝni hi*, 'a dented hat'; *mi ðo:θ o adra ag iʃo bu:yd arno vo*, 'he came home hungry'; *kǝulad ba:χ a i gwasgy n dyn* (*den*), 'a small armful, pressed well together'. (3) 'when, while, though, on condition of, considering that': *r o:ð ǝŋ gwilið iðo vo bëïdjo taly a gǝno vo ǥimmint o arjan*, 'it was a shame for him not to pay considering that he had so much money'; *pu:y vasa n meðul ǝ va:θ be:θ a vǝnta mor wasiad?*, 'who would have thought such a thing, considering that he is such a steady-going individual?'; *χǝmmun i lawar a ṭri:o i aχyb o*, 'I would not try and save him for a great deal'; *a minna ŋ govyn iðo vo am bëïdjo bo:d ǝn hi:r heb alu etto*, 'though I asked him to call again soon'; *a i gǝmmyd o i ǥi:d*, 'taking it all together'.

II. 'as', generally written 'ag' before vowels in Mod. Welsh. (a) before nouns, infinitives, or pronouns after *kin*, *mor*, 'as', *r y:n*, 'the same', etc.: *kin ḷuytlad a kalχan* (*χalχan*), 'as pale as a sheet' (lit. piece of lime); *mor hauð a tǝnny ḷa:u hyd ǝ gwynab*, 'as easy as winking'; (*gan mod i*) *mor hy: a govyn*, 'if I may make so bold as to ask'; *r y: va:θ a vi:* (*mi:*, *vinna*, *minna*), 'the same as I'; *daχi gǝstal kǝmro a vinna*, 'you are as good a Welshman as I am'. (b) before finite verbs. (Here *a* stands for ac+a, relative. Cf. W.B. col. 22. 20. kymeint ac a ercheist): *dim n agos kimmint a vǝða*, 'not nearly as many as there used to be'; *kǝntad a ·vǝðuχi m barod*, 'as soon as you are ready'. (c) before a clause: *t ǝdi r ta:n dim ǝŋ kǝnna kǝstal a pen vy:ð ǝ du:yð ǝn sy:χ*, 'the fire does not light so well as when the weather is dry'.

III. 'with'. In Old and Mid. Welsh 'a', 'ac'; in Mod. Welsh generally 'â', 'ag'. (a) expressing instrumentality: *tori a fiadyr*, 'to cut with a scythe'; *hiro sģidja a saim*, 'to grease boots';—after *gnĕyd:—be daχi wedi nĕyd a vo: (hɛvo vo)?*, 'what have you done with it?' (b) 'in company with, together with', used with verbs of motion to express bringing or taking: *dɵuχ a vo: i laur*, 'bring it down'; *mi a: i a vo: n i o:l*, 'I will take it back'; *do:s a vo: ļe Ќeïsti o*, 'take it back where you found it'; *Ќeɾuχ a glo: i vɔny ɔ grifa*, 'take some coal upstairs'. (c) in phrases like *i fur a vo:*, 'away he went'; *adra a vo:*, etc. (d) with certain verbs as *kwarvod*, 'to meet'; *ka:yl madal*, 'to get rid (of)'; *meθy*, 'to fail'; *pĕidjo*, 'to cease', as *pĕidjuχ a kɔboli (χɔboli)*, 'do not talk nonsense'; *daχi wedi kal madal a χ annuyd?*, 'have you got rid of your cold?'; *mi veθis a χa:l*, 'I failed to get'. (e) with certain adverbs as *bron*, *digon*, *dʒest*, *gwastad*, *kuderbyn (kɔverbyn)*, etc., q.v. Cf. also *ġid a*.

a, relative, a, D., 'who, which'. Scarcely used in popular speech, except in proverbs and a few other stereotyped expressions. It usually, however, leaves its trace in the mutation of the verb as *hɔnny na:θ i*, '(it is) this (which) she did'. When the omitted words are 'a'i' (i. e. relative +'ei' = 'his', 'her', 'it') there is no mutation, e. g. *hɔnny kodoð o*, '(it is) this (which) caused it'. Where literary 'a'i' or 'a'u' would occur before a verb beginning with a vowel, *h* is prefixed to the verb, as *ɾvo: horðroð hi*, '(it is) he (who) ordered it'.—Examples of *a* are: *beθ bɔnnag a neuχi (= beθ bɔnnag neuχi)*, 'whatever you do'; *mɵurθ a la:ð, ebriļ a vliŋ* (prov.), 'March slays, April flays'; *ɾ hɛ:n a u:yr a r ivaŋk a dɔbja* (prov.), 'the old man knows, and the young man thinks (he knows)'; *dy:n a i helpo!*, 'God help him!'; *dy:n a i stɔrjo!*, 'poor fellow!' (lit. 'may God consider him').

a, interj., ah, D., s.v. 'ehem'; 'ah!'

abal, adj., abyl, W.S.; abl, D.; cf. D.G. ccxxxix. 10; 'able': *dy:n abal*, 'able man' (= *gaļy:oġ*); *dim ɔn abal i ɔnniļ i tammad*, 'not able to earn their living'.

abar, s., aber, D., 'confluence'. Except in place-names this word is only used by fishermen, etc., when referring to the mouth of the river Saint at Carnarvon, e. g. *kɾöisi ɾ abar*.

abuyd, s.m., abwyd, D. (1) 'a bait for catching fish or setting a trap'; *may o wedi mynd a ɾ abuyd i ġi:d*, 'it (the fish) has carried off the whole bait'; *gosod abuyd i ðal ļuynog*, 'to set a trap for a fox'. (2) 'lugworms' (Arenicola piscatoria). Two varieties are distinguished, *abuyd dy:* and *abuyd ļu:yd*, the difference in colour depending on the nature of the shore; *abuyd melys*, 'large worms found in the sand of the sea-shore and used as bait' (Eunice sanguinea). (3) 'shred, particle, vestige': *t o:s na ðim abud o hono vo, may o wedi mynd*, 'there is not a trace of him, he has gone'; *mi gɔmmis i ðu:y valwan ðy: a dɔmma vi n dgobjo nu nes o:ð na ðim abuyd o ·honynu* (O.H.), 'I took two slugs and squashed them (in my hands) until there was not a whole particle of them left' (as a remedy for warts).—Cf. T.N. 169. 37.

a:d (I.W.; O.H.), *aid* (E.J.), *ja:d* (J.J.; W.H.), s.m., iâd, D., 'the vault of the head'.

adag, s.f., pl. *adega*, adeg, D., 'time, a stated time or season'; *r y:n adag daχi ŋ kɔmmyd brekwast vory ?*, 'will you have breakfast at the same time to-morrow?'; *adag ǩinjo, adag ie:*, 'dinner time, tea time'; *mi ðo:θ o r y:n adag a χi:*, 'he came the same time as you'; *t öyðun i ðim ɔŋ gubod pa: adag o:yð i, na ḷe: r öyðun i, na dim by:d*, 'I didn't know what time it was, nor where I was, nor anything'; *r adag ma vory*, 'this time to-morrow'; *daχi wedi penny r adag ?*, 'have you settled the time?'; *ar ɔr adag honno*, 'at that time'; *daχi ŋ gweld ɔr adag ɔn hi:r ?*, 'does the time seem long to you?'; *ma r adag ɔm paʃo ŋ gynt uθ i mi ðu:ad i ðëyd strëyon*, 'the time passes quicker when I come and tell stories'; *adag ·a·nivir jaun ar ɔ vluyðyn*, 'a very unpleasant time of year'; *may m buru ar adega*, 'it is raining at intervals'.

adan, s.f., adain, D., but aden, s.v. 'ala'—pl. *adenyð*: (1) 'wing' (but *asgaḷ* is commoner); *adenyð plug*, 'the feathers of a plug' (in slate-quarrying, etc.). (2) 'fin'. (3) = *stɔlan bri:ð*, 'mould-board of a plough'. (4) pl. *edyn, hedyn*, 'spoke'. (O. H. always uses this word, but *sboksan* is more generally employed.)

adar, s.pl., sing. *deryn*, m., adar, D., 'birds': *adar (ɔ) to:*, 'sparrows'; *adar (ɔr) ëira*, 'fieldfares (Turdus pilaris)'; *deryn korf = dɔḷy:an*, 'owl'; *deryn buŋ*, 'aderyn y bwn' 'bittern' (but remembered only as in use long ago as a term of reproach. O.H.); *adar penwaig*, applied to terns of all species = *gwenoljad ɔ mo:r*; *deryn sglɔvëyθys*, 'bird of prey'; *adar di:arθ*, 'migratory birds'; *deryn ɔn sevyḷ ar ɔ vrigan*, 'a bird sitting on the branch'; *mɔn deryn*, expletive; *gweḷ y:n deryn meun ḷa:u na day meun ḷu:yn* (prov.), 'a bird in the hand is worth two in the bush'; *ḷa:ð day ðeryn ag y:n erǵid* (prov.), 'to kill two birds with one stone'; *ma na adar dy:on ɔm ṃho:b tɔluyθ* (prov.), 'there are black sheep in every family'.

adëiljad, s.m., adeilad, D., s.v. 'aedificium'; 'building' (semi-literary = *bildin*).

adëiljady, v., adeiladu, D., s.v. 'aedifico'; 'to build' (semi-literary = *bildjo*).

adloð, s.m., adladd, D., 'aftermath'.

adnod, s.f., pl. *adnoda*, adnod, D., 'verse of the Bible': *plɔgy r adnod i r drevn*, 'to twist a verse of the Bible to make it fit the system'.

adra, adv., adref, D., 'home; at home': *mynd adra*, 'to go home'; *ədi o adra ?*, 'is he at home?'; *taly r exuyn adra*, 'to retaliate' = *taly r pu:yθ ən o:l.*

aduy, s.f., pl. *aduya, aduyon*, adwy, D., 'gap', e.g. for a way to pass through; *aduy i lidjart*, 'a gap for a gate'; *tori aduy i vildjo ty:*, 'to take down a piece of wall or hedge to build a house'; *kay aduy boljon, gnëyd aduy wry:sg*, 'to close a gap by means of fixing stakes in the ground and twining branches between them'. Fig. *may o əm mho:b aduy*, 'he is to be depended upon in any emergency'. Cf. *bulx.*

aduyθ, s.m., adwyth, D., 'hurt, disease': *ma: riu aduyθ arno vo ; may o wedi ka:l riu aduyθ.*

adyn, s.m., adyn, D., 'a poor wretch, a pitiable creature': *wedi ka:yl i adal ən y:n adyn ar i ben i hy:n ; adyn tryenys.*

aða, Adda, 'Adam'. *aða ǵ eva* (i.e. 'Adam and Eve'), a plant-name (O.H.). I am informed that this term is applied here to 'monkshood' (Aconitum Napellus), but in Anglesey it is applied to the 'cuckoo-pint' (Arum maculatum), and in S. Carnarvonshire to the 'early purple orchis' (Orchis mascula); *maip aða*, 'the roots of the black bryony' (Tamus communis); *dagra aða*, 'Sedum sieboldi'.

aðewid, s.f., addewid, D., 'promise': *tori, kadu aðewid*, 'to break, keep a promise'. Cf. *gaðo.*

aðod, addod, D.—*u:y aðod*, 'nest egg' (I.W.).

aðoli, v., addoli, D., 'adore, admire highly': *du i n lëikjo ka:l v aðoli*, 'I like to be admired'.

aðuyn, adj., addfwyn, D.; addwyn, W.Ll. liv. 89, 'gentle': *aðuyn vel o:yn.*

aðvad, adj., comp. *aðvettax*, addfed, D., 'ripe'.

aðvedy, v., addfedu, D., 'to ripen'.

afliu ; wafliu (O.H. frequently), s., affliw, S.E., 'shred, particle': *du i wedi losgi vo i gi:d, t o:s na ðim afliu o hono vo*, 'I have burnt it all, there is not a shred of it left'; *tori rubaθ ən afliu ;—dim afliu o wyni*, 'not a breath of wind'; *t o:ð o ðim əm brivo r y:n afliu*, 'it did not hurt in the slightest'; *t o:ð na ðim afliu o hono vo*, 'there were no signs of him (he had absolutely disappeared)'.

agan, s.f., pl. *aǵenna*, agen, D.. 'a natural cleft, e.g. in a rock or in the earth': *may o wedi tori agan ar i la:u*, 'he has cut his hand open'. Also *hagan* (O.H.).

agor, agoryd, v., agori, D., but egoryd, agor, s.v. 'aperio'. Fut. S. 1. *gora*, 2. *gori*, 3. *goriθ.* Pl. 1. *goran*, 2. *gorux*, 3. *goran.* Pret. *goris* (no pl.). Imperative, *agor ; gorux*, 'to open (in all senses)'. *agor dru:s, fenast, boks*, 'to open a door, window, box'; *agor ki:l dru:s*, 'to put a door ajar'; *agor ke:g*, 'to gape';

lǫŋ wedi agor ṭruiði, ' a ship completely split open '; *lǫŋ wedi agor ɔn ðu:y,* ' a ship split in two '; *mi goroð ɔ pot ɔn ðay,* ' the pot came in two '.

agor, s.m., pl. *agoryð,* (in slate quarries) ' the opening of a bargain ' : *y:n medrys o r agor i r kar,* ' a workman who is skilled in all the operations of a slate quarry (from the opening of a bargain to the tipping of the rubbish) '.

agorad, gorad, adj., agored, D., ' open ' : *weḷ i χi bẽidjo gadal ɔ fenast ɔn agorad,* ' you had better not leave the window open '; *ḷoft agorad,* ' loft open to the air '; *gaduχ ɔ dru:s ɔŋ ġi:l gorad,* ' leave the door ajar '; *ḷɔdan gorad,* ' wide open '; *hu:χ gorad = hu:χ vagy,* ' brood sow '.

agos, adv., comp. *(a)gosaχ,* agos, D., ' near, close; nearly ' : *isía, mynd, ɔn agos i r ta:n,* ' to sit, go, near the fire '; *mi vasa hɔnny n agosaχ i r gwi:r,* ' that would be nearer the truth '; *ɔn agos i bymp,* ' nearly five (o'clock) '; *er s n agos i ðu:y vlɔnað,* ' since nearly two years '; *planny n ṛhy: agos,* ' to plant too close '; *dim n agos kɔsial fort o wẽiθjurs,* ' not nearly such good workmen '.

ai, ai, D. (1) interrogative particle. Very often used in the expression *ai ˈjeʹl,* ' really!', ' you don't mean it!', e.g. *du i n mynd vory.* Ans. *ai ˈje!* Sometimes occurs also before nouns and adjectives as : *ai kany may o ?,* ' is he singing?'; *ai ko:χ di o ?,* ' is it red?', to express emphasis instead of the ordinary *ɔdi o ŋ kany,* etc. It is, however, far more often omitted in such cases. (2) in dependent questions, ' whether', in sentences of the form : *on i ðim ɔŋ gubod ai ˈrvo: o:yð o,* ' I did not know whether it was he '. (3) conj. representing the second ' ai ' in ' naill ai . . . ai ', Lat. ' an ', used only with *pẽidjo* to express ' orʹnot ' after ' whether' : *wyða hi ðim o:ð o ɔmma ai pẽidjo (fẽidjo),* ' she did not know whether he was here or not '.

ail, adj., ail, D., ' second ' : *ail u:r, ail wraig,* ' second husband, second wife '; *bo:b ɔn ail,* ' alternately ' (Anglo-Welsh, ' every other '); *bo:b ɔn ail durnod,* ' every other day '. Prefixed to verbs to express repetition of an action, e.g. ·*ail ·dri:o,* ' to try again '; ·*ail·dummo,* ' to warm up again '; ·*ail·nëyd,* ' to make again ', etc., e. g. *wedi ail i nëyd,* ' made over again '; *ṛhaid i mi ·ail·nëydʹo vory,* ' I must cook it again to-morrow '; *wedi ·ail·ga:l annuyd,* ' to have caught cold again '; *wedi ail i ga:l o,* ' to have caught it again '.

·*ail·veðul,* v., ' to change one's mind '.

ais, s.pl., sing. *ẽisan,* f., ais, D., ' laths, esp. those to which slates are attached on a roof, and which themselves are attached to the *sbarailf.*

akkar, s.m.f., pl. *aǩeri,* acr, T.N. 9. 39, ' acre ' : *akkar o di:r,* ' an acre of land '; *akkar o wair (di:r gwair),* ' an acre of hay '.

akku, when enclitic *aku, əku, ku,* adv. accw, D., 'there, yonder': *ə iy: akku daχi n veðul ?,* 'is it *that* house you mean?'; *·əluχi ə ·ty: aku ?,* 'do you see that house?'; *akku əm maŋgor,* 'over in Bangor'; *ə ru:m i vəny ku,* 'the room upstairs there'; *be sy ·g̣in ti ku ?,* 'what have you got there?'　　Often equivalent to 'at home': *syt ma: r tẽyly aku ?,* 'how are you all at home?'

ak·sẽis, s., 'exercise'.

aksẽiſo, v. (1) 'to exercise, drill'. (2) 'to challenge, incite by throwing the arms about', etc.: *aksẽiſo dy:n i gufjo,* 'to incite a man to fight'.

aksis, s., acsus, G.O. ii. 194. 21, Eng. (Dial.) access. Cf. Fr. accès. Only in the exp. *kṛənny r aksis,* 'a fit of the ague'. Cf. *kṛy:d.*

a:χ, s., pl. *aχa; ja:χ,* pl. *jaχa* (O.H.) ach, D.; iach C.C.M. 90. 24; 385. 26; G.R. 9. 10, generally used in the plural: 'origin, antecedents'. *·tasaχi ŋ gubod i haχa ·vasaχi ðim ən tṛoi n i my::sg,* 'if you knew their antecedents you would not associate with them'; *holi aχa vo,* 'to inquire about his antecedents'.

aχ, interjection implying disgust: *aχ (ə) boχi!* (used in speaking to children).

aχan, sometimes for *vaχgan,* 'my lad'.

aχlod, s.f., achlod, T.N. 322. 15, only in the interjection *r aχlod ·vaur!* implying surprise = nearly, *di:ar annul!*

aχlyst, s., achlust, R., 'report, vague rumour': *ka:l aχlyst = ka:l riu ꞵugrym, riu grap.*

aχos, s.m.; pl. *aχoſon,* achos, D., 'cause': *heb raid nag aχos iðo nẽyd o,* 'without any cause or necessity for him to do so'; *t o:s dim aχos i χi gwyno am mo:d i n hu:yr heno,* 'you have no cause for complaint because I am late to-night';—also in religious sense: *gweˑði:o am luɪðjant ar ər aχos,* 'to pray for success for the cause'.

Conj., 'because': *ma:y y:n o r sgoljon wedi χay aχos bo:d ə vre:χ go:χ o gumpas,* 'one of the schools has been closed because there are measles about'; *aχos bod nu ŋ kay gwẽiθjo,* 'because they won't work'. Cf. R.B. 114. 14; L.A. 158. 4.

aχosi, v., achosi, S.E., 'to cause'.

aχuyn, v., achŵyn, D., s.v. 'queritor'. Pret. *χuinis, χunis,* 'to tell tales': *ma: r plant ən aχuyn ə nail̥ ar ə lal̥,* 'the children tell tales about one another'; *ka:l bara me:l am aχuyn,* 'to get bread and honey for telling tales'; *pẽidjuχ aχuyn arno vo,* 'don't split on him'.

aχyb, v., achub, D. Pret. S. (1) *χibis,* (2) *χibist,* (3) *χyboð.* Pl. 3 *χyboson.* Imperative *χyba.* (1) 'to seize': *aχyb ə kəvlẽystra,* 'to seize the opportunity'; *aχyb ə bla:yn,* 'to anticipate, forestall'; *aχyb bla:yn ə r̥heuja,* 'to forestall the frost'; *aχyb i gam,* 'to defend oneself' *ne:s i aχyb ə ŋham hevo vo*, 'I defended myself from him (e.g. by striking first)'. (2) 'to save': *aχyb i vɐwyd*, 'to save his life'.

alarχ, s.m., pl. *elyrχ*, alarch, D., 'swan'.

ali, s., alei, W.S. [alley] 'passage between seats in a chapel'.

aljokar, s., 'yellow-ochre'.

altṛad, s.m., 'alteration'.

altṛo, v., altro, C.C. 88. 15; T.N. 187. 27, 'to alter, change' (either for good or bad): *may r dɐwyð wedi altṛo hëïðju—am la:u*, 'the weather has changed to-day—for rain'; *may o wedi altṛo n aru*, 'he has changed very much'; *altṛo i su:n*, 'to change its sound'.

aḷan, adv., allan, D., 'out': *mynd aḷan*, 'to go out'; *may o aḷan*, 'he is out'; *o:ð aḷan*, 'on the outside'; *aḷan o le:*, 'out of place, wrong', e.g. *ma na rubaθ aḷan o le:*;—*aḷan o r golug*, 'out of sight'; *ty: χwïθig aḷan*, 'wrong side out'.

a:ḷi [ga:ḷi].

aḷtidio, v., alldudiaw, C.Ch. 46. 5; alltudo, D., 'in exilium pellere'. Used as a threat with no definite meaning attached: *mi aḷtidja i di os gnëï di o* (O.H.).

am, prep., am. With pronouns: S. 1. *am dana (i)*, 2. *am ·danaí(i)*, 3. *am dano (vo)*, *am dani (hi)*. Pl. 1. *am ·danon(i)*, *am ·danan(i)*, 2. *am ·danoχ(i)*, *am ·danaχ(i)*, 3. *am ·danyn(u)*. Followed by the vocalic mutation, except in *am byθ*.

1. 'around, round': *klɔmmy am*, 'to twist round (of a creeping plant)'; *tɔnny ə kṛo:yn o:ð am rubaθ*, 'to take the skin or peel off something'; *mi ro:θ o bappyr am ə lyvr*, 'he put paper round the book'.—Esp. with regard to articles of clothing: *may hi ŋ gwisgo am dani*, 'she is getting dressed'; *rhaid i ni wisgo am danan*, 'we must get dressed'; *rhoid sgïdja am ə ṇrha:yd*, 'to put boots on'; *rhɐuχ ɔχ kap am ɔχ pen*, 'put your cap on'; *tɔnny ŋho:t o:ð am dana*, 'to take my coat off'; *mi dɔnnis i golar o:ð am i uðu vo*, 'I took his collar off'.

2. 'on the other side of': *may o m byu am ə parad a vi:*, 'he lives next door to me'; *am ə for a ni:*, 'on the other side of the road to us'.

3. 'about, concerning, of': *·glu:soχi so:n am dano vo ?*, 'have you heard (speak) of him?'; *dëyd ə gwi:r am dano vo*, 'to tell the truth about him'.

4. 'with regard to': *may o n lukkys am waiθ*, 'he is lucky with regard to (getting) work'; *r o:ð ɔn ḷe: da jaun am y:n pe:θ*, 'it was a very good place for one thing'. Cf. also the adjectives *·ano·bëïθjol am*, 'in despair at'; *garu am*, 'fond of, great at'; *ha:yl am*,

'generous with'; *ɑ̇a: am*, 'good at'; *wa:yθ am ɑ̇ano vo*, 'never mind'.

5. 'at (of time)': *am ꝺay* (*o r glo:χ*), 'at two (o'clock)'; *am vaint o r glo:χ ·gəmmuχi de: ?*, 'at what time will you have tea?'

6. 'for, for the space of (referring to time)': *am ɑ̇riꝺja*, 'for three days'; *gwëiłjuχ am vynyꝺ*, 'wait a minute'; *am vaint* (*ə*) *pariθ o etto ?*, 'how much longer will it last?'; *am byθ*, 'for ever'.

7. 'for, for the distance of': *mi auni am viłtir etto*, 'we will go (for) another mile'. Cf. *mynd am ɑ̇ro:*, 'to go for a walk'.

8. 'for' (of a number of times): *am ə ṭro: kənta.*

9. 'for' (of price): *be ɑ̇aχi ŋ godi am ə r̥hëi n ?*, 'how much do you charge for these?'

10. 'for, in exchange for, instead of': *ga: i ꝺay χwe:χ am su:łt ?*, 'may I have two sixpences for a shilling?'; *ka:l bara me:l am aχuyn*, 'to get bread and honey for telling tales'; *be di r kəm·ra:ig am . . . ?*, 'what is the Welsh for . . .?'

11. 'for' (indicating direction): *mynd am i garṭra*, 'to make for home'; *ṭroi i vəny am ə wla:d*, 'to turn up (out of a high road), to get into the country'; *mynd am vaŋgor*, 'to make for Bangor'.

12. without a verb of motion, implying a desire of getting something or of going somewhere, expressed sometimes in English by 'for', as 'are you for London?' = *ɑ̇aχi am lyndan ?*; *ɑ̇aχi am egluys, am gappal ?*, 'are you going to church, to chapel?'; *vel ka:θ am levriθ*, 'like a cat after milk'; *ɑ̇aχi am χwanag ?*, 'are you going to have some more?' (lit., 'are you for more').

13. followed by a verb, 'about to': *may hi am vuru*, 'it is going to rain'; *ɑ̇aχi am vynd ałan ?*, 'are you going out?'; *ɑ̇aχi am ꝺenig hëiꝺju ?*, 'are you off anywhere to-day?'; *t o:yd ne:b am venṭro*, 'no one would venture'.

14. without a verb expressed, implying an occurrence impending, especially in connexion with the weather: *may hi am la:u*, 'there's rain coming'; *may hi am χwanag o ëira*, 'there's more snow coming'; *may hi am ꝺurnod po:yθ*, 'it's going to be a hot day'.

15. 'for, for the purpose of': *pe:θ garu əɑ̇i darłan am godi if'o kəsgy*, 'reading is a dreadful thing for making one sleepy'; *mi ꝺo:θ o am venθig kəłaθ*, 'he came to borrow a knife'; *am ə gora*, 'in emulation' (Fr. 'à qui mieux mieux', Anglo-Welsh, 'for the best'), e. g. *r̥hedag ᴣno am ə gora*, 'to see who can get there first'; *mynd am ora ra:s hevo mi*, 'to run a race with me'; so also :—*gwëiꝺi am ər yχa*, 'to shout in emulation; to see who can shout the loudest'; *χwara am ə sala*, 'to play a rotten game'.

16. 'for, as far as concerns': *ta wa:yθ am hənny*, 'for the matter of that'; 'if that is anything' (lit. if it were worse as concerns that); *am un i*, 'as far as I know, for (what) I know'.

17. 'at the risk of': *kovja am də vəwyd !* 'mind you remember' (i.e. if you value your life).

18. 'because of': *am* (*ə*) *mo:d i n meꝺul*, 'because I thought';—

also used as a conjunction before *na*(*d*)—*am na vedrun ðu:ad ǝŋ gyní*, 'because I could not come sooner'.

19. with *ben*, 'over; at': *r o:ð hi n tavly du:r am ǝ ṃhenni*, 'she was pouring water over me'; *χwerθin am i benno*, 'to laugh at him'; *gnëyd sbort, ka:l hu:yl am i benno*, 'to make fun of him'.

20. after certain nouns as *di:olχ am*, 'thanks for'; *ovn am*, 'fear for', etc.

21. after certain verbs difficult to classify, as *·aŋ·hovjo am*, 'to forget about'; *dëyd uθ ru:in am . . .*, 'to tell somebody to . . .'; *disgul am*, 'to wait for'; *edraχ am*, 'to see (some one), to call upon, to look for'; *galu am*, 'to call for'; *gobëiθjo am*, 'to hope for'; *govaly am*, 'to take care of'; *govyn am*, 'to ask for'; *govyn i ru:in am . . .*, 'to ask some one to . . .'; *gwe·ði:o am*, 'to pray for'; *gweld bai am*, 'to blame for'; *gweld ǝ werðon am*, 'to wait long for, to long for'; *hirëyθy am*, 'to long for'; *kovjo am*, 'to remember about'; *χwiljo am*, 'to look for'; *morol am*, 'to bear in mind to'; *meðul am*, 'to think of', etc.

ambaḷ, adj. and adv., ambell, D., s.v. 'rarus'; 'now and then, occasionally' (but always with a substantive): *ambaḷ i ðy:n*, 'here and there a man'; *ambaḷ* (*i*) *dro:*, 'occasionally'; *ambaḷ y:n*, 'an occasional one'; *may hi m bra:v ambaḷ i ðurnod*, 'it is fine on occasional days'; *may hi n weḷ ambaḷ i usnos na i ǵilið*, 'it is better some weeks than others'; *may hi ŋ gnëyd ambaḷ i gavod*, 'there is a shower now and then'.

amdo, s.f., amdo, D., 'shroud'.

amðifin, v., amddiffyn, D. Fut. *amðifǝna*, 'to defend': *amðifin i blaid*, 'to stick up for his party'.

amðivad, adj., amddifad, D., s.v. 'orphanus'; 'destitute' (followed by the preposition *o*): *plentyn amðivad*, 'orphan'.

amðivady, v., amddifadu, D., s.v. 'orbo'; 'to deprive': *amðivady o jeχid, vǝwyd*.

amgorn, s.m., amgarn, D., 'a ring of metal round the handle of a scythe or knife where the blade meets it; round the end of the handle of a hammer; round the tip of a cow's horn', etc.; also 'ferrule': *amgorn ar vla:yn fon*.

am·hëyaθ, s.m., ammheuaeth, D., s.v. 'dubitatio'; 'doubt': *t o:s na ðim am·hëyaθ am dano vo*, 'there is no doubt about it'; *meun am·hëyaθ*, 'in doubt'.

am·hëys, adj., ammheus D., s.v. 'dubitosus'; 'doubtful': *may o n am·hëys o hona i*, 'he is doubtful of me'; *r o:ð o n ðistau, veḷy r o:ð o n am·hëys ·gǝnonu*, 'he was quiet, so they did not know what to make of him'.

·am·hosib, adj., ammhosibl, D., s.v. 'impossibilis'; 'impossible'.

·am·hosi·bilruyð, s.m., 'impossibility'.

amkan, s.m.; pl. *amkanjon*, amcan, D., (1) 'purpose, object':
ma: ǵin i riu amkan i vynd, 'I have some object in going'; *be
o:ð ʔχ amkan uθ vynd ?*, 'what was your object in going?'; *mynd
ʔno dan ʔr amkan o i weld o*, 'to go there with the object of seeing
him'; *may o wedi drʔsy ʔn i amkanjon bʔdol*, 'his affairs have
become embarrassed'; *wedi meθy i amkan*, 'to have failed in one's
object'. (2) 'conjecture, guess, inkling': *ma: ǵin i riu amkan pu:y
sy wedi ʔry o*, 'I have some idea who sent it'; *·uyδoχi amkan le
ma:y o ?*, 'have you any conjecture as to where it is?'. (3) 'conjecturing faculty': *amkan ʔ tᵣaur ʔdi i lʔgad o*, 'the conjecturing
faculty of the ploughman is in his eye'; so also *amkan go:*; *ʔ go:
ʔꬶ gwëïθjo uθ i amkan*; *amkan lʔgad*.

amkanys, adj., amcanus, M.A. ii, 255. 39, 'resourceful, deft':
may o n rëit amkanys, 'he has a very good idea how to set about
things', said e.g. of a beginner = *sǵilgar*.

amlug, adj., amlwg, D. (1) 'clear, evident': *may n amlug jaun
hëïðju*, 'it is very clear to-day' (of an object); *gweld ʔn amlug*, 'to
see clearly'; *may n amlug (= eglyr) i mi*, 'it is clear to me':
klu:ad ʔn amlug, 'to hear clearly'. (2) 'exposed': *le: amlug*; *le:
amlug i r gwynt*. Cf. G.R. 3. 12.

amlʔgy, v., amlygu, D. (1) 'to explain, make plain': *·vedruχi
amlʔgy vi ?* (for 'i mi'), 'can you enlighten me?' (2) 'to dis-
close': *paid ti amlʔgy dim am ʔ pe:θ du i n i δëyd*.

amma, v., ammau, D., s.v. 'dubito'. Pret. *amhëyis*. (1) 'to
doubt': *t ʔdu i δim ʔn amma na nëïθ i glirjo*, 'I don't doubt it will
clear up'; *t ʔdu i δim ʔn amma na gnëyd ʔn jaun δary o*, 'I don't
doubt he did right'; *t ʔdu i δim ʔn amma na nëïθ o m ono vo*, 'I
don't doubt he will not do it'.—With a person as direct object:
may o n v amma i, 'he doubts me'. (2) 'to suspect, expect,
imagine': *r ʔdu i n amma*, 'I dare say it is', 'I expect it is'.

ammal, adv., aml, D., comp. *amlaχ*, 'often': *may hi n diguð
ʔn ammal vely*, 'it often happens so'; *dʔna be glu:χi amla*, 'that's
what you hear most often', 'that is the expression generally used';
ᵣhan amla, 'for the most part'.

ammod, s.f., ammod, D. (1) 'agreement, covenant, condition':
gnëyd ammod i nëyd rubaθ, 'to make an agreement to do something': *ar ʔr ammod o δu:ad (iδo vo δu:ad) ʔn o:l am u:yθ*, 'on
condition of his coming back at eight'; *ammod pᵣjodas*, 'promise
of marriage'; *tori ammod pᵣjodas*, 'breach of promise'. (2) used
of a cow expected to calve: *ammod byuχ i δu:ad a lo:;—pᵣy:d may
i hammot i ?*, 'when is she expected to calve?'; *may hi bron ar
ben i hammod*. Cf. D.G. cx. 5.

ammuys, adj., amwys, D., 'ambiguous, equivocal': *riu air
ammuys ʔdi o*, 'it is an ambiguous expression', e. g. it need not
necessarily be taken in a bad sense. Also of persons: *dy:n*

ammuys jaun ədi o, dislau, ar i ben i hy:n, 'he is a man you can make nothing of, quiet, keeping to himself'.

ammyd, s., amyd, D., 'far, frumentum'; only in *bara ammyd*, explained by J.J. as bread made of wheat or barley as distinguished from that made of oats or rye.

amrant, s.f., pl. *amranta*, amrant, D., 'eyelid'.

amriu, amryw, D., 'several': *amriu o ëirja*.

amsar, s.m. (but *r amsar hunnu, honno*, or *hənny*), pl. *amsera, amseroð*, amser, D., 'time': *na i ðarļan o peŋ ga: i amsar*, 'I will read it when I have time'; *ə mhen amsar*, 'after a certain time'; *ma: r amsar dgest i ben*, 'the time is just up'; *may amsar garu*, 'there is plenty of time'; *vaint o amsar nëiθ o bara ?*, 'how long will it last ?'; *amsar kinjo*, 'dinner time'; *ar o:l i amsar*, 'late'; *o vla:yn i amsar*, 'early'; *i r amsar*, 'punctual', e.g. *daχi i r amsar hëiðju*, 'you are punctual to-day'; *mi ðo:θ ən þgad i amsar*, 'he came at the nick of time'; *bo:b amsar*, 'always', e.g. *may r vre:χ go:χ əŋ gadal rubaθ ar i ho:l bo:b amsar*, 'measles always leave some effect behind them'.

an-, an-: a negative prefix always bearing full stress. Before another 'n' the 'n' is doubled when the word is pronounced with unusual emphasis, as ·*an·nivir*,—otherwise ·*a·nivir*.

ana, s.m., anaf, D., 'deformity': ·*vəðanu ŋ kəmmyd ne:b a riu ana no vo*, 'they take no one who has any deformity'; *may ana arno vo er i enedigaθ*, 'he is deformed from birth'.

anadl, s.f., anadl, D., 'breath' (more often expressed by *gwynt*).

anadly, v., anadlu, D., 'to breathe'.

anair, s.m., anair, D., 'calumny': *rhoid anair i ru:in*, 'to calumniate some one, to blacken some one's character'.

·*an·ammal*, adv., anaml, D., s.v. 'raro'; 'seldom': *əm by:r* ·*an·ammal*, 'very seldom'.

·*ana·tirjol*, adj., annaturiol, C.C.M. 157. 31, 'unnatural'.

anavys, adj., anafus, D., 'painful': *ma nu n anavys jaun*; *ədi o n anavys jaun ġin ti ?* Cf. *navod, navy*.

andros, s., andras, D.G. ccxx. 42, mild equivalent of *djaul*, 'deuce': *mynd vel ər andros*, 'to go like the deuce'; *χwara r andros*, 'to play the deuce'; *ma r andros ən i gorði o*, 'the devil is in him'.

anduyo, v., amdwyo, M.Ll. i. 5. 1; and wyo, C.C. 148. 15; T.N. 47. 28; 138. 16 (Eng. 'undo'), 'to spoil, injure': *ma: r gwynt o:yr ma wedi handuyo nu*, 'this cold wind has spoilt them' (e.g. the flowers); *anduyo plentyn*, 'to spoil a child' = *dveθa plentyn hevo möyθa*.

anduyol, adj., andwyol, S.E., 'harmful, injurious': *ma na ðay be:θ ən anduyol i r y:d.*

·*a·neduyð*, ·*a·nəduyð*, adj., annedwydd, D., 'unpleasant, disagreeable', in the old saying *tṛi: fe:θ ·a·nəduyð—ty: məglyd, devni, gwraig riŋklyd* (O.H.), 'three disagreeable things—a smoky house, drops, and a scolding woman'. Cf. Prov. xxvii. 15; M.A. iii. 259 a. 31.

·*an·esmuyθ*, adj., anesmwyth, W.B. col. 59. 23. (1) 'uneasy, anxious': ·*an·esmuyθ ən və meðul ; mynd ən ·an·esmuyθ ar ə ŋhəunt i.* (2) 'uncomfortable': *kṛy:s ·an·esmuyθ.*

·*ane·smuyθo*, v., anesmwytho, R., 'to become uneasy, anxious'.

, ·*a·neθa*, adj., annethe, T. N. 4. 16; 73. 16; 405. 23; anneheu, D., s.v. 'sinister'; 'bungling' = *ḷəuχwiθ, χwiθog.*

·*an·favrjol*, adj., anffafriol, S.E.; anffafrol, C.C. 454. 31, 'unfavourable'.

·*anfor·tynys*, adj., anffortunus, S.E.*, 'unfortunate'. Seldom used = ·*an·lukkys.*

·*an·happys*, adj., anhappus, 2 Esd. xv. 59. Cf. D.G. cli. 15, 'unhappy'.

·*an·hebig*, adj., annhebyg, D., s.v. 'dissimilis'; 'unlike'.

·*an·hëïlum*, ·*an·hëïluŋ*, adj., annheilwng, D., s.v. 'indignus'. (1) 'dishonest': *mynd ən ·an·hëïlum a pe:θ.* (2) 'gained by dishonest means': *Ḱëinjog ·an·hëïlum ëïθ a du:y a hi:* (prov.), 'a penny dishonestly gained will take away two with it', i.e. 'honesty is the best policy'.

·*an·həustar*, s.m., anhawsder, D., 'difficulty'.

·*an·huyldab*, s.m., anhwyldeb, S.E. (1) 'a derangement of the functions of the body or mind': *riu ·an·huyldab oði vjaun iðo vo; ·an·huyldab ar ǵefyl.* (2) 'unpleasantness', e.g. such as might arise though a dispute: *pobol əŋ gnëyd ·an·huyldab ən ə gwaiθ.*

·*an·huylys*, ·*an·höylys*, adj., anhwylus, D. (1) 'difficult to manage or deal with': *dy:n, Ḱefyl ·an·huylys.* (2) said of tools, etc., which work badly: *gwëïθjo n ·an·huylys.* (3) 'inconvenient': *may n ·an·huylys jaun i mi vynd.* Cf. ·*aŋə·vlëys.*

·*an·hɔvryd*, adj., anhyfryd, D., s.v. 'insuavis'; 'unpleasant'.

·*a·niban*, adj., anniben, D., 'slow, dilatory': *Ḱerðad ən ·a·niban, ·a·niban ən dəsgy, ·a·niban i vynd i r kappal, gwëïθjo n ·a·niban ; —mendjo n ·a·niban,* 'to improve slowly (in health)'.

·*a·niðan*, adj., anniddan, D., s.v. 'illaetabilis'; 'dull, not entertaining': *dy:n ·a·niðan.*

·*a·niðig*, adj., anniddig, R., 'cross, bad-tempered, crabbed', esp. of children.

·a·niujol, adj., annuwiol, D., s.v. 'impius'; 'ungodly, profane'. Used also facetiously as an intensifying adverb as blï:n ·a·niujol, 'terribly peevish'.

anival, nival, s.m., pl. anivëiljad, nivëiljad, anifail, D., 'animal': may o vel nival, 'he is a brutish man'.

·a·nivir, adj., anifyrr, D., s.v. 'iniucundus'. (1) 'nasty, unpleasant': le ·a·nivir ar i ben i hy:n, 'an unpleasant lonely place'; durnod smit ·a·nivir, 'an unpleasant rainy day'; dy:n ·a·nivir, 'an unpleasant man'; = dy:n ka:s, dy:n blï:n. (2) 'uncomfortable (in mind)': o:n i n lëimlo n ·a·nivir jaun, 'I was feeling very uncomfortable'.

anjal, adj., anial, D., 'deserted, lonely': le: anjal.

anjaluχ, s.m., anialwch, D., 'wilderness', e.g. a place overgrown with trees in their wild state: dim ond anjaluχ a drɔsni; ko:yd ag anjaluχ. (Perhaps a scriptural reminiscence, but frequently used by O.H. Cf., however, the true popular form njaluχ.)

·anjo·δevol, adj., annioddefol, S.E., 'unbearable'.

·a·njolχgar, adj., anniolchgar, D., s.v. 'ingratus'; 'ungrateful'.

·an·luk, s.f., anlwcc, C.C.M. 43. 33, 'bad luck, mishap': ·an·luk o:yδ o.

·an·lukkys, adj., anlwccus, C.C.M. 451. 20, 'unlucky'.

·an·lɔgys, adj., anolyguś, D., s.v. 'indecens'; 'unsightly': bara ·di·olug, ·an·lɔgys; dy:n ·an·lɔgys ɔn dëbig i vugan brain, 'an ugly fellow like a scarecrow'.

·an·ɳhe:g, adj., annheg, M.A. i. 490 a. 28, 'unfair'.

annos, hannos, v., annos, D. (1) 'to set on': annos ki:. As compared with hɔfo, hannos ki: is to make a dog drive the sheep on (ɔn i blëyna) or away from some place, hɔfo is to make him catch hold of them (ga:l ɩδo vo gɔdjad ·ɔnynu). In the first case the dog barks, in the second he does not (O.H.). Cf. also kōiθi. (2) Also used of the act of driving, e.g. hannos nu alan o r ti:r pori, 'to drive them (by means of a dog) out of the pasture'.

·an·ɳrhevn, s., annhrefn, D., 'disorder'.

annuyd, s.m., annwyt, W.B. col. 6. 21; anwyd, D. (1) 'a cold': du i wedi ka:l annuyd (sometimes r annuyd), 'I have caught cold'; may o wedi ka:l annuyd ɔn o: drum, 'he has caught rather a bad cold'; annuyd ɔn i dru:yn, 'a cold in his nose'. (2) 'cold (generally)': krɔnny ǵin annuyd, 'to shiver with cold'; o:s naχi annuyd ?, 'are you cold?'

annuyl, adj., anwyl, D. (1) 'dear'. (2) 'pleasant, delightful, e.g. of weather'. (3) 'lovable, lovely': ma: na rubaθ annuyl jaun ɔn i forδ o. 'there is something very lovable in his ways': gwynab annuyl, 'a lovely face'. (4) with variations of the word dyu as an exclamation of surprise (cf. du lieber Gott!), *dyu annul!, dyuks annul!, di:ar annul!, pobol (bobol) annul!, ta:d annul!, taid annul!*, ' good gracious!' (The form in *u* occurs especially often in the last-named expressions.)

·*an·obaiθ*, s.m., anobaith, D., 'despair': *r ŏyδun i wedi mynd i ·an·obaiθ am ·danoχi*, 'I had begun to despair about you '.

·*ano·bëiθjo*, v., anobeithio, D., 'to despair'.

·*ano·bëiθjol*, adj., anobeithiol, D., 'hopeless': *wedi mynd ən ·ano·bëiθjol* (of a sick person), 'beyond hope of recovery'.

anoδ, hanoδ, adj., comp. *anos, ·an·hθuδaχ*, sup. *·an·hθuδa, ·an·hθusa*, anhawdd and anodd, D. (cf. anawd, L.A. 90. 26), 'difficult': *may kəm·ra:ig ən anos na fo:b jaiθ araḷ*, 'Welsh is more difficult than any other language'; *ma: n anoδ kodi ən ə bora*, 'it is difficult to get up in the morning'; *du i n anoδ ə ṃhḷeʃo*, 'I am difficult to please'; *anoδ tənny kast o he:n gefyl* (prov.), 'it is difficult to cure an old horse of tricks'; *anoδ tənny dy:n o:δ ar i dəluyθ* (prov.), 'what is bred in the bone will come out in the flesh'.

·*an·ʒhevnys*, adj., annhrefnus, D., 'disorderly; in disorder'.

·*an·ʒhëyθol*, adj., annhraethol, D., s.v. 'inenarrabilis'; 'inexpressible': *·an·rhëyθol o δry:d*, 'excessively dear'.

ansad, adj., ansad, S.E., 'unsteady' (e.g. of a vase): *ansad i veδul*, 'wavering of mind'.

·*ansa·θredig*, adj., ansathredig, S.E., *gëirja ·ansa·θredig*, ' out-of-the-way words'.

·*an·sbarθys*, adj., annosparthus, D. (1) 'turbulent' (of persons). (2) of something done in a rough, awkward, haphazard fashion: *tynnu gwla:n o:δ ar δavad ən ·an·sbarθys*.

·*anse·vədlog*, adj., ansefydlog, D., s.v. 'inconstans'; 'unsteady, unsettled': *ma: r dəwyδ ən ·anse·vədlog*, 'the weather is unsettled' = ·*an·wadal*.

·*an·stθwaḷt*, adj., anystywallt, D.; cf. also D., s.v. 'ferox', 'infrænus'; 'churlish, unmanageable': *dy:n ·an·stθwaḷt = anoδ i dri:n*.

·*an·stərjaθ*, s.m., anystyriaeth, B.C. 141. 4; 'thoughtlessness, heedlessness, inconsiderateness'.

·*an·stərjol*, adj., anystyriol, D., s.v. 'inconsiderans'; 'thoughtless, heedless, inconsiderate'. (Fr. étourdi.)

antirjaθ, s.f., anturiaeth, D., s.v. 'temeritas'; 'enterprise, venturesomeness, speculation': *antirjaθ i ventʒo pʒe:s*, 'venturesomeness in risking money'.

antirjo, v., anturio, D., 'to venture' = *mentʒo*: *antirjo i wla:d araḷ*, 'to go abroad as a speculation'.

antyr, s., antur, D., 'venture' in the phrase *ar antyr*, 'as a venture'.

anuydog, adj., anwydog, D., 'sensitive to cold'.

anuydys, anwydus, S.E., 'sensitive to cold'.

·*an·vantas*, s.f., anfantais, S.E.; anfontais, D.P.O. 30. 4, 'disadvantage'.

. ·*anvan·ïëiſol*, adj., anfanteisiol, S.E., 'disadvantageous'.

anvarθ, *anvaθ*, adj., sup. *verθa*, anferth, D., s.v. 'monstrum'; 'monstrous, enormous, terrible': *penſur anvaθ, gwynt a glaːu anvarθ, kaṛag vaur anvarθ ;—ṛ huːyl verθa weliſ i rïoːyd*, 'the greatest fun I ever saw'; *helynt verθa vyu*, 'a terrible row'.

·*an·vodlon*, adj., anfoddlawn, D., but anfodlon, s.v. 'offensus'; 'discontented'.

anvoð, s., anfodd, D., 'unwillingness' in phrase *o i anvoð*, 'against one's will'.

anvon, v., anfon, D., s.v. 'mitto'. Pret. S. *anvonis*, etc. No plural. Plup. *anvonsun*. Imperative S. 2. *anvon*. (1) 'to send' (more often *gṛy*). (2) 'to take, accompany' (Anglo-Welsh 'to send'): *anvon ruːin i r steſon*, 'to take some one to the station'.

·*an·wadal*, adj., anwadal, D., 'inconstant, changeable': *tuːyð ·an·wadal gwyːl̥t*, 'stormy, unsettled weather'; *dyːn ·an·wadal ṇ i waiθ*.

·*an·warað*, adj., anwaraidd, S.E., 'savage, uncivilized; wild (e.g. of untrained horses); brutal (e.g. of one who illtreats animals)'. (J.J., O.H., frequently.)

·*an·wedig*, adj., enwedig, D., s.v. 'praesertim'; anwedig, H.S. 25. 4; G.R. (3). 5; 57. 3: *ṇ ·an·wedig*, 'especially'.

·*an·wirað*, s.m., anwiredd, D., s.v. 'iniquitas'; 'falsehood, lie': *dëyd ·an·wirað* = *dëyd k̯eluyð*.

·*anwy·bodaθ*, s.f., anwybodaeth, D., s.v. 'inscitia'; 'ignorance'.

·*anwy·bodol*, adj., ? anymwybodol, S.E.; 'unconscious': *mi aːθ o n ·anwy·bodol o hono i hyːn*, 'he became unconscious'.

·*anwy·bodys*, adj., anwybodus, R.B. II. 392. 20, 'ignorant'.

·*anwy·bəðys*, adj., anwybyddus, S.E., 'unconscious': ·*anwy·bəðys o hono i hyːn* (O.H.).

·*an·yvyð*, adj., anufudd, D., s.v. 'inobsequens'; 'disobedient'.

·*anṇ·mynol*, adj., annymunol, S.E., 'unpleasant', esp. of persons; *dyːn ·anṇ·mynol* = *dyːn kaːs*.

anṇnad, adj., anynad, D., 'peevish, morose, crabbed' (understood, but seldom used).

aŋa, s.m., angau, D., 'death'. As distinguished from *marwolaθ*, *aŋa* is generally death more or less personified, but not always, e. g. *mi ðo:θ i aŋa ən sədyn jaun*. Cf. *marwolaθ*.

aŋal, s.m., pl. *aŋəljon*, angel, D., 'angel'.

aŋan, s.m., angen, D. (1) 'need, necessity': *may n aŋan r̥hoid i̯ði hi, may hi n djoða iſo*, 'it is a necessity to give to her, she is suffering from want'; *meun gwi:r aŋan am dano*, 'in real want of it'. (2) 'want': *l̥ugy o aŋan*, 'to be dying from want'.

aŋanr̥hëidjol, adj., angenrbeidiol, D., s.v. 'necessarius'; 'necessary'.

aŋgar, s.m., ager and agerdd, D., 'steam, vapour, exhalation': *pen ma nu ŋ gnëyd l̥e: i gadu gwair, ma nu ŋ gnëyd riu fnestri ba:χ, ga:l i r aŋgar vynd al̯an*, 'when they make a place to keep hay in, they make some small windows to let out the vapour'; *ma: na riu aŋgar o:yr əŋ kodi oði ar var̯ig nɛ avon*, 'there is a sort of cold vapour rising from hoar-frost or a river'; *po:b y:n ən i aŋgar i hy:n*, 'every one "stewing in his own juice"'; so, *aŋgar ə bobol*.

·*aŋ·hafal*, s.m., anghaffael, S.E.*, 'difficulty, hindrance, e. g. such as would prevent the carrying out of an engagement'; *os na ða:u riu ·aŋ·hafal*, 'if no difficulty arises'; *o:ys na riu ·aŋ·hafal arno vo ru:an ?*, 'is he in some difficulty now?' Cf. T.N. 305. 18.

·*aŋ·henys, aŋhennys*, adj., anghenus, D., 'needy'.

·*aŋ·höiljo*, v., anghoelio, D., s.v. 'dubito'; 'to disbelieve': *daχi n ·aŋ·höiljo vi ?*

·*aŋ·hovjo*, v., anghofio, D., s.v. 'obliviscor'. Pret. S. 1. ·*aŋ·hovis*, 3. ·*aŋ·hovjoð*. Imperative ·*aŋ·hovja*; ·*aŋ·hovjuχ*, 'to forget': ·*gu:soχi r sg̯idja ? na: ðo: wi:r, rëit ðru:g, ðary mi ·aŋ·hovjo n la:n. mi a: i vory, rëit ſu:r*, 'did you get the boots?' 'No, indeed, I am very sorry: I entirely forgot. I will be sure to go to-morrow'; *du i wedi ·aŋ·hovjo am ə l̯u:y*, 'I have forgotten the spoon'; ·*aŋ·hovjo ðary mi roi glo: arno vo*, 'I forgot to put coal on it'.

·*aŋ·hənnas*, adj., anghynnes, D., s.v. 'frigidus'; 'repulsive, loathsome'. Cf. P.G.G. 71. 22.

·*aŋ·həsbal̯*, adj., anghysbell, D., 'out-of-the-way, remote': *l̯e: ·aŋ·həsbal̯*.

·*aŋ·həsyr*, s.m., anghyssur, D., s.v. 'demissio'; 'discomfort'.

aŋlod, s.m., anglod, D., s.v. 'ignominia'; 'disgrace': *t o:ð hi ðim ən aŋlod i̯ðo vo*, 'it was no disgrace to him'. Emphasized: *y:n əŋ ka:l kl̯o:d a r l̯al̯ əŋ ka:l ·aŋ·ŷlho:d*.

·*aŋ·ŷhesol*, adj., anghynhesol, S.E., 'repulsive'.

aŋo, s., angof, D., s.v. 'obliuio'; in phrase *gul̯un aŋo* (i. e. gollwng yn angof), 'to forget'.

aŋor, s.m., pl. *aŋorjon*, angor, D., 'anchor'.

aŋori, v., angori, S.E.*, 'to anchor'.

·*aŋˑṛhedy*, v., anghredu, D., 'to disbelieve': *daχi n ·aŋˑṛhedy vi?*, 'do you disbelieve me?'

·*aŋˑṛhjadys*, adj., anghariadus, D., (Prov.) 'uncharitable'.

·*aŋəˑfredin*, adj., anghyffredin, D., s.v. 'rarus'; 'uncommon, extraordinary'. Often used adverbially to intensify an adjective, e. g. *əŋ gluːs ·aŋəˑfredin*, 'uncommonly pretty'. [Occasionally pronounced ·*aŋˑfredin*, with strongly breathed voiceless glide between *ŋ* and *f*.]

·*aŋəˑfərðys*, adj., anghyffyrddus; cf. angonffordd, W.S. [Disconfort], 'uncomfortable'. [For pronunciation cf. above.]

aŋəlas, s.f., angyles, G.I. xxiv. 53, 'angel' (as term applied to a woman).

·*aŋˑsyrys*, adj., anghyssurus, M.Ll. i. 115. 7, 'uncomfortable': *ḷeː ·aŋˑsyrys*.

·*aŋəˑvlëys*, adj., anghyfleus, Acts xxvii. 12, 'inconvenient': *ty: ·aŋəˑvlëys*, 'an inconvenient house, e. g. as to position' (but *ty: ·anˑhuylys*, 'inconvenient as to internal arrangements', etc.); *may n ·aŋˑvlëys i mi vynd*, 'it is inconvenient for me to go' (as to circumstances). Here ·*anˑhuylys* would imply, rather, bad communication.

appad [*attab*].

ar, prep. ar. With pronouns. S. 1. *arna* (*i*), 2. ·*arnat*(*i*), 3. *arno* (*vo*), *arni* (*hi*). Pl. 1. ·*arnon*(*i*), 2. ·*arnoχ*(*i*), ·*arnaχ*(*i*), 3. ·*arnyn*(*u*). Emphasized: *ərna iː*, etc. Pl. 2. *arnoˑχiː*, *arnaˑχiː*, 3. *arnyˑṇhuː*. Shortened enclitic forms: S. 1. *na i*, 2. *nati*, *ant*(*i*), 3. *no vo*, *ni hi*. Pl. 1. *nani*, 2. *noχ*(*i*), *naχ*(*i*), *aχi*, 3. *nynu*. (For the use of these see below, 1 (b).) Followed by the vocalic mutation; but *igjan*, 'twenty', takes *h* as *day ar higjan*.

1. 'on'. (a) 'on' (of rest or motion): *sevyḷ ar ə graig*, 'to stand on the rock'; *kodi ar i draːyd*, 'to stand up'; *ar ben*, 'on the top', as *ar ben r aːlḷ*, 'on the top of the hill'; *ar ə ðeː*, 'on the right'; *ar ə χwiːθ*, 'on the left'.—Where English usage requires 'in', as *ar i helu*, 'in his possession'; *ar i weði*, 'in his prayer'; *ar i bregaθ*, 'in his sermon'; *ṛhoi duːr ar ə ḷevriθ*, 'to put water in the milk'.—Where English usage requires 'by': *vaint i o r gloːχ ar əχ waiſ χiː?*, 'what time is it by *your* watch'. (b) after nouns expressing want, desire, hunger, thirst, fear, etc.: *be s aχi iſˑo?*, *be s naχi iſˑo?*, *be sy noχ iſˑo?*, i. e. beth sydd arnoch chwi ei eisieu?, 'what do you want?'; *ma na i iſˑo*, 'I want'; *aḷan sy no vo iſˑo mynd*, 'he wants to go out'; *os noχi iſˑo rubaθ?*, 'do you

want something?'; *ma na i iſo buːyd, diːod,* 'I am hungry, thirsty'; *ma na i ovn,* 'I am afraid'; *ma na i vlyːs o,* 'I have a great desire for it'; *oːs anti annuyd?,* 'are you cold?' (c) after nouns expressing colour, shape, taste, smell, etc.: *may gwaur laːs ar ər awyr,* 'the sky has a blue tinge'; *i oːs na ðim lyːn arno vo,* 'it has no shape'; *ma na vlaːs halan arno vo,* 'it tastes of salt'; *ma na hogla druːg arno vo,* 'it has a bad smell'. (d) after nouns expressing character, disposition, humour, state, etc.: *syt huːyl sy ·arnoχi heno?,* 'how do you feel to-night?'; similarly: *dəmma syt ə maːy arna iː,* 'that is how *I* am situated'. (e) after nouns expressing appearance : *may golug ëira arni hi,* 'it looks like snow'; *faſun olug oːð arno vo?,* 'how did he look?'; similarly: *vasun i ðim ən meðul hənny arni hi,* 'I should not have thought that by the look of her'. (f) after nouns expressing fault or blame : *ɣhoi bai ar,* 'to blame'; *arno·χiː ma r bai,* 'it is *your* fault'. (g) after nouns expressing hurt, illness, disease, defect, etc.: *be s anti?,* 'what is the matter with you?'; *i oːð dim byːd arno vo,* 'there was nothing the matter with him'; *may attal dëyd arno vo,* 'he stammers'. (h) after nouns expressing name, reputation, etc. : *i oːys dim enu arni hi,* 'it has no name'; *enu druːg ar ðənas,* 'a disparaging term for a woman'. (i) after nouns expressing duty, care, etc. : *govol ə ruːm oːyð arni hi,* 'she had to look after the room'. (j) after a verbal noun whether of transitive or intransitive force. In the former case this usage is restricted to negative clauses of the form *i oːys na ðim tɾoi arno vo,* 'he is a resolute man' (lit. 'there is no turning him'); *i oːys na ðim tusy na θagy arno vo,* 'he is impossible to deal with' (lit. 'there is no leading him nor choking him'). An example of the latter is *may muːy o vynd ·arnynu,* 'there is more demand for them' (lit. 'go on them').

2. with nouns expressing time or weather, considered in their relation to a person : *may hi wedi boːd ən hiːr jaun ƙin deχra ɣ haː ·arnoni,* 'the summer has been a long time coming'; *mi ëiθ ən noːs arno vo ƙin ðo vo ðuːad,* 'it will be night before he comes'; *dəmma hi n niul arna i,* 'I was caught in the mist'.

3. with certain adjectives : *may n druːg arˠ i ɣhieni,* 'it is hard on their parents'; *may n weḷ arno·χiː nag arny·ŋhuː,* 'you are better off than they are'; *kaːs jaun ·arnoχi,* 'very nasty for you'; *ma n vain jaun arno vo,* 'he is in very straitened circumstances'; *may n weḷ arno vo ruːan nag oːyð hi ri·oːyd,* 'he is better off now than he ever was'; *may hənny n o leːu arna i,* 'I am all right as far as that is concerned'.—Somewhat similar is the expression *may hi wedi darvod arno vo,* 'he is done for'.

4. 'on the point of': *du i ·ar ꝼarvod ruːan,* 'I am just finishing now'; *pen oːn i ·ar ·nëyt hənny,* 'when I was on the point of doing that'.

5. with an infinitive expressing potentiality : *dəna ḷeː vasa (basa) vo ar gaːl,* 'that is where it would be likely to be found'.

6. expressing an object for which a thing is intended: *ar osŏd*, 'to be let'; *ar werθ*, 'to be sold'.

7. expressing the means for the attainment of an end: *forð ar i hagor nu*, 'a way to open them'.

8. expressing debt: *vainĭ sy arna i?*, 'how much do I owe?'; *may arna i ðu:y g̃ēinjog i χi:*, 'I owe you twopence'.

9. of time or weather, 'on, at, in': *ar ɔr y:n adag*, 'at the same time'; *ar ðy ļy:n*, 'on a Monday'; *ar dɒwyð po:yθ*, 'in hot weather'.

10. 'on, of, concerning, about': *ʃarad ar*, 'to speak about'; *gnëyd ka:n ar*, 'to make a song about'.

11. 'for, as far as concerns': *wa:yθ boχĭ wedĭ kodĭ am u:yθ ar ðim r u:tĭ wedĭ nëyd*, 'you might just as well have got up at eight for anything you have done'.

12. in numerals before *de:g*, *pɔmθag* and *igjan*, as *ţri ar ðe:g*, *pedwar ar bɔmθag*, *pymp ar higjan*; *or* takes the place of *ar* in *y:n* or *ðe:g*, 'eleven'.

13. sometimes *ar* expresses the relation of a part to the whole: *r adag ɔmma ar ɔ vluyðyn*, 'this time of year'; *ɔn isla ɔ ʋan ma ar ɔ burð*, 'sitting at-this part of the table'.

14. where in English the direct object is followed by an adverb of quantity, etc., the latter is expressed by a substantive followed by *ar*, as *beruχ dippin arno vo*, 'boil it a little'; *na i iʃo kobļjo tippin ar ɔ sg̃idja*, 'I want to cobble my boots a bit'. The order may also be reversed, e. g. *berwi arno vo dippin.* Similarly: *daχi ðim wedi bytta ļawar arno vo*, 'you have not eaten much of it'. Cf. L.A. 51. 1.

15. in conjunction with nouns, forming prepositions or adverbs (or their equivalents), e.g. *ar i ben i hy:n*, 'alone'; *ar vry:s*, 'in a hurry'; *ar draus*, 'across'; *ar dɔd*, 'on the point of'; *ar ðamwain*, 'by chance'; *ar ganol*, 'in the middle of'; *ar garlam*, 'at full speed'; *ar gɒunĭ*, 'because of'; *(mynd) ar goļ*, 'lost'; *ar i ora*, 'in best form'; 'straining to the utmost (and barely succeeding)'; *ar gruydyr*, 'wandering'; *ar gɔvar*, 'against'; *ar gɔvyl*, 'near'; *ar hy:d*, 'along, throughout'; *ar laur*, 'down'; *ar i laur*, 'downwards'; *ar le:d*, 'breadthwise'; *ar le:s*, 'for the good of'; *ar o:l*, 'after, behind'; *ar orũwarad*, 'down'; *ar i vɔny*, 'upwards'; *ar vi:n*, 'on the point of, on the brink of'; *ar wëyθa*, 'in spite of'; *ar wi:b*, 'at a run'; *ar ɔ kɔnta*, 'at first'; *ar (ɔχ) injon*, 'straight on'; *ar ynwaθ*, 'at once', etc., etc.

16. after various verbs or verbs in connexion with nouns, e.g. *avlonɔðy ar*, 'to disturb'; *byu ar*, 'to live on'; *deχra ar*, 'to begin (something)'; *di:al ar*, 'to take vengeance on'; *divlasy ar*, 'to get tired of'; *dɔlanwady ar*, 'to have an influence on'; *edraχ ar*, 'to look at'; *eʃëiθjo ar*, 'to have an effect upon'; *galu ar*, 'to call, to wake'; *gnëyd misţar ar*, 'to master'; *bo:d ɔn g̃amblar ar*, 'to be skilful in'; *gnëyd ţrevn ar*, 'to set to rights'; *gwëïði ar*,

'to shout to'; *kay i ðurn ar*, 'to shake one's fist at'; *kodi kwilið ar*, 'to make ashamed'; *kodi ovn ar*, 'to frighten'; *koḷi arno i hy:n*, 'to lose control of oneself'; *kṛevy ar*, 'to implore'; *kɔmmyd manias ar*, 'to take advantage of'; *ḷa:ð ar*, 'to run down, depreciate'; *manteiſo ar*, 'to have the advantage over'; *nabod ar*, 'to know by'; *ṛhoi enu ar*, 'to name'; *ṛhoi ḱeryð ar*, 'to reprove'; *ṛhoi klek ar (ɔ maud)*, 'to snap (the fingers)'; *ṛhoi klep ar*, 'to bang'; *ṛhoi mi:n ar*, 'to sharpen'; *sbi:o ar*, 'to look at'; *tendjo ar*, 'to attend'; *toṛi ar*, 'to shorten, interrupt'; etc., etc.

a:r, a:yr, s., âr, D. (1) in *ti:r a:r*, 'ploughed land'. (2) (in the game of rounders) *ar ɔr a:yr*, 'at the post' (I.W.).

ara, adj., araf, D., 'slow' (generally with the addition of *de:g*): *mi ða:u hi n ara de:g*, 'she will come along slowly'; *ɔn ara de:g may mynd ɔ ṃheḷ* (prov.), 'slow but sure wins the race'; *kɔmma n ara* 'take your time'; *ɔn ara de:g l*, 'gently!'

arad, s.m., pl. *eryd*, aradr, D., 'plough'. (For parts of plough see *arnoð, ðurn, gwadan, kly:st, korn, kuḷtur, stɔḷan, su:χ*.) This word is used in Aber and Llanfairfechan, but *gwy:ð* takes its place in Pentir and Tregarth.

araḷ, occasionally *araθ* (I.W.), adj., pl. *eriḻ*, arall, D., 'other': *dy:n araḷ*, 'another man'; *ɔ dy:n araḷ*, 'the other man'; *i ben araḷ ɔ burð*, 'at the other end of the table'; *ḱimmint araḷ*, 'as many again'; *ru:in araḷ*, 'some one else'; *rubaθ araḷ*, 'something else'; —adverbially: *dim by:d araḷ*, 'nothing else'; *be nauni araḷ ?*, 'what else shall we do ?';—as pronoun: *wëiθja vel hyn, wëiθja vel araḷ*, 'sometimes one way, sometimes another';—*vel araḷ* = also 'otherwise': *ma: nu ŋ gnëyd vel araḷ, meðul vel araḷ*.

aran, s., pl., *renna*, aren, D., 'ren'; 'testicle ?'

araθ, s.f., araith, D. (1) 'speech, language': *ma: gɔno vo araθ ðru:g jaun, ɔŋ kably a ṛhegi*, 'he uses very bad language,—cursing and swearing'. (2) 'a speech': *gnëyd araθ*, 'to make a speech'. (3) 'delivery': *araθ dila, araθ wantan*, 'feeble delivery'.

arbad, v., arbed, D., 'to spare': *pëidjo arbad i hy:n*, 'not to spare oneself'; *ṛhaid i ti arbad dɔ hy:n ne mi laði di dɔ hy:n*, 'you must spare yourself or you will kill yourself'.

ardal, s.f., pl. *ardaloð*, ardal, D., 'district, neighbourhood': *ɔn ɔr ardal (= kɔmdogaθ) ɔmma*, 'in this neighbourhood'; *meun ardal wledig*, 'in a country district'.

arðal, v., arddelw, D., 'to acknowledge'; *na: i m o i arðal o*, 'I won't acknowledge it'; *gu:r bneðig ðim ɔn lëikjo arðal riu he:n gardottyn ḷaud sy m perθyn iðo vo*, 'a gentleman not liking to acknowledge some poor old beggar who is related to him'; *dyu ɔn arðal i waːs*, 'God acknowledging his servant' (i.e. by giving him unction).

arðeljad, s.m., arddeliad, S.E., 'unction' (e.g. of a preacher): *ſarad dan arðeljad nëylţyːol*, 'to speak with peculiar unction'.

arðerχog, adj., ardderchog, D., 'splendid, magnificent': *tɪwyð arðerχog*, 'magnificent weather'; *forð arðerχog i sëikļo*, 'a splendid road for cycling'.

arður, s.m., arddwr, D., 'ploughmaṅ' = *ţŗaur, iŗɐur*.

arëiθjo, v., areithio, D., 'to make a speech'.

arſad, s., arffed, D., 'pudenda' = *gwendid*.

argay, s., argae, D., 'dam': *ŗhoid argay ar draus ɔr avon*, 'to dam the river'. ·

argjan, s.f., in exclamations of astonishment, etc., as *ɔr argjan vaur l ; ɔr argjan annul, naːẞ i l ; ɔn enu r argjan vaur l*

argluyð, s.m., pl. *argluɪði*, arglwydd, D., 'Lord'.

arjan, arian, D. (1) s.m. 'silver': *arjan byu*, 'quicksilver'; *dail arjan*, 'silverweed' (Potentilla anserina). (2) s. pl., 'money': *arjan preːs* (= *arjan koːχ*, seldom used), 'copper coin'; *arjan gunjon*, 'silver coin'; *arjan melyn*, 'gold coin'; *arjan sɔxjon*, 'cash'; *wedi ɔnniļ arjan ne wedi kaːl rëi*, 'having made money or having obtained some'; *os byːð ģin ti arjan, paid a i siŋkjo nu n dɔ bokkad* (O.H.), 'if you have money do not let it lie by'; *ŗhoid arjan maur ɔn venθig tðo vo*, 'to lend him a large sum of money'; *may hi m byu ar i harjan*, 'she has private means, she lives on her own means'; *maː gɔno vo arjan ar ɔ tiːr*, 'he has a mortgage on the land'; *newid ɔn arjan maːn*, 'to change into small coin'; *knilo arjan, sbarjo arjan, tŗoi arjan hëibjo*, 'to save money'; *gwarjo arjan*, 'to spend money'; *gwastrafy arjan*, 'to squander money'.

arχ, s.f., pl. *ëirχ*, arch, D., 'coffin'.

arχoļ, s.f., pl. *arχoļjon*, archoll, D., 'wound': *may o wedi toŗi arχoļ vaur ar i ben* (O.H.). [The usual word for 'wound' is *briu*.]

arχva, s.f., archfa, B.C. 88. 15, 'a bad smell': *may na arχva ðruːg ɔn ɔ ruːm ma*, 'there is a bad smell in this room'; *daχi ŋ kluːad ɔr arχva ?*, 'do you notice the smell?'; *riu arχva drom*.

arχwaθ, s., archwaeth, D., s.v. 'gustus'; 'taste' in the sense *dim arχwaθ at vuːyd*, 'no taste for food'.

arlais, s., pl. *arlëiſ'a*, arlais, D., 'temple' (of the head).

arlöisi [*löisi*].

armal, s.m., armael, O.P.; S.E.; armel, S.E., 'the second milk at milking time'. Cf. *blëinjon, tikkal*.

arnoð, s.m., arnodd, D., 'plough-beam'.

aron, s., pl. *arons*, 'the common guillemot' (Urca troile).

aros, v., aros, D. Fut. S. 3. *ɣhosiθ*. Pret. *ɣhosis*. Imperative, *aros ;· ɣhosuχ*. (1) 'to stay, stop': *aros ən ə ty:*, 'to stop in the house'; *aros tan dy (δy) sadurn*, 'to stay until Saturday'; *wa:yθ ǵin i aros na fëidjo*, 'it is all the same to me whether I stay or not'; *aros dros ə no:s*, 'to stay overnight'. (2) 'to wait for': *ən aros i r δëyar gnesy*, 'waiting for the earth to get warm'; *breχtan i aros pɣy:d*, 'a piece of bread and butter to keep one going till a meal is ready'; *i aros*, 'meanwhile' (Anglo-Welsh: 'to wait').

ar:s (Eng. 'airs'), s., 'animal spirits': *ļaun a:rs*.

arsuyd, s.m., arswyd, D., 'terror': *ma na i (ǵin i) arsuyd mynd*, 'I am afraid of going'; *kodi arsuyd ar*, 'to terrify'; *t o:δ na i δim arsuyd ovn*, 'I had no fear'.

arsuydo, v., arswydo, D. (1) 'to be terrified': *wedi klu:ad rubaθ nes may o n arsuydo*. (2) 'to be filled with horror'; *kayl i arsuydo uθ weld riu δamwain.*

arsuydys, adj., arswydus, D., s.v. 'formidolosus'; 'terrible': *ma: n o:yr arsuydys*, 'it is terribly cold'; *o:δ əm beθ arsuydys*, 'it was terrible'.

arθ, s.f., pl. *ëirθ*, arth, D., 'bear': *vel r arθ wy:ļt o r ko:yd* (J.J.), 'like a wild bear out of the wood', i.e. raging.

arθas, s.f., arthes, D., s.v. 'ursa'; 'a noisy, surly woman, who shouts at one' (J.J.).

arθǵi, s.m., arthgi, S.E.*, 'a noisy, surly fellow, who shouts at one': *ta:u ɣ he:n arθǵi gwirjon* (O.H.).

arθjo, *harθjo*, v., arthio, S.E., 'to shout at, to speak loud and gruffly' = *gwëiδi n hvļ a fərnig* (O.H.); *may o n arθjo arna i ; paid ag arθjo*.

arθrag, s.f., i.e. arthwraig = *arθas*: *he:n arθrag o he:n δənas* (O.H.).

aruyδ, s.m., pl. *aruiδjon*, arwydd, D., 'sign': *aruyδ gla:u*.

arva, s.pl., sing. *ervyn*, arf, pl. arfau, D., 'implements'.

arvar, s.f., arfer, D., 'habit, custom': *ən o:l i harvar*, 'according to their custom';—adverbially: *may o n huyraχ nag arvar*, 'he is later than usual'.

arvar, v., arfer, D., s.v. 'consuesco'. (1) 'to be accustomed, to be used (to)': *r öyδun i n arvar kayl vannoδ nes bədun i dgest a mynd o ɣho:* (*la:s*), 'I used to get toothache so badly that it used nearly to drive me mad'; *du i n deχra arvar hevo vo*, 'I am beginning to get accustomed to it'. (2) Transitively: *arvar də hy:n i nëyt hənny*, 'get accustomed to do that'. (3) 'to use': *·t ədani δim n arvar ə gair əna*, 'we don't use that word'.

arverjad, s.m., arferiad, W.Ll. xlii. 98, 'custom': *he:n arverjad*, 'an old custom'.

arverol, adj., arferol, D., s.v. 'usualis'; 'usual': *vel arverol*, 'as usual'.

arvod, s.f., pl. *arvoda*, arfod, D., 'ictus teli'; 'what is cut by one sweep of a scythe reckoned forward' (cf. *gwana*): *mi doris i və hy:d ar dair arvod*, 'I have cut my length in three strokes' (so said an old man to O.H.); *kəmmar di arvod go veχan*, 'take a moderate sized stroke'.

arwain, v., arwain, D., 'to lead' (not very frequent, and semi-literary, cf. *iusy*); *arwain kany*, 'to lead singing'.

arwin, adj., ? gerwin, D., 'terrible' (as intensifying word): *r̥hiu glepjan arwin o hy:d* (J.J.), 'a terrible clattering continually' (Ô.H. does not know this word). For gerwin, cf. T.N. 222. 11, Dyna f'yntau 'n troi 'i fontin, tan ddiawlio yn erwin. Also 115. 29; 137. 13.

arwinol, adv., ?arwynol, W.Ll. (voc.), dihafarch. Cf. D. *arwynawl, 'terrible' (as intensifying word): *ma: n o:yr arwinol*, 'it is terribly cold'.

aryθrol, adj., aruthrol, D., 'terrible' (as intensifying word), 'extremely': *r o:δ ən warθ pr̥yt hənny aryθrol*, 'it was looked upon as a terrible disgrace at that time'; *ən δivrivol aryθrol*, 'extremely serious'; *aryθrol o va:n*, 'extremely small'; *ən yuχ i vəny peθ aryθrol*, 'ever so much higher up'.

as, er ys, *as talum*, 'long ago'.

asan, s.f., pl. *senna*, asen, D., 'rib; rib of a boat or basket': *dəna be seviθ at əχ senna χi*, 'that will set you up'; *asan vra:n, asan vra:s*, 'spare rib'.

asgaḷ, s.f., pl. *esg̊iḷ, asg̊eḷi, asg̊eḷoδ*, asgell, D. (1) 'wing' (this is the common word, cf. *adan*): *asgaḷ arjan*, 'chaffinch' (Fringilla coelebs) = *pu:ynt*; *ḷedy i esg̊iḷ*, 'to spread the wings': fig. 'to put on airs of importance, to show off'; *kodi esg̊iḷ*, 'to take wing'. (2) 'fin'. (3) *asgaḷ ə korδur*, 'the beater of a churn'. (4) 'sail' (of a windmill). (5) 'thistle' (corruption of 'ysgall'). (6) *asgaḷ ə wyntyḷ*.

asgan, s.f., ? asgen, D., 'noxa, laesio'. (1) 'tendency, natural inclination': *ma na riu asgan əno vo ri·o:d i δu:n* (O.H.), 'he has a kind of natural inclination to steal' (= *elvan*); *asgan gwëiθjo*, 'love of work' (I.W.). (2) *he:n δy:n əm pigo pobol* (O.H.). (3) *he:n asgan ədi o*, 'he is a tough customer' (I.W.). (4) 'a wiry person' (I.W.).

asgurn, s.m., pl. *esgyrn*, asgwrn, D., 'bone': *dim ond kro:yn ar ər asgurn*, 'nothing but skin and bone'; *may i esgyrn dg̊est tr̥u i gro:yn i̇ðo vo,* 'his bones are almost through his skin, he is like a skeleton'; *asgurn pen,* 'skull'; *asgurn ko:yl,* 'the bone of divination', i.e. 'the shoulder-blade of animals'—also of human beings (so called, according to E.J., because supposed to indicate whether a baby about to be born will be a boy or a girl), esp. 'the shoulder-blade of a sheep, formerly placed over the door of a house' (O.H., who, however, was unable to give any clear account of its supposed occult powers); *r esgyrn əŋ gustun,* referring to the hind hip-bones of a cow before calving; *asgurn pəsgodyn,* 'fish-bone'; *may o n asgurn o ðy:n,* 'he is a strong man'; *mən ər asgurn!,* asseveration; *may o wedi kayl asgurn i gravy arno n van na,* said of some one who has married a worthless wife, or has gone to live in some poor position.

aſad, s., asiad, D., s.v. 'ferrumen'; 'a join'.

aſo, v., asio, D., s.v. 'ferrumino'; 'to join'.

at, prep., at. With pronouns S. 1. *atta i,* 2. ·*attat(i),* 3. *atto (vo),* atti *(hi).* Pl. 1. ·*atton(i),* 2. ·*attoχ(i),* ·*attaχ(i),* 3. ·*attyn(u).* Takes the vocalic mutation. 1. 'to, towards': "denotes prox- imity, but not entrance; hence it is used before persons; and also before places and things, when entrance into them is not implied: 'i' = 'to', 'into', denotes motion towards a place or object, into which an entrance is made."—"'At' is opposed to 'oddi wrth'; 'i' is opposed to 'o'" (Rowlands, 'Welsh Grammar', 4 ed., pp. 213, 214, § 736). *mynd i r gwely,* 'to go to bed'; *mynd at ə gwely,* 'to go to the bed'; *mynd i r tṛe:n,* 'to get into the train'; *mynd at ə tṛe:n,* 'to go to the train'; *mynd i r mo:r,* 'to go to sea'; *mynd at ə mo:r,* 'to go to the sea'; *mynd i r dre:, mynd at ə dre:,* 'to go to the town'; *dəuχ əmma at ə ta:n,* 'come here to the fire'; *mi ëiſ i ən ne:s atto vo,* 'I went nearer him'; *kṛəsbas wlanan nesa at ə kṛo:yn,* 'a flannel shirt next the skin'; *tṛoi ə du:r at i velin i hy:n,* 'to turn the water to one's own mill', i.e. 'to turn something to one's own advantage'; *mi a:nu at i ǵilið etto,* 'they will make it up again'; *kṛëyðuχ at ə tattus,* 'reach to the potatoes', i.e. 'have some'; *hel at i ǵilið,* 'to shrink up, to huddle together'; *kayl ə ðay pen l̦inin at i ǵilið* 'to make two ends meet'; *ṛhaid i χi gayl meǵin atto vo,* 'you must get a pair of bellows to it'.

2. 'against a certain time, by': *huraχ mi ða:u i godi at ə pnaun,* 'perhaps it will clear up by the afternoon'.

3. 'for, as a provision for': *daχi iſo ǩi:g at ə sy:l?,* 'do you want meat for Sunday?'

4. 'for, for the purpose of, in the interests of, as a remedy for': *dim ən forðjo su:l̦t at rubaθ,* 'not being able to afford a shilling for something'; *ǩa:l pe:θ at vyu,* 'to get something to live upon'; *ṛhoid arjan at aχos da,* 'to give money for a good cause'; *may ən l̦yndan veðiǵinjaθ at bo:b pe:θ ond ṛhak hiraθ,* 'in London there is a remedy for everything except for l̦onging'.

5. 'about, round about, towards': *hogyn at v o:yd i*, 'a boy of about my age'; *hogyn at i vaint o*, 'a boy of about his size'; *at glaŋġëya*, 'about, towards the thirteenth of November'. Similarly, *kodi at ə tattus*, 'to earth up potatoes'.

6. 'up to, as far as', generally preceded by *d (hy:d)*: *dani wedi ka:yl tɐwyð da: d at hyn*, 'we have had fine weather so far'; *may o ŋ koχi (d) at i glistja*, 'he is blushing to the roots of his hair', lit. 'to his ears'; *mi ləχiθ ə tɐwyð ma at ə kro:yn*, 'this weather wets to the skin'; *r o:ð ər ëira n du:ad at gorn ə guðu*, 'the snow was up to the neck'.

7. preceded by *ty: ag*, 'towards, with regard to': *wedi gnëyd ə ŋora ty: ag atto vo*, 'having done my best for it'.

8. after certain verbs, as *dəχryn at*, 'to be frightened at'; *kovjo at*, 'to remember (somebody) to'; *sgwenny at*, 'to write to'; *sənny at*, 'to be astonished at'.

atebjad, s.m., atebiad, S.E.*, 'answer': *t o:ys na ðim atebjad*, 'there is no answer', e.g. to a note.

atebol, adj., atebol, S.E., 'answerable': *atebol drosto i hy:n*, 'answerable for himself'. Cf. *tebol*.

atgas, adj., atgas, D., s.v. 'execrabilis'; 'hateful, execrable': *ma: n atgas ġin i*, 'I can't bear him'; *may n taro n atgas*, 'it strikes (the ear) most unpleasantly'; *gwëiθrad atgas ; su:n atgas ; sunjo n atgas ;*—in a milder sense, 'sharp': *ən atgas ən i appad ; —nt o:ð turna hun a hun ən atgas?—tro: atgas*, 'an unpleasant experience', e. g. 'a disappointment': *wel, syt ma: hi, vaχgan ? wel, welis i rotʃun be:θ, mi ġe:s dro: atgas* (O.H.).

atgo, s., atgof, D., s.v. 'recordatio'; 'remembrance': *may hənny braið ən atgo ġin i ; may ġin i riu atgo 'am dano vo*, 'I have a slight remembrance of it'.

atgofa, v. tr., atgoffa, D., s.v. 'recordor'; 'to recall to mind': *atgofa he:n beθa ; atgofa hənny iðo vo*, 'to remind him of this'.

atgovjo, v. intr., atgofio, D., s.v. 'reminiscor'; 'to recall to mind': *ðary mi atgovjo*, 'it came back to my mind'.

atʃad, atʃas, in exp. *mynd i u atʃad o*, 'to come full upon him suddenly'; *mi ëis ən injon i u atʃas o ən nru:s ə kappal.*

attab ; appad (O.H. always), v., atteb, D. Fut. S. 1. *teba*, 2. *tebi*, 3. *tebiθ*, etc. Imp. *tebun*. Pret. *tebis*. No pl. Imperative *attab ; tebuχ*, 'to answer': *θeba vo ðim*, 'he would not answer'; *t ədi o ðim ən sa:l, ðary o v attab i*, 'he is not ill, he answered me'; *attab ə diban*, 'to answer the purpose'; *r o:ð ə peθa n attab i ġilið ən jaun*, 'the articles suited admirably, fitted in nicely'; *karag attab*, 'echo'.

attab, appad, s.m., pl. *atebjon*, atteb, D., 'answer'.

attal, v., attal, D., 'to impede, hold back': *t o:ys gəno vo ðim daint i attal i davod*, 'he always speaks out, says what would be better left unsaid' (rarely used except in this phrase).

attal, s., attal, D., 'impediment': *may attal dëyd arno vo*, 'he stammers'.

audyrdod, s.f., pl. *audyrdoda*, awdurdod, D., s.v. 'auctoritas'; 'authority'; *r audyrdoda*, 'the authorities'.

audyrdodol, adj., awdurdodol, T.N. 243. 24, 'authoritative, dictatorial'.

auχ, s.m., awch, D., 'sharp appetite, eager desire': *ma: d auχ ən vaur am vu:yd*, 'you have a sharp appetite'.

aur, s.f., pl. *orja*, awr, D., 'hour': *ma: r dy:ð ən məstyn aur erbyn kanol jonaur*, 'the days are an hour longer by the middle of January'; *χwartar aur, hannar aur*, 'a quarter of an hour, half an hour'; *hannar aur wedi day*, 'half past two' (but *χwartar wedi day*); *aur a hannar*, 'an hour and a half'; *gwaiθ aur*, 'an hour's work, an hour's walk'.

aust, s.m., Awst, D., 'August'.

avjaχ, adj., afiach, D., s.v. 'insalubris': 'unhealthy, unwholesome, sickly': *tɐwyð avjaχ*, 'unhealthy weather'; *baχgan avjaχ o:ð o əri:o:yd*, 'he was always a sickly youth'.

avjaθ, s., afiaith, D., 'lightness of heart': *sy daχi hëiðju ? du i n və avjaθ*, i. e. *du i wedi kayl bayχ o:ð ar ə ŋhɐvn* (O.H.); *mi ðɛydis i hənny ən və avjaθ*, 'I said that in the lightness of my heart' (O.H.).

avjeχid, s.m., afiechyd, D., 'unhealthiness, disease': *avjeχid ar ben gli:n*, 'a disease on the knee'.

avlan, adj., aflan, D., s.v. 'spurcus'; 'unclean'. (Scarcely colloquial but cf. *gavr*.)

avlavar, adj., aflafar, D. (1) 'unseemly of speech': *riu he:n sgurs avlavar* (O.H.). (2) 'discordant': *su:n avlavar, ļais avlavar*.

avlawan, adj., aflawen, D., s.v. 'illaetabilis'. (1) 'peevish, cantankerous'. (2) 'extremely': *ən o:yr avlawan* (I.W.).

avlonyð, adj., aflonydd, D., s.v. 'inquietus'; 'restless, fidgety': *kṛjadyr, plentyn, təmmar avlonyð*.

avlonəðy, v., aflonyddu, D., s.v. 'inquieto'; 'to disturb': *du i n du:ad i avlonəðy ·arnoχi*, 'I am coming to disturb you'.

avluyð, s., aflwydd, D. (1) 'bad luck': *r o:ð ər avluyð ·gənoni hëidju* (E.J.), 'we had bad luck to-day'. (2) 'defect, drawback, imperfection': *ma na riu avluyð arno vo* (J.J.), 'there is some imperfection in it'; *ma: ba:u (= χwyn) ən avluyð* (J.J.), 'weeds are a drawback, imperfection'. (3) as expletive: *be avluyð sy əno vo, du:χ ?* (E.J.), 'I wonder what on earth is the matter with it';

so, *be avluyð sy ·arnaχi ?*—Similarly *riu he:n ģerig ən avluyð o vydyr ; tattus ən avluyð o va:u ; ər y:d ən avluyð o əsgal̦ a χwyn* (all O.H.).

avol, s.m., pl. *vala*, afol, D., 'apple': *vala sirjon*, 'crab-apples'; *vala pe:r*, 'apples, as distinguished from crab-apples'; *avol ko:χ ə baχgan (əŋ go:χ i ģi:d drosto, melys)*, E.J.; *avol kro:yn ŕ hu:χ*, 'russet'; *avol χweru* (J.J.), 'bitter-sweet' (?); *avol pi:g ə glomman* (O.H.), term applied to apples with an excrescence at the stalk; *avol ə ro:* (so called from Ro Wen), O.H.; *avol deru*, 'oak-apple'; *köydan vala*, 'apple-tree'; *köydan vala sirjon*, 'crab-apple tree'; *diŋkod avol*, 'pips of an apple'; *plikjo avol*, 'to peel an apple'; *ma: r avol wedi gläiʃo*, 'the apple is bruised, rotten'; *te:u vel avol*, 'as fat as a dumpling'; *·vedruχi ðim ka:l əχ avol i χwara a:g i vytta* (prov.), 'you can't eat your cake and have it'; *ma r jëir əŋ kluydo r y: va:θ a vala ar bren* (E.J.), 'the hens are roosting like apples on a tree'; *kodi vala du:r*, 'the game of extracting apples from water with the teeth'.

avon, s.f., pl. *avonyð*, afon, D., 'river': *avon ðolennog*, 'a winding river'; *glan ər avon*, 'the bank of a river'; *mi:n ər avon*, 'the brink of the river'; *mynd i no:l du:r tr̦os avon* (prov.), 'to go a long way for something which can be got close at hand'.

avrad, adj., afraid (?), 'wasteful'. Only in the popular rime *by:m əm byu əŋ gənnil gənnil | a:θ y:n ðavad i mi n ðuivil | tr̦ois i vyu ən avrad avrad | a:θ ə ðuivil ən y:n ðavad.*—The word seems to be used in the same sense in C.C. 188. 23, Nâd i afraid ieungctid hala Bol mewn henaint i gardotta. Cf. afradlon, 'prodigal'.

avriolað, adj., afreolaidd, S.E., 'irregular' *ı ə galon ən mynd ən avriolað* (O.H.).

avriolys, adj., afreolus, D., s.v. 'perbacchor'; ·'unruly': *plant avriolys*, 'unruly children';—*kefyl avriolys ;—byu ən avriolys*, 'to live a dissolute life'.

avrosgo, adj., amrosgo, D., 'clumsy, unwieldy': *dy:n avrosgo*, 'a hulking fellow'; *pe:θ maur avrosgo*, 'a great, clumsy thing'; *ker̦ðad ən avrosgo.*

avrɵujog, adj., afrywiog, D., s.v. 'contumax'; 'churlish, crusty, harsh, unpleasant': *təmmar (tempar) avrɵujog*, 'a churlish temper'; *tɵwyð avrɵujog*, 'cold, stormy weather'; *golug avrɵujog*, 'a churlish, unattractive appearance'.

awal, s.f., pl. *awelon*, awel, D., 'breeze': *ma na awal ða: o wynt hëiðju*, 'there is a good breeze to-day'; *awal galad*, 'a stiff breeze'; *awal wnynl̦yd*, 'a biting wind'; *kal̦yn po:b awal o wynt* (fig.), 'to trim one's sails to every breeze'.

awan, s.f., pl. *(a)wenna*, awen, D., 'bridle-rein'. In the general sense of 'reins' only in such stereotyped expressions as *may r awenna n də laːu di*, 'the reins are in your hand', i. e. 'you have the upper hand'. [The usual word is *reːns*.]

awyð, s.m., awydd, D., 'desire': *heb awyð gnëyd dim*, 'no desire to do anything'.

awyðvs, adj., awyddus, D., 'eager, anxious'.

awyr, s., awyr, D. (1) m. 'air': *r awyr agorad*, 'the open air'. (2) f. 'sky': *r awyr laːs*, 'the blue sky'; *awyr goːχ*, 'red sky'; *ʈraːyθ awyr*, 'a formation of clouds like ribbed sand when the tide is out'.

aːyl, s.f., pl. *ëiija*, ael, D., 'brow': *pëidjuχ a k̑iχjo χ ëilja arna i*, 'don't frown at me'; *kuʃjo nes oːð o n waːyd ər aːyl*, 'to fight till his forehead was covered with blood' (I.W.); *i g̑eːg o n waːyd ər aːyl* (O.H.); *aːyl ə bryn*, 'brow of the hill'.

ayr, s.m., aur, D., 'gold': *nid ayr poːb peːθ melyn* (prov.), 'all is not gold that glitters'.

aːyr, s.m., pl. *ëyrod*, aer, W.Ll. ii. 9; B.C. 97. 14, 'heir'.

aːyr, s.m., aer, C.C. 396. 18, 'air': *tan r aːyr*, 'in the open air'; *mynd am newid aːyr*, 'to go for a change of air'.

b

babi, s.m., pl. *babis*, babi, C.C.M. 197. 21, 'baby'.

badlan, s.f., in such phrases as *s g̑in i r yːn badlan goːχ ə delyn*, 'I haven't a brass farthing'; *mi waris i boːb badlan goːχ* (O.H.); *du i n mëindjo r yːn badlan ·arnati*, 'I don't care a button for you'.

bag, s.m., pl. *bagja*, 'bag'.

bagal, s.f., pl. *bagla*, bagl, D. (1) 'crutch': *mynd uθ i vagla*, 'to go on crutches'. (2) 'handle': *bagal fon, əmba·rel, ɽhaːu, forχ*, 'handle of a stick, umbrella, spade, fork' (in this sense sometimes m.—*bagal maur*, O.H.). (3) 'drawback': *vyːð ən vagal garu (aru) ·arnati*, 'it will be a great drawback to you'. (4) m. in slate quarries, 'a corner at the entrance of each shed (*gwal*) where long siabs of slate (*klətja day hyːd*, etc.) are placed, ready to be divided into the proper lengths' [*gwal*].

bagal [*magal*].

bagaldjo, v., bragaldio, S.E.*; cf. bagaldio, M.F., 'to prattle, babble'. Said of children who are just beginning to talk, or of grown-up people who talk in an incoherent fashion'. Also *bagaldjo ʃarad*.

bagaḷʃ, s. (1) 'portable property' (in disparaging sense), 'lumber'

= *he:n dakla,—hel də vagatʃ a fur a ti:.* (2) as a term of reproach : *he:n vagatʃ o bobol ·ədynu.*

bagjad, s.m., pl. *bagëidja,* ' bagful '.

baglan, s.f., baglan, S.E.*= *bagal* in the sense of crutch. Also ' a snare ' : *baglan i ðal gwniŋan* (O.H.) = *magal.*

bagly, magly, v., maglu, D. (1) ' to catch ' (of the foot) : *bagly ə ṭro:yd meun rubaθ ; magly ə iṛa:yd ən i ġiliδ ;* also abs. *mi vaglis.* (2) ' to stumble ' : *magly uθ drawo ə ṭro:yd uθ gaṛag ;*—trans. ' to cause to stumble ' : *mi vagloδ drẽynan vi.* (3) ' to snare '.

bai, s.m., pl. *bëia,* bai, D. (1) ' fault ' : *arno·χi: ma r bai,* ' it's *your* fault ' ; *heb i vai heb i eni* (prov.), ' no one is without his faults ' ; *·r öyδati ar vai,* ' you were at fault ' ; *may r bai n sevyl ar i ṛhieni,* ' their parents are to blame ' ; *gweld bai,* ' to find fault ' ; *ma nu ŋ gweld bai ·arnoni os nauni durdjo nu,* ' they take it amiss if we scold them ' ; *ə kəθral əŋ gweld bai ar bexod* (prov.), ' the pot called the kettle black ' ; so also *hel bëia, kodi bëia ;—sərθjo ar i vai,* ' to acknowledge one's fault '. (2) ' blame ' (Anglo-Welsh ' fault ') : *əvo: sy ŋ ka:l ə bai,* ' he gets the blame ' ; *ṛhoi bai ar,* ' to blame '. (3) ' defect, blemish '.

bakjo; bagjo (O.H.), v., bacio, T.N. 474. 4, ' to back ' (said to horses) : *bakja !* ' back ! ' (*bag,* O.H.).

bakko, s.m., ' tobacco ' : *dgo:y o vakko əŋ ḡhi:l i vo·χ,* ' a plug of tobacco in his cheek ' ; *bakko main,* ' twist ' ; *bakko rega·reg,* ' plug tobacco ' (W.H.—App. not known at Llanfairfechan = *bakko kalad*) ; *blu·χ, purs, putʃ bakko,* ' tobacco-pouch '.

bakkun, s.m., bacwn, G.C. 128. 18 ; backwn twrch, W.S.; baccwn, D.; Mid. Eng. bacoun, ' bacon ' = *bekn, ḵi:g ·mo·χ.*

bakstandjo, v., ' to scold ' : *paid a bakstandjo n wirjon ; mi ḡe:s və makstandjo n aru.*

bakstreljo, v., ' to scold '.

bakʃa, s.pl., sing. *baksan,* f., bacseu, D. (1) ' a footless stocking ' : *ḵlokʃa a bakʃa,* ' clogs and footless stockings ' ; also, ' the legs of a stocking worn outside the boots in order to walk on ice '. (2) ' any old, worn-out stocking ' : *t o:ys na ðim ond he:n vakʃa am i dra:yd o,* ' he has nothing but old stockings on his feet ' ; *kadu arjan meun riu he:n vaksan,* ' to keep money in some old stocking ' (cf. T.N. 22. 35) ; *dim y:n baksan beni* (O.H.), ' not a farthing '.

bakʃog, adj., applied to horses and fowls which have long hair round the feet : *ḵefyl bakʃog, jëir bakʃog.*

ba·χ (rarely shortened as *hynna baχ !* ' so little as that ! '), bâch, D., adj., comp. *ḷai,* eq. *ḷëiad, ḷi:ad,* sup. *ḷëia, ḷi:a.* The radical is nearly always used after fem. nouns. (1) ' little ' : *hogyn, hogan ba·χ,* ' little boy, girl ' ; *tippin ba·χ,* ' a little bit ' ; *may pe:θ ba·χ ən diðany hi̇*, ' a little thing comforts her ' ; *gwëïljuχ am vynyd ba:χ*, ' wait a moment ' ; *hynna ba:χ o amsar daχi ŋ ga:l ?*, ' is that all the time you get ? ' ; *dy:n bəχan ba:χ te:u*, ' a tiny little fat man '. (2) term of endearment frequently used with proper names. (3) implying eulogy : *le: ba:χ divir*, ' a nice place ' ; *dy:n ba:χ klu:s ədi o*, ' he is a nice little man ' ; *dənas ba:χ ðel*, ' a nice little woman ' ; *gu:r bneðig ba:χ ɼhadlon*, ' a pleasant-spoken gentleman '. (4) implying pity : *kɼadyr ba:χ !*, ' poor fellow ! ' ; *peθ ba:χ !*, ' poor little thing ! ' (5) implying contempt : *welis i ri̇o:yd ðy:n ba:χ mor ·a·nivir a vo: !*, ' I never saw such a disagreeable man ' ; *he:n walχ ba:χ !*, ' you rascal ! ' (e.g. to a dog).

ba:χ, s.m., pl. *baχa*, bâch, D., ' hook ' : *ba:χ a dolan*, ' hook and eye ' ; *ba:χ sɡidja*, ' button-hook ' ; *ba:χ klikjad*, ' the hook which holds the latch of a door ' ; *stry:d vaχa* (J.J. ; O.H.), ' stilts ' ; cf. D., s.v ' grallae ', tudfachau, ystudfachau ; *baχa i bəsgotta*, ' fish-hooks ' ; *ɼhəuχ ə kɼoχon ar ə ba:χ*, ' put the pot on the hook '. Used of the hands : *meθy kadu i vaχa ən lonyð*, ' to pilfer ' = *may i la:u ən vlewog, may o n ladroni.*

baχal̥, s., bachell, D.F. [91] 16 : in *baχal̥ vorðuyd*, ' hollow of the thigh ' (J.J.) (the usual word is *ǩesal vorðuyd*) and *baχal̥ əsguyð*, ' the hollow between the shoulder-blades '. This word is a diminutive of ' bach ', ' a hollow ' ; cf. the place-name *ə va:χ* at Llandudno, now called ' The Happy Valley '.

baχgan, s.m., pl. *beχɡin*, bachgen, D., ' boy ' (more often *hogyn*) : *baχgan ivaŋk*, ' a young fellow ' ; *maχgan i*, ' my boy !, my lad ! '. Cf. *aχan !*

baχɡennyn, s.m., ' bachgennyn ', D., s.v. ' puellus ' ; ' a little boy '.

baχjad, s.m., pl. *baχjada*, bachiad, D., s.v. 'anfractus ', ' flexura '. (1) ' sheep's ear-mark ' [*no:d*]. (2) ' a certain flaw in slate ' : ' Mae rhyw fachiadau yn ochrau rhai o'r cerrig (clytiau) ; gan hynny mae yn gorfod marcio yn hollt yn yr ochr lle mae y bachiadau er mwyn ei chael ar ei hyd ' (J.J.)—' faults in the sides of the blocks '. (3) ' a bite ' (in fishing) (I.W.). (4) ' a job ' : *ɡe:sti vaχjad ?*, ' have you got a job ? '

baχog, adj., bachog, D., ' grasping ' : *dy:n baχog—am vaχy ə kubul i̇ðo i hy:n.*

baχur, s.m., bachwr, S.E., ' one who " buckles to ", who works with energy and persistence ' : *may o n ë:θa baχur*, ' he is a very good workman ' (O.H.).

baχy, v., bachu, D., ' to hook, catch ' : *ma: m̥hokkad wedi baχy,* ' my pocket has caught ' ; *r o:ð briga r ko:yd əm baχy ·arnoni*, ' the twigs kept catching in our clothes '.—Applied to harnessing a horse : *amsar baχy*, ' the time the horses are harnessed for work in the fields ' ; *pɼy:d ðary χi vaχy ?*

baldary:o, v.; cf. baldarddu, R., 'to talk nonsense'.—Also *paldary:o* (O.H.).

balir, s.m., pl. *balira*, = *baril*, ' barrel'.

balχ, adj., balch, D. (1) 'proud': *wedi gwisgo n valχ*, said of the sole of a boot which has worn through in the middle (O.H.); *ƙin valχad a ·lusifar, ƙin valχad a siŋgo* (O.H.). (2) 'glad': *r ǝdu i n valχ bo χi n weḷ*, 'I am glad you are better'; *r öyðun i ƙin valχad o hono a tasun i wedi ka:yl ᵇyuχ a ḷo:*, 'I was as glad of it as if I had got a cow and a calf' (E.J.).

balχtar, balχi̯ra, s.m., balchder, D. (1) 'pride': *ꭓ he:n valχtar hyḷ na*, 'that unpleasant kind of pride'. (2) 'joy, gladness': *sboŋkjo o valχi̯ra*, 'to leap for joy'.

bal·χi:o, v., balchio, D., 'to be proud': *paid a bal·χi:o dim*, 'don't be stuck up about it'.

balog, s.f., pl. *balogjon*, balog, D., 'perizoma'; 'the flap of the breeches': *du i wedi koḷi bottum ar ǝ valog ; kay dǝ valog.*

banadl, s.m., banadl, D., 'broom' (Cytisus scoparius).

bannog, adj., bannog, D., 'notatus, notabilis', in *morgaθ vannog*, 'spotted ray' (Raia maculata).

bant, s., mant, D., 'maxilla': only in *bant ǵëyad*, 'close', in the sense of keeping silent about something: *may nu n ðigon bant ǵëyad hevo rubaθ ·lëikjanu* (I.W.), 'they can keep their mouths closed well enough when they like'.

bant, s., 'band': *bant ǝ glo:s* (O.H.), 'band at the top of the breeches'.

banu, adj., pl. *bëinu* (J.J.; O.H.), banw, W.S.; banyw, D., female': *ka:θ vanu, marljod bëinu.*

baŋgljo [maŋgljo].

baŋgor, Bangor.

bar, s.m., pl. *barja*, barr, I.D. xxix. 9: 'bar, bolt'.

bara, s.m., bara, D., 'bread': *bara kaus* (χaus), 'bread and cheese'; *bara menyn* (= *breχtan*), 'bread and butter'; *du:y o vara menyn*, 'two pieces of bread and butter'; *bara sy:χ*, 'dry bread'; *bara fres*, 'new bread'; *he:n vara*, 'stale bread'; *bara bru:d*, 'bread fresh from the oven'; *bara pryn*, 'bought bread'; *tavaḷ o vara*, 'a slice of bread'; *ʃurud o vara*, 'scraps of bread' = *bara ma:n ; y:n o r bara*, 'one of the loaves of a baking',—so *saiθ o vara*, 'a batch of seven loaves'. See also *briuʃon, ƙilƙin, kḷuf, kꭓub, kꭓǝstyn, muidjon, torθ*, etc. Sorts of bread: *bara ammyd*, see *ammyd; bara bri:θ*, 'currant loaf'; *bara dan badaḷ*, 'bread baked in an oven with a pan over it', 'pan loaf'; *bara day vlaud*, 'bread made of wheat and barley'; *bara gweniθ, gwyn*, 'wheaten bread, white bread'; *bara haið,* 'barley bread'; *bara kan,* 'white bread'; *bara kanθrig = bara day vlaud*; *bara k̆eirχ,* 'oatcake'; *bara klalf,* 'bread badly risen, unwholesome, doughy, heavy bread'; *bara ko:χ = bara haið*; *bara k̢ri:,* 'bread made without barm'— usually cut into square pieces and practically the same as pastry; *bara kɔmmysg = bara day vlaud*; *bara levan,* 'bread made with a sponge or lump of dough left over from the last baking' (in common use fifty years ago, J.J.); *bara pëiljad,* 'a kind of cake like a muffin made on a frying-pan'; *bara rada̢l,* 'bread baked on a griddle on a peat fire with a pan over it and the whole covered with peat'; *bara r̢hiðjon,* 'bread made from wheat flour mixed with bran'; *bara r̢hɔnjon,* 'bread made of oats cleared of the husks'; *bara syrg̃ëirχ,* 'bread made, like lightcakes, of wheat or barley mixed with oatmeal and barm added' (J.J.).

bara, v., 'it is barred, forbidden'; *bara sɔm* (in playing marbles), 'moving is forbidden' (I.W.); *bara k̆iks,* 'another go is forbidden' (I.W.); *bara dokkyn [tokkyn].*

barbar, barbur, s.m., barbwr, I.G. 110 [55], 'barber'.

barbro, v., 'to do the work of a barber'; 'to dock trees' (I.W.).

bardun = mardun (J.J.).

barð, s.m., pl. *bëirð,* bardd, D., 'poet': *barð talkan slip,* 'a sorry rimester'.

barðonjaθ, s.f., barddoniaeth, D., 'poetry'.

bargan, s.f., pl. *barg̃ëinjon,* bargen, D., D.G. clvi. 6; pl. bargeinion, B.C. 146. 22, 'bargain', esp. a 'bargain in a slate quarry', i.e. 'a part of the rock, generally seven or eight yards wide, let on special terms to three men, who are called *k̢riu bargan*'.

barg̃ëinjo, v. bargeinio, D., s.v. 'depaciscor'; 'to come to terms, to settle a bargain': *daχi' wedi barg̃ëinjo?   na: ðo: wi:r, ma na χwëigjan 'r̢hɔŋθoni.*

bargod, s.f., pl. *bargodjon, bargoda,* bargod, D., 'eaves': *ma: r vargod ɔn dɔveryd,* 'the eaves are dripping'; *du:r bargod,* 'water from the roof'; *may hi n r̢hewi n r̢hɔujog, ag ma: n l̢ixjo l̢yuχ ɔn yuχ na r vargod* (E.J.), 'it is freezing hard, and the snow is drifting above the eaves' (an alliterative saying).

bargodi, v., bargodi, S.E., 'to project, overhang', e.g. of slates or the covering of a haystack.

barig, s.m., barrug, D., 'hoar-frost': *ma: r barig ɔŋ g̃en gwyn ar ɔ ðëyar,* 'hoar-frost is a white film on the ground'; *r oy:ð po: b man ɔn wyn o varig,* 'everything was white with frost'; *ma: r niul ɔŋ kodi o:ð ar ɔ barig,* 'the mist is rising from the frosty ground'.   Cf. *r̢he:u.*

baril, s.m., pl. *barila*, baril, D.; D.G. lxxiv. 41; O.F. baril, 'barrel'. Also *balir*.

barjaθ, s.m., bariaeth, D., 'greediness'.

barjo, v., barrio, M.Ll. i. 186. 32, 'to lock, bolt': *may ġ∂no vo gorjad i vynd ∂n i bokkad ond i ni bëidjo varjo vo oδi'veun*, 'he has a key to go in his pocket as long as we don't lock it (the door) inside'.

barkar, s.m., barcer, D., s.v. 'coriarius'; Acts ix. 43, 'barker'.

barǩid, s.m., barcut, D., 'kite' (but according to Forrest this word is always used in North Wales for the common buzzard, Buteo vulgaris): *mi' δo:θ o vel barǩid ar ġiu*, 'he came suddenly, unexpectedly'; also *disġin vel barǩid ar ġiu ;—barǩid gwynt*, 'kite' (artificial): *flëio barǩid*, 'to fly a kite'.

barkjo, v. 'to strip off bark, to do the work of a barker'.

barklod, s.m., pl. *barklodja*, barclod, C.L.C. ii. 21. 11; Eng. barm-cloth; 'apron'.

barklodjad, s., barclodaid, S.E., 'apronful'.

barkty, s.m., 'tan-house, barkery'.

barkyttan, s.f., barcutan, D.G. ciii. 10, 'kite' (but see *barǩid*); *barkyttan bappyr*, 'kite' (artificial).

barn, s.f., barn, D., 'judgment, opinion': *∂ varn gɷwir*, 'the just judgment'; *ɹhoi barn ar*, 'to judge of'; *∂n o:l marn i:*, 'in my opinion'; *daχi o r y:n varn a vi: ?*, 'are you of the same opinion as I?'; *·t ∂danu δim o r y:n varn ar ∂ pe:θ*, 'they are not of the same opinion about the matter'.

barnëiʃo, v., barneisio, W.S., 'to varnish'.

barnis, bernis, s., bernais, H.S. 20. 14; barnais, D.G. lxxvi. 25; D., s.v. 'encaustum'; 'varnish' (O.H.).

barny, v., barnu, D., 'to judge': *barny ∂n d∂nar, galad*, 'to judge kindly, harshly'.

barv, s.f., pl. *barva*, barf, D., 'beard': *tori barv*, 'to shave' (seldom used = *ʃevjo*); *barv ka:θ*, 'whiskers of a cat'; *barv deru* (J.J.), 'a kind of lichen growing on oak-trees'; *barv mo:r*, 'a kind of seaweed' (Desmarestia).

barvog, adj., barfog, D., 'bearded'.

barys, adj., barus, D., 'greedy': *plentyn barys*. When used with *ka:θ* the word implies a tendency to steal; *anival barys*, 'an animal which is perpetually wandering from field to field' (J.J.).

ba:s, adj., 'bass': *lais ba:s*.

basġad, s.f., pl. *basġedi*, basket, W.S.; basged, D., 'basket': *gwr∂δyn basġad*, 'the handle of a basket'; *gwëylod, ti:n basġad*, 'the bottom of a basket'; *senna basġad*, 'the ribs of a basket'; *gwaiθ basġad*, 'wicker-work'.

basġedjad, s.f., pl. *basġədëidja,* basgedaid, S.E., 'basketful'.

basn, s.m., pl. *basns,* 'basin'.

bastart, s., pl. *bastardjad,* bastart, S.G. 377. 11 ; bastardd, D. (1) 'bastard' : *bastart my:l,* pl. *bastardjad mɔlod,* 'mule'. Cf. T.N. 94. 30. (2) in slate quarries—'a kind of slate which is a mixture of pure slate and granite, and which does not admit of being split finely, but is often used for cheap roofing'. There are two varieties, *bastart galad* and *bastart rɵujog,* 'hard and soft greys'.

batjo, v., 'to use a mattock' (J.J.).

batl, s.f., pl. *bateloð* (O.H.), bateil, S.G. 113. 25 ; battel, W.S. ; pl. batteloedd, I.G. 216. [52], 'battle'.

battog, s.f., pl. *batoga,* 'mattock' (J.J.; O.H.). J.J. distinguished between *battog, kaib,* and *ho:v.*

ba:θ, s., a by-form of *ma:θ* used only in phrases like : *welis i ri·o:yd mo i ba:θ,* 'I never saw the like of her' ; *heb i ba:θ,* 'unequalled' (fem.). Also in pl. *·welsoχi ri·o:yd hogja o i baθa nu ?,* 'did you ever see such boys ?'

ba:u, s.m., baw, D. (1) 'dung' : *ba:u devaid, gwarθag, ḷuynog,* etc. ; *y:n ba:u ja:r a r ḷaḷ ba:u deryn,* 'six of one and half a dozen of the other' ; *ry:ð o mo i va:u i r k̃i:—weḷ gɔno vo roid ɔ garag arno vo,* said of a very niggardly person. (2) 'mud' : *ma: ho:yl ɔχ tra:yd m ɔ ba:u,* 'there are marks of your feet in the mud'; *tai ba:u,* 'mud houses'. (3) 'dirt, rubbish', e.g. in quarries = *rubal, sburjal ; karjo ba:u,* 'to cart away rubbish'. (4) 'weeds' = *χwyn.* (5) *vedra i nëyd dim ba:u o hono vo,* 'I can make nothing of it'.

baud, s.m.f., pl. *bodja,* bawd, D. (1) 'thumb, great toe': *baud maur ; day, du:y vaud ;—ɽhoi klek ar ɔ maud,* 'to snap my fingers'; *t ëi di vyθ yuχ la:u baud sɵudul ; vɔði di byθ yuχ baud na sɵudul,* 'you will never get on in the world' (cf. G.O. ii. 92. 5) ; *hevo ·bysabaud,* 'with finger and thumb'; *kadu dɔ vodja,* 'do not pick and steal'; *byu o r vaud i r ġena,* 'to live from hand to mouth'. (2) 'claw' (of a crab): *bodja kɽaŋkod.* (3) 'in slate quarries *bodja* (ḷa:yθ) are certain flaws which, when the slate is split, have the shape of thumb-marks and the colour of milk' (J.J.). Cf. *smotja ḷa:yθ* (the former affect the splitting and the latter do not). (4) in slate quarries the term *bodja* is also applied to the projections to which the ropes are attached which support a *burð* or hanging scaffold.

baujaχ, s.m., bawach, S.E., 'a worthless fellow': *he:n vaujaχ garu ɔdi o.*

bawa, v., bawa, S.E., 'cacare'. Cf. *ba:u* (1).

bawad, s.f., pl. *bawëidja,* mawaid, D., 'llonaid dwy law'. (1) 'handful': *dɔruχ i mi vawad o hono vo,* 'give me a handful of it'; *du:y váwad,* 'as much as can be held in both hands'. (2) 'as far as can be reached between finger and thumb in the game at marbles called *χwara tṛiθuḷ*' (W.H.).

bawað, adj., bawaidd, G.O. i. 162. 3, ' sordid, stingy '.

ba:y, s.m., ' bay ' (of the sea).

ba:yð, s.m., baedd, D., ' boar ': *danvon ər hu:χ at ə ba:yð ;—mi godis ə ɤwrəχyn vel ba:yð kənðëirjog* (J.J.), ' I bristled up like a mad boar '; *ba:yð gwy:ḷt* (J.J., O.H.), ' wild boar '; *vel ba:yð gwy:ḷt o r ko:yd* (J.J.), ' raging '. (Cf. *arθ*.)

bayχ, s.m., pl. *bëiχja*, baich, D.; bauch, M.Ll. ii. 40. 32 ; 109. 14 ; baych, W.Ll. lxxvi. 42 ; lxxvii. 29. 32 ; cf. G.R. 27. 1, ' a load, burden ': *bayχ maur o brikja*, ' a heavy load of firewood '.—Also fig. *may hi wedi mynd ən vayχ arno vo*, ' it has become a burden to him '.

ba:ys, adj.; comp. *bëysaχ*, bais, D., ' vadatio '; bâs, ' non profundus '; ' shallow ': *du:r ba:ys*, ' shallow water '.

be: [*be:θ*].

bed, s., pl. *bedja*, ' bed (in slate quarries) '.

bedlan, s.m., in phrase *ar hy:d ə bedlan*, ' all the time '; *may o n sunjan am i suppar ar hy:d ə bedlan*, ' he keeps grumbling for his supper '; *paid a bregljaχ ar hy:d ə bedlan* (E.J.), ' don't keep jabbering all the time '; *ḷuiðjannys ar hy:d ə bedlan* (O.H.), ' successful all along the line'.

bedu, s.pl., sing. *bedwan*, f., bedw, D., ' birches ': *briga bedu*, ' birch twigs '; *gjalam vedu*, ' birch rod '.

bedyð, s.m., bedydd, D., ' baptism ': *bedyð esgob*, ' confirmation '. Cf. L.A. 145. 8; Yny lhyvyr hwnn [30].

bedəðjo, v., bedyddio, D. Pret. Pass. *bedəðjuyd*, ' to baptize ': *ma: nu wedi ka:l i bedəðjo ǵin ər esgob*, ' they have been confirmed '.

be:ð, s.f., pl. *beða, beði*, D., ' grave ': *toṛi be:ð*, ' to dig a grave '.

begjo, v., begio, C.C. 163. 17, ' to beg ': *vegja vo ðim ˙arnoχi*, ' he would not beg from you '.

bëibil, s.m., pl. *bëibla*, bibl, D., s.v. ' biblion '; ' bible '.

bëiðgar, adj., beiddgar, D., ' daring ' (but cf. *mëiðjo*).

bëiχjo, v., beichio, D., ' to bellow ' (of a bull) = *py:o*. Also of human beings, ' to bellow, bawl ': *r o:ð oᵐm bëiχjo (kṛi:o) = gnëyd nada*.

bëiχjog, adj., beichiog, D., ' onustus, gravidus '; ' bulging ', e. g. of setts when not cut square (O.H.) = *boljog*.

bëili, s.m., pl. *bli:od*, bayli, W.S.; pl. bailîaid, B.C. 120. 30 ; Mid. Eng. baily ; ' bailiff, sheriff's officer ': *mor brəsyr a bëili meun saf'un*.

bëintin ; bëindin (W.H.), s.f., Eng. binding. (1) ' binding round the edges of an article of clothing ', etc. (2) ' what is given over and above the measure ': *ṛhoi hyn ən vëindin.*

bëio, v., beio, D., ' to blame ' : *nid ə bobol sy i vëio*, ' it is not the people who are to blame '.

bekkar, s.m., ' baker '.

bekkun, s.m., Eng. bed-gown, ' a woman's bodice ' (now seldom worn) : *pais a bekkun*.

bekkus, s.m., ' bake-house '.

bekn, s.m., ' bacon '. Also *bakkun*.

bekſo, v., fecsio, T.N. 22. 35 ; Eng. vex, ' to worry '.

bela, s.m., pl. *belod*, bele, D., ' marten ' (Mustela martes).

belifegor, s.m., Belphegor (name of demon. Cf. B.C. 143. 19 ; T.N. 457. 6.—' Beelphegor ' is the form in the Vulgate corresponding to ' Baal-peor ' in the A.V. Cf. Num. xxv. 3), term of reproach : *riu he:n velifegor dru:g*.

belax, adv., bellach, D., ' now, at last ' : *mi ðəljun inna ga:yl və suppar belax, axos r ədu i wedi gwëiljo digon*, ' it's time I had my supper too by this time, as I've waited long enough ' ; *rhaid i ni vo:d ən ðjolxgar am bo:b durnod bra:v belax ga:ni ru:an*, ' we must be thankful for every fine day we get now (from now onwards) ' ; *rhəux gora i χ su:n belax*, ' stop your noise now '.

bendiǵedig, adj., bendigedic, Gen. ix. 26. (1) ' magnificent, soul-inspiring ' (e. g. of an eloquent sermon or prayer). (2) ' excellent, splendid ' : *daxi wedi gnëyd tro: bendiǵedig*.

bendiθ, s.f., pl. *bendiθjon*, bendith, D., ' blessing '. Used ironically in *do:s, bendiθ ðyu i ti: !, do:s o: na, bendiθ ə ta:d i ti !, do:s, bendiθ ta:d !*, ' get away for goodness' sake ' ; *govyn bendiθ ar ə bu:yd*, ' to ask a blessing on the food, to say grace '.

bendiθjol, adj., bendithiol, S.E., ' beneficial ' : *tro: bendiθjol*, ' a beneficial turn '.

benθig, s.m., benthyg, D. ; cf. benthig, G.R. 57. 10, ' loan ' : *rhoi benθig a kəmmyd benθig*, ' to lend and to borrow ' ; *govyn benθig (am venθig) su:lt*, ' to borrow a shilling ' ; *ga: i venθig su:lt ·gənoxi ?*, ' will you lend me a shilling ? ' ; *dərux i mi venθig honna, s gwelux ən ða:*, ' lend me that, please ' ; *arjan benθig*, ' borrowed money ' ; *benθig rhuŋ la:u a la:u*, ' a loan without security '.

benθəkka, θəkka (O.H.), v., cf. benthygio, D., ' to borrow '.

bera, s.pl., berr, D. ; cf. T.N. 146. 4, ' legs ' : *səmmyd də vera*, ' stir your stumps ' ; *mi trawoð o nes o:yð a i vera i vəny*, ' he knocked him sprawling '.

berdjo, v., in phr. *berdjo klauð (kerig)*, ' to place thorns on the top of a wall and keep them in position by placing stones on them '.— *kerig ar vlëyna ə drain a r bona i vəny*.

berdyn, berdiŋ, s.m., 'thorns, etc., placed on the top of a waⅱ, with stones to keep them in position'.

bernis [*barnis*].

beru, s.m., berw, D. (1) 'boiling': *dəruχ ja:s o veru arno ve,* 'boil it slightly';—fig. *may hi n veru gwy:ḷḷ,* 'it is very lively (e. g. of a meeting)'. (2) 'foaming water'. (3) 'whim, fad, infatuation, muddle-headedness', i.e. *pen ma ru:in wedi kəmmyd riu y:n pe:θ ən i ben a dim ond hunna ;—ma na riu veru ən i benno.*

beru, berwi, s.pl., berwr, D. : *beru du:r,* 'water-cress' (Nasturtium officinale) ; *beru frëinig,* 'cress' (Lepidium sativum).

berva, s.f., pl. *ber·va:y,* berfa, D., 'wheel-barrow': *berva vrëiχja,* 'a wooden contrivance without wheels, with two handles at each end, for carrying stones, etc.'

ber·va:yd, s.f., pl. *bervëidja,* berfäaïd, S.E., 'wheel-barrowful'.

berwedig, adj., berwedig, D., s.v. 'assus'; 'boiling': *du:r berwedig,* 'boiling water'.

berwi, v., berwi, D. Pret. 3. *berwoð.* Imperative *berwa; berwuχ, beruχ,* 'to boil': *ma: r du:r əm berwi,* 'the water is boiling'; *ma: r teḱaḷ əm berwi,* 'the kettle is boiling'; *berwi ŋ grəχjas,* 'to boil furiously'; *u:y wedi berwi,* 'a boiled egg'; *tənnuχ ə teḱaḷ i laur ṛhag iðo verwi n sy:χ,* 'take the kettle off or else it will boil away'; *t o:ys dim berwi arno vo,* 'it won't boil'. Figurative uses : *may ṇrha:yd i m berwi,* 'my feet are tingling with heat'; *berwi i ben,* 'to take a fad about something, to get excited, talk excitedly';—'to swarm': *əm berwi o lay, o brṛvad,* 'swarming with lice, with insects';—*may r ḷe: əm berwi i ġi:d hevo nu,* 'the whole place is swarming with them'.

betjø, v., 'to bet'.

betjo, v., Eng. debate (?), with *pəsljo : pəsljo a betjo* (*p ṛ ynta nëiθ o ai pëidjo*), O.H., 'to rack one's brains, to be at one's wit's end (as to whether one will do a thing or not)'.

be:θ, be:, beθ, be, beth (for pa beth). (1) interrogative pronoun *be: ?,* 'what?', asking for the repetition of a remark (= *ṣyt?,* which is considered less polite), and in the other senses of the English word; *be di o ?,* 'what is it?'; *be sy: ?,* 'what's the matter?'; *be s ant i/o ?,* 'what's the matter with you?' (= *be hary ti ?*); *be may o n ðëyd?,* 'what does he say?'; *be:θ o:yð ə testyn ?,* 'what was the text?'; *i be: may hunna n ða: ?,* 'what's this for?'—With *i* understood 'why?': *be na: i helḱid o mor beḷ ?,* 'why should I lug it so far?'; *be r a: i a vo: ?,* 'why should I take it?';—*be stad, stid* = *be sy wedi du:ad,* e. g. *·be stad iðo vo ?,* 'what's the matter with him?'; *·be stad i r hogan ?; ·be stid i r dy:n ?* (2) introducing indirect question : *hidjuχ be vo, hidjux be vo vo:,* 'never mind'; *wa:yθ be* *vo*, ' it doesn't matter '; *dim ods be:*, ' it doesn't matter what '; *d un i δim be na: i, p ɣ ynta mynd ta pëidjo*, ' I don't know what to do, whether to go or not '; *may hun əm böyθaχ na d un i δim be:*, ' this is hotter than I don't know what '; *t o:δ i δim əɲ gubod be δëyda hi*, ' she did not know what to say '.—With *bənnag* (a) ' whatever ': *beθ bənnag nëiθ o*, ' whatever he does '; *goluχ ə gannuyl̦ be bənnag neuχi*, ' light the candle whatever you do '; (b) ' at any rate ' (Anglo-Welsh, ' whatever ').

beθma, y peth yma, ' what d'you call it? ': *r o:δ o n rëit beθma*.

bëydy, s.m., pl. *bə·dai*, beudy, D., ' cow-house, cattle-shed '.

bëyδy, v., baeddu, D. = *mëydy*, ' to maul, soil ': *dənjon əm bëyδy i ɡ̇iliδ ; plant əm bëyδy r ty:*; fig. *bëyδy kəmerjad dy:n*.

bëynyδ, adv., beunydd, D., ' quotidie '; ' continually ': *may o əmma bëynyδ əɲ kl̦ebran ;—byθ a bëynyδ*, ' for ever and a day '.

biδjol, adj., buddiol, D., ' advantageous, serviceable ': *dil̦ad biδjol ;—gwisgo n viδjol*, ' to wear serviceable clothes '.

bi:f, s.m., biff, W.S., ' beef '.

bigal, s.m., pl. *biɡ̇ëiljad*, bugaîl, non bigail, D., ' shepherd '. Often *bigal devaid*.

biɡ̇ëiljo, v., bugeilio, Cant. i. 7, ' to keep sheep ': *biɡ̇ëiljo devaid*.

bihavjo, bəhavjo, v., ' to behave ' = *əmδuyn*.

bik, call to a single pig (cf. *ɡ̇is*). Also an endearing expression to a pig : *bik ba:χ !* (O.H.).

bildjo, v., bildio, T.N. 407. 11, ' to build '. Cf. *adëiljady, kodi*.

bili dukkar, s., ' razor-bill ' (Alca torda). Also *bili dəuka, bili dukka*.

bilifudan, s., ' a kind of material ': *klo:s o vilifudan, pais vilifudan*. Also a term of reproach : *ɣ he:n vilifudan gwirjon* (O.H.).

bilug, s.m., pl. *biluks*, bilwc cau, W.S. (a hedgynge byll), ' bill-hook '.

bi:tʃ, s., pl. *ko:yd bi:tʃ*, ' beech ': *knay bi:tʃ*, ' beech-nuts '.

biumaras, bliumaras, ə bliu, Buwmares, W.Ll. lxvii. 22, ' Beaumaris '.

biusful, adj., Eng. abuseful ; ' cruel, harsh, apt to ill-treat '.

biuslyd, adj. = *biusful*.

biuʃo, v., biwsio, T.N. 300. 24 ; Eng. abuse. (1) ' to abuse, insult '. (2) ' to ill-treat ': *biuʃo anivëiljad ; be u:ti m biuʃo ml̦hant a i kyro nu ?*

bjogan (*pjodan* at Tregarth, I.W.). s.f., pl. *bjogannod, pjogod* (O.H.), pioden and piogen, D., s.v. ' pi '; ' magpie ' (Pica rustica) : *k̇in ʃoɲkad a r bjogan*. Also a term of reproach for a woman.

blagyr, s.pl., blagur, D., 'young sprouts or shoots': *tavly r blagyr*, 'to sprout'; *blagyr ədi r təuljad kənta*.

blagyro, v., blaguro, D., 'to sprout'.

blaið, s.m., pl. *blëiðja(i)d*, blaidd, D., 'wolf'. (For pl. cf. M.Ll. ii. 118. 7; D.P.O. 160. 35.)

blakkan, s., 'a black': *ǩin ðy:ad a blakkan*. Also a cow-name. Cf. T.N. 183. 5.

bla:s, s.m., blâs, D., 'taste': *may bla:s iṛi:og arno vo*, 'it tastes of treacle'; *nt o:ys na vla:s da: arno vo ?*, 'isn't it nice?'; *be di r bla:s dru:g sy ar hun ?*, 'what makes this taste so nasty?'; *wedi mynd aḷan o i vla:s*, 'to have lost its (proper) taste, to have become sour, high, etc.'—Fig. *may bla:s ar da:n heno*, 'a fire is pleasant to-night'; *χe:s i ðim bla:s ərï o:yd arno vo*, 'I never had any pleasure in it'; *χe:s i ðim bla:s ərï o:yd i wrando arno vo*, 'I never had any pleasure in listening to him'.

blasterog, adj., sometimes for *brasterog*, 'fat'.

blasys, adj., blasus D., s.v. 'sapidus'; 'tasty, savoury': fig. *pṛegaθ vlasys*, 'a taking sermon'.

blaſo, v., blasio, 'to taste' = *provi*: *t ədi o ðim ond i vlaſo vo*. Cf. Y genau sydd yn ffailio iawn flassio pob melysion, B. 1747.

b la:u = *heb la:u* [*heb*].

blaud, s.m., blawd, D., 'flour': *blaud gwyn = pëiljad*, 'wheat-flour'; *blaud ǩ̈eirχ*, 'oatmeal'; *blaud ḷi:*, 'saw-dust'; *gwerθy blaud*, 'to flatter'; *dal blaud wynab*, 'to put the best face on matters', 'to put up with what cannot be prevented'.

bla:yn, s.m., pl. *blëyna*, blaen, D. (1) 'front, fore-part, tip, point': *bla:yn ə tṛu:yn*, 'the tip of the nose'; *ar vla:yn ə tṛa:yd*, 'on tip-toe'; *ar vlëyna χ tṛa:yd*, 'on tip-toe'; *bla:yn ə gəḷaθ*, 'the point of the knife'; *blëyna ə bəsað*, 'the tips of the fingers'; *bla:yn ḷanu*, 'the turn of the tide'; *bla:yn newyð*, said of the .new moon: *mi ða:u penwaig hevo r bla:yn newyð* (O.H.), 'there will be herrings with the new moon'; *bla:yn ə mo:r*, 'the edge of the flowing or ebbing sea'; *deryn əɲ kaḷyn bla:yn ə mo:r*.—Common in place-names, e. g. *bla:yn ə ðalva* (between Pen Bryn Du and Y Drosgl); *bla:yn kḷənin* (i. e. Celynin—between Y Foel Fras and Pen y Dorth Goch). (2) 'priority' (of place or time): *pu:y ga:θ ə bla:yn ?*, 'who was first?'; *aχyb ə bla:yn*, 'to forestall'. (3) 'push': *t o:s dim bla:yn əno vo*, 'he has no push in him', 'he is not quick in furthering his own interests'. Cf. also *blëinjon*.

Adverbs and prepositions formed with *bla:yn* are the following :—

o vla:yn, prep., 'before' (of place, and sometimes of time): *ṛhoi kḷut o vla:yn ə ta:n*, 'to put a rag before the fire'; *ṛhoi ə drol o vla:yn ə ǩefyl*, 'to put the cart before the horse'; *toṛi iuḷ o vla:yn höylan*, 'to make a hole to put a nail in'; *un i ðim be ða:u o vla:yn ne ar i c:l o*, 'I don't know what comes before or after it'; *o vla:yn ə ty:*, 'in front of the house'; *o mla:yn i*, 'in front of me'; 'before me' (of time); *rheduχ o n bla:yn ni*, 'run on in front'; *o vla:yn ə gla:u*, 'before the rain'.

o r bla:yn, adv., 'before, ago': *p(ə)θevnos o r bla:yn ; r usnos o r bla:yn*, 'the other week'; *·vy:oχi əno o r bla:yn?*, 'have you been there before?'; *ə tro: o r bla:yn*, 'last time'.

rhag bla:yn, adv., 'at once, immediately': *may hi ŋ krəχy i dail rhag bla:yn*, 'its leaves shrink up immediately'; *gwerθy po:b pe:θ rhag bla:yn*, 'to sell everything at once'.

ə mla:yn, adv., 'forwards': *ən o:l ag ə mla:yn*, 'backwards and forwards, there and back, to and fro'; *keruχ ən əχ bla:yn*, 'go on'; *tyd ə mla:yn*, *ən də vla:yn*, 'come on'; *mynd ə mla:yn hevo r gwaiθ*, 'to go on with the work'.

ə mla:yn la:u, adv., 'in front of, in the sense of anticipating or forestalling a person or thing': *mynd ə mla:yn la:u iðo vo*, 'to forestall him' (cf. *blëynlau*).

bla:yn, adj., comp. *blëynaχ*, blaen, D., 'foremost, front': *ko:ys vla:yn*, 'fore-leg'; *daint bla:yn*, 'front tooth'.

bleðyn in *kleða bleðyn*, cleddyf Bleddyn, D., 'spleen'.

blëind, s.m., pl. *blëinds*, 'blind' (O.H. has *kərtan*).

blëinjo, v., blaenio, D., s.v. 'spiculo', 'to milk the first milk at milking-time'.

blëinjon, s., pl. blaenion, S.E., s.v. 'blaen'; cf. Neh. x. 37, 'the first milk at milking-time'.

ble:r, adj., afler, D., vulgo pro aflerw. (1) 'untidy': *ru:m vle:r ; du i n rhy: vle:r i vynd alan.* (2) 'untidy in work, wasteful, unmethodical, lacking in promptitude': *ma: nu ŋ gwëiθjo ə χwaral ən vle:r jaun*, 'they are working the quarry very wastefully'; *dənas vle:r ən i gwi:sg a i gwaiθ ;—·r öyðanu n vle:r jaun = hi:r əŋ kəχuyn* (E.J., speaking of the mourners at a funeral). (3) 'strange', implying the lack of something: *by:ð ən vle:r*, 'it will seem strange without you'.

bleruχ, vleruχ, s.m., aflerwch, S.E., 'untidiness, wastefulness'.

ble:u, s.pl., sing. *blewyn* m. (which is sometimes also used collectively), blew, D. (1) 'hair' (of persons, except of the hair of the head—cf., however, *blewyn o wa:lt*—and animals): *ma: r ga:θ əŋ koli ble:u*, 'the cat's fur is coming out'; *blewyn maur*, 'long hair', e.g. of cattle which can stand the weather; *ble:u ləgad*, 'eye-lashes'; *ble:u gëivr*, 'a peculiar formation of clouds' (J.J.); *mi ðëydif i am bo:b blewyn o wa:lt ən i fen i*, 'I told her over and over again'; *heb vlewyn ar i davod*, 'without mincing matters'; *tənny blewyn o i dru:yn o*, 'to anger him'; *rhaid tənny r gwinað o r ble:u*, 'one must set to in earnest = rhaid i χi vo:d uθi hi o ðivri, gimmint a ·vedruχi ; wedi nëyd o i dru:χ ə blewyn*, 'having done it to a nicety'; *blᴇwyn kam ən mynd i r ləgad*, 'an eyelash getting into the eye'. (2) used of grass: *blᴇwyn glaːs*, 'fresh spring grass, unwholesome for sheep' (J.J.); *mi gorfenniθ blᴇwyn glaːs ə gwanuyn i*, said of a sheep, because such grass picks out the weakest (O.H.); *bleːu glaːs* = also grass such as grows up in a path and has to be removed. (3) '(not) the least, (not) the slightest bit': *δary χi vrivo? naː, dim blᴇwyn* (O.H.), 'have you hurt yourself? No, not in the least'; *dim blᴇwyn o laːu* (O.H.), 'not a drop of rain'; *waːyθ i mi r yːn blᴇwyn bᴇidjo* (O.H.), 'I might just as well not every bit'; *waːyθ ǵin i hun δim blᴇwyn ən ə byːd* (O.H.), 'I should like that just as well'.

bleujaχ, s., pl. blewiach, D., 'hair (in a disparaging sense), down': *riu heːn vleujaχ ar i eːn o* (I.W.). Also 'small bones of fish' (I.W.).

blewemma, v. (?), blewyna, S.E., 'to hang about': *be uːti n i vlewemma* (O.H.—obsolete).

blewog, adj., blewog, D., 'hairy': *dylo blᴇwog*, see *laːu*.

blëynad, s., ? planed, D., s.v. 'planeta', in the sense of 'meteor' —in phrase *mynd vel blëynad*, 'to go hurriedly' (I.W.).

blëynbost, s., blaenbost, S.E., 'the post to which a gate fastens'.

blëynl̦au, adj., blaenllaw, D., s.v. 'praesignifico'; 'pushing, quick to further one's own interests'.

blëynl̦ym, adj., blaenllym, D., s.v. 'cuspidatus', 'samius', 'satyricè'; 'sharp-pointed' (more often expressed by *blaːyn main*).

blëynor, s.m., blaenor, D., 'an elder in a chapel'.

blëynori, v., blaenori, D., s.v. 'excedo', etc., 'to take a prominent position, to take a leading part' (*meun*).

bliːn, adj., blin, D. (1) 'peevish, bad-tempered, cross': *kradyr kaːs bliːn*, 'an unpleasant, peevish creature'; *plenłyn bliːn*. (2) 'tiresome, unpleasant': *heːn waiθ go vliːn ədi o*, 'it's a tiresome job'; *maːr dᴇwyδ ən δigon bliːn uθ δal vod o n syːχ*, 'the weather is rather unpleasant, considering it is dry'. (3) 'tired': *tᴇimlo n vliːn*.

blinedig, adj., blinedig, 'tired'.

blino, v., blino, D. (1) 'to be tired': *du i wedi blino*, 'I am tired'; *daχi wedi blino ar ǵiːg?*, 'are you tired of meat?'; *du i wedi blino əmma*, 'I am tired of being here' (Anglo-Welsh, 'I am tired here'). Fig. of land: *may r tiːr wedi blino*, 'the land is tired, used up as regards bearing crops'. (2) 'to tire'. (3) 'to annoy, aggravate, vex': *t ədi o m blino dim arna i*, 'it doesn't annoy me at all'.

bliŋo, v., blingo, D., 'to flay': *mᴇurθ a laːδ, ebrił a vliŋ* (prov.), 'March slays, April flays'; *bliŋo ə kiː (ə gaːθ) erbyn i gumfon (χumfon)*, 'to squander, to become poor through being too free with one's money'; *bliŋo r koːyd* (O.H.), 'to slice off the surface of wood', e.g. with an adze (*neδa*) in ship-building.

bli:θ, s., blith, D., 'lactans, lactarius, lac praebens': only in *degum ə bli:θ*, 'tithe on cattle, sheep, and poultry' (O.H.).

bloda, s.pl., sing. *blodyn*, m., blodeu, D., 'flowers': *ən de:u o vloda*, 'thick with flowers'; *ən i vloda*, 'flowering'; *bloda piso n ə gwely*, 'dandelions'. Cf. Fr. pissenlit.

blöiðjo, v., bloeddio, D., s.v. 'clamo'; 'to shout': *o:yð o m blöiðjo uθ farad; blöiðjo maur*.

blokkyn, s.m., pl. *blokja*. (1) 'block': *blokkyn pren*. (2) 'blockhead': *he:n vlokkyn*.—Also *plokkyn*, q.v.

blonag, s.m., bloneg, D., 'pig's fat, lard': *rhaid i mi vyu ar ə mlonag am usnos*, 'I must live on my own fat for a week' (being in straits); *hiro hu:χ de:u a blonag* (prov.), 'to give to one who already has plenty'.

blonhegan, s., blonhegen, D., 'fasciculus axungiae'; 'leaf' (of pork).

blonhegog, adj., blonegog, T.N. 15. 38, 'fat'.

blorjo, v. = *broljo* (E.J.).   Cf. S.J.E., p. 108.

blotjog, adj., plotiog, T.N. 12. 29, 'variegated, of various colours': *gəun blotjog, fro:g gotton vlotjog*.

blottyn, s.m., Eng. blot; 'speck, mark': *byuχ wen a blottyn dy: ar i θalkan i; blottyn dy: ar uymmad merχ, ar gi: gwyn*.

blo:yð, s.f., bloedd, D., s.v. 'clamor'; 'shout'.

blo:ysg, adj., bloesg, D., 'blaesiloquus, blaesus'; 'of thick utterance': *tavod blo:ysg; may i barabl o n vlo:ysg*.

bluiðjad, s.m., blwyddiaid, (pl.) Lev. xxiii. 18, 19, 'a yearling' (J.J.); adjectivally *devaid bluiðjad*, 'yearling sheep'.

blu:χ, s.m., pl. *bləχa; bləχod* (O.H.), blwch, D., 'box' (in fairly common use, but *boks* is more frequent): *blu:χ ə bigal*, 'a small, round, light wooden box formerly used by shepherds to hold butter, containing from a quarter to half a pound, carried with a piece of a loaf (in a wallet) and a can of buttermilk' (J.J.); *blu:χ bakko*, 'tobacco pouch'.

blu:yð, s.f., blwydd. (1) 'a year, in speaking of age': *be di o:yd o ? blu:yð a hannar*, 'how old is he? eighteen months'; *he:n wraig ən dair blu:yð i gant o:yd*, 'an old woman of ninety-seven'; *hannar blu:yð ədi o vory*, 'he is six months old to-morrow'; *pen i vlu:yð*, 'his birthday'; *dy sy:l duyθa o:ð hi ŋ ka:l pen i blu:yð ən y:n or ðe:g*, 'it was her eleventh birthday last Sunday'. (2) 'yearlings, things of a year old': *ma: r blu:yð ən ʃa:ð ə dəvluyð* (O.H.), '(frogs) of one year old kill those of two years old'.

bluyðyn, s.f., pl. *blənəðoð, blənəða*, blwyddyn, D., s.v. 'annus'; 'year' (not used after cardinal numbers except *y:n*): *y:n vluyðyn*, 'one year'; *may o wedi maru ɛr s blənəðoð*, 'he died years ago'; *vlənəða ar vlənɛða*, 'years upon years'; *kantoð o vlənəðoð ən o:l*, 'hundreds of years ago'; *bluyðyn nɛwyð ða: i χi ! ər y:n pɛ:θ (r y: va:θ) i χiθa*, 'a happy New Year to you! The same to you'.

bly:s, s.m., blys, D., 'longing, craving, desire': *ma na i vly:s o*, 'I am longing for it'; *ma na i vly:s govyn iðo vo*, 'I have a great mind to ask him'; *n ! o:s ˚arnoχi ðim bly:s aliŗo ?*, 'haven't you any desire to change?' (i. e. your manner of living); *r o:ð arno vo vly:s bildjo ty:*, 'he wanted to build a house'; *kodi bly:s*, 'to excite a desire'.

bləðar, s., pl. *bləðars*, Eng. plover (?), the 'grey plover' (Squatarola helvetica).

blənað, s.f., blynedd, D., s.v. 'annus'; 'year' (only used after cardinal numbers except *y:n*): *du:y vlənað, iair blənað, pedar blənað, pym mlənað, χwɛ blənað, saiθ mlənað, u:yθ mlənað, na:u mlənað, dɛ:ŋ mlənad, igjan mlənað, kan mlənað*.

blənəðol, adj., blynyddol, D., s.v. 'annuus'; 'annual'.

bləf'o, v., blysio, D., 'to long for' = *bo:d ən awyðys, ɒuχys*.

bləf'og, adj., cf. blysig, D., 'longing'.

bnavyd, bənavyd, v., bynafyd, S.E., 'to hurt, to hurt oneself' = *brivo:* *may o wedi bnavyd ən aru ;* *mi lasun i bnavyd o n ovnaduy*, 'I might have hurt him very badly'.—Tan frethyn yn dy frathu y Nifel i'th fynafu, A. (T. Ellis Roberts).

bnavys, adj., 'painful' = *anavys*.

bnɛðig, bṇhɛðig, adj., bonheddig, D., s.v. 'nobilis', only in *gu(:)r bnɛðig*, gwr bonheddig, 'gentleman'. Pl. *bonɛðigjon, bonɛðigjons, bðigjons*.

bnjawid, bənjawid, s.m., pl. *bnjawəda*, mynawyd, D., 'pricker, awl'.

bo: s.m., bo, S.E., 'bogey'.

boba, s.f., epithet applied to an old woman (practically obsolete). Cf. *ɛwa*.

bo:d ; *bod* (in rapid speech), v., bôd, D., 'to be'.

Present : S. 1. *ədu, du*, 2. *u:yt (u:t)*, 3. *ədi, di, i* ; *ma:y (may, ma:, ma)*; *o:ys (o:s, os, s)*. Pl. 1. *ədan, ədyn*, 2. *ədaχ, daχ, ədyχ*, 3. *ədyn* ; *(ə) ma:y nu*.

Present (Relative): *sy:ð, sy:, sy, s*.

Present (Iterative) and Future: S. 1. *bəða(v)*, 2. *bəði*, 3. *by:ð*. Pl. 1. *bəðan, bəðun*, 2. *bəðuχ*, 3. *bəðan*.

Imperfect: S. 1. *öyðun, o:n, on*, 2. *öyðat*, 3. *o:yð, o:ð*. Pl. 1. *öyðan*, 2. *öyðaχ*, 3. *öyðan*.

Imperfect (Iterative) and Conditional: S. 1. *bəðun*, 2. *bəðat*, 3. *bəða*. Pl. 1. *bədan*, 2. *bəðaχ*, 3. *bəðan*.

Imperfect (Impersonal) : *bədid.*

Preterite and Perfect: S. 1. *byːom, byːs,* 2. *byːost, ·byːoχti,* 3. *byː, byːo.* Pl. 1. *byːon,* 2. *byːoχ,* 3. *byːon.*

Pluperfect: S. 1. *basun,* 2. *basat,* 3. *basa.* Pl. 1. *basan,* 2. *basaχ,* 3. *basan.*

Present Subjunctive : S. 2. *boχti,* 3. *boː, bədo, boθo.*

Imperfect Subjunctive : S. 1. *baun,* 2. *baːt,* 3. *baːy, baː* (*pe baː vo*). Pl. 1. *baːn,* 2. *baːχ,* 3. *baːn.*

Imperative : S. 2. *byːδ,* 3. *boːyd, boːd.* Pl. 2. *bəduχ.*

The following shows the use of the Present in detail :—

(a) Affirmative : S. 1. *du i, r ədu i* [*ən duːad*], 2. *r uː(y)ti,* 3. (*ə*) *maːy o* (rarely *maːy vo*) ; (*ə*) *maːy hi.* Pl. 1. (*·ə*)*dani, ·r ədani,* 2. (*·ə*)*daχi, ·r ədaχi,* 3. (*ə*) *maːy nu.* The forms with *r* are often preceded by the particle *mi; r* is sometimes omitted as *mi du inna n duːad.*

(b) Negative: S. 1. (*t ə*)*du i δim* [*ən duːad*], 2. (*t*) *uː(y)ti δim,* 3. *t ədi o δim ; t ədi hi δim ;—t oː(y)s na δim,* 'there is not any' ; *s gini δim,* 'I have not any'. Pl. 1. (*·t ə*)*dani δim,* 2. (*·t ə*)*daχi δim,* 3. (*·t ə*)*danu δim.*

(c) Interrogative : S. 1. *ədu i* [*ən duːad*] *?* 2. *uː(y)ti?* 3. *ədi o ?, ədi hi ?* Pl. 1. *·ədani ?* 2. (*ə*)*·daχi ?* 3. *·ədynu ?—oːys na ?,* ' is there ? '

(d) Interrogative negative : S. 1. *nt ədu i* [*ən duːad*] *?,* 'am I not [coming] ? ', etc.; *nt oː(y)s na ?,* ' is there not ? '; *du i n duːad, nt ədu* (*i*) *?,* 'I am coming, am I not ? '

(e) Answering a question in the affirmative : S. 1. *ədu,* 2. *uːyt,* 3. *ədi.* Pl. 1. *ədan,* 2. *ədaχ,* 3. *ədyn,* 'I am, etc.', equivalent to ' yes '; *oːys,* ' there is ', ' yes '. The pronouns are very seldom used with the above, and then only for the sake of emphasis. S. 3. and Pl. 3. when emphatic become respectively *ədi, ə maːy o* (*oːys, ə maːy*) ; *ədyn, ə maːy nu.*

(f) Answering a question in the negative : S. 1. *naːg ədu,* 2. *naːg uː(y)t,* 3. *naːg ədi; naːg oːys.* Pl. 1. *naːg ədan,* 2. *naːg ədaχ,* 3. *naːg ədyn,* 'I am not, etc.', equivalent to 'no'. For pronouns cf. (e).

(g) Interrogative in answer to a statement, as in English : ' He is going. Is he ? ' S. 1. *ə\du ?, ədu \i ?* 2. *uː\yt ?, uː(y)\ti ?* 3. *ə\di ?, ədi \o ? ; ə maːy \o ?* (emphatic) ; *oː\ys.* Pl. 1. *ə\dan ?, ·əda\ni ?* 2. *ə\daχ ?, ə\dyχ ?, ·əda\χi ?* 3. *ə\dyn ?, ·ədy\nu ?* (\ indicates a rise in the voice in the following syllable). [*ai·\je ?* may be used instead of these when emphasis is required.]

(h) Interrogative negative in answer to a statement in the negative, as in English : ' He is not going.' ' Isn't he ? ' S. 1. *naːg ə\du ?* 2. *naːg uː\yt ?* 3. *naːg ə\di ?, naːg \oːys ?* Pl. 1. *naːg ə\dan ?* 2. *naːg ə\daχ ?, naːg ə\dyχ ?* 3. *naːg ə\dyn ?—naːg ədu, naːg ədu ?,* ' No, I am not, am I ? '; *naːg oːys, naːg oːys,* ' No, there is not, is there ? ' (*a* in the first *naːg* is longer than in the second).

The same with other tenses, e. g. Present Iterative or Future :—
(a) (*mɪ*) *vəða i̯*, *bəða i̯*, (b) *vəða i̯ ðim*, (c) *vəða i̯?* (d) *n vəða i̯?*
(e) *bəða(v)*, (*bəða iː*), (f) *naː vəða(v)*, (*naː vəða iː*), (g) *vəða(v)?*
vəða iː? (h) *naː vəða(v)?* [except with the Preterite and Perfect :
(d) *mɪ ˑvyːˑoxi̯ əmo, n ˋdoː?* (e) *doː*, (f) *ˑnaː ðoː*, (g) *ˋdoː?* (h) *ˑnaː ˋðoː?*]
The following are examples of the use of the tenses :

Present : *may o n ðuːr daː jaun; ðuːr daː jaun ədi o*, 'it is
very good water'; *vaint i (ədi) o r gloːx?*, 'what time is it?'; *yːn
o b leː di d vam?*, 'where does your mother come from?'; *maːy
m boːyθ hɛ̈ɪðju. ədi, ə maːy*, 'it *is* hot to-day'. Ans. 'yes, it is';
dim ə m̥heḷ wedi pedwar, ədi hiˉ?—deːŋ mynyd,—oː, ə maːy hi, 'not
much after four, is it?'—' Ten minutes'.—' Oh, it is, is it?'; *mynd
vory may o*, 'he is going to-morrow'; *mynd vory may ˋo?*, 'is he
going to-morrow?'; *sy daxi, s taxi, syt ər ˑədaxi, syt ər əˑdaxi?*,
'how are you?'; *əˋxiː di mistar dgoː(n)s? iːa*, 'are you Mr. Jones?'
Ans. 'yes'; *un i ðim be ma n i veðul ədu i*, ' I don't know what he
thinks I am'; *oːs na beθ?*, 'is there some?' (vocalic mutation).

Present Relative : *be syː?*, 'what's the matter?'; *be s naxi i̯ʃo?*,
'what do you want?'; *vaint syː oːð əmma i vaŋgor?*, 'how far is it
from here to Bangor?'; *veḷy s i̯ʃo gnɛ̈yd*, 'that's what you ought
to do'; *ə pe sy n jaun sy n jaun*, 'what's right is right'; *kəmˑraːig
go waːyl s g̊ini hi*, 'she speaks rather bad Welsh'.

Present Iterative : *r yː vaːθ a vyːð boːb dyːð*, 'the same as
usual'; *vel ə vam vyːð ə verx* (prov.), cf. 'like father like son';
vəða i byθ ən saːl, 'I am never ill'; *ḷeː bənnag bəða iː byːð ə k̊iː*,
'wherever I am the dog is'; *bða i n ovnys jaun ən ə noːs*, 'I am
very timid at night'; *ḷeː byːð peθ ər čïθ peθ* (prov.), 'money goes
where money is'.

Future : *kaðu k̊əunt vaint vyːð o boːb yːn*, 'count how many
there are of each'; *os na byːð dim axos əŋ kodi*, 'if no cause arises';
k̊əntad a ˑvəðuxi m barod, 'as soon as you are ready'.

Imperfect : *pen ðoːθ o adra r oːð o dgest a maru*, 'when he
came home he was nearly dead'; *mi redi̯ʃ nes oːn i wedi koḷi ŋwynt*,
' I ran till I was out of breath'; *r ˑöyðani wedi xloi hi*, ' we had
locked her up'; *kay berwi oːyð o*, 'it wouldn't boil'.

Imperfect Iterative : *r öyðun i n arvar kaːyl vannoð nes bəðun
i dgest a mynd o ɣhoː*, ' I used to get toothache till I was nearly
mad'; *dim n agos k̊immint a vəða*, 'not nearly as many as there
used to be'; *bəða g̊in ə n̥haid lawar jaun o strɛ̈yon*, 'my grandfather used to know a great many stories'; *mi ˑvəðanu n dɛ̈yd er s
talum, pen oːn (vəðun) i̯ n hogan*, 'they used to say long ago, when
I was a girl'; *mi vəða hunnu n duːad i gwell i*, 'he used to come
and see her'.—With conditional meaning : *pe baːy r wyðva ŋ
gaus vəða n haus kaːl kosyn* (prov.), 'if Snowdon were made of
cheese it would be easier to get some'; *mi vəða n ðigon am əx
höydal xi vynd əno*, 'it would be at the peril of your life for you to
go there'.

Preterite and Perfect : *ma: n bravjaχ ru:an na by: iṛu: r dy:δ*, 'it is finer now than it has been all day'; *ḷe: ·by:oχti ?*, 'where have you been?'; *dəmma ḷe ·by:onu n iṛoi bora ma*, 'this is where they have been ploughing this morning'; *mi vy:om i əmma o r bla:yn*, 'I have been here before'; *vy:o vo δim əmma er s iṛo: by:d*, 'he has not been here for a very long time'; *mi ·vy:osti n hi:r !*, 'you *have* been a long time !'; *by:o vo varu*, 'he died'; *vy:o ri:o:yd dru:g na vy:o n δjoni i ru:in*, 'it is an ill wind that blows nobody good'.

Pluperfect. The simple pluperfect sense has been entirely lost. The tense is used : (1) in optative phrases of the form *piḷḷi na vásun i əno !*, 'I wish I had been there !'. (2) to extenuate the force of a question, as *syt na ·vasaχi n dëyd rubaθ ən ə kwarvod ?*, 'why didn't you say something at the meeting ?'. (3) in conditional sentences, S. 1. *tasun* (=petaswn), 'if I had been, if I were', 2. *tasat*, 3. *tasa*; Pl. 1. *tasan*, 2. *tasaχ*, 3. *tasan*, e. g. *vel tasa*, 'as it were'; *·tasaχi n veŋaχ mi vasa n haus əχ dəsgy*, 'if you had been younger it would have been easier to teach you'; *tasa tippin o ëira n du:ad i laur, vasa ŋ gnesaχ wedyn*, 'if a little snow fell it would be warmer afterwards'; *mi vasa n δa: gin i tasa ṛ he:n δənas na n du:ad i χrogi, i ga:l darvod hevo hi*, 'I wish that old woman were coming (and be hanged to her), so as to be done with her'; sometimes the simple form is used, as *may hi n edraχ vel basa hi am la:u etto*, 'it looks like more rain'. (4) with conditional or pluperfect conditional sense. The following are examples in addition to those given in (3): *·vasaχi n lëikjo i mi ṛoi ta:n ar ə lamp ?*, 'would you like me to light the lamp ?'; *mi ·vasaχi n mynd əno tan χbjaŋy*, 'you would get there in a jiffy'; *r öyδun i n ovni ·vasaχi δim ən lëikjo nu*, 'I was afraid you would not like them'; *r ədu i n fu:r na vo: vasa ə mistar*, 'I am sure *he* would be the master'; *r on i ŋ gubod be vasa diwaδ ə ga:n*, 'I knew what would be the end of it'; *mi vasa hi n dëyd na χəmma hi δim doktor*, 'she would have said she would not have any doctor'.

Present Subjunctive : *da: bo: χi*, 'good-bye'; *ḷe bənnag ə bo:*, 'wherever it may be'; *be:θ bənnag bo: vo*, 'whatever it may be'; (*m*) *bo:yθ ə bo: vol*, 'may he be warm' (a curse); so, *bo:yθ ə bo: χti ! ; wa:yθ be vo (vo:)*, *hidjux be vo (vo:)*, 'never mind'; *vel bo: r la:u ən tuifad ə kṛo:yn*, 'so that the hand may be touching the skin'; *ḷinjo r gwadan vel bo: r iṛo:yd* (prov.), 'to cut one's coat according to one's cloth'; *dikka bo: r k̃ëiljog kənta ə ka:n* (prov.), 'the more angry a cock is the sooner he will crow' (said of people who sing to hide their anger); *kyro r hëyarn iṛə bəδo vo m bo:yθ*, 'to strike the iron while it is hot'; *voθo ra:s i ti, mi ·vy:osti n hi:r !*, 'good gracious! what a time you've been !'; *voθo ra:s i ti! ḷe: r u:ti wedi bo:d ?*, 'good gracious! where have you been?'

Imperfect Subjunctive : *vasa r kəujon δim haus uθ ga:l kṛəsiyn oni ba:y vo:d ər ja:r ən i vaḷy vo n δigon ma:n ·yδynu*, 'it would be no use for the chickens to get a crust of bread unless the hen made it small enough for them'; *mi ˑvasaχi n ˑaŋˑhovjo χ pen oni baː i voːd ən sæund ˑɔnoχi,* 'you would forget your head if it wasn't fastened to your shoulders';—in conditional sense (= *bədun, basun*), *am na baun i n medry,* 'because I should not be able';—in conditional clauses, S. 1. *taun,* 2. *taːt,* 3. *taːy, ta(ˑ), da(ˑ).* Pl. 1. *taːn,* 2. *taːχ,* 3. *taːn,* more rarely *pe baun,* etc., e.g. *mi gəsgaχ ta droija n mynd ˑdrostaχi,* 'you would sleep if carts were running over you'; *waːθ gin i taːti heb nëyd o am draguyδoldab a durnod dros ben,* 'I shouldn't care if you did not do it for ever and a day'; *ta (hə)ny n rubaθ, ta ny riu ods, ta vatlar am hənny, ta waːyθ (am hənny),* 'for the matter of that, if that be anything'; *mi aː i ta hi m buru heːn wragaδ a fyn,* 'I'll go though it be raining cats and dogs'. Cf. also the expressions *taun i byθ (vyˑθ) o r ˑvan ma !* (asseveration), 'so may I never move from this spot!'; also as exclamation, 'upon my word!', etc.—So also *taun i maru !, taun i lugy !*

Use of the infinitive : (1) to express the English 'that' : *boːd =* 'that … is (was)'; *boːd (na),* 'that there is (was)'.—With pronouns, S. 1. *moːd i,* 'that I am', 2. *voː ti,* 3. *voːd o, boːd o ; boːt i.* Pl. 1. *boːd ni,* 2. *boː χi,* 3. *boːd nu.* Examples : *oːys. naːg oːys, wiːr. r ədu i n dëyd boːd,* 'There are'. 'No there are not, indeed'. 'I say there *are*'; *maː n δaː gin i bo χi n weḷ,* 'I am glad you are better'; *r on i n meδul boːt i am laːu,* 'I thought it was going to rain'; *r on i n meδul boːd na lawar o vara ar ə burδ.* So also with (*v*) *eḷa, huraχ,* 'perhaps'; *ond,* 'but that, only'; *pitti,* 'it is a pity'; (*v*) *əḷa voːd o n ə tyː,* 'perhaps he is in the house'; *eḷa wiːr mai dəna be syː, ond bod ni δim əŋ gubod,* 'perhaps that is what it is, only that we don't know'; *pitti boːt i mor dæuyḷ,* 'it is a pity it is so dark'.—With *oni boː, oni baːy,* for examples see above.— With prepositions, to express conjunctions : *am i voːd (am voːd o), gan i voːd (gan voːd o),* 'because he is (was)'; *rhag i voːd,* 'for fear that he be'; *r̥hag boːd,* 'for fear that'; *t oːys dim moːδ i ubod gan boːt i wedi deʲid,* 'there are no means of telling as she has got away'. (2) The infinitive preceded by *i* is used in a variety of senses which do not correspond with the Eng. 'to be', e.g. *vel na may o i voːd,* 'that's how it should be'; *ma na saiθ i voːd,* 'there ought to be seven' (Anglo-Welsh, 'there are seven to be'); *may hi i voːd ən wastad,* 'it is supposed to be level' (but is e.g. warped); *daɲos i hyːn ən yuχ nag ədi i voːd,* 'to make oneself out to be above one's station'; *t oːδ merχaid δim i vòːd ɔno,* 'women were not supposed to be there'.

The verb *boːd* is also used in the sense of 'to live, to exist', e.g. *tr̥ə byːδ i vammo,* 'while his mother is alive'; *darvod a boːd* 'to be over', e.g. of a flower; *r oːδ o ˑən ˑboːd,* 'it *did* exist' (but does no longer), e.g. a word now obsolete) ; *du i δim əŋ kr̥edy vod o wedi boːd,* 'I don't believe he ever existed'; *dim əŋ kr̥edy bod dyu meun boːd,* 'not believing in the existence of God'.

bodan, s.f., cyffoden (?), D., 'sweetheart': *puy di də vodan ru:an ?*, 'who is your sweetheart now?'

bodjo, v., bodio, S.E.* (1) 'to thumb, to knead with the finger and thumb', e.g. putty; 'to play with something with the finger and thumb'. (2) 'to be slow in work' (J.J.).

bodlemma, v., cf. bedlema, M.F., Eng. bedlam, 'to wander aimlessly': *ḷcː ·byːosti m bodlemma ?* (O.H.).

bodlemman, s.f., term of reproach applied to a woman who wanders aimlessly: *hcːn vodlemman vydyr* (O.H.).

bodlon, adj., boddlawn, corruptè bodlon, D., but bodlon in D.G. lxxxviii. 28; D.F. 49. 7; D.P.O. 28. 34; P.G.G. 74. 2, etc. (1) 'content': *may o n vodlon ar ə peːθ sy gəno vo*, 'he is content with what he has'. (2) 'easy-going'—often in a bad sense;—(of horses), 'quiet': *ə kefyl muya bodlon welis i ri·oːyd (dim kast əno vo)*, O.H.

bodloni, v., bodloni, D., s.v. 'satisfacio'. (1) 'to please, content': *may n anoð jaun i modloni hevo buːyd*, 'it is difficult to please me as regards food'. (2) 'to come to an agreement', e.g. after a dispute.

bodlonruyð, s.m., bodlonrwydd, D., s.v. 'aequanimitas'; 'contentment'.

bodyn, s.m., bodyn (dim. of baud) in *bodyn ə mlinyð*, 'bib, pout, whiting-pout' (Gadus luscus).

boːd əg yːn, bod yg un, T.N. 116. 19, 'every one': *maː nu wedi mynd boːd əg yːn.*

boːð, s., bodd, D., 'delight, pleasure': *uθ i voːð, uθ voːð i galon*, 'to his heart's delight'; *may hi uθ i boːð hevo i θaid* 'it is her heart's delight to be with her grandfather'.

boði, v., boddi, D. Pret. Pl. 3. *boðson*; 'to drown, to be drowned': *r oːyð ə ḷ̣eyad wedi boði meun duːr, əŋ gorvað ar i hoχor— vel kuːχ*, 'the moon was drowned in water, lying on its side—like a boat' (J.J.); *boði ə mlinyð*, 'to drown the miller', 'to put too much water in the flour and so make it too wet to knead'; *boði kneya*, 'feast after carrying hay or corn'.

boðran, boðro, v., Eng. bother; 'to talk nonsense': *paid a boðran = paid a berwi də ben, kḷebran, sunjan* (E.J.).

bogal, s.m., pl. *bog̈eɪlja*, bogail, D., 'navel'.

boi, s.m., pl. *bois*, 'boy': *be ðydoð ər heːn voi*, 'what did the old chap say'.

boks, s.m., pl. *boksys*, 'box': *ṃynd i r boks*, "to kick the bucket".

bokſad, s.m., pl. *bokſeidja*, bocsiad, T.N. 99. 1, 'boxful'.

bo:χ, s.f., pl. *boχa*, bôch, D., 'cheek': *lëẏsy boχa*, 'to look surly, sulky' (W.H.).

boχgoχ, adj., bochgoch, S.E., 'red-cheeked'.

boχjo, v., bochio, S.E. (1) 'to bulge': *may r wal ən boχjo alan*, 'the wall is bulging'. (2) 'to eat in a noisy way, working the food from one cheek to the other': *may r moχyn əm boχjo bytta.*—Also trans. *boχjo bara.*

boχlas, adj., bochlaes, S.E. (1) 'flabby-cheeked' (W.H.). (2) 'sulky-looking' (I.W.).

bol, s.m., pl. *bolja*, bol, D., 'belly': *kəmmar lond də vol*, 'take your fill'; *magy bol*, 'to grow a protruding stomach'; *may hunna wedi ka:yl gormod ən i vol*, 'that fellow has had a drop too much'; *ƙin dulad a bol byuχ*, 'pitch dark'; *ka:yl ḷond i vol* (fig.), 'to get his full deserts'; *a i ḷəgad ən vu:y na i vol*, said of one who helps himself to more than he can eat; *ṛhoid rubaθ ar i vol* (= *ən i flat*), 'to lay something flat'; *bol graun*, 'hard roe'; *bol ḷaiθ*, 'soft roe'.

bolǵi, s.m., bolgi, S.E., 'glutton': *ṛ he:n volǵi kəθral.*

boljad, s., pl. *boleidja*, bolaid, D.G. cxlvi. 31, 'bellyful': *boljad ƙi: beriθ dridja* (prov. exp.), 'a dog's fill lasts three days'.

boljog, adj., boliog, D., s.v. 'ventriosus'; 'big-bellied, bulging'.

bo·lol, s.m., bolol, S.E., 'bogy': *may o vel ə bo·lol*, 'he is the very devil'; *may hi n dəuyḷ vel ə bo·lol, may hi vel bo·lol o dəuyḷ*, 'it is pitch dark'; *may r bo·lol ən i gorði o*, 'the devil is in him'.

bombran, s.m., bonbren, S.E. (1) 'double-tree, the wooden bar to which the traces are attached in ploughing with two horses, and which is itself fastened by a chain at each end to the centre of each *timbran* or single-tree'. (2) 'any piece of wood about the length of the above': *bombran pṛen* (O.H.), 'a wooden post'. O.H. also applies this word to the thatcher's instrument called 'aseth' by O.P., "a sharp-pointed spar to fasten thatch". (3) applied to persons, 'a good-for-nothing fellow' (O.H.).

bo:n, s.m., pl. *bona*, bonjon, bôn, D., 'the base of anything', 'the base of a tree—strictly speaking, the part between the roots and the stem': *os na fḷəǵi i r bri:g, ṛhaid i ti blegy i r bo:n* (prov.), 'if you do not bend to the branch (i. e. the birch rod) you will have to bend to the stem' (i. e. ? the gallows tree—supposed to be the stem of a birch, I.W.); *bo:n brayχ*, 'the upper part of the arm'; *bo:n ə gumſon*, 'the root of the tail'; *bonjon ər y:d*, 'stubble'; *bonjon (dannað)*, 'stumps (of teeth)'; *bona r bəsað*, 'the base of the fingers (toes)'; *bo:n ə gly:st* (cf. B.H. 135. 39), 'the roots of the ear': *taro ar vo:n ə gly:st*, 'to strike on the ear' (cf. *boŋklyst*); *bo:n ə gwa:ḷt*, 'the

E

roots of the hair'; *torɨ gwry:χ (kɫauδ) ən ə bo:n*, 'to cut down a hedge so as to let it grow again'; *kodɨ bona* (in slate quarries), 'to level a gallery and facilitate working at the further end of a bargain' (gwastatau y bongc a gwneyd y lle yn fwy parod erbyn mynd i'r pen, y rhan uchaf o'r fargain, J.J.).—*ən ə bo:n* is used figuratively for 'at bottom': *ma: n rëit δa: ǵin i o ən ə bo:n*, 'I like him very much at bottom'.

bonat, s.f., pl. *bonetti*, 'bonnet': *bonat kɫut, bonat hud*, 'sun-bonnet'.

bondeu, adj., bondew, S.E., 'thick at the base', e.g. of the arms.

b ond i grəbuɫ = na bo ond ei grybwyll, G.O. i. 9. 6, 'forsooth'.

bondo, s.f., bondo, D., 'eaves' (I.W.).

bondog, s.m., Eng. bond-dog. Cf. N.E.D., s.v. 'bandog'; 'a surly fellow' (I.W.).

bonδy, bonddu, S.E., in the exp. *ko:χ bonδy ; ko:χ vonδy* (O.H.), a fishing-fly sometimes called 'Marlow buzz'.

bonyn, s.m., bonyn, D., s.v. 'trunculus'; 'stump': *bonyn köydan*, 'the stump of a tree'.

boŋkɫyst, s.f., bonclust, D., 'a box on the ears'.

boŋkyf, s.m., boncyff, D., s.v. 'stipes'; 'a log to put on the fire' (O.H.).

bora, s.m., pl. *brëya*, bore, D., 'morning': *bora da:*, 'good morning'; *bora vory*, 'to-morrow morning'; *o vora dan no:s, o vora gwyn dan no:s*, 'from morning till night'; *bora gla:s*, 'dawn'; *ben ə bora, bora kɨnta*, 'the first thing in the morning'; *bem bora drannoθ*. 'the first thing next day'; *kodɨ χwe:χ ə bora*, 'to get up at six in the morning'. Fig. *əm mora i o:ys*, 'in his young days'.

bora, adj., comp. *brëyaχ*, bore, D., s.v. 'mane'; 'early': *kodɨ n vora*, 'to get up early'. Cf. *kɨnnar*.

bordor, s.f., bordyr, W.S.; bordr, W.Ll. lxxii. 52, 'border; flower-bed' (O.H.).

bos, s., 'stomach of birds; belly': *hel ən i vos*, 'to eat greedily' (I.W.).

bostjo, v., Eng. (Dial.), bost, 'to burst' (O.H.); cf. C.F., 1889, 678. 36 : *dgest a bostjo ǵin χwerθin*.

bostun, s.m., Eng. apostume; bystwn, D., 'whitlow'.

bottum, s.m., pl. *bətəma*, bwtwm, L.A. 95. 14; W.S.; bottwm, D.; M.E. botoun; 'button': *be daχi y kaɫyn hunna ? ɨ ədi o δim gwerθ kap bottum*. Cf. *bottum korn* [*korn*].

bo:θ, s.f., pl. *boθa*, bôth, D., 'nave of a wheel': *bo:n ə vo:θ*, 'the side of the nave towards the axle'.

bɐujog, adj., bywiog, D.; cf. bowiawg, G.R. 58. 10, 'lively'.

bɐulyd, adj., bawlyd, D., bowlyd, s.v. 'cacatus'; 'mean'.

bɐund, adj., 'bound' in sense of bound to do a thing, etc.: *may hiˑm bɐund o hono vo, os byːð o gumpas*, 'she is bound to catch it (i. e. an illness) if it is about'.

bɐuyd, s.m., pl. *bɐwəda*, bywyd, D., 'life': *t oːys na ðim maːθ o vɐwyd əno vo*, 'there's not a spark of life in him'; *bɐwyd ən i ləgad*, 'life, animation in his eye'; *kovja am də vɐwyd*, 'mind you remember'; *mɐwyd iˑ!*, exclamation of surprise.

braːd, s.m., brâd, D., 'treachery': *nëˑiθ o ðim braːd iˑ ncːb ;—braːd pɐudur*, 'Gunpowder Plot' (J.J.).

bradur, s.m., pl. *bradurs*, bradwr, D., 'traitor'.

bradəχγ̣, v., bradychu, D., 'to betray'.

braːg, s.m., brâg, D., 'malt'.

bragur, s.m., bragwr, T.N. 17. 39, 'maltster'.

bragy, v., bragu, S.E. (1) 'to make malt'. (2) formerly used in the sense of 'to sprout' (= *eǵino*) in speaking of corn (J.J.).

braið, adv., braidd, D. (1) 'rather, somewhat': *may n mynd ən oː oːyr. ədi, braið*, 'it's getting a bit cold'. 'It is, rather'; *mi vyːð na i braið own gwarθag*, 'I am rather afraid of cattle'; *daχi wedi kaːyl annuyd? doː, braið*, 'have you caught cold?' 'Yes, a little'. (2) 'almost': *braið ə ṃhen draːu r byːd*, 'almost at the end of the world'.

braint, s.f., pl. *brëintja*, braint, D., 'privilege': *χeːs iˑmoˑr vraint*, 'I never had the privilege'.

brak, adj., brac, C.L.C. ii. 20. 5, T.N. 133. 25, 'loose': *tiːr brak*, 'loose, soft, broken land' (= *tiːr ρhyːð—heb gledy*, opp. to *tiːr tṛum, kḷëiog, tyn*, J.J.); *dyːn brak iˑdavod*, said of a man who cannot keep a secret; *may o n m brak iˑdavod, ðydiθ o boːb peːθ*, 'he is always wagging his tongue : he will tell everything' (O.H.).

brakty, s.m., bragdy, S.E., 'malt-house'.

bran, s., bran, S.E., 'bran' = *ëˑisin*.

braːn, s.f., pl. *brain*, brân, D., 'crow, rook': *may r brain əŋ gwëˑiði*, 'the crows are cawing'; *kin ðyːad a r vraːn*, 'as black as a crow'; *mi nabun o əm ṃhiːg ə vraːn*, 'I should know him anywhere'; *riu vraːn ðyː ðëydoð uθa i*, 'a little bird told me'. *braːn dəðyn*, 'carrion crow' (Corvus corone). If one settles down on a farm it is supposed to bring good luck. Cf. W.M.M. s.v. 'bran-diddyn'; *bugan brain*, 'scarecrow'; *pyρρys brain* [*ρyρρys*]; *kṛavaŋk ə vraːn*, 'crow's foot' (Ranunculus bulbosus).

(2) 'contrivance for raising the body of a cart': *ɣhoi r drol ar i
bra:n* (*i ɣodi hi ar i θi:n*).

branar, s., braenar, D.; branar, L.G.C. 61 [45]. (1) 'fallow-
ground': *branar ha:*, 'land ploughed in the winter and left
fallow'. (2) 'a kind of disease in cattle which makes them eat
clothes, said to be caused by eating a certain herb': *ma: branar
ar ǝ gwarθag*. Cf. M.F. s.v. 'branar'.

bra:s, adj., pl. *brëiʃon*, brâs, D. (1) 'fat': *ki:g bra:s*, 'fat meat'
(not often used = *ki:g gwyn*). (2) 'rich' (in speaking of land): *ti:r
bra:s = ti:r nerθol, kɣy:*;—*may na le: bra:s ǝmma*. (3) 'big': *peθa
bra:s*, 'big lumps' (speaking e.g. of coal); *tǝla bra:s*, 'large holes'
(e.g. in a riddle); *brëiʃon ǝ sgri:n*, 'the larger stones which will
not pass through a screen or standing riddle'; *lyvr bra:s, wedi
brinijo n vra:s*, 'a book with big print'. (4) 'coarse': *breθyn,
barklod, li:an bra:s*, 'coarse cloth, apron, table-cloth'. Fig. *ʃarad
ǝn vra:s*, 'to use coarse, vulgar, unseemly, insulting language' =
*riu he:n ëirja fi:aθ, brǝnijon,—di:radjo pobol, sar ha:y,—ʃarad ǝn
ðru:g, ǝn isal* (O.H.).

brasbuyθ, s., brasbwyth, S.E., lit. 'a coarse stitch', in the phrase
du i ðim ond am roid riu hirbuyθ a brasbuyθ ǝno vo, 'I am only
going to put a few stitches in it'.

brasgammy, v., brasgamu, S.E., 'to stride: *dy:ar annul ! ma:y
o m brasgammy n aru !*, 'good gracious! how he strides along!'

·*bra:sʰholti*, v. (in slate quarries), 'to rough-split'.

·*bra:sʰholtur*, s.m. (in slate quarries), 'a rough-splitter'.

brasolt, adj. (in slate quarries): *ky:n brasolt*, 'a chisel for rough-
splitting'.

brastar, s.m., brasder, 1 Sam. xv. 22, 'fat', e.g. of meat or on
broth.

brasterog ; blasterog (E.J.), adj., brasderog, S.E., 'fat'.

brastod, s., brasdod, 'coarse, unseemly language': *ʃarad brastod*
(O.H.), cf. above *ʃarad ǝn vra:s*.

brat, s.m., pl. *bratja*, bratt, D.; Eng. (Dial.) brat. (1) 'rag' (not
in common use; for example see *brenin*). (2) 'pinafore'.

braθǵi, s.m., brathgi, S.E., 'a surly, irascible fellow': *ta:u r he:n
vraθǵi djaul !* (O.H.).

braθjad, s.m., brathiad, D., s.v. 'morsus'; 'bite', e.g. of a dog;
also 'nibble' (in fishing).

braθog, adj., brathog, G.O. ii. 189. 30, 'given to biting': *tǝnny la:u
hyd ǵi: braθog* (prov. exp.), 'to stroke, wheedle a dog given to biting'.

braθy, v., brathu, D. (1) 'to bite': *ki: braθy o:yð o, ǝɲ kǝvarθ
ar wynab paub* 'he was a biting dog who barked at every one';

paid a braθy r bensal, 'don't bite the pencil'. (2) 'to nip off a piece of flesh in shearing'. Cf. *pigo, pegjo*. (3) *braθy i ben tṛu: r dru:s*, 'to pop one's head in at the door'. Cf. D.F. [29] 28, [91] 19; G.R. 35. 6.

bra:u, s.m., braw, D., s.v. 'terror'; 'terror, fright': *mi ge:s i vra:u garu*, 'I had a terrible fright'; *pobol meun bra:u, ar ə bra:u*, 'people in terror'.

braud, s.m., pl. *brodyr*, brawd, D., 'brother'.

bra:v, adj., comp. *bravjax*, brâf, C.L.C. ii. 9. 1. (1) 'fine (especially of the weather), nice, pleasant'.—Does not mutate. *may (hi) m bra:v hĕiδju. ədi wi:r, may m bra:v jaun*, 'it's a fine day.' 'Yes, indeed, it is very fine'; *may hi m bravjax ən ə ty:*, 'it is better, pleasanter in the house'; *le: bra:v jaun i ista ədi əmma*, 'this is a nice place to sit'; *ta:n bra:v*, 'a nice fire'; *may m bra:v arno vo!*, 'he has a fine time of it!'; *may gwaiθ əm be:θ bra:v jaun*, 'work is a fine thing'; *u:ti n y:n bra:v !*, 'you're a nice specimen!' (2) 'fine' (in appearance, in person): *he:n wrĕigan bra:v*, 'a fine old woman'.

bray, adj., brau, D., 'brittle, tender': *may o n vray vel Ki:g Kiu*, 'it is as tender as chicken' (opp. *gwydyn*).

brayx, s.f., pl. *brĕixja*, braich, D., 'arm': *bo:n brayx*, 'the upper part of the arm'; *brayx tṛol*, 'shaft of a cart' (= *ḷorp*); *brayx ə mrayx, əm mrĕixja i giliδ*, 'arm in arm'; *ṛhaid i r vrayx wĕiθjo o r ĝesal*, 'the whole arm must be in motion' (i. e. hard at work); *kənnig ar hy:d brayx*, 'to offer something with the hope that it will not be accepted'; *brĕixja ər em, en*, etc. (J.J.), 'the up-strokes of an "m", "n", etc.'

brδwidjo, v., breuddwydio, D., 'to dream'.

brebog, s.f., 'a foolish, prattling woman': *ta:u ə vrebog wirjon* (J.J.).

brebul, s.m., brebwl, C.L.C. ii. 21. 9; T.N. 128. 10; Eng. brabble, 'to wrangle'; 'a foolish, prattling man' (J.J.).

bregljax, v., 'to jabber': *paid a bregljax ar hy:d ə bedlan*, 'don't keep jabbering all the time.'; *riu he:n vregljax farad*.

bregljax, s., 'jabbering'.

brĕib, s., breib, W.S., 'bribe'.

brĕibjo, v., bribio, W.S. (1) 'to bribe'. (2) 'to deal in an under-hand manner (telling tales, etc.) for the sake of gain'. (For the latter sense cf. C.C. 14. 17, Mae'r ffeiriaid yn loytran, mae'r barnwyr yn bribian).

brĕibjur, s.m., bribiwr, W.S.; pl. breibwyr, B.C. 19. 11. (1) 'one who bribes'. (2) 'an informer' = *dy:n əŋ karjo* (telling tales) *ag ən dëyd ·an·wiraδ am ga:l peθ* (O.H.).

brekḱi, s., brecci, D., 'cervisiae liquor incoctus': in phrases *ar i vrekḱi, meun brekḱi,* 'on the spree' (O.H.).

brekwast, s.m., brecffast, C.C. 8. 22 ; brecwest, T.N. 12. 33 ; cf. Eng. (Dial.) breckwist, Irel. Nhb.; brickwast, Nhb.; 'breakfast'.

brekwesta, v., 'to breakfast'.

bre:χ, s.f., y frêch, D.: *ə vre:χ go:χ,* 'measles'; *ə vre:χ wen,* 'smallpox'; *bre:χ ər jëir,* 'chicken-pox'.

breχtan, s.f., brechdan, D., 'a piece of bread and butter'; *breχtan dzam,* 'a piece of bread and jam'; *breχtan dena vel dëilan,* 'a piece of bread and butter as thin as a leaf'; *breχtan vaud,* 'a piece of bread on which the butter is spread with the thumb'; *klemman, taval, kləutan, kluf o vreχtan,* 'a big piece of bread and butter'; *breχtan i aros pry:d,* 'a piece of bread and butter to go on with till the next meal';—also fig. *breχtan i aros pry:d ədi honna,* 'he is only flirting with her'.

breḷi, s.pl., sing. *braḷan*, briallu, D., 'primroses' (Primula vulgaris).

brenhinas, s.f., pl. *breninesa*, brenhines, D., s.v. 'regina'; 'queen'.

brenin, s.m., pl. *brenhinoð*, brenhin, D., 'king': *ma: r durnod wedi mynd i r brenin,* 'the day has gone imperceptibly without getting anything done'; so also *mi ·roisoχi ðo:y i r brenin*; *ərenin maur !,* excl. of surprise; *brenin ə bratja a i dra:yd tru i sanna !,* excl.

brenʃaχ, in the exp. *brenʃaχ annul !,* excl. of surprise. Also *brenʃun*.

brest, s.f., pl. *brestja*, brest, I.D. xxxvi. 31 ; C.C.M. 80. 15 ; C.C. 150. 10 ; 432. 16 ; 'breast, chest' (of human beings or animals): *prəgeθy, gwe·ði:o o r vrest,* 'to preach, pray extempore'; *gwasga də vrest,* 'do not say a word';—as applied to land, 'a slope' = *ḷeχwað*.

brestjo, v., Eng. (Dial.) breast. *brestjo gwry:χ* is sometimes used for *tokjo gwry:χ,* 'to clip a hedge' (J.J.); but O.H. has *brestjo kḷauð tu:yrχ,* 'to renew a hedge-bank with fresh sods'.

bresyχ, s.pl., bresych, D., 'charlock' (Brassica Sinapis, etc.).

bresys, s.pl., sing. *bresan*, 'braces'.

brettyn, s.m. (dim. of *brat*), pl. *bratja*, brettyn, D., s.v. 'pittacium'. (1) 'rag' (not in common use = *raksan*): *t ədi o ðim ond pöiri ar i vrettyn i hy:n* (O.H.), 'he is only fouling his own nest'. (2) said of some one who has become weak through illness, etc.: *dy:n wedi mynd ən he:n vrettyn, wedi darvod ən y:n brettyn* (O.H.). (3) in moral sense 'a fellow without backbone' = *dy:n a dim fru:t ənovo, dim nerθ, dim əsbryd ; dy:n ·di:vəwyd* (E.J.).

breθyn, s.m., pl. *breθəna*, brethyn, D., 'cloth': *breθyn kartra,* 'homespun'.

brevy, v., brefu, D., 'to bleat, to low' (of sheep or cattle); also applied to children crying (O.H.).

brëyðuyd, s.m., pl. *brðwidjon*, breuddwyd, D., 'dream'.

brëyo, v., breuo, S.E., 'to become brittle or tender; to become rotten (of clothes)': *ma:r k̃i:g ən brëyo ; trəusys wedi brëyo—ən da: i ðim ond i vynd i r potjur* (O.H.)

bri:, s.m., bri, D., 'esteem, reputation': *r o:ð o meun bri: r amsar honno ;—meun bri: maur ;—koli i vri:*, 'to lose one's character'; *hel bri:*, 'to call witnesses to testify as to one's character'; *hel bri: ə nail ə lal = hel bëia*, 'to find fault with one another'.

bri:d, s.m., 'breed' (T.N. 88. 3): *may k̃iu o r bri:d (o vri:d) ən wel na frentis*, proverb implying that one who follows the calling of his father is better than an apprentice.

bri:g, s.m., brig, D. (1) 'top (especially of trees); topmost branches; tops (in the aggregate)': *ma: r plant ən driɲo i vri:g ə göydan*, 'the children are climbing to the top of the tree'; *bri:g ta:s*, 'the top of a haystack' (= *kri:b, pen*); also the tops or ears of corn: *ə sgyba ar i penna bri:g ə mri:g ; rhoid ə sgyba a i bri:g i vjaun ;*—'the tops of waves': *r o:ð ə mo:r ən vri:g gwyn* (O.H.). Cf. *brigun*. (2) 'twigs': *dail ar ə bri:g*.

briga, s.pl. (1) sing. *brigan*, 'branches': *du:y vrigan vaur vaur* (O.H.); *t o:ys na ðim digon o wynt i əsguyd ə briga*, 'there is not enough wind to move the branches'. (2) dim., sing. *brigin*, brigyn, D., 'twigs': *lɔvny hevo drain a briga bedu*, 'to harrow with thorns and birch twigs'; *r o:yð briga r ko:yd ən baxy ·arnoni*, 'the twigs used to catch in our clothes'.

brigo, v., barugo, C.C.M. 49. 32, 'to freeze', but only applied to hoar-frost, such as may come in a night and disappear with the first rays of the sun (cf. *ɤhewi*): *may n fu:r o rewi axos bo:t i wedi brigo n aru*, 'it is sure to freeze because there is a heavy hoar-frost'.

brigog, adj., brigog, D. (1) 'branchy, spreading' (of trees). (2) of corn, 'rich in grain' = *fruyθlon* (J.J.). Cf. *kribog* (Corwen) same sense.

brigun, s.m., brigwyn, 'white water on a rough sea': *brigun gwyn* (O.H.).

brikbyst, s.pl., 'horizontal poles at the top of scaffolding, secured in the wall and to the perpendicular poles' (O.H.).

briks, s.pl., sing. *briksan*, f. brics, D.G. xxxii. 32, 'bricks'.

brisin, s.m., 'breeze' = *awal farp ar vo:r ne lyn* (J.J.).

brits, *britf*, s.f., 'the figure of Britannia on the reverse side of copper coins'; only used in phrases connected with tossing coins:

p̦ g̦ yn ta k̦iŋ ta bri̵s? (O.H.), 'heads or tails'; so, *p̦ g̦ yn ta du:y g̦iŋ ta du:y brits?* (O.H.).

bri:θ, adj., brith, D., 'speckled, variegated': *byuχ vri:θ*, 'black and white, red and white cow, etc.', pl. *gwarθag briθjon*;— *bara bri:θ, torθ vri:θ*, 'currant bread, currant loaf'; *r o:δ ə mo:r ən vri:θ o go:yd* (O.H.), 'the sea was dotted with pieces of wood' (i.e. after a wreck).

briθgig, s.m., brith-gig, T.N. 59. 22, 'streaked bacon, meat', etc., i.e. lean and fat in alternate layers.

briθgo, s.. cf. brith goſ, M.F., 'a dim recollection': *may g̦in i vriθgo am dano* (J.J.).

briθil̦, s.m., pl. *briθil̦* and *briθil̦jaid*, brithyll, D., 'trout' (Salmo fario): *briθil̦ ə mo:r*, 'salmon trout' (Salmo trutta); *briθil̦ mair*, 'five-bearded rockling' (Motella mustela).

briθo, v., britho, D., 'to speckle': *r o:δ i wa:l̦t wedi briθo*, 'his hair had become speckled with grey';—in making butter: *may o n deχra briθo*, 'the butter is beginning to come' (in minute particles); —in met. sense: *ma nu ən briθo r wla:d*, 'the country is dotted with them'.

briθwyn, adj., brithwyn, S.E.*, 'of white and another colour': *byuχ vriθwyn*.

briu, s.m., pl. *briuja*, briw, D., 'a wound': *ig̦uſo, mendjo briuja*, 'to heal wounds'; *r o:δ g̦in i vriu ən hiraχ na hənny*, 'I had a wound longer than that'; *ma:y l̦o:sg ëira wëiθja n tori n vriuja*, 'chilblains sometimes break out into wounds'; *dan i vriuja*, 'wounded'.

briuljo, v., brwylio, W.S.; C.C. 180. 14; 469. 4; briwlio, B.C. 90. 21, Eng. broil, 'to cook, toast before a fire', e.g. bread, potatoes, fish, etc.

brius, s.m., Eng. brew-house; 'back-kitchen' = *k̦eg̦in g̦evn, k̦eg̦in ba:χ*.

briusin, s.m., briwsyn, S.E., 'a crumb, small piece': *dəruχ i mi vriusin ba:χ o vara*.

briuſon, s.pl., sing. *briuſonyn*, briwsion, D., 'crumbs': *heluχ ə briuſon o:δ ar ə l̦aur*, 'get the crumbs up off the floor'.

briuſoni, v., briwsioni, D., s.v. 'affrio', 'to crumble (trans. and intr.) of bread', etc.: *paid a briuſoni ə dorθ ; g̦haid i χi dlino r dorθ ən wel̦ ə ig̦o: nesa g̦hag iδi vriuſoni*.

briuſonl̦yd, adj., briwsionllyd, S.E., 'crumbly'.

brivo, v., briwo, D., 'to hurt, to be hurt, to hurt oneself': *may o wedi brivo*, 'he has hurt himself' [*may o wedi vrivo* = 'he has been hurt' is also used]; *may r hu:χ wedi vrivo vo*, 'the sow has hurt him'; *mi vrivi di hevo r̥ḧëi n*, 'you will hurt yourself with those'; *by:ð tavoda paub ∂m brivo*, 'they will all have sore tongues'; —also in a restricted sense, 'to rupture oneself': *may o wedi brivo* = *may o wedi tori i leŋǵid*.

briwar, s.m., bruwer, W.S., 'brewer'.

bro:, s.f., pl. *brovyð*, bro, D., 'neighbourhood, district' (not common): *i vro: enedigol*, 'his native district'.

brodjo, v., brodio, D.; D.G. xlvii. 50; brodrio, W.S. [Brauder], 'to darn': *brodjo sanna hevo n∂duy ðy:r sanna*, 'to darn stockings with a darning needle'.

brok, adj., broc, S.E., 'grey (with a tinge of red)', only in *k̯efyl brok*.

bro:χ, s., broch, D., 'foam': *∂ du:r ∂n tr̥oi ∂n vro:χ* (J.J.);—applied to persons of a rough, uncouth nature: *he:n vro:χ o rubaθ ∂di o* (O.H.).

broχi, v., brochi, D., 'to be angry, to bluster, chafe'.

broχlyd, adj., 'in a bad humour' (O.H.).

brol, s.f., brol, G.O. ii. 206. 21, 'a boast': *he:n vrol vaur*.

broljo; blorjo (E.J.), brolio, R.; Eng. brawl, 'to flatter, praise, speak well of': *broljo ru:in*, 'to praise some one'; *broljo i hy:n*, 'to boast'.

broljur, s.m., broliwr, R., 'boaster, braggart'.

brolog, s., Eng. prologue (from the old interludes), I.W., 'nonsense' = *lol*, e.g. *riu he:n brolog*, but never used now (O.H.). Cf. C.F. 1880, p. 331.

bron, s.f., pl. *bronna*, bron, D., 'breast': *bron k̯ëytys*, 'bronchitis'.

bron, adv., bron, S.E. 'almost': *r o:ð o bron a l̯eθy dano vo*, 'he was almost sinking under it'; *torθ bron wedi darvod*, 'a loaf almost finished'; *byuχ bron l̯o:*, 'a cow about to calve'.

bronwan, s.f., pl. *bronwennod*, bronwen, D., 'weasel'.

bronwaθ, adj., bronfraith, D., *deryn bronwaθ*, 'thrush', pl. *adar bronwaθ; k̯ëil̯jog bronwaθ, ja:r vronwaθ*.

br∂un, adj., 'brown', in *bara br∂un*, etc. Also as substantive, a kind of bird (sp.?) I.W.

bru:as, s.m., brwes, W.S.; browes, W.Ll. (Voc.), s.v. 'micas'; brywes, B.C. 74. 17; Eng. brewes, browes, 'broth' = *fru:yθ k̯i:g bra:s berwedig*;—*ka:l i vy:s meun bru:as paub, r̥hoi i vy:s ∂n ∂ bru:as*, 'to have one's finger in every pie', 'to meddle with other people's business'; · *bru:as menyn*, made by crumbling bread into a teacup, adding a lump of butter, and pouring boiling water over it (E.J.); *bru:as k̯ëirχ*, made by grinding oat-cake small, adding dripping, and pouring boiling water over it (E.J.); *bru:as ∂ bi:g, bru:as pi:g ∂ tekk̯al̯*, 'boiling water poured over bread and a little *gwɛran byp̯pyr* added'.

bru:d, adj., brŵd, D., s.v. 'fervens': *bara bru:d*, 'hot bread just out of the oven'.

bruinjad, s., pl. *bruinjaid*, brwyniad, D., 'smelt' (Osmerus eperlanus).

bruχan, s.m., ? D. bruchen, 'scatebra, scaturigo', cf. S.E., s.v. brychen, 'foam, froth': *kodi n y:n bruχan*, 'to rise in one mass of froth' (I.W.).

brumstan, s., brwmstan, D.; Eng. brumstone (14th–15th cent.); Mod. Sc. brumstane; s.v. 'sulphur', 'brimstone, sulphur'.

brunt, adj., fem. *bront*, pl. *brəntjon*, comp. *brəntaχ*, brwnt, D., s.v. 'sordidus'; 'cross, unkind, surly', opp. to *feind*: *may o n edraχ ən vrunt*, 'he looks cross, surly'; *ma: nu wedi bo:d ən vrunt ·uθaχi*, 'they have been unkind to you'; *ğëirja brəntjon*, 'cross words'; *r o:n i n tëimlo n vilan vrunt* (O.H.), 'I felt wild with anger'.

brus, bruʃ, s.m., pl. *brusis, bruʃis*, brwis, W.S., 'brush': *ko:ys brus*, 'the handle of a brush'; *brus ḷaur*, 'a floor brush (with a long handle)'; *brus dannað, diḷad, gwa:ḷt, gwinað, pa:ynt, witwaʃ (χwëitwaʃ)*, 'tooth, clothes, hair, nail, paint, whitewashing brush'.

bruʃo, v., 'to brush': *neuχi vruʃo χ ko:t k̆in mynd aḷan, ma na rubað wedi eḷun arno vo*, 'will you brush your coat before you go out, there is something spilt on it'.

bruydyr, s.f., brwydr, D., 'battle' (semi-literary).

bru:yn, s.pl., sing. *bruynan*, brwyn, D., 'rushes': *kannuyḷ vru:yn*, 'rushlight'.

bry:d, s., bryd, D., 'mind' in *ṛhoi i vry:d ar*, 'to set one's mind upon'.

bry:d, adv., pa bryd, 'when?': *bry:d dəuχi n χ o:l ?*, 'when will you come back?'; *bry:d vasa n ora i mi odro ?*, 'when had I better do the milking?'—also *pṛy:d*.

bry:χ, adj., fem. *bre:χ*, brych, D., 'brindled': *ə vry:χ vyχas (byχas) = siğil di:n ə gu:ys* (J.J.), 'wagtail', cf. D. brith y fuches, 'motacilla'.

bry:χ, s.m., pl. *brəχod*, brych buwch, D., 'afterbirth' (of all animals, but especially of cows): *may o n edraχ vel bry:χ*, said of one of a wretched, pinched, wizened appearance; *ṛ he:n vry:χ gwirjon* (O.H.); for pl. cf. T.N. 346. 24.

bryn, s.m., pl. *brənja*, brynn, D., 'hill' (cf. *ga:ḷt*).

bry:s, s.m., brŷs, D., 'haste': *t o:ys dim bry:s*, 'there's no hurry'; *daχi meun bry:s am de: ?*, 'are you in a hurry for tea?'; *kəχuyn ar vry:s maur*, 'to start in a great hurry'; *mi a:θ o ar vry:s guy:ḷt*, 'he went off in a terrible hurry'; *ma na i dippin o vry:s*, 'I am rather in a hurry'.

·*bry:sg·luini*, s.pl., prysglwyni, D., s.v. 'frutetosus'; brysglwyni, Job xxx. 4—*kaηhenna ən t∂vy i v∂ny o wi:al* (J.J.), 'new shoots growing upwards, e.g. in a hedge after cutting'.

br∂djo, v., brydio, D., 'to throb, tingle with heat' (used esp. of the feet).

br∂gɐuθa ; pr∂gɐuθa (O.H.), v., briwgawthan, C.C. 130. 7; brygawthan, R.; prygowtha, T.N. 242. 1; bragowtha, M.F. Cf. also pregethu prygothen, C.L.C. ii. 27. 24, 'to speak indistinctly'. See also *pr∂gɐuθan, pr∂gɐuθur*.
          ̥

br∂χa, s.pl., brych, pl. brychau, D., 'specks, small particles of dirt', etc.: *r o:yδ ∂ levriθ ∂n vr∂χa garu*, 'the milk was full of specks'; *hidlan i gadu r br∂χa*, 'a strainer to remove the specks'; *br∂χa gwla:n*, 'flock' (J.J.);—*kodi br∂χa* (fig.), 'to find faults, blemishes'.

br∂χedyn, s.m. Cf. brychiad, S.E., 'salmon trout'.

br∂χni, s., brychni, D., in exp. *br∂χni hayl*, 'freckles'.

br∂nary, v., braenaru, D., s.v. 'aro'; brynaru, Yny lhyvyr hwnn [7]; C.C. 404. 26, 'to lay out in fallow'.

br∂ntini, s.m., bryntni, D., 'sordes, squalor'; 'cruelty, unkindness'.

br∂ntuχ, s.m. = *br∂ntini*. This is the more usual form.

br∂ʃo, briʃo, v., brysio, D., 'to hasten': *br∂ʃuχ ! ; briʃuχ !*, 'make haste !, be quick !'; *br∂ʃuχ ∂mma etto*, 'come and see us again soon' (said to a visitor on taking his departure).

ˋ *br∂ʃog, briʃog*, adj., brysiog, S.E., 'hurried, hasty, in a hurry'.

bu:, in the exp. *bu: na be:—χe:ʃ i δim bu: na be: gino vo*, 'I could not get a word out of him'; *mi a:θ o o:δ ∂mma heb δeyd na bu: na: be:*.

bu:a, s.m., pl. *bu:a:y*, bwa, D., 'bow': *bu:a sa:yθ*, 'bow and arrow'; *t∂nny n i vu:a vo*, 'to pull at his bow', i.e. 'to provoke'; *kodi n y:n bu:a*, 'to rise in a curve' (speaking, e.g. of the flight of a cannon-ball).

bubaχ, s.m., bwbach, D., 'bogy, bugbear': *ma:y o n he:n vubaχ*, 'he is an old bugbear';—also used of one who keeps to himself and never says a word to any one (O.H.), *bubaχ o δy:n*.

buf, bwff, W.Ll. lxvi. 43, *l̥edar buf*, 'wash-leather'.

bufin [*pufin*].

bugan, s.m., pl. *buganod, b∂ganod*, bwgan, W.S., 'ghost, bogy': *bugan bra:n* (*brain*), 'scarecrow'; *gneyd bugan maur o bo:b peθ*, 'to make mountains of molehills, exaggerate little anxieties'; *∂ treθi ma ∂di r he:n v∂ganod*, 'it is these rates and taxes which are the old bogies'; *may o wedi valy n χwilvriu bugan*, 'it is torn to shreds'; *bugan o δy:n ·an·waraδ* (O.H.).

bugun i, for tebygwn i, 'I should think' (J.J.).

buguθ, bэguθ, s., pl. *bэgэθjon,* bygwth, D., 'threat'.

buguθ, bэguθ, bэguyθ, v., bygwth, D. (1) 'to threaten': *buguθ iaro ru:in,* 'to threaten to strike some one'; *ma hi m buguθ storom,* 'the weather looks threatening'. (2) 'to make as if (one were about to do something)': *wedi buguθ gwëiθjo a dim эŋ gnëyd.* (3) 'to insinuate': *buguθ bo χi wedi gnëyd peθ.*

bukkad, s.m., pl. *buǩedi,* bwcket, W.S., 'bucket': *bukkad glo:,* 'coal-scuttle'.

bukkul, s.m., pl. *bэkḷa,* bwckyl, W.S.; bwccl, D., 'buckle': *ḳloksan bukkul,* 'buckled clog'; *sǵidja bэkḷa,* 'buckled shoes'; *bukkul bresys,* 'the buckle of braces'.

buks, in such expressions as *mi ëiſ i m buks i veun,* 'I popped in suddenly'; *mi ëiſ i m buks i u wynab o,* 'I came right upon him suddenly'—(J.J.); *gnëyd rubaθ эm buks, gnëyd riu vuks o waiθ,* 'to do something in a hurry';—also *buts, dэna ņhu m buts*—(O.H.).

bukslyd, adj., 'hasty': *mi a:θ эm bukslyd jaun (i riu dramguyδ, heb gэnsidro ǩin mynd*); *dy:n эŋ gweld bai arno i hy:n am i vod wedi bo:d эn ṛhy: bukslyd*—(O.H.).

bukſo, v., 'to act hastily': *bukſo gwëiθjo* (Llanfairfechan). [O.H. has *ſukſo,* probably a confusion with *frukſo.*]

bu:χ, s.m., pl. *bэχod,* bwch, D.: *bu:χ gavr,* 'he-goat'; *edraχ vel bu:χ,* 'to look surly and disagreeable'.

buχan, s.f., epithet applied to an untrustworthy person: *riu he:n vuχan o ðэnas* (O.H.).

buχyn, masc. of above (O.H.).

bul, bulaiſ, s., bwlas, W.S. 'bullace' (Prunus insititia), *ëirin bul, ëirin bulaiſ.*

bulat, s.f., pl. *buledi,* 'bullet': *эn sy:θ vel bulat* (e. g. of a furrow), 'as straight as a die'.

bulfyn, s.m. (1) 'bullfinch' (Pyrrhula Europaea). (2) 'a fat man'.

buli, s.m., Eng. bully, 'prize-fighter': *rvo: di buli r by:d* (O.H.), 'he is the champion prize-fighter of the world'.

buljo, v., bwlio, T.N. 13. 3; Eng. bully. (1) 'to tease, annoy', e. g. *plant эm buljo he:n bobol,* by mimicking them. (2) 'to insult' = *kэmmyd ru:in эn эsgavn a dëyd gëirja fi:aδ uθo vo—paid di a muljo i:, du i m barny mod i gэstal a tiθa.* (3) 'to handle roughly, 'to "punish"' (e. g. in prize-fighting): *r u:ti wedi ka:l dэ vuljo n aru.*

bulχ, s.m., pl. *bэlχa,* bwlch, D., 'gap'. [As compared with *aduy, bulχ* is, generally speaking, an accidental gap which requires filling up, e.g. a gap made by sheep in a hedge or a piece of wall which has fallen, while *aduy* is a permanent gap made for a way to pass through.] (1) 'a mountain pass or any opening between two hills'. (2) 'gap, e.g. in a hedge or wall': *ma: r devaid wedi gnëyd bulχ ən ə klauð*, 'the sheep have made a gap in the hedge'; *χwalʸ bulχ*, 'to make a gap in a wall' (by pulling down the stones). (3) applied to a 'hare-lip': *bulχ ən ər e:n, bulχ ən ə wevys*. (4) of sheep's ear-marks : *bulχ bla:yn gwennol, bulχ klikjad, bulχ plʸ:g, bulχ iʳi θorjad [no:d]*. (5) fig. *vəða i ŋ gweld bulχ ar i o:l*, 'I miss him'. (6) 'defect': *t o:ys ne:b nad o:ys riu vulχ arno vo*.

bulragjur, s.m., 'bully-ragger': *he:n bulragjur gurjon* (O.H.).

buḷ, adj., corr. of *muḷ*, 'sultry' : *ma: r du:yð əm buḷ*.

buḷtid, s.m., 'swivel'.

bumbatʃ, ·buts·bats, ·butʃ·batʃ, adv., 'clumsily, anyhow' = *rusyt rusyt, ·stirim·stram·sirelaχ:*—*may o wedi gosod ə kḷut* (patch) *əm ·buts·bats*.

bundal, s.m., pl. *bundeli*, bwndel, T.N. 22. 38, 'bundle': *bundal o riubob*, 'a bundle of rhubarb'; *bundal o orjada*, 'a bunch of keys'.

buns, s., pl. *bunʃis*, 'bunch': *ko:yd hy:d ə forð a bunʃis maur ən hoŋjan o·ruθynu*, 'trees growing along the road with big bunches (of flowers) hanging from them'.

buŋ [adar].

buŋglar, s.m., bwngler, W.S.; D. (1) 'bungler': *o:ð dim ond luk buŋglar iðo nëyd* (O.H.), 'it was only a "fluke"'. (2) 'a worthless good-for-nothing fellow': *riu he:n ləmbar o he:n ðy:n, ən medry gnëyd ag əŋ kay—ḷaun o bo:b dru:g* (O.H.)—*paid a kaḷyn ʳ he:n vuŋglar na*.

buŋgul, s., 'bungle'.

burð, bur, s.m., pl. *bərða*, bwrdd, D. (1) 'table': *iro:yd burð*, 'leg of a table'; *gosod ə burð*, 'to lay the table'; *kḷirjo r burð*, 'to clear away'·;—fig. *ðo:θ ə gair na ðim i r burð o r bla:yn* (O.H.), 'we have never talked about that word before' (cf. Fr. 'mettre sur le tapis'). (2) *burð mortar*, 'mortar board'. (3) in slate quarries: a kind of scaffold suspended by ropes (cf. *baud*, 4) at about 15 yards from the ground, against the face of the rock, and large enough to hold three men who bore a hole for blasting (J.J.).

burjad, s.m., bwriad, W.S. [A cast], *burjad o la:u*, 'a shower of rain' (I.W.).

burjady, v., bwriadu, D., 'to intend'.

burn, s.m., bwrn, D.; Eng. (Dial.), burn, 'burden'; 'a burden on the stomach giving an inclination to vomit': *may hi ŋ kodi burn ·arnoχi*, 'it makes you feel sick';—also used figuratively, *t ədi o ðim ond burn ar ə wla:d* (J.J.), 'he is only a burden on the country';—also 'a weight on one's spirits'.

buru, v., bwrw, D. Imperative S. 2. *buru, burja*, 3. *burjad*; Pl. 2. *burjuχ*. Imperf. S. 3. *burja*. (1) 'to shed' (a) of rain, etc.: *buru gla:u*, 'to rain'; *buru ëira*, 'to snow'; *buru kenlʸsg* (*kenslʸs*), 'to hail'; *buru ëirlau*, 'to sleet'. Very frequently

without *gla:u*, ' to rain ' : *may hi m buru n jaun, ən drum, ən aru,*
' it is raining heavily ' ; *may hi m buru n ðu:ys,* ' it is raining
steadily ' ; *may n ṭreſ'o buru* (more rarely *stido buru*), ' it is pouring
with rain ' ; *may hi m buru he:n wragað a fyn, may hi m buru
sgrəmpja gu:yl ə gro:g, may hi m buru vel tasa hi n du:ad o gruk,*
' it is raining cats and dogs ' ; *may hi m pigo buru,* ' it is "spotting",
raining a few drops ' ; *may golug buru arni hi,* ' it looks like rain ' ;
burjad vaint vy:d vənno vo, burjad hənny vurja vo (O.H.), ' let it rain
as much as it likes ' ; (b) of corn which has become over-ripe and
is shedding the grain (= *koḷi, droni*); (c) ' to bring forth ' : *buru
ḷo:,* ' to calve ' ; (d) ' to lay eggs ' (of insects): *pṛəvaid glëiſ'on əm
buru ar ə devaid*; (e) fig. *buru və hiraθ,* ' to get over my longing,
to make me forget my home-sickness, etc.' ; *buru ə gwaiθ na ən
rhu:yð,* ' hurry up with that job ' ; *ən meθy buru i annuyd,* ' unable
to keep warm '. (2) ' to throw about ' (as of the limbs): *mi taroð
o nes o:yð o m buru i bədola,* ' he knocked him sprawling ' ; *buru
tṛuiði hi,* ' to speak at a great rate ', said e. g. of a drunken man or
of some one scolding. (3) ' to spend ' (of time): *buru sy:l,* ' to
spend Sunday, to stay for the week-end '. (4) ' to suppose ' :
burjuχ vo:d . . . , ' suppose that . . . , let us take, for instance, that . . .'.

busan, s., pl. *busys*, ' bush : the inner circle of the nave of a wheel
that encloses the axle ' (O.H.).

bustvil, s.m., pl. *bustvilod*, bwystfil, D., ' beast, animal '.

but, in phrase *mynd ən ful but*, ' to go full pelt ', I.W. (Eng.
full butt).

buṭri, s., bwtri, L.G.C. 28. [40]; C.C. 331. 11 ; W.S. [Buttrye];
T.N. 224. 29, ' pantry ' (seldom used).

buts [*buks*].

butſar, s.m., pl. *butſerja(i)d*; cf. bwtsiwr, C.C. 365. 21,
' butcher '.

butſas, s.pl.; sing. *butſasan*, bwtiasen, W.S.; bottas, D.; bwttias,
C.C.M. 105. 28 ; bwtiiws, T.N. 205. 36, ' top-boots ': *butſas
ə go:g,* ' wild hyacinths ' (Hyacinthus non-scriptus) ; cf. D.,
hosanau'r gog.

butti, s.m., bwtti, W.S. [Boty]: *ṛhoid i vy:s ən ə butti,* ' to meddle
with some one else's business ' ; *u:yti n ə butti ?,* ' are you in the
scrape ? ' ; *t a: i ðim i u butti nu,* ' I'm not going to be mixed up
with them '.

buttog, s.m., pl. *butoɡi*, ' boat-hook '.

buθlan [*muθlan*].

buθyn, s.m., pl. *buθənnod*, bwthyn, S.E.*, ' hut ' : *buθənnod kṛənjon*
(O.H.), in speaking of prehistoric round dwellings.

bu:yd, s.m., pl. *buydyð*, bwyd, D., ' food ' : *daχi ðim ən du:ad ən
o:l bu:yd ?,* ' you are not coming back for a meal ? ' ; *may hi n dəsgy*

huiljo r buːyd, 'she is learning to cook'; *dim posib gnëyd buːyd hevo voː*, 'it is impossible to cook with it (the coal)'; *ma na i iſo buːyd*, 'I am hungry'; *ɣhoid buːyd i ɡiː*, 'to feed a dog'; *buːyd lͽfaint*, 'toadstools'; *buːyd gwyδa*, 'goosegrass' = *gwlyːδ gëiru*.

buydo, v., bwydo, R., 'to feed': *buydo moːχ*, 'to feed pigs'.

buyran, böyran [*pabuyr*].

bwiː, s.m., bwi, W.S., 'buoy'.

byːan, adj., buan, D. (1) 'quick': *pͽsgodyn byːan*, 'a fish which swims fast'; *byːan ·vyoχi !*, 'you *have* been quick!'; *ma r merχaid ͽn rëit vyːan i weld bëia*, 'women are very quick at finding fault'. (2) 'fast' (of clocks): *maːr ḳlokja ͽn ͽ wlaːd driː χwartar aur ͽn vyːan*, 'clocks in the country are kept three-quarters of an hour fast'. (3) adv., 'soon': *mi ðaːu ͽn vyːan ruːan*, 'it will burn up soon now'; *maː r maun ͽn darvod ͽn vyːan χadal ͽ gloː*, 'peat burns quick compared with coal'; *ͽn vyːan ne ͽn huːyr*, 'sooner or later'.

byːarθ, s.m., pl. *byarθa*, buarth, D. (1) 'farm-yard'. (2) 'sheep-fold'. Cf. the place-names *byːarθ merχaid mavon* (or *anavon*), — *kum r avon goːχ*, — *anavon*, — *gorlan heːn*, — *ḷaːδ ͽ sais*, — *ͽ gaɾag*, — *nant ͽ kͽtja*, — *ͽ ḳevn*, — *kut ͽ moːχ* (between Aber and Llanfairfechan, O.H.); *byːarθ gwarχa*, 'a pound for strayed sheep'. Cf. W.S. buarth i warchau.

byːd, s.m., pl. *bͽda*, byd, D. (1) 'world': *diwaδ ͽ byːd*, 'end of the world', 'la fin du monde'; *pen draːu ͽ byːd*, 'end of the world', 'le bout du monde'; *may r byːd ͽn duːad i ben*, 'the world is coming to an end'; *ma lawar o wiːb wedi duːad ar ͽ byːd*, 'there have been great changes'; *vel na may r byːd ͽn mynd ͽ mlaːyn*, 'so the world wags', 'such is life'; *byːd druːg ͽdi o l*, 'it's a wicked world!'; *may r byːd wedi mynd ruːan*, 'things have come to a pretty pass'; *wedi gweld ḷawar tɾo: ar vyːd*, 'having gone through a great deal'; *gwyn dͽ vyːd l*, 'what a happy man you are!'—*ͽn ͽ byːd*, etc., used to intensify a statement: *t oːyδ o ŋ goːsb ͽn ͽ byːd*, 'it was no punishment at all'; *un i ðim ar wynab ͽ byːd maur ma be oːyδ o n veδul*, 'I have not the slightest idea what he meant'; *gora n ͽ byːd*, 'all the better';—esp. with superlatives in phrases of the form: *muya n ͽ byːd ·rutḷjuχi ar ͽ duːr, bytɾa n ͽ byːd ëiθ o*, 'the more you stir up water, the dirtier it gets'; *dikka n ͽ byːd voː r këiljog, kͽnta n ͽ byːd kaːn o* (prov.), 'the angrier a cock is, the sooner he crows'.—Similarly by itself, especially after *dim*: *ðaːu dim byːd pen vyːδ iſo vo*, 'nothing comes when it is wanted'; *t oːyδ dim byːd arno vo ond i vod o wedi bytta gormod*, 'there was nothing the matter with him, except that he had eaten too much'; *vyːom i ðim ͽno er s tɾoː byːd*, 'I have not been there for a long time'; *r oːδ mudral* (= *lot*) *byːd o ·honynu*, 'there were an immense number of them'; *pͽːθ* (*vyu*) *vyːd ·vͽnnoχi*, 'whatever you like'; *amriu byːd*, 'several'. (2) 'trouble, fuss': *maː byːd ovnaduy* (*bͽda garu*) *hevo χïi*, 'there's no end of trouble with you'; *ma: r by:d hevo nu*, 'they are a fearful nuisance'; *·r ədani meun by:d*, 'we are in trouble'; *daχi meun by:d ən ṭṛi:o kodi ən ə bora*, 'you have great trouble in trying to get up in the morning'; *mi g̈ëïf i vy:d garu i rustro vo*, 'I had a great deal of trouble in preventing him'; *may gəno vo lawar o vy:d hevo i arjan*, 'he makes a great fuss with his money'; *may bəda garu arno vo i vyu*, 'he has great trouble in making a livelihood'. Cf. *po:yn, iṛafarθ, helbyl*.

bydreði, s., budreddi, D., 'filth'.

bydäwaθ, s.f., cf. mudwraig, D.G. lxxxiv. 55; bydwraig, D., 'midwife'.

bydyr, adj., pl. *bydron*, comp. *byïṛaχ*, budr, D., 'dirty': *may r forð ən mynd ən vydyr*, 'the road is getting dirty'; *kleri bydron*, 'dirty collars'; *heluχ ə ḷestri bydron ar ə iṛc:*, 'take away the dirty things on the tray'; *he:n voχyn bydyr!*, 'you dirty pig!'—In the sense of stormy: *may r dəwyð wedi ṭṛoi ən vydyr jaun*, 'the weather has got very dirty'.

by:ð, s., budd, D., 'advantage, benefit': *ṭ o:s na ðim by:ð i gayl oruθo vo*.

byða, s.f., buddai, D., 'churn' (seldom used = *korður*): *byða gnok*, the old-fashioned type of churn, 'plunging churn'. Cf. *gorð*.

byχað, s., buchedd, D., 'life, way of living, character': *newid byχað*, 'to change one's way of living'; *y:n ·di:-vyχað = y:n ·di:-g̈ariktor*.

byχas, s.f., buches, D. (1) 'a number of cows together'. (2) 'the place where cows are milked when they are outside';—*bri:θ ə vyχas* (O.H.), *ə vry:χ vyχas* (J.J.), 'wagtail' (Motacilla—all species).

byr, adj., fem. *ber*, comp. *bəṛaχ*, byrr, D., 'short': *ə forð vəṛa*, 'the shortest way'; *dy:n byr*, 'a short man'; *·wyðosti be: r ədu i n də weld di n debig?*   *i r durnod (dy:ð) bəṛa—byr a bydyr*, 'do you know what I think you are like? The shortest day—short and dirty'.

byrgyn, s.m., burgyn, D. (1) 'the dead body of an animal' (O.H., but app. obsolete). (2) term of reproach: *he:n vyrgyn; byrgyn bydyr*. Cf. T.N. 207. 1.

byrym, s.m., burm, I.G. 629. [49]; burym, W.S.; Eng. birme (17th cent.); 'barm, yeast': *byrym sy:χ*, 'German barm'; *byrym gly:b*, 'brewers' barm'; *byrym gnëyd*, 'home-made barm, made of hops, sugar, etc.'

by:s, s.m., pl. *bəsað*, bŷs, D., 'finger, toe': *hevo ·bysabaud*, 'with finger and thumb'; *ṛhoi i vy:s ən ə bru:as*, 'to meddle with other people's business'; *kodi by:s aṭ ru:in*, 'to beckon to some one'; *may o ŋ kodi r by:s ba:χ*, 'he is addicted to drink'; *a i vy:s ar o:l paub*, 'spiteful, slandering'. The following is said to children, taking hold of each finger in turn, beginning at the thumb : *modryb vaur, a i by:s ən ər yud, kornal ə gogor, dik ən ə vëipan, by:s ba:χ a r ewin bəχan* (W.H.); *modryb ə vaud, by:s ər yud, hirvys, kutvys, bəχan kɔvruys* (I.W.).—*by:s ko:χ*, 'fox-glove' (Digitalis purpurea), also *by:s ər u:yð* (J.J.); *bəsað koχjon gunjon*, 'white fox-gloves'; *sunjan vel kakkun meun by:s ko:χ*, ' to buzz like a bumble-bee in a fox-glove ', i. e. ' to fume and grumble '; *by:s klok*, 'hand of a clock '; *by:s maur, by:s aur,* 'hour hand '; *by:s ba:χ, by:s mynyd,* 'minute hand '.

bysnas, s.m., pl. *bysnesa*, busnes, C.C. 110. 21 ; 158. 9, 'business': *bysnas da, gwa:yl,* ' good, bad business '; *may o əm mysnas paub, ən r̥hoid i vy:s əm mysnas paub,* 'he meddles with every one's business '.

bysnesgar, bəsnesgar, snesgar, adj., 'meddlesome '.

bysneslyd, adj., ' meddlesome ': *dy:n bysneslyd,* ' a busybody '.

bysnesy, bysnesa, snesy, v., ' to be a busybody, to be meddlesome with other people's affairs ': *y:n garu jaun ədi o am vysnesy.*

bystaχ, s.m., pl. *bystyχ, bystaχjad*, bustach, D., s.v. 'iuvencus '; ' bullock ' = *y:χ.* As term of reproach : *r̥ he:n vystaχ gwirjon.*

bystyl, s.m., bustl, D., 'gall '.

bytëig, adj., bwytteig, D., s.v. 'manduco '; 'voracious, given to eating much '.

bytta, v., bwytta, D. Imperf. S. 3. *bytta.* Pret. S. 1. *bittis,* 3. *byttoð.* Pl. 3. *bydson.* Imperative *bytta ; byttuχ* [O.H. has occasionally *bətta, bəttið*, etc.], ' to eat ': *haffo bytta,* ' to gulp ' = *ləukjo; may o ŋ kəbry bytta,* ' he gobbles his food '; *t ədi o ðim ən efëiðjo ar əχ bytta,* 'it doesn't affect your appetite '; *may o n y:n sa:l jaun i vytta,* 'he is a very bad eater '.—Fig. used of the sea encroaching on the land (= *ənni̯l ar*), or of a river undermining its banks.—Intransitively *o:nu m by̦tta ?,* ' were they good eating ?'

byttur, s.m., pl. *bytturs*, bwyttawr, D., ' eater ': *byttur maur,* ' a great eater '; *sglafjurs o vytturs,* 'voracious eaters ' (O.H.).

byθ, emphatic *by:θ*, byth, D. (1) ' ever ': *pryn he:n, pryn ëilwaθ, pryn newyð, ve bery byθ* (prov.), ' buy old and you must buy again, buy new and it will last for ever '; *am byθ,* ' for ever '; *byθ a bëynyð, byθ a hevyd,* ' for ever and a day '; *di:olχ byθ am hənny !,* ' thank Heaven for that ! '—Esp. with a negative ' never ', (a) with reference to present time : *nëiθ i byθ ðigja,* ' she never gets angry '; *vəða i byθ ən da:l̯l be vəðaχi n ðëyd,* 'I never understand what you say '; *vəða i byθ ən sa:l,* ' I am never ill '; (b) with reference to future time : *r̥haid i mi nëyd əmdraχ ne t a: i byθ i r əsgol,* 'I must

make an effort or I shall never get to school'; *neuχi byθ δəsgy,*
'you will never learn; *r o:n i n meδul vasun i byθ əŋ kəraδ əno,*
'I thought I should never get there'; *nëi di byθ ro:t ən χwe:χ.*
'you will never set the Thames on fire'; *welis i m ono vo byθ
wedyn,* 'I never saw him again'. (2) ' ever ', after adjectives and
adverbs in phrases of the following form : *ǩin dənnad byθ a ˑvedruχɪ
roid o,* 'as tight as ever you can tie it '; *kənta byθ ə medruχi,* ' as
soon as ever you can '; *kənta byθ ëif i əno, ǵida byˑθ ëif i əno,*
' as soon as ever I went there '; *ǩerδ ǵimmin vy:θ,* ' go as fast as
ever you can'. (3) After comparatives in phrases of the form:
mynd əm böyθaχ byθ, 'to get hotter and hotter '; *may hun ən lai byθ,*
' that is smaller still '. (4) ' ever since, still ', Fr. 'toujours :
may ə ǩi əno byθ, 'the dog is still there'; *byθ o r adag honno,*
' ever since '.

byu, v., byw, D. (1) 'to live' (in all senses): *le: may o m byu?,*
' where does he live?'; *byu meun gobaiθ o: hy:d,* 'to live always in
hope'; *ɤhaid byu a bo:d hevo r bobol,* ' one must live amongst the
people'; *wa:θ ǵin i ˈle: i vyu ond ka:l pe:θ ˑat vyu,* 'I don't care
where I live as long as I get something to live *on* '; *byu ar gənnyrχ
ə ti:r,* 'to live on the produce of the land '; *muya vy:δ dy:n byu,
muya we:l a muya glyu* (prov.), ' we live and learn'; *byu vel ku:n
a mo:χ,* ' to live a cat and dog life '; *t o:δ na byu na maru nad aun
i əno,* ' he would take no refusal as to my going there '; *byu bəwyd
vel δary o vyu,* 'to live a life as he did'. (2) 'to support life':
vəwiθ o δim by:d (O.H.), ' it (*syntyr*) will not support any life'.
(3) sometimes used substantively as *may na:u byu ka:θ əno vo,* ' he
has the nine lives of a cat '; so also *ən ə myu* is used to emphasize
a negative—'in the least' (cf. B.C. 83. 12): *un i ən ə myu be na: i,*
'I haven't the least idea what to do'; *he:n voχyn! he:n be:θ! vedra
i ən ə myu i δa:ḷl o l,* ' wretched thing! I simply *can't* understand it !'

byu, adj., byw, D., 'alive': *os byu ag ja:χ,* 'if all's well'; *may
o n vyu o gnonod,* 'it is alive with maggots '; *glo:yn byu,* ' butterfly'
(gloyn Duw, D.).—Used for the sake of emphasis: *pe:θ vyu vy:d
ˑvənnoχi,* 'anything you like '.

byujogi, bəujogi, v., bywiogi, R.; cf. Gen. xlv. 27, 'to enliven,
become enlivened'.

byuχ, s.f., pl. *byχod,* buwch, D., ' cow': *byuχ gəvlo,* 'a cow in
calf'; *byuχ a lo: uθ i θra:d,* 'a cow with a calf'; *byuχ ar i θrədyδ
lo:,* ' a cow which has calved three times '; *byuχ suynog,* 'a barren
cow'; *lvjad byuχ,* 'a tuft of hair on the forehead'; *byuχ go:χ,*
' a red cow', also ' a lady-bird ' (Coccinella): *vyuχ go:χ ba:χ ər
ëiθin, le: may karjad hun a hun?*—Cow-names are: *blakkan, briθan,
gwenno, koχan, luydan, möylan, muynan, penvan, seran.*

bədimja = mədimja, s.pl., cf. munud, mynud, D. (I.W.), 'grimaces'
= *stimja.*

bədjo, v., Eng. bud, 'to graft' (gardener at Bangor) = *impjo nimpjo*.

bədol, adj., bydol, D., 'worldly' : *dy:n bədol*.

bəðar, adj., byddar, D. (1) 'deaf' : *mor vəðar a fren* (J.J.). (2) 'pig-headed, self-willed', applied to people who will not hear : *mor vəðar a pen r̥ha:u, mor vəðar a po:st l̥idjart* (J.J.). (3) applied to people of an impassive, unimpressionable, inexcitable nature, e.g. a man who would not be put out by seeing a cow in his corn-field (J.J.). (4) applied to substances, soft in themselves, which offer a kind of 'dull' resistance to a blow, e. g. wool, sand (J.J.).

bəðary, v., byddaru, D., s.v. 'obsurdesco'; 'to deafen, to madden by continual talking'.

bəgəθjo, v., bygythio, S.E.*, 'to threaten'. Cf. *buguθ*.

bək̃edad, s.m., 'bucketful'.

bəχan, adj., fem. *beχan*, pl. *bəχɩn*, comp. *lai*, eq. *l̃iad (l̃i:ad)*, sup. *l̃ëia (l̃i:a)*, bychan, D., 'little' : *r o:ð o n r̥hy: vəχan i bëidjo kwiljo*, 'he was too little not to believe'; *t ədi hi ðɩm ən lëikjo i bot i n veχan*, 'she does not like being little'; *dy:n bəχan ba:χ tɛ:u*, 'a tiny little fat man'; *dëyd ən vəχan am dano vo*, 'to belittle him'; *tyd, meχan i*, 'come, little one' (e.g. to a cow).—Used substantively : *r̥hy: vəχan o da:n*, 'too little fire' (in his character); *əŋ ka:l r̥hy vəχan at i gadu*, 'getting too little to keep him'.

bəχany, v., bychanu, D., s.v. 'eleuo'; 'to belittle, decry'.

bəlχog ; bəlχjog (W.H., J.J.), adj., bylchog, D., s.v. 'filicatus'; bylchiog, s.v. 'laciniosus'; 'full of gaps', e.g. a wall or a range of mountains.

bəlχy, v., bylchu, H.S. 2. 1, 'to make a gap'.

bənnag, adv., bynnag, D., '-ever, -soever' : *pu:y bənnag*, 'who-ever'; *be:θ bynnag*, 'whatever', 'at any rate' (= Anglo-Welsh 'whatever'); *le: bənnag ə bo:*, 'wherever it may be'; *pu:y bənnag ·vəðanu*, 'whoever they may be'; *be:θ bənnag ðyda vo*, 'whatever he says'; *for bənnag ər ëiθ i*, 'whichever way she goes'; *ond pa: r y:n bənnag*, 'but however that may be . . .', 'but at any rate . . .'.

bəns, s.pl., sing. *bənsan*, f. bwnn bara, W.S. [A. bunne], 'buns'.

bərbuyl̥, adj., byrrbwyll, D., s.v. 'inconsiderantia', 'temerarius'; 'rash, hasty, thoughtless' : *dy:n bərbuyl̥*, 'one who acts without considering the consequences'.

bərbuyl̥tra, s.m., byrbwylldra, S.E., 'rashness, hastiness, thought-lessness' : *gnëyd peθa meun bərbuyl̥tra*.

bərdun, s.m., byrdwn, I.G. 362. [42]; burdwn, M.Ll. i. 183. 31; Eng. burden, and Dial. burdoun, Sc. ; 'burden, refrain of a song' (= *mərdun*).

bərðjo, v., byrddio, D., s.v. 'contabulo, contigno'. (1) 'to board over' (with planks) : *bərðjo r laur, bərðjo r loft*. (2) 'to lay' (a table) :, *du i wedi darvod bərðjo r burð* (O.H.). (3) 'to board' (a ship) : *bərðjo loŋ*, also *bərðjo i loŋ*, and abs. *ma nu wedi bərðjo*, 'they have gone aboard'. (4) 'to take forcible possession of' : *bərðjo iy:, farm*, etc. ;—*bərðja vo*, 'collar him' (for a talk), I.W. (5) 'to thrash' : *mi na: i də vərðjo di*, 'I will thrash you'; *du i n ðigon o ðy:n i χ bərðjo χi*, 'I am man enough to thrash you' (cf. C.F., 1890, 332. 4).

bər·ha:y, v., byrrhau, D., 'to shorten' : *may r ðy:ð əm bər·ha:y*, 'the days are drawing in'.

bərləmmy, bərləmjo, v., cf. W.S. bwlglymu val dwr [Bobyll]; bwrlymu, O.P., 'to bubble' : *may r du:r əm bərləmmy i vəny ; r o:ð ə du:r əm bərləmjo n fɲonna ;*—also *bərləmmy farad, paid a bərləmmy kluyða ;—mi bərləmma i di i draguyðoldab* (O.H.), a threat with no definite meaning.

bəstaχy ; bustaχy (W.H.), v., bustachu, D.F. [164] 14 [to check, restrain], 'to overstrain oneself, to work hard to no purpose' : *n daχi n wirjon əm bəstaχy vel hyn !*, 'how silly you are overworking yourself like this !'; *i be: u:ti m bəstaχy də hy:n a gnëyd dim tɾevn ar ə pe:θ ?*

bəstifol in *pel bəstifol* (I.W.), 'ever so far' = *gəstifol*. Perhaps connected with 'mistiff' = 'mischief'. Cf. T.N. 405. 14 Ca'dd lawer o fistiff yn ffoi rhag ei feistar.

bəstodi, v., 'to run about wildly' (of cattle in hot weather).

bətmant, s.m., 'abutment' (of a bridge) = *pentan*.

bɹ·θëid, bɹ·θëiod ; bɹ·θëig (O.H.), s.pl., bytheiad, D., 'hounds': *bɹ·θëig nəsvor* (O.H.), 'foxhounds'. ['There is . . . an old-established pack of foxhounds kept by Mr. Evan B. Jones, of Ynysfor, near Beddgelert, which has been hunted by members of the same family for about a century'.—Forrest, p. 25.]

bəθëirjo, v., bytheirio, D., 'to belch'.

bəθol, adj., bythol, D., s.v. 'sempiternus'; 'continual, everlasting' : *ko:yd bəθol wirðjon*, 'evergreens', *d*, for ' hyd ' in *d aī*, i.e. hyd at [*hyːd*].

d, for ' nid ', e. g. *d un i ðim* [*nid*].

d, for ' dy ', e.g. *dal d aval* [*də*].

daː, adj., comp. *gweḷ* eq. *kəstal, kəstlad*, sup. *gora*, da, D., ' good ': *dyːð daː*, ' good day '; *bora daː*, ' good morning '; *pnaun daː*, ' good afternoon '; *nosˑtauχ*, ' good night '; *bluyðyn newyð daː i χi*, ' a happy New Year to you '; *nosˑtauχ a daː ə boː χi*, ' good night and good-bye '; *pėidjuχ, daː χiː*, ' don't, that's a good fellow '; *daχi ɲ kluːad ə buːyd ən ðaː ?*, ' does the food taste nice ? '; *hogla daː*, ' a nice smell '; *sy daχi hëiðju ? rëit ðaː*, ' how are you to-day ? Very well '; *may hi meun ōydran garu ag edraχ mor ðaː*, ' she is a great age to look so well '; *may o n ðaː i jeχid*, ' he is well '; *daχi n rëit ðaː əχ ḷeː*, ' you have a very good place '; *os gweluχ ən ðaː (s gweluχ ən ðaː)*, ' please '; *dëyd ən ðaː am ruːin*, ' to praise some one '. Followed by prepositions : *am*, ' at ': *may o n yːn daːˑjaun am ðëyd ˑanˑwirað*, ' he is very good at telling lies ';—*ar* : *may hi n o ðaː ˑarnoχi*, ' you are pretty well off ';—*at*, ' for ' (implying remedy): *daː jaun at*, ' very good for, as a remedy for '; *at beː may o n daː ?* (I.W.), ' what is it good for ? '—*ġin* (sometimes *kin*, see below) : *ma n ðaː ġin i*, ' I am glad ', e.g. *ma n ðaː ġin i bo χi n weḷ*, ' I am glad you are better '; also, ' I like ', as *θaː (= ni dda) kin i m ono vo*, ' I don't like him '; *mi vasa n ðaː ġin i tasa ɣ heːn ðənas wedi mynd*, ' I wish the old lady had gone ';—*i*, ' for ' (implying purpose): *ˑt ədynu n daː i ðim*, ' they are good for nothing '; *i beː may hun ən daː ?*, ' what is this for ? ';—*r.hag*, ' as a remedy against, as a means of escaping ': *may baŋgor ən ḷeː rëit ðaː r.hag ëira*, ' Bangor is a very good place for escaping snow '.

daː s.m., da, D. (1) ' cattle ' (but practically obsolete): *r.haːd ar ə daːl* was an expression formerly used when a cow calved (J.J.; O.H.). Cattle and poultry are sometimes distinguished by the terms *daː kornjog* and *daː phyːog*. (2) ' goods ' (in general).

dabal, s., tabyl, W.S. [A. table], tabl, D. (1) ' the top of the wall of a house where the roof meets it ': *kay ə dabal* (O.H.), ' to fill up the space between the top of the wall and the roof '. (2) ' the outside of the roof corresponding to the spot where the wall meets it ': *kerig ar ə dabal*, ' stones placed on the roof as a protection against the wind'. (3) 'the part of the top of a hay-stack between the edge and the first rope running lengthwise' (J.J.).

da·da:, s.m., childish word for 'sweets'.

·dad·dgëintjo, v., 'to disjoint'.

dadl, s.f., dadl, D., 'dispute': *tori r ðadl*, 'to settle the dispute'.

dadla, dadly, v., dadleu, D., 'to dispute': *by:ð ɤhëi ǝn dadla m bo:yθ am i henwada*, 'some people dispute hotly about their religious denominations'; *dadly dros i blaid*, 'to argue in favour of one's party'; *dadla hevo i ǵilið (dadly ǝn erbyn i ǵilið)*, 'to dispute with one another, to quarrel'; *dadly am bri:s pe:θ*, 'to haggle about the price of a thing'.

·dad·luyθo, v., dadlwytho, D., 'to unload'.

dadmar, v., dadmer, D., 'to thaw'.

·dad·sgriujo, v., 'to unscrew'.

·dad·vlino, v., dadfiino, D., s.v. 'refocillo'; 'to get rid of fatigue'.

·dad·wrëiðjo, v., dadwreiddio, D., s.v. 'inextirpabilis'; 'to uproot'.

dadg, s. = *dadl* (O.H.), *mynd ǝn dadg*, 'to get into a dispute, quarrel'.

dadgo, v. (1) 'to chaff' (LW.). (2) 'to quibble' (W.H.): *dim ius i ñ ðadgo*, 'it is no use your quibbling'. (3) 'to dispute, haggle' = *dadly* (O.H.).

dafod, v., dattod, D. Pret. S. 1. *dafottis, dfottis, dafis:* 3. *dafottoð, dfottoð*. Pl. 3. *dafodson, dfodson*. Imperative S. 2. *dafod, dafotta, dfotta*. Pl. 2. *dafottuɤ, dfottuɤ*, 'to undo, untie': *may ǝ marklod wedi dafod*, 'my apron is undone'; *dafod ko:t*, 'to unbutton a coat'; *dafod klo:s*, euphemistically for 'ventrem exonerare'; *dafod eda o ri:l*, 'to unwind thread from a reel'.

dagar, s.f. (cf. dager, D., 'pugio'), *pe:θ i wasgy ǩe:g ǩefyl dru:g* (O.H.).

dagra, s.pl., sing. *dëigryn*, dagrau, D., 'tears': *r o:ð dagra ǝm pǝuljo o i lǝgad o*, 'tears were streaming from his eyes'; *gnëyd dagra*, 'to shed tears'.

dail, s.pl., sing. *dëilan*, dail, D., 'leaves': *may r dail ǝn disǵin*, 'the leaves are falling'; *kwymp, kwimpjad ǝ dail*, 'the fall of the leaves'; *krǝnny vel dëilan*, 'to tremble like a leaf'; *wedi kodi n i dail*, 'come up into leaf'; *may dëilan ar i davod o*, 'he speaks thick'; *heb ðëilan ar i davod*, 'without mincing matters'; *paid a hel dim dail hevo mi*, 'don't let me have any of your nonsense'; *dëilan plug*, see *plug*.—Used to distinguish a plant from the root, flowers, or fruit, e.g. *dail arjan*, 'silverweed' (Potentilla anserina); *dail dy:on da:*, 'knotty-rooted figwort' (Scrofularia nodosa); *dail gron*, ' pennywort ' (Cotyledon Umbilicus) ; *dail karn ebol*, ' colt's foot ' (Tussilago Farfara) ; *dail knay ə ðẽyar*, ' earth-nut ' (Conopodium denudatum) ; *dail krɑːχ, dail ḻuynog*, ' fox-glove ' (Digitalis purpurea) ; *(dail) kr̥iba sant fraid*, cribau S. Ffraid, D., ' betony ' (Stachys Betonica) ; *dail ḻorjad*, ' broad-leaved plantain ' (Plantago major) ; *dail ḻuːyn hydyl (hydyð)*, ' ribwort plantain ' (Plantago lanceolata) = *dail ᵏẽiljog* (Bangor) ; *dail r̥hokkos*, ' mallow ' (Malva silvestris, etc.) ; *dail tavol*, ' dock-leaves ' (Rumex obtusifolius) ; *dail vəðigad*, ' all-heal ' (Hypericum Androsaemum) ; *dail ə pẽils* = *ḻəgad ebril̥*, ' the lesser celandine ' (Ranunculus Ficaria).

daint, s.m., pl. *dannað*, dant, D., pl. daint, ' Quae vox apud Venedotas pro sing. passim vsurpatur ', pl. dannedd, ' tooth ' : *daint blaːyn*, ' front tooth ' ; *ᵏilðaint*, ' back tooth ' ; *daint ḻəgad*, ' eye tooth ' ; *tənny daint*, ' to draw a tooth ', ' to have a tooth out ' ; *may i dannað wedi pədry*, ' her teeth are decayed ' ; *may o wedi wasgy o a i ðannað*, ' he has bitten him ' ; *may n mynd tr̥u nannað i*, ' it sets my teeth on edge ' ; *grindzan i ðannað*, ' to grind one's teeth ' ; *t oːys gᵊno vo ðim daint i attal i davod*, ' he always speaks out, says what had better be left unsaid ' ; *daɲos i ðannað*, ' to show his fangs, to threaten ' ; *ma na riu ðaint r̥hᵊɲθo vo a voː*, ' there is no love lost between them ' ; *may gᵊno vo ðaint i mi (ðaint ən v erbyn)*, ' he has something against me ' ; *ᵏeluyð ən də ðannað !*, ' that's an absolute lie ! ' ; *du i kəstal (kəstlad) a tiða ən də ðannað*, ' I'm as good as you at any rate ' ; *mi ᵏeːs i o ar i wẽyθa vo n i ðannað*, ' I got it in the teeth of his opposition ' ; *mi r̥hois hi iði hi ən i dannað (= ən i gwymmad)*, ' I paid it back to her with interest, I got the better of her '.—In transf. senses *daint oːg, kribin*, etc. ; *dannað ə graig*, ' the jagged edges of the rock ' ; *daint ə ḻeːu*, ' dandelion ' (Leontodon Taraxacum).

dakja, interj., Eng. God ache : *dakja vo ᵊɲwaθ !*, ' drat him ! '

dakku, adv., dacw, D.G. lix. 16, Fr. voilà : *dakku voː !*, ' there he is ! '

dal, v., dal, D. Fut. S. 1. *dalja*, 3. *daliθ (ðẽil̥)*. Pl. 2. *daljuχ*. Imperf. *daljun*. Pret. 1. *dalis*. S. 3. *daljoð*. Pl. 3. *dalson*. Plup. *dalsum*. Imperative S. 2. *dal ;* *daljux*. Pret. Pass. *daljuyd*.
  I. tr. (1) ' to hold in the hand or arms ' : *puːy ðaliθ hun ?*, ' who will hold this ? '. (2) ' to hold ' (in possession) : *dal tiːr*, ' to hold land '. (3) ' to hold (something) so that it cannot fall or break loose ' : *rubaθ i ðal ə dgain ar ᵍevn ᵏefyl*, ' something to hold the chain on the back of the horse '. (4) ' to hold, contain ' : *ðẽil o ðuːr ?*, ' will it hold water ? ' ; *ᵏimmint a ðaliθ o, ðalja vo*, ' as much as it will hold, would hold '. (5) ' to break in ' (of a horse) : *dal ᵏefyl (= tor̥i i laur, tor̥i i veun*, J.J.). (6) ' to hold or keep in a certain position ' : *dal ən dyn*, ' to hold tight ' ; *dal ə ðesᵍil ən wastad iði hi*, ' to humour her ', lit. ' to hold the dish straight for her ' ; *ma nu n dal əχ tr̥aːyd ən sattaχ*, ' they

hold your feet firmer'; *vel ·tasanu n dal ə by:d uθ i ǵiliδ*, 'as if
they kept the world together'; i.e. 'as if the world could not get on
without them'. Similarly *dal i lais ən hi:r*, 'to lengthen out a
sound with the voice'. (7) 'to hold back': *ı o:s na δim dal arno
vo*, 'there's no holding him back'. Similarly *dal du:r*, 'to back
water' (in rowing): *y:n ən tənny a r lal̥ ən dal du:r* (O.H.), 'one
pulling and the other backing water'; *dal i wynt*, 'to hold one's
breath'. (8) 'to detain': *k̂e:s ə nal*, 'I was detained'. (9) 'to
catch': *gosod abuyd i δal l̥uynog*, 'to set a trap to catch a fox';
dal pəsgod, 'to catch fish';—'to catch up': *mi daljuχ o ar ǵevn əχ
bëik*, 'you'll catch him on your bicycle'. (10) *dal gaval*, 'to catch
hold (of), to hold on': *dal d aval əno vo rhag iδo sərθjo*, 'catch
hold of it to keep it from falling'; *dal d aval ən ə re:ns*, 'catch hold
of the reins'. (11) *dal sylu*, 'to notice': *mi ·daljuχi sylu ə tro:
nesa*, 'you will notice next time'; *erbyn dal sylu*, 'when you come
to think of it'. (12) 'to harness': *amsar dal*, 'the time for harnessing the horses to begin work' = *amsar baχy*. (13) 'to hold out':
dal də la:u, 'hold out your hand'. (14) 'to hold out against,
sustain, stand, endure, support, keep out': *may r gwarθag dy:on
əŋ glettaχ i δal ə dəwyδ*, 'black cattle stand the weather better';
meθy dal ru:in, 'to be unable to endure somebody'; *muy nɑ hənny
δëil ər he:n gorfyn* (O.H.), 'more than the body can endure'; *ı ədi r
sǵidja ma δim ən dal du:r*, 'these boots do not keep out the water'.
(15) 'to lay a wager, to bet': *mi δalja i χi su:l̥ı*, 'I'll bet you
a shilling'. Cf. the doggerel rime: *y:n day tṛi:, mi ro: nu i laur ən
fri: | mi δalja i am bëint o guru puy bənnag a δëil a mi: | nad oy:s
əmma na mu:y na lai ond injon igjan fri:* (E.J.).

II. intr. (16) 'to hold': *nëiθ o δal ru:an*, 'it will hold now'.
(17) 'to keep (in a certain direction)': *dal gormod ar ə δe:*, 'to
bear too much to the right'; *dal ar hy:d ə lo:n spel*, 'to keep along
the high-road a bit'; *dal i r χwi:θ, i r δe:*, 'to keep to the left, to
the right'. (18) 'to keep, continue': *may n dal i χuθy o hy:d*, 'it
keeps on blowing'; *may hi wedi dal ən hi:r heb δim gla:u*, 'it has
kept off raining for a long time'; *may r ta:n ən dal*, 'the fire keeps
in'; *may fair lambad ən dal* (O.H.), 'Llanbedr (y Cenin) fair still
continues'; *os δëil ə by:d i vynd* (O.H.), 'if the world goes on'.
(19) *dal ar*, 'to hold on (to)'—(fig.) 'to give heed, attend, mark':
dani wedi kl̥u:ad peθa da: jaun ond i ni δal ·arnynu a i gnëyd nu, 'we
have heard some very good things, if we only give heed to them and
do them' (cf. Jer. xxiii. 18; Acts xvi. 14);—'to pull up (some one)':
du i n dal arno vo peŋ glu:a i o (O.H.), 'I pull him up when I hear
him (making mistakes)'. (20) *dal aı rubaθ*, 'to stick to something,
persevere in something'. (21) 'to hold, maintain' (also *dal
al̥an*). (22) 'to begin' (connected with 11): *dal am hannar aur
wedi tṛi:*, 'to begin at half-past three'.

dalan, s.pl., danadl, D., only *dalan pöiθjon*, 'nettles' (Urtica dioica).

dalan [*dolan*].

daldun, dandlun, dandljo, v., ' to dandle '.

daljad, s.m., daliad, D.G. xlix. 23. (1) ' a keeping back, detention ' : *daχi wedi ka:yl daljad go hi:r hёiδju,* ' you have been kept rather long to-day '. (2) ' the time a team remains in the field to work '. The two *daljad* are from about 7 to 11 a.m. and from 1 to 5 p.m. (cf. *dal* 11).—Also of persons' working hours: *daljad dy:n* (on a farm) 6 a.m. to 5·30 p.m.; *daljad ə mёinar ədi u:yθ aur.*

dal̨, adj., pl. *dёil̨jon,* dall, D., ' blind ' : *dal̨ bo:s̨l,* ' stone-blind ' ; *dal̨a o baub na vyn welad* (prov.), ' none is so blind as he who won't see '.

·dal̨gёibjo, v., ' to speak beside the mark ' : *be u:t̨i n ·dal̨gёibjo am beθa d u:t̨i δim ən i da:l̨i nu* (O.H.) = *boδro, s̨lunf'o.* Cf. T.N. 29. 5, Nid yw'r holl gwbl ond dall geibio ;—also 32. 1.

dal̨inab, s.m., dallineb, D., ' blindness '.

da:l̨l ; dy:al̨ (O.H. nearly always), v., deall and dyall, D. ; deallt, D.G. ccxiv. 9 ; dealld, D.F. [vi.] 8, [xiii.] 9, etc. ; dallt, C.L.C. v. vi. 67. 23. Fut. S. 3. *dal̨liθ.* Imp. *dal̨tun.* Pret. S. 3. *dal̨loδ, dyal̨loδ; dəhal̨loδ* (O.H.). Pl. 3. *dal̨lson.* Imperative *dal̨la, da:l̨l ; dal̨lux,* ' to understand ' : *daχi n da:l̨l ?,* ' do you understand ? ' ; *vəda i byθ ən da:l̨l be ·vəδuχi n δёyd,* ' I never understand what you say ' ; *mi δo:ni i δal̨l əy ɡil̨iδ vesyl t̨ippin,* ' we shall come to understand one another by degrees ' ; *mi δal̨loδ mod i meun helbyl,* ' he (the dog) understood I was in difficulties '.

dal̨y, v., dallu, D., ' to blind ' : *ə gola n ə nal̨y i ən la:n.*

damχwal (J.J.), *dəmχwal* (O.H.), v., dymchwelyd, D., s.v. 'euerto '; ' to fall down ' : *bildin wedi damχwal* (J.J.), ' a building which has fallen down ' ; *dəmχwal dros ə dibin* (O.H.), ' to fall over the precipice '.

damwain, s.f., pl. *damwёinja,* damwain, D., ' accident ' ; *damwain vaur,* ' a bad accident ' ; *ar δamwain,* ' by chance '.

damwёinjol, adj., damweiniol, D., s.v. ' accidentalis ' ; ' accidental '.

dan, prep., dan, D., s.v. ' sub '. See *t̨an.*

danheδog; adj., dannheddog, D., ' toothed, serrated '.

danvon; daŋon (I.W.); *davnon, davny(d)* (O.H.), v., danfon, D., s.v ' mitto '. Pret. S. 3. *dvonoδ* (O.H.), ' to send, take, conduct ' : *danvon ər hu:χ al ə ba:yδ;—plismon ən davnon ru:in* (O.H.), ' a policeman taking some one to the lock-up ' ; *no:l a danvon ədu i l̨ru: r dy:δ,* ' I am fetching and carrying all day long ' ; *rhaid no:l a i danvon hi* (said of old people), ' she has to be tended everywhere ' ; *ga: i χ daŋon χi adra ?,* ' may I see you home ? '

daŋos ; daŋgos (O.H.), v., dangos, D. Fut. 3. *daŋhosiθ (deŋys).*

Pret. 1. *daŋhosis, daŋis,* 3. *daŋhosoð.* Imperative *daŋos ; daŋhosuχ.*
(1) tr. 'to show': *daŋos rubaθ i ru:in ;—daŋos gu:g al y:n,* 'to
frown, to look surlily at some one'; *daŋos i hy:n (hynan),* 'to show
off'; *daŋos i hy:n ən yuχ nag ədi i vo:d,* 'to make oneself appear
to be above what one really is'. (2) intr., 'to show': *ko:ys ən
daŋos, ə se:rs* (stars) *ən daŋos.* (3) 'to seem' (= ymddangos).

darbuylo, v., darbwyllo, S.E., 'to bring to reason'.

darja, in the exp. *o: darja !,* 'dash it !' :—*darja vo ynwaθ ; darja
də budin di.*

darlan, v., darllain, darllen, D. Pret. S. 3. *darlennoð,* Pl. 3.
darlenson. Imperative *darlan ; darlennuχ,* 'to read': *na i
ðarlan o peŋ ga: i amsar,* 'I will read it when I have time'; *lyvr
divir i ðarlan,* 'an amusing book to read'; *may o n darlan
po:b pe:θ ǵëiθ o aval əno vo,* 'he reads everything he can get
hold of'.

darlau, v., darllaw, D., 'to brew' :—fig. *may hi n i darlau hi er
s talum,* 'a storm has been brewing for a long time'.

darn, s.m., pl. *darna,* darn, D. (1) 'piece': *may o wedi kəmmyd
darn o mara i,* 'he has taken a piece of my bread'; *darn o graig,
bren, hëyarn,* 'a piece of rock, wood, iron'; *darn o gara,* 'a piece
of boot-lace'; *ən dri: darn,* 'in three pieces'; *may o wedi bildjo
r darn ma,* 'he has built this piece' ;—*darn kro:ys,* in old-fashioned
cottages of one story, a projecting piece partitioned off from the
rest and used as a bedroom. Its position was opposite the house
door by the side of the *simða vaur* (O.H.). Cf. *fambar.* (2) 'part':
darn kupanad, 'part of a cupful'. (3) used adverbially, 'partly':
ar i ðarn godi, 'partly raised'; *darn la:ð,* 'to half kill'.

darnjo, v., darnio, D., 'to divide into parts': *darnjo ty:, moχyn ;
pobol ən darnjo i hy:n uθ gufjo.*

darpar, s., darpar, D., 'praeparatio, apparatus': *darpar u:r,*
'fiancé'; *darpar wraig,* 'fiancée'.

darparjaθ, s.f., darparaeth, M.A. i. 348 b. 11, 'preparation': *dim
darparjaθ ar i gəvar.*

darpary ; dərpary (O.H.), v., darpar, darparu, D., 'to provide':
darpary prikja ar gəvar ə bora, 'to get firewood ready for the
morning'.

darvod ; davrod (often at Llanfairfechan), v., darfod, D. Fut.
S. 1. *darvəða,* 3. *darvəðiθ.* Imperf. S. 1. *darvun,* 3. *darva.*
Pret. 3. [*dary*], *darvəðoð.* Imperative *darvod, darvəða ; darvəðuχ.*
I. tr., 'to finish': *vely sy ifʼo gnëyd, darvod po:b dim,* 'that's the
way—finish (eat up) everything'; *du i 'ar ðarvod o ru:an,* 'I am
just finishing it (the book) now'; *rhaid i mi dri:o darvod ən o
vy:an i ga:l du:ad hevo χi,* 'I must try and get done pretty soon, so
as to come with you'. II. intr., (1) 'to come to an end, to be

finished, to wear out, to be over ' : *ma: r sǵidja ma wedi darvod,*
' my boots are worn out ' ; *may o wedi darvod,* ' it is finished ', also
' he has gone ', i. e. ' is dead ' ; *may hi wedi darvod arno vo,* ' it is
all up with him ' ; *mi ðəlis na ðarva vo byθ,* ' I thought it would
never wear out ' ; *ma: r maun ən darvod ən vy:an χadal ə glo:,* ' peat
burns away quickly as compared with coal '. (2) The uninflected
preterite form *dary,* i.e. darfu i (nearly always in the mutated form
ðary), is very frequently used as an auxiliary, instead of the inflected
form of the preterite in all persons, with all verbs except *bo:d,* and
especially in plurals the inflected forms of which consist of more
than two syllables : *ðary nu anvon,* ' they sent ' ; *ðary ni ðeχra,* ' we
began ' ; *ðary χi ðim kɹɹað,* ' you did not reach '. In S. 1. *ðary
mi* or *vi.* Sometimes *ðary* stands alone, the infinitive being
understood, as *ı̄ un i ðim ðary hi ai pëidjo,* ' I don't know whether
she did or not ' ; . . . *ag veḷy dary nu,* ' . . . and so they did '.
(3) In the phrase *be hary ti ?* (beth ddarfu i ti ?), this verb has the
sense of ' happened ', i. e. ' what is the matter ? ' So, by analogy,
un i ðim be hary o, ' I don't know what is the matter with him ' ; *be
sary ti ?* (by analogy with *be s anti ?,* i. e. beth sydd arnat ti ?) is also
occasionally heard, and *be:θ o.yð hary o ?*

darvodedig, adj., darfodedig, D., ' wasteful ' ; *menyn darvodedig,*
' wasteful butter ' ; *lëyly darvodedig,* ' a family that dies out rapidly '.

·*datˀbakjo,* v., ' to unpack ' : *ar o:l i χi orfan ·datˀbakjo,* ' when you
have finished unpacking '.

·*datˀbaχy,* v., dadbachu, ' to unharness '.

daun, s.f., dawn, D., ' gift ' : *daun madroð ḷiθrig,* ' the gift of ready
speech ' ; *may gʐno vo ðigon o ðaun ſarad* (= *ðaun dëyd*), ' he has
the gift of the gab '.

dauns, s.f., dawns, Psalm cl. 4, ' dance '.

davadan, s.f., dafaden, D., s.v. ' ovicula ' ; ' a single sheep ' : *ma:y
y:n ðavadan ar o:l* (O.H.), ' there is one sheep left behind ' (see
davod 1).

davadan, s.f., pl. *devaid,* dafaden, D., ' wart ' : *davadan wyḷt,*
' cancerous wart '.

davað [*eda*].

davn, s., pl. *davna ; devni* (O.H.), dafn, D., ' drop '.

davod, davad, s.f., pl. *devaid,* dafad, D., ' sheep ' : *haul pori
devaid a θoɹi maun,* ' the right of pasturing sheep and cutting peat ' ;
hel devaid, ' to collect sheep together ' ; *biǵëiljo devaid,* ' to look after
sheep ' ; *knëivjo devaid,* ' to shear sheep ' ; *knevin devaid,* ' a sheep
walk ' ; *ḱi: devaid,* ' a sheep dog ' ; *noda kḷisłja devaid,* ' sheep's
ear-marks ' ; *devaid gwlanog,* ' sheep with their wool ' ; *devaid
lɔmjon,* ' sheep after shearing ' ; *ma: ǵin i dair davad heb ðu:ad ag
u:yn leni,* ' I have three sheep which have not lambed this season ' ;

ma: kro:yn ər o:yn a kro:yn ə ðavad i welad mor ammal a i ġili̯ð ən ə varꭓnad (prov.), 'the lamb's skin and the sheep's skin are to be seen equally often in the market', i. e. 'the young die as well as the old' (cf. the literary form: Cyn ebrwydded yn y farchnad, croen yr oen a chroen y ddafad, D., cf. also M.A. i. 15 *a*. 23); *r o:yn ən dəsgy r ðavad bori* (prov. exp.), 'teaching one's grandmother'.

davod, davad, s.f., pl. *devaid*, 'wart' : *davod wy:l̥t*, 'cancerous wart'. Cf. *davadan*.

davyð, Dafydd, 'David' : *ən o:ys davyð*, 'in the Greek calends'; *davyð ðgo:ns*, 'the sea'; *asgwrn davyð!*, 'Good Heavens!'

day, s. and adj., fem. *du:y*, dau, D., 'two'. Both *day* and *du:y* are followed by the vocal mutation ; *day kant* is, however, the usual form for 200, and there are a few other exceptions, e. g. *day pen l̥inin*, in the phrase *ka:yl ə ðay pen l̥inin at i ġilið*, 'to make two ends meet'; cf. deupenn y llynynn, L.A. 96. 26; and words of English origin beginning with *g, ġ* as *du:y ġa:t*. With the article always *ə ðay, ə ðu:y* :— *ə ðay vurð*, 'the two tables'; *ə ðu:y gadar*, 'the two chairs';—*day ne dri: o ðərnodja*, 'two or three days'; *gəmmuꭓi r ðay?*, 'will you have both?'; *mi nëi̯θ ə ðay r y:n va:θ*, 'either will do'; *day a θair*, 'two (shillings) and threepence'; *gwerθ du:y*, 'two pennyworth'; *stamp du:y a dimma*, 'a twopence halfpenny stamp'; *ynwaθ ne ðu:y*, 'once or twice'; *ə mhen durnod ne ðay*, 'in a day or two'; *may r blaid wedi hol̥ti n ðu:y*, 'the party has split in two'; *may o r̥huŋ day veðul*, 'he can't make up his mind'; *·r ədani r̥huŋ day ola*, 'it is twilight'; *gwel̥ day meun bol na kant meun l̥a:u*, a proverb implying that it is better to have a small amount (of money) and know what to do with it than an unwieldy quantity.

dayuynebog, adj., dauwynebog, D., s.v. 'anceps'; 'two-faced, deceitful'.

de:, adj., deau and dehau, D. (1) 'right': *ə l̥a·u ðe:*, 'the right hand'—hence s.f. *ə ðe:*, 'the right'; *dal gormod ar ə ðe:*, 'to keep too much to the right'; *o ðe:*, 'right', opposite to *o ꭓwiθig*, 'wrong'; *du:y forð i nèyd po:b pe:θ—y:n o ðe:, y:n o ꭓwiθig*, 'two ways of doing everything—one right, one wrong'. (2) 'south': *iy: ðe:*, 'the south side'—also s.m. *ə ðe:*, 'the south' : *may n ꭓuθy o r ðe:*, 'it is blowing from the south'.

deduyð, adj., dedwydd, D., 'happy'.

deðvy, v., dyddfu, D., only in *deðvy gan wre:s* (O.H), 'to be overcome by the heat'.

defro, v., deffro, D., s.v. 'expergiscor'; 'to wake' (tr. and intr.).

de:g, de:ŋ, s. and adj., dêg, D., 'ten'; *de:ŋ* is the adjectival form: *de:ŋ mi:s, mlu:yd, ml̯ənað, mynyd, ewin, usnos ; de:ŋ waiθ*, 'ten times'; *de:g durnod* (beside *de:ŋ njurnod*) is, however, common, also *de:g k̯ëinjog*. In other cases the substantival *de:g o* has superseded it, as *de:g o vasġedi, vala, nəθod*, etc.

degum, s.m., pl. *degəmma*, degwm, D., 'tithe ': *ɨɾɛː r degum*, ' township '; *degum ə bliːθ*, ' tithe on animals '; *degum ər yːd*, ' tithe on corn '; *sgybor ðegum*, ' tithe barn '.

degvad, adj., degfed, D., ' tenth ' : *ə degvad ȧyːð; ə ðegvad ran*.

dëiğeinvad, adj., deugeinfed, D., ' fortieth '.

dëigjan, s. and adj., deugain, D.; deigian, C.C.M. 18. 6, ' forty '. For mutations see *igjan*.

dëiljo, v., deilio, D., 'to come into leaf': *maː r dgakmor ən deiljo n vyːan jaun*, ' the sycamore comes into leaf very early '.

dëiljo, v., deilio, C.L.C. ii. 12. 18, ' to deal ', e.g. at a shop ; also *dëiljo meun kəfəla ;—dëiljo uθi hi* implies an illicit connexion.

dëiljur, s.m., ' herbalist '.

dëiljur, s.m., ' dealer '.

dëimon, s., daimawnt, C.Ch. 56. 25, ' diamond or something shaped like a diamond ', e.g. in speaking of the meshes of a net.

dëintjo, v., deintio, D., s.v. ' denticulo, tango '; P.G.G. 224. 16, ' to go near, to enter ' : *paid a dëintjo at ə tyː*, ' don't go near the house ' (because of some suspicious circumstances connected with it) ; *dëintjo i meun*, ' to enter '.

dëintəðjaθ, s.f., deintyddiaeth, ' articulation ' : *may gəno vo ðëintəðjaθ ðaː*.

dëivis, s., deufis, D.G. iii. 7, ' two months ': *dëivis ne driː*, ' two or three months '.

dëivjo, v., deifio, D., ' to singe, blight, wither ' : *pen vəðuxi n ɽhoi klut o vlaːyn ə taːn may o n dëivjo ; maː gwyni ə duyran ən dëivjo ə kubul*.

dëivjol, adj., deifiol, S.E., ' nipping, blasting ' : *gwyni dëivjol*.

dekbuys, s., ' ten pounds ' (weight).

dekbyni, s., degpunt, T.N. 71. 24, ' ten pounds ' (sterling).

dekk̃in, dekk̃en, decyn in *dekk̃in i, dekk̃en i* = *debig k̃in i*, i.e. debyg genyf, ' I should think ' : *may o wedi mynd ruːan dekk̃in i*.

dexra, v., dechreu, D. Fut. S. 1. *dexra*, 2. *dəxriθ, dexrëyiθ*. Pret. S. 1. *dexris, dəxrēyis*, 3. *dexroð, dəxrëyoð*. Imperative, *dexra ; dexrux, dəxrëyux*. Pret. Pass. *dəxrëyud*, ' to begin ': *may n dexra tuly*, ' it is beginning to get dark '; *dexra o r dexra*, ' to begin at the beginning '; *ɽhaid i ni gaːyl ə druːg əna n jaun i ðexra*, ' we must set that to rights to begin with '; *dexra r taːn*, ' to light the fire ' (used of paper, sticks, etc.) ; *ədi r boks ma am gaːl i dori i ðexra r taːn ?*, ' is this box to be broken up to light the fire ? '; *dexra kany* (of the leader of a choir), ' to strike up, to give the note '. Nouns are often preceded by *ar*, e. g. *dexra ar ə gwaiθ*, ' to take up the task '.

dɛχra, s.m., dechreu, D., 'beginning': *ən ə dɛχra*, 'at first';
ən ə dɛχra kənta, 'at the very beginning'; *dɛχra a dïwað ə vluyδyn*,
'the beginning and end of the year'.

del, adj., comp. *delaχ*, dèl, D., 'protervus, morosus'; 'pretty,
nice': *ma: ·gənoχi da:n ba:χ del*, 'you have a nice little fire';
dənas ba:χ δel, 'a nice little woman'; *·ma:y o ŋ gweny n δel!*, 'he
does smile prettily!'; *may o ŋ gweḷa n δel*, 'he is mending nicely';
—as term of endearment, *del ba:χ!; ïyd e neḷi l ;*—ironically, *u:ti
n y:n del!*, 'you're a nice fellow!'

delu, s.f., delw, D. (1) 'image': *mi a:θ vel delu*, 'he stood stock
still with fright'. (2) 'cross': *delu ayr*, 'a gold cross' (O.H.).

delwi, v., delwi, D., 'to stand stock still with fright'.

de:n, s.m., 'dean'.

denig, dinig, deŋid, diŋid; dëiŋid (W.H.), v., diangc, D.;
dihengyd, C.C. 260. 23. Fut. 3. *diŋiθ* (I.W.), *dëiŋiθ* (W.H.).
Imp. *diŋun* (I.W.), *deŋun* (E.J.).   Pret. 3. *deŋoδ* (J.J.). *dëiŋoδ*
(W.H.). Imperative, *deŋ* (I.W., O.H.), *dëiŋ, dëiŋa* (W.H), 'to
make off, to escape': *daχi am δenig hëiδiu ?*, 'are you off anywhere
to-day?'; *dëiŋ(a) am də vəwyd*, 'escape for your life'.

deny(d), v., denu, D., 'to entice'.

deŋgar, adj., dengar, 'attractive, fascinating in manner'.

deŋwaθ, adv., dengwaith, D., s.v. 'decies'; 'ten times'.   Cf.
also *de:ŋ waiθ*.

de:r, s., 'a blow': *dəmma vi: a de:r ïδo vo nes o:δ o ŋ kany* (J.J.),
'I gave him a blow which made him sing out'; *χhoi de:r*, 'to
give a blow'.

derbyn, v., derbyn, D., s.v. 'recipio'.   Pret. 3. *derbənjoδ*.
Imperative, *derbyn; derbənjuχ*, 'to receive'.—In special sense,
'to receive into the world'.   Cf. D., s.v. 'obstetrico': *mi δerbənjoδ
hi χwe: χant*, 'she attended six hundred cases'.

derbənjad, s.m., derbyniad, D., s.v. 'ansa', 'excipulæ', 'mutulus';
'catch', e. g. on a door-post to receive the latch.

dernyn, s.m. (dim. of *darn*), dernyn, D., s.v. 'particula'; 'a
small piece': *dernyn da: jaun ədi hunna*, 'that is a fine piece'
(e. g. of poetry).

deru, s.pl., sing. *derwan*, f., derw, D., 'oaks':—*deru* is also used
for oak (the wood), *wedi nëyd o δeru*, 'made of oak';—and as an
adj. *kadar δeru*, 'an oak chair'.

derwinan, dərwinan, drəwinan, s.f., pl. *derwinod*, etc., derwreinien,
W.S. [Ryng worme]; derwreinyn, D., Lichen. Rectius Dyfrwreinyn;
ring-worm'.   Also *gwrinan*, cf. gwraint, D., sing. gwreinyn.
See also *drain gwynab*.

deryn [*adar*].

desgíl, s.f., pl. *desgla, dəsgla*, dysgl, D.; descyl, D.F. [xii.] 28; desgil, C.L.C. i. 23. 25; 'dish': *dal ə ðesgíl ən wastad* (*i*), 'to humour; to keep things straight between people who are on bad terms with each other'.

dest [*dgest*].

desílys, adj., destlus, D., 'neat, tidy'.

deθa, adj., deheu, D., 'skilful': *gnëyd po:b pe:θ o: ðeθa*, 'to do everything skilfully'; *y:n deθa jaun əi o i nëyd po:b pe:θ*, 'he is very skilful in everything'; *deθa hevo i gwaiθ*, 'skilful in her work'.

deur, adj., dewr, D., 'brave': *nt o:ð o n ðeur? mi χyboð ə dy:n*. 'wasn't he brave? he saved the man'; *may dy:n deur əm barod i roid i vəwyd i laur*, 'a brave man is ready to lay down his life'.

devni, s.pl., defni, D., s.v. 'davn'; 'drops'.

dewinjas, dʒwinjas, s.f., dewines, D., s.v. 'pharmaceutria'; dewinies, M.Ll. i. 235. 23; 'fortune-teller'.

dewinjaθ, dʒwinjaθ, s., dewiniaeth, D., 'fortune-telling': *dëyt tʒwinjaθ* (O.H.).

dewis, v., dewis, D., Imperative, *dewis, dʒwisa*, 'to choose': *dewis ə ty: kletla i r kļauð*, 'to choose the sheltered side of the wall'; *vel ·bəðuχi n dewis*, 'as you choose, as you like'; *dewis dewis ðay ðurn; dewis y:n, dewis hun (pa: r y:n gəmma i ont hun? I.W.), said by children asking some one to choose one of two closed hands in which something is held.

dewis, s., dewis, D., 'choice': *ar o:l i χi ga:yl əχ dewis*, 'after you have had your choice'.

dëyar, s.f., daear, D. (1) 'earth, world': *ə pe:θ gora ·gənoχi ga:l ar ə ðëyar*, 'the thing you like to get best in the world'. (2) 'earth, ground, soil': *tŗoi r ðëyar*, 'to turn over the earth' (esp. with a plough); *ən aros i r ðëyar gnesy*, 'waiting for the earth to get warm'. (3) pl. *dëyara*, 'earth' (of a fox).

dëyardor, s.f., daeardor, D.G. ccv. 47; cf. D., s.v. 'aestuarium', 'charadra', 'eluvies', 'labes'; 'land-slip'.

dëyargí, dyargí, s.m., pl. *dëyarguns*, daiargi, S.E., 'terrier' (O.H.).

dëyaru, v., daearu, D. (1) 'to cultivate' = *tŗi:n ə ðëyar* (O.H.). (2) 'to live, to "hang out"' (O.H.); cf. *dëyar ļuynog*.

dëyban, adj., deuben [*ǵelan*].

dëyblyg, adj., deublyg, D., s.v. 'duplicatò': *sərθjo n i ðëyblyg*, 'to fall doubled up' (seldom used).

dëyd; also *du:yd* (I.W.), v., dywedyd, D.   Fut. S. 1. *dëyda, ȧyda ; ȧuyda* (O.H.), 3. *dëydiθ, ȧydiθ ; ȧɹvyd* (O.H.).   Imp. S. 1. *dëydun, ȧydun*, 3. *dëyda ; ȧuyda* (O.H.).   Pret. S. 1. *dëydis, ȧydis*, 3. *dëydoð, ȧydoð* (*mi rydoð*, O.H.); Pl. 1. *dëydson*, 2. *dëydsoχ*, 3. *dëydson*.   Imperative S. 2. *du:ad ; ȧuyda* (O.H.); Pl. 1. *ȧydun*, 2. *ȧyduχ, dëyduχ, du:χ*, 'to say, tell': *dëyd k̃eluɹð*, 'to tell a lie'; *dëyd ɹ gwi:r*, 'to tell the truth'; *may hi n dëyd bo χi n edraχ ɹn. weḷ*, 'she says you look better'; *dyduχ* (*ȧydun*) *bo χi wedi gnëyd rubaθ i mi hëïðiu*, 'say (for example) that you have done something to me to-day'; *ma: nu n dëyd mai am aḷɹo iɹwɹð by:ð hi*, 'they say that it happens (i. e. corns hurt) when the weather is going to change'; *mi ðëydoð o ɹ do:y o*, 'he said he would come'; *mi ðëydi∫ i χa:χi ðim k̃injo hëïðiu*, 'I said you would not get any dinner to-day'; *mi ðëydoð hi ɹr a: hi*, 'she said she would go'; *mi ðydi∫i na vurja hi ðim*, 'I said it would not rain'; *t o:yð hi ðim ɹŋ gubod be ðëyda hi*, 'she did not know what to say'; *be naun i ond dëyd ɹ gwi:r a dëyd na naun i m ono vo?*, 'what should I do but tell the truth and say I wouldn't do it?'; *dëyd uθ ru:in am bëidjo*, 'to tell some one not to'; *wa:θ i mi ðëyd kaɹag a θuḷ na dëyd rubaθ uθ ɹ pḷant ma*, 'I might as well speak to a block of wood (lit. say stone with a hole in it) as speak to these children'; *dëyd padar uθ berson*, 'to teach one's grandmother'; *ɹn dëyd ar i beθ maur ɹnia*, 'swearing hard, "jurant ses grands dieux"'; *dëyd mu:y*, 'to exaggerate', e. g. *rois i swadan veχan iðo vo hevo k̃evn ɹ la:u a r hogyn ɹn dëyd mu:y* (O.H.), 'I struck him lightly with the back of my hand and the boy exaggerated'.—Imperative, *dyduχ, du:χ* at the end of a remark '-ever, I say, I wonder, let me see': *be hary r kaθod, dyduχ?*, 'whatever is the matter with the cats?'; *pu:y sy na, du:χ?*, 'I wonder who is there?'; *be ·vɹðani n alu vo, dyduχ?*, 'let me see, what used we to call it?'

dëydrod, s., deudroet, W.B., col. 22. 3, 'feet': *k̃erðad ar i ðëydrod*, 'to walk' (as opposed to riding, etc.).

dëyðag, s. and adj., deuddeg, D., 'twelve': *dëyðaŋ njurnod, mi:s, usnos, waiθ*.

dëyðegvad, adj., deuddegfed, D., 'twelfth'.

dëyðɹð, s., deuddydd, D., s.v. 'biduum'; 'two days'.

dëygant, dëykant, s., deücant, D., s.v. 'ducenti'; 'two hundred'.

dëynau, adj. and s., deunaw, D., s.v. 'duodeuiginti'; 'eighteen, eighteen pence'; *ǵenath ðëynau o:yd*.

dëynɹuvad, adj., deunawfed, D., s.v. 'duodeuicesimanus'; 'eighteenth'.

dëynɹð, s.m., pl. *devnɹðja*, defnydd and deunydd, D., 'material'. [*dëynɹð* is the popular form; *devnɹð* is a word of rather literary flavour used to translate Eng. 'use', as *gnëyd devnɹð o hono vo*, 'to make use of it'. So also *devnɹðjo*, 'to use'.]

dëysuḷḷ, s., deuswllt, G.O. ii. 138. 30, 'two shillings': *pisin deysuḷḷ*, 'a florin, two shilling piece'.

dëyvor, s., deufor, D., s.v. 'bimaris' = *day vo:r* in the phrases *ǩin haḷḷad a heli dëyvor* [*ha:ḷḷ*] *;—r o:n i vel dëyvor gǝvarvod*, 'I was all upset' (I.W.).

di:, pron. [*ti:*].

di:-. A negative prefix used with nouns and verbs and rarely with adjectives. A few of these are given below, but they might be almost indefinitely extended. The prefix is generally treated as a separate word bearing full stress. Where this is not the case the vowel is naturally shortened.

·*di:absan; di:absant* (O.H.), adj., diabsen, 'not given to slander': *dy:n ·di:absant jaun am nc:b.*

diadaḷ, s., diadell, D., s.v. 'grex'; 'flock': *ma na ludun dy: ǝm m̥ho:b diadaḷ* (E.J.), prov., 'there is a black sheep in every family'. Apparently only in this locution. [The usual word is *gyr*.]

·*di:aχos*, diachos, D., s.v. 'immeritò'; 'without cause': *melṭiθ ǝn ·δi:aχos ni δa:u* (prov.).

di:al, v., dial, D., 'to take revenge, avenge oneself': *arna i: by:δ o n di:al.* Also trans. *di:al i li:d*, 'to wreak one's vengeance' (cf. W.B., col. 121. 23); *di:al ǝ kam*, 'to avenge the wrong'.

dialaδ, dialedd, D., 'vindicta, vltio'; 'a great number': *may gǝno vo beθ dialaδ o δevaid; may gǝno vo aniveïljad ǝn δialaδ* (O.H.). Cf. Hugh Machno in M.Ll. ii. 311. 22; G.O. ii. 112. 5.

dialgar, adj., dialgar, C.C.M. 436. 28, 'revengeful'.

·*di:aḷy*, adj., diallu, D., s.v. 'impotens'; 'feeble, powerless'.

·*di:amkan*, adj., diamcan, S.E., 'aimless, random'.

di:an, n.pr.: *vel di:an* (f.) *a loli* (m.), 'like Dian and Loli' (Rowland), said of two bosom friends or an affectionate married couple. (Cf. 'Darby and Joan'.)

·*di:anav*, adj., dianaf, D.G. cci. 9, 'without blemish': *ǝn ja:χ a ·di:anav*, said of a new-born child ;—*wedi eni n ·δi:anav.*

di:ar, *dy:ar*, *di:a*, Eng. 'dear' in 'dear me!', etc.: *di:ar annul!, n eno r di:ar!, di:ar ba:χ!*, 'dear me!, good gracious!, my word!, etc.'; *dy:ar annul! ma:y o m brasgammy n aru!*, 'good gracious! how he strides along!'; *di:a! ma:y r δǝnas na ǝn dobjo ǝ plant ǝn aru*, 'my word! that woman does beat the children'.

·*di:arδal*, v., diarddel (diarddelw), S.E., 'to excommunicate, to strike off from membership in a chapel'.

di:arθ, adj., dieithr, D., s.v. 'extraneus'; dierth, D.F. [117] 21; M.Ll. i. 209. 4, 'strange': *dy:n di:arθ*, 'stranger'; *pobol δi:arθ*, 'strangers', term commonly applied to visitors at seaside resorts, etc.

·*di:·asgurn, di:·asgun,* adj., diasgwrn, S.E., ‘weak, feeble’: *dy:n* ·*di:·asgurn.*

·*di:·aval,* adj., diafael, S.E., ‘lazy, averse to work’: *dy:n di:·og,* ·*di:·aval.* Cf. *nëif o ðim gaval mi· hi,* ‘he won’t buckle to’.

·*di:·baid,* adj., dibaid, D., ‘continual, without break’.

diban, s.m., pl. *dibenjon,* diben, D., ‘purpose’: *i· riu ðiban,* ‘for some purpose’; *i· ðo:yθ ðibenjon,* ‘for some wise purpose’; *appad ə diban,* ‘to answer the purpose’.

·*di:·ben,* adj., ‘empty-headed’: *dy:n* ·*di:·ben.*

·*di:·ben·drau,* adj., di-ben-draw. (1) ‘interminable’: *ſurna* ·*di:-* ·*ben·drau.* (2) ‘mysterious’: *dy:n* ·*di:·ben·drau,* ‘a man one cannot “see through”’.

·*di:·berig,* adj., diberigl, P.G.G. 45. 7, ‘harmless, innocuous; safe’: *ma nu n holol* ·*ði:·berig,* ‘they are quite harmless’, e.g. patent pills ;—*ļe:* ·*di:·berig.*

dibin, s.m., dibyn, D.; dibin, M.Ll. i. 116. 14, ‘precipice’: *mynd, sərθjo dros ə dibin,* ‘to go, fall over the precipice’; *sərθjo n dibin dobyn,* ‘to fall headlong’.

·*di:·bluk,* adj., ‘without pluck, unenterprising’.

·*di:·bobol,* adj., di bobl, 2 Esd. xvi. 26, ‘uninhabited, sparsely inhabited.

·*di:·bo:yn,* adj., diboen, D., ‘comfortable, with mind at ease’: *wedi du:·ad ar i· ſurna m rëil* ·*ði:·bo:yn,* ‘having made his journey very comfortably’.

·*di:·bri:od,* adj., dibriod, S.E., ‘unmarried’.

dibris, adj., dibris, D., s.v. ‘abjectus’. (1) ‘wanting in self-respect’: *paid a bo:d mor ðibris arnat ti: də hy:n,* ‘do not lose your self-respect so’. (2) ‘reckless’: *r o:ð o n ɼhy: ðibris o lawar.* (3) ‘careless, not setting value on anything’.

·*di:·briſo,* v., dibrisio, D., s.v. ‘abjicio’, ‘despicio’, etc.; ‘depreciate’: *dy:n m* ·*di:·briſo i· hy:n,* ‘a man who has lost his self-respect; who has gone to the bad’;—also, ‘one who is reckless; who plunges needlessly into danger’.

·*di:·brovjad,* adj., dibrofiad, S.E., ‘inexperienced’.

dibuys, adj., dibwys, S.E. (1) ‘unimportant, immaterial’. (2) ‘with little cause’: *kwyno n ðibuys.*

·*di:·daro,* adj., didaro, D.P.O. 38. 3; 79. 11, ‘unconcerned, stolid’ = ·*di:·gənnur,* ·*di:·vatlar.*

·*di:·dëimlad,* adj., dideimlad, P.G.G. 63. 21, ‘unfeeling’.

·*di:·dor,* adj., didorr, D., s.v. ‘continuus’; ‘continuous, without break’.

·*di·́dorjad*, adj., didoriad, G.O. ii. 69. 12, said of one who has not been ' broken in ' when young, who has always had his own way, ' rude, unmanageable '.

·*di·́dramguyð*, adj., didramgwydd, D., s.v. ' inocciduus ', ' inoffensus '; ' not easily taking offence ': *dy·n ·di·́dramguyð*.

·*di·́drɛvn*, adj., didrefn, B.C. 87. 1, ' without order '.

·*di·́droi*, adj., di-droi, ' that cannot be turned aside ': *dy·n ·di·́droi*.

·*di·́drɜst*, adj., ' untrustworthy '.

diduyḷ, adj., didwyll, D., ' sincere '.

diða, adj., didda, W.S. [Wyth out goodes], ' without good ': *dy·n diðrug, diða*, ' a nonentity, a man with nothing in him '. Cf. B.C. 95. 28.

·*di·́ðal*, adj., di-ddal, ' unreliable, slippery ': *dy·n ·di·́ðal*.

diðan, adj., diddan, .D., ' amusing, pleasant, entertaining ': *he·n gumpēini diðan ɜdi o*, ' he is pleasant company '; *day ðy·n ɜn ðiðan hɛvo i g̓ilið*, ' two men on pleasant terms with one another '.

diðanuχ, s., diddanwch, D., ' the quality of being amusing, pleasant, or entertaining ': *may o n ḷaun diðanuχ*.

diðany, v., diddanu, D., ' to comfort ': *may pɛ:θ ba·χ ɜn i diðany hi*, ' a little thing comforts her '.

·*di·́ðarvod*, adj., diddarfod, ' unending; that never wears out; long in finishing ': *may o n ·ði·́ðarvod hɛvo i g̓ɜmuynas* (work).

·*di·́ðaun*, adj., di-ddawn, D.F. [85] 8, ' not gifted in speech '.

·*di·́ðerbyn·wynab*, adj., di-dderbyn-wyneb, ' not given to favouritism, not being a respecter of persons '.

·*di·́ðẹ̈yd*, adj., di and dywedyd, applied to one whom it is no use correcting, with whom it is useless to argue: *ɜ dy·n muya ·di·́ðẹ̈yd welis i ri·o·yd*.

diðig, adj., diddig, D., ' good-tempered ' (often applied to children).

diðim; ·di·́ðim (emphatic),adj., diddym, D.; diddim, W.Ll.xciv. 5; D.P.O. 50. 24; di-ddim, P.G.G. 153. 17, ' worthless, insignificant ': *dy·n diðim*, ' a man with nothing in him '; *ɜ dy·n muya ·di·́ðim welis i ri·o·yd*, ' the most insignificant man I ever saw '.

·*di·́ði·olχ*, adj., diddiolch, S.E., ' thankless '.

·*di·́ðjog̓i*, adj., diddiogi, S.E., ' active ': *may n ðy·n hoḷol ·di·́ðjog̓i*.

diðos, adj., diddos, D. (1) ' rain-proof, damp-proof ': *gnẹ̈yd ḷɛ: ɜn ðiðos*. (2) ' cosy '. (3) ' sober ': *dy·n diðos* (O.H.).

diðosi, v., diddosi, D., ' to make rain-proof, damp-proof '.

diðrug, adj., diddrwg, D.F. [103] 11, ' without badness ' [*diða*].

diðɜmmy, v., diddymmu, D., dyddymmu, D., s.v. ' annihilo ', ' to do away with '.

·di·refaθ, adj., dieffaith, S.E., 'without effect'; 'having lost its virtue' (e.g. of medicine).

·di·rguyδor, adj., diegwyddor, S.E., 'unprincipled'.

·di·renaid, adj., di-enaid, 2 Esd. iii. 5, 'soulless'.

difaθ, adj., diffaith, D. (1) of land, ti·r difaθ, 'wild, full of thorns, bogs', etc. (O.H.). (2) 'anything that causes disgust': he·n hogla dru·g ədi pe·θ difaθ (O.H.). (3) 'mischievous, bad': dyn difaθ = dy·n dru·g i gurs, dy·n am nëyd sbort.

·di·fa·yl, adj., diphael, G.R. 117. 18; diffael, G.O. ii. 184. 5, 'without fail'.

difig, s., diffyg, D., 'defect, insufficiency': difig ţrëiljad = kam-drëiljad, 'indigestion'; difig anadl, 'scantiness of breath'; difig govol, 'carelessness'.

difod, v., diffodd, D., s.v. 'extinguo'. Fut. 1. difotta. Imp. S. 1. difottun. Pret. S. 1. difottis, difis. Pl. 3. difodsun. Imperative difod, difa ; difottuχ. (1) tr. 'to extinguish, put out': difod ə lamp, 'to put out the lamp'. (2) intr. 'to go out' (of a light or fire): ma· r ta·n wedi difod, 'the fire has gone out';—fig. may hi wedi difod arno vo, 'he is done for'.

·di·frut, adj., 'without any "go", without stamina': dy·n ·di·frut = dy·n ·di·vəwyd, ·di·nerθ, di·og.

difruyθ, adj., diffrwyth, D., s.v. 'iners', 'flaccidus'; 'limp', e.g. of a child asleep: may i vrayχ o n δifruyθ, 'he has lost the use of his arm'.

difəgjo, v., diffygio, D., 'to be worn out with fatigue': difəgjo o dan i vayχ, 'to sink beneath his burden'; mi wëiθis nes on i wedi difəgjo n la·n.

di·g, s., dig, D., 'anger': gair i dənny di·g, 'a word to arouse anger'.

di·g, adj., sup. dikka, dig, D., 'angry': dikka n ə by·d vo· r ķëiljog, kənta n ə by·d ə ka·n o (prov.), 'the angrier a cock is the sooner he will crow', said of some one who sings to hide his temper, i.e. dim ŋ kany o χ kalon ond əŋ kany i la·δ ər əsbryd.

digalon, adj., digalon, D., s.v. 'iners', 'remissus'. (1) 'down-hearted, depressed': digon kula a digalon, 'rather poorly and dejected'. (2) 'depressing': may r dəwyδ ən δigalon jaun. (3) 'sad': pe·θ digalon.

digalonni, v., digalonni, D., s.v. 'demitto'; 'to make (one) despair, to dishearten'. Intr. 'to be disheartened'.

·di·ges, adj., di and Eng. guess, 'feckless, without ideas' (as to how to do a thing): ə dy·n muya ·di·ges am nëyd o welis i ri·o·yd.

·di·gevn, adj., digefn; C.C.M. 32. 29, 'defenceless'.

digjo, v., digio, D. (1) 'to anger, offend': mi δigis hunnu, 'I

made him angry'. (2) 'to be angry, offended': *may o wedi digjo*.
(3) 'to be tired (of)': *daχi wedi digjo uθ wy:a ˑ*, 'are you tired of
eggs?' (used facetiously).

·**di·goḷ**, adj., digoll; C.C.M. 90. 24. (1) 'without loss': *toṛi r
moχyn mor ·ði:ˑgoḷ ag sy m bosib*, 'to cut up the pig in such a way
as to cause the least possible loss'. (2) 'without defect, without
blemish': *bloḳḳyn o ðy:n solat ·di:ˑgoḷ*.

digon, digon, D. (1) s. 'enough': *o:ys na ðigon o bo:b pe:θ
·gənoχi ru:an ˑ*, 'have you enough of everything now?'; *may digon
o vi:n arno vo*, 'it is sharp enough'; *vəða i ðim əɲ kḷu:ad ən ða: ond
mi vəða i ɲ kḷu:ad ḷaun digon*, 'I do not hear well, but I hear quite
enough'; *ar ben i ðigon*, 'in clover'. (2) adv. (a) 'enough': *may
n ðigon a digalonni y:n*, 'it is enough to make one despair'; *by:ð
ən ðigon by:an at ə de:g*, 'it will be soon enough at about ten'; *mi
vəða n ðigon am əχ höydal χi vynd əno*, 'it would be as much as your
life is worth to go there'; (b) 'rather': *digon gwantan ədi o*, 'he
is in rather a poor state of health'; *digon ḷegaχ ; digon gwa:yl*,
'so so'.

digonað, s., digonedd, D., s.v. 'satias'; 'enough, 'sufficiency'.

·**di:ˑgəunt**, adj., di and Eng. account. (1) 'of no account':
mynd ən ·ði:ˑgəunt ġin baub. (2) 'making of no account, setting
no store by': *ən ·ði:ˑgəunt o i gartṛa, o i blant, o i wraig*.

·**di:ˑgəuntjo**, v., di and Eng. account, 'to make no account of, to
set no store by': ·*di:ˑgəuntjo i dëyly ; ·di:ˑgəuntjo i hy:n*, 'to lose
one's self-respect.' Cf. ·*di:ˑbriʃo*.

digri, adj., digrif, D., 'funny': *kəm·ra:ig go ðigri*, 'rather funny
Welsh'; *may o n dëyd peθa digri*, 'he says funny things'; *ḷe: digri·
jaun i vytta*, 'a funny place to eat in'; *he:n gradyr digri*, 'a funny
old character'.

digul, s., digwyl, D., s.v. 'feralia' (i.e. dydd gwyl); *digul
dommos*, 'St. Thomas's Day', i.e. Dec. 21.

diguyð, v., digwyddo, D. (1) 'to happen': *ma: n diguð ən
amal veḷy*, 'it often happens so'; *mi ðiguyðoð ə pedwar vynd i r
y:n ty:*, 'the four happened to go to the same house'. (2) 'to
expire' (of time): *ma i amsar wedi diguyð erbyn hyn* (O.H.), 'its
time has expired by now'.

·**di:ˑgwiḷð**, adj., digywilydd, D.; digwilidd, D.F. [47] 27,
'shameless': *mor ·ði:ˑgwiḷð a pen ṛha:u*, 'as shameless as the iron
of a spade'.

·**di:ˑgyro**, adj., diguro, S.E., 'which cannot be beaten, excelled'.

·**di:ˑgəfro**, adj., digyffro, D., s.v. 'inexcitus', 'placidus'; 'not
agitated or excited, placid'.

·**di:ˑgəχuyn**, adj., di-gychwyn, said of some one who has no 'go' in him, no 'grit', no initiative; 'feckless': *mor ·ðiːˈgᵊχuyn a malwan.*

·diːgᵊˈmuynas, adj., digymmwynas, G.O. ii. 19. 22, 'unpleasant (speaking of people); selfish'.

·diːˈgᵊnnig, adj., digynnyg. (1) 'not inclined to offer, to bid' (e.g. at an auction). (2) 'hesitating, in doubt': *ᵊn ·ðiːˈgᵊnnig naːy o ᵊ gwaiθ ai pëidjo,* 'in doubt as to whether he would do the work or not'; *r oːð o n ·ðiːˈgᵊnnig i nëyd ᵊ tuḷ.* (3) 'undesirable': *ḷeː ·diːˈgᵊnnig jaun,* 'a very undesirable situation'.

·diːˈgᵊnnur, adj., digynnwrf, D., s.v. 'inexcitus', 'mitis', 'placidus'; 'stolid, unconcerned, indifferent, easy-going, lackadaisical'.

·diːˈgᵊvri, adj., digyfrif, S.E., 'innumerable, incalculable': *riu bentur ·diːˈgᵊvri* (O.H.).

·diːˈhaḷgar [*dyaḷgar*].

·diːˈhaḷys [*dyaḷys*].

diharab, s.f., pl. *diarhebjon*, dihareb, D., s.v. 'prouerbium'; 'proverb'.

·diːˈhiːd, adj. (Eng. heed), 'unreliable'.

dihirin, s.m., dihiryn, D., s.v. 'inhonestus'; 'scamp, rascal'.

·diːˈhit, adj., 'unheeding, reckless, careless' (I.W.).

·diːˈhitjo, adj., 'heedless, unheeding': *r oːð i wraig ᵊn ðiːˈhitjo o hono vo,* 'his wife did not heed him, paid him no heed'.

·diːˈildjo, adj., di-ildio, 'unyielding'.

dik, 'Dick': *dik ʃon davyð,* i.e. Dick John David, 'snob' (esp. of a Welshman who, for the sake of 'respectability', apes English ways). From a ballad by J. Jones, Glanygors.

dikˈpennog [*ḅfant*].

dikᵣa, adj., diccra, D., 'cibi parcus'; cf. also D., s.v. 'fastidiosus'; (1) 'calm, stolid' = ·diːˈgᵊnnur, ·diːˈdaro, ·diːˈvattar. (2) 'slow': *may o n ðikᵣa hevo i vuːyd,* 'he plays with his food';—*dikᵣa o r buːyd, o i waiθ* (O.H.).

diktar, s.m., digter, D., 'anger'.

diχaḷ, s.f., pl. *diχeḷjon*, dichell, D., 'astuteness, cunning, craftiness': *diχeḷjon druːg,* 'malicious cunning';—*ḷaun o ðiχeḷjon ᵊ vaḷ* (O.H.); —*diχeḷjon ḷuynog* (O.H.).

diχeḷðrug; diχeḷrug (O.H.), adj., dichellddrwg, T.N. 207. 12, 'malicious, sly'.

diχeḷgar, adj., dichellgar, D., 'astute, deceitful'.

dil, s.m., pl. *dilja*, dil, D.—*dil meːl,* 'honeycomb';—*may r menyn ᵊn magy dilja vel knonod baːχ* (J.J.), meaning ?;—as excl. *dil annul!*

dilbo, s.m., term of reproach: *ə dilbo gwirjon !* (O.H.).

·*di·le:s*, adj., diles, D., s.v. ' frustra ', 'vacuus '; ' good for nothing': *dy:n ·di·le:s.*

·*di·lewyrχ*, adj., dilewyrch, S.E., ' not thriving, not flourishing ' (in appearance or otherwise): *dy:n krẏ: gwëiθgar, dim əŋ gwastrafy, dim puysa plant, ag etto n ·di·lewyrχ — dim by:d ən luyδo tðo vo ; he:n vẏuχ ar ə fair ən ·di·lewyrχ ɡin ə porθmon* (O.H.).

di·lëy, v., dilèu, D., ' to do away with ': *di·lëy po:b dru:g.*

dilidano (J.J.); *diridano* (I.W.; O.H.), adj., ' pleasant ': *rubaθ dilidano jaun.*

dilin, v., dilyn, D.; dilin, M.Ll. i. 140. 23. Fut. *diləna.* Imperative *dilin, diləna ; dilənuχ,* ' to follow ': *dilin i alwedigaθ,* ' to follow one's calling '; *dilin i ðəladsuyða, oriχwiljon,* ' to fulfil one's duties '; *dilin i waiθ,* ' to follow one's occupation '.

dilis, in the exp. *dilis ku:n,* ' sorrel ' (Bangor)· Cf. *krentʃ, syrans.*

di·liu, adj., diliw, S.E.*, ' colourless '.

diljo, v., ? dulio, D., s.v. ' supplodo '; ' to speak beside the mark ': *loljan a diljo.*

·*di·lol*, adj., ' without humbug, without nonsense '; ' without further ado ': *ðary mi agor ə dru:s ən ·ði:lol,* ' I opened the door without further ado '.

dilorni, v., diveiliorni, marginal gloss to ' dirmygy ' in 1 Tim. iv. 10 in Salesbury's New Testament (1567), ' to disparage, to be " down on " ': *may o n dilorni paub = may i gorn o dan baub, may i gorn ən ɲhi:n paub* (O.H.).

·*di·ly:n*, adj., dilun, S.E., ' untidy, shapeless '.

diḷad, s.pl., dillad, D., ' clothes '; sing. *diḷedyn,* ' garment, article of dress ': *diḷad gwely,* ' bed-clothes '; *ka:l mu:y na ḷond i ðiḷad,* ' to be too big for one's boots '; *diḷad ḱi:g a fudin,* ' Sunday clothes '.

dim, m (sometimes *tim* when emphatic), dim, D.,—s. ' thing, anything, (not) . . . anything, nothing ';—adj. ' no ';—adv. ' not '.

I. ' thing ' in a few expressions, as *po:b dim,* ' everything '; *gora o bo:b dim = gora o:ḷ,* ' best of all '; *ma: ḱi:g gavr kəstal a r y:n dim* (O.H.), ' goat's flesh is as good as anything ';—also used in some phrases to express ' the slightest particle, the slightest moment, etc.', e. g. *i r dim,* ' exactly, to a " t " '; *meun dim,* (of time) ' in a moment, in less than no time '; (of place) ' within a hair's breadth '; *ðəna vo meun dim i r drol,* ' there he was within a hair's breadth of the cart '; fig. *o:yð o meun dim i gal i la:ð,* ' he was within an ace of being killed '. Hence as substantive, (1) ' anything ': *weḷ ɡin i ðim na ka:yl və sommi,* ' I had rather anything than be disappointed '; *du i n lëikjo hi ən weḷ na dim,* ' I like it better than anything '; *wa:θ bo χti wedi kodi am u:yθ ar ðim r u:ti wedi nëyd*, 'you might as well have got up at eight for anything you have done';—so with *heb* : *heb ðim*, 'without anything'; *heb awyð gnëyt tim*, 'without a desire to do anything'. (2) '(not) . . . anything, (not) . . . any, nothing' (cf. French ne . . . rien) : *dim by:d* (i. e. dim yn y byd), '(not) anything in the world, nothing at all'; *dim ond*, '(not) anything but, only'; *t o:yð dim ar i gzvar o*, 'there was nothing ready for him'; *t o:s dim ly:n dim arno vo*, 'there is no form of anything on it', i. e. 'it is like nothing at all', 'it is all wrong'; *t öyðanu n meðul am ðim by:d ond am vynd alan a χadu ri:at*, 'they thought of nothing at all but of going out and making a disturbance'; *peθa nad ∂dyn ∂n ða: i ðim*, 'things which are good for nothing'; *dim amsar i ðim*, 'no time for anything'; *ma na i ovn nat o:ys na ðim*, 'I'm afraid there isn't any'; *welis i ðim by:d*, 'I saw nothing at all'; *mi vy:ð ∂n haus i χi vytta na dim by:d aral̦*, 'it will be easier for you to eat than anything else'; *s g̦ini ðim ond gro:t*, 'I have only fourpence'; *nëiθ dim y:n o ·honznu ðim ond gaðo*, 'none of them will do anything but promise'; *t o:ys na ·ðim ·ond mynd*, 'there is nothing for it but to go'. (3) followed by *o* in the form *m o*, lit. 'anything of', (a) used after negative verbs to express the logical direct object : *welis i m ono vo*, 'I did not see him'; *os na welsoχ χi: vi:, welis inna m ona χiθa*, 'if you did not see me, I did not see you'; *os na welis i: χi:, welsoχ χi: m ona vinna*, 'if I did not see you, you did not see me'; *wel̦ g̦in i ∂ dru:g ∂ gun i na r dru:g nas gun i m ono vo*, 'I prefer the evil I know to the evil I do not know'; *r̦hak ovn na ·welaχi m oni hi ∂n ·vannaku*, 'for fear you should not see it there'; *dëyd pe:θ na: ðëydiθ o m ono vo ∂n ∂χ gwynab χi*, 'to say something he will not say before your face. (b) as logical subject of a negative clause : *nëiθ m o hunna χwaiθ*, 'that won't do either'. (c) after the verb 'to be' : *t o:ys m o r help*, 'there is no help for it'.—The original sense being forgotten, *mo* is sometimes used pleonastically after *ðim*, as *χe:s i ðim mo r hy:d iðo vo*, 'I did not find it'; *rois i ðim mo r gal̦aθ arno vo*, 'I did not touch it with the knife'. (4) standing by itself *dim* = 'nothing' (so also *dim by:d*, 'nothing at all'), e. g. *be: s ·g∂noχi？ dim*, 'what have you got?' 'Nothing'. (5) without a preceding negative : 'nothing' : *o:ys ·g∂noχi ·ðim？* (*ðim* strongly emphasized), 'have you nothing?'; *mi pr̦joda i χi am ðim*, 'I will marry you for nothing'; *d∂χryn at ðim*, 'to be frightened at nothing'; *dim ond aur vy:om i n d∂sgy*, 'I only took an hour to learn'.

II. adjectively (*dim* is here, properly speaking, a noun followed by the genitive case), 'not . . . any, no'—emphasized by adding *∂n ∂ by:d* after the noun : *t o:ys dim djog̦i ∂n i gro:yn o*, 'there is no idleness in him'; *ma: nu n dëyd bo:d tɷwyd r̦he:u ∂n jaχaχ na dim tɷwyð aral̦*, 'they say that frosty weather is healthier than any (than is not any) other weather'; *pëidjo a gnëyd dim lol ∂n i gumpas o*, 'to make no nonsense about it'; *du:ad heb ðim pla:t*, 'to bring no plate'; *dim forð*, 'no road'; *dy:n a dim fru:t ɔno vo*, 'a man with no backbone'; *t o:ð ·gɔnonu m plant*, 'they had no children'. So in the phrases *dim ods*, 'no odds, no matter'; *dim posib* (*posib* used substantively), 'it is impossible', as :—*dim ods ǵin i*, 'it is all the same to me'; *t ɔdi o m ods*, 'it's all the same'; *t o:ys dim posib*, 'it is not possible'; *dim posib i ne:b vynd i veun*, 'it is impossible for any one to get in'. Similarly *dim y:n*, 'not a single one': *r o:yð ǵin i lawar jaun o wy:a ond ðary dim y:n o ·honynu ðy:or*, 'I had a great many eggs but not one of them hatched'.

III. adverb, 'not'; (a) in the form *ðim* after a negative verb, 'ni(d)' having disappeared, leaving as its only trace the vocalic or spirant mutation of the verb, or *t* if the verb begins with a vowel; cf. French ne . . . pas; *t ɔdi o ðim ɔn my:nd*, 'he is not going'; *t un i ðim*, (*t ɔ)du i ðim ɔɲ gubod*, 'I don't know'; *t a: i ðim alan vory*, 'I shall not go out to-morrow'; *vedar o m dɔsgy am ðim by:d*, 'he can't learn for anything'; *nëïθ o ðim kadu dim by:d*, 'he won't keep anything'. (b) in the form *ðim*, added for the sake of emphasis, 'not . . . at all': *wa:θ i χi vo:d ɔn ɔχ gwely ðim*, 'you might every bit as well stop in bed', lit. '(it is) not worse for you to be in your bed at all'; *mi ·ðɔljaχi na θoða menyn ðim ɔn i ǵe:g o*, 'you would think that butter would not melt in his mouth (at all)'. (c) before other adverbs: *dim mor grëÿlon a r ǵëïrja*, 'not so cruel as the words would seem to imply'; *dim n agos k̃immint a vɔða*, 'not nearly as many as there used to be'; *dim ɔn wel ̦ ɔdi o*, 'he is not better'.

dim, s., dim, R., *dim u:y*, 'the membrane which surrounds the inside of an egg-shell': *k̃in dɔny:ad a dim u:y* (J.J.).

dimbaχ, Dinbych; Dimbech, C.C.M. 134. 15; 'Denbigh'.

dimma, s.f., pl. *dim(ë)ya*, dimmai, D., 'halfpenny': *gwerθ dimma = mɛwaθ*, 'a halfpennyworth'; *tair r̥he:s o binna am ðimma*, 'three rows of pins for a halfpenny'; *su:l̦i a gro:t a dimma*, 'one and fourpence halfpenny'.

·*dinab·man* (LW.; E.J.), ·*dinad·man* (J.J.; O.H.), adj., dinôd and man (cf. *gwynab* and *gwymmad*), 'out-of-the-way': *l ̦c: ·dinab·man*, 'an out-of-the-way place'.

·*di:·nerθ*, adj., dinerth, D., 'weak, lifeless, without "go", without stamina'.

dinistr, s., dinystr, D., but dinistr, s.v. 'destructio'; dinustr is the mediæval form. Cf. Prof. J. Morris Jones in 'Y Beirniad' for June, 1912 (p. 124); 'destruction'.

dinistrjo, v., dinystrio, D., but dinistrio, s.v. 'destruo'; dinustrio is the mediæval form. Cf. *dinistr*; 'to destroy'.

dinistrjol, adj., dinystriol, D., dinistriol, B.C. 11. 3, 'destructive' (O.H.).

diniwad, adj., diniweid, D., 'innocent': *mor ðiniwad a r o:yn, a r glomman.*

diniwidruyð, dini·udruyð, s., diniweidrwydd, D., s.v. 'innocentia'; 'innocence'.

dinod, adj., 'not marked'; *o:yn dinod*, 'a lamb which has not been marked' (O.H.).

·*di·no:d*, adj., dinod, S.E., 'of no note, not remarkable, obscure': *le: ·di·nod.*

diŋkod, s.pl., dincod, D. (1) 'the pips of an apple': *diŋkod avol.* (2) *pen ðydiθ ru:in air go farp uθ ru:in aral, ma: nu n dëyd bod ə diŋkod arno vo* (O.H.). Cf. G.R. [195] 19; Jer. xxxi. 29.

di:od, s.f., pl. *diodyð, ajodyð,* diod, D., 'drink': *ma na i ifo di:od,* 'I am thirsty'; *kəmmux ði:od o de:,* 'take a drink of tea';—also for *di:od veðwol,* 'intoxicating drink'; *di:od daint ə le:u,* 'dandelion tea'; *di:od dail,* 'herb beer'; *di:od vain,* 'small beer'.

di:og, adj. (comp. *djokkax*), diog, D., 'lazy': *kena di:og,* 'lazy rogue'; *he:n gostog di:og, he:n rabust di:og, leban di:og.*

di:olx, s., diolch, D., 'thanks': *di:olx ; di:olx i xi,* 'thank you'; *di:olx ən vaur i xi,* 'thank you very much'; *di:olx am i xi ðëyd . . .,* 'thank you for saying . . .'; *di:olx bo xi wedi du:ad i gi:d ru:an !,* 'thank Heaven you have all come now!'; *di:olx byθ am hənny !,* 'thank Heaven for that !'; *di:olx byθ !,* 'hurrah !'; *di:olx mai ə·vo: sy n i xal hi ag nid ə·vi:,* 'I am glad he is getting it and not I'; *di:olx nad öyðun i əno,* 'I am glad I was not there'; *di:olx os nëiθ o,* 'I hope he will'; *di:olx ba:x i xi am wëiθjo n wel ə xivarlar nesa,* 'small thanks to you for working better next quarter', i.e. 'I dare say you will' . . ., 'likely enough you will';—With a sense of 'that will do, that's enough': *di:olx am ðigon o gyro n ə dru:s !,* 'I hope you've knocked at the door enough !'

di:olx, v., diolch, D., 'to thank': *ðary o ðim kimmint a di:olx i mi am ðu:ad a r ðavod,* 'he did not as much as thank me for bringing the sheep'.

·*di·olug,* adj., diolwg, D.G. xviii. 36. (1) 'plain, insignificant': *ər hogyn muya ·di·olug ən ər əsgol,* 'the plainest boy in the school'. (2) ·of unpleasant appearance': *bara ·di·olug, ·am·ləgys.* (3) 'unpromising, without prospect': *may n ·ði·olug jaun am dəwyð da: ; may hi n edrax ən ·ði·olug,* 'it looks unpromising'.

·*di·os,* adj., di-os, D., s.v. 'indubitanter'; 'without doubt': *ən ·ði·os.*

·*di:o·valux,* s.m., diofalwch, D., 'negligence, carelessness'.

·*di·ovol,* adj., diofal, D. (1) 'negligent, careless'. (2) 'safe': *may n ·ði:ovol i ni vynd for na,* 'it is safe for us to go that way'; ·*di·ovol ədi dim* (prov.), 'there is security in not possessing anything'.

·di··raðjo, v., diraddio, D., 'to speak evil of, run down, decry'.

·di··ra·s, adj., di-ras, C.C. (ed. 1776) 38. 24, 'graceless': *ə krjadyr muya ·di··ra·s welis i ri·o·yd.* Cf. Sian Robert gadd golled go gas, Sef dwyn ei cheiniogwerth o snisin, Gwnaeth hyn iddi regi'n ddi-ras. C.—'Marchnad Ca'rnarfon'.

·di··resum, adj., direswn, D., s.v. 'absurdus'; 'absurd'.

dirgal, adj., dirgel, D., 'secluded, secret': *le: dirgal*, 'a secluded spot'; *gnëyd pe:θ ən ðirgal*, 'to do a thing in secret'; *mynd i r dirgal i ðëyd peθ*, 'to go to a private spot to say something'.

dirǵeluχ, s.m., dirgelwch, D., 'mystery': *dəna r dirǵeluχ*, 'that's the strange thing about it'; *may hynna n ðirǵeluχ holol i mi syt ə kəmmoð hi o əri·o·yd*, 'it's a perfect mystery to me how she ever took him'.

diridus [dridus].

·di··riujo, v., dirywio, D., s.v. 'degenero'; 'to degenerate, come down in the world' = *mynd i laur.* Also trans.: *·di··riujo i hy·n*, 'to degrade oneself'.

·di·ri·vedi, s., dirifedi, D., s.v. 'innumerabilitas'; 'an immense number': *ma na ·ði·ri·vedi o ·honynu.* Also used adjectively, 'innumerable'.

dirjo, v., durio, D., 'to point (horse-shoes) with steel in time of frost to prevent slipping': *dirjo pədola.*

dirmig, s., dirmyg, D.; dirmig, G.R. 57. 9, 'contempt': *gosod dirmig arno vo*, 'to show contempt for him'.

dirnad, v., dirnad, D., 'to imagine, guess': *r öyðun i n meθy dirnad pa: adag o:yð hi*, 'I had no idea what time it was'; *ma na le i ðirnad bo:d . . .*, 'one might imagine that . . .'.

·di·rodras, adj., dirodres, D., s.v. 'inambitiosus'; 'unassuming'.

·di·roid, adj., di and rhoi, 'stingy'.

·di·ro:l, adj., 'unruly'.

·di·rym, adj., dirym, D., s.v. 'ignavus'; 'without force': *r o:ð ə gzvraθ wedi mynd ən ·di·rym*, 'the law had become a dead letter'.

dirwin, dirun, v., dirwyn, D., 'to wind': *dirwin davað*, 'to wind a skein'. Also intrans.: *dirwin i ben, dirwin i r pen*, 'to come to an end'.

·di·rəbyð, adj., dirybudd, D., s.v. 'subitus'; 'without warning, sudden'.

·di·rəmmy, v., dirymmu, S.E., 'to nullify'.

·di·sail, adj., di-sail, D.P.O. 205. 30, 'without foundation': *he·n stry·on ·di··sail*, 'groundless stories'.

·di:·se:l, adj., di and sel (zeal), 'slack ' (at work) : bo:d ən ·di:·se:l = ļẹ̈ysy i ðylo.

·di:·serχ, adj., di-serch, 2 Tim. iii. 3, 'unattractive'.

disgin, v., disgyn, D. Fut. S. 3. sgənniθ. Pret. S. 3. sgənnoð. Pl. 3. sgənson. Imperative, disgin ; sgənnuχ. (1) 'to descend, alight ', e. g. from a train or carriage. (2) 'to fall', generally of things : ma: r gorjad wedi disgin i dro:yd ə gadar, 'the key has fallen to the foot of the chair '; ma: r dail ən disgin, ' the leaves are falling '; may o n disgin i u le: bo:b kənnig, ' it drops into its place every time '; du:r ən disgin i laur ag ən tŗoi vel tŗoχjon, ' water falling and seething with foam ' (lit. like soap-suds) ;—also of persons : mi sgənnoð ar i wynab, ' he fell on his face '.

disglar, adj., disglair, D. (1) 'bright ': gola disglar. (2) ' comely ': dy:n disglar = gla:n i wymmad a i gorf ən appad (O.H.). Also ty: disglar, etc.

disglëirjo, v., disgleirio, D., 'to glitter ', e. g. of water in the sunshine.

disgul, disgwil, v., disgwyl, D., s.v. 'expecto '; disgwil, B.C. 32. 31 ; M.Ll. i. 6. 9, etc. ; P.G.G. 2. 9 and passim. Fut. (di)sgwilja. (1) 'to expect ': du i n disgul ən aru, 'I quite expect '; r öyðun i n disgul hi do:y a hëiðju, ' I was expecting her yesterday and to-day '; ł öyðun i ðim ən disgul vasun i n ə ty: mor vy:an, ' I didn't expect to be back so soon '; ŗhaid i χi wëiljad : r ədu i n i ðisgul o bo:b mynyd, ' you must wait : I am expecting him every minute '; ən disgul ən ðŗval am ləθyr, 'anxiously expecting a letter '; ma: gryfyð dgo:s ən disgul ķiu ba:χ o r gasag na, ' G. J. is expecting a foal from that mare '; pu:y daχi n ðisgul i r ru:m ma ?, 'whom are you expecting in this room ?'; mi vasun i n disgul rubaθ mģenaχ na hənny o·ruθaχi, ' I should have expected something better than that from you '. (2) 'to wait (for) ': mi ðisgwilja i ·uθaχi, 'I will wait for you '. (3) 'to hope (for) ': disgul am amsar gweļ, 'to hope for better days '.—Used substantively : ma na ðisgul maur oruθo vo, ' there are great expectations about him '.

·di:·sgurs, adj., ' taciturn '.

disgwiljad, s.m., disgwyliad, D., s.v. 'expectatio '; ' expectation ': hevo disgwiliad = hevo gobaiθ, ' I hope so '; mi ·ðẹ̈yθoχi aļan veļy ən weļ na r disgwiljad, ' so things turned out for you better than you expected '.

disgəbly, v., disgyblu, ' to discipline, exercise control ; excommunicate (from a chapel) ': ifo disgəbly ə bobol, ' the people must be disciplined '; ne:b ən disgəbly dim, ' no one exercising any control ' ;—meθy disgəbly i veðul.

·di:·so:n, adj., dison, R., ' not spoken of ': a:θ ən ·ði:·so:n am dano wedyn, 'nothing was heard of him afterwards '; also in good sense : *dy:n ·di·so:n am dano,* 'a man against whom there is nothing to be said'.

distau, adj., distaw, D., 'quiet, still, silent' : *ƙin ðistawad a lgodan,* 'as quiet as a mouse'; *r o:ð ən ðistau bora kənta,* 'it (the weather) was still the first thing this morning'; *niul tu:yl, distau,* 'a thick, still mist'; *ma: r van ma n le: rëil ðistau,* 'this is a very quiet place'; *o:ð o n rëil ðistau ar hənny,* 'he was very quiet about that matter'; *riu so:n distau am rubaθ,* 'a whispered rumour about something'; *klyun hi n agor ə fenast ən ðistau,* 'I heard her opening the window quietly'; *ən ðistau ba:χ,* 'silently'.

distewi, v., distewi, D., 'to be silent'.

distil, s., distyll, D., 'ebb-tide' : *may r lanu ar ðistil,* 'the tide is ebbing'; *pry:d ma: r du:r ən mynd ən ðistil ?,* 'when does the tide go down ?'; *may hi n ðistil,* 'it is low tide'.

distin, s.m., pl. *distja,* cf. dist, D., s.v. 'tignum'; 'beam', e. g. one of those supporting the planks of a floor.

distəuruyð, s.m., distawrwydd, D., 'silence'.

distriu, s., distriw, S.G. 302. 7; distryw, D., 'destruction'. (Scarcely colloquial. Cf. *dinistr*.)

distriujo, v., distrywio, D., 'to destroy'. (Scarcely colloquial. Cf. *dinistrjo, diva*.)

·di·stymmog, adj., di and stumog, 'without appetite'.

distərlyd, adj., diystyrllyd, S.E., 'apt to disparage, contemptuous, disrespectful; disparaging' : *farad ən ðistərlyd,* 'to speak disparagingly'.

distəruχ, s., diystyrwch, D.; distyrwch, G.R. [112] 18, 'contempt, disrespect'.

distəry, v., diystyru, D. (1) 'to treat with disrespect'. (2) 'to pass by (some one) pretending not to know him, to cut'. (3) 'to show disfavour towards' : *ta:d ən distəry y:n o i blant.*

·di·sutta, adj., diswtta, D., s.v. 'desubito', 'improvisè', 'subito'; 'sudden, abrupt' : *mi: a:θ i furð ən ·di·sutta (= sutta).*

·di·sylu, adj., disylw, S.E., 'not remarkable, insignificant, not attracting attention' : *le: ·di·no:d, ·di·sylu ;—rubaθ ·di·sylu ədi o,* 'he is a man of no presence'.

·di·syt, adj., disut, S.E.*, 'without tidiness or order'.

·di·səlwað, adj., disylwedd, S.E., 'without substance'. Applied to one who has 'nothing in him', 'no good stuff in him' : *plant ·di·səlwað.*

difa, s.pl., dis, D.; disieu, W.S.; B.C. 23. 15, 'dice'.

·di·fa:p, adj., 'shapeless'.

ditta, s.pl., 'dribblings from the mouth' (= *tida*).

dittal [*tikkal*].

dittan, s., titen, W.S.; diden, D., s.v. 'mamma', 'ruma', 'rumis'; 'teat' (= *tɛːθ*).

dittu, s.f. Cf. fy nitw, C.L.C. ii. 13. 17 (i.e. 'my pussy'), *dittu dommos laːs*, 'tom-tit' (Parus coeruleus).

diujol, adj., duwiol, D., 'godly'.

diva, v., difa, D., 'to destroy': *may r gwniŋod wedi diva ḷawar jaun o r knuːd*, 'the rabbits have destroyed a great deal of the crops'.

·diːvai, adj., difai, D.   (1) 'without fault': *kefyl ·diːvai ədi o*. (2) 'good enough': *may n ·ðiːvai iðo vo*, 'it is good enough for him'; or, more emphatically, *may n ·ðiːvai i u ðannað ;—oːyð ən ·ðiːvai enu arni hi*, 'it was a very good name for her'.

·diːvaχy, adj., di and bachu, 'slack (in working)': *dyːn ·diːvaχy. 'a man who cannot be induced to stick to anything'—dim ius i vaχy o, weiðiθ o ðim.*

·diːvalas, adj., difalais, I.G. 230 [59], 'innocent, well-intentioned'.

divalχ, adj., difalch, L.G.C. 76. 1; B.C. 15. 9, 'unassuming': *daχi wedi boːd mor ðivalχ a bytta hevo mi.*

·diːʼvantas, adj., difantais, S.E.*, 'unprofitable'.

divar, adj., edifar, D., in the phrase *may n divar ǵin i*, 'I am sorry, I regret': *may n divar ǵin i ·hyːd ər ·aur ·hon*, 'I regret it to this very hour'.   Also with *i*: *byːð ən divar i ti*, 'you'll be sorry for it'.

·diːvaʼteruχ, s., difaterwch, T.N. 285. 26, 'apathy, indifference; carelessness'.

·diːʼvattar, adj., difatter, B.C. 62. 4; P.G.G. 26. 12, etc., 'apathetic, unconcerned, stolid, indifferent, unperturbed'.   Cf. *·diːʼgənnur, ·diːʼdaro, ·diːʼgəfró, ·diːʼvëind.*

·diːvedar, adj., difedr, S.E., 'incapable'.

·diːʼveðul, adj., difeddwl, S.E.   (1) 'without thinking': *nëyd o n ·diːʼveðul ðary mi*, 'I did it without thinking'.   (2) 'indifferent, casual': *pëidjuχ a boːd mor ·ðiːʼveðul*, 'give your mind to it', 'don't be so casual'.

·diːʼvëind, adj., di and Eng. mind, said of a worthless, devil-may-care individual—*ən mëindjo ðim ən neːb.*

·diːʼvëys, adj., difeius, Eph. v. 27, 'faultless': *dyːn ·diːʼvëys* (O.H.).

·diːʼviːn, adj., difîn, D., s.v. 'retusus'; 'blunt'.

divir, adj., difyr, D.; difir, P.G.G. 11. 10, 'pleasant, amusing, entertaining': *sgurs divir*, 'entertaining conversation'; *yːn divir jaun i wrando arno vo*, 'one who is very interesting to listen to'; *ḷeː divir i blant*, 'a nice place for children'.

divja, s , difiau pro Dydd Iau, D. ; D.G. xxxiv. 11 ; cxxix. 15, ' Thursday ': *divja ǝ drǝχaval*, ' Ascension Day '.

divlanny, v., diflannu, D., ' to vanish ': *mi δivlannoδ o ɲolug i.*

divlas, adj., diflas, C.C. 453. 13 ; B.C. 26. 13, ' dry, uninteresting': *pͬǝgeθur divlas*, ' a dry preacher '; *ḻcː divlas*, ' a nasty, uninteresting place '.

·*diːˑvlaːs*, adj., diflas, D., ' tasteless ': *kiːg ·diːˑvlaːs = mervaδ.*

divlastod, s., diflasdod, S.E., ' coarse language ': *paid a ſarad divlastod ·anˑweδys.*

divlasy, v., diflasu, D. (1) tr. ' to disgust ': *may n δigon a divlasy ruːin*, ' it is enough to disgust any one '. (2) intr. ' to be tired of ': *du i wedi divlasy arno vo*, ' I am tired of it '.

divlin, adj., diflin, D., s.v. ' infatigabilis ' ; ' untiring '.

·*diːˑvlino*, v., difiino, ' to rest ': *sieδuχ i ·δiːˑvlino.*

·*diːˑvodi*, v., difodi, S.E., ' to do away with by removing, breaking to pieces, etc.': ·*diːˑvodi ǝsgol o r pluːy*, ' to do away with a school from the parish '; ·*diːˑvodi poːb peːθ sy ɲ gnēyd druːg.*

·*diˑvɐuyd*, adj., difywyd, D., s.v. ' inanimatus ' ; ' lifeless, inanimate '.

divrau, adj., difraw, D.F. [11] 1, 4 ; Isaiah xxxii. 10, ' fearless, cool, indifferent ': *dyːn divrau*, ' a cool customer '.

divri, adj., difrif, D., ' serious ': *oː δivri* (cf. B.C. 28. 21), *oː δivri kalon*, ' seriously '; *maː r taːn wedi kǝnna oː δivri ruːan*, ' the fire has burnt up properly now '; *ɼhaid i χi voːd uθi oː δivri*, ' you must set to in earnest '; *daχi n mynd aḻan oː δivri kalon boːb dyːδ*, ' you make a point of going out every day '; *ǝdi o n sais oː δivri kaḻon ?*, ' is he a real Englishman ? '

divrivol, adj., difrifol, D., s.v. ' tantopere '; ' serious ': *ſarad ǝn δivrivol*, ' to speak seriously'; *r oːδ o n δivrivol aryθrol ǝmma*, ' it (the storm) was extremely serious here ', ' it was a terrible state of things here '.

divrod, s.m., difrawd, D., ' destruction ', e.g. of property by a storm : *mi naːθ ǝ glaːu δivrod maur*, ' the rain made great havoc '.

divrodi, v., difrodi, D., ' to work havoc upon ': *r oːδ ǝr haiδ wedi kayl i δivrodi n δcχrmḻyd.*

·*diːˑvulχ*, adj., diuwlch, M.A. i. 389 a. 5, ' without flaw ' (of persons or things): *kǝmerjad ·diːˑvulχ*, ' a flawless character '.

·*diːˑvyːδ*, adj., difudd, D., s.v. ' inutilis ' ; ' unprofitable ': *pͬǝnny peːθ ·diːˑvyːδ.*

·*diːˑvǝnaδ*, adj., diamynedd, D.G. ccxv. 49, ' impatient '.

divǝruχ, s., difyrrwch, D., ' amusement '.

dívɚy, v., difyrru, D., ' to amuse '; ' to take pleasure in ' : *vəδa i n divɚy hevo r peθa na* (O.H.).

·*di:vytta*, adj., di and bwytta, ' without appetite '.

diwaδ, s.m., diwedd, D., ' end ' (in the immaterial, abstract sense): *ɘn ə diwaδ*, ' in the end '; *diwaδ ə mi:s ; mi δa:u diwaδ ə by:d tok*, ' the end of the world will come soon '; *o r diwaδ*, ' at last '.—As exclamation, euph. for *dyu*; in this sense, often pronounced *áywaδ*: *δiwad (áywaδ) annul!*

·*di:wa·hanjaθ*, adj., diwahaniaeth, T.N. 107. 17, ' without distinction ': *may o m prɘǵeθy hevo paub ɘn ·δi:wa·hanjaθ ; may dyu ɘn r̥hoid i baub ɘn ·δi:wa·hanjaθ.*

·*di:·waiθ*, adj., diwaith, Isaiah xxxii. 9. (1) ' unemployed ': *du i n ·δi:·waiθ er s talum jaun.* (2) ' lazy, averse to work ': *syt δy:n o:δ o? r o:yδ o n holol ·di:·waiθ.*

·*di:·wal̦*, adj., diwall, R., ' without imperfection ': *dy:n tr̦uyδo ·di:·wal̦.*

diweδar, adj., diweddar, D., ' late ': *vala diweδar*, ' late apples '; *ɘn δiweδar*, ' lately ' (but *kodi n hu:yr*, ' to get up late ').

diweδy, v., diweddu, D., ' to end '.

·*di:·wenwyn*, adj., diwenwyn, S.E.*, ' not jealous '.

·*di:·werθ*, adj., diwerth, S.E., ' worthless '.

·*di:·wëylod*, adj., di-waelod, Rev. xx. 1. (1) ' bottomless ': *mor ·δi:·wëylod a pul̦ k̦eris* (cf. *dyvn*). (2) ' unprincipled '.

diwid, adj., diwyd, D.; diwid, P.G.G. 42. 16; 43. 9; 105. 15, ' industrious '.

diwidruyδ, s.m., diwydrwydd, D., ' industry '.

diwigjad, s.m., diwygiad, D., s.v. ' correctio '. (1) ' a (religious) revival ': *kodi diwigjad*, ' to start a revival '. (2) ' conversion ' (in religious sense): *ka:yl diwigjad*, ' to be converted '.

·*di:·wrëidjo*, v., diwreiddio, D., ' to uproot '.

·*di:r̦madvarθ*, adj., diymadferth, D., s.v. ' iners '; ' helpless ', e.g. of an infant.

·*di:ɘm·δirjad*, adj., diymddiried, S.E., ' unreliable '.

·*di:ɘsbryd*, adj., diysbryd, D., s.v. ' excors, iners '; ' spiritless ': *dy:n ·di:ɘsbryd*, ' a man with no " go " in him '.

djagan : *mɘn djagan i!*, expletive.

djail, euph. for *djaul*: *djail a m pi:! pu:y o:δ ɘno ond ɘ·vo: ;— mɘn djail i!*

djaist: *djaist a minna!, mɘn djaist ti!*, expletives.

dja:n, expletive, ' upon my word!'

djauχ, expletive, euph. for *djaul*.

djaul, s.m., pl. *djøulad*, diawl, D., s.v. ' diabolus'; ' devil':
djaul a m sgybo i !, 'the devil snatch me!'; *djaul a i flamjo vo !;—
un i ðim be ðjaul s arno vo*, 'I don't know what the devil is the matter
with him'; *nid ən hi:r ə k̃ëidu r djaul i wa:s* (prov.), 'the devil does
not long preserve his dupe'; *aŋal pen forð, djaul pen pentan* (prov.),
said of one whose pleasant manners are only seen away from home;
may o vel djaul dan garag, 'he is continually nagging, grumbling';
χwara te:g i r djaul (prov.), 'the devil is not so black as he is
painted'; *rhuŋ ə djaul a i gumfon*, 'between the devil and the deep
sea'; *ba:u djaul*, 'asafœtida'.

djaus!, expletive, diawst, T.N. 115. 27 : *djaus! gwy:l̥t ! be u:ti
wedi gnëyd vel hyn ?*

djoða, v., dioddef, D. Pret. S. 3. *djoðoð*, 'to bear, endure, suffer':
vedra i ðim djoða nu, 'I can't bear them'; *·t öyðanu ðim ən djoða
if'o*, 'they used not to suffer want'; *may n wel djoða po:b pe:θ*, 'it
is better to put up with anything'; *du i wedi djoða lawar jaun oruθ
vannoð*, 'I have suffered a great deal from toothache'.

djoðevgar, adj., dioddefgar, D. (1) 'patient, not yielding to pain':
ma: rhëi ən tyχan pen ·vəðanu wedi brivo, a rhëi ən vu:y djoðevgar,
' some complain when they are hurt and some are more enduring'.
(2) of stone, etc. 'workable, not breaking when worked'. Opp.
farp.

djogal, adj., diogel, D., 'safe'.

djoǵi, s.m., diogi, D., 'laziness': *t o:ys na ðim djoǵi n i gro:yn o*,
' there is no laziness in him'.

djoǵi, v., diogi, D., 'to be lazy'.

djogyn, s.m., diogyn, O.P., 'a lazy fellow'.

djolχgar, adj., diolchgar, D., 'thankful': *rhaid i ni vod ən
ðjolχgar am dani hi*, 'we must be thankful for it'.

djolχgaruχ, s.m., diolchgarwch, D., 'thankfulness, thanksgiving':
kwarvod djolχgaruχ, 'harvest thanksgiving service'.

djoni, s.m., daioni, D.; cf. d'ioni, T.N. 163. 4ò, 'good': *mi
nëiθ o ðjoni maur*, 'it will do a great deal of good'; *wa:yθ be di o
os ədi ŋ gnëyd djoni i χi*, 'it doesn't matter what it is so long as it
does you good'; *vy:o rĩ:oyd dru:g na vy:o n ðjoni i ru:in* (prov.),
' it is an ill wind that blows no one any good'.

djotta, v., diotta, D., 'to tipple': *may o n djotta ar ə muya*.

djøuledig, adj., diawledig, C.C.M. 199. 10, 'devilish'.

djøuljo,v., diaw'lio, T.N. 222. 11, 'to swear': *ən rheǵi ag ən djøuljo*,
' cursing and swearing'. Said of human beings and of cats.

dle:d, dəlad, s.f., pl. *dledjon, dəledjon*, dyled, dylêd, dlêd, dylyed, D.;
dlêd, B.C. 83. 19; M.Ll. i. 143. 23. (1) 'debt': *taly i ðəledjon*,

'to pay one's debts'; *mynd i ðəlad*, 'to get into debt'; *may o n sup o ðleːd*, 'he is over head and ears in debt'. (2) 'obligation' : *tənny χi i ðəlad*, 'to put you under an obligation'; *ɩ oːs na ðim dəlad arna i*, 'I am under no obligation'.

dledog, adj., dyledog, D., 'in debt': *r̨hëi dledog ovnaduy ·ədynu*, 'they are fearfully in debt'.

doː, adv., do, D., 'yes': after verbs in the preterite or perfect tense, as ·*welsoχi o ?* (ðary χi weld o ?) *doː, na: ðoː*, 'did you see him? Yes'. 'No'. *daχi wedi weld o ?* *doː* (or *ədu*), 'have you seen him? Yes'; *mi ·gwelsoχi o, n doː ?* (*n toː ?*), 'you saw him, didn't you ?'

dob, s., 'lot': *mi dənna i dob puːy ëiθ i u wely gənta*, 'I will draw lots to see who goes to bed first'.

dobjo, dgobjo, v., dobio, T.N. 282. 1. Eng. (Dial.) dob ['to strike; to give a blow', s.Not.; 'to throw stones, etc., at a mark', w.Yks., s.Ches., Nhp., Cor.], 'to beat, strike'; 'to squash'; fig. 'to hammer in': *diːar !* *maːy r ðənas na n dobjo ə plant ən aru!*, 'my word! that woman does beat her children !'; *mi dobiʃ o a fastun*, 'I beat him with a stick'; *dobjo l̨god a χer̨ig*, 'to throw stones at mice'; *maː r glaːu ən dobjo ar ə gwynab*, 'the rain beats upon the face'.

dobyn [*dibin*].

dodran, s.m., dodrefn, D., 'furniture': *dodrevnyn, dodrenyn*, 'a single piece of furniture'.

doduy, dəduy, dəduy ; dəduyð (E.J.), v., dodwy, D., 'to lay (eggs)'.

döiθinab, s.m., doethineb, D., 'wisdom'.

dokkyn, s. [*tokkyn*].

doktor, s.m., pl. *doktorja(ɩ)d*, doctor, W.LL xx. 11, dokdor, v. 35, 'doctor'.

doktoras, s.f., pl. *doktoresa*,·'female doctor': *may hi n dippin o ðoktoras*.

dol, s.f., 'doll'. Also *babi dol*.

doːl, s.f., pl. *dolyð*, dôl, D., 'a level field in a low-lying valley'.

dolan, s.f., pl. *dolenna*, dolen, D., 'link, loop': *darn o hëyarn ən fyrvjo dolan* (J.J.),·'a piece of iron forming a link'; *pl̨gy n ðolan*, 'to bend into a link'; *dolan leː i laːu*, 'a loop to catch hold of'; *dolan r̨edag*, 'noose'.

dolan, s.f., pl. *dolenna, dlenna, dolenni, dalenni*, dolen llyfyr, W.S.; dolennau D.F. [120] 26. 28; dalen, D. s.v. 'pagina', 'leaf of a book, page': *tr̨oi r ðolan*, 'to turn over the leaf'; *tor̨i dlenna*, 'to tear out pages'; *r̨higo dolan*, 'to tear a page';—in speaking of clover, etc.: *dëilan bedar dolan*, 'four-leaved'.

dolðelan, Dolwyddelan.

dolennog, adj., dolennog, D., s.v. 'sinuosus'; 'winding' (of a river): *avon ðolennog*.

dolig, *mdolig*, s.f., Nadolig, D., 'Christmas': *ty: a dolig*, 'about Christmas time'; *dolig lawan a bluyðyn newyð ða: i χi*, 'a Merry Christmas and a Happy New Year to you'; *no:s dolig*, 'Christmas Eve'; *ky:f dolig*, 'yule log'; *mi vy::ð dolig ən ər ha: kin këi di o*, 'you won't get it till the Greek calends'; *gwilja mdolig*, 'Christmas holidays'.

dolirjo, v., dolurio, D., 'to wound', generally in fig. sense: *dolirjo i tëimlada*, 'to wound their feelings'.

dolyr, s.m., pl. *dolirja*, dolur, D., 'wound, hurt' = *briu:—gëif i bo:yn garu oruθ ə dolyr*, 'I had great pain from the wound'; *paub a i vy:s le bo: i ðolyr* (prov. exp.), 'each man knows where the shoe pinches in his own case'; *dolyr di:arθ*, said of something which will not heal, e.g. an ulcer.

dondjo, v., dondio, T.N. 46. 27, 'to scold' = *durdjo*. [J.J. always used *dondjo*, E.J. *durdjo*—'equally common', O.H.]; *may mam ən dondjo n aru*, 'mother is scolding terribly'.

donjol, adj., doniol, T.N. 118. 15. (1) 'funny, amusing': *y:n donjol ədi o*, 'he is a funny, amusing man'; *fadur donjol*, 'a witty, amusing speaker'. (2) 'gifted in speech': *prəgeθur donjol*.

do:r s.f., dôr, D., in old-fashioned cottages 'the inner of two doors, the outer one of which (*rhagðor*) is half the height of the door'.

dormaχ, s., ? torrmach, D., s.v. 'vadimonium';—*u:ti n dormaχ arna i*, 'you are a burden to me' (*ən əχ gwasgy χi ruvoð—ən rhoi bayχ 'arnoχi o hy:d*)—O.H.

dotjo, v., dotio, W.S. [Dote]; M.Ll. i. 207. 24; 264. 1; dottio, C.C. 12. 23. (1) 'to dote': *du i n dotjo 'attynu* (E.J.), 'I am very fond of them'. (2) 'to be astonished (at), taken (by)': *dotjo at ðənas harð*, dotjo *at i glendid hi* = *sənny* (O.H.).

·dəurdəu, adv., 'slowly, at one's ease': *mynd ·dəurdəu* = *mynd liŋkyn loŋkyn*, 'to go jogging along'; *mi ðois ən ·ðəurdəu o r van a r van*.

dəuka, duka, dukar, Eng. (Dial.) doucker, douker, i.e. 'ducker, diver', in *bili dəuka*, 'razor-bill' (Alca torda).

dəukjo, *dəukjan*, v., dowkio, W.S. [douke], Eng. (Dial.) douck, douk, dowk [to dive, plunge under water]. (1) 'to duck' (of ducks, geese, etc.). (2) 'to bob up and down', e.g. while bathing; of boats in rough weather; or of a horse walking in an unnatural way. (3) 'to dive': *mi dəukif i i r mo:r*.

dəukva, s.f., 'a ducking, wetting' (I.W.).

dəuχal, v., dymchwelyd, D. s.v. 'euerto'; 'to pour down' = *pistiljo i laur*. Cf. *damχwal*.

dɐunsrag, s.f., dawnswraig, S.E., ' dancer '.

dɐunſ'o, v., dawnsio, D., ' to dance.'

dɐunſ'ur, s.m., dawnsiwr, T.N. 345. 16, ' dancer '.

dɐunys, adj., dawnus, D.G. ccxli. 39, ' gifted in speech '.

do:v, adj., pl. *dovjon*, dôf, D., 'tame ': *kadu nu n δovjon*, ' to keep them tame '.

dovi, v., dofi, D. (1) tr. ' to tame ': *dovi anival gwy:ļ*, ' to tame a wild animal ' ; *dovi arno vo dippin*, ' to tame him a little '. (2) intr. ' to become tame '.

do:y, adv. and s. (generally δo:y), doe, D., ' yesterday ': *t ɔdu i δim wedi magy δo:y*, ' I wasn't born yesterday ' ; *mi ˑroisoχi δo:y i r brenin*, ' you got nothing done yesterday ' ; *hëïδju a do:y*, ' to-day and yesterday '.

do:yθ, adj., comp. *dɐyθaχ*, doeth, D., ' wise'.

drabja, s.pl. Eng. (Dial.) drab [small quantity], Yks., Chs., 'pieces': *maly n drabja ylu*, ' to chop into bits ' ; *drabja kiljon* (O.H. in speaking of bacon), ' thin slices '.

drabjo, v., ' to pull to pieces', lit. and fig., e.g. *drabjo diļad, kɔmerjad*. In shearing *drabjo* is to tear the fleece by working clumsily (O.H.).

drag, s.f. ; *may o wedi mynd i r δrag* (*dros i ben*), ' he has made a grave mistake (and so done himself an injury) '. O.H.

dragjo, v., dragio, W.S. [Rente]; D., 'lacerare, dilaniare ': ' to pull to pieces, tear, spoil ', e.g. ' clothes ': *pĕidjuχ a ļavnjo χ ģiliδ a dragjo χ diļad*; (fig.) *dragjo i hy:n*, ' to do oneself a (moral) injury '. Also ' to drag ', e.g. *dragjo iṛol* O.H. (but *ļysgo drain, keṛig, sle:d*, etc.).

drain, s.pl., sing. *dra:yn*, m., *drëynan*, f., draen, D., ' thorns': *drain dy:on*, 'black thorn'; *drain gunjon*, ' white thorn ' ; *drain morδy:on = drain meri*, ' brambles'; *ļɔvny hevo drain a briga bedu*, ' to harrow with thorns and birch-twigs'; *kļauδ drain*, 'thorn hedge' (used for the sake of distinction since *kļauδ =* 'hedge' and ' wall of loose stones') ; *tavly i enaid ar ɔ drain*, ' to be on thorns '. *drëynan* is generally 'a thorn-bush', 'a branch of thorn'.—*drain gwynab* (sing. *drëynan wynab*), ' sort of pimples on the face, out of which, when pressed, a kind of worm-shaped matter issues'. Cf. D. gwraint, sing. gwreinyn, ' vermiculus ', etc.

dra:χ, prep., drach, D., ' over', only in *dra:χ ɔ ɥhevn, dra:χ i ģevn*, etc., as in *edraχ dra:χ i ģevn*, ' to look over one's shoulder '.

draχt, s.m., dracht, T.N. 115. 25, ' draught, drink': *uti wedi kayl di:od ɔn aru ? na:, χe:s i δim ond y:n draχt ;—draχt o δi:od.*

draχįjo, v., drachtio, ' to drink': *paid a draχįjo r ļevriθ na, vy:δ na δim i ni i de:.*

drapja, interj., Eng. (Dial.) drab, s.Lin., Dev., only in *drapja vo* (*ynwaθ*) *!*, 'drat it!'

dratja, interj., only in *dratja vo* (*ynwaθ*) *!*, 'drat it !'

dra:u, adv., draw, D., s.v. 'ultra'; 'yonder': *pel dra:u*, 'far away over there'; *ə mhen dra:u r by:d*, 'at the end of the world'; *ən ne:s dra:u*, 'further on'; *kadu dra:u*, 'to keep off'; *ɪruyδo dra:u*, 'through and through'; *ly: dra:u i*, 'beyond'; *i bentir a dra:u*, 'to Pentir and beyond'.

drëidi, s.m., direidi, D., 'mischievousness': *drëidi dru:g, drëidi ·di·niwad*.

drëigja, s.pl., dreigiau (pl. of draig), B.C. 51. 21, 'sheet-lightning': *may hi ŋ glëyo drëigja*.

drëinjog, adj., dreiniog, D., s.v. 'dumosus'; 'thorny'.

drëivar, s.m., 'driver'.

drekf'un, s.m., Eng. direction; 'address' (of a letter).

drekljo, v., Eng. direct; 'to address' (a letter).

dreχtyn, s.m., drechtyn, T.N. 115. 22. Dim. of *draχt*, 'a little draught'.

dreŋ, adj., dreng, D. (1) 'stubborn, morose'. (2) 'rude': *rvi: sy n δreŋ uθa·χi: ən farad vel ·tasaχi n hogyn ba:χ ; paid di ag attab də da:d a də vam ən δreŋ* (O.H.).

dreŋgar, adj. (1) 'stubborn, morose'. (2) 'peevish': *may o n y:n dreŋgar* (= *bli:n, əŋ kri:o*), 'he (the child) is peevish, cross'.

dreŋlo, v., ymdreiglo, Jer. xxv. 34, 'to lie on the back and kick up the legs in the air (of horses) ; to wallow'.

dreŋys, adj. = *dreŋ*.

dreugi, s.m., drewgi, B.C. 118. 26, 'a filthy fellow': *ta:u ɼ he:n dreugi bydyr !*

dreulyd, adj., drewllyd, M.Ll. i. 135. 13, 'stinking': *wy:a dreulyd*, 'rotten eggs'.

drewi, v., drewi, D., 'to stink': *drewi vel ɡiŋgron, vel fulbart ; drewi o hogla kuru ; may o n drewi n fi:aδ*.

drëydys, adj., direidus, S.E., 'mischievous'.

drëynog, s.m., pl. *drëynogod*, draenog, D. (1) 'hedgehog'. (2) 'bass' (Morone labrax), Bangor = *dra:yn i:og* (O.H.).

·drib·drab, adv., 'bits, smithereens': *maly n ·drib·drab* (J.J.; O.H.); *wedi ka:l i nëyd ən riu ·drib·drab*. Also 'little by little, in driblets': *ma: nu n du:ad i vjaun ən ·drib·drab*, e.g. of money lent.

dridus ; diridus (W.H.); *dəridust* (Bangor), s.pl. and sing., drudwy and drudwen, D. Cf. drwdwst, M.F., 'starlings' (Sturnus vulgaris).

drinus, s.f.: *drinus ba:χ, drinus velan,* 'yellow-hammer' (Emberiza citrinella) = *dənas (dinas) benvelan.*

driŋo, v., dringo, D.   Pret. Pl. 3. *driŋson.*   Imperative *driŋ, driŋa,* 'to climb': *driŋo köydan,* 'to climb a tree'; *driŋo i vri:g ə göydan,* 'to climb to the top of the tree'.

driŋur, s.m., dringur, S.E., 'climber': *may r hogyn ən ðriŋur jaun i vəny r ko:yd.*

driu, s.f., dryw, D., 'wren' (Troglodytes parvulus)—generally *driu ba:χ.*   Does not mutate, e.g. *ə driu ;—driu wen,* 'whitethroat' [Forrest] (Sylvia cinerea).—*r o:ð ə ty: vel ny:θ driu,* said of a neat, cosy house.

drogan, v., darogan, D.   (1) 'to say beforehand, to express an intention': *du i n drogan mynd* (E.J.); *hu:y drogan gwaiθ na i nëyd* (prov.), 'it takes longer talking about, preparing to work than to do it'.   (2) generally in conjunction with *dru:g,* 'to forebode': *y:n garu jaun i ðrogan dru:g ədi v,* 'he is a terrible fellow for croaking, foreboding evil';—also of the weather: *may hi n drogan dru:g,* 'there's bad weather coming'.

drogan, s., apparently a corruption of crogen, D., 'gills of a fish' = *tagaḷ ;—ə drogan,* 'the gills', *i drogan,* 'his gills', imply a radical form *trogan,* but this is not in use.—(I.W.; J.J.)

drogan, s.f., pl. *drogod,* trogen, torrogen, D., 'ricinus', 'a kind of tick which adheres to the skin of cattle in summer', J.J. = *krogan* O.H.   Cf. T.N. 334. 36, i'r hyslaw a'r drogod.

droni, v., dironi, S.E., 'to shed grain' (= *buru, koḷi*).   Also trans. 'to spill grain' by handling the corn carelessly, etc.: *droni r y:d.*

dror, s.m., pl. *drors,* 'drawer'.

dros (rarely *tros*), prep., tros, D.   With pronouns.   S. 1. *drosta i,* 2. *·drostati,* 3. *drosto (vo), drosti (hi).*   Pl. 1. *·drostani,* 2. *·drostaχi,* 3. *·drostynu.*   Before vowels generally *drost :*—(1) 'over' (in all senses, both of place and time): *·vy:oχi drost ə bont?,* 'have you been over the bridge?'; *edraχ dros ə kḷauð,* 'to look over the wall'; *dros ə fri:ð ag ən sy:θ ar ẋ pen,* 'over the field and straight on'; *drost ə forð i* (= *gəverbyn a*), 'opposite, on the opposite side of the road to'; *dros ə rhinjog,* 'over the threshold'; *mi a:θ ə drol drosto vo,* 'he was run over by the cart'; *nëidjo dros ə kḷauð,* 'to jump over the wall'; *mynd dros ə ǵa:t,* 'to get over the gate'; *sərθjo dros ə dibin, ə dorlan,* 'to fall over the precipice, down the bank'; *ar o:l iði vrigo mi r o:ð na ru:d go de:u drosto vo,* 'after the frost there was rather a thick mist (over it)'; *aros dros ə no:s,* 'to stay over night'; *gnëyd ə gwair ən vədəla dros ə sy:l,* 'to gather the hay in heaps over Sunday'; *ðary hi sgreχjan drost ə ty:,* 'she shrieked (so as to be heard) all over the house'; *χwerθin dros bo:b man,* 'to laugh loud'.   With *i ǵi:d,* 'all over': *əŋ go:χ i ǵi:d drosto,* 'red all over'; followed by *ben*, 'over (the top)'; *mi nëidjoð ə ðavad dros ben ə ki:*, 'the sheep jumped over the dog'; *dros ben ə klauð*, 'over the wall'. (2) 'over, more than' (with numbers): *may o dros ðu:y la:θ o daldra*, 'he is over six feet in height'; *dros ðay gant*, 'over two hundred'; *may o drost i hannar kant*, 'he is over fifty'; *er s dros igjan mlənað*, 'for more than twenty years'; similarly *dros ðe:g*, 'after ten o'clock'. (3) 'for, on behalf of': *gweði:o drost i θa:d*, 'to pray for her father'; *ma: n ðru:g kin i ·drostaxi ag ən ðru:g ðuywaθ drosta vi: və hy:n*, 'I am sorry for you and twice as sorry for myself'. (4) 'for': *rhesum dros nëyd*, 'a reason for doing'. (5) *dros ben*, used adverbially, (a) 'exceedingly': *da: dros ben*, 'exceedingly good' (= *ən odjaθ o ða:*); (b) 'over and above': *am draguyðoldað a durnod dros ben*, 'for ever and a day'.

drosoð, drostoð, trosoð, adv., drosodd, D., s.v. 'superfero', etc.; 'over': *may po:b pe:θ drosoð*, 'it is all over'; *gəry trosoð ·atlynu*, 'to send over to them'; *mi nëidjoð ə taru drosoð*, 'the bull jumped overboard'; *er s trigjan mlənað a θrosoð*, 'sixty years ago and more'.

drovyn, v., darofun, cf. 'Y Beirniad' for June, 1912, p. 121, 'to intend': *ən drovyn mynd əno o hy:d*.

dru:g, adj., comp. *gwa:yθ*, eq. *gwëyθad*, sup. *gwëyθa*, drwg, D., 'bad': *hogla dru:g*, 'a bad smell'; *plant dru:g*, 'naughty children'; *sbrədjon dru:g*, 'evil spirits'; *gu:r dru:g*, 'the devil';—in rare cases *dru:g* precedes the noun: *sgərljo meun dru:g natlyr*, 'to scold when in a bad temper';—*o:yð o n ðru:g ?*, 'was it nasty' (e.g. the medicine); *may o y klu:ad ən ðru:g*, 'he is dull of hearing'; *dru:g odjaθ vy:ð ə dəwyð*, 'we shall have very bad weather'; *araθ ðru:g*, 'bad language'; *enu dru:g*, 'bad name, term of reproach'; *riu he:n gastja dru:g*, 'mischief'; *ki:, taru dru:g*, 'a dangerous dog, bull'; *may ə yhevn ən ðru:g jaun uθ gérðad*, 'my back is very bad while walking'; *a:θ ən ðru:g ·rhəŋθynu*, 'bad blood was stirred up between them'.—Followed by *ar*, 'hard upon': *may n ðru:g ar i rhi·eni*, 'it is hard on their parents'; followed by *gin*, 'sorry': *ma: n ðru:g jaun gin i vod o wedi difod*, 'I am very sorry it has gone out' (of a fire); *ma:n ðru:g kin i ·drostaxi*, 'I am sorry for you'.

dru:g, s.m., pl. *drəga*, drwg, D., 'matter, wrong, evil, hurt': *du i wedi ka:yl hy:d i r dru:g*, 'I have found out what is the matter'; *wedi kayl ə dru:g əna n jaun i ðexra mi vy:ð riu obaiθ*, 'after getting that right to begin with there will be some hope'; *dəna r dru:g*, 'that's the worst of it'; *ka:l dru:g*, 'to get the blame'; *gnëyd dru:g*, esp. as applied to women, 'to go wrong'; *vy:o ri·o:yd dru:g na: vy:o n ðjoni i ru:in* (prov.), 'it is an ill wind that blows no one any good'; *t o:s o r dru:g ond dru:g i ðisgul* (prov.) = nearly, 'honesty is the best policy'; *wel gin i ə dru:g ə gun i na r dru:g nas gun i m ono vo*, 'I should rather have the evil I know than the evil I do not know'; *mi geuxi ðru:g*, 'you will hurt yourself'; also

' you will get into a row '; *o:ð ðru:g i mi gay hun ?,* ' was I wrong in shutting this? '

dru:s, s.m., pl. *drəsa,* drŵs, D., ' door': *klikjad ə dru:s,* ' door-latch '; *durn ə dru:s,* ' door-handle '; *dru:s ə frənt,* ' front door '; *dru:s ə Ḱevn,* ' back door '; *r̥hoi klep ar ə dru:s, kay ə dru:s əŋ glep,* ' to bang the door '; *may r dru:s əŋ klepjan,* ' the door is banging '; *r̥hoi klo: ar ə dru:s,* ' to lock the door '; *kyro, knokjo ən ə dru:s,* ' to knock at the door '; *may o ən ə dru:s,* ' he is at the door '; *sevyl ar ben dru:s,* ' to stand at the door ' (often implying ' to gossip '); *ir̥oi o dros ben dru:s,* ' to turn him out '.

dry:d, adj., drûd, D., ' fortis, strenuus, audax '; comp. *dryttaχ,* ' dear ' (of price); *Ḱin ðrytiad a pyppyr,* ' as dear as pepper ' (O.H. —obs.).

drym, s.m., pl. *drəmja,* trùm, D.; cf. also D., s.v. ' lira '. (1) ' ridge ' (in general, e.g. between two watersheds) = *top ə ti:r.* The term *ə drym* is applied especially to the long ridge extending from the western side of Bwlch y Ddeufaen to the further slopes of Carnedd Ddafydd. (2) ' the top of a ridge in ploughing ' = *kanol Ḱevn.*

drəgað, s.m., drygedd, D., s.v. ' malignitas '; ' evil '.

drəgjoni, s.m., drygioni, D., ' evil '.

drəgy, v., drygu, D., s.v. ' vexo '; ' to degenerate, deteriorate '. Also *drəgy i hy:n,* ' to harm, injure oneself ' (morally), e. g. *hevo di:od.*

drəḰinlyd, adj., dryghinllyd, S.E., ' stormy': *may na olug drəḰinlyd jaun arni hi,* ' it looks like very bad weather '.

drəḰinog, driḰinog, adj., dryc-hinog, D., s.v. ' tempestuosus ', ' stormy '.

drəkḰin, drikḰin, s.f., pl. *drəḰinoð,* driḰinoð, dryg-hin, D., s.v. ' vireo '; ' bad weather ': *may hi n ðrəkḰin ovnaduy (ðrəkḰin vaur),* ' it is terribly bad weather '; *Ḱi: drəkḰin,* ' a partial rainbow '.

drəχaval, s.m., dyrchafael, D.; cf. drychafal, W.B., col. 128. 14, ' ascension '. Only in *divja ə drəχaval,* ' Ascension Day '.

drəljo, v., dryllio, D., ' to tear, break ' (not often used): *ə gwynt ən drəljo to:, ta:s.—paid a drəljo də ðiḷad uθ hel nəθod adar,* ' do not tear your clothes by bird-nesting '.

drəljog, adj., drylliog, D., ' apt to break ' (only used in fig. sense): *may n ðrəljog jaun ən i dëimlada,* ' he has very tender feelings— breaks down easily '; *may n ðrəljog jaun ar i linja,* ' he gives way to his feelings when praying '; *o:ð o n ðrəljog jaun dan ə bregaθ,* ' he was much affected by the sermon '.

drəmjo, v. (1) ' to make a noise like a drum ': *sərθjo nes·bədanu ən drəmjo ar ə ḷaur* (O.H.). (2) ' to pummel ': *mi də ðrəmja i di.*

drəntol, s.f., dryntol, D., 'a bent piece of wood with a piece of iron fastening the two ends, and a rope fastened to the iron, for carrying burdens' (O.H.).

drəsgol, place-name : *ə drəsgol* = Y Drosgl—name of a mountain.

drəslyd, adj., dyryslyd, 'wandering in mind ; muddled in the head ; entangled '.

drəsni, s.m., dyrysni, Gen. xxii. 13 ; drysni, P.G.G. 180. 6, ' thicket': *anjaluχ a drəsni* (O.H.).

drəsuχ, s.m., dyryswch, D.; cf. drysswch, G.C. 144. 22 ; 152. 17. (1) ' the state of being wandering in mind'. (2) 'puzzle, perplexity' : *may hunna n ðrəsuχ ara̦ḻ i mi̦.* (3) ' confusion '.

drəsy, v., dyrysu, D. Intr. (1) ' to become entangled ', e.g. of the hair. (2) ' to be embarrassed, to get into a muddle'; *may o wedi drəsy ən i amkanjon bədol,* ' his affairs have become embarrassed' ; *mi ðrəsis ən la:n,* ' I went entirely astray'. (3) ' to be beside oneself, to be driven distracted' : *r öyðun i dgest a drəsy,* ' I was almost beside myself '. (4) ' to lose one's wits, to become weak in the head ', e.g. of old people ; ' to go crazy, to become delirious ' : *may o wedi drəsy hevo r diwigjad,* ' he has gone crazy over the revival ' ; *may o wedi drəsy ən i snuyra,* ' he is delirious '. (5) ' to be wrong'. Trans. (6) ' to entangle '. (7) ' to interfere with, upset '; ' baffle, balk': *may n drəsy r gwaiθ,* ' it interferes with the work '. (8) ' to drive out of one's wits ', e.g. by continual talking = *muydro, bədary.*

du:ad, v., dyfod, D.; dwad, G.R. (5) 12. Fut. S. 1. *do:(v)*, 2. *doi̦,* 3. *da:u, doi̦f [de:l̦]*. Pl. 1. *do:n,* 2. *dəuχ,* 3. *do:n.* Imp. S. 1. *dəun, döyðun,* 2. *do:ț,* 3. *do:y, do:.* Pl. 1. *ðёyðan,* 2. *ðёyðaχ,* 3. *dёyðan.* Pret. S. 1. *dois,* 2. *doisț,* 3. *do:θ, da:θ.* Pl.1. *dёyðon, dёyson,* 2. *dёyðoχ, dёysoχ,* 3. *dёyðon, dёyson.* Imperative S. 2. *tyd,* 3. *do:yd.* Pl. 2. *dəuχ.* (1) ' to come ': *dəuχ.* Ans. *do:(v), na ðo:(v),* ' come. (Ans.) Yes '. ' No '; *ðəuχi̦ ? do:v, mi ðo:v heno,* ' will you come? Yes, I will come to-night'; *do:yd a ðe:l,* ' come what may ' (O.H.); *ðo:y o ðim dros i grogi̦,* ' he would not come on any account' ; *o b le: daχi n du:ad ?,* ' where do you come from ?'; *dəuχ i edraχ ta os na 'χöi̦lju̦χi̦,* ' come and see then if you don't believe ' ; *kənta ·dёyðonu,* ' as soon as they came ' ; *nes do:y o adra,* ' until he came home ' (habitually); *nes ·dёyðonu ən i hola,* ' until they came back '; *erbyn da:u o,* ' by the time he comes '; *ða:u o ðim țruy de:g,* ' he cannot be won over by kindness ' ; *ðy ly:n ðo:θ ə kəujon ba:χ,* ' the chickens were hatched on Monday ' ; *may n du:ad i r y:n van,* ' it comes to the same thing '; —of plants: *du:ad* or *du:ad a̦lan,* ' to come up ' ;—of fire ' to burn up ' : *mi ða:u ən vy:an ru:an,* ' it will burn up soon now ' ;—followed by *i* and a noun or pronoun = ' let ', the idea of motion being often entirely absent : *dəuχ i mi weld,* ' let me see '; *tyd i mi ga:l o,* ' let me have it ';—where English usage requires ' get ' : *may hi n du:ad i drevn*, 'it is getting into order'; ·*vedruχi ðu:ad o: na ?*, 'can you get out from there?'; *dəuχ i r gadar ma*, 'get into this chair'; *wedi ·du:ad ɪ weḷ sevəḷva*, 'having got into a better position';—to come to the acquisition of a certain faculty: *mi ðəuχi i ſarad ən jaun*, 'you will get to speak right'; *may o n du:ad i ſarad* (of a child), 'he is beginning to talk';—similarly of the weather, 'to begin, to come on', etc.: *may hi·n du:ad i vuru*, 'it is coming on to rain'; *may hi·n du:ad ən hayl*, 'the sun is coming out'; *huraχ mi ða:u i godi aɩ ə pnaun*, 'perhaps it will clear up by the afternoon';—'to do' (= *gnẽyd ə ɩro:*): *mi ða:u vel na hevyd*, 'it will do that way too';— impersonally with *hevo*, 'to get on': *syɩ ðo:θ i hevo χi ?*, 'how did you get on?'—with *a*, 'to bring': *dəuχ ag əmba·rel hevo χi*, 'bring an umbrella with you'; *dəuχ a ḷu:y i godi·r pudin ma*, 'bring a spoon to help this pudding'; *dəuχ a vo: i laur*, 'bring it down'; *dəuχ a hi: ən o:l i r van ma*, 'bring it back here'; *ma: ġin i dair davod heb ðu:ad ag u:yn leni*, 'I have three sheep which have had no lambs this year';—the preposition is often omitted and the verb used transitively: *ɩyd i mi χwanag o de:*, 'bring me some more tea'; —with *hy:d aɩ, hy:d i*, 'to find': *mi ·ðẽyθonu o hy:d ɩðo vo rusyɩ*, 'they found it out somehow'. (2) 'to become' (from bad to good): *mi sɩeðis i laur ɩan ɩði ðu:ad ən de:g*, 'I sat down till it cleared up'.— with *o* 'to become of': *be vasa n du:ad o ·honoχi ?*, 'what would have become of you?'; *be ðo:θ o hono vo ɩəbad ?*, 'what has become of it, I wonder?'

dubin, s., dwbing, W.S. [Dawbinge]; 'cow-dung or other substance formerly used for closing up the chinks of an oven' (O.H.).

dubjo, v., dwbío, W.S. [Daube]; 'to stop up the chinks of an oven' [see above].

dubul, adj., dwbl, D.; D.G. iv. 12; 'double': *ən i ðay ðubul*, 'doubled up'.

dudljan, v., 'to loiter, potter about' (Bangor).

duðy, v., dowyddu, dywyddu, etc., D., (of cows) 'to swell with milk before calving, to spring': *pa bry:d vy:ð ə vyuχ ən du:ad a ḷo: ? vy:ð hi ðim ən hi:r ru:an, may hi·n deχra duðy*, 'how long will it be before the cow calves? She won't be long now, she is beginning to spring'.

duibig, adj., dwybig, D., s.v. 'bidens'; G.O. ii. 58. 17, 'having two points': in phrase *ɩroi ən ə ɩɽesi a χwara fon ðuibig* (W.H.), said of some one who is cornered and tries to escape by double-dealing.

duiðjad, s.f., nodwyddiad, 'needleful': *duiðjad o eda*.

dul, adj., dwl ne hurt, W.S. [Dull], 'misty, hazy (opposite of clear): *ma: r dəuyð ən ðul*, 'the weather is hazy';—of persons, 'ignorant'.

dulni, dəlni, s.m., 'mistiness, haziness';—of persons, 'ignorance'.

dumpjan, v., pendwmpian, D., s.v. 'titubanter' : *dumpjan kɔsgy,*
' to doze, to nod the head when sleeping '. Also *pendumpjan.*

dundro, v., dwndrio, B.C. 24. 9, 'to make a noise ' = *kadu turu.*

dundur, s., dwndwr, B.C. 57. 25; P.G.G. 314. 14 ; T.N. 224. 32 ;
dwnndwrr, M.Ll. i. 232. 6 ; Eng. (Dial.) dunder [a loud rumbling
noise like thunder; a reverberating sound], Sc. ' noise, uproar,
hubbub '.

du:r, s.m., pl. *dɒvroð,* dwfr, dwr, D., ' water ' : *du:r kodi,* ' spring ';
du:r lonyð, ' stagnant water ' ; *du:r rhedegog,* ' running water' ; *dur
newyð,* ' spring tide ' (?) J.J. ; *rhedva, rhedjad du:r,* ' watershed ';
du:r berwedig, ' boiling water' ; *ı ədi r sgidja ma ðim ən dal du:r,*
' these boots are not watertight', *rhoi du:r i r arð,* ' to water the
garden' ; *rhoi du:r o:yr am ben peθ,* ' to throw cold water over
something ' (fig.) ; *a ı ben dan ðu:r,* ' in low water ' (fig.) ; *mynd ı
no:l du:r dros avon, kɔrχy du:r dros avon* (prov. exp.), ' to go a long
way for something which can be got close at hand' ; *ı bant ə rhe:d
ə du:r* (prov.), ' money goes where money is '.—*du:r po:yθ,* ' heart-
burn ' : *may du:r po:yθ arna i.*

durdjo, v., ystwrdio, D., s.v. 'objurgo' ; dwrdio, Judges viii. 1,
' to scold' (= *dondjo*) : *durdjo ə bu:yd a ı vytta* (prov. exp.).

durn, s.m., pl. *dɔrna,* dwrn, D. (1) ' fist ': *gwasgy r durn,* ' to
clench the fist'; *gwasgy dɔrna o gumpas ə mhen a sgnɔgy dannað ;—
kay r durn,* ' to close the hand': *kay ı ðurn ar ə pe:θ s gɔno vo
ən ı la:u,* also ' to clench the fist: *paid a kay də ðurn arna i ;—
durn k̆ëyad,* 'clenched fist ' ; *lond durn,* ' handful' ; *χwerθin ən ı
ðurn,* ' to laugh in one's sleeve ' ; *r o:ð ə ŋwynı ən ə nurn i,* ' my
heart leapt to my mouth'. (2) ' handle ' of a door, of a plough, etc. :
dɔrna ə bladyr, ' scythe handles'—*ə durn yχa,* nearest the mower,
ə durn isa, nearest the blade.

durnod, s.m., pl. *dɔrnodja, nodja,* diwrnod, D., ' day': *day ðurnod*
(not *day ðy:ð*), ' two days ' ; *day ðurnod ar o:l i ɡilið,* ' two days
running ' ; *day ne dri: o ðɔrnodja,* ' two or three days ' ; *saıθ njurnod,
nurnod,* ' seven days '; *durnod (ə) varχnad,* ' market day'; *durnod
golχi,* ' washing day' ; *durnod gu:yl,* 'holiday'; *ə durnod duyθa o r
mi:s* ' the last day of the month'; (ə) *durnod o r bla:yn,* ' the other
day ' ; *ə durnod bɔra,* ' the shortest day ' ; *ə durnod hira, huya,* ' the
longest day ' ; *durnod kɔnta r ha:,* ' the first day of summer ', i.e.
May 1 ; *durnod ə knebrun,* ' the day of the funeral '; *durnod bra:v,
po:yθ,* ' a fine, hot day ' ; *ə durnod ə ganuyd vi:,* ' the day I was
born ' ; *vyo vo ðim əmma er s nodja,* ' he has not been here for
days ' ; *əŋ ŋhorf ə durnod,* ' in the course of the day ' ; *ka:yl arjan
heb roid durnod te:g o waiθ am dano vo,* ' to get money without
having done a fair day's work for it '; *gora bo: r durnod gora bo: r
gwaiθ* (prov.), ' the better the day the better the deed '; *rhaid i nı*

vyu meun gobaiθ o hy:d, mi δa:u o n weḷ riu δurnod, ' we must live always in hope; things will be better some day '.

dusin, s.m., pl. *dusina, dusiya*, dwsing, G.O. ii. 30. 16 ; 144. 16, ' dozen': *dusin o ëirja*, ' a dozen words'; *hannar dusin*, 'half a dozen'.

duyaur, s.f., dwyawr, W.Ll. xliii. 108, ' two hours '.

duyfon, s.f., dwyffon, ' two sticks ': *mynd ar ə nuyfon*, ' to walk supported by a stick in each hand' (O.H.).

duylaθ, s.f., dwylath, ' two yards '.

du:yn, dugyd, v., dwyn, D. Fut. S. 1. *duyna, duga*. Pret. S. 1. *dugis, duinis*, 3. *dugoδ, duynoδ*. Pl. 3. *dukson, duynson*. Imperative *duga, duyna ; duguχ, duynuχ*. Pret. Pass. *dəgud* (J.J.), *dugud* (O.H.). (1) ' to bear ', only in a few semi-literary or stereotyped phrases as *du:yn enu*, ' to bear a name '; *du:yn se:l*, ' to show, have zeal '. (2) ' to bring ', also as above : *du:yn i go:*, ' to bring, call to mind '; *anoδ du:yn* (= *tənny*) *dy:n o:δ ar i dəluyθ* (prov.), ' what is bred in the bone comes out in the flesh '. (3) ' to steal ': *mi dənnis i golar o:δ am i uδu vo ṛhag i ru:in δu:yn o*, ' I took his collar off for fear some one should steal it '; *taly ṛ he:n a du:yn ə neμyδ* (prov. exp.), ' to pay for the old and steal the new ', i. e. ' to pay for goods bought previously and take the present purchase on credit '.

duyno, v., difwyno, diwyno, D. ; dwyno, D.F. [vii] 13, [125] 4 ; ' to dirty ' (= *mëyδy*), but scarcely used except euphemistically for small children ' messing ' their clothes. Cf. D., s.v. ' imbulbito '.

duyran, s.m., dwyrain, D., ' east ': *gμynt ə duyran*, ' east wind '; *os kyḷ ə gla:u | o r duyran ə da:u, | os kyḷ ər himδa | o r duyran da:u hiθa ;—duyran am dridja, duyran am dair usnos*,—weather proverbs.

du:ys, adj., dwys, D., ' intense, deep, reserved ': *may m buru n δu:ys*, ' it is raining continuously ' (of fine rain); *tëimlad du:ys*, ' deep feelings '; *y:n du:ys distau*, ' a quiet, reserved person '; *dənas δu:ys*, ' a reserved woman ', e. g. who keeps grief to herself.

duyθa, adj., diwethaf, R.B. 54. 16 ; diwaethaf, D.F. [100] 4, etc. ; diweddaf, D. ; ' last ': *dy gwenar duyθa*, ' last Friday '; *ə tṛo: duyθa*, ' last time '; *r usnos duyθa*, ' last week ', Fr. ' la semaine dernière ', —or ' the last week ' (= *r usnos ola*), Fr. ' la dernière semaine '; *ə durnod duyθa y:n*, ' the very last day '; *r o:yδ ọ m merθyr δuyθa*, ' he was in Merthyr last '.

duyvrayχ, adj., dwyfraich, ' having two arms ': *kadar δuyvrayχ*, ' arm-chair ' (seldom used).

duywaθ, adv., dwywaith, D., s.v. ' bis '; ' twice '; *d o:ys dim duywaθ*, ' there is no doubt about it.'

dy:, interjection expressing surprise.

dy:, adj. and s., pl. *dy:on*, du, D., ' black ': *gwarθag dy:on*, ' black cattle '; *muyar δy:on* 'blackberries'; *gwa:ḷt dy:*, ' dark, black hair '; *kin δy:ad a r vra:n, a r simδa, a χroχon, dy: vel məunan, vel ə radaḷ*, 'as black as a crow', etc. ; *dy: la:s*, 'dark blue, purple' : *gwynab dy: la:s ;*—'dark' : *ma: r g̊ëya dy: ən əmmyl ;—ə dəðja dy:on ba:χ*, 'the days each side of December 21' ;—*may hi meun dy:*, 'she is in mourning'.

dy:aḷ [da:ḷ].

dyalgar ; ·di:·halgar (O.H.), adj., dyallgar, D., 'intelligent'.

dyaḷturjaθ, s., d(e)alldwriaeth, D., s.v. 'intelligentia' ; 'an understanding'.

dyaḷys ; ·di:·halys (O.H.), adj., dyallus, D., 'intelligent'.

dy:ð, s.m., pl. *dəðja*, dŷdd, D., 'day'. Days of the week : *dy sy:l ; dy ḷy:n ; dy maurθ (məurθ) ; dy merχar ; dy:ð jay, divja ; dy gwenar ; dy sadurn.*—*dy ḷyn*, 'on Monday'; *ar ðy ḷyn*, 'on a Monday'; *ə dy:ð huya, bəṛa*, 'the longest, shortest day'; *dy:ð da: i χi*, 'good day'; *ar hy:d ə dy:ð, tṛu: r dy:ð, o hy:d tṛu: r dy:ð*, 'all day long'; *uθ liu dy:ð*, 'by daylight'; *bo:b dy:ð*, 'every day'; *dy:ð g̊ëyavol*, 'a wintry day'; *may r dy:ð ən məstyn, bər·ha:y*, 'the days are getting longer, shorter'; *hannar dy:ð*, 'mid-day'; *adag ə dəðja dy:on baχ*, 'the season of the short, dark days', i.e. on each side of December 21 ; *may o wedi gweld gweḷ dəðja*, 'he has seen better days'.

dygoχ, adj., dugoch, B.C. 65. 15, 'dark red'.

dyḷ, s.m., pl. *diḷja*, dull, D., 'manner, form' : *dyḷ o farad*, 'a manner of speaking, façon de parler'; *mo:ð a dyḷ*, 'way and manner'; *dyḷ gwla:d o farad*, 'a way of speaking in the country'; *wedi nëyd r y:n dyḷ*, 'made in the same manner'; *ən medry newid dyḷ i la:u*, 'able to change his handwriting'; *riu he:n ðyḷ pryðað sy arno vo*, 'he has a melancholy manner'.

dy:n, s.m., pl. *dənjon*, dŷn, D., 'man' (=homo). As distinguished from *gu:r*, *dy:n* is a term of less respect, as e. g. in *he:n u:r* and *he:n ðy:n.*—*dy:n ba:χ kḷu:s (= del) ədi o*, 'he is a nice little man'; *lump o ðy:n te:u*, 'a big fat man'; *dy:n bəχan ba:χ te:u*, 'a tiny little fat man'; *kḷamp o ðy:n maur*, 'a great big man'; *may o n verχ o ðy:n*, 'he is an old woman'; *by:ð ə dy:n ən ḷugy os na vrəfuχ*, 'the fellow will starve if you are not quick'.—Used indefinitely, 'one, people' : *ma: dy:n ən drum ar o:l ḳinjo*, 'one is heavy after dinner'; *dəna ðay ðy:n wedi gləχy n domman ag wedi mynd i u gwla:y*, 'there are two people (both women) who have got wet through and gone to bed'; *kynt (kəvervyθ) day ðy:n na day vənyð* (prov.), 'two people will meet sooner than two mountains', i. e. 'perhaps we shall meet again'.—As euphemism for *dyu* :—*dy:n a i help(j)o !*, 'God help him !'; *dy:n a stərjo !*, 'poor fellow !'; *n eno dy:n !*, or simply *dy:n !*, exclamation of surprise.

dyntyr, s.m., tentur brethyn, W.S. [A tentar]; deintur, D., 'Dentale, instrumentum ad extendendos pannos' ; 'an instrument

consisting of poles for stretching materials after they have been
fulled, tenter' (O.H.); *kay r dẏntẏr* is a place-name at Llanfairfechan.

dẏ:o, v., duo D., ' to blacken ; to become black '.

dẏ:o ; dëyo (Bangor), v., ? diduo, D., ' Dimovere, domo privare ',
' to shell ' (of beans and peas).

dẏ:or, v., dëor, D., ' to hatch ': *r o:yð ǵin i lawar jaun o uẏ:a,
ond ðary dim y:n o ·honynu ðẏ:or,* ' I had a great many eggs, but
not one of them hatched '; *kәvri ә kәujon ǩin ·yðynu ðẏ:or,* ' to count
the chickens before they are hatched '.

dẏ:r, s.m., dûr, D., ' steel ': *nәduyð ðẏ:r,* ' needle '; *höiljon dẏ:r.*
' steel nails put in horse-shoes to grip the ice '.

dẏrol, adj., durawl, D.G. lxiv. 38. (1) ' very strong ': *dẏ:n dẏrol.* (2)
' hard ': *bara dẏrol,* ' hard, stale bread ': *may r bara ma wedi mynd
әn he:n jaun, may o n vu:y dẏrol o lawar.* Hence ' durable, not
wasting ': *menyn dẏrol* (opp. to *darvodedig*).

dẏ:sg, s., dŷsg, D., ' learning ': *may dẏ:sg i u ga:yl o i vedyð i u
ve:ð* (prov.), ' one lives and learns '.

dẏsu, interj.: *dẏsu ba:χ !, dẏsu annul !,* ' good gracious '.

dẏu, s.m., pl. *diuja*, Duw, D., ' God '.

dẏuǩs, interj. (euphemism for *dẏu*), *dẏuǩs !, dẏuǩs annul !*

dẏ:uχ, s.m., ' blackness '.

dẏvn, adj., fem. *devn*, pl. *dәvnjon*, comp. *dәvnaχ*, dwfn, D., ' deep ':
fo:ys vaur ðevn, ' a large deep ditch ' (O.H.); *ǩin ðәvnad a puḷ ǩeri:s,*
' as deep as Pwll Ceris ' (in the Menai Straits); fig. *y:n dẏvn әdi o !,*
' he is a deep one '.—Used also substantively as a ' depth ' of
something, especially in slate quarries. Cf. *te:u.* So also in such
expressions as *trodvað o ðẏvn,* ' a foot in depth '; *rubaθ tebig i
laθan o ðẏvn,* ' something like a yard in depth '; *ḷe: may r dẏvn
muya,* ' where the depth is greatest '.

dә, adj., dy, D., ' thy ': *may dә vam d iſo di,* ' your mother
wants you '; *ar dә o:l di,* ' after you '; *hel ar d o:l !,* ' fetch back !'
(to a sheep-dog) ; *dә da:d a d vam,* ' your father and mother ';
i dә dẏ:, ' to your house '. (Forms like ' a'th ' and ' i'th ' do not
occur in the colloquial language except in stereotyped expressions.
The only example I have heard is *ka:n di benniḷ mu:yn i θ nain,
mi ga:n dә nain i tiθa* (prov.), ' one good turn deserves another '.)
dә is frequently used before finite verbs to reinforce the ensuing
pronoun *di*, as *mi dә gyra i di !,* ' I'll beat you '.

dәbryd, adj., dybryd, D., ' terrible, awful ': *pe:θ dәbryd ; kam-
gәmerjad dәbryd.*

dәd, in *ar dәd,* ' on the verge of ': *ar dәd gnĕyd rubaθ (a dim әn
i nĕyd o).*

dәðjo, v., dyddio, W.S. [Day], ' to dawn '.

dəðjol, adj., dyddiol, S.E., 'day': *əsgol ðəðjol*, 'day school'.

dəðordab, s.m. Cf. didordep, M.A. ii. 346. 28. A book word, recently revived in the form 'dyddordeb' (cf. O.P.), but used quite frequently as an equivalent of 'interest' in such phrases as *kəmmyd dəðordab meun*, 'to take an interest in'.

dəðorol, adj., dyddorol, S.E., 'interesting'. See above.

dəfëia, v., 'I defy', in the phrase *mi dəfëia i di i nëyt hənny*, 'I defy you to do it'; also 'I assure', as *mi dəfëia i di mai rvi: pi:a hi*, 'I assure you that it is mine.'

dəfryn, s.m., pl. *dəfrənnoð*, dyffryn, D., 'valley': *lili r dəfryn*, 'lily of the valley'.

dəgado, in phrase *dəgado paub !*, i. e. 'Duw gadwo (gato) pawb !', excl. of surprise (J.J.).

dəgyn, adj., dygn, D. ; dygyn, P.G.G. 101. 18; 106. 26; 'persistent': *dy:n dəgyn diwid*, 'a persistent, industrious man'; *gwëiθjo n ðəgyn tui r hy:d ə dy:ð* (O.H.), 'to stick to it hard all day';— *gwëiθjo n ðəgyn o ola i ola*.

dəgəmmod, v., dygymmod, D. (1) 'to suit, agree with': *t ədi o ðim ən dəgəmmod a vi:*, 'it does not agree with me' (e. g. of food); *ədi o n dəgəmmod a i le: ?*, 'is he suiting himself to his position?' (2) 'to make the best of': *may r dəwyð ən ·a·nivir, ond rhaid i ni ðəgəmmod a vo:*.

dɐ·hëig, adj., deheuig, D., s.v. 'dexter', 'rotundè'. (1) 'skilful, dexterous': *dy:n dɐ·hëig am i waiθ = gnëyd po:b pe:θ o: ðeθa*. (2) 'tactful, politic'.

dəhëyol, adj., deheuol, D., s.v. 'meridionalis'; 'southern': *r oxor ðəhëyol*.

dɐ·ka·y, s.m., Eng. decay, 'consumption': *nëiθ o ðim magy dɐ·ka·y*, said of a healthy, cheerful person.

dəksun = təbəksun, v., tebygaswn: *dəksun i*, 'I should think'.

dəxməgy, v., dychymmygu, D., 'to imagine': *dəxməgy bo xi ŋ gweld dy:n*.

dəxryn, v., dychrynu, D. Pret. *dəxrənnis*, *xrənnis*, 'to terrify, startle'; 'to be terrified, startled': *dəxryn atto vo*, 'to be frightened of him'; *ðary xi nəxryn i n ovnaduy*, 'you startled me terribly'; *mi xrənnis*, 'you gave me a fright'.

dəxryn, s.m., pl. *dəxryn·vëyð*, dychryn, D., 'a terror': *r o:ð o n ðəxryn i baub*.

dəxrənlyd, adj., dychrynllyd, T.N. 208. 20, 'terrible': *golug, nada dəxrənlyd ;—dəxrənlyd o o:yr*, 'terribly cold'.

dəxəmmig, s.m., pl. *dəxməgjon*, dychymmyg, D., 'imagination, delusion'.

dəlad [dle:d].

dəlanwad, s.m., dylanwad, D., s.v. 'influentia'; 'influence'.

dəlanwady, v., dylanwadu, S.E., 'to influence': *ma: r dɤwyð ən dəlanwady ·arnynu rusyt*, 'the weather exercises an influence over them somehow'.

dəledsuyð, dledsuyð, s., pl. *dəledsuyða*, dyledswydd, D., s.v. 'officium'; 'duty': *dilin i ðəledsuyða*, 'to fulfil, perform one's duties'; *dəledsuyða ïëyly:að*, 'family prayers'; *kadu dledsuyð*, 'to have family prayers'.

dəlivo, v. dylifo, D., 'to stream': *r oy:ð ə χwy:s ən dəlivo vel gla:u iṛana*, 'the perspiration was streaming down like thunder rain'; *may nu n dəlivo i r kɤvarvød*, 'a stream of people are going to the meeting'.

dəljun, v.   Imperfect of obsolete dylu, D., 2. *dəlat*, 3. *dəla*. Pl. 1. *dəlan*, 2. *dəlaχ*, 3. *dəlan*. 'I ought'; Plup. *dəlsun, lasun*, 'I ought to have, I ought': *mi ðəla gəχun ne mi ëïθ ən no:s arno vo*, 'he ought to start or he will be caught by the darkness'; *dəna vel ə dəla vo:d*, 'that is how it ought to be'; *mi ðəljun inna ga:yl və suppar beḷaχ*, 'it is quite time I had my supper too'; *mi ðəla χïθa nëyd sylu ono vo*, 'you ought to pay attention to him too'; *ma: peθa vel na n darvod a darvod ðəlan hevyd*, 'things like that are dying out and they ought to die out too'; *mi ·ðəlsanu roid i χi ðigon*, 'they ought to give you enough'; *mi ·lasanu i roid o iðo vo heb iðo vo ovyn*, 'they ought to have given it to him without him having to ask for it'; *t oy:ð o ðim əŋ ka:yl ə peθa lasa vo ga:yl*, 'he did not get what he ought to have got'.

dəly, v., 'to become hazy' (of the weather): *may hi n dəly*.   Cf. *dul.*

dəly:an, s.f., pl. *dəlyanod;* (*də*)*ḷy:od* (O.H.), dylluan and tylluan, D.; cf. W.B., col. 109. 28–31, 'owl'; also called *deryn korf: r o:yð ər he:n bobol ən arvar mynd i gəmmyd i kəmmyn uθ glu:ad ə ðəḷy:an əŋ gwiχjan* (J.J.), 'old people used to go and receive the sacrament when they heard the owl hooting'.—Used of human beings, men or women, 'one who wanders about at night' or 'one who is always asleep' or merely 'a fool': *ḷy:od o ðənjon* (O.H.).

dəmma (often *təmma*), adv., dyma, 'here is, here are', Fr. 'voici': *dəmma ḷe ·by:onu n ṭoi ə bora ina*, 'this is where they were ploughing this morning'; *dəmma gənnur maur am roi tippin o lo: ar ə ta:n !*, 'what a fuss about putting a bit of coal on the fire !';—often used in graphic narration, e. g. *dəmma ðëydoð o . . ., dəmma o:yð o n dëyd . . .*, 'here he was saying'; *dəmma hi n niul arna i*, 'here I was, caught in the mist'; *dəmma vo atta i*, 'here he comes up to me'; *dəmma r ḷëidar i vjaun i r ḷoft*, 'up comes the thief into the bedroom'; *dəmma ðənas i vjaun i r kwarvod gweði, a dəmma hi ar i glinja*, 'in comes a woman into the prayer meeting and down she goes on her knees'.

dəmyno, v., damuno, rectius dymuno, D., 'to wish'.

dəmynol. adj., dymunol, D., 'desirable, charming, comely' : *ə verχ ivaŋk harð ðəmynol,* 'the good-looking, charming young woman' ;— *golug dəmynol ar ə wyhyr.*

dəna (often *tə̃na*), *na,* adv., dyna, D., 'there is, there are', Fr. 'voilà' : *dəna r inig resum sy ǵin i,* 'that is the only reason I have' ; *dəna vo:, dəna hi:,* 'that's it' ; *ela wi:r mai dəna be sy: ond bod ni ðim əŋ gubod,* 'perhaps that is what it is, only that we don't know' ; *dəna r dru:g,* 'that's the worst of it' ; *dəna ǵimmint a sy:,* 'that is all there is' ;—often used in graphic narration, e. g.—*a dəna vo ŋ gwiḷljo,* 'and there he was, in a rage'.

. *dənas,* s.f. [pl. *merχaid*], dynes, C.C.M. 142. 1, 'woman' (less polite than *gwraig*): *dənas ba:χ ðel,* 'a nice little woman' ; *dənas aḷy:og,* 'a capable woman' ; *dənas (dinas) benvelan,* 'yellowhammer' (Emberiza citrinella).

dənewad, s., pl. *dənewid,* dyniewed, D., s.v. 'juvencus' ; 'a young heifer or bull between one year and eighteen months old '.

dənwarad, dəwarad, v., dynwared, D., 'to imitate' (but rather in the sense of 'to mimic' than in a good sense). Cf. *gwatar.*

dənyn, s.m., dynyn, S.E.*, 'a conceited fellow' : *may hun a hun ən he:n ðənyn garu ; r u:ti n daŋos də hy:n ən he:n ðənyn garu.*

dərməgy, dirməgy, v., dirmygu, D., 'to mock, make fun of' = *sbẽitjo, gwatwor, dənwarad, ǵambljo.*

dərnad, s.m., dyrnaid, D., 'handful' : *dərnad o bre:s,* 'a handful of money'.

dərnod, s.f., dyrnod, D., 'a blow with the fist' : *dərnod ar vo:n ə gly:st ;—dərnod gəlaθ,* a sheep's ear-mark, so called.

dərnol (I.W.; J.J.), *dərnwil* (I.W.), *dərnil* (O.H.), s.pl. ; sing. *dərnolan* (J.J.), *dərnol* (O.H.), dyrnfol, D., pl. dyrnfyl, but dyrnfolau, s.v. 'manica'; 'gloves used while cutting thorns': *pa:r o ðərnil* (O.H.).

dərnur, s.m., dyrnwr, D., 'thresher'. Also 'threshing machine'.

dərnwað, s.f., pl. *dərnveði,* dyrnfedd, D., s.v. 'bipalmis'; 'hand' (about four inches) used in measuring the height of horses: *du i n meðul ə gnẽiθ i ŋ glos jaun i ðərnwað ar bəmθag,* 'I think she'll be very nearly sixteen hands'.

dərny, v., dyrnu, D., 'to thresh': *indʒan ðərny,* 'threshing machine'.

dərwinan [*derwinan*].

dərys, adj., dyrys, D., 'perplexing, complicated'.

dəsǵẽidjaθ, s.m., dysgeidiaeth, D., 'doctrine'.

dəsglad, s.f., pl. *dəsglẽidja,* dysglaid, S.E.*, dyscled, M.Ll. i. 140. 16, 'dishful'.

dəsgur, s.m., dysgwr, S.E.*, 'learner'.

dǝsgy, v., dysgu, D. Pret. S. 1. *dǝsgis, disgis.* Imperative *dǝsga.*
(1) 'to teach': ·*tasaχi n veŋaχ mi vasa n haus ǝχ dǝsgy,*' if you
were younger it would be easier to teach you '; *r o:yn ǝn dǝsgy r
δavad bori* (prov. exp.), "teaching one's grandmother". (2) 'to
learn ': *dǝsgy o r gwraiδ,* 'to learn thoroughly '; *dǝsgy i greft,* ' to
learn his trade '; *dǝsgy aḷan,* 'to learn off, to learn by heart '.

dǝtſas, s.f., Eng. duchess, 'an imperious woman ': *he:n dǝtſas
ovnaduy.*

dǝvais, s.f., defeys, W.S. [Deuyse]; dyfais, M.Ll. ii. 39. 19 ;
D.P.O. 54. 10. (1) 'device, invention, contrivance ': *dǝvais δa:
jaun,* 'a very good invention '. (2) 'intent '; 'contriving faculty ':
dǝvais δru:g, 'evil intent '; *iuſo i δǝvais i δrǝgjoni,* 'to contrive
evil '.

dǝval, adj., dyfal, D., 'persistent, steady, unremitting ': *χwiljo n
δǝval ;—dǝval uθ hel arjan ;—ǝn disgul ǝn δǝval am lǝθyr,* 'anxiously
expecting a letter '.

dǝvaluχ, s.m., dyfalwch, D., 'persistence'.

dǝvaly, v., dyfalu, D., 'imagine, conjecture ': *welis i rotſun δǝvaly
a dǝvëiſo,* 'I never saw such cudgelling of brains '; *vedrun i δim
dǝvaly be o:yδ o n i veδul,* 'I could not imagine what he was
thinking of '.

dǝvary, v., edifaru, D., 'to regret ': *δary mi δim dǝvary,* 'I did
not regret it '.

dǝvëiſo, v., dyfeisio, G.R. (5) 12 ; B.C. 15. 1. (1) 'contrive,
devise ': *dǝvëiſo pu:y forδ i χ ṛhuydo χi,* 'to contrive how to ensnare
you '; also, *dǝvëiſo peθ.* (2) 'invent ': *dǝvëiſo pe:θ gweḷ nag o:yδ
·gǝnynu o r bla:yn,* 'to invent something better than they had before ';
ma: nu n dǝvëiſo po:b ma:θ o beθa ǝ dǝδja ma, 'they invent all kinds
of things these days '. (3) 'to make up ': *dǝvëiſo stori heb vo:d ǝn
wi:r.* (4) 'imagine ': *vedra i δim dǝvëiſo ḷe ma:y hi,* 'I can't
imagine where it is '. Cf. also *dǝvaly.* (5) 'to think of ': ·*tasaχi
m peryd i mi dǝvëiſo nu,* 'if you made me think of them for myself
(they would not come to my mind) '. (6) 'guess ': *tṛi:o dǝvëiſo n
hi:r jaun,* 'to try and guess a long time'.

dǝverol, diverol, adj., diferol, Cant. v. 13, 'dropping, dripping ':
ǝn ly:b dǝverol.

dǝveryd, diveryd, v. diferu, D., 'to drop ': *ma: r vargod ǝn dǝveryd,*
'the eaves are dripping '; *ma: nu n dǝveryd o χwy:s,* 'they are
streaming with perspiration ';—used very frequently in an adverbial sense: *may o wedi glǝχy n dǝveryd,* 'he is wet through ';
r o:δ ǝ ŋwa:ḷḷ ǝn ly:b dǝveryd, 'my hair was dripping wet '; *ma: nu
ŋ gwëiθjo n χwy:s dǝveryd pen ·vǝδuχi ǝn ǝ golug,* 'they work till they
are streaming with perspiration so long as you are in sight '.

dǝveryn, diveryn, s.m., pl. *dǝverjon,* diverjon, diferyn, G.O. ii.

276. 25, 'drop': *d ɔvoð o ðim dɔveryn wedyn,* 'he never drank a drop (of intoxicating liquor) afterwards'; *po:b diveryn,* 'every drop'; *heb ðɔveryn o la:u.*—Cf. *devni.*

dɔveθa, dveθa, v., difetha, D., s.v. 'consumo'; 'to waste; to spoil': *paid a dveθa matſis,* 'don't waste matches'; *dveθa plentyn (hevo möyθa),* 'to spoil a child'; *may y:n o ·honynu wedi kubul ðiveθa,* 'one of them is quite spoilt'.

dɔveθdod, veθdod, s.m., difethdod, 'destruction, waste'.

dɔveθgar, veθgar, adj., difethgar, 'wasteful': opp. to *kɔntṛivjol, forðjoL*

dɔvluyð, adj., dwyflwydd, D., s.v. 'biennis'; 'two years old': *ɔn ðɔvluyð o:yd.*

dɔvndur, s.m., dyſnder, D.; dyfndwr, C.C.M. 120. 32, 'depth': *r o:ð na ðɔvndur o igjan ḻa:θ,* 'there was a depth of twenty yards'.

dɔvndgun, s.m., dyſn, influenced by Eng. dungeon ?, 'a deep hole or ravine; gulf, abyss' (but more familiar than the English words): *sɔrθjo i r dɔvndgun;—dɔvndgun plum,* 'a yawning gulf'. Cf. *ĕigjon.*

dɔvn·ha:y, v., dyfnhau, D., 'to deepen'.

dɔvny, v., diddyfnu, D., 'to wean'.

dɔvrduyst, s., dyfrdwst, 'a disease of cattle, strangury' (J.J.).

dɔvrği, s.m., pl. *dɔvrguns,* dyfrgi, D., 'otter': *ɔn ly:b vel dɔvrği,* 'like a drowned rat'.

dɔvrjo, v., dyfrio, 'to water' (of the eyes).

dɔwalği, dualği, s., *ɔmlað vel dɔwalği,* 'to fight fiercely' (LW.).

dɔwedjad, s.m., dywediad, S.E.*, 'saying': *he:n ðɔwedjad,* 'an old saying'.

dga:d, s.f., Eng. jade, opprobrious epithet for a woman: also *dgadan.*

dgak, Eng. Jack, *dgak sboŋk = robin sboŋkjur,* 'grasshopper': *dgak lantar,* 'will-o'-the-wisp', also called *dgak sboŋk* (J.J.); *dgak do:,* 'jackdaw' (Corvus monedula).

dgakmor, s.m., 'sycamore'. (O.H. always uses *sarnan.*)

dgaŋglar, s.m., pl. *dgaŋglars,* 'one who gossips, a loiterer at a street corner, etc.'

dgaŋgljo, v., Eng. (Dial.) jangle; O.F. jangler, 'to gossip, loiter': *dgaŋgljo o gumpas.*

dgar, tſar, s.f., 'jar'.

dgarjad, s.f., 'jarful'.

dgebo, s., 'the devil, bogy': *mɔn dgebo.*

dgegyn, s. Cf. Eng. (Dial.) jag [a small load of coal, hay, etc.], 'a small load', e.g. *dgegyn o dail.*

dgëinjo, v., 'to join'.

dge:l, s.f., geol, W.B. col. 172. 16; G.C. 132. 5; géol, D.; siêl, B.C. 34. 11; géol, D.; 'jail, prison'.

dgelaiſ, s.pl., gellhesg, D., 'flags' (Iris pseud-acorus). For other forms cf. *kelaiſ*.

dgeljo, v., 'to put in jail'.

dgelus, adj., 'jealous'.

dgempar, s.f., pl. *dgempars*, 'jumper': an instrument used in slate quarries for boring holes. There are two kinds—*dgempar uru* and *dgempar vanu*.

dgerman, *dgermon*, s.m., Eng. journeyman, 'a man employed by the day by quarrymen for splitting and dressing slates'.

dgero, s.m., 'a tough customer', I.W. = *heːn walχ* (J.J.); *riu heːn dgero gurjon* (O.H.).

dgest, *dest*, *gest*, adv., Eng. just. Cf. Eng. (Dial.) jest, Shr., Oxf., Som. (1) 'on the point of, all but': *du i dgest am vynd i laur*, 'I am just going down'; *r ədu i dgest əm barod*, 'I am just ready'; *dgest i lond o*, 'just full'; *may r amsar dgest ar ben*, 'the time is just up'; *r ədu i dgest a ɫeθy*, 'I am almost sinking' (with the weight); *r ədu i dgest a gola iſo diːod*, 'I am almost ablaze for a drink'; *ruːan dgest*, 'just now'. (2) 'exactly': *dgest r y: vaːθ*, 'just the same' (= *ən injon*).

dgëynar, s.m., pl. *dgëynerja(ı)d*, 'joiner'.

dgëynt, s.f., pl. *dgëintja*. Cf. Eng. geynt(t)e, 15th cent., Dial. jeint, 'joint': *rhoi karag dros ə dgëintja*, in building.

dgilifriſ [*ˌsilifriſ*].

dgob, s.f., pl. *dgobsys*, 'job': *gwëiθjo ar dgob*, 'to work by the piece'.

dgob, s., '? mass': *sərθjo n yːn dgob*, 'to fall flop, to fall full length'; —*maː r plant wedi gnëyd ə davað ən yːn dgob i ɡiːd*. Cf. 'Nes âi 'r ddwy lob yn job i'r jail'. C.—Annogaeth i bawb feindio ei fusnes ei hunan.

dgob, *dgobyn*, s., siobyn, D., 'apex, apiculus'; 'a tuft' (of hair, etc.): *riu dgobyn ar i dalkan o* (I.W.).

dgobjo, v., Eng. job = *dobjo*.

dgokki, s.m., Eng. jockey, 'a horse-breaker' = *torur kəfəla*. ['Jockey' is so used in Shropshire.]

dgoχ, s.m. (1) 'a drink, draught, gulp': *dgoχ o levriθ*, 'a drink of milk'; *i laur a voː yːn dgoχ*, 'down with it at one gulp'. (2) 'a spurt of liquid': *təwaɫt dgoχ o hono vo*;—*dgoχ o böiri*.

dgoχjo, v. (1) 'to spill, spurt over': *may r duːr ən dgoχjo*, 'the water is spilling, spurting over'. (2) 'to squirt': *dgoχjo duːr o i ɡeːg am ben ə bobol*, 'to squirt water from one's mouth over people' (O.H.). (3) 'to gulp': *dgoχjo bytta* = *ɫeukjo* (O.H.).

dgolihəutjo, *dgolihöitjo*, v., 'to fool about, to gallivant'.—*mynd i laur i r dreː i əgolihəutjo*. Cf. *gwilihoban*.

dgolpan, s.f., 'a silly wench': *ha:n dgolpan wirjon.*

dgolpjo, v., 'to play the fool' (of women).

dgo:y, s.m., Eng. chew (?) (cf. *ʃo:y*, Eng. shew), 'lump': *dgo:y o gɔvlaθ*, 'a lump of toffee'; *dgo:y o vakko ɔŋ ýhi:l i vo:χ*, 'a plug of tobacco in his cheek'; *du i ẟɩm ɔn maljo dgo:y o vakko ɔno vo*, 'I don't care a fig for him'.

dgu:al, s.m., pl. *dgu:als*, 'ear-ring'.

dgug, s.f., pl. *dgugja*, 'jug'.

dgɔgjad, s.f.; pl. *dgɔğёidja*, 'jugful'.

dgɔkko, call to poultry.

e

e, e:, in *na:ʃ e*, nag ё, D.; Mid.W. nac ef; cf. W.B. col. 67. 17, 'no' [*na*]; and in *nɩ e: ?*, *ɩ e: ?*, onid ё ?, used in interrogations expecting the answer 'yes' [*nɩ*].

e:, interj., *ɔdi o n ẟa: ?*   *e:, odjaθ o ẟa !*

ebi̥l, s.m., pl. *ebiljon, pi̥ljon*, ebill, D., 'borer, drill' (used in quarries, etc.).—Sometimes a greenhorn at a quarry is sent to ask for an *ebi̥l dёydu̥l.*

ebol, s.m., pl. *boljon*, ebol, D., 'foal' (after weaning): *r u:ti vel ebol blu:yẟ !*, said of some one who frisks and plays about like a child; *dail karn ebol*, 'colt's foot' (Tussilago Farfara).

ebra, v., eb, heb, D.; cf. heb yr ynteu, R.B. 245. 13; eb yr mi, W.S. [Quod I]; heb 'r ef, D.F. [172] 9; ebr, B.C. 7. 13; 10. 9, etc.; in *ebra vi, ebra vo*, 'said I, said he' (only used by old people).

ebri̥l, s., Ebrill, D., 'April': *mɐurθ a la:ẟ, ebri̥l a vliŋ* (prov.), 'March slays, April flays'; *ɩ ɔdi ёïra ɔn ebri̥l ẟɩm ɔn sevy̥l mu:y na seviθ u:y ar ben ebi̥l* (*ɩɟosol*), 'snow in April lies no longer than an egg will lie on the top of a drill (crowbar)'; *sai ёïra ɔn ebri̥l mu:y na ɟhɔnjon mɐun ɟhidi̥l* (O.H.), 'snow in April lasts no longer than oatmeal in a sieve'; *li̥gad ebri̥l = dail ɔ pёils*, 'the lesser celandine' (Ranunculus Ficaria).

ebuχ, s., ebwch, D.; B.C. 56. 12; C.C.M. 163. 17; 'a strong effort': *daχi ẟɩm ɔn ɩɟi:o, daχi ẟɩm ɔŋ gnёyd ebuχ i nёyd o*, 'you are not trying: you are not making a real effort to do it';—*mi ẟo:θ vel ebuχ ag mi ɩɟawoẟ hi i laur* (O.H.), expressing a sudden unex-pected action.

eda, s.f., pl. *davaẟ*, edau, D., 'thread; woollen yarn': *eda ẟy:, ʒwen*, 'black, white thread'; *eda nɐduyẟ*, 'thread'; *eda gɔvrodaẟ,* 'linen thread'; *eda drislig, eda dair gaiŋk,* 'thread of three strands'; *davað gwëy,* 'wool', e. g. for knitting; *davað gwaun,* 'gossamer'; *dirwin davað,* 'to wind a skein'; *matja davað,* 'woollen mats'; *dɘuχ a nɘduyð ag eda i mi roi bottum arno vo,* 'bring a needle and thread for me to put a button on it'; *ɾhouχ ɘr eda ɘn ɘ nɘduyð,* 'thread the needle'; *wedi gwisgo at ɘr eda,* 'threadbare'.

edliu, v., edliw, D.   Pret. S. 3. *edliujoð,* 'to reproach, upbraid': *edliu i ðyːn am . . ., edliu drɘgjoni dyːn.*

ednod, s.pl., ednogyn, D., 'culex, musca', and s.v. 'scabro'; 'eggs of flies' (in meat, etc.) (J.J.): *buru ednod,* 'to lay eggs' (of insects) (O.H.).

edraχ, v., edrych, D.   Fut. S. 1. *drɘχa.*   Imperative *edraχ, drɘχa* ; *drɘχuχ.*   (1) 'to look (at), to throw glances, to glance': *edraχ ɘn aru arni hi,* 'to look intently at her'; *may r plant ɘn driŋo i vɘny ag ɘn edraχ dros ɘ klauð,* 'the children are climbing up and looking over the wall'; *edraχ tɾuː r gwryːχ,* 'to look through the hedge'; *edraχ dan i sgavaḷ,* 'to knit the brows, to frown (upon)'; *edraχ ɘn ḷɘgad ɘ gëinjog,* 'to weigh every penny carefully'. (2) 'to look, appear': *daχi n edraχ ɘn weḷ,* 'you look better'; *may r oraing ɘn edraχ ɘn syːr,* 'the orange looks sour'; *may hi meun öydran garu ag edraχ mor ðaː,* 'she looks very well considering her great age'. (3) 'to make inspection, to see': *dɘuχ i edraχ ta, os na ·χöiljuχi,* 'come and see then if you don't believe'; *wedi tɾiːo gnëyd poːb peːθ edraχ naːnu godi,* 'having tried to do everything to see whether they would get up'; *edraχ ar ɘχ oːl χi ɘdu i, i edraχ sy daχi n bihavjo oði kartɾa,* 'I am looking after you to see how you behave yourself away from home'. (4) with *am,* 'to see, visit': *mynd i edraχ am dano vo,* 'to go to see him'; *mi ðoːθ o i edraχ am ɘ nhaid,* 'he came to see my grandfather';—also 'to look for' (= *χwiljo am*).   (5) with *ar oːl,* 'to see after, look after': *may o n edraχ ar oːl i breːs ɘn jaun,* 'he looks well after the money'.

edrɘχjad, s.m., edrychiad, D., s.v. 'facies'; 'appearance': *o ran edrɘχjad,* 'as far as appearances are concerned'.

efaθ, s.m., pl. *efëiθja,* ephaith, G.R. [194] 14; effaith, R.; 'effect'.

efëiθjo, fëiθjo, v., epheithio, G.R. [194] 14; effeithio, S.E., 'to have an effect upon, to affect': *maː r ḷëyad ɘn efëiθjo ar anivëiljad* (J.J.), 'the moon has an effect upon animals'; *i ɘdi o ðim ɘn efëiθjo ar ɘχ bytta,* 'it does not affect your appetite'; *may o wedi fëiθjo n aru arno vo,* 'it has had a great effect upon him'.

efëiθjol, adj., effeithiol, S.E.*, 'effectual': *wedi weḷa vo n efëiθjol.*

efro, adj.. effro, D., 'awake': *may o n efro ;—ɾhuŋ kɘsgy ag efro,* 'between sleeping and waking'.

egar, adj., egyr, W.S. [Aeygre] ; eger, C.L.C. ii. 23 ; egr, D.,
' bad, rough, cold ' (applied esp. to weather): *durnod egar jaun*,
' a very cold, rough day'; *dɜrnod egar*, 'a painful blow ' ; *ſarad ɜn
egar*, ' to speak roughly, saucily '.

eǵin, s.pl., sing. *eǵinin*, egin, D., ' sprouts, shoots ' : *eǵin main ɜr
y:d*, ' tender shoots of corn ' ; *eǵin krɔvjon*, ' healthy sprouts ', e. g.
of potatoes appearing above the ground.

eǵino, *ǵino*, v., egino, D., ' to sprout ', e. g. of corn.

egluys, s.f., pl. *egluisi*, *egluysyð*, eglwys, D., ' church ': *daχi n
mynd i r egluys ?*, ' do you go to church?'; *may o wedi iroi i r
egluys*, ' he has gone over to the church ' ; *ǩin dlottad a ļgodan
egluys*, ' as poor as a church mouse '.

egluysrag, s.f., eglwyswraig, S.E., ' churchwoman '.

egluysur, s.m., eglwyswr, D., ' churchman '.

eglyr, adj., eglur, D., ' clear ' : *ſarad ɜn eglyr*, 'to speak clearly ' ;
may n eglyr (= *amlug*) *i mi*, 'it is clear to me '. Cf. *amlug*.

eglyro, v., egluro, D., ' to explain '.

egni, s., egni, D., ' effort, vigour ' : *gnëyd i egni*, 'to do one's
best ' ; *a i ho:ļ egni*, *nerθ i egni*, ' with all one's might '.

egras, s.m. Eng. (Dial.), ee-grass, ea-grass, eye-grass, hay-
grass, bee-grass [aftermath, after-grass]. Cf. also N.E.D., s.v.
' eegrass '. Applied to grass, etc., one year old : *ka:y o egras
blu:yð ; devaid ɜm pori r egras ɜn ɜ gwanuyn.* Also used adjectively,
gwair egras, ' hay one year old ' ; *kļovar egras.*—(J.J.; O.H.)

egry, v., egru, D., s.v. ' muceo '; 'to go sour ': *may r ļevriθ
wedi egry*, ' the milk has gone sour '. Also ' to go bad ' (of
butter, etc.).

egryn, s., (?) *egryn, D., ' timor, tremor, trepidatio '. Cf. M.F.,
s.v. *i o:ys na ðim egryn o wynt hëiðju* (O.H.) = *evlyn*.

eguyd, s.m., pl. *eguydyð*, egwyd, D., ' fetlock '.

eguyl, s., egwyl, R., ' lull ': *mi a: i ɜn ɜr egul ma*, 'I will go
during this lull '; *tasa eguyl i mi vynd*, ' if the storm abated
sufficiently for me to go '; *na:θ i ðim egul o himða hëiðju i nëyd
dim*, ' there has not been a moment's lull in the weather to-day to
do anything '.

egwan, adj., egwan, D., ' weak, delicate ': *plant egwan*.

ëidjon, s.m., pl. *ëidjona*, eidion, D., ' bullock '.

ëidrol, s., eidral, D. (Bot.) : *dail r ëidrol*, ' ground ivy ' (Glechoma
hederacea).

ëiðil, *iðil ; yvyl* (O.H.), adj., eiddil, D., ' spare, slender, frail '.

ëiðo, s.m., eiddo, D., ' property ': *dy:n ag ëiðo gɜno vo*, ' a man of

property'; *may o wedi kayl kэmmyd i ëiðo o:ð arno vo*, 'he got
deprived of his property'; *gwasgary r ëiðo ar o:l maru*, 'to dissi-
pate (some one's) property after his death'; *ëiðo i vi эdi o*, 'he is
my property'.

ëigjon, s.m., eigion, D., 'depths': *i ëigjon isa r mo:r*, 'to the
depths of the sea'; *эɲ ɲwëylod ëigjon э mo:r ; wedi sэrθjo i r ëigjon,
wedi sэrθjo dros graig i r ëigjon ;—mi ɪɽawa i o i ëigjon r avon ma*,
'I'll knock him to the very bottom of the river'; *эɲ ɣhanol (эm
mhervað) ëigjon э mэnэðoð*, 'in the very heart of the mountains'.
(All O.H.).

ëil, s.f., in *ëil vaun*, 'a shed near a house for keeping peat'.

ëilðyð, s., eilddydd, 'second day': *bo:b dy:ð ne bo:b эn ëilðyð*
(O.H.).

ëiljad, s.m., eiliad, 'moment': *meun ëiljad*, 'in a moment'.

ëiljan, dyw gwyl Elian, W.S. [Hyllarys day]: *aur vaur kalan* (or
jonaur), *du:y u:yl ëiljan a θair u:yl vair, os na by:ð hi n bedair*, 'the
days lengthen by a good hour by the first of January, two by
St. Elian's day, three if not four by the Annunciation'. (*ëiljan*
I.W.; *ëirjal* O.H.).

ëiljo, v., eilio, D., 'to wattle'.

ëilwaθ, adv., eilwaith, D., 'a second time': *pɽyn he:n, pɽyn
ëilwaθ, pɽyn newyð, ve bery byθ* (prov.), 'buy old, buy again : buy
new, it will last for ever'.

ëinjos, s., einioes, D., s.v. 'vita'; 'life': *эn vэ ëinjos (myu) welis
i э va:θ be:θ o r bla:yn*, 'I never saw such a thing before in my
life'.

ëira, s.m., eira, D., 'snow': *buru ëira*, 'to snow'; *may hi n
magy ëira*, 'snow is coming'; *may r ëira n de:u, druχys, may hi n
ëira maur*, 'the snow is deep'; *may n plyo ëira maur*, 'it is snow-
ing large flakes'; *du i ɲ kovjo tɽi ëira maur*, 'I remember three great
snow-falls'; *ar ëira maur*, 'in time of deep snow'; *pel̦an ëira*,
'snow-ball'; *kasag ëira*, 'a (rolled) snow-ball'; *knu:d o ëira*, 'a
fall of snow'; *kodan ëira*, 'puff-ball'; (côd euraid (?) D., coden
hyred, O.P.); *adar (эr) ëira*, 'fieldfares' (Turdus pilaris); *χwiljo
am ëira l̦onað*, 'to be on a fruitless quest'.

ëirin, s.pl., sing. *ëiran*, eirin, D. (1) 'plums': *ëirin mo:χ*, 'haws'
(Bangor); *ëirin perθi, ëirin ba:χ tagy*, 'sloes'. (2) 'testicles'.

ëirjas (*ëirjos* O.H. sometimes), s., eirias and eirias-dan, D., a word
without definite meaning, expressive of heat or flame: *tendja di,
may n ëirjos bo:yθ* (O.H.), 'mind, it is burning hot' (but not
necessarily red-hot); *. . . a vo n ëirjas o r ta:n* (O.H.), '. . . though
it was hot from having been just taken out of the fire'; *эn y:n
ëirjas o da:n* (O.H.), 'one mass of fire' (speaking of the phosphor-
escent sea); *ma na ëirjas o da:n*, 'there is a splendid fire' (i.e. in
the grate).

ẽirjaθ, s., aeriaeth, C.C.M. 214. 7, 'inheritance' = *pe:θ ar o:l ru:in*.

ẽirjo, v., 'to air'.

ẽirlau, s.m., 'sleet'.

ẽisin, s., eisin, D., (in bolting) 'the roughest part of the flour' = *bran; ẽisin si:l*, 'husks produced in purifying oats'.

ẽiθa, adj., adv. eithaf, D. (1) before a noun or adjective, 'very good, excellent, splendid; very, perfectly': *may n ẽiθa kaŋor*, 'it is very good advice'; *mi vasa n ẽiθa pe:θ i ti vynd mo*, 'it would be a splendid thing for you to go there'; *ẽiθa gwaiθ a vo:*, 'serve him right'; *may hanny n ẽiθa gw:ir*, 'that is very true'; *ẽiθa le:g*, 'perfectly fair'; *may hanny n ẽiθa da: ond . . .*, 'that is all very well, but . . .'; so with *ģin* and a pronoun: *mi o:δ an ẽiθa ģin i nad o:yδ*, 'I was very glad it was not'. (2) standing by itself 'pretty good, well enough': *o:δ o n ẽiθa*, 'it was pretty good'; *edraχ an ẽiθa*, *gubod an ẽiθa*, 'to look, to know well enough'.—Substantively: *welis i ẽiθa vo*, 'I have seen his worst'.

ẽiθin, s.pl., sing. *ẽiθinan*, eithin, D., 'gorse': *lu:yn ẽiθin*, 'gorse-bush'; *tumpaθ ẽiθin*, 'a dwarfed rounded gorse-bush—the effect of having been cropped by sheep' (so O.H., but the latter is often used for gorse-bush in general, I.W.); *silod ẽiθin*, 'small stunted gorse'.

ẽiθinog, adj., eithinog, L.G.C., 52 [40] 'abounding in gorse'.

ekṛuχ, s.m., ecrwch, T.N. 10. 2, 'roughness' (esp. of the weather): *ekṛuχ garu jaun*. Cf. *egar*.

ekstro, s.m. Cf. exdro, C.C.M. 174. 3; acstro, W.Ll. (Voc.), s.v. 'echel'; 'brace and bit' (carpenter's tool).

eχal, s.f., pl. *eχela, eχelyδ*, echel, D., 'axle': *mynd o:δ ar i eχal*, 'to lose one's temper'; *paid a i danny o o:δ ar i eχal*, 'don't upset him'.

eχely, v., echelu, 'to place on an axle': *dim wedi eχely n jaun* (speaking of a cart-wheel).

eχnos, s. and adv., echnos, R., 'the night before last'.

eχloy; eχloδ (E.J.), s. and adv., echdoe, D., 'the day before yesterday'.

eχuyn, s.m., echwyn, D., 'loan': *neuχi roid eχuyn o dorθ i mi?*, 'will you lend me a loaf?'; *taly r eχuyn adra*, 'to pay the loan back; to retaliate'.

eli, s.m., eli, D., 'salve, ointment': *ma: nu ŋ gosod nu meun padaḷ i χusy, ag wedyn ma: nu ŋ gwasgy nu ag aŋ gnẽyd eli hevo nu*, 'they put them in a pan to "sweat", and then they press them and make a salve with them'; *damma eli aχ kalon an du:ad ruan*, 'here's the delight of your heart coming now', i.e. tea; *mi ro: i ti eli!*

(ironically, to crying child), 'I'll make it better!'; *tori mhen a rhoid i mi eli* (prov. exp.), 'to do me an irreparable injury and then offer a slight atonement'; *eli r indja*, 'zinc ointment' (I.W.).

elor, s.m., elor, D., 'bier'.

elu, s.m., elw, D., 'gain, profit': *hurax gna:nu elu go ða: i xi*, 'perhaps they will bring in a good deal of profit for you'; *o bo:b gwaiθ da:u elu* (prov.), 'every work brings gain'. See also *helu*.

elvan, s., elfen, D. (1) 'element': *may o ən i elvan*, 'he is in his element'. (2) 'natural inclination, tendency': *ma na riu elvan ri·o:d əno vo i ðu:yn* (O.H.), 'he has a kind of natural tendency to steal' (= *asgan*); *magy elvan əno vo*, 'to excite a tendency in him'.

ela, adv., ſe allai, 'perhaps' [*galy*].

embyd, adj., enbyd, D., 'periculosus'; embyd, B.C. 51. 25, 'dangerous'; 'enormous'; also 'extremely, excessively': *basun i n lëikjo n embyd*, 'I should like extremely'.

embədys, adv., enbydus, W.S. [Dangerouse], 'extremely, excessively': *r o:ð o n valx embədys*, 'he was excessively proud'.

enaid, s.m., pl. *enëidja*, enaid, D., 'soul': *uθi hi nerθ enaid a xorſ*, 'at it might and main'.

enlyn, s.m., enllyn, D., 'anything eaten with bread, as butter, meat, cheese, etc.': *i o:ys ǵin i ðim enlyn*, 'I have nothing to eat but dry bread'.

ennil, ənnil, v., ennill, W.B. col. 167. 5; ynnill, D.; M.LL. i. 193. 1, 3, 4; W.Ll. ii. 64, 65, 67, 70. Fut. *nila*. Pret. *nilis*. Imperative *nila*; *niluxi*, 'to gain, win, earn': *enil serx*, 'to win affection'; *wa:yθ i xi ǵëinjog ·sbarjuxi na ǩëinjog ·niluxi*, 'a penny saved is a penny gained'; *os na ·ventruxi beθ ·niluxi ðim*, 'nothing venture, nothing have'; *rvo: niloð*, 'he won'; *ma:y r mo:r ən ənnil ar ə ti:r*, 'the sea is encroaching';—of a watch: *ənnil ta koli ma hi ?*, 'does it gain or lose?'

ennil, s., pl. *niljon*, ynnill, D., 'gain': *wedi gwastrafy i niljon*, 'having squandered his savings'.

entryx, s., entrych, D., 'the highest point of the heavens', esp. *entryx ər awyr.—ma:y r deryn wedi mynd i r entryx* (O.H.), 'the bird is soaring up to the sky'; *dy:n wedi kal i xuθy ǵin bəudur i r entryx i vəny* (O.H.), 'a man blown up by gunpowder'. (Frequently used by O.H.)

enu, henu (eno), s.m., pl. *enwa*, enw, henw, D., s.v. 'nomen'. (1) 'name': *be di d enu di ?*, 'what is your name?'; *sy daxi n sunjo·x enu ?*, 'how do you pronounce your name?'; *i oy:s dim enu arni̦ hi̦*, 'it has no name'; *to̦ri̦ enu*, 'to sign one's name'; *n eno r ta:d l*, *n eno r ta:d (annul) l*, exclamation of surprise. (2) 'reputation (good or bad)': *ɔŋ kayl ɔr enu o vo:d* . . ., 'having the reputation of being . . .'.

envys, envysg, henvysg, s.f., enfys, D., Passim Enfysg, 'rainbow'.

enwad, s., pl. *enwada*, enwad, O.P., 'sect': *by:d r̦hëi̦ n dadla m bo:yθ am i̦ henwada*, 'some people dispute hotly about their religious beliefs'.

enwi̦, v., enwi. D. Imperative Pl. 2. *enwuχ* (O.H.). Pret. Pass. *ennuyd*, 'to name'.

enwog, adj., enwog, D. (1) 'conceited, vain'. (2) 'famous'.

enwyn, adj., enwyn, D., only in *ɫa:yθ enwyn*, 'buttermilk'.

eŋan, s.f., eingion and einion, D.; eingon, W.B., col. 490. 9, 'anvil': *mor beŋgalad ag eŋan go:*, 'as hard-headed (i.e. obstinate) as an anvil'; *ki̦ŋ glettad ag eŋan*, 'as hard as an anvil'.

eŋlyn, s.m., pl. *eŋlɔnjon*, englyn, D., s.v. 'epigramma'; 'englyn'.

eplas [*heplas*].

eplesy, v., eplesu, heplesu, 'to ferment'.

er, prep., er, D. (1) 'since': *er nëiθjur*, 'since last night'; *er pen may hi̦ wedi̦ glëyo*, 'since it was light';—*er s, ar s, as*, er ys, 'for (of past time), since, ago': *er s mëiti̦n*, 'since some little time', 'some little time ago'; *er s talum*, 'since a good time', 'a good time ago'; *er s talum jaun*, 'since a long time', 'a long time ago'; *er s tr̦o:*, 'lately, for some time'; *er s tr̦o: by:d*, 'a very long time ago, since a very long time'; *er s amsar maiθ*, 'for, since a long time'; *vy:o vo ðim ɔmma er s talum jaun*, 'he has not been here for a long time'; *ma:y o ɔmma er s dɔrnodja*, 'he has been here for days'; *mi̦ weli̦s i̦ o er s ṫair blɔnað*, 'I saw him three years ago'. (2) 'in spite of': *er i̦ hoɫ gɾvoyθ t ɔdi̦ o ðim ɔn happys*—so 'although': *er i̦ðo nëyt hɔnny nëiθ o ðim ɫuyðo*, 'although he did that, he will not succeed'. (3) with *mu:yn*, 'for the sake of, in order to': *er mu:yn po:b pe:θ gneuχ hɔnny*, 'do that by all means'; *er mu:yn po:b pe:θ pëidjuχ a gnëyt hɔnny*, 'don't do that, whatever you do'; *mɔmryn o ðu:r po:yθ er mu:yn i̦ðo vo ga:yl i̦oði̦*, 'a drop of hot water to make it melt'.

erbyn, prep., erbyn, D. (1) 'against, in opposition to' (preceded by *ɔn*), *tr̦i:o ka:yl rubaθ ɔn ɔχ (h)erbyn χi̦*, or *i̦ χ (h)erbyn*, 'to try and rake up something against you'; *ʃarad ɔn i̦ erbyn*, 'to speak against him'; *daχi̦ n erbyn mynd ?*, 'do you object to go?' (2) 'against, implying contact with' (preceded by *ɔn*): *taro i̦ ben ɔn erbyn ɔ parad*, 'to strike one's head against the wall' (usually expressed by *ɔn ɔ parad*); *sevyɫ ɔn erbyn ɔ wal*, 'to lean against the wall'. (3) 'against, for, as a provision for' (= *ar gɔvar*); *r̦hostjo gu:yð erbyn dolig,* 'to roast a goose for Christmas'; *vəða i ŋ gorvod kəmmyd peθ heno erbyn vory,* 'I am obliged to take some to-night for to-morrow morning';—as a conjunction : *erbyn da:u hi etto,* 'for when she comes again'. (4) 'for, to wait for': *kodi saχad ar ben klauð erbyn i drol baʃo,* 'to put a sack on the top of a wall to wait for a cart to pass ("against" the passing of a cart)'. (5) 'by, by the time': *mi ðo: i n o:l erbyn ƙinjo,* 'I shall be back by dinner-time'; · *erbyn hyn,* 'by this'; *erbyn hənny,* 'by that time'; *erbyn du:ad ən i ho:l,* 'by the time she was back';—used as a conjunction : *erbyn ·bəðuχi gariƫa,* 'by the time you are home'. (6) 'from, to' (a resisting object): *hoŋjan erbyn ƫraust,* 'to hang to a beam' (speaking of a human being). (7) 'by' (preceded by *ən*): *mi tənna i di: ən erbyn də gly:st ti,* 'I'll pull you by the ear'; *i θənny hi n erbyn gwa:lƫ i fen,* 'to pull her by the hair of her head'.

ergid, s.f., pl. *ergədjon,* ergyd, D. (1) 'a blow'. (2) 'a blast', e.g. in a quarry. (3) 'shot', such as is used in a gun. (4) 'shot' (the sound).

eri·o:yd, əri·o:yd, ri·o:yd, adv., erioed, D.; yrioed, W.Ll. lxxii. 26 ; 'riod, B.C. 66. 31. (1) 'in the course of one's existence': *mi ƙe:s i lawar ƫroχva eri·o:yd* (O.H.), 'I have had many a soaking in my life'. (2) 'ever' (referring to past time): *welis i eri·o:yd dy:n ba:χ mor ·a·nivir a vo,* 'I never saw such a disagreeable man'; *ə ƙi:g gora glu:is i eri·o:d,* 'the best meat I ever tasted'; *vy:om i ri·o:d ən ə ŋwely am ðurnod,* 'I never spent a day in bed'; *welis i rotʃun* (= erioed ffasiwn) *be:θ (eri·o:yd) !,* 'I never saw such a thing !' (3) 'always', i.e. since his birth, since its beginning, etc.: *baχgan avjaχ jaun oy:ð o eri·o:yd,* 'he was always a sickly youth'.

erχuyn ; eχuyn (W.H.), pl. *erχwinjon,* s.f., erchẃyn and erchwynn, D., 'side of a bed (where one gets out)': *ƚe: daχi ŋ ƙəsgy ? uθ ə parad ia uθ ər erχuyn ?*

erχyƚ, adj., erchyll, D., 'terrible': *turu erχyƚ;—ƫo: erχyƚ* 'an abominable, shameful action'.

ernas, s.f., ernes, D., 'earnest-money': *su:ƚt o ernas.*

erθyl, s., erthyl, D., 'abortion'.

ervyn, v., erfyn, D., 'to entreat': *ervyn arno vo (i).*

ervyn [*arva*].

eru, s.f., erw, D., 'acre' (I.W.). O.H. considers the word obsolete.—Common in place-names, e.g. *eru vair* (in Bangor), *eru gron, eru gregog* (in Llanfairfechan).

eryr, s.m., pl. *erərod,* eryr, D. (1) 'eagle'. (2) 'shingles' (disease). [Certain people were supposed to be able to cure it by blowing on it. To acquire the power they were supposed to eat the flesh of eagles, or it was supposed that their ancestors had done so.]

erəri, s.pl., eryri, D., 'shingles', see above (2).

esgíd, s.f., pl. *sgídja,* esgid, D., 'shoe, boot': *paːr o sgídja,* 'a pair of boots'; *truːyn esgíd,* 'toe of a boot'; *ǩevn esgíd,* 'uppers'; *kara esgíd,* 'boot-lace'; *gwaltas esgíd,* 'shoe-welts'; *rhɐuχ əχ sgídja am əχ traːyd,* 'put your boots on'; *tənny sgídja,* 'to take off boots'; *ļnaːy sgídja,* 'to clean boots'; *glöivi sgídja,* 'to polish boots'; *hiro sgídja a saim,* 'to grease boots'; *kay, dafod sgídja,* 'to lace, unlace boots'; *klem o dan esgíd,* 'a patch underneath a shoe'; *may r esgid ma n doːst ar ə ŋhorn,* 'this shoe hurts my corn'; *may ǩevn ər esgíd ma əm brivo nɾhoːyd i,* 'this boot hurts my instep'; *na i iſo kobljo tippin ar ə sgíaja,* 'I must mend my shoes a bit'; *sodli a gwadny sgídja,* 'to sole and heel boots'; *t ədi r sgídja ma ðim ən dal duːr,* 'these boots let in water' = *may r sgídja ma əŋ koļi duːr ; paː sgídja daχi am wisgo hëiðju ?,* 'which boots are you going to wear to-day ?'; *du i ŋ gwisgo və sgídja ar ər oχra,* 'I wear out my boots on the sides'; *d euχi byθ i və sgídja iː,* 'you will never get into my shoes'; *may o n ļond i sgídja,* 'he is a pompous man'.

esgís, s.m., pl. *esgísodjon, esgiſon, sgíſa,* esgus, and esgusod, D., 'excuse': *hel esgís,* 'to find an excuse'.

esgísodi, v., esgusodi, D., 'to excuse': *neuχi v esgísodi vi ?,* 'will you excuse me ?'

esgob, s.m., pl. *esgobjon,* esgob, D., 'bishop'.

esgor, v., esgor, D., 'to bring forth'.

esiθ, s., 'wattle made of hazel to strengthen the eaves and the top of the thatch: *gwiːal əm pļeθy truː r sbaratſ* (O.H.). D. has aseth, 'scolops';—'a sharp pointed spar, to fasten thatch' (pl. esyth), O.P. Cf. however D.G. cxl. 31, 'Da nithiodd (i.e. y gwynt) dy do neithwyr ! Hagr y tores dy essyth.'

esmuyθ, adj., comp. *smuyθaχ,* esmwyth, D. (1) 'soft, pleasant': *esmuyθ dan droːyd* (J.J.), 'soft for walking on, pleasant under foot'; *leː esmuyθ i gerðad,* e.g. *mənyð ļyvn, gwastad* (O.H.)—also *gëirja esmuyθ.* (2) 'comfortable', e.g. of a garment. (3) 'easy in mind': *un i ðim syt ə may o n esmuyθ ən i groːyn,* 'I don't know how he can be at ease in his mind'; *esmuyθ guːsg, pottas maiþ* (prov.), 'tranquil sleep, turnip pottage', i.e. 'it is better to be contented with little than to live luxuriously on ill-gotten gains'. [The origin of the phrase (so the story goes) was as follows: Two families, equally poor, lived in neighbouring cottages, but whereas one lived on the poorest fare, the other had plentiful supplies of mutton. The reason was at length made clear when the head of the latter family was hanged for sheep-stealing.] (4) 'easy' (of some one who has been in pain). (5) 'mild' (of the weather).

estron, s.m., pl. *stronjaid,* estron, D., 'stranger'.

eslyn, əslyn, v., estyn, D., but ystyn s.v. 'porrigo'; ystynn R.B.

229. 17. Fut. *stənna*. Pret. *stənnis*. Imperative *esiyn, əsiyn, sənna ; stənnux*. (1) 'to stretch out': *esiyn i go:ys*, 'to stretch out one's leg'; fig. 'to die', "to kick the bucket". (2) 'to reach, to get': *esiyn glo:*, 'to get coal'; *stənnux lu:y ən ḷe: hon*, 'get a spoon instead of this'.

esys, *ëy∫os*, adv., eisoes, D.; eusys, D.F. [6] 26; B.C. 24. 5, 25. 29, 28. 23; P.G.G. 328. 22, 'already': *may o ëy∫os wedi darvod*, 'he has finished already'.

etto, adv., etto. D. (1) 'again': *brə∫ux əmma etto*, 'come and see us again soon'; *mi δa:u o ə pnaun ma etto*, 'he will come again this afternoon'; *na: i roid ṟhëi ni ən i hola etto ar o:l i χi orfan*, 'I'll put these back again when you've finished'; *veḷy etto*, 'ditto'. (2) 'yet, still': *δary mi δim gnëyd mistar arni hi etto*, 'I have not mastered it yet'; *mi δo: i hy:d atto vo etto*, 'I shall find him yet'; *may na dippin o forδ etto*, 'it is some way still'.—Often used like French 'encore' where English usage requires 'another' or 'more' as : *gəmmuχi gupanad etto ?*, 'will you have another cup?'; *y:n bur etto i∫'o i glirjo*, 'one more table to be cleared'. (3) 'another time' (Anglo-Welsh 'again'): *mi δëyda i ·uθaχi etto*, 'I'll tell you another time'.

eur, s., Mid.W. efwr (cf. examples in notes to B.B.C. p. 136), 'cow parsnip' (Heracleum sphondylium).

eval, s.f., pl. *gɔvëiljad*, gefail, D., 'smithy'.

eval, s.f., pl. *gɔvëiljad*, gefail, D., 'tongs', also *eval da:n*, for the sake of distinction; *eval bədola* (*bədoli* J.J.), 'pincers'; *eval gnay*, 'nut-crackers'; *eval ∫ugur*, 'sugar-tongs'; *eval gu:n*, 'dog-tongs' (used in Llanfairfechan church in the time of the grandfather of the present sexton, O.H.); *kəmala r eval*, 'the joints of the tongs' (O.H.); *ko:ys r eval*, 'leg of the tongs'.

evaḷ, s.m.f. pl. *gɔvëiljad*, gefell, D., Non Gefaill vt aliis placet. Est enim pl. Gefelliaid. 'twin': *day (du:y) evaḷ ·ədynu*, 'they are twins'; *day o:yn evaḷ*, 'twin lambs'.

eveṅil, s.f., efengyl, D., 'gospel': *ḱin wirad a r eveṅyl*.

evlyn, s.: *dim evlyn o wynt*, 'not a breath of air' (O.H. frequently).

evra, s.pl., efrau, D., s.v. 'zizania'; O.F. evraie, 'couch-grass' (Triticum).

ewa, ewa, O.P., a polite term used in addressing old men. Cf. *boba*. Practically obsolete.

ewaχ, s., ewach, O.P., 'a small wizened person': *he:n ewax sa:l, he:n ewaχ o he:n δy:n*.

ewas, fem. of *ewa* (O.H.).

ewin, s.f., pl. *wina(δ)*, *gwina(δ)*, ewin, D., 'nail' (of the hand or foot); 'claw' (e. g. of a cat); 'hoof' (of a cow): *nerθ ewin ag esgyrn*, 'tooth and nail'; *nerθ ə deːŋ ewin*, 'hard work'; e.g. *be sy gəno vo aı vyu ˀ dim ond nerθ ə deːŋ ewin ;—χeːs i ðim ḱimmint a ḷṛuːχ v ewin gəno vo, χeːs i ðim ḱimmint a sy dan v ewin*, 'I could get nothing out of him'; *heb ðim dan i ewin*, 'without a penny'; *ṛhaid tənny r gwinað o r bleːu*, 'one must set to in earnest'; *gwina r gaːθ*, 'the crooked yellow stonecrop' (Sedum reflexum); *ǵewin moχyn*, a kind of shell said to be fairly common in the district, but the specimen shown appeared to be a foreign species (Crepidula unguiformis); *gwina garḷag*, 'cloves of garlic'. Cf. *ǵewin*.

ewyn, s., ewyn, D., 'foam', seldom used = *froθ*.

ewyrθ, s.m., pl. *ewəθrod*, ewythr, D., 'uncle'.

ĕylod, s.f., pl. *loda*, aelod, D., 'limb, member': *du i wedi kaːyl annuyd ḷṛuː ə loda i ǵiːd*, 'I have got cold in all my limbs'; *mynd ar i bedar ĕylod*, 'to go on all fours'. In the sense of 'a member of a community', *ĕylod* may be either gender.

ĕyluyd, s.f., pl. *ĕyluydyð*, aelwyd, D., 'hearth': *may hi ar ər ĕyluyd ar hyːd ə dyːð*, 'she (the cat) is on the hearth all day'; *hauð kənna taːn ar heːn ĕyluyd* (prov.), 'it is easy to light a fire on an old hearth', i. e. 'an old friendship easily returns'.

ĕyog, adj., euog, D., 'guilty': followed by the prep. *o*.

ĕyraχ, s.m., pl. *ṛjaχod*, eurych, D. (1) 'tinker': *əmlað vel ṛjaχod, vel day ĕyraχ*, 'to fight like tinkers'; *fryːo vel ṛjaχod ḷanarχəˑməð* (O.H), 'to quarrel like the tinkers of Llanerchymedd';—as term of reproach: *heːn ĕyraχ* (O.H). (2) 'emasculator' = *kwĕirjur*.

ĕyras, s.f., pl. *ĕyresa*, aeres, C.C.M. 170. 7; 214. 6; 'heiress'.

ĕyron, s.pl., in *ḅgaid r ĕyron*, 'cranberries' (Vaccinium Oxycoccos); cf. llygad eirian, D., and aeron, 'fruit'.

ĕyru, s.m., pl. *ruyon*, aerwy, R. (1) 'a kind of chain attached to a piece of wood for fastening up cattle'. (2) 'a cord for fastening panniers to a pack-saddle: *baχy ə ḱewyḷ ar gyrn ə strodyr hevo ĕyru* (J.J.).

ĕyſos [*esys*].

f

fa:, s.pl., sing. *fëyan*, f. ffa, D., 'beans': *ρhe:s o fa:*, 'a row of beans'; *dy:o fa:*, 'to shell beans'; *fa: korsyð*, 'marsh trefoil' (Menyanthes trifoliata), called 'bog-bean' in parts of England.

fadin, adj., ? Eng. fading (originally name of a dance, see N.E.D.): *ṭρo: fadin*, 'a mean turn, a shabby trick'; *wedi gnëyd ə ṭρo: muya fadin ·welsoχi ri·o:d* (O.H.); *y:n go fadin ədi o*, 'he is a poor sort of creature'.

faga (J.J., O.H.), s.pl., sing. *fagan* (O.H.), 'old worn-out boots': *riu he:n faga o sǵidja; esǵid wedi mynd ən fagan; mi drawis i ρ he:n fagan am ə ηρho:yd*—all O.H. Cf. *fagoda, faχla, flaχod*.

fagal, s.m., pl. *fagla*, ffagl, D., 'faggot' of straw, gorse, bracken, heather, etc., but not wood (O.H.): *he:n fagal gwy:lṭ ədi o*, 'he is a very hasty, short-tempered man'.

fagjo, v. (1) 'to be tired, "fagged"': *wedi fagjo n la:n* (O.H.). (2) 'to trample down', e.g. young shoots in a field or garden: *fagjo o dan dra:yd* (J.J., O.H.). (3) 'to walk in a slovenly manner, treading down the heels' (J.J.).

fagly, v., ffaglu, D., 'to flare up': *ma: ρ glo: n fagly n aru ;— nëïθ glo: sa:l ðim fagly, a ρ laḷ ən fagly gormod* (O.H.).

fagoda, s.pl., 'old worn-out boots' (I.W.).

fagud, s., term of reproach: *ρ he:n fagud*—applied especially to children (O.H.).

fair, s.f., pl. *fëirja*, fair, W.S. (1) 'fair': *fair vaηgor hannar ha: ; fair lambad*, i.e. Llanbedr y Cennin; *fair ρen təmmor*, 'fair at the end of the season when farm-servants are hired' (Nov. 13); *fair gəvloǵi*, 'hiring fair'; *fair ve:l*, 'honey fair'—a fair at Conway so called; *fair okʃun*, 'auction'; *may hi wedi bo:d ən fair hevo vi hëïðju*, 'I have been very busy to-day'. (2) 'exchange': *fair bemban*, 'a perfect exchange'. (3) 'negotiation as to terms, bargaining': *guθjo ə fair ən i bla:yn ρhuη ə ðay*.

faiθ, s.f., pl. *fëïθja*, ffaith, O.P., 'fact'.

fakiρi, s.f., pl. *fakiρis*, 'factory': *fakiρis i nëyd davað*, 'woollen yarn factories'.

faχla, s.pl., 'old worn-out boots' (E.J., J.J.).

fals, adj., pl. *fëilſon*, ffals, S.G. 18. 19; D. (1) 'given to flattery': *dy:n fals*, 'flatterer, toady'. (2) 'treacherous': *fals vel ə ga:θ*.

falstar, s.m., falster, W.S. [Falsenesse]; ffalsder, B.C. 28. 7; 'treachery; flattery'.

falstra, s.m. = *falstar*, 'treachery; flattery'.

falſo, v., 'to flatter'; "to suck up".

falſur, s.m., ffalswr, D.G. ccxxvi. 31, 'flatterer, toady'.

fansi, s.m., ffansi, M.Ll. ii. 24. 3; P.G.G. 265. 23; phansi, B.C. 6. 9; 'fancy': *peθa fansi*, 'fancy articles'; *sərθjo meun fansi*, 'to fall in love'.

fan·si:o, v., phansio, Ecclus. xxxiv. 5, 'to fancy'.

fardjal, s., pl. *fardjals*, fardial, W.S. [A fardell]: *ŗ he:n fardjal !*, term of reproach applied to an old man; *pëidjuχ fardjal ſarad*, 'do not talk nonsense'; *riu he:n fardjal o ġerðad*, 'a slouching gait'—O.H.

fargod, s.m., ffargod, T.N. 405. 6; O.P. [a big paunch]: *he:n fargod o he:n ðy:n, r y:n hy:d a r y:n le:d* (O.H.).

farjər, s.m., Eng. farrier, 'veterinary surgeon'.

farm, s.f., pl. *fermyð*, ferm, W.S. [A ferme], 'farm': *ty: farm*, 'farmhouse'.

farmjo, v., 'to farm'.

farmur, s.m., pl. *farmurs*, fermwr, W.S. [A fermour]; ffarmwr, T.N. 12. 11, 'farmer'.

faro, s.m., Pharaoh: *he:n faro o ðy:n*, 'a cruel man' (W.H.).

farwel, *far·wel*, s., ffarwel, M.Ll. i. 3. 11, 'farewell, good-bye': *na i ðëyd far·wel i χi ru:an* (O.H.), 'I will say good-bye to you now'; *wedi kany far·wel i r by:d* (W.H.), 'having bid farewell to the world'; *kany farwel* (O.H.); *farwel ha:*, 'Michaelmas daisy'.

farweljo, v., 'to say good-bye': *noson farweljo* (O.H.), 'a "send-off"', 'an evening entertainment to celebrate some one's departure'.

fasno, v., 'to fasten'.

fast, adj., ffast, C.C. 68. 26, 'fast, quick': *berwi n fast*—also used of the wind, clocks, etc.

faſun, s.m., pl. *faſma*, ffasiwn, C.L.C. ii. 35. 17; ffassiwn, C.C.M. 105. 23. (1) 'fashion': *gra:t he:n faſun*, 'an old-fashioned grate'. (2) = pa ffasiwn?, 'what kind?': *faſun sta:t o:yð arno vo ?*, 'in what kind of state was he?'; *faſun y:n ədi o ?*, 'what kind of one is it?'; *faſun liu ?*, 'what colour?' (3) = ə va:θ, 'such': *o:yð faſun gre:d gəno vo ən i da:d*, 'he had such trust in his father'; *welis i rotſun* (erioed ffasiwn) *bc:θ,* 'I never saw such a thing'.

faſənol, adj., 'fashionable'.

fat, s.f., ffat, D., 'slap'.

fatjad, s., 'a slap': *mi rois i fatjad hevo r ḷa:u agorad.*

fatjan, v., cf. ffattio, C.C.M. 94. 30; 'to strike softly': *fatjan dərny = dim ən dərny n jaun.*

fatſ, s., 'an unfair advantage': *tendjuχ ido vo ga:l fatſ ·arnoχi,* 'take care he does not get an opportunity for revenge', equivalent to 'he is only biding his time'.

fattan, s.f., dim. of *fat*, 'a light slap': *rois i riu fattan ido vo.*

favar, s.f., pl. *favra*, favwr, L.G.C. p. 24. 14; fafyr, W.S.; ffafor, D.; ffafr, M.Ll. i. 99. 19; B.C. 15. 17; D.P.O. 59. 8; ffafer, B.C. 85. 14; 'favour': *mynd i favar ru:in*, 'to get into some one's favour'.

favrjaθ, s., ffafriaeth, 'favouritism'.

favrjo, v., fafrio, W.S.; ffafrio, D., s.v. 'faueo'; 'to favour'.

favrjol, adj., ffafriol, 'favourable'.

fawyð, s.pl., ffawydd, sing. ffawydden, D., 'fagus'; 'fir-trees; deal': *fawyð ko:χ, gwyn, melyn.*

fedog, s.f., pl. *fedoga*, arffedog, D., 'apron'. (Rarely used = *barkḷod.*)

fedogad, s.f., arffedogaid, S.E., 'apronful'. Cf. *fedogad ə gəuras*, in Bwlch y Ddeufaen, Llanfairfechan.

feg, s., Eng. fog, feg, 'hay which has been left to wither as it stands'; also 'grass which grows out of cow-dung, which the cattle will not eat'.

fẽi, interj., ffei, D., *fẽi honol !*, 'fie upon you !, for shame !'

fẽia, v., Eng. defy, in *fẽia i o*, 'I'll warrant'.

fẽil, s.f., 'file'.

fẽind, adj., comp. *fẽindjaχ*, ffein, C.C. 483. 2; ffeindiach, T.N. 118. 7. Eng. fine with epenthetic 'd'; cf. *vend* = fen (men); also perhaps influenced by Eng. 'kind'. (1) 'fine', e. g. of the weather = *bra:v.* (2) 'kind', *dy:n fẽind (uθ) ; prəgeθur fẽind*, a euphemism for a bad preacher.

fẽindruyð, s.m., 'kindness'.

fẽinjo ; finjo (O.H.), v., 'to fine'.

fẽintjo, v., fayntio, W.S.; ffeintio, M.Ll. i. 247. 15, 'to faint'.

fẽirjo, v., ffeirio, W.Ll., liii. 77, 'to exchange, barter': *mi fẽiris o hevo vo*, 'I exchanged it with him'; *·lẽikjaχi fẽirjo ə ðu:y dorθ ma ?,* 'would you like to exchange these two loaves?'; *fëirjo kəmdëiθas hcvo pobol*, 'to mix in society'.

fëiθjo [*efëiθjo*].

fel, adj., ffel, D., 'sharp' (of a child) = *parod i appad, i farad ; witti*, (O.H.). ['Fell' has a similar sense in Scotland.]

fenast, s.f., pl. *fnestri*, ffenestr, D., 'window': *may r fenast əŋ klepjan* (*klekjan*), 'the window is rattling'; *edraχ tru: r fenast*, 'to look out of the window''; *r o:ð hi ən ə fenast*, 'she was at the window, looking out of the window'; *fivl ə fenast*, 'window-sill'.

fendjo, v., ffeindio, T.N. 122. 12. Cf. Eng. fende (15th cent.). 'to find': Imp. *fendjun*, sometimes used with preterite meaning.

fe:r, s.f., pl. *fera ; feri* (O.H.), ffêr, D., 'ankle-bone': *meun du:r ai və feri*.

ferins, feris, s.pl., Eng. fairings, 'sweets': in phrase *du:ad a feris o r fair*, 'to bring back sweets from the fair'.

ferlyd, adj., fferllyd, D., s.v. 'algidus'; 'benumbed'.

feṭy, v., fferru, D., 'to congeal, become cold': *may i wa:yd o wedi feṭy ;—dy:n wedi feṭy i varwolaθ*, 'a man who has died from cold'.

feryn, s.m., pl. *ferəna*, offer, sing. offeryn, D., 'tool, implement'; 'instrument', e.g. organ, harmonium; cf. *arva* (sing. *erṿyn*), *ke:r, ge:r* (sing. *keryn*).

fettys, adj., fetus W.S. [Fayctouse]; ffetys R. [subtil]; Mid. Eng. featous ; fetis [pretty, well made]; O.F. fetis, feitis, faictis, 'pert, ready with an answer': *dy:n fettys = dy:n farp i appad* (O.H.).

fi:að, adj., ffiaidd, D. (1) 'abominable': *drewi n fi:að*. (2) 'contemptuous': *fi:að o lariṣ*, 'contemptuously proud'; *drəχoð ən fi:að arna i*, 'he looked contemptuously at me'.

fi:d, s., Eng. 'feed': *ṛhoi fi:d i r kefyl = l̦i:θ*.

fidil, s.f., fidyl, W.S.; ffidil, B.C. 42. 18, 'fiddle': *ṛhoi fidil ən to:*, 'to give up as a bad job, to throw up the sponge': *wa:yθ i χi roi fidil ən to: r y:n tippin*, 'you might just as well give it up'.

fidjo, v., 'to feed, supply': *r o:ð o n fidjo l̦anvar ag abar hcvo glo:*, 'he used to supply Llanfairfechan and Aber with coal'.

fidlar, s.m., fiddler, B.C. 42. 16, 'fiddler'.

fidljo, v., 'to play the fiddle'.

fi·ëiðjo, v., ffieiddio, D., 'to be disgusted with': *fi·ëiðjo və hynan*.

filot, s., filet W.S. [A fyllet], ffiled, W.Ll. lxiv. 64, in *filot fair* (= ? Fair), 'variegated grass'.

·filfi·falfaχ (W.H.); *filfin·falfo* (O.H.), s.m., 'a toady'.

filt, fild, in *fo:l filt*, 'Paisley shawl' (I.W.).

·fil̦·fal̦, adj., 'finicking': *kerad ən ·fil̦·fal̦*, 'to walk with mincing steps, to walk in a finicking way' (W.H.).

filjan, v., 'to bustle about' (I.W.): *ən filjan ŗhedag, ən filjan ar hy:d ə forð.* Cf. *fy:ļt.*

finihadan, finjadyn, s., Eng. finnan-haddie, 'haddock'.

finjo [*fëinjo*].

fiŋgl, s.f., 'unfair dealing' (I.W.): *he:n fiŋgl wirjon* (J.J.).

fiŋglo, fiŋgljo, v., 'to deal unfairly' (J.J.); 'to shilly-shally': *fiŋglo hevo də waiθ ; be u:ti n fiŋgljo vel na?* (O.H.)

fistjo, v., ffiustyaw, L.A. 39. 22 ; fustio, W.S. [Thresshe] ; ffiusto, D., 'to strike, thrash': *mi fistja i di = mi dərna i di.*

fistjon, s., fustion, W.S., 'fustian'.

fit, adj., comp. *fitjaχ,* fiitt, C.L.C. ii. 38. 22, 'fit': *os by:ð ə dɜuyð ən fit,* 'if the weather is fit'; *t ədi hi δim ən fit i χi vynd,* 'it is not fit for you to go'.

fit, s.f., pl. *fitja,* 'fit': *mi ġëiθ o fit,* 'he will have a fit'.

fitjo, v., 'to fit'.

flag, s.f., pl. *flagja,* 'flag' (banner).

flakjo, v., 'to flag': *flakjo r ļaur.*

flaks, s.pl., sing. *flaksan,* f., 'flag-stones'.

flaks, s.pl., sing. *flaksan,* f., Eng. (Dial.) flag, a form of flake [Sc., Nhb., Yks.], 'soot'.

flaχjad, s.m., pl. *flaχjada,* fflachiad, S.E., s.v. 'flash'; 'flash': *flaχjad o veļtan,* "a flash of lightning'; *mynd ar flaχjad,* 'to go like a flash'.

flaχjo, v., fflachio, S.E., s.v. 'flash'; 'to flash': *me:ļt ən flaχjo ; flaχjo mynd,* 'to go like a flash'.

flaχod, s.pl., cf. ffollach, D., 'cothurnus, calceamentum, pero', ffallach, s.v. 'sandalium', ffellych, s.v. 'baxeae'; 'old worn-out boots'.

flam, s.f., pl. *flamja,* fflam, W.B., col. 168. 36 ; D., 'flame': *wedi mynd vel flam (flamja),* 'gone like a flash'.

flamgoχ, adj., fflamgoch, W.B., col. 475. 36, 'fiery red'.

flamjo, v., fflamio, D., 'to flame'; *flamjo mynd,* 'to go like a flash'; so *flamjo n i blëyna ; r o:yð ļəgod maur ən flamjo o gumpas ; r o:yð ə ga:θ wedi mynd əŋ gənδëirjog, ag ən flamjo iŗu: r ty:.*

flamļyd, adj., fflamllyd, Psalm civ. 4, 'flaming, apt to burn quickly': *glo: flamļyd;*—also of persons 'apt to fly into a passion'.

flat, s.m., pl. *flatja,* 'an iron' (kitchen utensil).

flat, adj. (1) 'flat';—as subst.: *ŗhoid rubaθ ar (ən) i flat,* 'to lay something flat' = *ar i vol.* (2) 'dull, sultry, close, relaxing': *ļe: flat,* 'a dull place'; *tɜuyð flat,* 'close, sultry weather'. (3) 'low-spirited': *ïëimlo n flat jaun.*

flatʃo, v., cf. Eng. (Dial.) flosh [to splash, dabble, plunge about in bathing,—to agitate or splash water] and flash [a pool, sheet of water, etc.], O.F. flache, 'to splash': *paid a flatʃo də draːyd ən ə duːr, flatʃo uθ ǵerðad, flatʃo ǩerðad.*

flatʃur, s.m., 'splasher': *flatʃur o ǵerður.*

flegan, s.f., pl. *fleǵennod*, iar flegain, S.E., s.v. 'brood', a disparaging term applied especially to fowls: *heːn flegan o heːn jaːr*, 'a dilapidated-looking hen, with its feathers turned the wrong way'; also applied to cows (O.H.).—said of an untidy woman: *heːn flegan = dənas vleːr ən i gwiːsg a i gwaiθ.*

fleïo, fliːo, v., 'to fly'.

flemp, adj., in exp. *tro: flemp*, 'a shabby trick, a mean turn', e.g. a broken promise: *mi naːθ hun a hun dro: flemp hevo mi.*—A stronger term than *tro: gwaːyl, tro: saːl* (W.H.; O.H.).

flempan, s., in exp. *mi rois i flempan iðo vo* (i.e. *hevo ɲhavod*), 'I made him hold his tongue' (O.H.).

fliŋ, s., *rhoid fliŋ iðo vo*, 'to fling it'.

flippan, s.f. (1) 'a piece cut off': *flippan o garag = sgolpyn.* (2) 'anything worthless': *flippan o ðavad, o ðənas—*(O.H.).

flippan, adj., Eng. flippant: *mynd ən flippan = dëyd gair druːg heb iʃo* (O.H.).

flodjat, flodjart, s., 'flood-gate'.

flogjo, flokjo, v., 'to flock, crowd up'.

flonʃ, adj., 'cheerful, spirited' (of a sick person): *may o n edraχ ən o flonʃ; may o n rëit flonʃ ruːan.*

flonʃo, v., 'to become cheerful and spirited' (of a sick person).

fluːar, s., pl. *fluːars*, 'flower' = *blodyn*: *pot fluːars*, 'flower-pot'.

fluʃ, ? adj.;—as subst.: *təvy ən i fluʃ*, 'to grow close together' (O.H.).

flyːt, s., 'fleet': *flyːt o loŋa.*

flyuχ, s. ? ffliuwch, D., 'coma, suggestus comae': *mynd vel flyuχ*, 'to go like a flash'.

fodrum, fotrum, s.f. Eng. (Dial.) fodderum, Yks., Lan., Der., Lin., 'an open passage along the heads of stalls from where the cattle are supplied with fodder'.

foglyd, adj., ffoglud, T.N. 67. 14, 'bloated': *golug foglyd arno vo.*

foi, v., ffoi, Gen. xvi. 8. Fut. S. 3. *fyː, foiθ.* Pret. S. 3. *foːθ.* Imperative *foː*, 'to flee': *foi am i höydal*, 'to flee for his life'; *gwiɫtjo ruːin ag wedyn foi i furð*, 'to anger some one and then run away'; *poːb poːyn wedi foi*, 'all pain having disappeared'.

foːl, adj., fol, W.B., col. 125. 2; ffôl, D., 'foolish'.

folaδ, s., ffoledd, D., 'folly'.

foli, v., ffoli, O.P., 'to befool': *foli merχaid.*

folinab, s., ffolineb, D., s.v. 'stultitia'; 'foolishness .

folog, s.f., ffolog, Prov. xiv. 1, 'a foolish woman'.

folaχ, s., ? ffollach, D. (see *flaχod*), 'an insignificant person'. Cf. *slandi(n)folaχ*, which is a stronger term :—*r he:n folaχ kaχy* (O.H.).

fon, s.f., pl. *fyn*, ffon, D. (1) 'stick, walking-stick': *fon bigal*, 'shepherd's crook'; *fon davl*, 'sling. catapult'; *bagal fon*, 'handle of a stick'; *buru he:n wragaδ a fyn*, 'to rain cats and dogs'; see also *duyfon*. (2) 'bar' (of a grate). (3) 'rung' (of a ladder).

fond, adj., comp. *fondjaχ*, 'fond' (followed by *o*).

fonjad, s.f., 'a blow with a stick': *mi rois i riu fonjad veχan iδo vo.*

fonnog [*kumfonnog*].

forδ, s.f., pl. *fyrδ*, ffordd, D. (1) 'way, road': *forδ* (= *lo:n*) *bo:st, forδ vaur*, 'high road'; *dy:n ə forδ vaur*, 'high road inspector'; *forδ garjo maun*, 'a road for carrying peat'; *forδ əsgavn, drum (drom)*, 'easy, heavy road'; *ə forδ gənta, vəra*, 'the shortest way'; *for auni gənta i . . .?*, 'which is the shortest way to . . .?'; *vedar hi ə forδ əmma?*, 'does she know the way here?'; *ar ə for i vynd i r pentra*, 'on the way to the village'; *drost ə forδ i r ty:*, 'opposite the house'; *kerδad ə δu:y forδ*, 'to walk both ways'; *le: may r forδ əmma n mynd*, 'where does this road go to?'; *for ma*, or (generally more emphatic) *for ·hyn*, 'this way'. (2) 'way, direction': *əy gweld bo:b for*, 'looking every way'; *ty: a r for na du i ŋ kredy ma:y hi*, 'I think it is somewhere over there'. (3) 'way, manner': *for ma*, 'this way, like this'; *ma: nu n rhy: yχal i for*, 'they are too high and mighty'; *for δigri, rəvaδ*, 'an odd way' (about him); *meun forδ o farad*, 'so to speak'; *·t öyδaχi δim ən i gəmmyd o n ə for jaun*, 'you did not take it in the right way', i.e. 'you did not understand it rightly'; *du:y forδ i nëyd po:b pe:θ, y:n o δe:, y:n o χwiθig*, 'two ways of doing everything, one right, one wrong'; *forδ ar i hagor ιu*, 'a way to open them'.

forδjo, v., fforddio, D., 'in via aliquem dirigere': (fig.) *dənjon ən forδjo plant ar ə forδ jaun, a r leil ən i forδjo nu ar forδ δrəgjonys ; ən forδjo nu i δrəgjoni.*

forδjo, v., fforddio, T.N 4. 27; Eng. afford, influenced by fforddio (above). (1) 'to afford': *dim ən forδjo su:li at rubaθ*, 'not being able to afford a shilling for something'; *mi δëydoδ hi vedra hi δim forδjo*, 'she said she could not afford'. Impersonally: *gnëyd mu:y o wleδast nag ədi hi n forδjo ·yδynu* (O.H.). (2) 'to permit, allow' (in speaking of the law). Cf. the popular rime: *by:m əy kary du:y r y:n enu,* | *dg:en verχ ivaŋk a dg:en wraig weδu ;* | *gwyn vy:d na forδja r gəvraθ* | *i mi brjodi r δu:y ar ynwaθ.*

forðjol, adj., 'managing well, economical': *may y:n ən med̦ry gnëyd kimmint hevo pəmθag su:l̦t a nëiθ y:n aral̦ hevo pynt,—may o mor forðjol*, 'one is able to do as much with fifteen shillings as another can do with a pound,—he manages so well'.

forðol, s.m., pl. *forðoljon*, fforddolion (pl.), Psalm lxxxix. 41, etc. (1) 'road-mender' (in general). (2) (in slate quarries) 'platelayer, whose duty it is to keep the lines clear, to make repairs or new lines'.

forfad, s., fforffed, D., s.v. 'publicatio', 'sectio'; D.G. xxxvii. 1, Eng. forfeit, 'damage': *el̦iθ nëyd forfad əno*, 'perhaps he will do some damage there', e. g. by going into a dark room without a light (W.H) ;—*wedi mynd ən forfad* (*hevo*), 'to be utterly abandoned (to), to give oneself up entirely (to)'; *wedi mynd ən forfad hevo r merχaid;—wedi mynd ən forfad hevo r ṛhəδvrəduyr*, 'to be an out and out radical'; *wedi mynd ən forfad veδu*, 'strongly addicted to drink'; *wedi mynd ən forfad ylu*, "gone to the dogs", "gone to pot".—(O.H.)

fork, s.f., pl. *fyrks*, 'fork' (for the table).

forχ, s.f., pl. *fyrχ*, fforch, D. (1) 'fork with four prongs for digging potatoes, etc.': *tṛo:yd forχ*, 'handle of a fork'. Cf. *pikwarχ*. (2) a sheep's ear-mark so-called [*no:d*]. (3) 'fork of a tree', etc.

forχi, v., fforchi, O.P. (1) 'to fork', e. g. of a road, branch, etc. (2) 'to use a fork': *djaul a də forχo di!* (3) 'to make a *forχ* on a sheep's ear'.

forχjad, s.f., pl. *forχëidja*, fforchaid, O.P., 'as much as is lifted with a fork, either a *forχ* or *pikwarχ*'.

forχog, adj., fforchog, D., 'forked': *may kol̦yn nëidar ən forχog ;— o: forχog*, 'astride'.

fors, s.f., 'force, might, pressure, impetus': *t o:ys dim digon o fors ən ə tapja*, 'there is not enough pressure in the taps'; *sərθjo ar i ben ən i fors* (O.H.), 'to fall on his head with full force'; *ṛhoid fors əni hi*, 'to put force into it', e. g. in striking; *ə tṛo:yd ən o:l i nëyd fors*, 'the foot behind to gain an impetus' (= *i ga:l pu:ar*).

fortjun, s.f., cf. fortun, W.S.; fforten, C.C. 33. 20, 'fortune'.

fortynys, adj., fortunus, W.S., 'fortunate'. Seldom used = *lukkys*.

fo:s, fo:ys, s.f., pl. *fosyδ*, ffos, D., 'small stream, ditch': *fo:s a foŋkan*, 'a stream and the corresponding rise'; *be ëiθ ən vu:y ar o:l tori ben ?, fo:ys*, 'what becomes bigger when its end is cut off? A ditch'; *agor fo:ys*, 'to clear the mud, etc., out of a ditch'.—Also 'groove'.

foiṛum [*fodrum*].

fɵukyn, dim. of Ffowc : *ail ɘdi hyukyn i fɵukyn,* 'six of one and half a dozen of the other'.

fra:m, s.f., pl. *framja,* ffrâm, B.C. 14. 10, 'frame' : *fra:m dru:s, piktjur, igol,* etc.

fra:y, s.f., ffrae, W.S. [Affraye], W.Ll. xlv. 49 ; B.C. 20. 2, 'quarrel' : *ar fra:y,* 'quarrelling' ; *a:θ ɘn fra:y rhɘŋθa vi: a vo: ar gɵunt* . . ., 'we got into a quarrel about . . .'.

fra:yθ, adj., ffraeth, D., 'talkative, glib' : *ɘn fra:yθ i davod.*

frëinig, adj., Ffrengig, D., 'Gallicus'; *knay frëinig,* 'walnuts'; *beru frëinig,* 'cress'; *l̨godan frëinig,* 'rat'.

fres, adj., ffres, C.C.M. 157. 1 ; C.C. 73. 13, 'fresh' : *penwaig fres, menyn fres ; bara fres,* 'new bread'.

frëyo, fry:o, v., ffraeo, W.S. [Make an affray], 'to quarrel' : *ma: nu n frëyo hevo i gilið o hy:d ;—fry:o m bemban,* 'to be at loggerheads' ; *frëyo vel ku:n a mo:χ.*

fri:, adj., ffri, C.C.M. 46. 33 ; C.L.C. v. vi, 68. 26 ; T.N. 73. 1. (1) 'free, gratis'. (2) 'free with one's money, liberal' : *r öyðun i n fri: pen vɘða gin i bre:s ɘn ɘ m̨hokkad.*

fri:ð (Bangor, Tregarth, Pentir) ; *fri:θ* (Aber, Llanfairfechan), s.f., pl. *fri̬ðoð, fri̬θoð,* ffrith and ffridd, D., 'enclosed rough mountain pasture'.

frigud, s.m., ffrwgwd, B.C. 43. 21 ; ffrygwyd, C.L.C. iv. 19. 23, 'squabble' : *dim ond riu frigud gwirjon,—riu but o fra:y.*

frind, s.m., pl. *frindja,* ffrind, W.S., 'friend' : *ma: nu n frindja (garu) hevo i gilið.*

fri:o, v., ffirio, D., 'to fry' : *padal̨ fri:o,* 'frying-pan' ;—*may r gwynt ɘn fri:o r gannuyl̨,* 'the wind is making the tallow run down the candle'.

fritjan, v., 'to play in the rain' : *fritjan ɘn ɘ gla:u.*

frog, s.f., pl. *frogja,* frock, W.S. [Frocke], Mid. Eng. frog, 'frock'.

froml̨yd, adj., ffromllyd, 'testy', 'quick-tempered'.

frostjo, v., ffrostio, R., 'to boast'.

froθ, s., 'foam, froth' : *froθ (ɘ) mo:r,* 'meerschaum'.

fro:yn, s.f., pl. *fröyna,* ffroen, D., 'nostril; power of smell' : *may fro:yn jaun gɘno vo at bo:b pe:θ* (speaking of a dog).

fru:d, s.f., pl. *frɘdja,* ffrŵd, D., 'brook, stream'.

fruks, s., 'flurry' : *t o:ð o ðim am fruks,* 'he was not to be flurried'.

fruksl̨yd, adj., 'flurried'.

frukſo, v., 'to be flurried, to act hastily' : *pĕidjuχ frukſo hevo vo, may iſo kəmmyd muːy o amsar.*

fruːst, s.m., ffrwst, D., s.v. 'acceleratio'; 'hurry' : *may o wedi mynd ar fruːst (gwyːḷi).*

frut, s.m., ffrwt, T.N. 172. 17. (1) 'vigour' : *t oːs dim frut əno vo.* (2) " a quick impulse " (O.P.) : *riu frut o fraːy*, 'a bit of a squabble' (O.H.) ; *doːs ar frut i noːl piserad o ðuːr i mi* (O.H.). Also adjectively : *duːad ən frut* (O.H.).

frutfrut, s., 'sound of porridge boiling'.

frutjan, v. (1) expressing the sound of porridge boiling : *may r yud ən frutjan berwi.* (2) 'pedo', also *frutjan reχan.* (3) 'to walk quickly' : *ˑwelisti hun a hun ? doː, n frutjan mynd rĕit brəsyr ; —uːti n frutjan vel gwyðal.* (All O.H.)

fruydro, v., 'to explode'.

fruːyn, s.f., pl. *fruyna*, D., 'bridle' : *fruːyn duːyḷ* (i.e. dywyll), 'blinker'; also, 'the piece of iron extending from the corner of the blade of a scythe to the handle' = *gjalam hĕyarn.*

fruyno, v., ffrwyno, D., 'to bridle'; also, fig. *fruyno i davod, i nuyda*, etc., 'to bridle one's tongue, one's passions'.

fruːyθ, s.m., pl. *fruyθyð*, ffrwyth, D. (1) 'fruit'. (2) 'that which is distilled by boiling, etc.' : *bruːas = fruːyθ kiːg braːs berwedig ; sikkan = fruːyθ ə gĕirχan* (O.H.). (3) 'vigour, power' : *koḷi fruːyθ i loda*, 'to lose the use of his limbs'.

fruyθlon, adj., ffrwythlawn, D. (1) 'fruitful' : *haː fruyθlon.* (2) 'full of sap, juice, nutriment, etc'.

frədjo, v., ffrydio, D., s.v. 'defluo'; 'to gush (out)' : *gwaːyd ən frədjo ; duːr ən frədjo aḷan o r ðĕyar ne graig.*

frəmmy, v., offrymmu, D., 'to make an offering at a funeral'. [*ofrum.*]

frənt, s.m., 'front' : *druːs ə frənt*, 'front door'.

frəntjo, v., 'to face' (of a house, etc.) : *frəntjo r forð*, 'to face the road'.

fudan, s., ffwdan, D., s.v. 'festinatio'; 'haste' : *nĕis i doṟi o meun fudan* (O.H.) ; also 'fussiness'.

fudanḷyd, adj., ffwdanllyd, O.P., 'fussy, bustling' : *may hunna ŋ grjadyr fudanḷyd—dim əŋ kəmmyd amsar i nĕyd dim byːd.*

fudanys, adj., ffwdanus, D., 'fussy' : *yːn fudanys jaun ədi o.*

fuːl, s.m., pl. *fəlja(d)*, fwl, W.S. ; ffŵl, B.C. 38. 19 ; D.G. app. vii. 40, 'fool'.

fulbart, s.m., ffwlbart, L.G.C. p. 470. 4 ; D. ; Eng. foulmart, 'polecat' : *drewi vel fulbart ;*—as opprobrious epithet (E.J., J.J.), *heːn fulbart bydyr.*

fulbri, s. (1) 'foolishness': *na δigon o fulbri*, 'that's enough of this foolishness'. (2) 'a foolish, talkative fellow': *ꭅ heːn fulbri gwirjon* (J.J.).

ful but, adv., Eng. full butt: *mynd ən ful but*, 'to go full pelt'.

fulkyn, s.m., 'fool': *ꭅ heːn fulkyn meδu*, 'the old drunken fool' (W.H.).

fulpyn, s.m., 'fool'.

fulian, s.f., 'fool': *fulian o δənas* (a mild way of expressing it, O.H.).

fundro, fəundro, v., ffwndro, T.N. 68. 15; Eng. founder, 'to lose one's bearings', 'to be in perplexity': *dyːn wedi fundro = dyːn wedi koḷi forδ ;—mi fundris ən laːn: mi ëiꭅ i r tyː: nesa ən ḷeː duːad i hun*, 'I lost my bearings entirely: I went to the next house instead of coming to this one'; *kaptan loŋ ən fundro ən ə noːs ag ən mynd a i loŋ ar ə graig ən ə niul* (O.H.), a ship-captain losing his bearings in the night and running his ship on to a rock in the mist'; also trans. 'to perplex, muddle'.

fundrys, adj., 'confused, perplexed', "mithered".

fundur, s., ffwndwr, T.N. 15. 14. (1) 'agitation, commotion': *be di r fundur ? be ma pobol ən ꭅhedag ?* (O.H.) = *helynt*. (2) 'perplexity': *r oːn i meun fundur lawar gwaiθ am ləgodan*, i.e. as to whether it was a mouse or not (O.H.).

furδ (in full, *i furδ*), adv., ffwrdd, C.C.M. 421. 16, 'away': *ḷeː may ə loːn ? ən ə druːs fur*, 'where is the road? Away outside the door'; *iꭅo i dənny vo i furδ i lnay o, ḷuːx sy arno vo*, 'it must be taken away to be cleaned: there is dust on it'; *pꭅen wedi dori furδ*, 'a piece of wood cut away'; *gnëyd i furδ a rubaθ*, 'to do away with something'; *aː i a ꭅhëi n i fur ?*, 'shall I take these things away?'; *mynd furδ*; 'to go away'; *i furδ a vo*, 'off he goes'; *fur tiː!, fur a tiː!*, 'away with you!'; *hel də garkas (hel də brenja, hel də druːyd, hel də bak, gnaː də bak) a fur a tiː!* (O.H.).

furn, s.f., ffwrn, D., 'furnace'.

furnas, s.f., pl. *furnëiꭅa*, fwrneis, W.S.; ffwrnas, C.C. 359. 26; ffwrnes, B.C. 91. 23, 'furnace': *furnas o daːn*, 'a raging fire' = *goδaθ o daːn, wemfiam*.

fyːδ, s.f., ffydd, D., 'faith': *r oːyδ ǵin ər heːn bobol fyːδ ovnaduy meun ꭅhoi prokkar ən ə taːn er muːyn iδo vo gənna*.

fyːḷt, s., ffull, D., 'acceleratio, festinatio'; 'trot': *ar riu diːθ ne fyːḷt* (O.H.). Cf. *filjan*.

fyḷiyθ, s., 'trot': *ar ə fyḷiyθ* (O.H.).

fynyd, s., ffunud, D., 'form, manner, appearance': *may o r yːn fynyd a i vam*, 'he is the very image of his mother' (of face or character).

fyrad, s.m., pl. *fyrada*, firet, W.S. [A feret]; ffured, W.Ll. lxiv. 65; O.F. furet, 'ferret'.

fyrkan, s., Eng. firkin, 'a wooden vessel generally made of oak and containing the eighth part of a barrel': *darḷau ḷond fyrkan o guru;*—as term of reproach, *ła:u ꞃ he:n fyrkan fauyծ* —(O.H.).

fyrv ; fᵊrv (sometimes J.J.), adj., fem. *ferv*, eq. *fᵊrvad (frᵊvad*, O.H.) ; pl. *fᵊrvjon*, ffyrf, D., 'stout, substantial, bulky': *korłyn fyrv*, 'a stout cord' ; *pen fᵊrva i fon*, 'the thicker end of a stick'.

fyrv, s., ffurf, D., 'form'.

fyrvjo, v., ffurfio, D., s.v. 'formo'; 'to form'.

fy:sł, s.f., pl. *fisłja*, ffust, D., 'flail': *ȶro:yd ᵊ fy:sł*, 'handle of the flail'. Cf. also *siy:al, peᵑǵiuχ, kaꞃa (łe:p̊)*.

fᵊծlon, adj., ffyddlon, D., s.v. 'fidelis'; 'constant in religious observance'.

fᵊծlondab, s.m., ffyddlondeb, D., s.v. 'fidelitas'; 'regular attendance at religious observances'.

fᵊnnon, s.f., pl. *fᵊnonna, fᵊnonnyծ*, ffynnon, D., 'spring, fountain': *ḷᵊgad fᵊnnon*, 'spring-head', 'fountain head.'

fᵊrdur, s.m., ffyrfder, D., s.v. 'soliditas'; 'thickness' (= *ȶꞃu:χ*), e. g. of a stick.

fᵊrliᵑ, s.f., pl. *fᵊrliᵑod*, ffyrling, D., 'farthing'.

fᵊrnig, adj., comp. *fᵊrnikkaχ*, ffyrnig, D. (1) 'fierce, ferocious, implacable, fiery-tempered, raging, truculent': *may golug fᵊrnig arno vo*, 'he has a truculent aspect' ; *may o wedi mynd ᵊn fᵊrnig uծa i*, 'he has become enraged with me' ; *ǵelyn fᵊrnig*, 'a deadly enemy'. (2) of things, 'fierce, deadly': *may r ła:n ᵊn ḷosǵi n fᵊrnikkaχ ar dᵊwyծ o:yr*, 'fire burns more fiercely in cold weather'; *may n ꞃhᵊwi n ꞃhy: fᵊrnig i bara*, 'it is freezing too hard to last'; *may ǵin ᵊ dra:yn i:og biga fᵊrnig ᵊn ᵊr esǵiḷ*, 'the bass has formidable spikes in the fins' (O.H.). (3) used of a material which is hard to work: *kaꞃag fᵊrnig*.

fᵊrnigo, frᵊnigo, v., ffyrnigo, D., 'to become fierce, to get into a rage'.

fᵊrnigruyծ, s.m., ffyrnigrwydd, D., s.v. 'crudelitas'; 'fierceness, violent temper, rage'.

fᵊrnoχi, v., 'to be angry, to snort with rage' (W.H.).

gadal, v., gadael, D.   Fut. S. 1. (*ga*)*dewa*, 3. (*ga*)*dewiθ*.   Pl. 1.
(*ga*)·*daun*.   Imp. S. 1. (*ga*)·*daun*, 3. (*ga*)·*dawa*.   Pret. S. 1. (*ga*)-
dewis, (*ga*)*dawis*, 2. (*ga*)*dewist*, 3. (*ga*)*dawoδ*, *gadoδ*.   Pl. 3. (*ga*)-
dɐuson.   Plup. (*ga*)*dɐusun*.   Imperative : *ga:d ; gaduχ*, (*ga*)·*deuχ*.
Pret. Pass. *ga·daud.*   (1) 'to leave' : *gadal rubaθ ən ə loft*, 'to leave
something upstairs' ; *gadal əχ arjan ar əχ o:l*, 'to leave your money
behind you' ; *gadal riu air ar o:l*, 'to leave some word out' ; *mi*
(*a*)*dauni o n ə van əna*, 'we will leave it there' (e. g. an argument) ;—
with *lonyδ*, 'to leave alone' : *dawa m ono vo n lonyδ*, 'he would not
leave him alone' ;—with *i*, 'to leave alone' : *ga:d ɩðo vo*, 'leave
him alone' ;· *mi daun i ɩðo vo taun·i χi:*, 'I should leave him alone
if I were you' ; so with *lonyδ*: *pam daχi ŋ gadal lonyδ i hunəna ?*,
'why do you leave that man alone?'   (2) 'to let, allow' : *pëidjuχ
a gadal ɩði hi sərθjo*, 'don't let her fall' ; *ga·deuχ ɩðo vynd i grogi*,
'let him go and be hanged'.

gaðo, v., gaddaw & gaddewid, corruptè pro addewid, D.   Fut.
S. 1. *ðawa*, 3. *ðawiθ*.   Pret. *ðawis*.   Imperative *gaðo*, 'to promise' :
ðary nu aðo i gəry hi, 'they promised to send it' ; *nëiθ dim y:n o
·honynu ðim ond gaðo*, 'none of them will do anything but promise'.

gair, s.m., pl. *ǵëirja*, gair, D.   (1) 'word' : *ǵëirja maur*, 'long
words' ; *ǵëirja həljon*, 'bad language' ; *tori ǵëirja*, 'to articulate
clearly' ; *ɩri:o tori ǵëirja ag ən meθy* (e. g. of small children) ;—*dim
gair da: am ne:b*, 'not a good word for any one' ; *wa:yθ y:n gair
(mu:y) na χant*, 'one word is as good as a hundred', i. e. 'I'll tell
you once for all' ; *hannar gair i gal* (prov.), 'half a word to the
wise', 'le sage entend à demi-mot'.   (2) 'report' : *mi ðo:θ ə gair
ar le:d*, 'the report got abroad'.   (3) 'reputation' : *gair· gwa:yl
syδ ɩði hi.*

galar, s., galar, D., 'mourning' : *ma na alar ən ə ty:.*

galary, v., galaru, D., 'to mourn'.

galarys, adj., galarus, D., 'mournful' : *ma: r tëyly n alarys jaun
ar o:l ə babi ba:χ ;—su:n galarys*, 'a mournful sound'.

galu, v., galw, D.   Fut. S. 1. *galwa*, 3. *galwiθ*.   Pl. 1. *galun*,
2. *galuχ*, 3. *galwan*.   Pret. S. 3. *galwoδ*.   Pl. 3. *galson*.   Imperative
galu ; galuχ.   (1) 'to call, shout' (= *gwëiði*) : *os by:δ iʃo rubaθ*

ɣhaid i χi alu, ' if you want anything you must call '. (2) also with *ar,* ' to call ' (by name): *galu (ar) ru:in,* ' to call some one ' ;—also, ' to call, to wake ': *neuχi alu arna i (ɣalu i) ən ə bora,* ' will you call me in the morning '. (3) ' to call, name ': *be daχi ɳ galu hun ?,* ' what do you call this ? (4) ' to call (together) ': *os na vy:ð dim aχos əɳ kodi i alu ə kəɳor əɳ gynt,* ' if no cause arises to call the council sooner '. (5) with *am,* ' to call ' (alluding to some need): *t o:ys dim by:d əɳ galu am ˙danoχi,* ' there is nothing you have to do '. (6) with *hevo,* ' to call upon, visit '.

galuyn, s.m., pl. *galuini,* galwyn, G.R. 43. 14; D., ' gallon ': *govyn am aluyn o guru.*

galwad, s.f., galwad, D.. ' call, invitation ': *ar i alwad o ëif i əno,* ' it was at his invitation that I went there '; also the ' call ' of a minister.

galwedigaθ, s.f., galwedigaeth, D., ' calling ': *dilin i alwedigaθ,* ' to follow one's calling '.

ga:ɬ, a:ɬ, s.f., pl. *ǵeɬyð, eɬyð.* [In place-names always *gɒ:ɬ,* e.g. *ga:ɬ ə blëyna,—ə guyndy,—təðyn ɣhonuyn,—ty: he:n,—bryn gola,— ə ɣhiuja—all in Llanfairfechan.] allt and gallt, D. (1) ' hill ', i.e. ' cliff, steep slope, side of a valley ': *tori ko:yd ar ə ǵeɬyð,* ' to cut down trees on the steep slopes; *ga:ɬ ə mo:r,* ' cliff '; *ɬuybyr ən mynd uθ ben ga:ɬ ə mo:r.* (2) ' hill ', i.e. ' a steep piece of road, etc.' (Fr. ' côte '): *i vəny, i laur ər a:ɬ,* ' up, down the hill '; *ma: r aɬ ma n drom jaun,* ' this hill is very steep '; *ga:ɬ rəular* (in quarries), ' roller incline '.

galy, v., gallu, D. Fut. S. 1. *gaḷa,* 2. *ǵeḷi,* 3. *ǵeḷiθ, gaḷ, ǵeiḷ.* Pl. 1. *gaḷun,* 2. *ǵeḷuχ, gaḷuχ,* 3. *gaḷan.* Imp. S. 1. *gaḷun, ǵeḷun,* 2. *galat, ǵeḷat,* 3. *gaḷa, ǵeḷa.* Pl. 1. *gaḷan, ǵeḷan,* 2. *gaḷaχ, ǵeḷaχ,* 3. *gaḷan, ǵeḷan.* Pret. S. 1. *ǵeḷis,* 2. *ǵeḷist,* 3. *gaḷoð.* Pl. 1. *gaḷson,* 2. *gaḷsoχ,* 3. *gaḷson.* Plup. S. 1. *gaḷsun, (mi) lasun,* 2. *gaḷsat, (mi) lasat,* 3. *gaḷsa, (mi) lasa.* Pl. 1. *gaḷsan, (mi) lasan,* 2. *gaḷsaχ, (mi) lasaχ,* 3. *gaḷsan, (mi) lasan.* Pres. Sub. S. 3. *gaḷo.* Pl. 1. *gaḷon,* 2. *gaḷoχ,* 3. *gaḷon.* Fut. Pass. *ǵeḷir ;* Imp. Pass. *ǵeḷid ;* Plup. Pass. *ḷesid,* ' to be able ': *gaḷsun i nëyd o n ëiθa pe kəusun i,* ' I could do it well enough if I might '; *mi lasun i vnavyd o n ovnaduy,* ' I might have hurt him very badly '; *pe gaḷsa mi ḷuga vi,* ' he would starve me if he could '; *ə pe:θ lasa vo ðëyd,* ' what he might have said '; *du i ðim ən amma na lasa vo,* ' I do not doubt he could ': *gora gaḷ,* ' as well as he can ' = *gora gaḷo vo ; gora ˙gaḷoni, ˙gaḷoχi,* ' as well as we can, you can '; *gaḷa r dy:n gora vod ən ə ḷe: sala,* ' the best man might be in the worst place '.—*(ǵ)eḷiθ (vo:d)* and *(ǵ)eḷa (vo:d)* are used to express ' perhaps ': *un i ðim, eḷiθ vo:d,* ' I don't know, perhaps so '; *eḷa na ða:u o ðim,* ' perhaps he won't come '; *eḷa mai ifo du:r sy arno vo,* ' perhaps it wants water '; *eḷa da:u o hevo r y:n tre:n ə dois i:,* ' perhaps he will come by the same train as I did '. Ans. *eḷa,* ' perhaps so '.

galy, s.m., pl. *galy:oδ*, gallu, D. (1) 'power': *po:b pe:θ ən əχ galy χi*, 'everything in your power'; *gwëiθjo mu:y na i aly*, 'to overwork'. (2) 'natural mental power or capacity' (as distinguished from acquired capacity). Cf. *medar*. (3) 'sense': *ə pym galy*, 'the five senses'.

galy:og, adj., galluog, D., 'able': *may r medrys ən iuſ'o ə peθa ə may r galy:og wedi fendjo.*

ga:m, s., 'game': *ma: nu i vəny a fo:b ǵa:m = riks.*

ǵambl, s., 'sport, amusement, fun'; 'gambling' (playing for money).

ǵamblar, ǵemblar, s.m., Eng. gambler. (1) 'a skilful person, a master-hand': *may hi ŋ ǵemblar ar i gwaiθ* (= *ən vistar ar i gwaiθ*). (2) 'a smart fellow': *ma nu ŋ ǵemblars garu.*

ǵambljo, v., gamblo, T.N. 4. 31, 'to sport, make game; make game of; gamble (play for money)'.

ǵamjo, v., 'to sport; make game of': *paid ti a ŋamjo vi.*

ǵamlyd, adj., 'inclined to jeer, mock, make game of'.

ǵamstar, s.m., Eng. gamester, 'a skilful person, a master-hand': *may o ŋ ǵamstar ar hənny.* Cf. C.F. 1890, 332. 30.

gan, conj., gan, D., 'inasmuch as, because': *gan bo χi·am ·vynd*, 'inasmuch as you *are* going'; *gan mod i mor hy: a govyn*, 'if I may make so bold as to ask'.

gar, s.m., pl. *gara*, garr, D., 'poples'; 'the ham or hind part of the knee': *a i glos am ben i ara*, 'his trousers down to his knees': *gara k̃ëimjon*, 'bandy legs'; *kamma gar* [*kammaδ*].

ǵard, s.f., pl. *ǵards*, gard, W.S. [A garde], 'watch-chain'.

gardas, s.f., pl. *gardəsa*, gartys, W.S. [A garter]; gardes, D.F. [xvii] 27; gardas and gardys, D., 'garter': *du:y ardas.*

gardjo, v., gardio, W.S., s.v. 'kribo' [Carde]; R.; T.N. 408. 5. Cf. gardiau, D., s.v. 'strideo'; 'to card' (wool): *ə kəθral əŋ gardjo n ə fakiṛi* (O.H.). Also *kardjo*, q.v.

gardnar, s.m., 'gardener'.

garδ, gar, s.f., pl. *ǵerδi*, gardd, D., 'garden': *iṛi:n garδ*, 'to garden'.

garδjo, v., 'to garden'.

garδun, s.m., pl. *garδərna*, arddwrn, D., 'wrist': *ne:s pnelin na garδun* (prov.), 'the elbow is nearer than the wrist', i.e. 'blood is thicker than water'.

garlag, s., garlleg, D., 'garlic': *gwina garlag*, 'cloves of garlic'.

garíra, adv., gartref, 'at home' (domi); 'home' (domum): *ədi o garíra ?*, 'is he at home?' (more rarely *adra*); *gneuχ vel ·iasaχi garịra*, 'make yourself at home'; *may o wedi mynd garịra*, 'he has gone home' (more commonly *aðra*).

garθ, s.f., garth, D., 'a jutting piece of hill' = *ịru:yn mənyð*. Very common in place-names and not quite obsolete in current speech. I have heard O.H. use the word twice, i.e. *sərθjo ðros garθ*, and *o r nail garθ i r lal*, the latter alluding to the jutting hill on each side of the entrance to the Aber valley.—With the article in place-names always *ə garθ*.

garu, adj., pl. *g̈ẹiru*, comp. *garwax*, garw, D. (1) 'rough, severe': *isuyð garu*, 'rough weather'. (2) 'rough, hardy' (opp. to *rhɵujog*); used substantively: *tori r garu* (fig.), 'to break the ice'. (3) (with *g̈in*) 'sorry': *may n aru g̈in i*, 'I am sorry'. (4) used with various meanings of an intensive nature: *y:n garu ədi o*, (in good sense) 'he is a splendid fellow'; (in bad sense) 'he is a shrewd, grasping fellow'; a terrible fellow';—in fem. *y:n garu ədi hi ;—y:n garu daxi !*, 'what a fellow you are!' (in either sense) ;—followed by *am*, 'fond, (a) terrible (fellow for)': *garu am dani ədi o !*, 'he is a terrible fellow for business'; *may hi n aru am vala*, 'she is fond of apples'; *may hi n y:n aru am əm·droi i laur əno*, 'she is a dreadful one for loitering down there'; *dy:n garu am ə by:d ma*, 'a grasping man';—*may o n aru əm mho:b pe:θ*, 'he takes an energetic part in everything'; *r ədaxi n y:n garu i wisgo x sg̈idja*, 'you are very bad at wearing out your boots'; *pe:θ garu ədi darlan am godi if̣o kəsgy*, 'reading is a dreadful thing for making one sleepy'; *may by:d garu hevo vo*, 'he gives a great deal of trouble'; *he:n vaujax garu ədi o*, 'he is a worthless old creature'; *may amsar garu*, 'there is plenty of time'; *may g̈in i bo:yn garu ən ə mhen*, 'I have a terrible pain in my head'; *pilti garu !*, 'what a pity!' (5) adverbially, 'much', 'very', "awfully", etc. (often = *ovnaduy*): *du i n disgul ən aru*, 'I quite expect'; *daxi wedi mendjo n aru xadal ·öyðaxi ðo:y*, 'you are much better than you were yesterday'; *may n debig aru i la:u*, 'it is very like rain'; *mi vy:ð na bobol ən aru ə durnod hunnu*, 'there will be a great many people that day'; *edrax ən aru arni hi*, 'to look intently at her'; *may hi wedi kodi n wynt garu jaun*, 'it has become very windy'.

g̈as, s.f., 'gas': *r öyðun i n dal sylu bod ə g̈as wedi ka:yl i θroi*, 'I noticed the gas was turned on'.

ga:st, s.f., pl. *g̈ẹist*, gâst, D., 'bitch': ·*ga:staxun*, 'bitch and puppies'.

g̈a:t, s.f., pl. *g̈atja*, 'gate': *du:y g̈a:t*, 'two gates'; *po:st ə g̈a:t*, 'gate-post' (of wood or a single stone); *pilar ə g̈a:t*, 'gate-post' (built of stone or brick).

gaval, v., gafaelu, D. Fut. S. 1. *g(a)vẹyla*, 2. *g(a)vẹili*, 3. *g(a)vẹiliθ*, *veliθ*. Pl. 1. *g(a)vẹylun*, 2. *g(a)vẹylux*, 3. *g(a)vẹylan*. Imp.

g(a)vëylun, gavun. Pret. S. 1. *g(a)vëilis, gavis,* 2. *g(a)vëilisʃ, gavisʃ,* 3. *g(a)vëyloð, gavoð, veloð.* Pl. 3. *gavson.* Plup. *gavsun.* Imperative, *gaval, gava ; g(a)vëyluχ, gavuχ,* 'to lay hold (of)', 'to catch (of fire)', 'to take root': *gaval ən ə re:ns, gaval y:n bo:b ḷa:u,* 'take hold of the reins, take one in each hand'; *paid a gaval əna i.* 'don't take hold of me'; *nëif o ðim gaval əni,* 'he won't buckle to'; *may hi ɲ gaval ən ə gla:u,* 'the rain is setting to in earnest'; *gaval am ə mëiɲgevn,* 'to catch round the small of the back'; *may r gwynʃ əɲ gaval ·moχi,* 'the wind is piercing'; *may hi wedi gaval a i dannað əno vo,* 'it bit him'; *os by:ð hi wedi gaval ən jaun,* 'if it has taken root properly'.—Cf. *kədjad.*

gaval, s.f., gafael, D., 'hold, grasp': *dal, ka:yl gaval (ən),* 'to catch hold (of), to keep hold (of)'; *koḷi, guḷuɲ gaval,* 'to lose hold (of)'; *dal d aval əno vo r̄hag iðo sərθjo,* 'catch hold of him to keep him from falling'; *ðary mi ga:l gaval əno vo,* 'I caught hold of him'; —fig. *may r diwigjad wedi ka:yl gaval ən drum əno vo,* 'the revival has caught hold of him strongly'; *ma: gin baub aval meun byu,* 'every one clings to life'; *koḷi r aval,* said of a dying man; *r̄hedag, gwëiθjo nerθ i aval,* 'to run, work to the utmost of one's power'; *mynd i aval ə gərvraθ,* 'to get within the arm of the law'; *koḷi r aval ən i waiθ,* 'to be turned off';—*bo:b gaval,* 'every time': *meθy·, gweḷa bo:b gaval.*

gaval, adj., pl. *gavëiljon,* in the exp. *karag aval,* pl. *kerig gaval, kerig gavëiljon,* 'a stone fixed fast in the ground' (J.J.).

gavëylgar, vëylgar, velgar, adj., gafaelgar, D. (1) 'tenacious': *pry: gavëylgar jaun,* 'a very tenacious insect', i.e. one which keeps a tight hold, e.g. on the hair of cattle (J.J.); *dy:n gavëylgar = dy:n əɲ gaval ən i waiθ* (O.H.)—opp. to ·*di:·aval.* (2) 'arresting the attention': *pr̄egaθ avëylgar.*

gavl, s.f., pl. *gavla,* gafl, D. (1) 'fork' (of human beings or animals): *ki: a i gumfon ən i avl,* 'a dog with his tail between his legs' (= *ki: swaʃ*). The expression *a i gumfon ən i avl* is also used of human beings = 'cowed', 'crestfallen'. (2) 'legs': *dy:n a gavl hi:r, gavla hirjon,* 'a long-legged man' (O.H.); *ḷedy i avla,* 'to stand with one's legs wide apart' (O.H.). (3) 'lap': *plenʃyn ən i gavl ʃr̄u: r dy:ð,* 'a child in her lap all day' (O.H.).

gavljo, v., 'to place the legs wide apart': *dy:n əɲ gavljo o vla:yn ə ʃa:n,* 'a man sitting with his legs wide apart before the fire'.

gavlog, s.m., gaflog, S.E., s.v. 'forked'; 'a long-legged man' (J.J., O.H.).

gavr, s.f., pl. *gëivr,* gafr, D. (1) 'goat, she-goat': *bu:χ gavr,* 'he-goat'; *vel gavr ar drana,* 'like a goat in a thunderstorm', said of some one in a state of great excitement; *gëivr fi:r gnarvon,* epithet of the people of Carnarvonshire; *r̄ he:n avr avlan!,* term of reproach for a woman (O.H.); *məɲ gavr!,* expletive. (2) 'a small bundle of corn, etc., such as can be easily grasped by the hand, and tied loosely together'. [The word in this sense is perhaps the same as the Eng. (Dial.) 'gavel', 'a sheaf or quantity of corn ; a bundle or sheaf of rush used in thatching '—Nrf.]

gavrjo, v., gafriaw, O.P., 'to tie corn, marram-grass (*morait/*), etc., in small loose bundles and place them to stand leaning against one another in threes to dry' (O.H.).

ǵëirwir, adj., geirwir, D., s.v. 'verax', 'verus'; 'truthful': *gonast a ǵëirwir.*

ǵelaχ, s.m., gelach, O.P., 'a small, wiry individual' (I.W.)—as term of reproach = *hogyn dru:g ag ən ðiχelðrug dəχrənlyd* (O.H.): *le: ·by:osti, r he:n elaχ kaχy ?* (O.H.).

ǵelan, s.f., pl. *ǵelod*, gêl, D., 'leech'; also *ǵelan bendul* (I.W.) ; *ǵelan ðëyban, ǵelan ridul* (O.H.): *uθi hi vel ǵelan*, 'at it like a nigger'.

ǵelyn, s.m., pl. *ǵelɔnjon*, gelyn, D., 'enemy': *ǵelyn fərnig, ǵelyn gla:s*, 'a deadly enemy'; *ə ǵelyn gla:s* is also an epithet of death.

ǵelɔnjaθ, s.m., gelyniaeth, D., 'enmity'.

ǵelig (O.H.); *ǵerlig* (E.J., J.J.), s.pl.; sing. *ǵeligan* (O.H.), *ǵerlɔgan* (W.H., E.J., J.J.) ; *gərligan, garlag, garlɔgan* (J.J.), gellyg, D., 'pears': *köydan ǵelig, elig* (O.H.), *köydan ǵerlig, erlig* (J.J.), 'pear-tree'; *ǵelig keθin*, 'a worthless kind of pear' (O.H.).

ǵe:n, s.f., gên, D., 'jaw': *klikjad ǵe:n*, 'jaw-bone'; *ər e:n isa, yχa*, 'the lower, upper jaw'; *wëyθa ən i e:n*, 'in spite of him' (O.H.).—Also 'chin': *may r levriθ wedi rhedag ar əχ ǵe:n.*

ǵena, s.m., pl. *ǵenëya*, genau, D., 'mouth' (= *ke:g*); *ǵena tul*, 'the mouth of a hole'; *əŋ ǵena r avon*, 'at the mouth of the river'; *dan ə ǵena* often = 'chin'; *əŋ ǵena r sa:χ ma:y knilo* (prov.), 'economy should begin at the mouth of the sack'—i.e. when a new supply is begun, not when it is all but finished ; *ǵena gla:n i ogany* (prov.), 'one who finds fault should be without fault himself';—*ǵena go:g (go:yg)*, genau goeg, D., 'lizard'.

ǵenaθ, s.f., pl. *(g)neθod*, geneth, D., 'girl'. The more usual word is *hogan.*

ǵenedigaθ, s., genedigaeth, D., 'birth'.

ǵenedigol, adj., genedigòl, D., s.v. 'nativus'; 'native': *r o:ð o n enedigol o bulheli*, 'he was a native of Pwllheli'; *le: ǵenedigol, bro: enedigol*, 'native place'.

ǵeni, v., geni, D. Pret. *ganuyd* [no other inflected forms are used], 'to be born': *əmma ganuyd a maguyt i*, 'it was here that she was born and brought up'; *ə durnod ə ganuyd vi*, 'the day I was born'; *ə durnod ǵesti də eni*, 'the day you were born'; *·wyðoχi m o χ ǵeni i r by:d*, 'you do not know what trouble is'; *man ǵeni*, 'birth-mark'.

ǵenḷi goːχ, s.f., cenlli goch, D., s.v. 'cenchris'; the generic term for 'hawk',—properly speaking 'kestrel', Forrest, (Falco tinnunculus.) Cf. *ḱidiḷ*.

ǵenwar, s.f., pl. *ǵenwëirja*, genwair, D., 'fishing-rod' (O.H. frequently) = gjalam *bəsgotta*, gjalam *vöïrjo;—tɔvar*, *ǵenwar a gun nëïθ uːr boneðig ən ḷum* (prov.); *pɔy: ǵenwar*, 'earth-worm'.

ǵeːr, *ǵeːrs*, s.pl., sing. *ḱeryn*, q.v., cer, D., s.v. 'gerræ'; 'gear, stuff': *ǵeːr(s) kəfəla*, 'harness'; *ǵeːr boːn* is used to distinguish from *ǵeːr redig*, 'ploughing gear'; *heːn ǵeːr*, 'old stuff' (O.H. speaking of antiquities dug up);—also tools, instruments. Cf. *ervyn, feryn*.

ǵerjan, v., geran and gerain, D., 'to whine' (of children), generally *ǵerjan kɔiːo*. Also, 'to quarrel, bicker': *ǵerjan ar i ǵiliθ*.

ǵerḷan, s.f., only in *ǵerḷan goːχ* (W.H.) = *ǵenḷi goːχ* (?), 'hawk' —not known to O.H. (This word occurs in an article on the birds of Anglesey in the 'Clorianydd' for Feb. 22, 1912.)

ǵernjal, ǵernjo, v., ymgernial, O.P.; S.E., s.v. 'wrangle'; 'to talk loudly, wrangle'.

ǵeruyn, s.f., cerwyn, D., 'brewing-tub'—made of brass or copper (O.H.).

ǵes, s.f. (1) 'guess': *ə ǵes, riu ǵes veχan*. In slate-quarries, in taking a bargain, 'the estimate as to how much will be worked in a month' (J.J.). (2) 'idea': *i oːð gəno vo ðim ǵes i naðy*, 'he had no idea how to trim' (sc. slates).

ǵesʿo, v., 'to guess' = *dɔvëiʿo, kafjo*.

ǵewin, s.m., pl. *ǵewina, ǵewəna*, gewin, D. (1) 'sinew, muscle': *r oːð ə ǵewin wedi kutjo*, 'the sinew had shrunk'. (2) a by-form of *ewin*, 'nail': *may ǵewin o ðyːn ən werθ mənyð o ðənas ; gweḷ ǵewin o vaːb na mənyð o verχ* (prov.). In these proverbs *ewin* is often heard instead of *ǵewin*.—Cf. Exod. x. 26.

ǵëya, s.m., gayaf, L.A. 54. 9; gaeaf, G.R. [94]. 8; gauaf, D., 'winter', i.e. November, December, and January: *maː r ǵëya dyː ən əmmyl*, 'gloomy winter is approaching'; *kḷaŋǵëya* = calan gauaf, 'the winter calends', i.e. Nov. 13.

ǵëyavað, adj., gauafaidd, D., s.v. 'hyemalis'; 'wintry': *r oːð hi n ëyavað jaun hëïðju*.

ǵëyavol, adj., gayafawl, M.A. i. 42 b. 7, 'of or belonging to the winter': *dyːð ǵëyavol*, 'a winter's day'.

ǵid, always in conjunction with *a*, prep. gydâ, gyd ag, D., s.v. 'cum'; gida, G.R. 2. 15; D.F. [25]. 27. (1) 'with', only used in certain locutions—otherwise *hevo*. Sometimes the two expressions are interchangeable. *mi ʿeïθ ǵid a mənað*, 'it will go (e. g. into the box) with patience'; *ǵid a govol*, 'with care'; *ǵid a χ ḱennad*, 'by your leave'; *ǵid a ḷaːu*, 'by the bye'; *ǵid a hənny*, 'in addition to this '; *hu:i ǵid a r k̆i: a hu:i ǵid a r ga:θ*, ' to run with the hare and hunt with the hounds ';—*ǵid a hyn*, ' presently ' : *na: i ðeχra ǵid a hyn*, ' I shall begin presently ' ; *ǵid a r no:s*, ' in the evening '. This expression is also used substantively : *ty: a ǵid a r no:s*, ' towards evening ' ; *tru:y ǵid a r no:s*, ' all the evening '. (2) ' along ' : *ḷuybyr ən troi i laur ǵid a r avon*, ' a path turning down along the river ' ; *ku:χ ən mynd ǵid a r avon*, ' a boat floating down the stream ' ; *riu viḷtir ǵid a r avon i laur*, ' a mile or so down the river ' ; *ǵid a r tai*, ' along the houses '. (3) used as a conjunction, ' as soon as ' : *ǵid a do:nu*, ' as soon as they come ' ; *ǵid a ·bəðanu wedi paſo*, ' as soon as they have passed ' ; *ǵid a kḷu:oð o hənny*, ' as soon as he heard that ' ; *peθ kənta ǵid a ·kodanu ðy sy:l*, ' as soon as they are up on Sunday '. Cf. y gyt ac y doethant rac bron Kynan, R.B. ii. 113. 22 (S. § 206); gyt ac y bu nos, W.B., col. 71. 12; gyt ac y kyuodes ef, W.B., col. 52. 20.

ǵi:d, only in *i ǵi:d*, i gŷd, D., s.v. ' insimul ' ; ' all, altogether ' : *daχi wedi du:ad i ǵi:d ru:an*, ' you have all come now ' ; *·r ədani n ail nëyd ə ty: i ǵi:d*, ' we are reconstructing the whole house ' ; *rχi: ga:θ ə ḷəθəra i ǵi:d hëiðju*, ' you got all the letters to-day ' ; *r o:ð hi ŋ ǵe:g i ǵi:d*, ' she was a great chatterbox ', lit. ' she was all mouth ' ; *əŋ go:χ i ǵi:d drosto*, ' red all over ' ; *r o:ð ə ta:n wedi mynd i laur i ǵi:d*, ' the fire had gone quite low ' ; *dim əno i ǵi:d*, ' not all there, crazy '.

ǵildjo, v., gildio, W.Ll. xxi. 88. (1) ' to yield, give way '. (2) of corn ' to yield well, to produce good grain ' (J.J.). (3) of corn ' yielding the grain easily when threshed ' (J.J.).

ǵildjo, v., Eng. geld; (Dial.) gild, w.Som., ' to clean (herrings) before salting, etc., by removing the entrails ' : *ǵildjo penwaig* (O.H.).

ǵilið, gilydd, D., s.v. ' mutuus ' ; gilid, W.B., col. 9. 3 ; 12. 13 ; gilidd, G.R. 28. 20 ; D.F. [6] 28, [24] 5, [38] 23 :—always preceded by a pronominal adjective, ' each other, one another ' ; *ma: r pəsgod əŋ gwëy tru i ǵilið*, ' the fish are threading in and out between one another ' ; *ma: nu n frëyo hevo i ǵilið o hy:d*, ' they are always quarrelling with one another ' ; *t ədi r beχǵin ðim mor ðo:yθ a i ǵilið*, ' the young fellows are not all equally wise ' ; *mi ðo:ni i ða:ḷt əŋ ǵilið vesyl tippin*, ' we shall get to understand one another little by little ' ; *pym ty: ən sæund uθ i ǵilið*, ' five houses in a row ' ; *kayl ə ðay pen ḷinin at i ǵilið*, ' to make two ends meet ' ; *la:yθ wedi hel at i ǵilið*, ' curdled milk ' ; *mynd i ǵilið*, ' to shrivel, to shrink ' ; *ma: rhëi pobol ən meðul bod nu n dal ə by:d uθ i ǵilið*, ' some people think they hold the world together ' ; *du:y noson ar o:l i ǵilið*, ' two nights running ' ; *əŋ knokjo uθ ə dru:s vel ·tasanu am godi r by:d ə mhen i ǵilið*, ' knocking at the door as if they were going to set the whole world topsy-turvy ' ; *mi a:nu at i ǵilið etto*, ' they will come together again ', i.e. ' they will make it up ' ; *hel nu ŋ griu at i ǵilið*, ' to drive them together into a mass ' ; *syt ə may əχ plant χi i kəmmyd nu at i ǵiliδ ?*, ' how are your children taking them all together ? ' ; *uθ roi po:b durnod at i ǵiliδ*, ' on the average ' ; *may ɣhëi n medry ə δu:y la:u vel i ǵiliδ*, ' some people can use both hands equally well ' ; *dim mor anoδ i baub a i ǵiliδ*, ' not equally difficult to all ', ' not so difficult to some as it is to others '.

ǵin, ǵen, ǩin, prep., gan, D. ; gen, G.R. 22. 2 ; 35. 17. With pronouns S. 1.*ǵin i,ǵen i* ; 2.*ǵin ti, ǵen ti* ; 3. *ɡəno vo, ǵeno vo, ǵino vo* ; *ɡəni hi, ǵini hi*. Pl. 1. ·ɡənoni, ·ǵinoni, ·ǵenoni ; 2. ·ɡənoχi, ·ɡənəχi, ·ǵinoχi, ·ǵenoχi ; 3. ·ɡənonu, ·ɡənynu, ·ǵenynu, ·ǵinonu. (1) with *bo:d* to denote possession : *may ʝais main ɡəno vo*, ' he has a shrill voice ' ; *oy::s ǵin ti vəmryn o vakko ?*, ' have you a scrap of tobacco ? ' ; *may ǵin i bedar jaiθ*, ' I know four languages ' ; *r o:yδ ɡəno vo vəδul maur o hono vo*, ' he thought a great deal of it ' ; *may ǵin i gy:r ən ə ᵐhen*, ' I have a headache ' ; *may ǵin i gwiliδ ʃarad o χ bla:yn χi*, ' I am shy of talking before you ' ; *ko: da: ǵin i!*, ' what a memory I have ! ' (2) after various adjectives denoting their relation to a person : *may n δa: ǵin i*, ' I am glad ' ; *may n δru:g ǩin i*, ' I am sorry ' ; (also without *ma:y* : *da: ǵin i, dru:g ǩin i*) ; *θa: ǩin i m ono vo*, ' I don't like him ' ; *weʝ ǵin i*, ' I would rather ' (cf. *weʝ i mi*, ' I had better ') ; *wa:yθ ǵin i, dim ods ǵin i*, ' it is all the same to me ', ' I don't care ' ; *may n ɣhy: bo:yθ ǵin i*, ' it is too hot for me ' ; *peθ həla ǵin i ədi gweld . . .*, ' there is nothing I hate more than seeing . . .' ; *debig ǩin i*, ' I suppose ' ; *may n haus ǵin i veδul*, ' I am rather inclined to think ' ; *may n hu:yr ǵin i gwelt hi n mendjo*, ' I am longing to see her get better ' ; *ə pe:θ gora ·ɡənoχi ga:l ar ə δëyar*, ' the thing you like to get best in the world ' ; *i ədi hi δim ən ɣhy: vy:an ·ɡənoχi ŋweld i ?*, ' you don't think it too soon to see me ? '—also after a predicative noun with *ən* : *may ŋ gwestjun ǵin i ·vedruχi godi vory*, ' I rather doubt whether you will be able to get up to-morrow '. (2) ' by ', expressing the agent after a passive verb : *δary o ga:yl i la:δ* (= *mi ʝaδuyd o*) *ɡəno vo*, ' he was killed by him '. (3) where English usage requires ' from ' in cases like the following : *ga: i venθig su:ʝ ·ɡənoχi ?*, ' will you lend me a shilling ? ' ; *χeuχi mo r gwi:r ɡəno vo*, ' you can't get the truth out of him ' ; *ǵin bu:y ·prənnisti o ?*, ' from whom did you buy it ? ' (4) after *ka:yl*, with a person from whom permission is obtained : *os ǩëiθ o ǵin i da:d*, ' if his father will let him '. (5) ' with, because of ' : *krənny ǵin annuyd*, ' to shiver with cold ' ; *meθy gweld ə ko:yd ǵin brenʝa*, ' not to see the wood for the trees '. (6) rarely in phrases of the form : *ɣ he:n fu:l ɡəno vo!*, ' the old fool ! ' ; *ɣ he:n grjadyr ǵin ə ŋhaid*, ' my old grandfather '.

ǵini, s.m., pl. *ǵinis*, gini, T.N. 4. 30, ' guinea ' : *day ǵini*, ' two guineas ' ; *pentur o ǵinis anvarθ*, ' an immense heap of guineas '.

ǵino, v. [*eǵino*].

ǵiŋrom, s. [*ǩiŋgron*].

g̓is, Eng. (Dial.) gis, giss, Sc. and N. Eng., a call to pigs (to make them come to the speaker). According to O.H. *bik* was formerly said to one, *g̓is* to a number, but now *g̓is* is used in both cases.

gjalam (W.H.; I.W.; O.H.), *gwialam* (O.H.); *gwalan* (J.J.), s.f., pl. *gjalams, gwialams, gwialyms.* Cf. also *gwi:al.* With the article *ə wjalam*, gwialen, D., 'rod': *gjalam vedu*, 'birch rod'; *gjalam (bə)sgotta, vuirjo (vöirjo)*, 'fishing-rod'; *gjalam hëyarn* [*fru:yn*]; *gjalam ayr*, 'agrimony' (Agrimonia Eupatoria); *gjalam arjan*, kind of plant (sp. ?)—Also 'penis'.

gjalχan, galχan ; g̓i:alχ (I.W.), s.f., pl. *gjalχod.* With the article *ə wjalχan*, mwyalchen, D., 'blackbird' (Turdus merula).

glan, s.f., pl. *glennyð, glanna*, glann, D. (1) 'shore, bank': *glan ə mo:r*, 'sea-shore' (pl. *glanna moroð*); *glan ər avon*, 'the bank of the river': *may r avon wedi tori dros i glennyð.* 'the river has overflowed its banks'; *ar lan ə be:ð*, 'on the brink of the grave'. (2) the place is a quarry where the slates are dressed, and in general the sides of the quarry as compared with the *tuḷ* or deep workings.

gla:n, adj., glân, D. (1) 'clean': *du:r gla:n*, 'clean water'; *kḷeri gla:n*, 'clean collars'. (2) 'pure': *kəmro gla:n (glöyu)*, 'a pure Welshman'. (3) 'good-looking, beautiful': *merχ la:n əsiuyθ*, 'a fine sprightly girl'. (4) 'utterly, entirely': *mi ·aŋ·hovis ən la:n nëiθjur*, 'I clean forgot last night'; *meθis ən la:n (löyu)*, 'I failed utterly'; *ovnaduy la:n*, "awfully"; *kodi n la:n ar* (imp.), 'to cease entirely': *mi godoð ən la:n arna i i vynd ə mla:yn hevo farad sëisnag*, 'I entirely gave up speaking English': *mi godoð ən la:n arno vo ar ganol i bregaθ*, 'he utterly broke down in the middle of his sermon'.

glandag, adj., glandeg, D., s.v. 'mundus'; 'good-looking': *əy:n glandag.*

glanwaθ, adj., glanwaith, D., s.v. 'mundus'; 'clean and neat': *r o:ð na rubaθ digri əni hi ond r o:ð hi n rëil dut, ən rëil lanwaθ* (O.H.), 'there was something funny about her, but she was quite tidy, quite clean and neat'; *dgob lanwaθ dëidi meun mynyd* (O.H.), 'a clean, neat job, all in a minute';—*farm lanwaθ.*

glanwëiθdra, s., glanweithdra, D., s.v. 'munditia'; 'cleanliness and neatness'.

gla:s, s.m., pl. *glasys*, 'glass, tumbler'; 'looking-glass'.

gla:s, adj., pl. *glëif'on*, glâs, D. (1) 'blue': *r awyr la:s*, 'the blue sky'; *karag la:s*, pl. *kerig glëif'on*, 'slate'; *krogan la:s*, pl. *kreg̓in glëif'on*, 'mussel'. (2) 'green': *ti:r gla:s*, 'lawn, grass-plot'; *kḷut gla:s o vla:yn ə ty:*, 'a green patch before the house'. (3) implying youth: *riu la:s hogan*, 'a young girl'; cf. glaslangc, D., s.v. 'adolescens', 'iuuenculus'. (4) 'grey': *ḵefyl gla:s*, 'a grey horse'; *byuχ la:s*, 'a grey cow'; cf. *glasy* (of the hair); *bora gla:s*, 'dawn'; cf. W.B., col. 73. 29.   (5) epithet of death, *ə ģelyn glaːs*; cf. C.C. 12. 13,—also *ə glaːs*, 'death';—*ģelyn glaːs* = also 'a deadly enemy'; cf. D.F. [75]. 3.   (6) with intensive meaning or the like: *ovnatsan laːs !* 'extraordinary!'; *yːn glaːs ədi o*, 'he is a tough customer';—*gwalχ glaːs ədi o*, *may o n wydyn vel korŀyn*;— *r uːyti n yːn glaːs !*, 'you're a fine fellow!' (ironically); *may n huːyr glaːs i mi vynd*, 'it is high time for me to go'; *ar i wẽyθa glaːs*, 'in spite of him'.

glasan, s.f., pl. *glasennod*, glasen, 'young girl'.

glasrau, s., glasrew, D.G. l. 21, 'rain fallen and congealed' (Fr. 'verglas').

·glaːs·rewi, v., glasrewi, *may hi wedi ·glaːs·rewi*, 'the ground is covered with a coating of ice'; 'the rain has frozen as it fell'.

glastur, s.m., glasdwr, Sion Tudur in G.R. [370]. 13; cf. glastwfyr, W.B., col. 203. 10, 'cold water and buttermilk'; fig. of something flimsy, of a milk-and-water character: *syt maː nu m pɹəģeθy ? nẽiθ ə ðay ðim glastur.*

glastura, v., 'to work in a lazy, dawdling fashion': *paid a glastura hevo də waiθ* (O.H.).

glasturað, adj., 'flimsy, milk-and-water': *pɹegaθ lasturað*. (W.H.).

glaswyn, adj., glaswyn, W.Ll. lxv. 5, 'greyish white': *byuχ laswan.*

glasy, v., glasu, D.   (1) 'to turn green': *may poːb man əŋ glasy*, 'everything is turning green' (in spring); *may r gwair əŋ glasy ən ə daːs*, 'the hay turns green in the stack'.   (2) 'to turn grey' (of the hair): *gwaːɫt əŋ glasy.*

glaʃad, s.m., pl. *glaʃëidja*, 'a glassful': *glaʃad o guru*, 'a glass of beer'.

glaʃad, s.m., glasiad, 2 Kings vii. 7, 'the peep of day'. Cf. *bora glaːs.*

glaːu, s.m., pl. *glawogyð*, glaw, D., 'rain': *buru glaːu*, 'to rain'; *may n debig aru i laːu*, 'it looks very like rain'; *may hi am laːu vory*, 'it is going to rain to-morrow'; *may n tɹoi n laːu*, 'it is turning to rain'; *may hi n hel glaːu*, 'rain is coming on, the clouds are gathering for rain'; *may hi wedi kay am laːu*, 'it has set in for rain'; *gobëiθjo nẽiθ i ðim glaːu*, 'I hope it won't rain'; *may hi wedi gnẽyd glaːu maur (glaːu garu)*, 'it has rained very heavily'; *ɹhak ovn iði hi gaːyl glaːu iði hi*, 'for fear of it getting wet' (in the rain); *may hi wedi dal ən hiːr heb ðim glaːu*, 'we have had no rain for a long time'; *may na voːr o laːu etto*, 'there is any amount of rain to come yet'; *ðary mi moχal ə glaːu ən oχor ə kĺauð*, 'I sheltered from the rain behind the wall'; *mynd ən oːl ag ə mlaːyn i r glaːu*, 'to go in and out into the rain'; *may χuθjad (χwiʃjad) gla:u əni hi heno,* 'the wind promises rain'; *smukkan o la:u, gla:u ma:n, gla:u bəχan,* 'drizzle'; *may hi m pigo gla:u,* 'it is " spotting " rain'; *gla:u tɾana,* 'thunder rain'; *gla:u gola,* 'rain when the sky is bright towards the east'—looked upon as a bad sign (Llanfairfechan); *gla:u mi:s mai,* 'May rain' (*ma: nu ŋ gadu vo tɾu r vluyδyn, may o n δa: ɾhag ə gavod a ḷay meun anivẽiljaid,* O.H.).

glaujo, v., glawio, D., 'to rain' (= *buru gla:u, buru*): *may hi ŋ glaujo,* 'it is raining'; *δary hi laujo n drum* (= *n aru*) *nẽiθjur,* 'it rained heavily last night'; *mi lawiθ os gostegiθ ə gwynt,* 'it will rain if the wind drops'; *glaujo n δu:ys,* 'to rain steadily'; *may na i ovn na glaujo nẽiθ i tɾu: r dy:δ,* 'I am afraid it will rain all day'; *may hi n du:ad i laujo,* 'it is coming on to rain'.

glawog, adj., glawog, D., 'rainy': *ar δurnod glawog.*

glẽini, s.m., goleuni, D.; goleini, C.C.M. 14. 7, 'light': *s aχi iʃo glẽini?,* 'do you want a light?'

glẽiʃad, s., gleisiad, D., 'sewin' (I.W.).

glẽiʃo, v., gloesio, D., 'to vomit': *pu:ys glẽiʃo,* 'inclination to vomit'.

glendid, s.m., glendid, D., 'beauty': *doḷo at i glendid hi.*

gleny, glenyd, v. [*glɔny*].

gle:u, adj., pl. *gleujon,* glew, D. (1) 'hearty, well': *kəχuyn rẽil le:u δary mi,* 'I started heartily enough'. Very common in answer to inquiries about health in the form *go le:u,* 'pretty well': *sy daχi hẽiδju? n o le:u.—go le:u* is also used adjectively or adverbially in the sense of 'fair, rather, pretty well' in such cases as the following: *r ədaχi wedi hel tippin go le:u o ve:l i r ku:χ,* 'you have feathered your nest pretty well'; *ma: honna n o le:u o harδ,* 'that is rather pretty'; *daχi wedi kaʃjo n o le:u, ond daχi δim ən jaun,* 'you have guessed pretty well, but you are not right'. (2) 'pertinacious, persistent, tenacious':—*ɾ he:n deklyn gle:u;* esp. 'tenacious as regards money': *pobol ən meδwi ag ən mynd ən leujon,* i.e. one can get nothing out of them. (3) 'grasping': *dy:n gle:u jaun ədi o.* Cf. T.N. 308. 30, Mae gwyr o gyfraith yn bethe glewion, Hwy wnant am arian yn ddi feth Ar ʃeinioes y peth a fynon.

glewa, v., glewa, O.P., 'to be grasping'.

glẽyad; glẽyod (J.J.), s.m., glaiad, D., 'dried cow-dung used as fuel'.

glẽyadan, s.f., glaiaden, D., 'a piece of dried cow-dung'.

glẽyo, gly:o, v., goleuo, D. Fut. *glẽya.* Imperative *glẽya; glẽyuχ.* (Forms from this verb are used indiscriminately with those from *gola.*) (1) 'to light': *glẽyuχ ə ta:n,* 'light the fire'. (2) 'to lighten': *may hi ŋ glẽyo me:ḷt,* 'it is lightning'; *may hi ŋ glẽyo drẽigja,* 'it is sheet lightning'. (3) 'to glow, to shine': *pɾəvaid ba:χ sy ŋ glẽyo,* i.e. glow-worms. (4) 'to become light': *er pen may hi wedi glëyo*, 'since is was light'; *may ŋ glëyo dippin*, 'it is getting a bit lighter'. (5) 'to enlighten, explain'. (6) 'to go away suddenly, quickly', in the expression *glëya hi n də vla:yn*, 'off with you' = *glöivi*.

glidjo, v., gludio, D., s.v. 'hæreo'; 'to adhere, stick': *ba:u əŋ glidjo ag əŋ gleny ; ba:u əŋ glidjo ən əχ gwymmad χi ; ə ku:yr wedi glidjo n i glistja*.

gli:n, s.m., pl. *glinja*, glin, D., 'knee': *pen gli:n*, 'the top of the knee; knee'; *padal pen gli:n* (O.H.), 'knee-cap' = (?) *pelan pen gli:n* (J.J.); *avjeχid ar ben gli:n*, 'an affection of the knee'.

glivirin, glɔvinir, s., pl. *glivirjad*, gylfinhir, D., 'curlew' (Numenius arquata).

glo:, s.m., glo, D., 'coal': *gwaiθ glo:, pul glo:*, 'coal-mine'; *kut glo:*, 'coal-shed'; *bukkad glo:*, 'coal-scuttle'; *klap o lo*, 'lump of coal'; *glo: ma:n* (= *sleks*), 'slack' (opp. *glo: bra:s*); *glo: gwy:lt*, 'coal which burns away quickly' = *glo: flamlyd*.

glöivi, v., gloywi, D. (1) 'to polish': *glöivi sgidja*, 'to polish boots'; *glöivi ge:r*, 'to polish harness'; *glöivi kəfəla*, 'to groom horses'; *glöivi hi*, 'to run away'; *pe ·gwelati o n i glöivi hi !*, 'you should have seen him take to his heels!' (2) 'to pour away a liquid and leave the sediment' (cf. *glöyvon*);—also used of potatoes: *glöyvuχ ə du:r oði ar ə tatius, ne mi ·vəðanu wedi muyglo*, 'pour away the water from off the potatoes or they will be all in a mush'. (3) 'to improve in appearance, to look smart and spruce': *ma: hun a hun wedi glöivi n aru* (= *gwela i olug*), e.g. after having had money left him, or having become sober (O.H.). (4) 'to become thin or clear' (of liquids).

glo:yn, glöyun ; glöyvyn, gluyvyn (O.H.), s.m. and pl.—only in *glo:yn* (etc.) *byu*, 'butterfly', gloyn Duw, D.

glöyu, glëyu, adj., pl. *glöyvon, gluyvon*, gloyw, D. (1) 'clear, bright': *glöyu vel grisal*, 'clear as crystal'; *kin löyvad a du:r*, 'as clear as water';—often used to intensify *gla:n*, e.g. *kəmro gla:n glöyu*, 'a thorough Welshman'; *drəsy n la:n löyu de:g*, 'to be utterly confused'. (2) 'polished': *sgidja gluyvon*. (3) 'spruce', etc.' (cf. *glöivi*, 3): *r o:ð o n edraχ ən löyu jaun ;—ə we:ð muya glöyu ən ə pɾëimin*, 'the smartest team in the show'. (4) in the exp. *tida gluyvon*, 'dribbling from the mouth' (O.H.) = *glɔvëirjon*.

glöyvon, glöivjon, s.pl., gloewon, O.P., "the clear of a liquid": *glöivjon la:yθ*, 'whey' (O.H.);—*ɔvad ə glöivjon a kadu r kaus* (O.H.).

gluvar, s.m., glwfer, T.N. 17. 17, Eng. glover, 'tanner' = *dy:n əŋ gnëyd ledar ag ən tɾi:n ə kɾu:yn*.

gly:b, adj., fem. *gle:b*, pl. *glɔbjon*, comp. *glɔppaχ*, gwlyb, D., 'wet': *ən ly:b vel dɔvrgi*, 'like a drowned rat'; *ən ly:b dɔveryd* 'dripping wet' = *ən ly:b soppan dail domman ; ma: r dɛʉʸð ən ly:b*, 'the weather is wet'; *lo: gly:b*, 'an unweaned calf'; (fig.) 'a raw youth', 'a dull person'; *pobol ləbjon*, 'soakers'.—Substantively: *gly:b a gwely*, 'hot water and milk, and lodging'.

glybanjaθ, s.m., gwlybaniaeth, D., 'wetness, dampness, moisture': *hi:r lybanjaθ, hi:r səχtur* (weather proverb).

glybur, s.m., gwlybwr, D., 'wetness, dampness, moisture'.

gly:d, s.m., glûd, D., 'viscous matter in the ears, wax' = *ku:yr* (O.H).

glyn, s.m., pl. *glənnoð*, glyn, D., 'valley'.

gly:n [ə ·*γly:n*].

gləχy, v., gwlychu, D., 'to wet'; 'to be wet': *ma:y ifo gla:u i ləχy ə ðěyar dippin*, 'rain is wanted to wet the ground a little'; *may o wedi gləχy n dəveryd ; wedi gləχy n domman* (= *soppan dail domman*); *wedi gləχy n ļibrin*, 'he is dripping wet', 'he is wet through'; *ðary χi ləχy ?*, 'did you get wet?'

gləny(*d*) ; *gleny*(*d*) (E.J., J.J., O.H.), v., glynu, D., 'to stick': *may o γ kay gləny*, 'it won't stick'; *ma: r bara γ gləny ən əχ ǩe:g χi*, '(badly-baked) bread sticks to your mouth'; *he:n snavad əγ glənyd ən i ģilið*, 'slimy matter sticking together' (e. g. on a pond).

gləvěirjo, v., glyfoeriaw, O.P., 'to slobber, slaver, dribble'.

gləvěirjon, s.pl., glafoerion, D., 'dribblings from the mouth, slaver': *buru* (*guļun*) *gləvěirjon*, 'to slobber'.

gləvnjad, gləvinad ; glivinad (O.H.), s., gylfinaid, lit. 'beakful': *gləvnjad o levriθ*, 'a mouthful of milk'.

gnēyd, v. Fut. S. 1. *gna:*(*v*), 2. *gnēï*, 3. *gnēiθ, gnēif*. Pl. 1. *gnaun*, *gna:n*, 2. *gneuχ*, 3. *gna:n*. Imperf. S. 1. *gnēyθun ; gnaun*, 2. *gnēyθai ; gna:yt, gna:t*, 3. *gnēyθa ; gna:y, gna:*. Pl. 1. *gnēyθan ; gna:n*, 2. *gnēyθaχ ; gna:χ*, 3. *gnēyθan ; gna:n, gna:yn*. Pret. S. 1. *gne:s, gnēis*, 2. *gnest, gnēist*, 3. *gna:θ*. Pl. 1. *gnēyθon, gnēyson*, 2. *gnēyθoχ, gnēysoχ*, 3. *gnēyθon, gneyson*. Pres. Subj. S. 3. *gnelo*. Pl. 1. *gnelon*, 2. *gneloχ*, 3. *gnelon*. Imperative *gna: ; gneuχ*. Fut. Pass. *gnēir*. Pret. Pass. *gnaud*, gwneud, D.G. ccv. 14 (gwneuthur, D). (1) 'to make' (in various senses): *may nu wedi gnēyd ka:n arno vo*, 'they made a song about him'; *gnēyd ta:n*, 'to make a fire'; *nid po:b ko:yd nëiθ drol*, 'not every wood will make a cart'; *wedi nēyd o go:yd*, 'made of wood'; *gnēyd ļeχi i doi tai*, 'to make slates for roofing houses'; *gnēyd gwely*, 'to make a bed'; *gnēyd hu:yl am ben ru:in*, 'to make fun of some one'; *gnēyd nada*, 'to scream'; *gnēyd padar* (= *stori*) *o hono vo*, 'to make a long story of it'; *gnēyd pas arno vo*, 'to take him in'; *gnēyd pre:s*, 'to make money'; *gnēyd stu:r*, 'to make a noise'; *gnēyd stimja*, 'to make grimaces';

gnĕyd sylu (= *dal sylu*), 'to pay attention', 'take notice'; *gnĕyd tro:yd i davarn*, 'to set foot in a public house'; *gnĕyd* (= *kadu*) *turu*, 'to make a noise'; *gnĕyd əmdraχ*, 'to make an effort'; *gnĕyd ən vaur o*, 'to make much of', 'to make the most of': *ŗhaid gnĕyd ən vaur o bo:b durnod braːv gaːni ruːan*, 'we must make the best of every fine day we get now'. Cf. G.R. (2) 8.—with noun as appositive complement: *gnĕyd ə gwair ən vədəla dros ə sy:l*, 'to gather the hay in heaps over Sunday';—with adjective as appositive complement: *r ədu i wedi nĕyd o ŋ grəvaχ hëiðju*, 'I have made it stronger to-day'; *ma: r dəwyð tamp ma əŋ gnĕyd ruːin ən flat*, 'this damp weather makes one feel dull'; *puintjo moːχ* = *gnĕyd nu n deujon; gnĕyd ļinja o vaːχ i vaur*, 'to enlarge photographs'; *gnĕyd əχ hyːn ən vəχan*, 'to make yourself small', i.e. 'to crouch down'; similarly: *gnĕyd i hyːn vel ər oːyð o*, 'to make himself as he was';—followed by *i*, 'to make', i.e. 'to force, compel': *ŗvoː naːθ i mi χwerθin*, '*he* made me laugh';—of weather, cf. Fr. 'faire': *may hi ŋ gnĕyd təwyd gly:b jaun*, 'it is very wet weather'; *huraχ ə gnĕif hi gavod*, 'perhaps there will be a shower'; *may hi wedi gnĕyd glaːu maur*, 'there has been heavy rain'.

(2) 'to do': *be nesti hevo vo ?*, 'what did you do with it?'; *ən meθy gubod be ·nĕyθuni*, 'not knowing what to do'; *gneu·χiː, na: iː ðim*, '*you* do it, *I* won't'; *be naun i ond dĕyd ə gwiːr a dĕyd na naun i m ono·vo ?*, 'what should I do but tell the truth and say I wouldn't do it ?'; *ruːan daχi wedi gnĕyt i !*, 'now you've done it !'; *beθ bənnag ·nelonu*, 'whatever they do'; *beθ bənnag a nĕiθ o*, 'whatever he does'; *·vedrani ðim gnĕyd day waiθ ar ynwaθ*, 'we can't do two things at once'; *os oːyd ŗiu ðruːg wedi nĕyd*, 'if some evil had been done'; *daχi ŋ gnĕyd gwerθ əχ buːyd ?*, 'does what you do make up for your keep?'; *ədi o wedi gnĕyd djoni* (= *ļeːs) ?*, 'has it done any good?'; *gnĕyd i ora*, 'to do one's best'; *gnĕyd kam hevo*, 'to wrong'; *gnĕyd ə troː*, 'to do, to answer the purpose'; *gnĕyd heb*, 'to do without'. Other senses are: (a) 'to do (with), concern': *rubaθ nelo vo ðim a vo*, 'something which does not concern him'; *be sy ·neloχi a ni: ?*, 'what have you to do with us?'; *t oːs na ðim ·neloχi a vi:*, 'you have nothing to do with me'. (b) 'to do', 'to be good, seemly': *nĕiθ hon i vytta ?*, 'is this good to eat?' (c) 'to cheat' (Eng. to "do"): *gnĕyd ruːin*. (d) 'to cook': *gnĕyd buːyd ; gnĕyd ə suppar*, 'to cook, get ready the supper' (Anglo-Welsh 'to make the supper'); *na: i nĕyd χwanag ·arnynu*, 'I will do (cook) them more'; *na i nĕyd nu vory gaːl ni kaːl nu n oːyr ŗ usnos nesa*, 'I'll cook them to-morrow so as to have them cold next week'.

(3) as auxiliary: (a) used with the infinitive instead of the synthetic forms of the verb: *na i garjo vo ?*, 'shall I carry it ?'—Ans. *iːa ; na i wĕiði n saiθ muːy*, 'I'll shout seven times louder'; *t ədu i ðim ən amma na nĕiθ i glirjo*, 'I do not doubt it will clear up'; *ma na i ovn na glaujo nĕiθ i tŗu: r dy:ð*, 'I am afraid it will

rain all day ' ; *vaint o amsar nëiθ o bara ?*, ' how long will it last ? ' ; *nëyθa hi δim mynd for araḷ*, ' it wouldn't go any other way ' ; *nɛːs i δim gləχy*, ' I didn't get wet '. (b) as polite form of the imperative : *neuχi aros əmma ?*, ' will you wait here ? '—Ans. *gnaːv*, ' Yes '; *naː na (i)*, ' No '—[with the verbs *mynd* and *duːad* the answer is generally *aːv, doː(v)*]; *neuχi roi ṛhëi n ə ṃhen araḷ ə burδ ?*, ' will you put these things at the other end of the table ? '. (c) to avoid repetition of the same verb : *χmasun* (= *χəmsun*) *i lawar a χerδad i gonuy heno a χmasa χiθa χwaiθ, na nëyθaχ ?*, ' I wouldn't walk to Conway for a great deal to-night and you wouldn't either, would you ? '; *mi gadwiθ ə duːr əm böyθaχ ən ə teḳaḷ nag ən ə dzug, əŋ gnëïθ ?*, ' the water will keep hotter in the kettle than in the jug, won't it ? '; *neuχi gany pen δoːnu, əŋ gneuχ ?*, ' you will ring when they come, won't you ? '; *mi δëydoδ hi uθa i, " ḳeruχ i noːl gloː i mi", " naː na, wiːr ", meδa vi*, ' she said to me, " go and fetch some coal for me ". " No, I won't ", said I '; *diːolχ os nëïθ o*, ' I hope he will '; *δary mi ovyn iδo vo vynd ond naːθ o δim*, ' I asked him to go, but he didn't do so ' (Anglo-Welsh ' he didn't *do* ').

(4) verbal noun used as attributive genitive : *byrym gnëyd*, ' home-made barm '.

go: (long only when emphatic), adv., go, D., (emphatic) ' very '; (not emphatic) ' rather, pretty, fairly ': *vedar o gəmˑraːig ? goː χədig*, ' does he know Welsh ? Very little '; *kəmˑraːig go waːyl s gəno vo*, ' his Welsh is rather poor '; *byːδ go χədig o amsar*, ' there won't be much time '; *du i wedi boːd am droː go δaː:*, ' I've been for a pretty good walk '; *dənas go vaur*, ' a good-sized woman '; *sy daχiˑhëïδju ? n o lɛːu*, ' how are you to-day ? ' ' Pretty well '.

goː, s.m., pl. *govaint*, gôf, D., ' smith ': *r oːδ o n oː*, ' he was a smith '.

gobaiθ, s.m., pl. *gobëïθjon*, gobaith, D., ' hope ': *byu meun gobaiθ o hyːd*, ' to live always in hope '; *may gobaiθ noswëïθja gola n vyːan ruːan*, ' there is hope of light evenings soon now '; *hevo gobaiθ*, ' I hope so '; *oːys ˑgənoχi rëï nad oːys dim gobaiθ ˑyδynu δəsgy byθ ?*, ' have you some for whom there is no hope that they will ever learn ? '; *gobaiθ magy*, ' in the family way '; *ma gəni hi obaiθ magy o hono vo*, ' she is pregnant by him '.

gobëïθjo, v., gobeithio, D., ' to hope ': ' I hope ' is often expressed simply by the infinitive : *gobëïθjo na nëïf hi δim para n hiːr*, ' I hope it won't last long '; *gobëïθjo ə parïθ o dros dolig*, ' I hope it will last over Christmas; *gobëïθjo r taːd* (= *r annul*)*!*, ' I hope to goodness ! '

gobëïθjol, adj., gobeithiawl, O.P., ' hope-inspiring ': *ədi o n obëïθjol ?*, ' is there hope of recovery ? ' (from the injury); *dyːn gobëïθjol*, ' a promising man '.

gobennyð, s.m., pl. *gobenaðja*, gobennydd, D., 'bolster': *ka:s gobennyð*, 'bolster case' (= *tyðad*).

godakja, i.e. God ache: *godakja χi!*, 'drat you!' (more often *dakja*).

godra, s.m., godre, D. (1) 'skirt, bottom part of a dress or any garment': *koduχ odra χ trousys*, 'turn up your trousers'; *kodi godra* (of a woman), 'to lift the skirts', and fig. *kodi i godra hi*, 'to show her up, to expose her failings'. (2) 'skirt, bottom' (e.g. of a mountain): *manyð a i odra gorlewinol an a mo:r*, 'a mountain whose base is washed by the sea on the western side'.

godrapja, 'drat' (generally *drapja*): *godrapja χi!*

godro, v., godro, D., 'to milk': *sto:l odro*, 'milking-stool'; *gwarθag godro*, 'milch cattle'; *pry:d vasa n ora i mi odro?*, 'when had I better do the milking?'

goðaθ, s., goddaith, D., in phrase *goðaθ o da:n = furnas o da:n* (J.J.), 'a mass of flame, a blazing furnace' (said of a great fire). Cf. *kolkarθ, wemflam*.

goðav, v., goddef, D., 'to bear' (with): *goðav iðo vo*, 'to bear with him'; *daχi ŋ goðav i mi ðëyd peθa rhwvað*.

go:g, s.f., pl. *koga*, côg, D. (1) 'cuckoo': *kin lonad a r go:g*, 'as blithe as a lark', 'as bright as a button', 'as right as a trivet'; *hëiðju vel go:g, vory vel taru*, 'to-day as bland as a dove, to-morrow raging like a bull' (of people of changeable character); *mi welis i go:g*, 'I saw a cuckoo'; *bu:yd a go:g*, 'wood sorrel' (Oxalis Acetosella).

gogany, v., goganu, D., 'to speak evil of': *gogany dy:n an i gevn;— gena gla:n i ogany* (prov.).

gogarθ, Gogarth, cf. D., s.v. 'garth'; only in the place-name *a gogarθ*, 'Great Orme's Head': *pen a gogarθ* is the extremity of that promontory.

goglað, s.m., gogledd, D., 'north': *gogla ðuyran*, 'north-east'.

goglas, s.m., goglais, D., 'itching': *ma: nu n oglas i gi:d*, 'they are itching all over'; *kodi goglas arno vo*, 'to tickle him'.

goglas, v., goglais, 'to tickle': *paid a ŋoglas i*, 'do not tickle me'; fig. *goglas a tëimlada*, 'to tickle the feelings'.

gogleðol, adj., gogleddol, D., s.v. 'borealis'; 'northern': *glëini gogleðol*, 'northern lights'.

goglëiſol, adj., gogleisiawl, O.P., 'ticklish' (J.J.).

gogonjant, s.m., gogoniant, D., s.v. 'gloria'; 'glory'. Used as excl. of delight.

gogor, s.m., pl. *gogra*, gogr, D., 'sieve': *gogor rhaun* (= *gogor hidil*), 'hair sieve', 'strainer' (for milk); *may o vel gogor hidil*, said of one who cannot keep a secret; *gogor pyro* (O.H.), used for

corn ;—*gogor* is also used for ' riddle ' for riddling cinders = *r̥hidil̥*.
[*gogor* is the generic term ; *r̥hidil̥* = ' riddle ' only.]

gogro, v., gogro, ' to sieve '.

gogrun, v., cf. gogrynu, D. (1) ' to sieve '. (2) ' to squander ' :
may o ŋ gogrun ə kubul, ' he squanders everything '. (3) ' to sway
from side to side as one riddling ' : *gogrun mynd*.

goχal, v., gochel, D., ' to beware, take heed' : *goχal r̥hag i bc:θ
δu:ad ;—ə nc:b sy m byu meun ty: gwydyr goχelad liχjo k̬erig* (prov.),
' people who live in glass houses should not throw stones '.

gola, s.m. (pl. goljada), goleu, D., ' light ' : *r̥hoi gola ar ə gannuyl̥*,
' to light the candle '; *dal̥ gola i ru:in*, ' to hold a light to some one ';
·*r ədani r̥huŋ day ola*, ' it is twilight ', i. e. ' between daylight and
artificial light '; *gwëiθjo n δəgyn o ola i ola*, ' to work hard from
dawn till nightfall '; *may hi n lu:yd ola*, ' it is dusk '; fig. *ka:yl gola
ar rubaθ*, ' to get enlightenment on some question '; *riu δru:g ən
du:ad i r gola*, ' some evil coming to light '.

gola, adj., comp. *glëyaχ*, goleu, D. (1) ' light' : *noswëiθja gola*,
' light evenings '; *may hi n ola am hannar aur wedi χwe:χ*, ' it is
light at half-past six '; *r o:δ ə l̬ëyad ən ola*, ' the moon was shining '.
(2) ' clear ', of the air (opp. to *dul̥*). (3) ' light ', of colours : *pry:d
gola*, ' a light, fair complexion '; *gwa:l̥ gola*, ' fair hair '. (4) ' well
versed ' : *dy:n gola ən i vëibil*, ' a man well versed in the Bible '.

gola, v., goleu. Pret. *golis*. Imperative, *gola*; *goluχ* (cf.
glëyo), ' to light ' : *gola matʃan, k̬etlyn, kannuyl̥, ta:n*, ' to light a
match, pipe, candle, fire '; *may r gas əŋ gola ru:an*, ' the gas will
light now '; *du i dgesl a gola iʃo di:od*, ' I am almost on fire for
want of a drink '.

gold mair, s., gold Mair, D., ' marigold ' (Chrysanthemum
segetum).

goldyn, s., goldyn, D.G. li. 38, ' a gold coin ' : *ən velyn vel goldyn*
(W.H.); also applied to persons : *ə goldyn lartʃ, ə goldyn fi:aδ*
(O.H.).

golχ, s.m., golch, D., ' urine ' (formerly kept for cleaning
purposes) : *r̥hoid gjalam vedu ən ə golχ*, ' to put a rod in pickle '.
(Cf. *irδrug*.)

golχbran, s.m., golchbren, R., ' beetle ' (washing instrument
formerly in use) = *kolbran* (J.J.).

golχi, v., golchi, D. Imperative *golχa*. (1) ' to wash ': *golχi
dil̥ad, golχi (= molχi) dylo ;—golχi l̬estri suppar*, ' to wash up the
supper things '; *golχi ə l̬aur*, ' to clean the floor '; *golχi ə l̬əgaid
meun du:r oy:r*, ' to bathe the eyes in cold water '; *kruk golχi*,
' washing tub '; *tr̥oχjon golχi*, ' soap-suds '. (2) ' to thrash ' =
r̥hoid kwëir.

golχjon, s.pl., golchion, D., 'proluvies'; 'pig's food; dish-water'.

golχrag, s.f., golchwraig, D., ' washerwoman ; washer': *may hi n olχrag rēit ða:*, 'she is a very good washer'.

golχva, s., golchfa, D., s.v. 'lauatrina'; 'a thrashing'.

golug, s.m.f., golwg, D. (1) 'sight' (in various senses): *nabod ar ə golug, uθ ə golug*, 'to know by sight'; *r o:yð o wedi koḷi i olug*, 'he had lost his sight'; *ðary o ðim kodi i olug*, 'he did not raise his eyes'; *be u:ti n dal d olug arna i ?*, 'why are you staring at me?'; *meun golug, ən ə golug*, 'in sight'; *aḷan o r golug*, 'out of sight'; *wedi mynd o r golug*, 'disappeared'; *d o:ys na ðim golug arno vo ru:an*, 'it is nowhere to be seen'; *koḷi golug ar*, 'to lose sight of'; *r o:ð ·gənonu olug am lu:yθ o ģerig*, 'they had some inkling they would get a cargo of stone'. (2) 'appearance': *may golug da: jaun ·arnynu*, 'they look very well'; *faſun olug o:yð arno vo ?*, 'how did he look?'; *may golug buru arnɪ hi*, 'it looks like rain'; *ən o:l po:b golug*, 'to all appearances'.

goləgys, adj., golygus, D., 'fine', 'of prepossessing appearance', 'of good presence': *dy:n, ḱefyl goləgys; golug goləgys jaun o:ð arno vo.*

gonast, adj., comp. *gonestaχ*, onest, D.; gonest, B.C. 70. 28, 'honest': *gonast a ģëirwir*, 'honest and truthful'.

gonestruyð, s.m., gonestrwydd, I.G. 540. 12; onestrwydd, D., s.v. 'bonitas'; 'honesty'.

go:r, s.m., gôr, D., 'matter, pus': *gwasgy ə go:r aḷan o hono vo.*

gora, adj., goreu, D., 'best': *ə ḱi:g gora glu:is i erï·o:yd*, 'the best meat I ever tasted'; *kovjon gora at*, 'kindest remembrances 10'; *ə gora o r o:ḷ, ə gora o r y:n*, 'the best of all'; *gora po:b dim*, 'the best thing of all'; *gora pen ora*, 'so much the better': *u:ti ɲ gnēyt i n o le:u ?—ədu—wel, gora pen ora;— gora n ə by:d*, 'all the better'; *ɪṛo:yd gora ə mlëyna*, 'best foot foremost'; *gora peɲ gənta*, 'the sooner the better'; *gora pen vuya*, 'the more the better'; *gora bo: r durnod, gora bo: r gwaiθ*, 'the better the day, the better the deed'; *gnēyd ə gora o r gwëyθa*, 'to make the best of it'; *ə gora welis i a ḷgad ə ṃhen əri·o:yd*, 'the best I ever set my eyes on'; *ə bəwyd gora o r y:n*, 'the best life of all';—followed by *ģin* (cf. *may n ða: ģin i*): *p ṛyn di r gora ģin ti ?*, 'which do you like best?'; *be di r gora gəno vo ga:l ?*, 'what does he like to have best?';—as substantive: *r ədu i wedi gnēyd ə ɲora*, 'I have done my best'; *gnēyd i ora gla:s*, 'to do one's level best' (cf. T.N. 90. 27);—*am ə gora*, 'in emulation, Fr. 'à qui mieux mieux' (Anglo-Welsh, 'for the best')*; *mrəson am ə gora*, 'to vie with one another'; *ən mynd am ə gora i vo:d əɲ gənta*, '(each one) trying to get first';—*ar ə gora* occurs in the expression *mi na: i ar ə gora a χi !*, 'I will be even with you yet !';—*ar i ora*, (a) 'in one's best form': *may o m brəǵeθur da: jaun pen vy:ð o ar i ora*, 'he is a very good preacher when he is in his best form'; (b) 'straining to the utmost (and barely succeeding)': *may o ar i ora ʒŋ ka:l ə ðay pen l̦inin at i ǵilið*, 'he strains to the utmost to make two ends meet';—*o r gora*, (a) 'all right'; (b) 'well!' (Fr. eh bien !); (c) 'perfectly well': *du i ŋ gubod o r gora bo χi n dëyd k̯elwyð*, 'I know perfectly well that you are telling a lie';—*r̦hoi gora*, (a) 'to give in': *r̦hoi gora ið o vo*, 'to give in to him'; (b) 'to cease': *r̦hoi gora i gufjo*, 'to cease fighting';—*du i wedi r̦hoi gora i ðarl̦an o*; (c) 'to give up': *mi ro:θ gora i r verχ*, 'he gave up the girl'; *may nu wedi r̦hoi gora i ly: nu n l̦yndan*, 'they have given up their house in London'.—Cf. D.F. [151] 1. Canys eu harfer ydyw ffrostio . . . nad rhaid iddynt roi'r goreu i ni mewn dim.

gorad, s.f., pl. *gorjada*, koret, W.S. [A were]; cored, D., 'cataracta' and s.v. 'excipulae'; 'a space on the sea-sands enclosed on three sides by a wattled hedge, used for catching fish; a weir'. Near Bangor occur the names *gorad ə ǵil̦, ə gorad vaur, ə gorad dre: kasțal̦* and *ə gorad go:χ*.

gorad, adj. [*agorad*].

gordro, ordro, v., 'to order'.

gorð, s.f., pl. *gyrð*, gordd, D., 'sledge-hammer; mallet': *gorð hëyarn* (in slate quarries), 'a sledge-hammer from 15 to 18 pounds in weight to drive in a *ky:n k̯raig*, to loosen the rock'; *gorð bren* (in slate quarries), 'a small wooden mallet used with a *ky:n manol̦i*'; *gorð byða* (E.J.), 'churn-staff' = *gorð gorði* (O.H.).

gorðrus, s., gorddrws, R. [a threshold, a hatch], 'the upper part of a double door' (J.J.).

gorfan, v., gorphen, D. Fut. S. 1. *gorfenna*, 3. *gorfenniθ*. Pret. *gorfennis, gorfis*. Imperative *gorfan, gorfenna*, 'to finish': *daχi wedi gorfan ?*, 'have you finished?'; *dani wedi gorfan korði*, 'we have finished churning'; *daχi wedi gorfan* (= *darvod*) *hevo r̦hëi n ?*, 'have you finished with these ?'; *hogyn, dy:n heb i orfan*, 'an unlicked cub', 'a freak'.

gorfenna, s.m., Gorffenna, Yny lhyvyr hwnn [13]; Gorphenhaf, D., 'July'.

gorfennol, adj., gorphenawl, O.P., 'in a finished state': *döuχ for ma, ma hun ən vu:y gorfennol*, 'come this way, this (house) is in a more finished state'.

gorfuys, s., gorphwys, D., 'rest'.

gorfuyso, gorfuys, v., gorphwyso, D. Imperative *gorfuysa ; gorfuysuχ*, 'to rest'.

gori, v., gori, D., s.v. 'suppuro'. (1) 'to suppurate, gather':

may vә myːs әŋ gori (= *kasgly*), 'my finger is gathering'. (2) 'to sit' (of a hen) : *may r jaːr әŋ gori.*

goriχwiljaθ, s.f., gorchwyliaeth, Num. iv. 16 : 'duty, occupation, task' : *dilin i oriχwiljaθ,* 'to follow one's occupation'.

gorivәny, gorifynu; gorufynu, B.C. 43. 8.—in phrase *ar orivәny,* 'upwards'.

goriwarad, s.m., gorwaered, D. ; goriwared, Micah i, 4, 'slope': *pen ә goriwarad,* 'the top of the slope' ; *ar oriwarad,* 'down' ; *may ә ḷeː i ǵiːd ar oriwarad,* 'the whole place is sloping, on the slope' ; *ar ә goriwarad,* 'on the downward grade'.

gorjad, s.m., pl. *gorjada,* agoriad, D.; cf. goriadeu, B.C. 6. 4 ; 16. 5, 'key' ; *tuḷ gorjad,* 'key-hole'; *bundal o orjada,* 'a bunch of keys' ; *gorjad moːr,* any shell of the genus Turritella.

gorχast, s.m., pl. *gorχestjon,* gorchest, D., 'excellentia'. (1) 'exploit, feat, achievement' : *t oːð hәnny dim gorχast әn ә byːd,* 'that was no feat at all' ; *may n χhiu orχast әni hi,* 'she does it out of bravado' ; *gnēyd χhiu orχast o rubaθ,* 'to make a show of doing a great deal'. (2) 'conceit, vanity' : *i orχast sy n i ðәveθa vo.*

gorχestol, adj., gorchestol, D.F. [ix]. 27 ; [23]. 3 ; Gen. xxx. 8 ; B.C. 18. 16, 'conceited, vain' : *dyːn gorχestol = dyːn baːχ әŋ kṛedy mai ᵃvoː sy ŋ gwelad ә kubul,—wela vo neːb әn debig iðo vo i hyːn* (O.H.).

gorχesty, v., gorchestu, O.P., 'to boast, to vaunt' : *r oːyð o n arvar gorχesty am i voːd wedi vagy n yːn o saiθ meun gwely peswyn,* 'he used to boast that he had been brought up one of seven in a chaff bed'.

gorχuyl, s.m., pl. *goriχwiljon,* gorchwyl, D., 'work, duty, task' : *may χ gorχuyl әn deχra,* 'your task is beginning'.

·gorḷanu (so O.H. always) ; *gorḷan,* s., gorllanw, D., 'high-tide': *may hiˑ m ben ·gorḷanu,* 'it is high-tide'; *top gorḷan,* 'high-water mark' ; *top ·gorḷanu marður* (neap), *sbriŋ.*

gorḷewin, s.m., gorllewin, D., 'west' : *muːy әn ә gorḷewin na . . .,* 'more to the west than . . .' ; *goglað orḷewin, deː orḷewin,* 'north-west, south-west'.

gorḷewinol, adj., gorllewinawl, D., s.v. 'occidentalis' ; 'western'.

gorḷyd, adj., gorllyd, D., s.v. 'purulentus'. (1) 'exuding matter'. (2) of fowls, 'inclined to sit' : *jaːr orḷyd,* 'a broody hen'. (3) of eggs, 'for hatching' : *uːy gorḷyd.*

gormod, gormod, D., 'too much'. (1) adverb: *dal gormod ar ә ðeː,* 'to keep too much to the right'; *r oːyð әm buru gormod i mi ðuːad a voː i vәny,* 'it was raining too much for me to bring it up' ; *r oːyð o n tṛәstjo n ormod ar i enu,* 'he trusted too much to his reputation'. (2) substantive : *gormod o duru,* 'too much noise';

gormod o budin daǵiθ ǵi: (prov.), 'too much pudding will choke a dog', i.e. 'one can have too much of a good thing'; *may hunna wedi ka:yl gormod ǝn i vol,* 'that fellow has had a drop too much'.

gormodaδ, s.m., gormodedd, D., s.v. 'excelsus' (sic); 'excess, superfluity': *may o wedi ṟhoi̯ mȫyθa iδi hi̯ i ormodaδ,* 'he has spoilt her to excess'; *ǝvad i ormodaδ.*

gorur, s.m., agorwr, i.e. 'opener': *gorur westras, gorur ḵreǵin,* 'oyster-catcher' (Hæmatopus ostralegus).

gorvaδ, v., gorwedd, D. Fut. *gorveδa.* Pret. *gorveδis; veδis* (O.H). Imperative *gorva(δ). gorveδa,* 'to lie': *gorva i laur* (to a dog), 'lie down'; *ǝɳ gorvaδ vel ḵlut,* 'lying like a log'; *δary ṟ hu:χ orvaδ ar ǝ mo:χ,* 'the sow overlaid the young pigs'; *r o:δ ǝ lȅyad ǝɳ gorvaδ ar i̯ hoχor,* 'the moon was lying on its side'; *may hi̯ wedi gorvaδ am bedwar mi:s,* 'she has been laid up for four months';—also used of corn, etc., which has been laid by the rain ;—*ǝn i orvaδ,* 'lying down'; 'sloping, slanting': *may ṟhȅi n ǝn sǝθaχ, dim ǝn i gorvaδ ḵimmint,* 'these are standing straighter, not sloping so much'.

gorvod, v., gorfod, D., 'to be obliged, to have (to)': *daχi̯ wedi gorvod gwȅiljad tippin ba:χ ru:an ?,* 'have you had to wait a bit just now?'; *wedi gorvod tǝnny ǝ ḵlo: i̯ fur i̯ ga:yl ǝ gorjad,* 'having had to take the lock off to get the key'.

gorvodaθ, s.m., gorfodaeth, D., 'obligation': *t o:ys na δim gorvodaθ,* 'there is no obligation (to do so)', 'it is not obligatory'.

gorvolaδ, s.m., gorfoledd, D., 'religious ecstasy'.

gorvoleδy, v., gorfoleddu, D., 'to lose control of oneself and give full vent to religious emotion'.

goryχavjaθ, s.m., goruchafiaeth, D., 'supremacy': *daχi̯ n tȅimlo n happys ar o:l ka:yl goryχavjaθ ar rubaθ,* 'you feel happy after getting the best of something' (e. g. arriving at the solution of some question).

gosod, v., gosod, D. (1) 'to set, place' (not commonly used except in certain locutions = *ṟhoi*): *gosod ḵaṟag ar i̯ fen,* 'to set a stone on its end'; *gosod abuyd,* 'to set a bait'; *gosod burδ,* 'to lay a table'; *gosod i̯ hy:n,* (a) 'to make oneself smart': *may o wedi gosod i̯ hy:n ǝn nȅis;* (b) 'to put on airs'; (c) 'to put oneself in a position (to)'. (2) 'to let': *gosod ty:,* 'to let a house'. (3) verbal noun used as attributive genitive: *dannaδ gosod,* 'false teeth'; *gwisǵo gwa:ḷt gosod,* 'to wear false hair'. Cf. D., s.v. 'galericulum', and 'bara gosod', 1 Sam. xxi. 6, etc. (='bara dangos') 'shew-bread'.

gosod, s.m., gosod, D. (1) 'an amount placed', in the exp. *gosod o wair i̯ r gwarθag,* 'a feed of hay for the cattle'. (2) 'a letting, contract': *ar osod,* 'to be let';—in slate quarries, 'a con-

M

tract between the contractor and the men as to the pay to be given for a day's work '.

gosodjad, s.m., gosodiad, L.G.C. 421, 22; Iolo MSS. 229. 28; D., s.v. ' constructio '; ' demeanour, bearing ': *dy:n kləvar o ran i osodjad*, ' a man of fine bearing '; *dy:n o osodjad balχ*, ' a man of proud bearing '.

gostag, s., gosteg, D., ' silence ': *gostag !*, ' silence ! '

gostegy, v., gostegu, D. (1) ' to silence, appease ': *ən vy:an am ostegy rɐu*, ' quick at appeasing a squabble '.—Also intr. *mi stegoð ə rɐu*. (2) ' to fall ' (of the wind): *os gostegiθ ə gwynt*,—trans. *gostegy r gwynt ən ə stymmog*.

gostəŋedig, adj., gostyngedig, D., s.v. ' humilis '; ' humble '.

gostəŋeiðruyð, s.m., gostyngeiddrwydd, D., s.v. ' humilitas '; ' humility '.

gɐun, s.m., pl. *gɐuna*, gown, W.S.; C.C.M. 160. 29; gŵn, D., ' gown, dress '.

govaly, v., gofalu, D., ' to take care, to look after ': *r ədu i ŋ govaly am hənny*, ' I see about that '; *may r blodyn ən tɪvy a nc:b əŋ govaly am dano*, ' the flower grows though no one looks after it '.

govalys, adj., gofalus, D., ' careful ': *govalys am*, ' careful about '.

govar, s.m., pl. *goveryð*, gofer, D., ' outlet of a spring, stream ': *may fənnon a i govar i r de: ən jaχysol, meða ɹ he:n bobol* (J.J.), ' a spring with its outlet running towards the south is wholesome, old people used to say '.

govi, s.m., ? Eng. cove, ' wag '. Only in the expression *he:n govi* (W.H.).—I am informed that this was a nickname given to an old Bangor character, and is not in general use.

govid, s.m., gofid, D. (1) ' grief '. (2) ' pain, irritation ': *i dorᵢ riu ovid ne bo:yn*, ' to allay some irritation or pain '; *o:s na lawar o ovid ən ə briu ?* (O.H.), ' does the wound give much pain ? ' Cf. D., gofidio, s.v. ' vlcero '.

govidjo, v., gofidiaw, D., ' to grieve ': *ə galon əŋ govidjo*.

govidys, adj., gofidus, D., ' full of grief ': *dy:n govidys i veðul*.

govol, s.m., pl. *govalon*, gofal, D., ' care ': *ǵid a govol*, ' with care '; *govol ə ru:m o:yð arni hi*, ' she had to look after the room '; *kəmmyd govol*, ' to take care '; *kəmmuχ ovol* (= *tendjuχ, gwiljuχ*) *i goli o*, ' take care not to lose it '; *ɹhaid i mi gəmmyd govol ɹhag i χi glu:ad və hanas i ǵi:d*, ' I must take care you don't hear my whole life's history '; *may n fu:r o gəmmyd govol o hono vo*, ' he is sure to take care of it '.

govyn, v., gofyn, D. Fut. S. 1. *govənna, vənna*. Pret. S. 1. *govənnis, vənnis*. Pl. 3. *govənson*. Imperative *govyn, govənna ;*

govənnuχ, 'to ask': *govənnuχ ·yδynu δu:ad*, 'ask them to come'; *nëiſ i ovyn ·yδynu be ·δëydsonu*, 'I asked them what they said'; *may hi ŋ govyn ·vasaχi n lëikjo ka:yl χwiadan δy sy:l*, 'she is asking whether you would like a duck on Sunday'; *may hi ŋ govyn p ŗ yn ta vory ta drennyδ daχi am vynd furδ*, 'she is asking whether it is to-morrow or the day after that you are going'; (*gan mod i*) *mor hy: a govyn*, 'if I may be so bold as to ask'; *govyn benθig su:ļļ*, 'to borrow a shilling';—of animals maris appetentes: *ma: ŗ hu:χ əŋ govyn ba:yδ*. Cf. D., s.v. 'equio'.

govyn, s.m., pl. *govənjon*, gofyn, D. (1) 'requirement'. (2) 'debt': *o:s ·gənoχi lawar o ovənjon ?*, 'have you many demands upon you?'

gradaļ, s.f., gradell, W.S. [A gyrdyron], 'griddle': *kļy:sl ə radaļ*, 'the handle of the griddle'; *bara radaļ* (i.e. bara ar radell), 'bread baked on a griddle'. Cf. *ırəbaδ*.

graδol, adj., graddol, W.S. [graduate], 'gradual': *nəχy n raδol*, 'to be sinking gradually'.

grafıjo, v., 'to graft'. [As distinguished from (*n*)*impjo*, *grafıjo* means to graft two branches together at their ends, (*n*)*impjo*, to insert small shoots by raising the bark on the sides of the end of the stock.]

granar, s., 'granary'.

gra:s, s.m., grâs, D. (1) 'grace': *voθo ra:s i ti !*, excl. 'upon my word !'; *dyu po:b gra:s !*, excl. (2) 'grace (before and after meals)', *gra:s ƙin, ar o:l bu:yd*. (3) n. pr. 'Grace'.

gra:t, s.m., pl. *gratja*, grât, W.Ll, (Voc.), s.v. 'alch'; 'grate': *ſon ə gra:t*, 'bar of the grate'.

gratjad, s.m., 'as much as fills a grate': *gratjad maur o da:n*, 'a blazing fire'. Cf. *tanļuyθ*.

gratjo, v., 'to grate': *pε:θ i ratjo ſinſir*, 'a thing to grate ginger'.

gratyr, s.m., gratur, W.S., 'grater': *gwynab ə gratyr*, 'very rough face'.

graun, s.m., grawn, D. (1) 'grain' (in collective sense). Cf. *gronyn*. (2) 'spawn of fish': *bol graun*, 'hard roe'.

graval, s.f., grafel, W.S.; grafael, C.C.M. 121. 14, 'gravel'; also the disease so called.

gravëiljo, *grəvëiljo*, v., grafaelio, W.S. [To grauell], 'to wear the sole of the foot to the raw as sheep-dogs sometimes do in wet weather'; 'to make a sore by chafing'.

gravëiljog, *grəvëiljog*, adj., 'gravelly'.

gravyn, v., gwarafun, vulgo gorafun, D., 'to grudge': *t a: i δim, riu ravyn o:yδ o roid o benθig o r bla:yn*, 'I won't go: he lent it rather grudgingly last time'; *ədi hi ŋ gravyn bakko i χi?*, 'does she grudge you tobacco?'

grawys, s.m., Grawys, D., 'Lent'.

gra:yn, s.m., graen, D.G. lxxxvii. 10; W.S. [Grayne]. (1) 'grain' in wood, stone, etc.: *ən erbyn ə gra:yn*, 'against the grain'; *for may i gra:yn hi?*, 'which way does the grain run?'; *t u:ti ðim ar i gra:yn hi*, 'you are not working with the grain'. (2) 'finish': *wedi rhoid gra:yn arno vo*, 'having put a finish to it'; *t o:s dim gra:yn ar əχ gwaiθ*, 'there is no finish to your work'.

grëifan, v., cf. Eng. (Dial.) grince [to grind the teeth], Nhb., 'to grind' of the teeth (W.H.) = *grindgan, krinfan*.

gresyn, s.m., gresyn, D., in *gresyn garu*, 'a great pity'. (Seldom used = *pitti*.)

grëyan, s.f., graian, D., 'gravel': *may r gla:u wedi kodi ə lo:n nes may hi n rëyan*, 'the rain has churned up the road into gravel'.

grëynys, adj. (1) of persons, animals, etc., 'in good condition': *may golug grëynys arno vo*. (2) of work, etc., 'with a finish', e. g. one can see a man is a good workman because his work is *grëynys* [*gra:yn*].

gridus, gridust, v., grydwst, D. = grydian, 'grunnire'; cf. also D., s.v. 'grunnitus', 'musso'. (1) 'to jump about in pain' (I.W.). (2) 'to make a slight sound', e.g. of a child in the cradle when waking (Bangor)—said also of a whispered report: *pobol əŋ gridust hevo i ɡilið bod na rubaθ əm bo:d—t ədanu ðim ən fu:r ond bod na ridust* (O.H.).

griðvan, v., griddfan, D., 'to groan': *griðvan o dan i vayχ, meun po:yn, ar o:l perθənas sy wedi maru; griðvan uθ varu—* (O.H.); also 'to grumble': *griðvan am la:u*.

grift, s., grifft, D., s.v. 'gyrinus'; G.O. ii. 136. 9, 'frog-spawn'.

grindil (O.H.); *grindi̦l* (I.W.), s.m., cf. alch gridyll, W.S. [A gyrdyron], 'gridiron'.

grindjo, v., ? greidiaw, O.P. (1) 'to roast' (O.H.): *grindjo ki:g* (obsolete). (2) in the phrase *r o:n i ŋ grindjo na vasun i n i ga:l o*, 'I was mad that I could not get it' (Bangor).

grindgan, v., 'to grind', of the teeth = *grëifan, krinfan*.

grifa, s.pl., sing. *grifin*, grisiau, D., s.v. 'gradatio'; 'stairs': *ar ben ə grifa*, 'at the top of the stairs'; *əŋ ŋwëylod ə grifa*, 'at the bottom of the stairs'; *i vəny, i laur ə grifa*, 'upstairs, downstairs'; *may o i vəny ə grifa (= ən ə loft)*, 'he is upstairs'.

grifal, s., grisial, D., 'crystal': *glöyu vel grifal*, 'as clear as crystal'.

gro:, s., gro, D., 'gravel': *gro: əŋ ŋwëylod ə nant*, 'gravel at the bottom of the stream'; *gro: ma:n*, 'shingle', e. g. on a beach.

gronyn, s.m., pl. *gronɘnna*, gronyn, D. (1) 'a single grain': *gronyn o wenɩθ*, 'a grain of wheat'. (2) 'scrap': *byttoð ɘ lɘgod o boːb gronyn*, 'the mice ate every scrap of it'; *dim gronyn o sɘnnuyr*, 'not a grain of sense'; *hɩljo dim gronyn ɘno vo*, 'not to care a jot for it'.—Cf. *graun*.

groːt, s.m., pl. *grotja*, grod, W.Ll. xvi. 79; grôt, C.C. 465. 28, 'a groat, fourpence': *suːḷi a groːt*, 'one and fourpence'; *ɩnoχyn groːtʲ*, term of reproach, e. g. to a dog; *nëi di byθ roːt ɘn χweːχ*, 'you will never set the Thames on fire'.

grottan, s.f., grottan, G.O. ii. 22. 19, dim. of above: *oːs ǵin ɩi breːs ? naːg oːys, s ǵin ɩ r yːn rottan* (O.H.).

grɵud, s., 'crowd': *χwaly r grɵud; ma na rɵud garu van ma* (O.H.).

grɵudi, s., 'crowd': *grɵudi o blant; be daχɩ n nëyd ɘɲ grɵudi hɛvo χ ǵɩlɩð ?* (O.H.)

grɵudi, s., in *kany grɵudi [krɵudi]*.

grɵudjo, v., 'to crowd together': *plant wedi grɵudjo at ɩ ǵɩlɩð; wedi grɵudjo ɩ χwara* (O.H.).

grɵus, s., 'grounds', e. g. of beer (O.H.).

grugnaχ, grugnaχy, v., grwgnach, D., 'to grumble': *paid a grugnaχ*.

grugnaχlyd, adj., grwgnachlyd, O.P., 'given to grumbling'.

grɤːal, griual, s.m., 'gruel'.

grɤːd, gryt, s.m., grut, D.G. ccv. 25; D., 'grit, fine sand'.

grɤːð, s.f., pl. *grɩðja*, grûdd, D., 'cheek': *t oːs na ðim gweːn ar ɩ ryːð*, 'he never smiles'; *dagra ar ɩ rɩðja*, 'tears rolling down his cheeks'.

grɤːg, s.m., grûg, D., 'heather': *ɘsgyb gryːg*, 'heather broom'.

grygog, adj., grugawg, O.P., 'overgrown with heather': *mɘnyð grygog; friːθ rygog*.

grym, s.f., grym, D., 'force': *oːys grym ɘn hun vory ?*, 'does this hold good (is it in force) to-morrow?'; *ṛhiːθ o grevyð heb i grym*, 'an appearance of religion without its reality'. As expletive: *grym vaur ! r uːḷi n yːn hyḷ !; grym annul ! dakku i ti hogan gluːs ! gryt [gryːd]*.

grɘmmys, adj., grymmus, D., 'powerful': *pr̥ɘǵeθur grɘmmys; pr̥egaθ rɘmmys*.

gubod; gubad (O.H.), v., gwybod, D. Pres. S. 1. *gun*, 2. *gwyðost*, *gwyst, gust*, 3. *guːyr.* Pl. 1. *gwyðon*, 2. *gwyðoχ*, 3. *gwyðon.* Imperfect. S. 1. *gwyðun*, 2. *gwyðaɩ*, 3. *gwyða.* Pl. 1. *gwyðan*, 2. *gwyðaχ*, 3. *gwyðan*, 'to know': *ːwyðoχɩ ?* Ans. *gun, naː un i*, 'do you know?' Ans. 'Yes, no'. *(d)un i ðim, (t ɘ)du i ðim ɘɲ gubod*, 'I don't know'; *am un i*, 'as far as I know'; *am un i bo:d o*, 'perhaps he is'; *gun i am ru:in*, 'I know of somebody'; *un i ən ə myu be na: i*, 'I haven't a notion what to do'; *t öyðun i ðim əŋ gubod* (= *wyðun i ðim*) *bo χi wedi du:ad*, 'I did not know you had come'; *t o:yð hi ðim əŋ gubod be ðĕyda hi*, 'she did not know what to say'; *mi wyðun nad ·ĕyθaχi ðim*, 'I knew you wouldn't go'; *u:yr ne:b ar ə ðĕyar ḷe: χ ka:l χi*, 'no one knows where to find you'; *heb ubod iðo vo*, 'without him knowing'; *heb ubod i χi: χ hy:n*, 'unconsciously'; *gubod dim oruθo i hy:n*, 'to be in a state of absolute unconsciousness'.—Pres. S. 1. with the pronunciation *myun* is often used to express 'I am sure', 'I should think', 'I dare say', 'I suppose', 'about': *o:ð hi· n u:yθ, myun*, 'it was eight o'clock, I dare say'; *ǩin yχad a hun, myun*, 'as high as this, I dare say'; *ədi, myun*, 'it is, I am sure';—*os gun i*, 'I wonder': *ədi o wedi du:ad, s gun i?*; *s gun i beθ o:ð no vo iſo*.

gudan, s., gwden, D., 'withe, generally of oak or hazel, placed round a chisel to hold it while working on a hard substance' (O.H.).

guðu, s.m., pl. *gəðva*, gwddf vulgo gwddw, D., 'neck': *korn ə guðu*, 'wind-pipe' or loosely 'throat': *r o:ð ər ĕira n du:ad at gorn ə guðu*, 'the snow was up to one's neck'; *hevo r tavod əŋ ŋhorn ə guðu*, 'mum, silent, shy'; *dolyr guðu*, 'sore throat'; *may gəno vo uðu vèl kḷaguð*, 'he has a neck like a gander'; *uθ i gəðva i ǵiḷið*, 'at one another's throats'; *guðu pottal*, 'the neck of a bottle';—so, also,·of a narrow piece of land.

gu:g, s.m., gŵg, D., 'a surly look'; *daŋos gu:g at y:n*, 'to look surlily at some one'; *dy:n heb dənny gu:g ne:b*, 'a man who has incurred no one's displeasure'; *welis i m o i u:g ərio:yd*, 'I never excited his displeasure'; *dənas a gu:g arni hi*, 'a surly-looking woman'; *mynd heb na hu:g na gu:g* (O.H.), 'to go away empty-handed' (M.F. has 'heb na hŵg na dŵg').

gugan, s., 'whirligig' (I.W.). Cf. D. chwirli gwgon [*χurlĭbugan*].

gugys, adj., gygus, D., 'surly': *golug gugys*.

guḷun, goḷun, gəḷun, ǵeḷun, ǵiḷun, v., gollwng, gellwng, gillwng, D., gyllwng, D.F. [7]. 9. Fut. S. 3. *ḷ·ŋiθ*. Pret. S. 3. *ḷ·ŋoð*. Imperative *guḷun, ḷəŋa*. (1) 'to let loose': *guḷun i aval*, 'to loose one's hold'; *gəḷun ə vyuχ*, 'to let out the cow'; *gəḷun ə ga:θ aḷan o r ku:d*, 'to let the cat out of the bag'; *guḷun kəfəla*, 'to unharness horses'; *goḷun i hy:n*, 'to forget oneself, lose one's self-respect'; *əŋ guḷun i davod heb iſo vo*, 'letting his tongue wag unnecessarily'; 'letting out a secret'; *guḷun aŋo* (i. e. gollwng yn angof), *guḷun dros go:*, 'to forget'. (2) 'to let fall': *guḷun ťida, gləvĕirjon*, 'to dribble'; *ḷəŋoð o o i la:u*, 'he dropped it'; *neuχi vruſo χ ko:t ǩin mynd aḷan ; ma: rubaθ wedi eḷun arno vo*, 'will you brush your coat before you go out; there is something spilt on it'.—Intransitive: (3) 'to run, leak': *may r tebot əŋ guḷun ; may r teǩaḷ wedi mynd i elun.* (4) 'to give way', e.g. a roof, stones, a cliff which is being eaten away by the sea, etc.

gumman, s.m., gwmmon, gwimmon, D., 'sea-weed': *gumman melys, gumman bytta*, 'edible sea-weed'; *gumman kodog ma:n,* 'bladderwrack' (Fusus vesiculosus); *gumman kodog bra:s* (Ascophyllum nodosum); *gumman ledar*(?).

gun, s.m., pl. *gənna*, gwnn, D., s.v. 'scloppus'; D.G. xliv. 36, 'gun'.

gundun, s.m., gwndwn, Yny lhyvyr hwnn [7]; gwynndwnn, rectiùs gwynndonn, D.; 'lay land, land which has never been ploughed': *redig gundun*, 'to plough a piece of land which has never been ploughed before'; *gwair gundun* (as distinguished from *gwair rho:s*), 'lay hay, hay from meadow-land'.

gunnin, s., gwynning, D., 'the outside or sappy part of timber' as opposed to the heart (*rhiðin*).—O.H.

gunnuy, s.m., gwynnwy, D., s.v. 'leucoma', 'volua'; 'the white of an egg'.

gunny, v., gwynnu, D.; gwnnu, W.Ll. xlvi. 13, 'to turn white', e.g. of ripening corn; said also of the hair. Cf. *glasy.*

gu:r, s.m., pl. *gwy:r*, gŵr, D. (1) 'man' (vir): *gu:r bneðig,* 'gentleman'; *he:n u:r*, 'old man' (more respectful than *he:n ðy:n*); *ə gu:r dru:g*, 'the devil': *may r gu:r dru:g i lond o*, 'the devil is in him';—as plant name *he:n u:r*, 'southernwood' (Artemisia Abrotanum); *bottum gu:r ivaŋk*, 'bachelor's button', i.e. 'large double red (or white) garden daisy' (Bellio perennis hortensis). (2) 'husband'. (3) 'a married man': *laŋk ta gu:r ədi o?*, 'is he a bachelor or a married man?'; *gu:r ivaŋk*, 'bridegroom'. (4) 'innkeeper': *r o:n i n rēit gbəðys hevo r gu:r.*

gurdənny, v., 'to thrash': *mi gurdənnis o n jaun ; gurdənny ki:,* etc. (O.H.).

gurol, adj., gwrol, D. (1) 'brave, manful': *edraχ ən urol = edraχ ən dalgry.* (2) 'vigorous': *təvy n urol.*

guroldab, s.m., gwroldeb, D., s.v. 'virosus'. (1) 'bravery, manliness'. (2) 'vigour': *ma na uroldab ən ə tu:*, 'there is vigour in the growth' (O.H.).

gurtaθ, s.m., gwrtaith, D., 'manure'. Not in ordinary use (cf. *tail*), but common in the proverb *gurtaθ da: ədi gwenwyn* [*gwenwyn*].

gurθ, s.m., gŵth, D., 'a push': *mi ro:θ o urθ i mi.*

gurθban, s.m., gwrthban, D., 'a kind of sheet formerly used for threshing upon' (O.H.). In the sense of 'blanket', still remembered, but long since obsolete = *plaŋkad.*

gurθglau(δ), s.m., gwrthglawdd, D., s.v. 'agger'; 'an opposing wall', e.g. directly opposite a gap, or the outside wall of the curve in a sharp turn of a road': *tṛol ən mynd tṛuy aduy a faft ə drol ən mynd ən erbyn ə gurθglauð am vo:d ə forð ən ṛhy: gy:l* (O.H.);—*mi drawis ə ṇṛhu:yn ən ə gurθglau,* e. g. in darkness or mist (O.H.).

gurθjo, guθjo, hurθjo, huθjo, hufjo, v., gwthio, D., 'to push': *guθjo tṛol.*

gurθjol, adj., gwyrthiawl, O.P., 'miraculous'.

·*gurθ·nebjad,* ·*guθ·nebjad,* s.m., gwrthwynebiad, O.P.; gwrth'nebiad, T.N. 230. 7, 'opposition, objection': *t o:s ǵin i ðim* ·*guθ·nebjad,* 'I have no objection'.

gurθod, v., gwrthod, D., 'to refuse': *mi gurθodoð hi,* 'he refused it'; *mi gurθodoð vi,* 'he refused me'; *gurθod y:n forð a kəmmyd forð aral̦,* 'not to take one road and take another'.

·*gurθ·wynab,* ·*guθ·wynab,* s.m., gwrthwyneb, D., 'contrary': *i r* ·*guθ·wynab,* 'on the contrary'.

·*gurθwy·rneby,* ·*guθwy·rneby,* v., gwrthwynebu, D., 'to oppose': ·*guθwy·rneby o,* 'to oppose him'.

gurθyn, adj., gwrthun, D., 'offensive'; *may nu n urθyn i weld,* 'they are offensive to the eye'; *r u:ti ar vai dẽyd ər he:n air gurθyn na uθo vo,* 'you are to blame for using that offensive word to him'; *jaiθ urθyn,* 'offensive language';—*he:n walχ gurθyn ; he:n dga:d urθyn.*

guṛu, adj., pl. *gərvod, gəvrod,* gwrryw, D., 'male': *kaθod gərvod,* 'tom cats' (I.W.); *u:yn gəvrod,* 'male lambs' (O.H.); *he:n be:θ uṛu ədi hi,* 'she is a virago'.

guryd, s.m., gwrhyd, D.; gwryd, I.D. xliv. 29, 'fathom'.

gustun, gəstun, v., gostwng, D. Fut. *(gu)stəŋa.* Pret. *(gu)stəŋis.* Imperative *gustun, stəŋa.* (1) 'to go down, abate': *nẽiθ o ustun,* 'it will go down' (of a swelling); *may r gwynt wedi gəstun,* 'the wind has gone down'; *ṛhẽi əŋ kodi a ṛhẽi əŋ gustun,* 'some going up in the world and some going down'. (2) trans.: *i godi a i ustun o,* 'to move it up and down'; *mi stəŋiθ ə gwynt,* 'it (the rain) will make the wind drop'; *mi vasa kavod ən nobl i əstun ə l̦u:χ,* 'a shower would be a splendid thing to lay the dust';—in knitting stockings, 'to decrease'.

gustyl, s., gŵystl, D., 'surety': *ṛhoid peθ ən ustyl* (O.H.).

guθjo [*gurθjo*].

gu:yð, s.f., pl. *gwyða,* gŵydd, D., 'goose': ·*r ōyðanu ŋ gwẽiði r y: va:θ a gwyða,* 'they were cackling like geese'; *køujon gwyða,* 'goslings'; *mi a:θ ə ṇṛho:yn i vel kṛo:yn gu:yð,* 'I went all goose-flesh'.—Cf. *klaguð.*

gu:yð, s., gŵydd, D., 'presence': *ən i u:yð o,* 'in his presence'; *əŋ ŋu:yð,* 'openly' (opp. to *ən ðirgal̦*).

gu:yl, s.f., pl. *gwilja,* gŵyl, D., 'feast-day, holiday': *gu:yl ẽiljan*

[*ëiljan*]; *gu:yl vair*, ' Lady Day '; *gu:yl ivan*, ' Midsummer's Day ';
gu:yl ə gro:g, ' Holy Cross Day ' [*sgrəmpja*]; *gu:yl (vi)heŋal*,
' Michaelmas '; *durnod gu:yl*, ' a holiday '; *gwilja mdolig*, ' Christmas holidays '.

gwadan, s.m. (O.H.); s.f. (W.H.; I.W.), pl. *gwadna*, gwadn,
D., ' sole ': *gwadan ə tro:yd, ər esǵid*, ' sole of the foot, the boot ':
ðary mi gyro vo nes o:ð o dros i ðay wadan i vəny, ' I knocked him
sprawling '; *ļinjo r (g)wadan vel bo: r tro:yd*, ' to cut one's coat
according to one's cloth '; *gwadan su:χ*, ' the lower removable part
of a ploughshare, the sole of a plough ' (cf. D. gwadn yr aradr,
s.v. ' dentale '); *gwadan tŗol*, ' the foundation of a cart '.

gwadny, v., gwadnu, D., ' to sole ': *sodli a gwadny sǵidja*, ' to
sole and heel boots ';—*gwadna hi*, ' get away '; *may o wedi
gwadny hi*, ' he has taken to his heels '.

gwady, v., gwadu, D., ' to deny ': *gwady arjan ən ļe: taly*, ' to
deny a debt instead of paying '; *gwady nad o:ð o wedi gnēyd*, ' to
deny that he had done it '.

gwa:ð, v., gwahodd, D.; gwadd, B.C. 38. 31; 39. 3. Fut. *gwahoða*.
Pret. *gwahoðis*. Imperative *gwa:ð*, ' to invite ': *gwa:ð ru:in i
suppar*, ' to invite some one to supper '.

gwa:ð, s.m., gwahodd, D., ' invitation ': *gwa:ð i ǵinjo*, ' an
invitation to dinner '; *gwa:ð maur*, ' a pressing invitation '.

gwa:ð, s.f., gwâdd, D., ' mole ': only in *pri:ð ə wa:ð*, ' mole-hill,
mole-hills '. Sometimes corrupted into *pri:ð ə wa:l, prıðwal*. (Otherwise ' mole ' = *turχ dēyar*.)

gwaðod, s.m., gwaddod, D., ' sediment '.

gwaðodi, v., gwaddodi, O.P., ' to deposit a sediment '; ' to settle ':
ma: r kuru ŋ gwaðodi.

gwa:g, adj., pl. *gwëigjon*, gwâg, D. (1) ' empty ': *ļestri gwëigjon*,
' empty vessels '; *y:n wa:g s aχi ifo?*, ' is it an empty one you want? '
(2) in such expressions as *kam gwa:g*, ' a false step ' in the sense of
expecting to find a footing and not doing so ; so also of the hands,
kaf gwa:g. (3) ' hollow '.

gwagað, s., gwagedd, D., ' vanity ': *kany gwagað*.

gwagan, wagan, s.f., pl. *gwaǵeni, waǵeni*, gwageni (pl.), T.N.
18. 2, ' waggon ': *gwaǵeni gwëigjon*, ' empty waggons '. In slate
quarries *gwagan* is a truck with sides, as opposed to *kar* or *sle:d*,
a truck without sides.

gwaǵenad, s., pl. *gwagənëidja*, ' waggon-load '.

gwagjo, v., gwagio, ' to empty '.

gwagla, s.m., gwâg-le, 2 Macc. xiv. 44; gwagle, B.C. 86. 13, ' a
gap in the ground, a hollow ': *pontjo dros wagla*, ' to bridge a gap ';
ma na wagla n i χanol hi, ' it is hollow inside '.

gwa·ha:n, s., gwahan, D., in the exp. *ar wa·ha:n*, 'apart': *ar wa·ha:n i hun*, 'apart from this'; *ma na gasgljad ·gᵊnonu ar wa·ha:n*, 'they make a collection apart'.

gwahanjaθ, gwanjaθ, s.m., pl. *gwanjẹyθa*, gwahaniaeth, D., 'difference': *may ḷawar o wahanjaθ ɽhuɳ ᵊ wla:d a r drc:*, 'there is a great deal of difference between the country and the town'; *klyuχ ᵊ gwahanjaθ hogla*, 'smell the difference'.

gwahanol, adj., gwahanawl, G.R. 42. 17 [separate]; cleifion gwahanol, St. Matt. xi. 5 [lepers], 'different': *meun gwahanol lcvyδ*, 'in different places'; *gwahanol liuja*, 'different colours'; *ᵊn wahanol*, 'otherwise'.

gwahany, v., gwahanu, D., 'to separate'.

gwair, s.m., pl. *gwẹirja*, gwair, D., 'hay': *ḷa:δ, toɽi gwair*, 'to cut hay'; *χwaly gwair*, 'to toss hay'; *tẹyny gwair*, 'to spread hay'; *ɽhcɳkjo gwair*, 'to put hay in windrows'; *gnẹyd ᵊ gwair ᵊn vᵊdᵊla*, 'to gather the hay into cocks'; *tɽi:n, kwẹirjo gwair*, 'to make hay'; *karjo gwair*, 'to carry hay'; *knẹya gwair*, 'hay-harvest'; *ta:s wair*, 'haystack'; *gwair sy:r*, 'sour hay'; *gwair ḷu:yd*, 'mouldy hay'—the result of being stacked when damp; *gwair wedi koχi*, '"burnt" hay', i. e. hay which has been stacked while green and has deteriorated through fermentation; *may r gwair wedi klɛdy*, 'the hay has settled down in the stack'; *maly gwair*, 'to chop hay'; *kadu ka:y ᵊn wair*, 'to keep a field for hay'; *gwair egras, gwair ivaɳk, gwair blu:yδ*, 'hay of the first year used for grass the first time'; *gwair gundun*, 'lay hay' = *gwair meδal, ᵊstuyθ, fruyθlon, ᵊn tᵊvy meun dolyδ isal* (J.J.); *gwair ɽho:s*, 'rough hay, growing in damp places, generally at a high elevation' = *gwair kalad ᵊn tᵊvy ar lc: gly:b* (J.J.); *gwair mᵊnᵊδoδ*, rougher than the latter and mixed with *kɽᵊuk*;—*le: ·by:osti n hel gwair i dᵊgu:n ?*, 'where have you been off to?', said to some one who has been away, no one knows where, without saying a word to any one.

gwaiθ, s.m., gwaith, D.   (1) pl. *gwẹiθja*, 'work': *gwaiθ eda a noduyδ*, 'needlework'; *he:n waiθ bli:n* (= *ka:s*) *ᵊdi o*, 'it is nasty work'; *gwaiθ aur*, 'an hour's work', what takes an hour to do, e. g. 'an hour's walk'; *may paub ᵊn i laun gwaiθ*, 'every one is hard at work'; *t o:ys na δim osgo gwaiθ ᵊno vo*, 'he does not look like working'; *ɽhoi durnod te:g o waiθ*, 'to do a good day's work'; *tɽoi o o i waiθ*, 'to discharge him'; *·vedrani δim gnẹyd day waiθ ar ynwaθ*, 'we cannot do two things at once'; *dy:δ gwaiθ*, 'week-day'; *noson waiθ*, 'week-night'; *ɽhoid rubaθ ar waiθ*, 'to make use of something', e. g. *may dyu ᵊn ɽhoid kᵊvran i bo:b y:n, ond t ᵊdi paub δim ᵊn i roid o ar waiθ*.— Expressing reiterated or habitual action: *ᵊn ᵊ ɽwaiθ ᵊr ᵊdu i n dẹyd uθi hi i bot i m berwi r wy:a n ɽhy: galad*, 'I am continually telling her she boils the eggs too hard'; *pu:y godoδ ᵊ sgo:l ma ? r·vo:, nt* *ədi n i waiθ kodi sgo:ls ?*, 'who made this disturbance? He did: isn't he always making disturbances?'; *ḷa:ð adar may honna ən i gwaiθ*, 'it is its nature to kill birds' (speaking of a hawk). (2) pl. *gwëyθyð*, 'works, mine, etc.': *gwaiθ glo:*, 'coal mine'; *gwaiθ ayr*, 'gold mine'; *gwaiθ du:r*, 'waterworks'; *gwaiθ sebon*, 'soap works'; *gwaiθ sets*, 'quarry for obtaining sets'.

gwaiθ, s.f., pl. *gwëiθja*, gwaith, D., 'time' (Fr. 'fois'): *ḷawar gwaiθ*, 'many a time, often'; *ynwaθ ne ðu:y*, 'once or twice'; *ə drədyð waiθ*, 'the third time'; *saul gwaiθ ?*, 'how many times?' (also in indirect questions); *ambaḷ i waiθ*, 'occasionally'; *mi do:θ o ər y:n waiθ a χi:*, 'he came the same time as you did'; *mi ḷaðuyd o ar y:n waiθ (= ən ə van)*, 'he was killed on the spot'.— Adverbially in the form *wëiθja*, weithiau, D., s.v. 'interdum'; 'sometimes': *wëiθja vel hyn, wëiθja vel araḷ = wëiθja bo:b syt*, 'sometimes one way, sometimes another'. Cf. *tro:*.

gwaχal, gwaχḷyd, gwaχyl, adj., gwachul, D., 'feeble, poorly': *may o n ðy:n gwaχal.*

gwal, wal, s.f., pl. *gwalja, walja*, gwàl, D. (1) 'wall': *gwal ġerig*, 'stone wall'. Cf. *kḷauð, parad*. (2) in slate quarries: 'a shed in which slates are worked'. The *gwalja* stand in rows; the entrance to each is separated from the entrance to the next one by a projecting partition, usually formed by a single large piece of slate standing on end. Each side of this partition forms a corner which is called *bagal*.

gwa:l; gwa:yl (O.H.); *gwa:y* (J.J.), s.f., gwâl, D., 'lair of a beast', esp. 'the form of a hare'.

gwalan [*gjalam*].

gwaldras, s., gwaldras, M.F., 'a blow with a stick across the shoulders' (*gwar*).

gwaljo, v., (g)walio, T.N. 477. 9, 'to wall'; 'to build a wall': *gwaljo vel bigal*, 'to build a wall in a bungling way', e.g. *karag ar garag* instead of *karag ar ə dgëintja*. Also 'to form (e.g. stones) into a wall'.

gwaljur, s.m., gwaliwr, 'wall-builder': *may o n waljur da:*.

gwalk, s.f., gwalc, D., 'coma, cæsaries, capillitium'; 'a turning up': *het ḷair gwalk*, 'a three-cornered hat';—also *kwalk* (Bangor).

gwalkjog, adj., gwalciawg, O.P., 'turned up': *het walkjog*.

gwalχ, s.m., pl. *gwëiḷχ*, gwalch, D. (1) 'a kind of hawk (the colour of which was *gla:s*) now extinct in the district, but formerly common' (O.H.).—Apparently the Peregrine Falcon (Falco peregrinus). (2) 'rogue': *·kəmmuχi ovol, gwalχ!*, 'take care, you rogue!'; *he:n walχ ba:χ*, 'you rogue'; *gwalχ dru:g*, 'a wag'; *gwalχ gla:s ədi o* (O.H.), 'he is a tough customer'.

gwalĭas, s., pl. *gwalĭesi*, gwaldas, O.P., cf. W.S. gwalt [A welte], 'welt': *gwalĭas esg̈id.*

gwalva, s.f., gwalfa, B.C. 65. 26, 'a strewing, litter' (J.J., who used the word of the cockle-shells which formerly lay outside all the cottages at Aber).

gwaḷ, s.m., pl. *gwaḷa*, gwall, D., 'defect, weak spot': *kodi gwaḷa ar baub*, 'to speak disparagingly of every one'; *may r kəθral wedi ka:yl i waḷ arno vo*, 'the devil has found out his weak spot'.

gwaḷa, gweḷa, s.m., pl. *gweḷë̆ivja*, gwellaif, D.; guelleu, W.B. col. 483. 11, 'shears for shearing sheep'. Used also for any kind of shears, e.g. for cutting hedges; but these are always called *sisurn* by farmers.

gwaḷgo, adj., pl. *gwaḷgovjon*, cf. gwallgof, D., 'insanitas'; 'mad': *hannar gwaḷgovjon*, 'half crazy'.

gwaḷgovruyδ, s., gwallgofrwydd, 'madness'.

gwaḷgovys, adj., gwallgofus, D., s.v. 'insanus'; 'mad'.

gwa:ḷt, s.m., gwallt, D., 'hair' (of the head): *gwa:ḷt gola*, 'fair hair'; *gwa:ḷt iꞷwyḷ*, 'dark hair'; *gwa:ḷt ko:χ*, 'red hair'; *gwaḷt wedi gunny*, 'white hair'; *may i wa:ḷt o ŋ glasy*, 'his hair is turning grey'; *may i wa:ḷt o n mynd ən vaur*, 'his hair is getting long'; *tori gwa:ḷt*, 'to cut one's hair', 'to have one's hair cut'; *pu:y he:n vyuχ sy wedi kropjo də wa:ḷt di ?*, 'what old cow has been cropping your hair?' (said to some one whose hair has been cut badly); *i gwa:ḷt am ben i dannaδ*, 'her hair all over her face'; *mi δydif i uθo vo am bo:b blewyn ən i wa:ḷt o (am bo:b blewyn o wa:ḷt ən i benno)*, 'I told him explicitly';—*gwa:ḷt ə vorwyn*, 'maiden-hair' (Adiantum capillus-Veneris).

gwaḷtog, adj., gwalltog, D., 'hairy' (of the head): *po:b koppa waḷtog o ·honynu* (cf. Psalm lxviii. 21), 'every man-jack'. Sometimes corrupted into *koppa waḷgo*, e.g. *mi a: i a nu i r gwarχa bo:b koppa waḷgo o ·honynu*, 'I will take them to the pound every man-jack of them'.

gwamaly, v., gwammalu, D., 'to act with levity, to make fun, to be frivolous'.

gwammal, adj., gwammal, D. (1) 'fickle': *mor wammal a r gwynt*. (2) 'frivolous': *hogan wammal*.

gwan, adj., pl. *gwë̆injaid*, gwann, D. (1) 'weak': *ḷgada gwan, ḷəgaid gwë̆injaid*, 'weak eyes'; *ma na rubaθ ən wan əno vo*, 'there is some weakness, defect, in him'. (2) 'pale': *gla:s gwan*, 'pale blue'; *ko:t la:s gwan*.

gwana, s.f., pl. *gwanë̆ivja*, gwanaf, D. (1) 'as much as can be cut breadthwise with one sweep of the scythe' (cf. *arvod*). (2) 'a row of mown hay; swathe'. (3) 'the breadth between the ropes used in securing a haystack' (J.J.).

gwan·ha:y, v., gwanhau, D., 'to weaken'.

gwanjaθ [*gwahanjaθ*].

gwanjĕyθy, v., gwahaniaethu, O.P., 'to differ; discriminate'.

gwanḷyd, adj., gwanllyd, T.N. 73. 19, 'weak, sickly'.

gwantan, adj., gwantan, T.N. 27. 36; gwentan, C.F. 1890, 332. 13. (1) 'unsteady, unreliable'. (2) 'weak, feeble, poor': *may o m by:r wantan*, 'he is a poor specimen'; *y:n go wantan ϩdu i*, 'I am rather poor' (e.g. at explaining); *araθ gwantan jaun o:yδ gϩno vo*, 'he was a poor speaker'.

gwanuyn, gwanun (old people), but generally *gwanwyn*, s.m., gwanŵyn, D., 'spring': *may gwenwyn ϩn hayl ϩ gwanwyn* (prov.), 'there is poison in the spring sunshine'; *hirlum ϩ gwanwyn*, i.e. March and April.

gwaŋk, s.f., gwangc, D., 'greediness, insatiable desire': *may na waŋk am vu:yd gϩno vo*, 'he has a voracious appetite';—*gwaŋk am verχaid, arjan;—may ϩ waŋk arno vo = may o n ḷŋky ϩ kubul* (O.H.); *gwaŋk aŋa*, 'a voracious appetite sometimes preceding death'.

gwaŋkys, adj., gwangcus, D., 'voracious'.

gwar, s.f., pl. *gwaɾa*, gwarr, D., 'the part of the back across the shoulders, where e.g. a yoke is carried'; *magy gwar*, 'to stoop' (acquire a natural stoop); *may r pun ϩn sϩrθjo ar i waɾo*, 'the pack is falling forward on to his (the horse's) shoulders'.

gwarad, v., gwared, D., 'to deliver', in the exclamations *gwarad ni! gwarad ϩ ŋhalon i!*, 'save us!'; also *ka:yl gwarad o beθ*, 'to get rid of a thing'.

gwarant, s.f., pl. *gwaranta*, gwarant, D.; D.G. x. 19, 'warrant': *kodi gwarant ar*, 'to take out a warrant against'. Cf. *gwranta*.

gwaredigaθ, s.f., gwaredigaeth, R., 'deliverance'; *ḵe:s i waredigaθ heno*, 'I got a load off my mind to-night'.

gwargammy, v., gwargammu, 'to stoop in the shoulders' (as old people do). Cf. *gwargrϩmmy*.

gwargloδ [*gwergloδ*].

gwargrϩmmy, v., gwargrymu, O.P.; cf. gwarrgrwm, D., s.v. 'incuruiceruicus', 'to stoop in the shoulders' (as old people do): *ma: ɾ he:n δy:n na wedi gwargrϩmmy n aru* (O.H.). Cf. *gwargammy*.

gwarjo, v., 'to stoop': *may o n gwarjo n aru*.

gwarjo, v., gwario, D., 'to spend': *gwarjo arjan*, 'to spend money'; *nĕiθ o δim i gwarjo hi nes ḵeiθ o rubaθ am dani hi*, 'he

won't spend it till he gets a good equivalent for it'; *y:n garu jaun
ədi o am warjo i bre:s*, 'he is a terrible spendthrift'.

gwarχa, s.m., gwarchae, D., 'a pound for strayed sheep or other
animals'. Also *by:arθ gwarχa*.

gwarχa, v., gwarchae, D., 'to impound'. Cf. above.

gwarχod, v., gwarchod, D., 'custodire, observare'. (1) 'to keep
house': *du i ŋ gwarχod ən δa:*, 'I do the housekeeping well'.
(2) in the exclamations *gwarχod paub! gwarχod ni!* (for Duw
gwarchod ni!); *ə nevoδ (= ia:d) vo ŋ gwarχod!* 'Heaven help us!'

gwarọg, adj., gwarrog, 'stooping': *dy:n gwarọg*, 'a man with
a stoop'.

gwarθ, s.m., gwarth, D., 'shame, disgrace': *o:δ ən warθ pryl
hənny aryθrol*, 'it was looked upon as a great disgrace at that
time'; *o:δ ən warθ i δənoljaθ i groǵi o*, 'it was a disgrace to
humanity to hang him'.

gwarθag, gwarθaig, s.pl., gwartheg, D., 'cattle': *gwarθag dy:on*,
'black cattle'; *gwarθag godro*, 'milch cattle'; *gwarθag hespjon*,
'dry cattle'; *mi a: i ta gwarθag ən ə gweniθ*, 'I will go whatever
happens'.

gwarθys, adj., gwarthus, D.F. [169]. 6, 'shameful'.

gwa:s, s.m., pl. *gwëiʃon*, gwâs, D., 'servant', esp. 'a farm servant'
(fem. *morwyn*): *pen gwa:s*, 'the farm hand who follows the first
team'; *ail wa:s*, 'the farm hand who follows the second team';
usnos gwa:s newyδ, a phrase alluding to the diligence of a
new servant or to the popularity of a new man *r nëiθ o δim para n
usnos ə gwa:s newyδ arno vo o hy:d*, nearly equivalent to 'a new
broom sweeps clean'; also 'people will get tired of him when the
novelty has worn off'; *gwa:s i ŋwa:s i a ŋwa:s inna n djoǵi*, said
to a servant who shifts work on to others' shoulders; *gwa:s ə go:g*,
'meadow-pipit' (Anthus pratensis); *gwa:s ə nëidar*, 'dragon-fly'.
(2) equivalent to 'my boy', 'old fellow', etc.: *wa:s, wa:s i*, 'my
boy'; *tyd əmma wa:s*, 'come here, old fellow' (e.g. to a dog);
ʃ he:n wa:s, euphemism for the devil.

gwasanaθ, s.m., gwasanaeth, D., 'service', esp. in religious sense.

gwa:sg. s.f., gwâsg, D., 'press', e.g. 'cheese-press'.

gwa:sg, s.m., gwâsg, D., 'waist'.

gwasgary, v., gwasgaru, D., 'to scatter, separate'; 'squander':
day δy:n wedi ka:yl i gwasgary oruθ i ǵiliδ, 'two people separated
from one another'; *gwasgary i ëiδo*, 'to squander one's property'.

gwasgy, v., gwasgu, D., 'to press': *ksulad ba:χ a i gwasgy n
dyn (den)*, 'a small armful pressed well together'; *gwasgy a r
brëiχja*, 'to hug'; *gwasgy r durn*, 'to clench the fist'; *ədi r sǵidja
ŋ gwasgy χ tra:yd?*, 'do the boots pinch your feet?'; *gwasgy a r
dannaδ*, 'to bite'; *may ʃ hu:χ wedi wasgy o a i dannaδ*, 'the sow

has bit him '; *gwasga dǝ veǵin (dǝ vrest)*, ' keep your lips closed ',
' do not say a word '.

gwastad, adj., gwastad, D. (1) ' level, even, straight ' : *kin
wastattad a r ǵëinjog ;—forð wastad*, ' level road ' ; *karag wastad*,
' a flat stone ' ; *kluṱ gwastad te:g*, ' a nice flat piece of ground ' ;
klauð gwastad, ' an even wall ' ; *ka:l po:b pe:θ ǝn wastad*, ' to get
everything straight ' ; *ǝn wastad a hun*, ' in a straight line with that ' ;
sbi:a n wastad (= ǝŋ guderbyn) a dǝ dru:yn, ' look straight in front
of your nose ' ; *r ǝdu ɪ n ṱri:o i dal hi n wastad ǝm mho:b man*, ' I try
and humour every one ' (cf. *dal ǝ ðesǵil ǝn wasiad*) ; *os na: vy:ð
poppeθ ǝn wastad ·rhǝyoni*, ' unless everything is straight between
us '; ' unless we are on good terms '. (2) ' steady ' : *mynd ǝn hǝrðjog
ǝn le: mynd ǝn wastad*. (3) ' staid, sedate ' : *pu:y vasa n meðul ǝ va:θ
be:θ am dano vo a vǝnta mor wastad !*, ' who would have thought it
of him, considering that he is such a steady-going individual ! '
(4) adv., ' always ' : *ǝn wastad (te:g)*.

gwasta·ta:y, gwas·ta:y, sta:y, v., gwastattau, D. (1) ' to make
level ' : *gwasta·ta:y o gumpas ty:*, ' to level the ground round a
house ' ; *sta:y tippin arno vo*, ' to level it a bit '. (2) ' to pacify ' :
ṱhaid gǝry ru:in i sta:y nu. (3) ' to settle up ' : *gwasta·ta:y kʋʋrivon*,
' to settle accounts ' ;—in slate quarries : to make up the number
of slates at the end of a month ; e.g. *gwasta·ta:y nu n hannar kant*.

gwastattað, s.m., gwastadedd, D., ' plain '.

gwastraf, s.m., gwastraff, O.P., ' waste, extravagance '.

gwastrafy, v., gwastraffu, D., ' to squander '.

gwatar, v., gwatwar, D., ' to mimic, imitate '.

gwatfad, gwatfo, watfad, watfo, v., ' to watch '.

gwaud, s.m., gwawd, D., ' mockery, derision ' : *ṱ o:ys dim ond
gwaud gǝno vo*, ' he takes nothing seriously, makes fun of everything ' ; *o ran gwaud*, ' in mockery '.

gwaul, gwaun, s.m., gwawn, D., in *ṱhafa gwaul (kwaul*, J.J.),
' gossamer ' ; also in *davað gwaun,—may hun wedi nǝðy kin vëinad
a davað gwaun*, ' this is spun as fine as gossamer '.

gwaur, s.f., gwawr, D. (1) ' dawn '. (2) ' tinge ' : *may gwaur
la:s ar ǝr awyr*, ' the sky has a blue tinge ' (sign of the weather
clearing) ; *vy:o na ðim ḷawar o waur arno vo wedyn*, ' he succeeded
but ill afterwards ' (cf. Eng. ' off colour '). Cf. D. s.v. ' defloresco '.

gwa:y, interj., gwae, D., ' woe ' : *gwëiði gwa:y*, O.H. (of a supposed ghost) ; *gwa:y i χi os gneuχi hǝnny !*, ' woe to you if you do
that ! '

gwa:yd, s.m., gwaed, D., ' blood ' : *gwa:yd ǝn frǝdjo (sboŋkjo)*,
' blood spurting out ' ; *kǝmro o wa:yd*, ' a Welshman by birth ' ; *m
arno vo ovn ṱruy wa:yd i galon*, ' he is beside himself with fear ' ;

köysa wedi mynd əŋ goχjon i əmmyl gwa:yd, 'legs chafed to the raw' (e.g. by drifting sand) ; *r o:ð hi ən i gwa:yd ar ə ḷaur,* 'she was wallowing in her blood on the floor'; *kynt ə tummiθ gwa:yd na du:r* (prov.), 'blood is thicker than water'.

gwaydģi, s.m., pl. *gwaydguns,* gwaed-gi, D.P.O. 39. 9, 'blood-hound' = *ķi: gwa:yd* ;—as term of reproach : *ta:u ŗ he:n waydģi gwirjon (waydģi bydyr),* said to some one who takes things wrongfully.

gwa:yl, adj., gwael, D. (1) 'ill' (= *sa:l*): *may o wedi mynd ən wa:yl,* 'he has been taken ill'; *may golug dy:n gwa:yl arno vo,* 'he has the look of a sick man'. (2) 'bad, mean, sorry': *kəm·ra:ig gwa:yl,* 'bad Welsh'; *peθ ba:χ gwa:yl,* 'a thing of no importance'; *ṭŗo gwa:yl* (= *sa:l*), 'a shabby trick'; *ru:m wa:yl,* 'a room of mean appearance'.

gwa:yθ, adj., adv., gwaeth, D., 'worse': *mi lasa vod ən wa:yθ,* 'it might be worse'; *ən wa:yθ o r hannar,* 'half as bad again'; *mynd ən wa:yθ wa:yθ o hy:d,* 'to get worse and worse'. Introducing a clause *wa:yθ* implies before it a suppressed negative, e.g. *wa:yθ i mi bëidjo, na: wa:yθ I?* Ans. *na: wa:yθ (ðim),* 'I might just as well not, mightn't I?' Ans. 'Yes'; *wa:yθ ar ə ðẽyar be:θ,* 'it doesn't in the least matter what'; *wa:yθ ·yðynu bëidjo ŗhedag ðim,* 'they might just as well not run'; *wa:yθ boχti wedi kodi am u:yθ ar ðim r u:ti wedi nẽyd,* 'you might just as well have got up at eight for all you have done'; *wa:yθ be di o os ədi o ŋ gnẽyd djoni i χi,* 'it doesn't matter what it is so long as it does you good'; *wa:yθ y:n gair na χant,* 'one word is as good as a hundred'.—Followed by prepositions : *am,* 'as regards': *wa:yθ am dano vo,* 'not worse as regards it', i.e. 'never mind'; *ta wa:yθ (am hənny),* 'if that is anything, for the matter of that':—*ģin,* e.g. *wa:yθ ģin i,* 'not worse in my estimation', i.e. 'I don't care'; *wa:yθ ģin i be ðydiθ o,* 'I don't care what he says'; *wa:yθ ģin i vaint nẽiθ o sbẽiljo arna i, t ədi o ðim əm mhary dim arna i,* 'I don't care how much he makes fun of me, he doesn't do me any harm'; *be o:yð gwa:yθ ģino vo be vo nu ?,* 'what did he care for them?'; *wa:yθ gəno vo r y:n ḷammad,* 'it made absolutely no difference to him';—*i,* 'for' (for another example see above): *wa:yθ i χi:,* 'not worse for you', i.e. 'what does it matter to you?'; *wa:yθ i mi ðẽyd uθ ðarn o bren nag ·uθy·nhuθa,* 'I might as well speak to a block of wood as to them' (cf. *wa:yθ i mi ðẽyd kaŗag a θuḷ*); *wa:yθ i ti be vo nu,* 'never mind them'; *dəmma vi n dẽyd uθo vo nat o:yð wa:yθ iðo vo heb,* 'I told him that it was no use his doing it'; *wa:yθ i ti heb na θri:o* (= *heb ðim ṭṛi:o*), 'it's no use your trying'.—Used substantively : *ŗhag i χi ga:l gwa:yθ,* 'for fear you get something worse'; *be wayθ be vo ?,* 'what does it matter?'

gwe:, s.f., gwe, D., 'web': *may o wedi drəsy ŗ we:,* 'he has upset the plans'; *gwe: pŗy: kop,* 'spider's web'.

gwɛ:ð, s.f., pl. *gweði*, gwêdd, D., 'team': *may gwɛ:ð nobl jaun gɘno vo*, 'he has a fine team of horses'; *pen wɛ:ð*, 'the best team on a farm'; *r ail wɛ:ð*, etc.; *gwɛ:ð vain*, 'a team drawing tandem'.

gwɛ:ð, s.f., gwêdd, D., 'appearance, aspect': *bvuχ a gwɛ:ð ða: arni hi ; may na wɛ:ð ða: ·arnaχi ;—da: jaun o ran pɾy:d a gwɛ:ð*, 'good-looking';—of the face, 'colour, complexion', alluding to temporary modifications, such as paleness, etc.: *gwɛ:ð i wynab*. Cf. Dan. iii. 19, a gwêdd ei wyneb ef a newidiodd, "and the form of his visage was changed".—Fig. *ɾhoi gwɛ:ð aral ar beθa*, 'to put a new aspect on affairs'.

gweði, s.f., pl. *gwɛ·ði:a*, gweddi, D., 'prayer': *mi ðẽydoð o ar i wedi*, 'he said in his prayer'.

gweðil, s.m., gweddill, D., *ɘ gweðil*, 'the rest'.

gwɛ·ði:o, v., gweddio, D., 'to pray': *gwɛ·ði:o ãrost i θɑ:d*, 'to pray for her father'; *mi doroð hogyn i wɛ·ði:o ar ganol ɘ bregaθ*, 'a boy broke out into prayer in the middle of the sermon'; *gwɛ·ði:o am luiðjant ar ɘr aχos*, 'to pray for the success of the cause'.

gweðol, adj., gweddol, D., 'moderate, reasonable': *hogyn gweðol*, 'a moderate sized boy'; *sy daχi hëïðju ? ɘn weðol*, 'how are you to-day?' 'Pretty well' (= *sɘmmol*).

gweðu, adj. and s., pl. *gweðwon*, gweddw, D., 'widowed': *gu:r (dy:n) gweðu*, 'widower'; *gwraig weðu*, 'widow'; *du i n weðu er s dëïgjan mlɘnað*, 'I have been a widower for forty years'.

gweðwi, v., gweddwi, D., 'to put aside widow's weeds': *may hi ɲ gweðwi n aru* implies 'she is looking out for another husband'. Also used similarly of a widower.

gweðys, adj., gweddus, D., 'proper, decent, seemly': *dɘro vo n weðys*, 'give it properly' (e.g. to a child handing something to some one in an unseemly way).

gweǵil, s.m., gwegil, D., 'the nape of the neck': *linin ɘ gweǵil*, 'the spinal cord'; *may o wedi toɾi linin i weǵil*, 'he has broken his neck'; *r o:n i n meðul bod na rubaθ ɘn ɘχ gweǵil χi*, 'I thought you were offended with me about something' (O.H.).

gwegjan, v., gwegian, R., 'to totter': *r o:ð o ɲ gwegjan ar i göysa ;—r o:ð ɘ ɲhöysa ɲ gwegjan dana i*, 'my legs bent under me'.

gwegni, gweǵi, s., gwegi, D. (1) 'emptiness': *ɾhoid i dro:yd ar wegni*, 'to make a false step'; *sgavnaχ na gweǵi*, 'lighter than air'. (2) 'levity': *dy:n ɘn laun o wegni*.

gwēïði, v., gweidi, R.B. 174. 18; L.A. 82. 27; gweiddi, M.Ll. i. 116. 6; D.P.O. 298. 30; gwaeddi, D. Pret. S. 3. *gwẽyðoð*, 'to shout, to call'; 'to squeal' (of a pig), etc.: *os by:ð i/fo pe:θ ɾhaid i χi wëïði (alu)*, 'if you want anything, you must call'; *gwēïði ar i g̃iliδ*, 'to shout to one another'; *na: i wĕiδi n saiθ mu:y*, 'I'll shout seven times louder'.

gwĕini, v., gweini, D., 'to be in service': *may gəno vo y:n verχ əŋ gwĕini əm maŋgor*, 'he has one daughter in service in Bangor'.

gwĕisin, s.m., dim. of *gwa:s*, 'farm-servant': *iyd əmma ŋwĕisin* (O.H.).

gwĕiljad, gwĕiljo, v., gwa(i)tio, W.S. [Wayte]; gwaetio, T.N. 309. 5, 'to wait': *gwĕiljuχ am vynyd, am vynyd ba:χ*, 'wait a minute, a moment'; *gwĕiljuχ, vəða i δim χwiŋkjad na vəða i m barod*, 'wait, I shall be ready in a moment'; *mi a: i n ara de:g i χ gwĕiljad χi*, 'I'll go slowly on, for you to catch me up'; *gwĕiljo irɛ:n*, 'to wait for a train'; *əŋ gwĕiljad am i θa:d adra*, 'waiting for her father to come home'; *gwĕiljad nu ən i ho:l*, 'to wait till they come back'.

gwĕiθgar, adj., gweithgar, D., s.v. 'affabrè', 'fabrè'; 'hard-working'.

gwĕiθjo, v., gweithio, D. (1) 'to work': *gwĕiθjo i hoχor hi*, 'to work with all one's might'; *gwĕiθjo vel la:δ nadroδ (= nēidar)*, *vel bustvil, vel k̃efyl, vel negar; gwĕiθjo n δubul drebal, n δubul pu:ar*, 'to work like niggers'; *gwĕiθjo n χwy:s dəveryd*, 'to work till one is all in a perspiration'. (2) 'to work, to be in motion': *r̃haid i r vrayχ wĕiθjo o r g̃esal*, 'the arm must work from its socket', i.e. 'one must work hard'. (3) 'to froth, to foam; to ferment' (cf. Jonah i. 11, 13).—Transitive (4) 'to work': *may n haus i gwĕiθjo, t ədi r k̃erig δim mor søund*, 'it is easier to work it: the slate does not cling together so'; *ma: nu ŋ gwĕiθjo ə χwaral ən vle:r ru:an*, 'they are working the quarry wastefully now'. (5) 'to act as a purgative upon': *gwĕiθjo ru:in pen vy:δ o wedi r̃hummo; —ka:l i wĕiθjo*, 'to have his bowels moved'.

gwĕiθjur, s.m., pl. *gwĕiθjurs*, gweithiwr, D. (1) 'workman'. (2) 'worker': *ədi r k̃efyl ən wĕiθjur da: ?*

gwĕiθrad, s.f., pl. *gwĕiθredoδ*, gweithred, D. (1) 'deed'. (2) 'deed' (in the legal sense).

gweld (more rarely *gwelad*), v., gweled, D. Fut. S. 3. *gweliθ*, *gwe:l*. Pl. 2. *gweluχ, gwəluχ (·øluχi, ·əluχi, əχi)*. Pret. S. 1. *gwelis*, 2. *gwelist*, 3. *gweloδ*. Pl. 1. *gwelson*, 2. *gwelsoχ*, 3. *gwelson*. Imperative *gwe:l; gweluχ, gwəluχ, øluχ*. The future is very frequently used with present meaning. Sometimes the imperfect (*gwelun*) is used with preterite meaning, e.g. *ə pe:θ kənia ·welani*, 'the first thing we saw'. (Cf. *klyun*.) (1) 'to see': *·weluχi r dy:n aku ?*, 'do you see that man ?'; *wela i m ono vo*, 'I don't see him'; *pu:y wela vo ond . . . ?*, 'whom should he see but . . . ?'; *mi vy:δ ən hi:r jaun k̃iŋ ·gweluχi o etto*, 'it will be long before you see him again'; *i edraχ be ·weluni*, 'to see what we *shall* see'; *gweld po:b for*, 'to see in every direction '; *may o wedi gweld gwel̦ dəðja,* ' he has seen better days '; *əŋ kəmmyd po:b pe:θ we:l o,* ' taking everything he sees ' (O.H.); *muya vy:ð dy:n byu, muya we:l a muya glyu* (prov.), ' we live and learn '. (2) with *ka:yl,* ' to see ', i. e. ' to obtain information through the course which events take ': *rhaid i χi ga:l gweld,* ' you must see '; *kaun weld etto,* ' we shall see '; *g̈ei di weld be g̈ei di ar o:l d ewyrθ,* ' you will see what your uncle has left you '. (3) ' to look ': *gwəluχ!, əluχ!, ɐluχ!,* ' look ! '; *gweluχ be nëif i godi ar ə lo:n nëiθjur,* ' look what I picked up on the road last night '. (4) ' to see ' = ' to understand ': *daχi ŋ gweld? ·əluχi, ·ɐluχi, ɐχi,* ' do you see ?, you see ' (often used, as in English, as a kind of expletive at the end of a statement). (5) followed by an adjective or adverb = ' to seem ': *daχi ŋ gweld ər adag ən hi:r ?,* ' does the time seem long to you?' (Anglo-Welsh: ' do you see the time long ?'); *r öyðun i n i weld o n vaur jaun,* ' he seemed to me very big '; *·wyðosti be: r ədu i n də weld di n debig ?,* ' do you know what I think you are like ?'—similarly *os ·gweluχi n ða: (s gweluχ ən ða:),* ' if it seems good to you ', i.e. ' please '. (6) ' to see ' = ' to visit ': *mi vəða hunnu n du:ad i gwel̦ i,* ' he used to come and see her '. (7) ' to see ' = ' to live until ': *may m bosib i ni bëidjo gweld r amsar honno,* ' it is possible we shall not see that time '.—Phrases : *gweld bai,* ' to blame ' [*bai*]; *gweld i g̈i:l ðannað,* ' to experience the utmost of his unkindness '; *gweld ə werðon am dano,* ' to be sick of waiting for it '.

gwelu, adj., gwelw, D., ' pale ' (as result of illness—seldom used = *l̦u:yd*): *r o:ð golug gwelu a gwa:yl arno vo* (J.J.).

gwelwi, gweuli, v., gwelwi, O.P., ' to turn pale '.

gwely, s.m., pl. *gwla:y* (cf. gwlau, D.P.O. 317. 23), gwely, D. (1) ' bed ': *gwely wensgod,* ' four-poster with curtains ' (J.J.), but cf. *wensgod; gwely py:st bərjon,* ' bed with short legs used when the ceiling is sloping, thus affording little space ' (J.J.); *gwely peswyn,* ' chaff bed '; *mynd i r gwely,* ' to go to bed '; *daχi n mynd i χ gwely ŋ gynt ru:an,* ' you go to bed earlier now '; *may nu wedi mynd i u gwla:y,* ' they have gone to bed '; *wa:yθ i χi vo:d ən əχ gwely ðim,* ' you might just as well be in bed '; *may n haus mynd i r gwely na χodi o hono vo,* ' it is easier to go to bed than to get up '; *vy:om i ri·o:yd ən ə gwely am ðurnod,* ' I never spent a day in bed '; *kwëirjo, tɹi:n, gnëyd gwely,* ' to make a bed '; *wedi ka:yl i gwely,* said of a woman in childbed, ' to be brought to bed '. (2) used e.g. of a stone which lies well in the mortar: *may g̈ini hi wely da:* (O.H.); similarly: *may r gwair wedi kəmmyd i wely n jaun,* ' the hay (in the stack) has settled down nicely '. (3) ' flower-bed ' = *gwely bloda* (cf. D., s.v. ' area ', gwely mewn gardd). (4) ' bed of a river '.

gwel̦, adj., gwell, D., ' better ': *may o wedi gweld gwel̦ dəðja,* ' he has seen better days '; *amsar gwel̦,* ' better days '; *ma: nu n wel̦ l̦e*

ma: nu, ' they are better where they are '; *daχi n edraχ ən weḷ,*
' you look better ';—with *ǵin* as *weḷ ǵin i,* ' I had rather ': *weḷ*
·gənoχi i ·rjaun ta aḷan ?, ' would you rather be inside or outside ? '—
with *i* as *weḷ i mi,* ' I had better ': *weḷ i ni aros əmma am vynу́d,*
' we had better wait here a minute '; *weḷ i ni ga:l tippin ba:χ ar ə*
ta:n, ' we had better have something on the fire '.

gweḷa, v., gwella, D., ' to improve ; to get better (in health) ' :
os medri di weḷa də hy:n, ' if you can better yourself'.

gweḷa, s. [*gwaḷa*].

gweḷjant, s.m., gwelliant, R., ' improvement ': *may hynna n*
weḷjant maur.

gwe:ḷt, s.m., gwêllt, D., ' straw': *gwe:ḷt gla:s,* ' grass ' [*gweḷtglaitʃ*] ;
sometimes *gwe:ḷt* alone is used in this sense as *səp o we:ḷt,*
' a tuft of grass', e. g. left by cattle;—*to: gwe:ḷt,* ' thatched
roof'; *het we:ḷt,* ' straw hat'; *rha:f we:ḷt,* ' straw rope';
pottal (= *suppyn*) *o we:ḷt,* ' bundle of straw'; *gu:r gwe:ḷt,* ' a
kind of guy formerly left on *no:s glaŋǵēya,* as an insult, at the
house of a girl by a rejected lover; sometimes tied to the top
of a tree where it could be seen by the neighbours before it could
be taken down ' (O.H.); *may r durnod wedi mynd i r gwe:ḷt,* ' the
day has gone by without anything being accomplished ' (cf. *wedi
mynd i r brenin*);—also used of persons ' he is a failure '; also
gəry i hy:n i r gwe:ḷt.

gweḷtglaitʃ, gweḷtglatʃ, gwestglaitʃ (J.J.; O.H.); *gwestglas ;
gwesglas* (E.J.), *gwe:ḷt gla:s,* s.m., gwelltglas, D., ' grass '.

gweḷtog, adj., gwelltog, D., (of corn) ' rich in straw '.

gweḷtуn, s.m., gwelltуn, D., ' blade of grass; a straw '.

gwe:n, s.f., pl. *gwena,* gwên, D., ' smile ': *t o:s na ðim gwe:n ar
i ry:ð o ; ·weluχi byθ we:n ar i ry:ð o,* ' you never see him smile ';
tippin ba:χ o wena, ' a little cheerfulness '; *gwe:n ar i ena,* ' a smile
on his lips '; *mi ðēydoð hənny ǵid a i we:n ar i wynab,* ' he said that
with a smile on his face '.

gwenar, s., Gwener, D., *dy gwenar,* ' Friday '; *no:s wenar,*
' Friday night '; *dy gwenar ə grogliθ,* ' Good Friday '.

·gwe:n·de:g, adj., ' pleasant spoken but insincere ': *y:n ·gwe:n·de:g
ədi o, y:n ·we:n·de:g ədi hi.*

gwendid, s.m., pl. *gwendida,* gwendid, D. (1) ' weakness ': *ma:
gwendid ən ə top gəno vo,* " he is a bit off it "; *tru mo:d i ən ə уwendid,*
' as I was in a weak state '; *χwiljo (kodi) gwendida,* ' to seek out
weak points '. (2) ' pudenda ': *ka:l slap ən i wendid.*

gwenhiθan, s.f., gwenhithen, M.Ll. i. 240. 26, ' a grain of wheat '
gweniθ, s.m., gwenith, D., ' wheat '.

gwennol, s.f., pl. *gwenoljad,* gwennol, D. (1) ' swallow ': *gwennol ə mo:r*, term applied to all species of tern (Sterna fiuviatilis, etc.) = *deryn penwaig*, χ*widlur penwaig*. Cf. D., s.v. 'cypsellus', 'drepanis'; morwennawl, R.B. 102. 26. (2) 'shuttle'; also in making nets, 'needle, an instrument for holding and netting the material' (O.H.).

·*gwe:n·ple:s*, adj., 'affable': *r o:ð o n ·we:n·ple:s jaun hevo mi* (generally implying that the affability was a mere blind; cf. ·*gwe:n· de:g*).

gwenwisg, s.f., gwenwisg, D., 'surplice'.

gwenwyn, s.m., gwenŵyn, D. (1) 'poison': *ma: r dy:n wedi kəmeryd gwenwyn*, 'the man has poisoned himself'. (2) 'envy, jealousy, spite', cf. B.C. 17. 17; *may i wenwyn ən i la:ð o*, 'his jealousy is the undoing of him'; *gurtaθ da: ədi gwenwyn*, a proverb implying that envy often profits those towards whom it is shown. Cf. *may li:d a χənvigan ən la:ð i perχennog*.

gweny, v., gwenu, D., 'to smile': ·*ma:y o ŋ gweny n ðel!*, 'he does smile prettily!'—of sunshine: *ꞃ hayl ən tunny ag əŋ gweny n nobl*.

gwenyn, s.pl., sing. *gwenənan*, gwenyn, D., 'bees': *haid, hatʃad o wenyn*, 'a swarm of bees'; *kəχjad gwenyn*, 'a hiveful of bees'; *gwenyn mëirχ (mëiχ)*, 'wasps'.

gwep, s.f., gwep, D., 'vultus, facies, rostrum'. (1) 'face': *tꞃo: də wep ga:l i mi roid y:n i χti* (O.H.), 'turn your face for me to give you a slap'. (2) 'mouth': *kay də wep!*, 'shut your mouth'; *ꞃ he:n wep!* (= *ꞃ he:n ge:g!*), said of some one who cannot keep a secret.—[The word is only used in a facetious sense.]

gwe:r, s.m., gwêr, D., 'animal fat such as that about the entrails of sheep and cattle' (*gwe:r ə pervað*); 'tallow': *wa:st ə gwe:r*, 'droppings of tallow from a candle'.

gweran, s.f., gweren, D., 'caul or fatty membrane investing the intestines, epiploon, omentum'; cf. y weren fol, D., s.v. 'omentum', 'peritonæum'; also 'suet' = *lu:yn*, now generally *ʃiuat*;—*gweran byppyr*, 'a dish made by melting suet, adding pepper and salt, mixing it with bread crumbs in a bowl, and pouring boiling water over it' (O.H.).

gwergloð, gwargloð, s.f., pl. *gwergloðja, gwargloðja*, gweirglodd, D.; gwerglodd, M.LL i. 116. 3, 'meadow'. The following *gwergloðja* formerly existed on the low-lying land along the sea at Llanfairfechan on each side of the river: *gwergloð ə ly:s, — syrdan, — ba:χ, —kay r onnan, —ben ə bryn, — tan r a:ll ba:χ, —tan r a:ll yχa, — vydyr, —vaur, — lu:yn gugan, —ə gilvaχ. —ə welsman, —ər henar, — ə doldir* (O.H.);—*brenhinas ə wergloð*, 'meadow-sweet' (Spiræa Ulmaria) = χ*wy:s arθyr*.

gwerin, s.f., gwerin, D., 'the common people';—also *ə werin bobol*.

gwern, s.pl., sing. *gwernan*, gwern, D., ' alders '.

gwers, s.f., pl. *gwersi*, gwers, D., ' lesson '.

gwerθ, s., gwerth, D. (1) verbal noun, ' sale ': *ar werθ*, ' on sale '. (2) ' worth, value ': *ṛhoid i baub ən o:l i werθ*, ' to give to each according to his worth '; *rubaθ sy a gwerθ əno vo*, ' something of value '; *daχi ŋ gnëyd gwerθ əχ bu:yd ?*, ' does what you do cover your keep ? '; *i o:s na δim ḷawar o werθ əno vo*, ' it is not worth much '; *ˑgəusoχi werθ əχ pṛc:s nëiθjur ?*, ' did you get your money's worth last night ? '; *gwerθ dimma*, ' a halfpennyworth ' (= *mewaθ*); —preceded by *dim*, ' not much ' (but *dim o werθ*, ' nothing of value '): *ˑχəmsoχi δim gwerθ o budin*, ' you have not taken much pudding '; *vedar hi δim gwerθ*, ' she can't (talk) much (Welsh) '; *δary mi gəsgy δim gwerθ nëiθjur*, ' I did not sleep much last night '; *i ədi hi δim ən weḷ δim gwerθ*, ' she is not much better '; *dim gwerθ o forδ*, ' not far '; *vəδa i δim gwerθ ən i nëyd o*, ' I shan't be long doing it '; *d ədi o δim gwerθ*, ' he is not much good ';—as adjective : *mi vasa n werθ i χi gweld nu*, ' it would be worth your while to see them '; *i ədi o δim gwerθ i reǵi*, ' he is not worth swearing at '.

gwerθol, s.f., pl. *gurθavlja, gurθalva, gwerθolja*, gwrthafl, D. ; gwarthol, D.F. {84}. 8 ; gwarthal, C.Ch. 56. 37, ' stirrup ': *dəro də dro:yd ən ə werθol*, ' put your foot in the stirrup '.

gwerθur, s.m., gwerthwr, D., s.v. ' vendaχ '; ' seller ': *gwerθur pəsgod*, ' a seller of fish '.

gwerθy, v., gwerthu, D. Imperative *gwerθ, gwerθa*, ' to sell ': *i o:ys na δim n agos ǩimmint o werθy ˑarnynu ru:an*, ' there is not nearly such a good sale for them now '.

gwerθyd; gwarθyl, gwerθyl (O.H.), s.f., gwerthyd, D. (1) ' spindle '. (2) ' the iron rod which unites the power to churns, to water-wheels, etc.'

gwestyn, s.m., ' a thin wiry man ' (I.W.)—often used as an endearing term, *ṛ he:n westyn bəχan* (of a child) ; *o: ŋwestyn ba:χ !* (to a dog) —O.H. Cf. Ar lleidar gwesdyn drwg i gasdie, A.—(Ellis Roberts).

gweuluyd, adj., gwelwlwyd, ' pale ' (O.H.).

gwevl, s.f., pl. *gwevla, gwelva*, gwefl, D., ' lip '—used both of human beings and animals : *gwelva tena*, ' thin lips '; *ḷedy* (= *estyn, lëysy*) *i welva*, ' to pout ' (cf. CC. 18. 9) ; *paid ag əsguyd də wevla arna i*, ' do not say a word '. Cf. *gwevys*.

gwevlgammy, v., gweflgammu, ' to make a wry mouth ' (O.H.).

gwevrjo, v., gwefrio, G.O. ii. 242. 20. in phr. *dest a gwevrjo*, ' to be on fire for anything ' (I.W.).

gwevys, s.f., pl. *gwevəsa*, gwefus, D., ' lip ': *gwevəsa mëinjon*, ' thin lips '. Cf. *gwevl*.

gwëy, v., gweu, D., s.v. ' textim '. (1) ' to weave ; to knit ':

gwēy sanna, ' to knit stockings '; *ko:t wēy*, ' jersey '; *k̯r̯ɔsbas wēy*, ' a jacket with sleeves worn by workmen underneath a coat '. (2) of rapid motion in and out : *ɔ pɔsgod ɔŋ gwēy ir̯u i ǵiliδ*. Cf. D.G. xlvii. 30.

gwēydlyd, adj., gwaedlyd, D. (1) ' bloody, blood-stained '. (2) ' revengeful ' : *dy:n gwēydlyd = dy:n djalgar :—r̯ he:n ǵena gwēydlyd djalgar* (O.H.).

gwēydlyn ; gwēydlyd (I.W.), s.m., gwaedling, gwaedlif, D., ' fluxus sanguinis '; ' bleeding from the nose ' : *kayl ɔ gwēvdlyn ;—l̯ɔ̯fa r gwēydlyn = milδail*, ' yarrow ' (Achillea Millefolium). Cf. Eng. (Dial.) ' stanch-girss '.

gwēydwyl̯l̯, adj., gwaedwyllt, D., s.v. ' impetuosus ', ' temerarius '; ' passionate ' : *gwy:l̯l̯ wēydwyl̯l̯*.

gwēydy, v., gwaedu, D., ' to bleed '.

gwēylaδ, s.m., gwaeledd, D., s.v. ' leuitas '; ' sickness ' : *ɔŋ kodɩ o:δ ar wēylaδ*, ' arising from sickness '.

gwēylod, s.m., pl. *gwēylodjon*, gwaelod, D. (1) ' bottom ' : *ɔŋ ŋwēylod ɔ grifa*, ' at the bottom of the stairs '—(*ɔn wēylod* also occurs ; cf. yn waylod eigion, C.L.C. v. vi. 51. 22) : *ɔŋ ŋwēylod ɔ dil̯ad, ɔ du:r, ɔr avon*, etc. ;—*ɔ gwēylod isa*, ' the very bottom '. (2) fig. ' bottom ' : *ɔn ɔ gwēylod*, ' at bottom '; *dim ɔn ɔ gwēylod,—ɔŋ kogjo bo:d ar ɔ gwynab*, ' not really,—looking as if he was, pretending to be '. (3) ' grounds ' : *gwēylod blaud k̯ēir̯χ wedi berwi*, ' grounds of boiled oatmeal ';—also in pl. : *gwēylodjon baril ; gwēylodjon golχi ɔn ɔ k̯ruk*.

gwēyly, v., gwaelu, O.P., ' to become poorly, infirm ' : *may hi ŋ gwēyly n aru er s riu δay vi:s*, ' she has been getting very infirm the last two months or so '; *may hi wedi gwēyly l̯awar*, ' she has been pulled down very much ' (by her recent illness).

gwēyrod, s.pl., cf. gwyryng, D., ' vermiculi in dorsis boum '. (1) ' worms that breed under the skin of cattle ', i.e. ' the maggots of the warble-fly ' (Hypoderma bovis), called gweryd, gweryrod in Medd. An. p. 89. (2) ' ship-worms ' : *gwēyrod meun ko:yd l̯oŋ* (O.H.). Cf. W.S. gwyran aderyn gwyllt ' A bernacle '.

gwēyθa, adj., gwaethaf, D., ' worst ' : *may r adag wēyθa wedi pafo*, ' the worst time (of year) has passed '; *wedi mynd i r l̯e: gwēyθa*, ' gone to the bad '; *vel may gwēyθa mo:δ*, ' I am sorry to say ';—used substantively : *ar wēyθa*, ' in spite of '; *ar i wēyθa (ar hy:d i wēyθa) δo:θ o*, ' he came in spite of himself, against his will '; *ar i wēyθa vo n i δannaδ*, ' in the teeth of his opposition ', also *ar i wēyθa vo n i e:n*.

gwēyθdy, s.m., gweithdy, D., s.v. ' lithotomia '; ' workshop ' : *gwēyθdy sa:yr*.

gwēyu, s.m., gwayw, D. (1) ' spear ', in the plant-name *dail bla:yn ə gwëyu* (O.H.).—G. has (p. 4) Ranunculus Flammula, Lesser Spearwort, Blaen gwaew lliaf, and R. Lingua, Greater Spearwort, Blaen y gwaew mwyaf. (2) 'a shooting pain': *gwëyu ən i χevn ;—mi a:θ gwëyu i go:ys y:n 'onynu ;—vedra r doktor ðim tori r gwëyu.*

gwi:al, s.pl., gwial and gwiail, D., 'rods': *gwi:al mëinjon, əstuyθ,* 'slender, pliable rods'; *ḳru:θ sgotta wedi nëyd o wi:al,* 'a fishing basket made of rods, osier'. Cf. *gjalam.*

gwi:al̯, s.pl., sing. *gwia̯lan*, f. gwaell, pl. gweyll, gwehyll, D., 'knitting needles'; *gwia̯lan wa:l̯i,* 'hair-pin'.

gwi:b, wi:b, s.f., gwib, D., 'vagatio'. (1) 'a run': *gnëyd, kəmmyd wi:b* (O.H.), 'to take a run' (before a jump); *mi na:θ wi:b a̯lan,* 'he rushed out'; *ar wi:b,* 'post haste'. (2) 'wandering, peregrination': *wedi mynd ar i wi:b,* 'gone off on his wanderings'. (3) 'spirit of unrest': *may riu wi:b garu əni hi* (= *riu vynd, riu ·an·sevəd·logruyð*), 'she is always gadding about', 'she cannot settle down' ;—*may riu wi:b əno vo am vynd o hy:d ;—pen drawa r wi:b arna i* (*ar ə ṃhenni*), 'when the wandering spirit came upon me'; *may o ŋ kəmmyd ə wi:b ən i ben ag̯ i fur a vo:,* 'he gets the wandering instinct on the brain and off he goes'; *ma: l̯awar o wi:b wedi du:ad ar ə by:d,* 'the world is full of unrest'.

gwibdaiθ, s.f., gwibdaith, 'flying visit, hurried journey': *may o wedi kəmmyd i wibdaiθ ; may o wedi mynd ar i wibdaiθ.*

gwibjo, v., gwibio, D., 'to be given to wandering, to be unable to settle down'; 'flighty'.

gwibjog, adj., gwibiog, D., s.v. 'vagabundus'; 'given to wandering, roaming about': *wel wi:r, r o:n i n wibjog jaun pen o:n i n ivaŋk—ən mynd ar ol merχaid ;—seran wibjog,* 'falling star'.

gwig̯il, adj., gwygyl, O.P., 'sultry': *may r dəwyð ən wig̯il* (= *mul̯, marwaið*).

gwi:χ, s.f., pl. *gwiχja*, gwich, D., 'squeak'.

gwiχjad, s.pl., sing. *gwiχin, gwiχan*, gwichiad, D., 'periwinkle'. Also called, for the sake of distinction, *gwiχan vylta ; gwiχjad mo:χ,* 'whelk' (Fusus); varieties are *gwiχjad mo:χ melyn* and *ko:χ ; gwiχan ḳi:* (Littorina littoralis), *gwiχan arjan,* apparently a shell of the genus Trochus worn to a silvery colour.

gwiχjan, v., cf. gwichio, D., 'to squeak'; 'to creak' (e.g. of boots); 'to screech' (of fowls and owls): *gwiχjan χwerθin,* 'to giggle' (applied especially to girls).

gwiχlyd, adj., gwichlyd, O.P., 'creaking': *sg̯idja gwiχlyd.*

gwilihoban, v., gwilhobain, O.P. [to gallop], 'to gallivant, to fool away one's time' = *dgolihəutjo,—may hi wedi mynd i wilihoban a̯lan ;—l̯e: may r hogyn ? may o ŋ gwilihoban ar o:l ər he:n neθod na.*

gwiljad, gwiljo, v., gwylio, gwyliaid, gwilio, gwiliaid, D., gwylat, W.B., col. 74. 18 ; gwilied, D.F. [166]. 12 ; B.C. 34. 2 ; D.P.O. 56. 28. (1) ' to watch ': *du i ŋ gwiljad i səmidjada* (J.J) ;—*rhaid i wiljo vo* (O.H.). (2) ' to mind, take care ': *gwiljux sərθjo,* ' mind you don't fall '.

gwiljad, s., in the phrase *ar wiljad ə dy:ð = ə waur gənta n tori* (O.H.). Cf. *gwyl.*

gwiḷḷinab, s.m., gwylltineb, D., ' fury ': *gnēyd k̑igëïðdra ən i wiḷḷinab (wirjondab)* (O.H.), ' to commit an act of cruelty in a moment of passion '.

gwiḷḷjo, guḷḷjo, v., gwylltio, D. (1) ' to fly into a rage ' (*hevo*). (2) ' to go wild ', e.g. with excitement : *·t ədynu ðim əŋ gwiḷḷjo ru:an, ma: nu wedi syvylo,* ' they are not in wild excitement now, they have quietened down '. (3) ' to take fright ': *mi wiḷḷjoð ə kefyl.* Trans. (4) ' to make angry '. (5) ' to frighten ': *gwiḷḷjo r adar;* (of a sheep-dog) *gwiḷḷjo r devaid i vəny.*

gwi:n, s.m., gwin, D., ' wine '.

gwina, adj., gwinau, D., ' bay ' (of horses).

gwinjo, v., gwynio, D., ' to throb ' (I.W.).

gwiŋo, v., gwingo, D. ; B.C. 31. 11. (1) ' to quiver, twitch ' (of an animal on the point of death). (2) ' to set one's limbs in motion, exert oneself ': *may rhëi əŋ gwiŋo hənny vedranu a mynd dim kam ən i blëyna ;—rhaid i ti wiŋo am də dammad ;—dy:n əŋ gwiŋo gwëiθjo.*

gwi:r, adj., gwir, D., ' true ': *k̑in wirad (wirjad) a fadar,—a r eveɲjil,—a bo:d bara meun torθ,* ' as true as the gospel ' ;—*ən wi:r,* ' really, truly ': *ən wi:r dlaud,* ' really poor '; also ' indeed ' (here *ən* is generally omitted): *i:a wi:r,* ' yes, indeed '; *na: na, wi:r,* ' I will not, indeed ', i.e. ' no, I won't '; *eḷa wi:r mai dəna be sy:,* ' perhaps, indeed, that is what it is '; *veḷy wi:r, dəna be o:yð o,* ' just so, that was it '; *veḷy wi:r ! = ai je !,* ' really !', ' you don't mean it !'—As substantive ' truth ': *gwi:r a χeluyð,* ' truth and falsehood '; *dēyd ə gwi:r,* ' to tell the truth '; *mi vasa hənny n agosaχ i r gwi:r,* ' that would be nearer the truth '; *du i wedi dēyd ḷawar o stry:on ·uθaχi, a ḷawar o wi:r ·ənynu,* ' I have told you a great many stories, and there is a great deal of truth in them too '; *g̑in ə gwirjon k̑ëir ə gwi:r* (prov.), ' from the innocent is obtained the truth '; *χeuχi m o r gwi:r gəno vo,* ' you can't get the truth out of him '; *t ədi o ðim əŋ kayl ə gwi:r,* ' he does not get justice, get his due ' (in good sense); *ar əχ gwi:r ? ar ə ŋwi:r, taun i maru r mynyd ma !,* ' Really ? ' ' Really, upon my life and soul ' (lit. ' were I to die this minute '.

gwirðjo, v., gwyrddio, ' to become green ': *may r ko:yd əŋ gwirðjo.*

gwirjon, gurjon, adj., gwirion, D.   (1) 'simple (in good sense), innocent' : *r o:ð o mor wirjon !,* 'he was so simple !'; *ə pe:θ ba:χ gwirjon !,* 'poor little thing !'   (2) 'stupid, foolish' : *ǩin wirjonad a i gəsgod,* 'as foolish as can be'; *he:n lob (lolyn, bembul,* etc.) *gwirjon,* 'old fool'; *he:n ḋgolpan wirjon daχi !,* 'you silly idiot !'; *wedi mynd ən wirjon he:n,* 'in his dotage'; *paid a gnëyd də hy:n ən wirjon,* 'don't make a fool of yourself'; *ən daχi n wirjon əm bəstaχy vel hyn !,* 'how stupid you are to overwork yourself like this !'; *mi es i n wirjon gadal ə matʃis ən ə lọft,* 'it was stupid of me to leave the matches upstairs'.

gwirjonað, s.m., gwirionedd, D., 'truth' : *dëyd ə gwirjonað ;—may hi m berfaθ wirjonað,* 'it is perfectly true ';—*wirjonað inna !,* 'dear me !'

gwirjondab, gurjondab, s., gwiriondeb, D., 'innocentia'; 'foolishness' : *gnëyd ǩiǵëïðra ən i wirjondab (wiḷtinab),* O.H., 'to commit an act of cruelty in a moment of passion '.

gwirjoneðol, adj., gwirioneddawl, O.P., 'true, real' : *ən wirjoneðol sa:l.*

gwirjoni, gurjoni, v., gwirioni, O.P., 'to play the fool'; also trans.: *gwirjoni ǵenaθ,* 'to make a girl love one madly'.

gwi:sg, s.f., pl. *gwisgoð,* gwîsg, D., 'dress, clothes ; covering, husk, etc. ': *dənas vle:r vydyr ən i gwi:sg a i gwaiθ,* 'a slatternly woman'; *ǩëïrχ wedi tənny i wi:sg,* 'oats with the husk taken off'; *gwi:sg ər arad,* 'part of a plough opposite the mouldboard', 'side of a plough'.

gwisǵi, wisǵi, adj., gwisgi, D., 'nimble' : *may o n wisǵi i dro:yd, gwisǵi ar i dro:yd.*

gwisgo, v., gwisgo, D.   (1) 'to dress' : *may hi ŋ gwisgo am dani,* 'she is getting dressed'; *may hi ŋ gwisgo am dani hi,* 'she is dressing her '.   (2) 'to dress' (implying style of clothes worn): *gwisgo n syvyl,* 'to dress plainly'.   (3) 'to wear' (transitive): *gwisgo r bais a r klo:s,* 'to wear the breeches' (of a woman);— intransitive : *may o ŋ gwisgo n ða:,* 'it wears well '.   (4) 'to wear out' (trans.): *ɖu i ŋ gwisgo və sǵidja ar ər oχra,* 'I wear out my boots on one side ';—intr. 'to wear out, wear away, grow thin ', used of other objects as well as clothes, e.g. *may r garag wedi gwisgo,* 'the stone is worn away'; *wedi gwisgo i r eda,* 'threadbare '. —used also of persons.

gwiθan, s.f., pl. *gwiθenna,* gwythen, D., 'vein'; also 'vein of slate, etc.'

gwiẅ, s.f., pl. *gwivja,* gwîf, D.; pl. gwifiau, s.v. 'palangæ'; 'a large crowbar used esp. in slate quarries to move a block (*ply:g*) after blasting '.

gwla:d, s.f., pl. *gwledyð,* gwlâd, D.   (1) 'country' (Fr. 'pays '): *dim ond burn ar ə wla:d,* 'only a burden on the country'.   (2)

'country' (Fr. 'campagne'): *ən ə wla:d*, 'in the country'; *mɣnd am dro: i r wla:d*, 'to go for a walk into the country'; *dyl̥ gwia:d o farad*, 'a manner of speech in the country'.

gwladaδ, adj., gwladaidd, D. (1) 'of the country', 'rustic': *ma na olug gwladaδ jaun arni hi.* (2) 'of a kindly disposition', 'pleasant to deal with' = *hauδ i dri:n, kəmdëiθasol, kəmuɣnasgar, əŋ gnëyd ən de:g a faub, meun amoda da: a faub* (O.H). Cf. B.C. 13. 23.

gwla:n, s.m., gwlân, D., 'wool'.

gwlanan, s.f., pl. *gwlanenni*, gwlanen, D., 'flannel': *krɔsbas wlanan*, 'flannel shirt'; *pais wlanan*, 'flannel petticoat'; *gwlanan o δy:n*, 'a man of weak character, without backbone', so *r he:n wlanan !* [This term was once applied by a preacher to the Almighty through the mouth of Jonah, when the destruction of Nineveh was not carried out. W.H.]

gwlanennur, s.m., gwlanennwr, 'wool-buyer, flannel-maker'. Cf. Yn union daw'r gwlanenwr, Iawn brynwr yn ei bryd. C.— 'Cerdd yr Edau Wlan'.

gwlasbant, s., gwylmabsant, O.P., 'feast of the patron saint of a church, wake': *gwlasbant lanvar, abar, duygɤvɔlχi*—died out about 1832 (O.H.).

gwlasbanta, v., gwylmabsanta, O.P., 'to frequent wakes, make merry at a wake' (O.H.).

gwledig, adj., gwledig, D., 'rural': *ardal wledig*, 'a rural district'.

gwle:δ, s.f., pl. *gwleδoδ*, gwlêdd, D., 'feast': *kadu gwle:δ*, 'to have a feast'.

gwleδast, s.f., gloddest, D., 'revelling, carousing, riotous living' (O.H.).

gwlesta, v., gloddesta, D., 'to carouse'.

gwli:θ, s.m., gwlîth, D., 'dew'.

gwliθlau, s.m., gwlithlaw, D., s.v. 'psecas'; 'fine drizzle'.

gwliθo, v., gwlitho, D., 'to fall' (of dew): *may hi ŋ gwliθo*, 'dew is falling'.

gwly:δ, s.pl., sing. *gwliδin*, gwlŷdd, D., 'sprouts', e.g. of potatoes coming up—further advanced than *egin*: *gwly:δ dom*, 'chickweed' (Stellaria media); *gwly:δ ḡëiru = bu:yd gwyδa*, 'robin-run-in-the hedge, goosegrass, cleavers' (Galium Aparine).

gwly:χ, s.m., gwlŷch, D., 'liquid'; 'gravy' (I.W.).

gwnadyr, gwnjadyr, s.m., gwniadur, D., 'thimble'.

gwnedyn, s.m., pl. *gwnjada.* Cf. gwyniad, D., s.v. 'sario'; 'salmon-trout' (Salmo trutta)—I.W.; young salmon (O.H.).

gwneppryd, s.m., wynebpryd, D., s.v. 'facies'; 'countenance';
gwneppryd brunt əsgavn.

gwnidog, s.m., pl. *gwenidogjon,* gweinidog, D., 'minister'.

gwniŋan, niŋan, s.f., pl. *gwniŋod, niŋod,* cwningen, D.; O.F.
conin, connin; Anglo-French, coning, 'rabbit': *ə wniŋan.*

gwniŋǵi, niŋǵi, s.m., gwenwyngi, 'a jealous man'; 'a peevish
man'.

gwni:o, v., gwnío, D. Fut. S. 1. *gwni:a,* 3. *gwni:θ, gwni:f.* Pret.
3. *gwni:oδ.* Imperative, *gwni:a ; gwni:uχ,* 'to sew'.

gwniθvan, s.m., gwenithfaen, G.O. ii. 177. 6, 'granite'—a
common word in slate quarries. Four varieties are distinguished:
gwniθvan gla:s, gwyn, dy:, and *ko:χ.*

gwni:ur, s.m., gwnîwr, O.P., 'one who sews'.

gwnjadrag, s.f., gwniadwraig, D., 'sempstress'.

gwnjadur, s.m., pl. *gwnjadurs,* gwnîadwr, O.P., 'one who sews'
(O.H).

gwnynlyd, adj., gwenwynllyd, D.   (1) 'poisonous'. (2) 'malignant', e. g. of an ulcer = *ḷidjog.*   (3) 'keen': *ma: r gwynt ən
wnynlyd.*   (4) 'spiteful, mean': *r o:δ o n ɣhy: wnynlyd iδo vo ga:l
kur o r əmba·rel,* 'he was too spiteful to let him have a corner of
the umbrella'.   (5) 'jealous, envious'.

gwnyno, v., gwenwyno, D.   (1) 'to poison'. (2) 'to be jealous'.

gwobr, s.f., pl. *gwobra,* gwobr, D., 'reward, prize'.   (Rather
literary, but common in connexion with eisteddfod competitions, etc.)

gwəudjo, v., gwawdio, D., s.v. 'ludo'; 'to mock, make game
of': *mi gwəudjoδ vi,* 'he made game of me'.

gwəudjur, s.m., gwawdiwr, B.C. 38. 17, 'mocker, jester'.

gwəudlyd, adj., gwawdlyd, D., 'mocking, derisive; inclined to
jeer'.

gwəurjo, v., gwawrio, 2 Pet. i. 19.   (1) 'to dawn'. (2) 'to
improve': *may o n deχra gwəurjo* is said e. g. of one who has been
in bad circumstances, when things are beginning to improve.

gwraiδ, s.pl., sing. *gwrĕiδin,* m., gwraidd, sing. gwreiddyn, D.;
gwreiddin, D.G. clxxv. 25, 'roots'; *kodi o r gwraiδ,* 'to root up';
gwraiδ witf, 'twitch, couch-grass'.

gwraig, s.f., pl. *gwragaδ,* gwraig, D.   (1) 'woman' (more
complimentary than *dənas*); *gwraig ə ty:,* 'lady of the house';
buru he:n wragaδ a fyn, 'to rain cats and dogs'. (2) 'wife': *u:yθ
o blant o r wraig gənta,* 'eight children by the first wife'; *gwraig
ivaŋk,* 'bride'; *gwraig weδu,* 'widow'.

gwra:χ, s.f., pl. *gwraχod,* gwrach, D., 'hag': *ko:yl gwra:χ ar o:l bytta yud.* 'an old wives' fable'. (For similar expressions cf. D.F. [x]. 11, [45]. 12.) *bréyδuyd gwra:χ ən o:l i hulys*, "the wish is father to the thought"; *iṛc:χ du:y wra:χ nag y:n* (prov.), "two heads are better than one". Used also of men: 'an owl';—*gwra:χ ə lydu = gwra:χ ə tukka*, 'woodlouse', gwrach y lludw, D., 'cutio, porcellio'.

gwraχan, s.f., pl. *gwraχod*, gwrachan, D., s.v. 'anicula'. (1) 'hag', as term of reproach: *ta:u ṛ he:n wraχan !* (2) This term is applied indiscriminately to all kinds of sea-bream and wrasse: *gwraχan ȯy:*, 'black sea-bream' (Cantharus lineatus). Two other varieties are distinguished: *gwraχan go:χ* and *gwraχan wen*. Cf. also *pəsgodyn arjan, pəsgodyn ayr.—gwraχan ə ba:u*, 'a small fresh-water fish about four inches long, of a reddish colour, which lives in still water' (O.H.), '? minnow' (Leuciscus phoxinus);—*gwraχan ba:χ*, 'a kind of bird'. Cf. gwrach y cae (O.P.), 'hedge-sparrow', i. e. Accentor modularis.

gwrando, v., gwrando, D. Imperative *gwrando, gwranda ; gwranduχ*, 'to listen': *gwrando ar ə pe:θ sy arno vo*, 'to brood over one's illness'.

gwranta, v. (Fut. S. 1), warantaf, S.G. 94. 36; wrantaf, S.G. 42. 30; cf. D.G. cxxiv. 31, cxxx. 27: *mi gwranta i di*, 'I'll warrant you'.

gwregys, s.m., pl. *gwregəsa*, gwregys, D., 'truss' (apparatus used in cases of rupture).

gwrēiδjo, v., gwreiddio, D., 'to take root': fig. *may o wedi gwrēiδjo n δa: jaun*, 'he has remained long in his situation'.

gwrēiδjol, adj., gwreiddiol, D. (1) 'thorough, from the root': *dəsgy n wrēiδjol*, 'to learn thoroughly'. (2) 'reliable, true': *may r pe:θ ədu i wedi δēyd əm berfaiθ wrēiδjol.*

gwrēigan, s.f., gwreigan, D., s.v. 'vxorcula'; 'a little woman': *may hi n he:n wrēigan bra:v*, 'she is a fine little old woman'; also 'wife': *ə wrēigan aku*, 'the old woman at home'.

gwrēiχjon, s.pl., sing. *gwreiχjonan*, gwreichion, D., 'sparks'.

gwre:s, s.m., gwrês, D., 'heat': *may r ta:n ən ṛhoi gwre:s*, 'the fire is hot'; *may hi ɲ kodi n wre:s*, 'it (the weather) is getting hot'.

gwresog, adj., gwresog, D. (1) 'hot, heat-giving': *may r glo: n wresog*, 'the coal gives out a great deal of heat'. Also applied to the weather,—a stronger term than *tesog.* (2) 'cordial'.

gwri:d, s.m., gwrîd, D., 'ruddiness, flushing of the face': *ə gwri:d wedi mynd o r boχa.*

gwrido, v., gwrido, D., 'to blush': *gwrido d at i glistja, gwrido at vo:n ə gwa:lt*, 'to blush to the roots of one's hair'.

gwrinan, s.f.   Cf. gwirin, D., s.v. 'verminatio'; and gwraint, sing. gwreinyn, 'ring-worm': *ə vrinan* (O.H.).   Cf. *derwinan*.

gwrilgoχ, adj., gwridcoch, D., s.v. 'ruber'; 'ruddy, rosy-cheeked'.

gwrodan, s.f., gwaroden, S.E., s.v. 'switch'; 'rod': *gwrodan ðeru ne goḷan i walájo* (O.H.)—thicker and tougher than *ŗhodan*.

gwry̆ːχ. s.m., pl. *gwrəχod*, gwrўch, D., 'hedge'.   (Seldom used = *ḳlauð*, but *ḳlauð gwry̆ːχ* is in fairly common use to distinguish from *ḳlauð ḳeŗig*, etc.); *pḷəgy gwry̆ːχ*, 'to bend a hedge'.

gwry̆m. s.m., pl. *gwrəmja, gwrimja*, gwry̆m, D., 'a small ridge; a weal': *r oːð ə ɲhevn i n wrəmja maur vel ə my̆ːs* (J.J.), 'my back was covered with weals as big as my finger';—also 'a pleat', e.g. of a stocking.

gwry̆ːsg. s.pl., sing. *gwrysgan*, gwry̆sg, D., 'small branches cut off': *gnĕyd ḳḷauð gwry̆ːsg*, 'to make a hedge by inserting poles in the ground and entwining branches between them'; *gnĕyd aduy wry̆ːsg [aduy]*.

gwrəðyn, gwryðyn, s.m., 'withe' (?): *gwrəðyn basġad*, 'handle of a basket'.

gwrəχyn, s.m., gwrychyn, D., s.v. 'seta'.   (1) 'bristles': *kaːθ əɲ kodi i gwrəχyn*, 'a cat arching its back' (*kodi i χry̆ːχ* is also heard); *mi godis ə ɲwrəχyn vel baːyð kənðĕirjog*, 'I bristled up like a mad boar'.   (2) 'blades of grass left standing after the scythe' (O.H.); *gwrəχyn arvod*, 'such blades left standing between each sweep of the scythe forward'.

gwrəmjog, adj., gwrymiog, D., s.v. 'fimbriatus'; 'full of ridges, ribbed', applied e.g. to the sand of the sea-shore when the tide is low (J.J.).

gwybad, s.pl., sing. *gwybedyn*, gwybed, D., 'flies'.

gwydro, v., gwydro, D., 'to glaze'.

gwydrur, s.m., gwydrwr, D., 'glazier'.

gwydyn, adj., sup. *gwyína*, 'tough', applied to meat, hay, etc. (opp. *bray*)—fig. *may o n y̆ːn gwydyn* (*ən wydyn vel kortyn*), 'he is a tough customer'.

gwydyr, s.m., gwydr, D., 'glass': *lamp wedi toŗi i gwydyr*, 'a lamp with a broken chimney'; *paːyn* (= *kwaral*) *o wydyr*, 'a pane of glass'.

gwy̆ːð, s.m., pl. *gwəðjon*, gwŷdd, D., 'arbusta, arbores, caules'; gwydd aradr, s.v. 'aratrum'; cf. also W.LL lvi. 101, 'plough' (Pentir, Tregarth, and the neighbourhood of Bangor).   Cf. *arad*.

gwy̆ːð, s.m., pl. *gwəhiðjon*, gwŷdd pro gwehydd, D., 'weaver'.

gwyðal, s.m., pl. *gwyðelod*, Gwyddel, D., 'Irishman'.—As term of reproach: *gwyðal hy̆ḷ*.

gwyδelas, s.f., Gwyddeles, 'Irishwoman': *baŋk r̥ he:n wyδelas*, name of a sand-bank.

gwyδelig, adj., Gwyddelig, 'Irish': *tro: gwyδelig*, 'a shabby trick'.

gwy:χ, adj., gwŷch, D., 'splendid, fine, smart': *gwy:χ o be:θ ; ma na olug gwy:χ ar ə gwarθag ; dy:n gwy:χ ; gwëiθjur gwy:χ ; ma na olug gwy:χ ar i waiθ.*—Not often used : English words such as *kr̥and, nëis, smart* tend to take its place.

gwylaδ, adj., gwylaidd, S.E., s.v. 'modest'; 'modest'.

gwylan, s.f., pl. *gwlanod*, gŵylan, D., 'sea-gull': *gwylan benδy*, 'black-headed gull' (Larus ridibundus); *gwylan vre:χ*, 'herring-gull' (Larus argentatus); *gwylan wen*, 'common gull' (Larus canus); *gwylan kevn dy:*, 'black-backed gull' (Larus marinus).

gwyl̥, s., gwyll, D., in phrase *gid a gwyl̥ ə no:s = r̥huŋ day ola* (O.H.). Cf. D., s.v., 'Yngwyll y nôs, Crepusculo vespertino'. Cf. also *gwil̥jad*.

gwy:l̥, adj., pl. *gwil̥tjon*, gwyllt, D. (1) 'wild = not tamed': *dovi anival gwy:l̥*, 'to tame a wild animal'; *mo:χ gwil̥tjon*, 'wild boars'; *kaθod gwil̥tjon*, 'wild cats'; *kefyl gwy:l̥*, 'a horse that has not been broken in'. (2) 'wild, growing wild': *mavon gwil̥tjon*, 'wild raspberries'; *pyppys gwil̥tjon*, 'vetch'; *sa:yds gwy:l̥*, 'wood sage';—similarly *gwy:l̥ luini*, 'thick, almost impenetrable bushes'; *gwa:l̥ gwyl̥*, 'hair which stands straight up in spite of brushing'. (3) applied to what has never been cultivated (of land): *ti:r gwy:l̥*. (4) 'wild, stormy, raging': *tu:yδ amwadal gwy:l̥*, 'wild, unsettled weather'; *du:r gwy:l̥*, 'a strong current'; *may hi n veru gwy:l̥*, 'it is in a wild state of excitement', e. g. a meeting; *may o n holiks gwy:l̥*, 'he is in a terrible temper'. (5) 'of anything that burns quickly or bursts suddenly into flame, inflammable': *glo: gwy:l̥*, 'coal that burns quickly'; *dy:n gwy:l̥ vel matfan*, 'one who flares up in an instant like a match'. (6) 'quick tempered': *dy:n gwy:l̥* (cf. the last example); *gwy:l̥ wëydwyl̥*, 'passionate'. (7) 'hasty, apt to act in a hurry'. (8) 'malignant': *davad wy:l̥*, 'a cancerous wart'. (9) *tra:yθ gwy:l̥*, 'quicksand' (O.H.).

gwymmad [*gwynab*].

gwyn, adj., fem. *gwen*; comp. *gunnaχ*, pl. *gunjon*, gwynn, D.; comp. gwnnach, L.A. 16. 14; G.R. 31. 18; pl. gwnnion, D.F. [viii] 22. (1) 'white': *may hi n vy:d gwyn*, 'it is a white world' (after a fall of snow); *ə mənəδoδ ən i kr̥əsa gunjon*, 'the mountains covered with snow'; *bəsaδ koχjon gunjon*, 'white fox-gloves'; *menig gunjon*, 'white gloves'; *r o:yδ po:b man ən wyn o varig*, 'everything was white with frost'; *mi vy:δ əχ pen ən wyn pen ·weluχi hənny*, 'your hair will be white by the time you see that'; *o r bora gwyn dan no:s*, 'from early morning till night'; *ki:g gwyn*, 'fat meat'; *gwyn ə gwe:l ə vra:n i χiu* (prov.). (2) 'white-hot'.

(3) 'blessed', in phrase *gwyn dǝ vy:d !*, 'what a happy man you are'; similarly: *gwyn po:b pc:θ newyδ* (prov.).—As substantive: (1) 'fat'.   (2) 'silver coins': *o:ys ·gǝnoχi̦ χwe:χ o bre:s ǝn ḷc: χwe:χ o wyn ?*, 'have you six coppers for a sixpenny piece'. (3) 'desire': *gweld i̦ wyn arno*, 'to like it' (I.W.).

gwynab, rarely *wynab ; gwymmad, wymmad* (O.H. always) (A by-form *χwynab, χwymmad* also exists, e. g. *ǝ i̦y: χwymmad i̦ vǝny*, 'face upwards'; *dim ar χwymmad ǝ δëyar*, 'nothing on earth'), s.m., pl. *gwyneba*, wyneb, D.   (1) 'face': *ka:l rubaθ gǝno vo mor hauδ a tǝnny ḷa:u hyd i̦ wynab*, 'to get something from him as easily as stroking his face', i. e. 'for the mere asking'; *ṛhoid wynab agorad ar baub*, 'to act frankly towards every one'; *dëyd rubaθ ǝn ǝχ gwynab*, 'to say something before your face' (opp. *ǝn ǝχ k̆c:n*, 'behind your back'); *dëyd rubaθ ǝn ǝχ gwynab no:yθ*, 'to say something before your very face'; *gnëyd rubaθ ǝn wymmad ǝ gɀraθ* (O.H.), 'to do something in the face of, against the law'; *dal gwynab (i̦)*, 'to make believe': *i̦ o:δ o δim ǝn lëikjo vo o gubul, ond r o:δ ǝn dal gwynab iδo vo ;—dal blaud gwynab [blaud] ; tǝnny gwyneba*, 'to make faces'; *tǝnny gwynab hi:r*, 'to pull a long face'; *sǝrθjoδ i̦ wynab*, 'his countenance fell'.   (2) as term of reproach, implying ugliness: *ṛ he:n wynab !* (3) 'surface': *ar wynab ǝ mo:r*, 'on the surface of the sea'; *un i̦ δim ar wynab ǝ δëyar*, 'I have no notion'; *gwynab ǝ dorθ*, 'the surface of the loaf': *ṛhǝuχ bla:t ar i̦ wynab o*, 'put a plate over it' (i.e. over another plate).

·*gwynab·galad ; ·gwymmad·galad* (O.H.), adj., gwynebgaled, 'bare-faced, impudent' (= *talog*): *may o mor ·wymmad·galad na nëiθ ṛhesum m o i̦ droi o.*

·*gwynab·gleduχ*, s.m., gwynebgaledwch, 'barefacedness, impudence'.

gwyneby, v., wynebu, D., 'to face': *θala fon δim i̦ wyneby taiθ ǝn ǝr he:n amsar*, 'a stick would be useless to face a journey in old times'.

gwynera: *may na fitja gwynera arno vo*, 'he is changeable' (I.W.).

gwynlasy, v., gwynlasu, O.P., 'to turn deadly pale'.

gwynt, s.m., pl. *gwyntoδ*, gwynt, D.   (1) 'wind': *gwynt ǝ duyran*, 'east wind'; *gwynt maur*, 'high wind'; *gwynt tros ǝ ti:r*, 'land wind' (on the sea); *may na awal δa: o wynt hëiδju*, 'there is a good breeze to-day'; *i̦ o:s na δim χwa: (= evlyn) o wynt*, 'there is not a breath of wind'; *i̦ o:ys na δim digon o wynt i̦ ǝsguyd ǝ briga*, 'there is not enough wind to move the branches'; *i̦ ǝdi̦ r gwynt δim ǝm buguθ*, 'the wind is not boisterous'; *may r gwynt ǝn vain (= wnynḷyd)*, 'the wind is piercing, keen'; *may hi̦ y kodi̦ n wynt*, 'the wind is rising'; *may hi̦ wedi̦ kodi̦ ywynt ǝn aru jaun*, 'it has got very windy'; *may r gwynt wedi̦ mynd i̦ laur (tori̦ i̦ laur, huiljo i laur, gostegŗ, gusŗun, ļëŗˑhaːy*), 'the wind has dropped'; *may r gwynt wedi troi,* 'the wind has changed'; *r oːð ə gwynt ən ə ŋɥevn,* 'the wind was behind me'; *əŋ ŋɦəsgod ə gwynt,* 'sheltered from the wind'; *kiŋ gəntad a r gwynt,* 'as swift as the wind'; *ſarad i r gwynt,* 'to talk nonsense'; *mynd a i ben ən ə gwynt,* 'to be at a loose end, to be harum-scarum, to flaunt about'; *gwynt teːg ar d oːl diˑ!,* 'good riddance!' (2) 'breath': *du i wedi koļi ŋwynt,* 'I have lost my breath'; *kaːl gwynt,* 'to get one's breath; to have a moment's rest'; *a i wynt ən i uðu,* 'breathless'; *r oːð ə ŋwynt ən ə nurn i,* 'my heart leapt to my mouth'; *kəmmuχ əχ gwynt,* 'take your breath'; *miˑ ləŋkoð ə kuru ar yːn gwynt,* 'he swallowed the beer at one gulp';—fig. *may o n ļaun o wynt,* 'he is a frothy man'. (3) 'draught'. (4) 'wind' (in the stomach): *gwynt əŋ kasgly.* (5) 'inclination': *t oːs gin i ðim gwynt i vynd əno,* 'I don't feel much inclined to go there, I don't much care about going there'; *χədig iaun o wynt sy gin mam iðo vo,* 'mother doesn't much care for him'.

gwyntog, adj., gwyntog, D., 'windy'.

gwyntyļ, s.f., gwyntyll, D., s.v. 'vannus'; 'winnowing fan': *ə wyntyļ i ļnay ər yːd* (O.H.).

gwyrð, fem. *gwerð,* pl. *gwərðjon, gwirðjon,* adj., gwyrdd, D., 'green'.

gwyrðlas, adj., gwyrddlas, D., s.v. 'virido'; 'green': *may r kaːy ən wyrðlas.*

gwyrðlesni, s., gwyrddlesni, D., s.v. 'viriditas'; 'greenness', esp. of grass.

gwyro, v., gŵyro, D., 'to stoop, bend': *vedruχi ðim mynd ən əχ sevyļ, ŗhaid i χi wyro; gwyruχ uθ ben əχ plaːt,* 'lean over your plate'.

gwyrθ, s.f., pl. *gurθja,* gwyrth, D.; pl. gwrthyev, L.A. 83. 6; gwrthiau, M.Ll. i. 94. 9, 'miracle'.

gwyvo, gwywo, v., gwywo, D., s.v. 'flacceo'; gwyfo, C.L.C. ii. 37. 26; T.N. 74. 2, 'to fade'.

gwyvyd, s.m., gwyddfid, D.: *ļɀfˑa r gwyvyd,* 'honeysuckle' (Lonicera Periclymenum).

gwyvyn, s., gwyfyn, D., 'moth'. Seldom used.

gwəhiljon, s.pl., gwehilion, D., 'dregs' (literal and figurative).

gwəhəry, v., gweryru, D., 'to neigh; to guffaw'.

gynt [*kynt*].

gyr, s.m., pl. *gəroð,* gyrr, D., 'flock, drove': *gyr o ðevaid, voːχ, warɓag, gəfəla, wyða,* etc.

gytto, pet name for 'Griffith'.

gəflog [*kəfəlog*].

gənna, adv., gynneu, D., 'just now'.

gərnat, s.m., 'gurnard': *gərnat grε:*, *gərnat sbotjog*, 'grey gurnard' (Trigla gurnardus); *gərnat ko:χ*, 'red gurnard' (Trigla lineata).—Cf. *χurnur.*

gərur, s.m., gyrrwr, D., s.v. 'exactor'; 'driver': *robin ə gərur*, 'gadfly';—also 'drover'—properly the assistant of a *porθmon.*

gəry, v., gyrru, D. (1) 'to drive': *gəry ə wε:δ*, 'to drive the team'; *gəry moχyn*, 'to drive a pig'; *əχi: δary ɲəry vi ar ə kwestjun*, 'you made me ask the question'; *may o ɲ gəry ar i dri: mi:s*, 'he is nearly three months old'. (2) 'to send' (= *anvon*): *gəry ləθyr*, 'to send a letter'; *gəry govyn*, 'to send an invitation'; *gəry irosoδ ·atiynu*, 'to send over to them'; *gəry morwyn ar negas*, 'to send a maid on an errand'.

gəstifol, in *peļ gəstifol*, 'ever so far': *ma: nu wedi mynd əm beļ gəstifol* (O.H.) = *bəstifol.*

h

ha:, s.m., hâf, D., 'summer': *durnod kənta ɼ ha:*, 'the first day of summer' (i. e. May 1); *hannar ha:*, 'midsummer'; *fair vaŋgor hannar ha: ;—ɼ ha: ba:χ*, 'St. Luke's summer' (but applied to the end of September).

ha:d, s.m., hâd, D., 'seed' (in the aggregate). Cf. *hadan, hedyn.*

hadan, s.f., pl. *hada*, haden, O.P., 'a single seed': *hadan o dε:*, 'tea-leaf' (O.H.).

hady, v., hadu, D., 'to seed'.

hadyd, s.m., hadyd, M.Ll. i. 169. 1, 'seed-corn'; also 'potatoes kept for planting'.

hafjad, s., haffiad, 'handful': *dəro i mi hafjad o wε:ļt, o brikja.*

hafjo, v., haffio, T.N. 47. 10; 225. 5; 300. 35. (1) 'to snatch, snatch at, jump at' (= *kəθry i bε:θ, nĕidjo i bε:θ*, J.J.); *ku:n ən hafjo ar i ɡiliδ ;—paid a hafjo arna i*, 'don't jump down my throat'. (2) 'to gulp': *hafjo bytta* (of human beings or animals) = *ļɒukjo.*

hafla, s.pl., affleu and *hafflau, D. (1) 'grasp': *ļond i hafla*, 'as much as can be grasped by the two hands and arms'. (2) 'clutches': *r o:δ o ən i hafla ; a:θ ən injon i u hafla ; a:θ o i hafla ɼhag bla:yn ; kadu aļan o hafla ɼ hε:n blismon na.*

hagan [*agan*].

hagar, adj., hagr, D., 'ugly' = *hyļ* (but the latter is the ordinary word); *tɾu:y dε:g ne hagar*, 'by fair means or foul'.

hagry, v., hagru, O.P., 'to make ugly, become ugly '.

hai, in the expression *hai luk !* an exclamation equivalent to ' may it be so, indeed ', e.g. *gobëiθjo by:ð hi vely—wel, hai luk !*

haid, s.f., pl. *hëidja*, haid, D., ' swarm ' (of bees) ; ' flock' (of birds) ; ' shoal ' (of fish) ; ' pack ' (of hounds), etc.

haið, s.m., haidd, D., ' barley'.

haint, s., pl. *hëintja*, haint, D., ' epidemic ' : *may gëva gla:s ən dəbəkkax o hëintja*, ' a green winter is more likely to bring epidemics with it '.

hak, s.m., pl. *hakja*, Eng. hack, ' a cut, cleft ' : *mi doris hak ar ə ļa:u ;—hak ən ə graig*, ' a cleft in the rock '. (Cf. *agan.*)

hakjo, v., haccio, C.G.M. 95. 23, Eng. hack, ' to notch, to cut marks in a stick '—the old-fashioned way of keeping accounts.

halan, s.m., halen, D., ' salt ' : *pinfin o halan*, ' a pinch of salt ' ; *ǩettog (halan)*, ' salt-box ' ; *ǩalan o halan*, ' bar of salt ' ; *mi ro: i halan ən i bottas o !*, ' I'll be even with him !', ' I'll have it out with him !' = *mi ro: i halan ar i vriu o.*

hald, s., ? hald, D., ' succussio ' ; R. [the trotting or jogging of a horse] in the phrase *ar i hald* as *ðo:θ ar i hald*, ' he came un-expectedly,—as the whim led him ' ; *mi ðo: i riu ðurnod etto ar və hald*, ' I shall be turning up again some day '.

·haldi·war, s., ' a ruffian ' (I.W.).

haldjo, haldjan, v.; cf. haldian, D., s.v. ' nuto ' ; ' to reel' (of a drunken man) ; *haldjo o r y:n oxor i r ļaļ.*

haljo, v., ' to haul ' : *haljo ku:x.*

ha:ļt, adj., pl. *hëiltjon*, hallt, D., ' salty, salt ' (intensified *xweru ha:ļt*) : *du:r ha:ļt*, ' salt water ' ; *ǩin haļtad a heli trimor (dëyvor, day vo:r)*, ' as salt as the water of three seas ' ; *daxi n i glu:ad o n ha:ļt ?*, ' does it taste salty to you ? '—fig. *may n ha:ļt gin ə ŋhaļon ðëyd*, ' it grieves me to say '.

halty, v., halltu, D., ' to salt '.

ham, s.f., pl. *hams*, ' ham '.

hambəgjo, v. (1) ' to humbug ' (trans.). (2) ' to play the fool ' (*uθ bexy, veðwi, vyu n avradlon*, etc.). (3) ' to play the deuce with ' : *hambəgjo i jexid.* (4) ' to overwork ' : *hambəgjo i hynan = bəstaxy.* (5) ' to ill-treat '. (All O.H.)

hamðan, s.f., hamdden, D., ' leisure '.

hamðenol, adj., hamddenawl, O.P., ' leisurely ' : *gnëyd rubaθ ən hamðenol ; y:n hamðenol jaun di o*, ' he takes it easy '.

hampar, s.f., *hampar o enaθ*, ' a romping girl ', ' a tom-boy ' ; *he:n hampar (vydyr) !* (Cf. M.F. rhampen.)

hamport (O.H.); *hamburt* (Bangor), s.m., ? Eng. hand-board; 'a kind of tray formerly placed on the table to hold the tea things, with one leg supported by three feet and generally made of oak' (O.H.)—also 'tray'.

hanas, s.m., pl. *hanefʼon*, hanes, D., 'story, history': *dëyt hanas*, 'to tell a story'; *mi driːʃ i gaːyl ər hanas gəno vo m bersonol ond mi veθiʃ,* 'I tried to get the story from him personally, but without success'; *tasa ṛ heːn sgidja ma n medry ʃarad mi ˙gøusani dippin o i hanas o,* 'if these old boots could speak we should hear a bit of his history';—*dim hanas ono vo,* 'no signs of him'.

handi, adj. (1) 'handy, convenient'. (2) 'quick': *dəruχ lump o gaus ən i ġcːg o, mi˙gnoiθ hunna n o handi,* 'put a lump of cheese in his mouth, he'll chew that quickly enough'.

handlan, s.f., pl. *handls,* 'handle', e. g. of a can or bucket. Also *handl.* Cf. *koːys, ṭṛoːyd, klyːst, gwrəðyn.*

hanesyn, s.m., hanesyn, O.P., 'a little story'.

hannar, s.m., hanner, D., 'half': *hannar kant o bynna,* 'fifty pounds'; *may o drost i hannar kant,* 'he is over fifty'; *əŋ gant a hannar oːyd,* 'a hundred and fifty years old'; *bluːyð a hannar,* 'eighteen months of age'; *hannar aur wedi yːn or ðeːg,* 'half-past eleven'; *hannar dyːð,* 'midday'; *hannar noːs,* 'midnight'; *hannar koron,* 'half a crown'; *hannar ḷanu, hannar ṭṛai,* 'half tide'; *hannar kimmint araḷ,* 'half as much again'; *muːy o r hannar,* 'half as big again'; *maː nu n ṛhyː vaːn o r hannar,* 'they are too small by half'; *weḷ gin i o r hannar,* 'I had far rather'; *bron wedi darvod, nag ar i hannar nag ar i χwartar χwaiθ,* 'nearly finished, neither half finished nor quarter finished either'; *r oːð na helynt a hannar,* 'there was a terrible row'; *ṭori ən i hannar (ṭṛu i hannar),* 'to break, to tear in two';—as adverb: *hannar kiŋ grəvad a hiː,* 'half as strong as she'; *wedi hannar i lugy,* 'half-starved'; *mi aːθ a r kiː ar hannar bytta,* 'he took the dog away when he had only half finished eating'; *hannar pan,* "not all there".

hannos [*annos*].

hanny, v., hanfod, D., 'to originate, come originally (from)': *puːy dëyly ədi o? may o n hanny aḷan o hun a hun; hanny aḷan o ʃiːr voːn* (O.H.).—Somewhat literary.

hanoð [*anoð*].

hantiks, s., Eng. antics, (Dial.) hantics: *mynd ṭṛu i hantiks, daŋos i hantiks,* 'to show his naughty tricks'; 'to make an exhibition of himself'.

haŋkas, haŋkatʃ, s.m., pl. *haŋketʃi,* 'handkerchief': *haŋkas pokkad.*

haŋkəpjo, haŋkəfjo, v., 'to handcuff'.

haŋkəps, s.pl., 'handcuffs'.

haŋla, s.f., 'a scolding': *ɽhoi haŋla i ðy:n* (I.W.).

hapnjo, v., cf. hapio, W.S., 'to happen': *ðarɣ mi hapnjo i weld o = diguyð.*

happys, adj., happus, D., 'happy'.

hapysruyð, s., happusrwydd, D.F. [138]. 28; P.G.G. 63. 7, 'happiness'.

harbur, s.m., harbwr, C.L.C. iv. 33. 24, 'harbour'.

harð, adj., hardd, D., 'pretty': *merχ ivaŋk harð ðəmynol*, 'a pretty, comely young girl'; *maɣ hənnɣ n o le:u o harð*, 'that is rather pretty'.

harðy, v., harddu, Rev. xxi. 19, 'to beautify'.

harjo, v., hario, Eng. harry. (1) 'to be tired' (stronger than *blino*): *du i wedi harjo n la:n*, 'I am dead tired'. (2) 'to tire': *mi haris i nu i ǵi:d*. (3) 'to spoil': *maɣ gwynt ə duyran ən harjo, ən dveθa po:b pe:θ.*

harḷig, adj., haerllug, D., s.v. 'importunus', 'impudens'; 'impudent, audacious; hard, grasping', e.g. of one who drives a hard bargain.

harθjo [*arθjo*].

harɣ [*darvod*].

hasart, s., Eng. hazard, 'risk': *hasart garu jaun*, 'a great risk'.

ha:st, s.f., hast, C.C. 214. 11, 'haste': *mynd ar ha:st vaur.*

hastys, adj., 'hasty, apt to do things hurriedly'.

hatlin, s., hatling, St. Mark xii. 42, 'mite': *s ǵin i ðim hatlin*, 'I have not a brass farthing'.

hatʃad, s.f., 'hatch': *hatʃad o gəujon ; hatʃad o wenyn*, 'a swarm, hiveful of bees'; *hatʃad o vo:χ*, 'litter of pigs'.

hauð, adj., comp. haus, *həuðaχ*, sup. *həusa, həuða*, hawdd, D., 'easy': *mi vy:ð ən haus i χi vytta na dim by:d araḷ*, 'it will be easier for you to eat than anything else'; *ɽhoi diḷad meun du:r ga:l nu vod ən haus i golχi*, 'to put clothes to soak so as to make them easier to wash'; *pe ba:ɣ r wyðva ŋ gaus mi vəða n haus ka:l kosyn* (prov.), 'if Snowdon were made of cheese it would be easier to get one', i.e. 'if ifs and an's were pots and pans, there'd be no trade for tinkers';—with *ǵin*: *maɣ n haus ǵin i veðul*, 'I am inclined to think'. —Comparative with the verb to be: *pu:ɣ haus ·vəðuχi ?*, 'what will it avail you ?'; *vasa r kəujon ðim haus uθ ga:l krəsiyn oni ba:ɣ vod ər ja:r ən i valɣ vo n ðigon ma:n yðynu*, 'the chickens would be none the better for getting a crust unless the hen made it into small enough bits for them'; *be du i n haus a mynd ru:an a r ire:n wedi kəχuyn ?*, 'what is the use of me going now when the train has started ?'; *be o:yð o haus a ɽhoid kwëir iðo vo ?*, 'what was he the better for giving him a thrashing?'; *vy:o vo dammad haus*, 'he was none the better for it'; 'it was of no avail'.

haul, s.m., pl. *həulja*, hawl, D.   (1) 'right': *haul pori devaid a θori maun*, 'the right of pasturing sheep and cutting peat'.   (2) 'principal': *byu ar ər haul*, 'to live on the principal'; *lo:g a haul*, 'interest and principal'.

havaδ, adj., hafaidd, D., 'summery'.

havlig, s., haflug, D., 'abundantia, copia'; 'a number', generally in a derisive sense: 'troop, crew, bevy'; *havlig o fipfuns*, 'a troop of gipsies';—*r he:n havlig!*

havn, s.f., pl. *havna*, hafn, F.N. 5. (5).   A by-form of *kavn*, with the meaning 'hollow'.

havog, s., hafog, D.F. [74]. 21, 'havock'.—Often implies 'a sudden mishap': *mi δo:θ ən havog o la:u sədyn, a ninna n əmmyl ka:l ər y:d* (O.H.).

hay; hëy (J.J.; O.H.), v., hau and heu, D., 'to sow'.

hayl, s.m., haul, D., 'sun': *may r hayl ən tunny*, 'the sun is shining'; *may r hayl əŋ kodi*, 'the sun is rising'; *may r hayl ən mynd i laur, ən mynd dan g̈ëyra, ən maxlyd*, 'the sun is setting'; *may hi n du:ad* (= *kodi*) *ən hayl*, 'the sun is coming out'; *ən bgad* (= *əŋ ŋhe:g*) *ər hayl*, 'in the sun'; *p1ədra r hayl*, 'rays of the sun'; *py:si hayl*, 'sun rays seen descending from clouds in the distance'; cf. W.Ll. (Voc.), s.v. 'terydr'; *klip ar ər hayl*, 'eclipse of the sun'; *da:u hayl ar vryn etto*, 'better days will come'; *hayl tommos əwan*, 'the moon'.

ha:yl, adj., hael, D., 'generous, liberal': *ha:yl vy:δ həwal ar burs ə wla:d* (prov.), 'he cutteth large thongs from another man's leather', 'he is liberal at other people's expense'.

ha:yls, s.pl., Eng. (Dial.) hail [small shot, pellets], Sc., Irel. 'small shot'.

ha:yn, s.f., pl. *hëyna*, haen, D., 'layer, film, veneering': *du:r wedi rhewi n ha:yn o re:u arno vo*, 'water with a film of ice over it'; *ha:yn ar ha:yn*, 'layer on layer'.

heb, prep., heb, D.   With pronouns: S. 1. *hebδa i*, 2. *·hebδat(i)*, 3. *hebδo (vo), hebδi (hi)*.   Pl. 1. *·hebδon(i)*, 2. *·hebδox(i)*, 3. *·hebδyn(u)*. Followed by the vocalic mutation, 'without': *heb i vai heb i eni* (prov.), 'no one is without his faults'; *heb raid nag axos*, 'without any reason whatever'; *heb vlewyn* (= *δëilan*) *ar i davod*, 'without mincing matters'; *χëir m o r melys heb ə χweru* (prov.), 'every rose has its thorns'; *heb amsar i δim by:d*, 'no time for anything'; *mi g̈ëïθ o vod hebδo vo*, 'he shall do without it';—with *δim*, 'without any': *bara heb δim kodjad*, 'bread that has not risen';—after *mynd* and *du:ad*, negative of *mynd a, du:ad a*, e.g. *mi ëif i heb ə* *pappyr,* 'I never took the paper'; *wedi du:ad heb ər y:n ə may o,* 'he has not brought one';—with verbs (1) 'without': *heb ubod: χi χ hy:n,* 'unconsciously'; *r öyðun i am ðu:y noson heb dənny ə sgiája o:ð ar ə ŋrha:yd,* 'I was two nights without taking off my boots'; *mi gwelis i hi heb veðul i gwelt i,* 'I saw her accidentally'; *mi ·lasanu roid o iðo vo heb iðo vo o·vyn,* 'they might have given it to him without him asking for it'. (2) 'unless': *i ëyθun i ðim heb i χi daly,* 'I wouldn't go unless you paid me'. (3) where in English a simple negative or 'and . . . not' or 'who, which . . . not' would be more usual: *may r korn heb vynd etto,* 'the horn has not sounded yet'; *mi· ro:θ ə ki: meun kuppurð heb roi tammad o vu:yd iðo vo,* 'he put the dog in a cupboard and gave him nothing to eat'; *këirχ heb i valy,* 'unground oats'; *gwarθag ivaŋk heb gəra ð dɔvluyð o:yd,* 'young cattle under two years old'; *heb vod ən vaur, heb vod ən va:χ,* 'neither large nor small'; *dy:n heb vedry farad əŋ gröyu,* 'a man who cannot speak plain'; *wa:yθ ǵin i ta:ti heb nëyd am draguyðoldab a durnod dros ben,* 'I should not care if you did not do so for ever and a day';—*b la:u* (= heb law) = 'besides, but': *may rubaθ ən ə ɤhadu i b lau klo: a χlikjad,* 'something keeps me besides lock and latch'; . . . *a ɟawar b la:u nu,* '. . . and many others besides'; *pu:y o:ð ən ə van na b la:u plismon,* 'who should be there but a policeman'.

hedag, v., ehedeg and hedeg, D.   Fut. S. 3. *hediθ,* 'to fly': *i ədi gu:yð vra:s ðim ən hedag ə ṃheḷ* (prov.), i.e. 'a man of worth does not go far to be appreciated';—also 'to run to seed': *kabaitf wedi hedag.*

hedjad, s.m., hediad and ehediad, D., 'flight': *do:s ar d injon vel hedjad bra:n,* 'go straight as the crow flies'.

hedyð, s.m., pl. *hedəðjon,* hedydd, D., 'lark': *hedyð ə mo:r,* 'ringed plover' (Ægialitis hiaticula).

hedyn, s.m., pl. *hada,* hedyn, D., 'a (single) seed': *hada marχ meri,* 'hips'; *po:b hedyn o hono vo,* 'every scrap of it'.

heðuχ, s.m., heddwch, D., 'peace': *χëiθ o ðim mynyd o heðuχ nes kodiθ o,* 'he won't have a minute's peace till he gets up';—*prənna heðuχ = kay də ǵe:g;—əstys heðuχ,* 'justice of the peace'; *ḳreǵin heðuχ,* 'money'.

hefar, s.f., pl. *hefrod,* heffer, W.S. [Hecforde], 'heifer'.

hegal, s.f., pl. *hegla,* hegl, D., 'crus, tibia'; 'foot, leg': *mi· ro:θ ər he:n vyuχ ǵik i mi a i hegal.*   Generally used in the plural, implying large, clumsy feet combined with lankiness of limb, esp. in a semi-facetious sense, as *tyn də hegla attat o:ð ar for,* 'take your legs out of the way'; *səmmyd də hegla o: na; paid a hel də hegla bydron hyda i; maθry gwely bloda hevo i hegla.*

heglog, adj., heglawg, O.P., 'long-legged': *ən heglog ovnaduy ag ən vaur* (O.H., speaking of a dragon-fly). Also applied to a person with large awkward feet, e. g. turning too much in or out.

hegly ; hegljo (O.H.), v., heglu. (1) 'to be off', "to hook it", "to kick the bucket" : *may o wedi hegly hi*, "he has hooked it" ; *may o dgest a i hegly hi*, 'he is on the point of death' ; *r o:ð hi dgest wedi hegljo*, 'she was on the point of death'. (2) 'to come to grief, to fail in one's object' : *may o wedi hegljo = wedi meθy i amkan ; may o wedi hegljo hi*, e. g. *deχra bysnas ag ən meθy.*

hëïbjo, heibio, D., adv. 'past, over, aside' : *mi sgyboð hëïbjo*, 'he rushed past' ; *may hi wedi troi hunna hëïbjo*, 'she has given that fellow up' ; *troi arjan hëïbjo*, 'to put money by' ; *he:n sgidja wedi troi hëïbjo*, 'old boots thrown aside'.—prep. 'past' : *mynd hëïbjo ru:in*, 'to go past some one'.

hëïdjo, v., heidio, D., s.v. 'examino' ; 'to swarm' : *may r ḷe: n hëïdjo o bəsgod.*

hëïðan, s.f., haidden, D., 'a grain of barley'.

hëïðjannol, adj., haeddiannol, D., s.v. 'meritissimè' ; 'deserved ; deserving' : *sgurva hëïðjannol*, 'a well-deserved thrashing' ; *u:ti n hëïðjannol ?*, 'are you deserving ?' (O.H.)

hëïðjant, s., haeddiant, D., 'deserts' : *may o wedi ka:yl i hëïðjant*, 'he has his deserts'.

hëïðju, adv. and s., hediw, W.B., col. 26. 23 ; heddiw, G.R. 65. 19 ; heiddiw, C.C.M. 34. 13 ; 128. 11, 13, 17, etc. ; C.L.C. ii. 28. 27 ; heddyw, D., 'to-day' : *usnos i hëïðju*, 'a week to-day'.

hëïljonys, adj., St. James i. 5, 'liberal, bountiful'.

hëïni, adj., heinif and heini, D., 'brisk, vivacious, active' : *may o n y:n hëïni ar i dro:yd*, 'he is nimble on his legs' ; *gu:r hëïni*, 'a fine, brisk man' ; *ḷavn o ðy:n hëïni, kaŋan o hogan hëïni.*

hel, v., hel pro hely, D. Fut. *helja*. Pret. S. 3. *heljoð*. Pl. 3. *helson*. Imperative *helja ; heljuχ, heluχ*. (1) 'to chase, drive, drive away' : *hel nu o: na !*, 'drive them away from there !' (e. g. to a sheep dog) ; so, *hel ar d o:l !*, 'drive (it) back' ; *hel alan*, 'to drive out' ; *heljuχ r adar i fur*, 'drive the birds away'. (2) 'to drive together, to collect', esp. *hel devaid*, e. g. for the purpose of shearing. (3) 'to drive' : *hel (= gəzy) moχyn.* (4) 'to collect together and remove' : *hel də bak !*, 'off with you !' ; *hel kerig*, 'to remove stones from a field' ; *heluχ ə briuſon*, 'get the crumbs up' ; *heluχ ə ḷestri bydron ar ə tre:*, 'take away the dirty things on the tray'. (5) 'to collect' (in full *hel at i ġïlïð*) : *may o n hel poppeθ ġëïθ o aval ·mynu o he:n beθa*, 'he collects all old things he can lay hands on' ; *hel ə dre:θ*, 'to collect taxes' ; *hel arjan* (or simply *hel*), 'to collect (money), in a place of worship or otherwise'. (6) 'to collect' (intr.), e. g. of matter : *hel at i ġïlïð*, 'to form into a compact mass': *peθ gwair wedi hel ai i gíliδ*; also of persons, 'to huddle oneself, to crouch'. (7) 'to gather': *hel bloda*, ' to gather flowers'; *hel kokkos*, ' to gather cockles'; *daχi wedi hel tippin go lɛːu o veːl i r kuːχ*, 'you have feathered your nest pretty well'. (8) various phrases : *hel də garkas a fur a tiʹ,* 'be off with you !', so *hel də draːyd ! ; hel də brenja !* (i. e. " stumps "); *may hiʹ n hel glaːu,* 'there is rain coming'; *hel ḷanasṭ,* ' to turn everything topsy-turvy'; *hel meδəlja druːg,* ' to take a pessimistic view of things ' ; *hel stryːon,* ' to gossip ' ; *ən hel ag ən iṛiːo kaːl rubaθ am dana i,* ' trying to rake up something about me ' (i. e. against me) ; *ən hel ag ən iṛiːn,* ' to scold ' [*hel* by itself in some parts, e. g. Llanuwchllyn, means ' to scold '] ; *iʹ oːs na δim hel a voː,* 'one can do nothing with him '; *paid a hel də δylo hyda iʹ,* ' don't touch me !'.

hela, v., hely, hela, D., s.v. 'venor' [only in the infinitive], 'to hunt': *mynd i hela,* 'to go hunting ' ; *kuːn hela,* ' hounds'.

helaθ, adj., helaeth, D., ' abundant'; ' extensive '.

helbyl, s.m., pl. *helbylon,* helbul, D., 'trouble': *meun helbyl* (= *poːyn, byːd, ṭrafarθ*), ' in trouble, in difficulties '; *meun helbyl bliːn* (O.H.) ; *ṭruːy helbyl,* 'with a great deal of trouble'; *wedi iənny ə mëïχja iʹ helbyl,* ' after getting the surety into trouble ' ; *iənny peniur o helbyl,* 'to draw upon oneself a load of trouble '.

helbylys, adj., helbulus, D., ' troubled, in trouble '.

heli, s., heli, D. (1) 'salt water': *heliʹ r moːr ;—K̓in haḷiad a heliʹ iṛimor,* ' as salt as three seas '. (2) ' brine ' (for pickling).

helig, s.pl., sing. *helɔgan,* f., helyg, D., ' willows ': *helig melyn, helig ḷuːyd.*

heljur, s.m., heliwr, D., s.v. 'venator'. (1) ' hunter '. (2) ' gatherer ': *heljur χwedla,* ' gossip-monger, slanderer'; cf. D. heliwr chwedlau, s.v. ' delator '; *heljur raks,* ' ragman '.

helk, s., ' limp ': *may na helk ən i g̓erδad o* (W.H. ; J.J. ; O.H.). Cf. *heŋk, herk.*

helk̓id, v., helcyd, helgyd, D. (1) ' to chase, drive ': *kayl i helk̓id,* 'to be driven from pillar to post'. (2) 'to drag, lug ': *be naː i helk̓id o mor beḷ a baŋgor ?,* ' why should I lug it all the way to Bangor ?';—*be maː peθa vel hyn wedi helk̓id mor beḷ?* (3) 'to search': *helk̓id* (= χwiljo) *am arjan* (O.H.). (4) 'to speak evil of': *dyːn ən helk̓id pobol eriḷ* (O.H.);—as substantive : 'trouble, difficulty ': *may o meun riu helk̓id o hyːd* (O.H.).

helkjan, v., 'to limp' (W.H.). Cf. *heŋkjan, herkjan.*

helm, s., pl. helma, helem, C.C. 372. 13 ; Eng. (Dial.) helm [a shed in the fields for the shelter of cattle when turned out to pasture ; a hovel or hut], n.Cy., Yks., Lin.; ' shed for storing hay consisting of four supports and a roof'.

help, s.m., help, D., 'help': *ɩ oːys na δim help* (*ɩ oːys m o r help*), 'there is no help for it'; *ɩ oːs g̣in i δim help*, 'I can't help it'.

helpjo, helpy, v., helpu, D., s.v. 'auxilior'; helpio, St. Luke x. 40, 'to help': *may hi n medry helpy dippin arno vo*, 'she is able to be of some help to him'; *dy:n a i helpjo !*, 'Heaven help him!';— *dvu a m helpo i !*

helu, s. Cf. bod ar helw un, 'possideri', D., s.v. 'elw'. A by-form of *elu*, only used in phrases of the form *ɩ oːys g̣in i δim fərliŋ ar və helu*, 'I do not possess a farthing'.

helva, s.f., pl. *hel·vëy·δ*, helfa, O.P., 'a certain portion of mountain land from which the sheep are collected periodically at one great drive'.

helynɩ, s.f., pl. *heləntjon*, helynt, D., 'iter, venatio'. (1) 'trouble': *diwaδ ər helynɩ ma*, 'the end of this trouble' (i.e. the strike at Bethesda); *may r helynɩ drosoδ*, 'the trouble is over'; *be di r helynɩ sy ·arnoχi ruːan ?*, 'what is troubling you now ?'; *ɩ oːs na δim vaur o helynɩ arni hi*, 'there is nothing much the matter with her'; *heləntjon ə byːd ma*, 'the troubles of this world'; *mi vyːδ helynɩ əmma heno*, 'there will be trouble (a fuss, a bother) here to-night'; *vyːδ ən helynɩ ·arnoχi !*, 'you'll get into a row!'; *mi ·vasaχi meun helynɩ braːv vory !*, 'you would find yourself in a pretty pickle to-morrow!' (2) 'state' (of health, affairs, etc.): *gaduχ i mi gluːad ə ŋhylχ əχ helynɩ*, 'let me hear about you'. Cf. G.R. (2). 5.

heːn, adj., comp. *hyːn, hənaχ*, eq. *hənad*, sup. *həna*, hên, D., 'old': *heːn uːr, heːn δyːn, heːn bobol, heːn grjadyr*;—*du i n hyːn o gurs maur na vo:* (O.H.), 'I am much older than he'; *pëidjuχ a kodi heːn beθa*, 'do not rake up old sores'; *wedi mynd ən wirjon heːn*, 'in his dotage'; *wedi heːn gʌvino*, 'after long habit'; *r̝ heːn a uːyr a r ivaŋk a dəbja* (prov.), 'the old man knows, and the young man thinks (he knows)'; *ɩaly r̝ heːn a duːyn ə newyδ [duːyn]; pɽyn heːn pɽyn ëilwaθ [ëilwaθ]*;—used very frequently in a derisive or derogatory sense, or sometimes merely in an intensive sense: *heːn g̣iː baːχ !*, 'the wretched dog!'; *heːn beŋki ədi r hogyn na*, 'that boy is a stubborn fellow'; *heːn voχyn bydyr !*, 'you dirty pig !'; *pëidjuχ a mynd ar gʌvyl planɩ ɩy: nesa, maː nu n heːn blanɩ r̝hy: δruːg*, 'don't go near the children next door, they are too ill-behaved'; so of various depreciatory epithets male and female, as *heːn walχ, soppan, wep, wlanan, χwislan, bembul gwirjon, grimpin*, etc., etc.; *heːn furna ovnaduy*, 'a terrible journey'; *heːn waiθ kaːs ədi fevjo*, 'shaving is an unpleasant business'; *may r moχyn wedi gnëyd heːn lanasɩ əmma*, 'the pig has made a nice mess here'; *heːn hogla druːg jaun ədi hunna*, 'that's a very nasty smell'; *heːn beθa gwirjon*, 'stupid things'; *heːn lol*, 'nonsense'; *heːn droːl*, 'what a nuisance !'; *riu heːn guɩ baːχ o heːn dyː*, 'an old hovel of a house'; *gnëyd riu heːn suːn druːg*, 'to make a nasty noise'; *riu heːn gasija druːg*,

' mischief'.—Sometimes *hen* when not emphatic, especially in the secondary sense.

henaint, s.m., henaint, D., ' old age': δa:*u henaint δim i hynan* (prov.), ' old age does not come alone ', i.e. brings evil in its train.

hendra, s., hendref, D. (no meaning given), ' low-lying inhabited country '; ' lowlands as distinguished from the mountain pastures where the sheep are in the summer ': *mynd a r devaid o r hendra i r mənyδ* (J.J.).

henëiδjo, v., heneiddio, D., ' to become old '.

heno, adv. (used also substantively), heno, D., ' to-night ': *may n noswaθ brav heno*, ' it is a fine night '; *mi δa:u o heno ne vory*, ' he will come to-night or to-morrow '; *mi nëiθ ə ʈɾc: am heno*, ' it will do for to-night '.

henu [*enu*].

heŋgaḷ. adj., hengall, ' old-fashioned ' (applied to children), J.J.; O.H.; *di:ar annul! nt ədi n edraχ ən heŋgaḷ!* (J.J.).

heŋk, s.; cf. M.F. hengc; Eng. (Dial.) henk [to limp; to dance awkwardly], Sh., I., ' limp ': *may heŋk əno vo* (J.J.).

heŋkjan, v.; cf. M.F. hengcian: *heŋkjan ǩerδad* (J.J.).

hepjan, v., heppian, D., ' to doze '.

hepḷas, epḷas, s.m., heples, R., ' sponge ' (in making bread). Cf. *epḷesy*.

heppil, s.f., beppil, W.B., col. 31. 7; D., s.v. ' concubo '; P.G.G. 254. 7; hepil, W.Ll. xx. 70; eppil, D., ' family ', but only used in a derogatory sense : ' brood, crew '; ' a pack of rascals ': *hun a hun a i heppil; ɤhe:n heppil!, heppil ·ōyδanu əri·o:yd* (J.J.); *riu he:n heppil ·aɤ·hɯnnas,—ga:s,—aru* (O.H.). Cf. *piljo*.

her, s., hyrr and herr, D., ' a provoking '; ' a challenge ': *du i wedi derbyn də her di*, ' I have accepted your challenge '.

hergud, s., hergwd, O.P., ' a push ': *mi rois i hergud iδo vo nes iδo vo sərθjo ar laur*, ' I gave him a sudden push and knocked him down '.

herjan, herjo, v., hyrrio, ymherrio, D., s.v. ' prouoco '; herian, T.N. 89. 7. (1) ' to provoke, to nag at ': *may o n herjan (=plagjo) arna i* (J.J.); *herjan ar i giliδ (= kodi kneks, əmǵerjan, E.J.); herjan ru:in nes gwiḷtiθ o* (O.H.). (2) ' to challenge '. (3) ' to warrant ': *mi də herja (= dəfëia) i di mo:d i n jaun* (O.H.).

herjog, adj., heriog, G.O. i. 8. 28, ' contumacious ' (O.H.).

herjur, s.m., ' one who challenges '.

herk, s.f., herc, O.P. [A jerk forward], ' limp ': *may herk əno vo, əχədig o herk əno vo, herk veχan* (O.H.; so also I.W.; J.J. had *heŋk*, not *herk*. Cf also *helk* ;—*herk* appears to be the most usual form). Cf. C.C. 173. 19. Nac un herc na allom roddi Gownt oi blegid heb gwilyddio—which is possibly the same word. It is glossed, however, in the margin by ' gweithred'.

herkjan, v., hercian, O.P. [to reach forward quickly], ' to limp, hobble' (of a lame man or old people); ' to slouch': *dakku vo n mynd dan herkjan*, ' there he goes hobbling along'. (J.J. had also *heŋkjan*.)

herko, s., hanercof: *r̨ heːn hannar herko gwirjon!*, 'the daft fellow!'

herļyd, adj., herllyd, ' contumacious': *ən herļyd ag əŋ ġekr̨ys* (O.H.).

herob [*nerob*].

herwa, v., herwa, D., 'profugere, exlex vivere'; R.B. 57. 11 ; D.G. ccxxii. 40, ' to wander at night' (of cats): *kaθod ən mynd i herwa*.

hɛsban, s.f., hespen, D., 'fibula'; Eng. hasp; (Dial.) hesp, ' a piece of iron for fastening a door on the outside, secured by a piece of wood inserted through a staple'.

hesbin, s.f., pl. *sbərnjad* (J.J.), hespin, D., s.v. ' ovicula'; ' a ewe of a year old'.

hesbinuχ, s.f., pl. *moːχ hesbinuχ*; hesbinhwch, O.P.: *huːχ ivaŋk heb dor̨i arni* (J.J.).

hesburn, s.m., pl. *sbərnjad*, hespwrn, D., s.v. ' ovicula'; ' a sheep of a year old'.

hɛːsg, s., hêsg, D., ' sedge'.

het, s.f., pl. *hetja*, hett, D.; D.G. vii. 10 ; lxxxv. 1, ' hat': *koryn, kantal het*, ' crown, brim of a hat'; *het wɛːlt*, ' a straw hat'; *het silk*, ' a top hat'; *kaːyl l̨eː i roi het ar hoːyl*, ' to get a place to hang up one's hat', i. e. ' to marry a woman and live with her parents or in her home'; *rhoi i het am i ben*, ' to put one's hat on' ;—as term of reproach: *ər heːn het wirjon!*

heθ, s.f., cf. M.F. heth, term applied to cold, windy, snowy weather, *ëira, r̨heːu a gwynt ən sgəθry poːb peːθ ag ən l̨ixjo l̨yuχˑvëy̆ð dros ben ə kl̨oðja* (O.H.); *may ən heθ vaur jaun* (J.J.). Cf. *jaːθ.*

heul, s.f., heol, D.; hewl, C.C. 30. 6, ' farm-yard' = *byːarθ* (O.H., who frequently uses the word): *heul ər eval*, ' an enclosed space where horses are placed preparatory to being shod' (O.H.).

hevo ; hr̨vo (J.J. frequently), prep., hefo, efo. Originally ef a, ' he and'. Cf. L.A. 79. 2, ' ef a barnabas'; ' with'. (1) ' in company with, together with': *duːad hevo χi*, ' to come with you'; *duːad hevo* (= *a*) *r δavod*, ' to bring the sheep'; *aːθ o hevo r ḵiː*, ' he took the dog away'; *may o wedi mynd a r vasġad hevo vo*, ' he has taken the basket with him'; *naː i δim mynd a vo hevo mi*, ' I shan't take it with me'; *ɣhaid i χi ga:yl sgurs hevo vo*, 'you must have a talk with him'. (2) 'with' in an attributive sense, introducing an adjectival or adverbial clause (generally expressed by *a*): *dy:n hevo hel vaur am i ben*, 'a man with a large hat on'. (3) 'with' (followed by a word expressing instrument or means), 'by': *mi doroδ i by:s hi n sy:θ hevo krəmman*, 'he cut her finger clean off with a sickle'; *mi vrivi di hevo ɣhëi n*, 'you will hurt yourself with those'; *bara wedi nëyd hevo haiδ a gweniθ*, 'bread made of barley and wheat'; *hiruχ hi n rëil δa: hevo hun*, 'smear it well with this'; *hevo 'bysabaud*, 'with finger and thumb'; *hevo kannuyl*, 'by candlelight'; *mynd hevo r tre:n*, 'to go by train'. (4) 'with, with respect to': *ma: by:d ovnaduy hevo χt:*, 'there is no end of trouble with you'; *syt δo:θ i hevo χi?*, 'how did you get on?'; *daχi wedi gorfan (= darvod) hevo ɣhëi n?*, 'have you done with these?'; *vedrun i ən ə myu nëyd dim hevo vo*, 'I could do absolutely nothing with him'; *may r amsar ən mynd əm bo:yn hevo nu*, 'time becomes a burden to them'; *may hi wedi bo:d ən fair hevo mi hëiδju*, 'I have been very busy to-day'; *pen 'vəδaχi ar laur hevo menyn nε rubaθ*, 'when you run short of butter or anything'; *mi ëif i lerpul hevo ɣlhyu*, 'I went to Liverpool about my hearing'.

hevran, v., Eng. (Dial.) haver [to talk in a foolish, incoherent manner; to talk nonsense], Sc., Irel., Nhb., Cum., 'to speak evil of': *dy:n ən hevran dənas ən i χevn* (O.H.).

hevyd, conj. and adv., hefyd, D., 'also': *mi δa:u vel na hevyd*, 'that will do too'; *mi δa:u əχ adag χiθa hevyd*, 'your time will come too'; *byθ a hevyd*, 'for ever and a day'.

hevys, s.pl.; cf. Eng. heave, 'swell' (at sea): *ə mo:r ən riu hevys maur ar o:l storom* (O.H.). Also Bangor. Cf. Py ceit i riw hefis go rymus i roch, Dy ddiwedd rwi'n coelio fudd cario nod coch. B.—(Ellis Roberts).

hëy [*hay*].

hëyarn, haiarn, Non Haearn aut Hayarn aut Hauarn, D., s.m. (1) 'iron': *hëyarn buru*, 'cast iron'; *vel hëyarn sba:yn o galad*, 'as hard as Spanish steel' (said of a man who cannot be turned aside from his intention). (2) applied to various instruments made of iron: *hëyarn knula*, 'snuffers'; *hëyarn (hëyyrns) ta:n*, 'fire-irons'; *hëyyrn kwik*, 'curling tongs' (O.H.); *hëyarn guθjo*, 'an instrument for clearing away the top layer of peat when bringing peat-land under cultivation'; *hëyarn tɣoi* (in slate quarries), 'an instrument used when a flaw (*klystan*) appears in pillaring, in order to keep the line, if possible, from slanting off to one side' (J.J.); 'a piece of rail which is placed over another and forms a kind of point by which trucks can be diverted on to another tramway'. (3) adjectively: 'iron, made of iron'.

hēyðy, v., haeddu, D., 'to deserve': *may o n hēyðy i grogi,* 'he deserves to be hanged'.

hëylo, v., heulo, D., 'to shine' (of the sun): *may hi n hëylo,* 'the sun is shining'; *may y kodi i hëylo,* 'the sun is coming out'.

hëylog, adj., heulog, D., s.v. 'apricus'; 'sunny'.

hëynan, s.f., 'film'. Cf. *ha:yn.*

hëyntys, adj., heintus, O.P., 'infectious': *may hi n hëyntys,* 'it is infectious'.

hëyry, v., haeru, D., 'to affirm, assert': *paid a hëyry keluyð,* 'do not persist in what is an obvious lie'.

hëyur, s.m., hauwr, St. Matt. xiii. 3 ; héwr, D., s.v. 'seminator': 'sower'.

hi:; not stressed *hi,* often *i*; conjunctive form *hiθa,* emphatic ·*hi:,* pron., hi, 'she, it': *mi ëif i χwarvot i,* 'I went to meet her'; *gwelt i,* 'to see her'; *gnēyt i,* 'to do it'; *mi ðo:θ i,* 'she came': *hi* (sometimes *o*) is also used for impersonal 'it': *may hi m bra:v,* 'it is fine'; so also *dəna hi(:)* (often *i*) = *dəna vo(:),* 'that's it'. As complement to *i* 'her': *i θa:t i, i gu:r (h)i, i m̥ha:p i, i fen (h)i,* 'her father, husband, son, head'.

hidil. adj., hidl, D., 'dropping as out of a sieve': *r o:ð o y kri:o n hidil ðagra,* 'he was weeping copiously'; so *r o:ð hi n tu:alt dagra ən hidil, dagra o r l̥gaid ən hidil;—may o vel gogor hidil,* said of a man who cannot keep a secret.

hidjo, hitjo, v., G.O. ii. 140. 1 ; hidio, T.N. 22. 37, 'to care, heed': *hitjo dim ən ne:b,* 'not to care a jot for any one'; *hidjo r y:n blewyn (r y:n tattan),* 'not to care a jot'; *du i ðim ən hitjo hənny ·moχi,* 'I don't care *that* for you' (snapping the fingers); so *klep ar ə maud ! be du i n hidjo əno vo ? ;—hidjuχ be vo,* 'never mind it'; *hidjuχ be vo vo:,* 'never mind him'; *vy:ð hi ðim ən hidjo i ne:b smokjo əmma,* 'she doesn't care for any one to smoke here'; *hidjun i ðim govyn iðo vo,* 'I have a great mind to ask him'; *du i n hitjo dim l̥awar am dano vo,* 'I don't care much for it'.

hidlan, s.f., cf. hidl, D., 'strainer' (for milk, etc.).

hidlo, v., hidlo, D., 'to strain': *hidlo r l̥a:yθ ;*—fig. 'to be unable to keep a secret'.

hiðig, s.m., huddygl, hiddygl, D.; hiddigl, B.C. 95. 26, 'soot': *may o wedi du:ad vel hiðig i bottas,* 'it has come like soot into the broth', i.e. suddenly, unexpectedly; so *mi ëiθ vel hiðig i bottas.*

hik, s.f., pl. *hikja,* Eng. (Dial.) hick, a form of hack. [The latter has in Sc. the meaning 'a mark, notch; a deep cut, a fissure'.] 'slit, crack' applied to the narrow holes for ventilation in barns, a crack in a door, the hands, etc.; *r o:ð i dylo n hikja i gid,* 'her hands were cracked all over ': *os gnëiθ i hik·ənynu mi baran ən hu:y*, 'if she makes a slit in them (the flower stalks) they will last longer'; *du:y hik ə mla:yn ə gly:sl*, describing a sheep's ear-mark.

·*hik·hak*, adv., 'jagged': *tori pappyr ən ·hik·hak* (E.J.), 'to tear paper in a clumsy manner so as to give it a jagged edge'; of speech) 'slow and blundering' (I.W.).

hikjo, v., 'to split, crack': *r o:ð i hel wedi hikjo a mëyðy* (E.J.).

hikKin, s.m., 'slit' (E.J.).

hi:l, s., hîl, D., 'suboles, proles, posteri', in the phrase *hi:l ǵerð*, as *ṛhëi dru:g ·ədynu o hi:l ǵerð*, 'badness runs in the family', 'evil is inbred in them'; *du i n nabod nu o hi:l ǵerð*, 'I know the stock they come from'.

hiljo, v., hulio, Prov. ix. 2; hilio, D.F. [92]. 7. 22; Eng. (Dial.) hill [to cover up or over, etc.], 'to cover', only used of a table spread: *pen ëi∫ i əno r o:ð ə burð wedi hiljo* (J.J.), 'when I went there the table was spread'.

hiljogaθ, s.m., hiliogaeth, D., 'stock': *pu:y hiljogaθ ədi o ?*, 'of what stock is he?'

himða, s.f., hindda, D., 'fair weather': *os kyḷ ə glau | o r duyran ə da:u, | os kyḷ ər himða | o r duyran da:u hiθa*, 'if the rain is lost it comes from the east; if the fine weather is lost it also comes from the east'; *na:θ i ðim ton (= egul) o himða hëiðju* (O.H.), 'there has not been the slightest lull in the bad weather to-day'; *kodi n himða*, 'to clear up'.

hi:n, s.f., hîn, D., 'weather' (rare = *tu:yð*): *may n ðrəkKin ovnaduy, l ədi o ðim ən fil i χi vynd; ṛhosuχ tan by:ð hi n hi:n ða:*, 'the weather is extremely bad: it is not fit for you to go. Wait until the weather clears'; *newid ər hi:n*, 'change in the weather'.

hindgin, s., 'hinge'.

hinsauð, s.f., hinsawdd, 'climate'.

hi:r, adj., comp. *hu:y, hiraχ*, eq. *ky:d*, sup. *huya*, hîr, D., 'long': *ky:d a hun*, 'as long as this'; *ky:d a hëiðju ag əvory*, 'as long as to-day and to-morrow' (used facetiously of something very long); *fariθ o ðim ky:d*, 'it will not last so long'; *kin bo hi:r*, 'before long'; *ə ṃhen hi:r a hu:yr*, 'at last, at long last'; *gobëiθjo na nëi∫ hi·ðim para n hir*, 'I hope it won't last long'; *may n hi:r əŋ knesy*, 'it (the weather) is long getting warm'; *daχi ŋ gweld ər adag ən hi:r ?*, 'does the time seem long to you?'; *vy:ð hi ðim ən hi:r ru:an*, 'she won't be long now'; *ə dy:ð huya*, 'the longest day'.

hirad, irad, s., iraid, D., 'grease for greasing axles, etc.'

hiraθ, s.m., hiraeth, D., 'longing': *may ən ḷyndan veðiǵinjaθ al bo:b pe:θ ond ṛhak hiraθ*, 'there is in London a remedy for everything except to keep off longing'; *may gɘno vo hiraθ ar i hola nu*, 'he misses them'; *hiraθ am garîɽa*, 'home-sickness'.

hirbuyθ, s., hirbwyth, i.e. 'long stitch', in the exp. *du i ðim ond am roid riu hirbuyθ a brasbuyθ ɘn hun*, 'I am only going to put a few hurried stitches in this'.

hirðyð, s.m., hirddydd, G.R. 2. 10, 'long day': *o:ð ɘn hirðyð ɘn ɽ ha:*.

hirëyθy, v., hiraethu, D., 'to long': *hirëyθy ar o:l i garîɽa*.

hirgrun, adj., hirgrwn, D., s.v., 'cylindrus'; 'long and round, oval', often applied to stones, and generally in a somewhat disparaging sense: *îyːd ma a r yːn hirgrun na ; maː ɽ heːn beθ hirgrun na n ðigon hiːr i vynd îɽuiði hî* (i.e. the wall);—applied also to persons: *riu heːn ðyːn hirgrun.* (All O.H.)

·*hir·heglog*, adj., hirheglawg, O.P., 'long-shanked'.

hirlum, s., hir and llwm, in the phrase *hirlum ɘ gwanwyn*, applied to March and April :—*may hirlum ɘ gwanwyn wedi duːad* (O.H.).

hirnos, s., hirnos, B.C. 73. 20, 'long night': *ar hirnos ɘ gëya*, 'on a long winter's night'.

hiro, iro, v., iro, D., 'to grease': *hiro sǵidja a saim*, 'to grease boots'; fig. *hiro dylo*, 'to bribe' (= *ɽhoi kiːl durn*).

hirîjo, v., hurtio, D., 'to lose one's senses; to be dazed, "mithered"; to become weak in the head': *du i dgest a hirîjo*, 'I am almost driven out of my senses'.

hirvain, adj., hirfain, 'slender': *dɘnas hirvain*.

hirvys, s.m., hirfys, 'middle finger' [*byːs*].

·*hiːr·wyntog*, adj., hirwyntog, 'long-winded'.

hislan [*hɘslay*].

hiîjo, v., Eng. heed [*hidjo*].

hiîjo, v. (1) 'to hit': *may o n i hiîjo hî boːb kɘnnig*, 'he hits it every time'; *mi hiîja i di nes bɘði di m pɘuljo*, 'I'll knock you sprawling'. (2) 'to happen': *hiîjo boːd ɘno*, 'to happen to be there'. Cf. T.N. 134. 3. Os hitiais i siarad yn rhy ffest.

hiθa, pron., hithau. Conjunctive form of *hiː*, 'she also': *mi roîs i o îði hî, ag mi roːθ hiθa hun i minna*, 'I gave it to her and she gave this to me'.

hivjo, v., hifio, D. (1) 'to heave': *hivjun l*, 'pull away, lads!' (O.H.). (2) 'to pluck off, to cut off (esp. wool) clumsily, with difficulty': *tɘnny r gwlaːn oːð ar ɘ ðavad ɘn ansbarθys — hivjo ɘn ḷeː knëivjo am voːd ɘ gwaḷa heb viːn* (J.J.); *hivjo heːn ðavad wedi maru* (O.H), 'to pluck the wool off a dead sheep'.

hob, s. = *hobad* (O.H.).

hobad, s.m., hobaid, D., 'modius'; 'a measure of corn, about 244 lbs.' (O.H) = *saχad ; pedwar talbo* (*talbo* = about a quart) = *χwart maur ; pedwar χwart maur = kibin ; uy:θ gəbənnad = hobad fi:r gnarvon, hobad baŋgor ; day hobad baŋgor = ṭṛi hobad konuy ne abargela = pegad* (O.H.).

·*hobɪdɪ·hoɪ*, excl. of delight (O.H.).

hobl, s., Eng. hobble ; *meun hobl*, 'in a scrape, in an awkward predicament'.

hofol, adj., hoffol, = *hofys*, which is the commoner form.

hofys, adj., hoffus, 'lovable, attractive, taking': *r o:yδ rubaθ hofys əno vo*, 'there was something lovable in him'.

hog, s., in phr. *na:nu δim hog*, 'they will not do a stroke'.

hogan, s.f., pl. *gennod*, hogen, R., 'girl' (the usual word;—*genaθ* is less common): *hogan ivaŋk*, 'young girl up to the age of about 21'.

hogi, v., hogi, D. Imperative *hoga*, 'to whet': *kalan hogi*, 'whetstone'.

hogla (rarely *ogla*), s.m., arogleu, L.A. 52. 11. = 'odorem'; 81. 15; S.G. 10. 14 ; D., s.v. 'rentifolia', 'spiritus'; B.C. 55. 2 ; 'rogle, C.C. 26. 20; aroglau, M.Ll. i. 81. 4. (D. has arogl in the W.–L. part, but this is a 'learned' formation), 'smell': *hogla da:, hogla dru:g*, 'pleasant, bad smell'; *daχi ŋ klu:ad hogla bakko ?*, 'do you smell tobacco?'; *klyuχ ə gwahanjaθ hogla*, 'smell the difference'.

hogla, v., 'to smell' = *klu:ad*.

hoglaŋk, s.m., hoglangc, G.O. i. 124. 1 ; 158. 10, 'a young fellow up to the age of about 21'. The preceding stages are *kṛub* and *kṛumfast*.

hoglĕyo, v., arogleuo, cf. M.A. i. 25a. 18, 'to smell' (trans. and intr.) ; intr. generally used of a bad smell, 'to stink'.

hogyn, s.m., pl. *hogja*, hogyn, R., 'boy' (the usual term ;—*baχgan* is not often used in this sense) ; *kṛumfast o hogyn*, 'a big strapping lad'.

hoi, s., Eng. (Dial.) hoy [in wrestling, the throw of an adversary], Nhb., *ṛhoi hoi*, 'to administer punishment in a playful manner, generally by two men holding the culprit by the arms and another by the legs, and a fourth smacking him behind' (O.H.): *ṛhoi hoi i ru:in am regi ; kal hoi hevo ṛha:u*, etc.

höiljo, v., hoelio, D., 'to nail'.

hoit, s., cf. hoit, M.F. ; Eng. (Dial.) hoyt [a long rod or stick], Lan., 'a whip with a long handle and long lash used when driving a coach with three or four horses'.

höitin, s.m., cf. Eng. (Dial.) hoit [a foolish, awkward, clumsy

P

person ; a fool, simpleton, etc.], Sc., Nhb., Yks., Lan., ‘a foolish fellow’ ; *höilin meðu,* ‘a drunken sot’.

höiljo, v., hoetio, T.N. 329. 3, ‘to play the fool’, esp. of an old man who goes after women : *he:n ðy:n ən höiljo am verχaid ; mynd i höiljo ġin wirjoni.*

ho:l, ho:yl, s.m., pl. *(h)oljon,* ol, D., ‘mark, trace, track’ : *be di r ho:l na sy ar də wymmad di ?,* ‘what is that mark on your face ? ’ ; *may ho:yl əχ ļa:u ar ə pappyr,* ‘there is a mark of your hand on the paper’ ; *ho:l bodjo,* ‘thumb-mark’ ; *may ho:l əχ tro:yd ən ə ba:u,* ‘there is a mark of your foot in the mud’ ; *ho:yl k̦ri:o maur arno vo,* ‘the marks of much crying on his face’.

holbran, s.f., pl. *holbrenni,* rholbren, R., ‘rolling-pin’. Of two kinds, one smooth for making pastry, the other rough for grinding oat-cake in order to make *fot.* As term of reproach for a woman : *r̦ he:n holbran wirjon.*

holi, v., holi, D. (1) ‘to ask questions’ : *holi (ən ər əsgol),* ‘to ask questions round a class’ ; *holi am,* ‘to ask about’ ; *holi a stiljo,* ‘to inquire persistently, to cross-examine’. (2) ‘to sue’ : *holi meun ļy:s.*

holiks, s. : *may o n holiks gwy:ļi,* ‘he is in a terrible temper’ ; *by:ð ən holiks ·arnati* ‘you are in for it’.

holma, kolma, holmjan, holmjo, kolman, kolmjo, v. (1) ‘to potter about’ : *wedi bo:d ən rula ən holmjo ; wedi mynd i holmjo i rula.* (2) ‘to talk nonsense’ : *paid a holmjo.*

holmyn, s.m., cf. holmun, C.F. 1890, p. 333. 11, ‘a worthless good-for-nothing fellow’ ; *he:n holmyn gwirjon ;—wedi mynd ən holmyn gla:n,* e.g. through drink.

holo; also *holuy* (I.W.), adj., ‘hollow’. Sometimes expressed by *gwa:g, gwagle.*

holpjo, v., ‘to talk incoherent nonsense’ : *holpjo farad ən wirjon,* said of a drunken man.

holpyn (J.J.; O.H.); *hylpyn* (I.W.; O.H.), s.m., fem. *holpan, hylpan,* cf. holpyn, M.F., ‘fool, sot’ : un yn cerdded o amgylch heb amcan yn y byd ganddo (J.J.) ; *y:n wedi ka:l kam—basa vo n jaun tasa vo wedi kal i warëiðjo* (O.H.); *he:n holpyn meðu,* ‘drunken sot’ (O.H.) ; *hylpyn penχwiban* (I.W.).

ho:ļ, adj., holl, D„ ‘all, (the) whole’ ; *ər ho:ļ vy:d, ər ho:ļ usnos* (more often expressed by *i ġi:d, ar hy:d,* etc.—Sometimes *ho:ļi* as *i ho:ļi aļy.*

holol, adv., hollawl, D., s.v. ‘omnino’ ; ‘quite, entirely’ ; *ən holol wahanol,* ‘quite different’.

ho:ļi, s.m., pl. *holta,* hôllt, D. (1) ‘cleft, split, slash’ : *ho:ļi meun stəlan,* ‘a cleft in a plank’ ; *du i wedi tori ho:ļi ar ə ywynab,* ‘I have cut my face open '. (2) a sheep's ear-mark so called : ' a horizontal slit at the tip of the ear ' [*no:d*]. (3) in slate, etc., ' cleavage ' : *may ho:ļ! ar ə garag.*

holļan, s.f., hollten, dim. of above.

holļi, v., hollti, D.   Fut. S. 3. *holļiθ, hy:ļ!*.   Imperative *holļa*, ' to cleave, split ' : *holļa i benno*, ' cleave open his head ' ; *mi holļoð i galon* (fig.), ' he broke his heart ' ; *holļi ļexi*, ' to split slates ' ; *holļi blewyn* (fig.), ' to split hairs ' ; *ma: r blaid wedi holļi n δu:y*, ' the party is split in two '.

holļur, s.m., holltwr, O.P. (in slate quarries), ' splitter ', i. e. one who splits *kļəlja* into *sglodjon* by means of a *ky:n manoļ!*.

honfyst, s.f., cf. hunffost M.F. and (?) honffest, ' pais ', W.Ll. (Voc.), term of reproach for a woman : *weli di be u:ti wedi nëyd, ɾ he:n honfyst vaur i ti!* (O.H.).   Cf. *həmfost*.

honni, v., honni, D., ' publicare ' ; ' to assert ' : *du i n honni bod ən ·rhy:δ·vrədur*, ' I acknowledge myself a Liberal ' ; *δary o δim honni r y:n gair am ə pe:θ*, ' he had not a particle of information to give as to the matter ', e. g. when asked a question.

hoŋjan ; hoŋgjan (O.H.), v., hangian, W.S. (? read hongian); hongian, C.C. 334. 33 ; O.E. hongian beside hangian, ' to hang ' (in all senses except on the gallows = *kɾogi*) : *ko:yd a bunɟis maur ən hoŋjan o·ruθynu*, ' trees with large clusters (of berries) hanging from them ' ; *hoŋjan erbyn ṭraust*, ' to hang to a beam ', e. g. with the hands ; *hoŋjan ar i dra:yd* (= *uθ ben i dra:yd*), ' to reel ', e. g. of a drunken man or one who is weak through recent illness. Cf. W.S. hangian val dyn meddw yn profi kerddet.

hoŋlad, s., applied to objects of a rambling, clumsy, inconvenient nature, esp. *riu hoŋlad o he:n dy:*.

hopjar, s.f., ' copse ' : *hopjar ko:yd.*

hopɾan, s.m., pl. *hopɾod*, hoppran, D., ' infundibulum ' ; hopran, M.Ll. i. 249. 5 ; ' hopper ' : *r u:ti vel hopɾan melin*, i. e. noisy. Also facetiously, ' mouth ' : *kay də hopɾan.*   Cf. B.C. 66. 6.

horn, s., *mynd i r horn*, ' to sulk ' (used esp. of children).

hornjo, v., ' to sulk ' : *be u:ti n hornjo ?*, ' what are you sulking about ? ' ; *hornjo kɾi:o*, ' to cry from temper ' = *straŋkjo.*

hors, s.f., pl. *horsys*, cf. hobi-hors, D.G. cxxii. 29, ' clothes-horse '.   Also ' a platform of a scaffold with its supports '.

horslau, s.m., ' pouring rain ' : *horslau maur na welis i m o i drəmmax əri·o:yd.*

horuθ ; horuyθ (O.H.), s.m., ' a fat fellow ' : *ta:u ɾ he:n horuyθ gwirjon* ; also applied to animals : *horuyθ o voxyn, o ǵefyl*, etc.

hos, s.   (1) ' a hoisting ' : *ɾhoit hos i vəny* (O.H.).   (2) ' show ' (*həs* O.H.): *tippin ba:x o hos ən ə fenasṭ ;—gnëyt hos*, ' to show off '.

hosan, s.f., pl. *sanna*, hosan, D., cf. also W.B., col. 68. 2 ; D.G.
xvii. 26 ; xlvi. 47 ; cxxxiii. 29, 'stocking' : *ṛhoid hosan ar ə gwi:al*
(= *masga*), ' to put a stocking on the needles ' ; *gwëy sanna*, ' to knit
stockings ' ; *kṛo:θ, mëiluŋ hosan*, ' the thick and thin part of the
leg of a stocking ' ; *bla:yn, tṛu:yn hosan*, ' the toe of a stocking ' ;
ən ṇrha:yd i sanna, " in his stocking feet " ; *sanna sisurn*, ' stockings,
the feet of which are past repair, and are mended with pieces cut
from another pair '.

hoſo, v., ' to hoist ' : *hoſo moχyn i vəny* (O.H.).

həual ; hu:al (O.H.), Hywel, ' Howell '.

həuðgar, adj., hawddgar, D., s.v. ' amabilis ' : ' amiable, lovable '.

həuljo, v., hawlio, ' to claim '.

ho:v, s.f., pl. *hovja*, ' hoe '.

hoval (J.J. ; O.H.) ; *höywal* (W.H. ; I.W.), s.f., Eng. (Dial.) hovel
[a shed for cattle or pigs, an outhouse of any kind], ' a shed with
three walls and the remaining side open ' : *hoval drolja*, ' cart shed ' ;
hoval i bədoli kəfəla, ' shoeing shed ' ; *hoval vo:χ*, ' a shed for weigh-
ing pigs landed from vessels ', before the railway was made (O.H.).

hovjo, v., ' to hoe '.

höydal, s.f., hoedl, D., ' life ' : *mi vəδa n δigon am əχ höydal χi vynd
əno*, ' it would be at the peril of your life for you to go there ' ; *r ədu
i am və höydal ən i gadu vo ṛhag gnëyd dru:g*, ' I do my very best to
keep him out of mischief ' ; *χmasun (χəmsun) i m o və höydal a
mynd əno*, ' I wouldn't go there to save my life ' ; *ən ſoi am i höydal*,
' fleeing for his life ' ; *höydal o annuyd*, ' a very bad cold '.

ho:yl, s., pl. *höiljon*, hoel, D., ' hat-peg ' : *ṛhoi het ar ho:yl [heſ]*.
ho:yl [ho:l].

höylan, s.f., pl. *höilja*, hoelen, O.P., ' nail ' : *toṛi tuļ o vla:yn
höylan*, ' to make a hole for a nail ' ; *kyro höylan*, ' to hammer a
nail ' ; *kodi höylan*, ' to pull out a nail '.

höynys, adj., hoenus, R., ' full of life '.

höytan, s.f., hoeden, C.C.M. 76. 28, Eng. hoiden, ' a silly girl '.

höyu, hëyu, adj., hoyw, D., ' nimble ' = *ſonk, gwisġi*.

höywal [hoval].

hub, s., hwpp, D., ' conatus, molimen ' ; hwp, s.v. ' impetus ' ;
hwb, S.E., s.v. ' hop '. (1) ' hop ' : *hub, kam a nëid*, ' hop, skip and
jump ' (children's game). (2) ' limp ' : *r o:δ na riu hub əno vo n
natirjol*. (3) ' a lift up ', e. g. over a wall : *ṛhəuχ hub i mi*.

hubjan, hubjo, v. (1) ' to rise in the stirrups ' : *hubjuχ !* (W.H.).
(2) ' to hobble ', e.g. of an old man or one who has been ill ;
·*weluχi hunna n hubjan mynd ?—riu he:n hubjan gwëiθjo*, said of
slovenly work. (3) ' to give a lift up ' : *hubjun o i vəny !*, ' up with
it, lads ! ' (O.H.).

huda. hudjuχ, hwde, D., 'here' implying 'take', Fr. 'tiens', *huda di !;—huda vreχtan i ti,* 'look, here's a piece of bread and butter for you'.

huf, s. (E.J.; O.H.), Eng. (Dial.) huff [haste, hurry], Sh. I., 'hubbub, scuffle, flurry': *welsoχi ri·o:yd faſun huf ag c:yδ ar ə stemmar* (E.J.), 'you never saw such a hubbub as there was in the steamer'.

hufjan. hufjo, v., Eng. (Dial.) to huff away [to get on smartly with one's work], Peb., 'to work hard and hurriedly for a short time' (O.H.).

hu:g, in phr. *mynd heb na hu:g na gu:g,* 'to go away empty-handed' (O.H.). Cf. *gu:g.*

hu:i, hwi, R.; C.L.C. ii. 14, 17; cf. Eng. (Dial.) hooy [a call of encouragement to a dog], Yks., 'a call to a dog at a distance to make it drive sheep'.—In quasi-verbal sense: *hu:i ǵid a (hevo) r ǩi: a hu:i ǵid a r ga:θ* (prov.), 'to run with the hare and hunt with the hounds'. Cf. *həs.*

·*hu:i·hu:i,—may o n ·hu:i·hu:i rula,* 'he is far away somewhere'; —also as lullaby: *si: ·hu:i·hu:i luli.*

huiljo, v., hwylio, D., 'dirigere, præparare'. (1) 'to sail': *dakku loŋ ən huiljo n huylys | hëibjo r pu:ynt ag at ər ənys, | huilja sidan ko:χ (gwyn) syδ arni,* 'there is a ship sailing apace past the point (Gallow's Point) and towards the island (Puffin Island); her sails are of red silk'; *huiljo ar le:d,* 'to sail to foreign parts'. (2) 'to prepare': *ma: n anoδ huiljo r bu:yd heb δim popty,* 'it is difficult to cook without an oven'; *huiljo i vynd i r kappal,* 'to get ready for chapel': *huiljo i vynd i fur, huiljo i vynd at i waiθ.* (3) in phrase: *may r gwynt ən huiljo i laur,* 'the wind is falling'. (4) 'to amuse'.

huiljo, v., 'to wheel': *kəmmyd berva a huiljo (rubaθ) ar hy:d ə ka:y.*

huiljog, adj. hwylioc, Exod. xxi. 36. (1) 'lively, funny, witty': *may o n huiljog jaun (= may na hu:yl garu hevo vo),* 'he is very funny';—*he:n δy:n huiljog ovnadsan.* (2) 'lively, amusing, pleasant': *noson huiljog.* (3) 'lively, amused': *mi kadwoδ nu n huiljog,* 'he kept them amused';—·*r öyδanu n huiljog i u rəveδy.* (4) 'lively, animated', e. g. owing to a large concourse of people: *by:δ ə dre: ən huiljog ;—kwarvod huiljog,* 'a lively meeting'. (5) of preaching, 'with the *hu:yl* ': *prəģeθur huiljog, prəģeθy n huiljog.*

hu:χ, s.f., pl. *həχod,* hŵch, D., 'sow': *hu:χ vagy, hu:χ gorad,* 'brood sow'; *r u:ti vel hu:χ meun haiδ,* i. e. 'very destructive'; *hu:χ di:n gutta,* a bogy to frighten children.

hulpyn [*holpyn*].

hun, fem. *hon,* neut. *hyn,* pl. (*n*), hwn, D., 'this'. (1) adjective: *hun* and *hon* are very seldom used, and then only for the sake of emphasis in certain stereotyped expressions. The only instances I have heard are : *may n divar ǵin i hyd ǝr ·aur ·hon*, 'I regret it to this very hour'; *ǝŋ gnëyd dim ar ǝ ðëyar ·hon*, 'doing absolutely nothing'; *ǝ pe:θ kasa ǵin i ar ǝ ðëyar ·hon*, 'the thing I hate most in the whole world'; *θalsun i ðim ar ǝ ðëyar ·hon*, 'I would *never* pay'. Otherwise their place is taken by *ma* (*yma*).—*hyn* is, however, frequently used with certain words as *ǝ van ·hyn*, 'this place, here'; *ǝ forð ·hyn* (*for ·hyn*), 'this way'. This form is more emphatic than the commoner (*ǝ*) *·van ma*, (*ǝ*) *·for ma*.—The plural only occurs in the form *n* in (*ǝ*) *r̨hëi n*, y rhai hyn, 'these'. (2) pronoun (masc.) : *ga: i helpy χi i beθ o hun ?*, 'may I help you to some of this ?'; *hun ǝ may o ifo ?*, 'is this what he wants ?' : *mi čif i r ty: nesa ǝn l̨e: du:ad i hun*, 'I went into the next house instead of coming into this'; *ǝn wastad a hun*, 'level with this'; *i euχi m o hun hevo χi*, 'you won't take this with you'; *ðary mi osod ǝ ty: i hun a r l̨al̨*, 'I let my house to this, that, and the other'; *hun a hun*, 'such and such a person';—(fem.) *nëiθ hon i vytta ?*, 'is this good to eat ?'—(neut.) *hyn a hyn o rubaθ*, 'such and such an amount of something'; *k̨in hyn*, 'before this'; *ǵida hyn*, 'presently'; *wëiθja vel hyn, wëiθja vel aral̨*, 'sometimes in this way, sometimes in another'.—The plural is not used.

hunakku, pron., fem. *honakku*, neut. and pl. *hynakku* (all often *nakku*), hwnnaccw, G.R. [121]. 7, 'that (yonder)'. Often used in the sense of "the old man, the old woman (at home)".

hunna, pron., fem. *honna*, neut. *hynna* (pl. *r̨hëi na*), hwnna, 'that' (of a person or thing within reach of the senses, or an abstract idea under discussion : *he:n hogla dru:g jaun ǝdi hunna*, 'that is a very bad smell'; *may hunna wedi kayl gormod ǝn i vol*, 'that fellow has had a drop too much'; *may hi wedi t̨roi hunna hëibjo*, 'she has given that fellow up'; *paid a tǝnny hunna o dǝ ǵe:g*, 'don't take that out of your mouth'; *i be: may hunna n da: ?*, 'what's the good of that ?'; *nëiθ hunna m o r t̨ro: χwaiθ*, 'that won't do either' : *mi gammoð honna ǝn l̨e: mynd i vjaun*, 'that (nail) bent instead of going in'; *may honna n o le:u o harð*, 'that one is rather pretty'; *hynna ba:χ o amsar daχi ŋ ga:l ?*, 'is that all the time you get ?'; *amsar k̨in hynna*, 'a time before that'.

hunnu, fem. *honno, no*, neut. and pl. *hǝnny, ny, ni*. (Sometimes *hunu*, etc., when not emphatic, e. g. *ǝ ·wraighono*, 'that woman'.) hwnnw, D., 'that' (of a person or thing not within sight, hearing, or the senses generally, except *hǝnny*, which is used of things within sight, etc. or not). (1) adj. : 'that' : *by:ð na bobol ǝn aru ǝ durnod hunnu*, 'there will be a great many people that day'; *l̨e: ma: r ·brus hunu ?*, 'where's that brush ?'; *ǝ p̨ren hunu sy ŋ kadu ǝ t̨rëifa r̨hag k̨ravy oχor ǝ k̨efyl*, 'that piece of wood which keeps the traces from chafing the side of the horse'; *ǝ van honno*, 'that place'; *r amsar honno, r amsar no, r amsar hunnu, p̨ry:t hǝnny*, 'that time';

rhëi ni̦, ' those ' (= y rhai hynny). (2) pron., ' that one, that ' : *mi̦ r o:ð ǵini hi̦ garjad, ag mi̦ vəða hunnu n du:ad i gwelt i*, ' she had a lover, and he used to come and see her ' ; *dim oni hunnu?*, ' nothing but that? ' ; *hənny ba:χ !*, ' is that all ! ' ; *mi̦ gadwiθ hənny vo ɟ gənnas*, ' that will keep him warm ' ; *hənny sy i̦ſo o sëisnag*, ' all the English needful ' ; *di:olχ byθ am hənny !*, ' thank Heaven for that ! ' ; *mynd hənny vedar o*, ' to go as fast as he can ' ; *du i uθi hənny vedra i*, ' I am at it as hard as I can ' ; *ḱin hənny*, ' before that ' ; *erbyn hənny*, ' by that time ' ; *ar o:l hənny*, ' after that ' ; *ta ny n rubaθ, ta ny riu ods*, ' if that is anything, for the matter of that '.

huniṛo, v., cf. hwndro, M.F., ' to lose one's bearings entirely ' (through stormy weather or darkness), J.J. = *fundro*.

huntu, s.m., cf. hwyntwyr (pl.), G.O. ii. 125. 6, " South Walian " : *may hunna ty hu:ynt i huntu ag may huntu ty hu:ynt i r kəθral*, ' he is worse than a " South Walian ", and a " South Walian " is worse than the devil '.

hunəna, pron., fem. *honəna* ;—also *nəna, nona* ; hwnnyna, G.R. [121]. 7, ' that (person or thing) in sight or hearing ' : *pu:y di hunəna ?*, ' who is that? '

hu:r, s.f., hwr, W.S. [a Hore], ' whore '.

huraχ (more rarely *uraχ*), *huyraχ*, adv., nid hwyrach, D., s.v. ' forte ' ; ' perhaps ' : *huraχ mi̦ ða:u i̦ godi at ə pnaun*, ' perhaps it will clear up by the afternoon '. Ans. *na: huraχ*, ' perhaps '.

hurdgo ; urdgo (O.H.), v., Eng. urge, ' to push goods ' (for sale) : *hurdgo i dattus ; may o n hurdgo n aru*.

hurð, s.f., pl. *hərðja*, hwrdd, D., ' a short and sharp spell of briskness ' : *hurð o olχi̦*, ' a spell of washing ' ; *gwëiljuχi̦, mi̦ ro: i̦ hurð i χi̦ meun mynyd*, ' wait, I will give you a turn (i.e. a helping hand) in a minute ' ; *r o:ð na hurð vaur ən ə varχnad*, ' the market was very brisk ' ; *may hərðja arno vo*, ' he does things by fits and starts ' ; *hurð mammaθ*, ' a short brisk period of work which a mother makes the best of while the baby is asleep ', so a farmer might say to his men : *dəmma riu he:n hurð mammaθ i χi !* (O.H.).

hurǵi, hurjur, s.m., ' fornicator '.

hurjo, v., hwrio, T.N. 13. 32, ' to fornicate '.

·hurli·burli, s., Eng. hurly-burly : *r o:ð o meun ·hurli·burli*, ' he was in a state of agitation '.

hurḷyd, adj., ' given to fornication ' : *ḷəmǵi hurḷyd*.

hu·ro:, s.m., Eng. (Dial.) hoo-roo [a hubbub, noise, tumult], Yks., Lan., Chs., Der., War. : *vy:ð na hu·ro: maur ;—mi̦ nëiθ riu hu·ro: am rubaθ*, ' he will make a fuss about a thing '.

hursan, s.f., ' whore '.

hurθjo, v., 'to push': *hurθjo ə plani oruθ ə burδ* = *guθjo*.

husġip, s. (1) 'a toss up' (of coins): *mi roː i husġip i weld ədi o ŋ ġiŋ ta brits*, 'I will toss up to see whether it is heads or tails'. (2) 'scramble' (see below).

husġipjo, v. (1) 'to toss up' (a coin). (2) 'to throw things for children to scramble for'.

husmon, s.m., pl. *husmyn*, hwsmon, D.G. cxcvii. 22 ; D., 'farm-bailiff, chief servant on a farm'.

hutjo, v., hwttio, D., 'exibilare, explodere' ; 'to hoot at ; to drive off by shouting, etc., to shout at'.

huθjo [*gurθjo*].

huːyl, s.f., pl. *huilja*, hwyl, D. (1) 'sail': *kuːχ huilja*, 'sailing-boat' ; *loŋa huilja*, 'sailing-ships'. (2) 'spirit, animation, "go"', Fr. 'entrain': *daχi ŋ kaːyl huːyl ar əχ gwaiθ hëıδjuˀ*, 'do you feel in good trim for your work to-day?', 'do you feel "fit", "in good form"' ; *may o meun huːyl*, (and more emphatic) *may o n i huilja gora*, 'he is in his best form'; *mi ġëiθ o huːyl uθ δëyd ər hanas*, 'he will enjoy telling the story'; *t ədu i δim wedi kaːl huːyl ar δarlan barδonjaθ*, 'I never found any pleasure in reading poetry'; *syt huːyl ·guːsoχi ꞎ faſun huːyl ·ġëyθoχi ꞎ*, 'how did you get on?';— so, in preaching, etc., *kaːyl huːyl*, 'to become warmed in one's subject, to be carried away', hence (3) 'a peculiar kind of musical intonation used in Welsh preaching': *əna o dippin i beːθ mi aːθ ə prəġeθur i r huːyl*. (4) 'liveliness, funniness, wittiness': *may na huːyl garu hevo vo*, 'he is very funny, lively'. (5) 'fun': *gnëyt huːyl am ə m̥henni*, 'to make fun of me'; *ġeːs i lawar jaun o huːyl hevo vo*, 'I got a great deal of fun out of him'. (6) 'temper': *maːy huːyl δaː arno vo*, 'he is good tempered'; *may hi alan o i huːyl*, 'she is in a bad temper'.

huylys ; *höylys* (O.H.), adj., hwylus, D. (1) 'convenient': *ə noson huylysa* (= *muya huylys*), 'the most convenient night'; *t oːyδ hi δim ən huylys i mi vynd*, 'it was not convenient for me to go'; *hənny ·vedranu vynd a voː n huylys heb goli dim*, 'as much as they could conveniently carry without dropping any'; *may fon ən huylys ən ə noːs*, 'a stick is convenient in the night'. (2) 'easy', e. g. of a key turning in a lock. See also ex. under *huiljo*.

huːynt, adv., hwnt, D., s.v. 'trans'; hwynt, D.P.O. 30. 29: *ty huːynt*, 'beyond'. See ex. under *huntu*.

huːyr, s., hwyr, D., s.v. 'vesper'; 'evening'—not generally in use = *ġid a r noːs*, but the word occurs in the exp. *huːyr a bora*, 'morning and evening'.

huːyr, adj., hwyr, D., 'late' (of time or persons, etc.): *daχi wedi kodi n o huːyr bora ma*, 'you have got up rather late this morning';

vy:ð hi ðim mor hu:yr arna i heno ag o:yð hi nēiθjur, 'I shan't be so late to-night as I was last night'; *gwel hu:yr na huyraχ*, 'better late than never'; *ma:y n hu:yr ǵin i*, 'I long', e. g. *ma:y n hu:yr ǵin i gwelt i n mendjo*, 'I long to see her get better'.

hy:, adj., hŷ, D., comp. *həvaχ*, 'bold': *o b le: ðaχi n du:ad (gan mod i) mor hy: a govyn?*, 'where do you come from, if I may be so bold as to ask?' Also 'impudent, forward'.

hy:d, s., pl. *həda*, hyd, D., 'length': *ər y:n hy:d a r y:n le:d*, 'as broad as long'; *hy:d ə dorθ*, 'the length of the loaf, a whole round of bread'; *mi doris i və hy:d ar dair arvod*, 'I cut my length (of grass) in three strokes (of the scythe)'; *ən ðu:y la:θ o hy:d*, 'two yards in length'; *ar i hy:d*, 'at full length'; *sərθjo ar i hy:d i laur*, 'to fall full length';—more emphatically *ar i hy:d gy:d*, 'at full length'; 'from one end to the other' (cf. D., s.v. 'porrigo'): *gorvað ar i hy:d gy:d;—wedi kayl i drawo nes may o ar i hy:d gy:d ar laur;—kovjo r bregaθ ar i hy:d gy:d*, 'to remember the sermon from one end to the other';—of a length of time: *am riu hy:d*, 'for some time'; *·t ədanu ðim əŋ kayl byu am ðigon o hy:d.*—Pl. *həda, hədoð, hədjon*, in such phrases as *am hədjon, er s hədjon*, 'for a long time': *t oy:s dim hy:d ən mynd tru i ðylo vo, may o ar s hədjon əŋ gnēy'd i waiθ* (O.H.), 'he has been at it for a long time, but there is nothing to show for it';—also in the phrase *alan o hədoð (həda, hədjon)*, 'out of all proportion, all reason'.—*hyd ə no:d, hyd no:d, hyd nod*, hyt ynn oet, L.A. 34. 24, now written hyd yn oed, hyd yn nod, hyd y nod, hyd yn od [see note to above passage, p. 254], adv. 'even'.—As preposition (1) for *ar hy:d* (see below).—With pronouns *hyda i*, etc., 'along': *hy:d ə klauð*, 'along the wall, hedge'; *təvy hy:d ə forð*, 'to grow along the road'. (2) 'as far as, to': *do:s hy:d ə kəθral*, 'go to the devil'. (3) of time, 'until' (generally expressed by *tan*)—as conjunction 'as long as': *mi ǵeuχi aros ən əχ gwely hy:d ə ·lēikjuχi vory*, 'you can stop in bed as long as you like to-morrow'.

ar hy:d, r hy:d (of time or place). 'along, the length of, all through': *mynd ar hy:d ə forð*, 'to go along the road'; *ar hy:d pen ə wal*, 'along the top of the wall'; *may təlaθa n rhedag ar hy:d ə ru:m a trəustja ar le:d*, '"tylathau" run the length of a room and "trawstiau" across'; *ar hy:d ag ar draus*, 'in all directions, anyhow'; *ar hy:d ə dy:ð*, 'all day long'.

o hy:d, 'continually, without intermission, all the time': *byu meun gobaiθ o hy:d*, 'to live continually in hope'; *ma: r klok əŋ koli o hy:d*, 'the clock keeps losing'; *may hi n farad o hy:d*, 'she is always talking';—*du:ad o hy:d i*, 'to find'.

hy:d at (often *d at*): *d at i glistja, d at gorn i uðu*, 'up to his ears, his neck'; *d at hyn*, 'so far, up till now'; *du:ad hy:d at*, 'to find'; *mi ·ðēyθonu hy:d atto rusyt*, 'they found out somehow'.

hy:d i, 'up to', esp. in *ka:yl hy:d i*, 'to find': *gavoð o hy:d iðo vo?*, ' did he find it?'; *du i wedi ka:l hy:d i r dru:g*, ' I have found out what is the matter'; *χe:s i mo ᵣ hy:d iδo vo*, ' I did not find it '.

hydo, v., hudo, D., ' to entice': *hydo ru:in i r mɔnyδ*, ' to entice some one to the mountain'; *hydo i bre:s o*, ' to do him out of his money'.

hy:δ, s.m., hŷdd, D., ' hart'. Only in the plant-name *tavod ɔr hy:δ*, ' hart's tongue' (Scolopendrium vulgare).

hyδo, v., huddaw, O.P., in the exp. *hyδo r ta:n*, ' to cover the fire', i.e. by covering the peat with ashes for the night.

hygan, s.f., hugan, D., ' a covering', e.g. a sack, old garment, etc., for want of something better, put over the shoulders in cold or rainy weather (J.J.; O.H.): *tavl riu he:n hygan drostat* (J.J.).—As term of reproach: *ta:u ᵣ he:n hygan gɔθral !* (O.H.).

hylaχ, s.m., cf. hulach, M.F., ' a soft-headed fellow' (J.J.; O.H): *dim ɔno n solat, dim ɔno i ǵi:d, ɔn dëyd riu beθa gwirjon, ɔn huiljo paub* (O.H.);—*may o n he:n hylaχ δigon digri ;—ta:u ɔr he:n hylaχ gwirjon !*

hylbost, s.m., ' a fool' (I.W.).

hylpyn [*holpyn*].

hylyn, s.m. (fem. *hylan*). ' a fool': *ᵣ he:n hylyn gwirjon ! ;— ᵣ he:n hylan ! = ᵣ he:n gɔbolan !* (O.H.).

hyl̦ (sometimes *hyl̦t*), adj., pl. *hɔljon*, comp. *hɔl̦aχ*, hyll, D., ' ugly': *he:n δy:n hyl̦*, ' an ugly old man'; *ǵëirja hɔljon*, ' bad language'; *ɔ peθ hɔl̦a ǵin i ɔdi gweld pobol ɔŋ ᵏerδad ɔ dre:*, ' there is nothing I hate more than seeing people pacing up and down the town ;'—of weather: *may n edraχ ɔn hyl̦ jaun hëiδju*, ' it looks very stormy to-day'.

hy:n, s., hun, D., ' self': *ko:d dɔ hy:n*, ' get up'; *troi ɔ du:r at i velin i hy:n*, ' to turn matters to one's own advantage'; *kol̦i arno i hy:n*, ' to lose one's head'; *ar i ben i hy:n*, ' alone, all by himself'; *l̦e: ·a·nivir ar i ben i hy:n*, ' an unpleasant, lonely place'; *tɔnny peθ ɔn i ben i hy:n*, ' to bring down something on one's own head'; *pam nad euxi χ hy:n atto vo?*, ' why don't you go to him yourself?'; *o honyn i hy:n*, ' of their own accord'.

hy:n, s., hun, D., ' sleep', only in the phrase *tru:* (= *dru:*) *i hy:n*, ' in one's sleep': *may o n ſarad tru: i hy:n*, ' he talks in his sleep': *δary χi ri·o:yd godi dru: χ hy:n?*, ' did you ever walk in your sleep?'

hynan, s., pl. *hynain*, hunan, W.B., col. 2. 8, ' self' (rarer than *hy:n*); *ɔdi o i hynan?*, ' is he by himself?'

hynl̦a, s.f., hunlle, D., ' nightmare'. As term of reproach: *ᵣ he:n hynl̦a !*, ' the old bore !'

hynt, s., hynt, D., iter: *ᵣhu:yδ hynt i χi*, ' a pleasant journey to you' (Bangor). Cf. *hɔnt*.

hyrt, adj., hurt, D., 'silly, stupid, dazed, weak in the head': *ən he:n ag ən hyrt*, 'old and foolish'.

hyrtyn, s.m., hurtyn, D., s.v. 'blennus', 'idiota', 'morio'; 'a fool': *hyrtyn penχwiban*, 'a whimsical fool'.

hyrtys, adj., hurtus, 'in one's dotage'.

hy:sb, adj., fem. *he:sb*, pl. *həsbjon*, *hesbjon*, hŷsp, D., 'dry, not giving milk' (of cattle): *byuχ hy:sb (he:sb); gwarθag həsbjon (hesbjon)*.

hytlaχ, s.m.f., cf. hudlach, M.F., 'an idle, good-for-nothing person': *he:n hytlaχ lonyδ ; he:n hytlaχ vanu* (O.H.).

hvu, hvus, 'Hugh, Hughes'.

hyukyn, Huwcyn (dim. of *hyu*): *ail ədi hyukyn i føukyn*, 'like father, like son'; *hyukyn ən ə ləgad*, 'sleepy feeling in the eyes', "dusty miller"; *may hyukyn lonyδ ən du:ad*, said of a baby who is just going to sleep.

hyvan, s.m., hufen, D., 'cream'.

hyvenny, v., hufennu, D., 'to cream'.

hyvr, s.m., hyfr, D., s.v. 'caper'; hyfrod (pl.), G.O. i. 105. 2 ; Eng. (Dial.) haiver, Sc., Cum.; hever, Cum. [a he-goat after he has been gelded]; O.E. hæver [' buck, he-goat']: 'a gelded he-goat'.

hyvran, s.f., term of reproach for a woman : *ta:u ꝛ he:n hyvran gəθral!*

həbjan, həbjo, v., 'to improve in health': *may o n həbjan ən rëil δa: ; may o n həbjo i vəny n jaun.*

hədar, s., hyder, D., 'fiducia, confidentia, audacia': in phr. *ar i hədar*, 'on the off-chance': *mi a: i ar və hədar i dri:o*, e.g. *dy:n ifo peθ ag ən meδul bod o 'gənoχi ar werθ* (O.H.).—Cf. G.O. ii. 115. 28.

həfis, s., cf. hyffis, M.F., 'a long narrow purse formerly used by women': it had five or six partitions made of linen or silk (J.J.).

həχjan, əχjan, v., hychian, O.P., 'to grunt' (of a pig). Also of human beings: 'to quarrel, snap at one another': *ma: nu n həχjan ar i ̇gìliδ.*

həlau, adj., hylaw, D., 'generous, kind, obliging'.

həltod, s., hylldod, B.C. 150. 13. (1) 'ugliness'. (2) 'practical jokes, nonsense': *may o n ḷaun həltod ;—ən və həltod δary mi δ̇eyt hənny*, said e.g. when excusing oneself for having given offence (O.H.). Cf. *avjaθ*. (3) pl. *həltoda, həltodoδ*, 'quantity', in the phrase *həltoda o beθa.*

həm, s., 'hint': *roif i həm ìδo vo, χe:f i δim həm* (W.H.).

həmfost, s.f., 'a rough untidy girl' (I.W.). Cf. *honfyst.*

həmjan, v.: *həmjan kany*, 'to hum'.

hənod, adj., hynod, D., 'remarkable, strange, extraordinary':
t ədi o ðim ən edraχ ən hənod jaun, 'he does not look very remarkable'; *hənod o vaur,* 'extraordinarily large'.

hənt, s., hynt, D. (influenced by Eng. hunt (?)), in phrases: *pen
vyð: ər hənt arna i,* 'when I feel inclined'; *mi ëiʃ i ar və hənt,* 'I
happened to go'; *mi welis i hun a hun ar və hənt,* 'I saw such and
such a one by chance'. Cf. *hynt.*

həntjo, v., 'to hunt' = *hela.*

hərðjo, hurðjo, v., hyrddio, D. (1) 'to butt' (of a ram). (2) 'to be
changeable' (now brisk, now slack): *ma: r varχnad ən hərðjo ;—
hərðjo uθ wëiθjo ;—hurðjo mynd = mynd am sbel a ravy* (O.H.).

hərðjog, adj., hyrddiog, 'changeable' (now brisk, now slack):
*ma: r varχnad ən hərðjog ;—mynd ən hərðjog ən ḷc: mynd ən wastad
= mynd am hurð a stopjo mynd* (O.H).

həs, hys, R. ; G.O. i. 217. 2, said to a dog to make it drive
sheep.—In quasi-verbal sense *həs hevo r ḱi: a həs hevo r ga:θ:* (O.H.).
Cf. *hu:i.*

həsbjo, v., 'to become dry', esp. of cattle which have ceased
giving milk : *os na·odruχi r vyuχ ən la:n mi həsðiθ hi ;—ma r fənnon
wedi həsbjo,* 'the spring has dried up'.—Also trans. *həsbjo byuχ,* 'to
cease milking a cow for about two months before calving, to dry
a cow'.

həslay, s.pl., sing. *hislan,* hislau, sing. hisleuen, D., 'sheep-lice'.

həʃjo, haʃjo, v., hysio, D., s.v. 'exibilo', hyssio, s.v. 'incito', 'to
set on a dog';—also *həʃo dy:n i guʃjo,* 'to incite a man to fight'.
Cf. *annos.*

hətṛaus, 'aslant', in phr. *ar hətṛaus.*

hətṛav (so O.H. always); *hədrav,* s., Hydref, D., 'October'.

həvdra, s., hyfdra, Phil. 8, 'boldness'; *kəmmyd ər həvdra (ar
nëyd rubaθ),* 'to have the effrontery to, to make so bold as to'.

həvryd, adj., hyfryd, D., 'pleasant, delightful': *nt ədi m bra:v !—
o:, may n həvryd !,* 'Isn't it fine !—Oh, it's delightful !'

i

i (sometimes *i:* when stressed), prep., i, D. With pronouns :
S. 1. *i mi(:),* 2. *i ti(:),* 3. *iðo vo(:),* ðo vo, ə vo, iðo ; iði hi(:), iði.
Pl. 1. *i ni(:),* 2. *i χi(:),* 3. *yðynu, yðyṇhu:* (cf. udunt, W.B., col. 161.
7, 22, 24 ; so always in Mid. Welsh). With pronominal adjectives :
S. 1. *i və,* 2. *i də,* 3. *i u, i:* (cf. W.B., col. 179. 1). Pl. 1. *i n,* 2. *i χ,*
3. *i u, i:.* Takes the vocalic mutation except in the case of *mi(:),
ti(:), tiθa, də,* and sometimes *meun (mjaun).*

I. with the general idea of direction. (1) motion towards,
'to'. (a) of a material object: *mynd i r dre:*, 'to go to the town ';
mynd i vaŋgor, ' to go to Bangor; *mynd i r knebrun*, 'to go to the
funeral '; *driŋo i vri:g ə göydan*, 'to climb to the top of the tree ';
ma: r ḷanu n du:ad i r lan, 'the tide is coming in '; *o r y:n van
i r ḷaḷ*, ' from one place to another '; *o r naiḷ dy: i r ḷaḷ*, ' from
one side to the other ';—verb omitted, *dəmma r bobol i g̣:d i ben
ə kloδja*, ' up went all the people on to the top of the walls '.
(b) where the object is more or less abstract: *du:ad i drevn*, ' to
get into order '; *mynd i r δe:, i r χwi:θ*, ' to go to the right, the
left '; *dirwin i ben*, ' to come to an end '; *mynd i δǝlad*, ' to get
into debt '; *du:ad i r golug*, ' to come into sight '; *mynd i dippin
o öydran*, ' to be getting on in life '; *mynd i arᵒobaiθ*, ' to despair ';
du:ad i r y:n van, ' to come to the same thing '; *o dippin i be:θ*,
' gradually '. (2) as distinguished from *at*, *i* implies motion towards
a place or object into which entrance is made (cf. Rowlands,
Welsh Grammar, p. 213, § 736): *mynd i r əsgol*, ' to go to school '
or ' into the school ', but *mynd at ər əsgol*, ' to go to the school '
(for other examples see *at*); *mynd i r mo:r*, ' to go to sea ' or ' into
the sea '; *mynd i r gadar*, ' to get into the chair '; *sᵣθjo i r du:r*,
' to fall into the water '; *mynd am dro: i r wla:d*, ' to go for a walk
into the country '; *a:nu iδo vo ?*, ' will they get into it ? ' (e.g. of
papers into a box); *d euχi byθ i və sg̣idja i*, ' you will never get
into my shoes '; *ḳefyl ən mynd i r drol*, ' a horse going into the
shafts '; *o r badaḷ fri:o i r ta:n*, ' from the frying-pan into the
fire ';—elliptically (without a verb of motion) *maly bara i guppan
de:*, ' to crumble bread into a tea-cup '; *du i n disgul hi i r ty:*,
' I am expecting her home '. (3) implying an object or purpose:
gᵣy morᵘyn i negas, ' to send a maid on an errand '; *gwa:δ i g̣injo*,
' an invitation to dinner '. (4) expressing the direction which
a person or thing faces: *fenast ən frᵣntjo i r lo:n*, ' a window facing
the high road '; also *fenast i r lo:n*;—similarly *may r ḷe: n amlug
i r gwynt*, ' the place is exposed to the wind '. (5) denoting the
exact coincidence of an action with a point of time: *r o:δ hi i r
mynyd hevo po:b pe:θ*, ' she was punctual (to the minute) with
everything '; *du:ad i r mynyd*, ' to come to the minute '. (6)
denoting extent to which: *·meθadis i r karn*, ' a Methodist to the
backbone '; *dəna vo: i r dim*, ' that 's he exactly '. (7) *i meun
(veun, mjaun, vjaun)*, adv. ' in ': *deuχ a vo: i mjaun*, ' bring it in ';
ḷiχjo nu i meun, ' to throw them in ';—also of rest: *ədi o i veun ?*,
' is he in ? ' (see *meun*). (8) *i vəny, i laur*, (a) adv. *gorvaδ i laur*,
' lie down '; *ən yuχ i vəny*, ' higher up '; *ista i laur*, ' to sit down ';
—also of rest, *i vəny, i laur ə gri∫a*, ' upstairs, downstairs '. (b)
prep. *mynd i vəny, i laur ə gri∫a*, ' to go upstairs, downstairs ';
i vəny, i laur ər a:ḷt, ' up, down the hill ' (see *ḷaur, vəny*). (9)
i fur(δ), ' away ': *i fur a vo: !*, ' off he goes ! '; *mynd i furδ*, ' to
go away ' (see *furδ*). (10) after verbs of motion before an infinitive :

i

(a) where the idea of motion or arrival at a certain state is predominant : *mi ðəuχi i farad ən jaun*, 'you will get to speak properly'; *huraχ mi ða:u i godi ai ə pnaun*, 'perhaps it will clear up by the afternoon'; *may r iekal wedi mynd i elun*, 'the kettle runs'; *paid a mynd i χwara də riks ru:an*, 'none of your tricks now'.
(b) where the idea of purpose is more or less implied : *troi i galyn po:b awal o wynt*, 'to be fickle, variable, to turn with every wind'; *du:ad i glirjo r burð*, 'to come and clear the table'; *mynd i edraχ am dani hi*, 'to go and see her'; *ðəuχ i veun ən ə van ma i ista*, 'come in here and sit down'; *mi ëif i χwarvot hi*, 'I went to meet her'.

II. denoting purpose. 1. before an infinitive. (1) after verbs : (a) with active meaning, 'in order to' : *mi a:θ dan ə göydan i moχal ə gla:u*, 'he went under the tree to shelter from the rain'; *rhaid i mi dri:o darvod ən vy:an i ga:l du:ad hevo χi*, 'I must try and get finished soon so as to be able to come with you'; *may if o gla:u i ləχy ə ðëyar dippin*, 'rain is wanted to wet the ground a little'; *ma: nu n mantëif o ar bo:b peθ i nëyd pre:s*, 'they take advantage of everything to make money'; *ədi r boks ma am ga:yl i dori i ðeχra ta:n ?*, 'is this box to be broken up for lighting fires?';—similarly 'as a reason for' : *os na by:ð dim aχos əŋ kodi i alu ə kəŋor əŋ gynt*, 'if no cause arises to convene the council earlier'. (b) with passive meaning : *mynd a diḷad i ḷnay*, 'to take clothes to be cleaned'. (2) after nouns : (a) denoting an object for which something is designed : *ḷu:y i droi r yud*, 'a spoon for stirring the porridge'; *peθ i godi bara*, 'something to make bread rise'; *ḷeχi i doi tai*, 'roofing slates'; *ḷe: i gadu bu:yd*, 'a place for keeping food'. (b) expressing an object for which something is fitted or adapted : *ḷe bra:v i ista*, 'a nice place to sit'; *ḷyvr divir i ðarḷan*, 'an interesting book'; *ḷe jaun i luynog leχy*, 'a good place for a fox to lurk in'; *mi veθis a χa:l dy:n i nëyd o*, 'I couldn't get a man to do it'.—With passive meaning : *nëiθ hon i vytta ?*, 'is this good to eat?'; *vedruχi ðim ka:yl ər avol i χwara a:g i vytta*, 'you cannot have the apple to play with and to eat', i.e. 'you cannot eat your cake and have it'. (c) expressing an object which conduces towards a certain purpose : *rubaθ i godi χ kaḷon χi*, 'something to cheer you up'; *may na ðu:y forð i nëyd po:b pe:θ*, 'there are two ways of doing everything'; *t o:ys na ðim digon o wynt i əsguyd ə briga*, 'there is not enough wind to shake the branches'; *i aros, i wëitjad*, 'meanwhile; until, to last until' : *breχtan i aros pry:d*, 'a piece of bread and butter to last until a meal'; *ən lodgo i aros ka:yl ty:*, 'taking lodgings until one can find a house'; *i ðeχra*, 'to begin with'. (3) after adjectives : denoting adaptability for a certain purpose : *may gwarðag dy:on əŋ gletḷaχ i ðal ə dəwyð*, 'black cattle are hardier for standing the weather'; *mi vy:ð ən de:g i vynd i r kappal*, 'it will be fine for going to chapel'; *may hi n haus i drëiljo*, 'it is easier to digest';

huvlys i garjo r y:d, 'convenient for carrying the corn'; *ma: r dre: ən wel i vyu*, 'the town is better to live in': *mi vasa kavod ən nobl i əstun ə lu:χ*, 'a shower would be splendid for laying the dust';—especially with *rhy:*: *may n rhy: o:yr i vynd əm bennoθ alan*, 'it is too cold to go out bareheaded'; *du i n rhy: vle:r i vynd alan*, 'I am too untidy to go out'; *ma: nu n rhy: lartʃ i farad kəm·ra:ig*, 'they are too proud to speak Welsh'. 2. before nouns: (a) 'for the purpose of': *dim amsər i ðim*, 'no time for anything'; *i be: may hənny n da: ?*, 'what is the good of this?'; *d ədi o n da: i ðim*, 'he is good for nothing'.

III. before an infinitive, after adjectives and nouns of various other senses such as those of skill, capacity, habitual inclination, desire, etc., generally expressed in English by 'at': *deθa i nëyd pe:θ*, 'skilful in doing a thing'; *y:n da: jaun ədi o i nëyd kampja*, 'he is good at all sorts of tricks'; *y:n sa:l i vytta*, 'one who is very bad at eating'; *·a·niban jaun i nëyd i gwaiθ*, 'very slow at doing their work'; *daχi n y:n garu jaun i wisgo χ sǵidja*, 'you are very bad at wearing out your boots'; *awyð i wëiθjo*, 'a desire to work'.

IV. before an infinitive dependent upon another verb, as *dal i vytta*, 'to continue to eat'; *krevy ar ru:in i ðu:ad*, 'to beg some one to come'; *luyðo i nëyd rubaθ*, 'to succeed in doing something'; *para·toi i vynd*, 'to prepare to go', etc.

V. before an infinitive of passive meaning, denoting potentiality: *ma: kro:yn ər o:yn a kro:yn ə ðavad i welad mor ammal a i ǵilið ən ə varχnad* (prov.), 'the lamb's skin and the sheep's skin are to be seen equally often in the market'; *ə ma:y tippin o hu:yl i ga:yl*, 'there is a bit of fun to be got'.

VI. before an infinitive of passive meaning, denoting necessity, expediency, etc.: *nid ə bobol sy i vëio*, 'it is not the people who are to be blamed';—similarly with *bo:d*: *may gwraig i vod ən yvyð i u gu:r*, 'a wife should be obedient to her husband'; *may hi i vo:d ən wastad*, 'it should be, it is supposed to be flat' (but is e. g. warped); *ma na dri: i vo:d*, 'there ought to be three'.

VII. between two nouns, denoting the relationship of one person or object to another as regards position: *ty n o:l i χi*, 'behind you'; *drost ə forð i r ty:*, 'on the opposite side of the road to the house'; *ə ty: kletta i r klauð*, 'the sheltered side of the wall'; *ər oχor aral i r avon*, 'the other side of the river'; *meun rhiu viltir i abar*, 'within a mile or so of Aber'.

VIII. denoting possession: *ëiðo i vi: ədi o*, 'it is my property'; esp. as regards debts: *may arna i ðu:y ǵëinjog i χi:*, 'I owe you twopence'. Similarly, denoting kinship: *merχ i u m̥ha:p i*, 'her son's daughter'.

IX. denoting the complement required to complete a certain number: *he:n wraig ən dair blu:yð i gant o:yd*, 'an old woman ninety-seven years old'; *meun tair i bedwar igjan*, 'seventy-seven';

—so, of the time of day : *vaint ədi i χwe:χ ?*, 'how long is it till six o'clock'; *igjan mynyd i y:n or δe:g*, 'twenty minutes to eleven'; *χwartar i bymp*, 'a quarter to five'.

X. denoting some point in past or future time, considered in its relation to some other point of time : *tair usnos i hëiδju*, 'three weeks to-day'.

XI. after adjectives or adverbs denoting likeness, proximity, etc. (1) 'likeness': *may nu n debig i u ǵiliδ*, 'they are like one another'. (2) 'proximity': *ən agos i bymp*, 'nearly five o'clock'; *ən agos i r ta:n*, 'near the fire'. (3) 'an attitude of mind towards'; *ən drəmp i ǵiliδ*, 'true, loyal to one another', etc.

XII. after nouns, adjectives, and adverbs—with the main idea of advantage or disadvantage, expediency, possibility, or necessity—generally represented in English by 'for'. (1) nouns : *by:δ hunna m be:θ mëyθyn i mi*, 'that will be a treat for me'; *ply:an i χ gu:r ədi o*, 'it is a feather in your husband's cap'; *huraχ gna:nu elu go δa: i χi*, 'perhaps they will bring you in a good deal of profit'; *may ŋ goḷad i χi*, 'it is a loss for you'; *may m bry:d i χi vynd i χ gwely*, 'it is time for you to go to bed'; *dim posib i ne:b vynd i veun*, 'nobody can get in'; *ṛhaid i χi wëiδi*, 'you must call'; *heb raid nag aχos i χi nëyd o*, 'without any cause or necessity for you to do it'. (2) adjectives and adverbs: *ədi hi n du:ad ən əstuyθ i χi ru:an?*, 'is it getting easier for you now?'; *basa n werθ i χi gweld nu*, 'it would be worth while for you to see them'; *weḷ i mi*, 'I had better'; *wa:yθ i mi*, 'I might as well'.

XIII. the so-called "ethic dative" (extremely common): *may n fu:r i χi*, 'certainly'; *ma: r a:ḷt ma n drom jaun i χi*, 'this hill is very steep'; *dəna i χi ·an·luk !*, 'that's very unlucky!'; *by:o n wa:yl jaun i χi*, 'he was very ill'.

XIV. to bring a person or thing into relation with a statement made concerning them. (1) in adjectival phrases : *ty: ag y:n dru:s iδo vo*, 'a house with one door'. (2) in a simple statement : *may y:n ḷa:u ən vu:y na r ḷaḷ iδi hi*, 'one of her hands is bigger than the other'; *bluyδyn vy:δ pa:r o sǵidja əm para i ṇha:d*, 'my father's boots last a year'.

XV. 'for, on behalf of': *kay ə dru:s iδo vo*, 'to shut the door for him'; *du i wedi gnëyd kamp i χi heno*, 'I have done something difficult for you to-night which you could not'; *na: i ḷnay nu i χi* 'I will clean them for you'.

XVI. *i* followed by a noun or pronoun and infinitive. (1) in a subject phrase, with the verb 'to be': *o:δ dru:g i mi gay hun?*, 'was I wrong in shutting this?' ('was my shutting this wrong?'). (2) when in a sentence of the form *may o ŋ gobëiθjo du:ad* the action of the verb is transferred to a person or thing other than the subject, e.g. *may o ŋ gobëiθjo iδo vo δu:ad*, 'he hopes that he will come'; *may hi i∫o* (i.e. 'mae arni hi eisieu', equivalent to 'mae hi yn dymuno') *i χi vytta hunna,* 'she wants you to eat that'; *may r doktor iſˑo ıðo vo gaːyl tippin o sëïbjant,* 'the doctor wants him to have a little rest'. (3) in sentences of the form: preposition + *i* + noun (pronoun) + infinitive: *diːolχ am i χi ðëyd boːd . . .,* 'thank you for saying that . . .'. (4) in sentences of the form: preposition + *i* + noun (pronoun) + infinitive where the whole has the force of: conjunction + subject + finite verb, e.g. *er ıðo vynd,* 'in spite of his going' = 'though he went': *ar oːl i χi orſan gwëïθjo,* 'when you have finished working'; *kodi saχad ar ben klauð erbyn i drol baſˑo,* 'to put a sack on the top of a wall to wait for a cart to pass'; *du i wedi gnëyd ə taːn er muːyn i r duːr dummo,* 'I have lit the fire to heat the water (for the water to warm)'; *mi vyːð digon o bobol heb ıði hiː vynd,* 'there will be plenty of people without *her* going'; *heb ıðo ubod,* 'without him knowing' (but *heb ubod ıðo,* 'unconsciously'); *kin i r glaːu ðuːad,* 'before the rain comes'; *rhag ıðo dori,* 'for fear of it breaking'; *rhak ovn ıði vuru,* 'for fear it rains'; *ər yχa yːn ar ə forð uθ i χi vynd i bentir,* 'the highest one on the road when you go to Pentir'; *miŧir wedi i χi adal lyn ogwan,* 'a mile after you leave Llyn Ogwen'. (5) in sentences of the same type as (4) where *i* stands for *er muːyn* or *rhag i*—*dəuχ a nəduyð aǵ eda i* (= *er muːyn i*) *mi roi bottum arno vo,* 'bring me a needle and thread for me to put a button on it'; *·tendjuχi sərθjo,* for 'tendiwch (rhag) i chwi syrthio', 'take care you don't fall'. (6) where a conjunction takes the place of the preposition before *i*. (a) *gaːyl* (used as a conjunction for *i gaːyl,* cf. II. 1): *rhaid i χi gəχuyn kin hannar aur wedi uːyθ gaːl i χi voːd ən ſuːr o i weld o,* 'you must start before half-past eight so as to be sure of seeing him'; *pitti na vasun iː ən mynd ıno gaːyl i mi gaːyl guːr,* 'what a pity I'm not going there so as to get a husband'. (b) *nes*—*nes ·yðynu ðuːad ən i hola,* 'until they come back'. (c) *ond*—*dani wedi kluːad peθa da jaun ond i ni ðal ·arnynu a gnëyd nu,* 'we have heard some very good things if we only give heed to them and do them'.

XVII. denoting the indirect object: *rhoi tammad i r gwarθag,* 'to give the cattle a bit of food'; *mi rhoiſ i o ıði hi ag mi roːθ hiθa hun i minna,* 'I gave it to her and she gave this to me'; *dəruχ i mi venθig honna,* 'lend me that'; *mi roːθ gora i r verχ,* 'he gave up the girl';—elliptically: *dəmma vi a deːr ıðo vo nes oːð o ŋ kany,* 'I gave him a blow which made him sing out';—*gosod ə tyː ıðo vo,* 'to let the house to him'; *kınnig buːyd i ruːin,* 'to offer some one food'; *maða ido,* 'to forgive him', etc., etc.

XVIII. after nouns expressing a wish, thanks, etc. (verb understood): *bluyðyn newyð ðaː i χi !,* 'a Happy New Year to you !'; *dyːð daː i χi,* 'good day'.

XIX. after verbs of causal meaning: *əvoː naːθ i mi χwerθin,* 'it was he who made me laugh'; *may hənny m peri i mi χwerθin,* 'that makes me laugh'.

XX. after *ambaļ* and *ammal* as *ambaļ i δy:n*, 'here and there
a man'; *ammal i gnok dyr garag* (prov.), 'dropping water wears
away a stone'.

i: (unstressed *i*), pron., i, 'I'. (1) as subject to a verb and
following it: *d un i δim*, 'I do not know'; *mi δydis (δydiſ) i*,
'I said'; *mi gwela i o*, 'I see him'. (2) as object after an infinitive ending in a consonant: *δary o ŋweld i*, 'he saw me';—but
not after a finite verb as *kovjuχ vi aʈ əχ mam*, 'remember me to
your mother'; *mi gweloδ vi ; mi gwelson vi ;*—or when a subject
ending in a consonant follows the verb. e.g. *mi gripjoδ ə ga:θ vi
hevo i ſawan*, 'the cat scratched me'; *mi vagloδ δrëynan vi*,
'I tripped over a bramble'. (3) as complement to *və, ə*, 'my';
vi never occurs in this connection except after vowels, and even
then rarely. See also *mi:, vi:*.

i, adj., ei, D.,—but always i (y) before Salesbury, and still written
'i' in 'i gyd',—'his'; *i u, i*, 'to his'. Takes the vocalic
mutation, the complement being *o(:)* or *vo(:)*; *i dad* = 'pater
suus'; *i da:d o* = 'pater ejus'. *i* is often omitted before an
infinitive, leaving only the vocalic mutation, as *δary o weld o*, 'he
saw him'; *be daχi n δëyd ?*, 'what do you say?' This is, of
course, especially the case after a word ending in *i*, e.g. *dani wedi
weld o*, 'we have seen him'; *δary ni weld o*, 'we saw him'. For
'a'i' before a verb see *a* (rel.).

i, adj., ei, D. (but cf. above), 'her'; *i u, i*, 'to her'. Takes the
spirant mutation: *m* becomes *m̦h*, *n* becomes *n̦h*, as *i m̦ha:p i*, 'her
son'; *i n̦hain hi*, 'her grandmother'. Words beginning with
a vowel take *h*, as *i hewyrθ*, 'her uncle'. For *i* preceding an
infinitive cf. *i* ('his'). Examples are *δary o θaro hi, δary ni θaro hi,
dani wedi θaro hi*. For 'a'i' before a verb see *a* (rel.).

i, adj., eu, D. In Mid. Welsh eu and i (y), 'their'; *i u, i*, 'to
their'. Takes the radical, but *m* becomes *m̦h*, *n* becomes *n̦h*, and
words beginning with a vowel take *h*, as *i m̦ham*, 'their mother';
i n̦hain, 'their grandmother'; *i hewyrθ*, 'their uncle'. The complement is *nu* (emphatic *n̦hu:*). Often omitted before an infinitive,
as *δary o hattab nu, δary o gweld nu, dani wedi gweld nu*. For
'a'u' before a verb see *a* (rel.).

i for e in *na:ǯ i*, nag ê, D., for Mid. Welsh nac ef, 'no'.

i:a, adv., ie, D., 'yes', 'it is so': *i r dre: ·ëyθoχi ? i:a*, '(is it) to
the town you went?' Ans. 'it is so', i.e. 'did you go to the town?'
'Yes'; *iɛwyδ maur, t e: ? i:a wi:r*, 'rough weather, isn't it?'
Ans. 'Yes'; *ty: bra:v ədi hunna. i:a, nt e: ?*, 'this is a fine house'.
Ans. 'Yes, isn't it?'

iðau, s.m., pl. *iðewon*, Iddew, rectius Iuddew, D. (but Iddew
always before Salesbury. Cf. B.B.C. 102. 2 ; G.C..144. 23 ; L.A.

19. 4; 136. 4; C.Ch. 5. 3; Rom. ii. 9, 10, 17), 'Jew': *ia:n iðau.* iddwſ, tán iddwſ, D., 'erysipelas'.

iðau, s.m., eiddew, D., 'ivy'. Cf. also *irugl, jorug, jurug, jurugl, murigl, murugl, njurigl, urogl.*

·igam·ogam, ·miga·moga, ·iga·moga, adv., igam ogam, 'zigzag, in a jagged fashion': *paid a i doṛi o ·miga·moga* (E.J.), 'do not cut it in a jagged fashion'; *agor ṛhe:s ɔn ·igarmoga* (O.H.), 'to dig a furrow (e.g. for potatoes) crooked, zigzag'.

iğëinvad, adj., ugeinſed, D., s.v. 'vicesimus'; igieinſed, C.C.M. 1. 3; 'twentieth'.

igjan, s. and adj., pl. *ğëinja*, ugain, D.; igien, C.C.M. 3. 1; vgian, 5. 12; 'twenty': *y:n ar higjan*, '21'; *χweːχ igjan*, '120' (= *kant aǵ igjan*); *saiθ igjan*, '140'; *y:n igjan ar ðeːg a ſedwar*, '224'; *pɔmθag igjan*, '300'; *meun ſair i bedwar igjan*, '77 (years old)'; *er s dros igjan mlɔnað*, 'for over twenty years'; *ğëinja o wëiθja*, 'scores of times'; *ğëinja o viloð*, 'scores of thousands'; *igjan durnod*, 'twenty days'; *igjan o ðevaid*, 'twenty sheep'. Cf. *dëigjan, χwëigjan, trigjan.*

il, pron., ill, D., 'they' (before numerals, of two or three persons): *il day*, 'they two'. Also transferred to the first or second person plural: *rni: il tri:oð*, 'we three'.

impin (J.J.), *nimpin* (O.H.), s.m., impin, W.S. [An impe]; impyn, D., s.v. 'surculus'; 'a shoot for grafting'.

impjad (J.J.), *nimpjad* (O.H.), s., impiad, D.G. clxii. 22: D., s.v. 'emphyteusis'. (1) 'shooting' (of leaves): *nimpjad ɔ dail* (O.H.). (2) 'grafting' (by inserting shoots).

impjo (J.J.), *nimpjo* (O.H.), v., impio, W.S. [Graffe]; Rom. xi. 23; D.P.O. 295. 14. (1) 'to shoot' (of trees or leaves): *may r ğöydan ɔn impjo rëit nëïs* (J.J.); *may r dail ɔn nimpjo* (O.H.). (2) 'to graft by inserting shoots into a stock'.

indja, 'India': *eli r indja*, 'zinc ointment'.

indgan, s.f., pl. *indgans*, 'engine, machine': *indgan maly gwair*, 'hay-chopping machine'; *indgan ðɔrny*, 'threshing machine'; *indgan da:n*, 'fire-engine'; *indgan wni:o*, 'sewing machine'.

inig, adj., unig, D., 'alone'; *ɔn inig*, 'only'.

injon, adj., union, D., s.v. 'rectus'. (1) 'straight': *ḱin injonad a hayl dru:y dul; ḱin injonad a sa:yθ*, 'as straight as a die, as an arrow'; *tɔnny ku:ys injon*, 'to make a straight furrow'; *ar ɔχ injon*, 'straight on'. (2) 'just, exactly': *r y: va:θ ɔn injon*, 'just the same'; *dɔna χi: n injon*, 'just so'; *χweːχ o r glo:χ ɔn injon*, 'six o'clock exactly'; *ɔn injon o ·danani*, 'just below us'; *may o n aḱtjo vo n injon*, 'he takes him off exactly';—also *ɔn injon de:g.*

(3) 'presently' (esp. in the form *ən injon deːg*): *mi gaun i χwanag o laːu n injon*, 'we shall have more rain presently'.

injoni [*njŏnɪ*].

inna, pron., inneu, Rev. iii. 21 (cf. inheu, W.B. col. 2. 19; innheu, col. 3. 2). Conjunctive form of *iː*, 'I, me': *du inna n mynd aḷan*, 'I am going out too'; *ǩeruˑχiː əna ŋ gənta, mɪ ðoː inna əna tok*, 'you go there first; I'll come presently'; *ɪ̞rawa diː viː, mɪ ɪ̞rawa inna diθa*, 'you strike me, and I'll strike you'; *wela inna m ono vo*, 'I don't see it either'.

iŋk, s.m., ingc, D.G. cxciii. 12; Jer. xxxvi. 18, 'ink'.

iŋkum, s.m., inkwm, W.S., 'income'.

iːog, s., eog, D. This word seems to occur in *draːyn iːog* (O.H.), 'bass' (Morone labrax). This fish is, however, called *drëynog* at Bangor. Cf. W.S., 'draenoc pysc' [base]—cf. also *siːl ə goːg*. The word for 'salmon' is *sammon*.

irað, adj., iraidd, D., 'of succulent growth'; 'full of vigour'; 'supple': *köydan, dyːn, hogan, ǩefyl irað; sǥidja əstuyθ irað*.

irdrug, s., ir and trwngc (?), cf. irdrw'c, M.F., 'urine kept formerly for various purposes, such as dyeing, fulling cloth, etc.' Also used formerly for dipping beans and wheat before sowing, with the intention of making them unpalatable to mice, birds, etc. (J.J.). Cf. *golχ*.

iro [*hiro*].

irugl, s.m., eiddiorwg, D., s.v. 'eiddew'; iorwg, R., 'ivy'. Cf. *ɪðau*.

iːs, is, D., only in *iːs laːu*, prep., 'beneath': *iːs laːu sylu*, 'beneath notice'.

isal, adj., comp. *iːs*, eq. *isad*, sup. *isa, isela*, isel, D., 'low': *may r taːn wedi mynd ən isal*, 'the fire is low'; *tɪppɪn iːs i laur*, 'a little lower down'; *may n ðigon isal arno vo*, 'he is in rather low water, rather badly off'; *ər cːn isa*, 'the lower jaw'; *may o n isal i əsbryd*, 'he is low-spirited'; *jaiθ isal*, 'low, unseemly language'.

iseldar, s., iselder, D., 'lowness': *iseldar əsbryd*, 'lowness of spirits, dejection'.

ista, v., eistedd, D.; cf. eiste, W.B. col. 16. 35; 226. 32; iste occurs in B.B.C. 59. 7. Pret. S. 1. *steðɪs*, 3. *steðoð*. Pl. 3. *steðson*. Imperative *ista, steða; steðuχ*, 'to sit':—used substantively: *kodi ar i ista*, 'to sit up' (cf. Fr. 'sur son séant').

iſ'o, s., eisiau, D. (1) 'want, destitution', Fr. 'misère': *djoða iſ'o*, 'to suffer want'. (2) 'want, need', Fr. 'besoin', followed by the preposition *ar* when the pronoun is expressed: *ma na i iſ'o buːyd*, 'I am hungry'; *ma na i iſ'o diːod*, 'I am thirsty'; *be s ant iſ'o ?* (i.e. beth sydd arnat ti ei eisieu?), 'what dost thou want?';

be s aχi iʃo?, *be s noχi iʃo?*, 'what do you want?'; *ma na i iʃo i χi vynd*, 'I want you to go'; *huraχ mai iʃo duːr sy arno vo*, 'perhaps it wants water'; *mi ðoːθ o aðra ag iʃo buːyd arno*, 'he came home hungry';—when the noun is expressed *ar* is often omitted : *may də vam d iʃo di*, 'your mother wants you';—used absolutely : *ðaːu dim byːd pe vyːð iʃo vo* (i. e. 'pan fydd ei eisieu '). 'nothing comes when it is wanted '; *hynny sy iʃo o seysnag* (i. e. ' sydd ei eisieu '), ' all the English necessary'; *t oːs na ðim iʃo vo ruːan*, 'it is not wanted now ';—used in a kind of appositive sense : *mi ëiʃ i ʃop a sǵidja iʃo i truʃo*, 'I went into a shop with some boots which wanted mending'; *yːn bur etto iʃo i glirjo*, 'one more table that wants clearing';—from such expressions as *be s aχi iʃo?*, the transition is easy to *be daχi iʃo?* Thus instances like the following are frequent : *du i ðim iʃo vo*, 'I don't want it'; *·öyðaχi iʃo vo?*, ' did you want it?' The original form, however, always occurs in answers to questions, e. g. *daχi iʃo hun?*, 'do you want this?' Ans. *oːys*, 'yes'. Cf. the use of *ovn*.—The verb 'to be' is often omitted in quick speech, e.g.: *iʃo noːl o alan*, 'I want to fetch it out '; *iʃo karθy kut ə varlan*, 'I want to clean out the pony shed '; *iʃo taly?*, ' do you want to pay?'

iʃt, interj., ust, D. ; ist, B.C. 33. 29, 'hush'.

iu, s.f., yw, D., ' yew' : *köydan iu, koːyd iu*.

ius, s., ' use' : *dim ius aros ən ə tyː*, ' it is no use stopping in the house'; *vasa ðim ius i mi veðul mynd Kim belad*, ' it would be no use for me to think of going so far'; *kəmmyd rubaθ er muːyn kaːyl ius ə ɣhorʃ*, 'to take an aperient'.

iuʃo, v., iwsio, C.L.C. ii. 22. 3, ' to use'.

ivan, Ifan, 'John' : *guːyl ivan*, 'Midsummer's Day' : *ləʃa ivan*, 'mugwort' (Artemisia vulgaris).

ivans, 'Evans'.

ivaŋk, adj., comp. *veŋaχ* (rarely *jeŋaχ*), eq. *veŋad*, sup. *veŋa*, pl. *iviŋk*, ieuangc, D. ; cf. ifangk, K.H. 19. 27, 'young' : *ərviː ədi r veŋa*, 'I am the youngest'; *pobol ivaŋk, iviŋk*, 'young people '; *gwarθag ivaŋk*, 'young cattle'.

j

jaː [*jaːθ*].

jaːd [*aːd*].

jaiθ, s.f., pl. *jëiθoð*, iaith, D. (1) 'language', Fr. 'langue': *may ǵin i bedar jaiθ*, 'I know four languages'; *ər jaiθ vain*, 'English'. (2) 'language', Fr. 'langage': *jaiθ ðruːg, jaiθ isal*, etc., ' bad language, low language, etc.'

jaːχ, adj., comp. *jaχaχ*, iâch, D. (1) 'healthy' : *kin jaχad a* χnëyan, ja:χ vel ə g̊ëirχan, "as right as a trivet", "as sound as a bell"; os byu ag ja:χ, 'D.V.' (2) 'healthy, conducive to health': ḷe: ja:χ jaun ədi baŋgor, 'Bangor is a very healthy place'. (3) 'wholesome'.

janto, pet name for 'Ifan'.

jaŋy, v., ehengu, D.; cf. iangwr pro eangwr, D.; ianged (= ehanged), C.C. 102. 21, 'to extend, to widen': jaŋy əχ sənjada (E.J.), 'to widen your ideas'; jaŋy ə ti:r ; jaŋy ka:y, garð (O.H.).

ja:r, s.f., pl. *jëir*, iâr, D., 'hen': magy jëir, 'to rear poultry'; may r ja:r əŋ gori, 'the hen is sitting'; may r jëir əŋ kḷuydo, 'the hens are roosting' (cf. also kokjan, ṭresi);—kuṭ jëir, 'hen-coop'; mynd vel ja:r i ðəduy, 'to go like a hen to lay', i.e. 'to go off suddenly'; r u:ti vel ja:r ar ə gla:u, 'you run off like a hen when rain comes'; ən mynd vel ja:r əŋ k̊erðad ar varwor ta:n, 'treading gingerly' (cf. B.C. 6. 21); vel ja:r dan badaḷ 'glum, disconsolate'; also 'disproportionate', e.g. of a hat too big for the head; ɽ he:n ja:r !, term of contempt for a man, 'a busybody'; mugud ər jëir, 'blind man's buff'; ja:r ðu:r, 'moor-hen' (Gallinula chloropus); ja:r ə mənyð, 'grouse' (all species); ja:r vo:r, 'lump-sucker' (Cyclopterus lumpus); also a kind of shell-fish (Aporrhais pes-pelicani).

jard, s.f., pl. *jerdyð*, 'yard'.

ja:s, s.m., pl. *jasa* ; *afa* (O.H.), iâs, D. (1) 'shiver': afa öirjon ṭruyðo vo i g̊i:d, 'cold shivers all over'. (2) 'a touch of cold or heat': may ja:s digon o:yr hëiðju, 'there is rather a cold touch in the air to-day'; may ëira n du:ad.—syt daχi ŋ gubod ?—du i n ṭëimlo ja:s ən ə ɽhu:yn i, 'snow is coming. How do you know? I feel the cold in my nose' (O.H.); dəruχ ja:s o veru arno vo, 'give it a touch of boiling'.

ja:θ, s.f., iaeth, D., 'glacialitas'; 'frosty, still, snowy weather': may ja:θ o:yr jaun heno, may hi n ɽhewi ;—may n ja:θ drom (J.J.) O.H. has ja:—may r ja: ma n o:yr.

jaun, iawn, D. Adjective: 'right, suitable, good': ər amsar jaun, 'the right time'; ər enu jaun, 'the right name'; wedi kayl ə dru:g ma n jaun, 'having got that evil righted'; kəmro jaun ədi o, 'he is a good Welshman'; er s mëiṭin jaun, 'since a good long time';—also in various intensive senses: may hi m buru n jaun o hy:d, 'it keeps on raining hard'; may hi ŋ gwëiði n jaun, 'she is shouting loud'.—Adverb: 'very': maur jaun.

jaun, s., iawn, D., 'compensation': ka:l jaun ;—gnëyd jaun am ə kam, 'to atone for the wrong'.

jay, Iau, D., s.v. 'difiau', dyw ieu, L.A. 130. 5, in dy:ð jau, 'Thursday' = divja.

jay, s.m., afu, au, D., 'liver': da: vel jay, ṭori vel jay is said of slates easily split.

jay, s.f., pl. *jĕya*, iau, D., ' yoke ' ; also, ' yoke over the shoulders for carrying milk, etc.'

jeχïd, s.m., iechyd, D., 'health' : *ar le:s d jeχïd*, ' for the good of your health ' ; *jeχïd da !*, ' your good health !' ; *jeχïd i χ kalon χi !*, expression of approval nearly equivalent to ' bravo !'

jeχɔdurjaθ, s.f., iechydwriaeth, D., s.v. ' iachawdwriaeth ' ; Psalm lii. 2, etc., ' salvation '.

jeŋktïd, s., ieuengctid, D., s.v. ' iuuentus ' ; ieungctid, C.C. 105. 1 ; 106. 14, ' youth '.

jĕyo, v., ieuo, D., ' to yoke '.

jogyn (J.J.) ; *okkyn* (O.H.), s., ogyn, ' a turn with a harrow' : *basa n weḷ rhoi jogyn drosto etto* (J.J.).

jonaur, s., Ionawr, K.H. 38. 35, ' January'.

jurχ, s., iwrch, D., ' caprea mas' [roebuck]. (1) known as name of an animal (O.H.). Cf. the place-name *pant ɔr jurχ*. (2) as term of reproach : *he:n jurχ o he:n ðy:n ɔdi hun a hun,—brunt, parod i rɐu* (O.H).

jurugl (L.W.) ; *jurug* (I.W. ; O.H.) ; *jorug* (O.H.), s.m., eiddiorwg, D., s.v. ' eiddew ' ; iorwg, R., ' ivy '. Cf. *ïðau*.

k

kabalatſo, v., cf. calarlatsio, C.F. 1890, p.314. 1, 'to talk nonsense ' (I.W.) = *ſarad ar draus pen a kḷistja* (O.H.).

kaban, s.m., caban, D. (1) ' small cottage, cabin ': *r u:ti wedi gnëyd kaban rëil gly:d ;—kaban krubi* was formerly the name of a small cottage at Llanfairfechan (O.H.).—Not in general use in this sense. (2) ' cabin ' (of a ship). (3) ' eating-shed ' (in quarries).

kabarðiljo, v., cabarddulio, T.N. 295. 24, ' to talk nonsense ' (I.W.).

kabatſ, kabaitſ, s.pl., sing. *kabatſan*, f., cabets, T.N. 173. 10, ' cabbages': *kabatſ koχjon*, ' red cabbages '; *kabatſ gunjon*, ' green cabbages ' (for the sake of distinction); *kabaitſɔ ḷaur* (J.J.), ' broad-leaved plantain ' (Plantago major) = *dail ḷorjaid*.

kabatſo, v., ' to cabbage, to crib ' (W.H.): *kabatſo po:b pe:θ arna i r o:ð o ;—kabatſo kluyða = kḷatſo kluyða* (O.H.).

kablur, s.m., cablwr, 1 Tim. i. 13, ' blasphemer '.

kably, v., cablu, D., ' to blaspheme ': *kably dyu ;—kably a rhegi*, ' to curse and swear '.

kadaχ, s.m., pl. *kadaχa*, cadach, D., ' a cloth ': *kadaχ gli:n* (in slate quarries), ' knee-rag, fastened round the knee with a buckle, to protect the clothes when trimming slates'; *kadaχ guδu*, 'neck-cloth'; *kadaχ ḷaur*, 'floor-cloth'; *kadaχ ḷestri*, 'dish-cloth'; *kadaχ pokkad*, 'handkerchief' (seldom used = *haŋkatſ pokkad*); *kadaχ gwlanan*, 'a flannel'.

kadar, s.f., pl. *kadëirja*, cadair, D., 'chair': *kadar vrëiχja*, 'arm-chair'; *kadar siglo*, 'rocking-chair'; *tro:yd kadar*, 'leg of a chair'.

kadarn, adj., pl. *kedyrn*, cadarn, D., 'solid, firm': *dy:n kadarn ar i garn* (O.H.), 'a man of his word'; *dy:n kadarn ar i vargan* (O.H.), 'a man who sticks to a bargain'; *may r wal ən r̥hy: simsan, iſo gnëyt i ŋ gadarn*.

kadi, Cadi, D.G. cxcix. 1; T.N. 5. 11, pet name for 'Catherine = katr̥in;—he:n gadi* (of men), 'an old woman; one who is continually meddling with other people's business and finding fault with everything and everybody'; *kadi ģenod*, 'a boy who goes after girls'.

kadlas, s.f., pl. *kadlëiſa* (?), cadlais and cadlas, D., 'rick-yard': *may gwa:s əŋ ka:yl i nabod uθ i gadlas* (prov.).

kadu, v., cadw, D. Fut. S. 2 *kadwi*, 3. *kadwiθ, kadiθ* [*këidu*]. Pret. S. 1. *kadwis*, 3. *kadwoδ*. Pl. 3. *kadson*. Pres. Subj. [*katto*]. Imperative *kadu; kaduχ*. 'to keep'. (1) Transitive (a) 'to keep, maintain': *kadu gwa:s, k̄i:, ſop*, 'to keep a servant, dog, shop'. (b) 'to keep, preserve (in a particular place)': *ḷe: i gadu gwair*, 'a place for keeping hay'. (c) 'to keep' as opposed to throwing away, squandering, etc. : *os na χadwi di δim vy:δ ģin ti δim*. (d) 'to keep, reserve' (for a particular purpose): *kadu ka:y ən wair*, 'to keep a field for hay'. (e) 'to keep' (in the memory): *kadu kəunt vaint vy:δ o bo:b y:n*, 'to keep count how many there are of each'; *kadu i gəmra:ig*, 'to keep up one's Welsh'. (f) 'to keep, keep safe, protect': *may r̥hubaθ ən əŋ kadu ni b lau klo: a χlikjad*, 'something keeps us safe besides lock and latch'; *nid ən hi:r ə k̄ëidu r djaul i wa:s ; dru:g ə k̄ëidu r djaul i wa:s* (prov.), 'the devil does not long preserve his dupe'; *katto paub ḷ; dyu katto* (*gatto*) *paub ḷ* excl. of astonishment, 'good gracious!', i.e. 'God preserve us all' (not common = *gwarχod ni:ḷ gwarχod paub ḷ*). (g) with *r̥hag*, 'to keep from': *ə pr̥en hunu sy ŋ kadu ə tr̥ëiſa r̥hag kravy oχor ə k̄eſyl*, 'that piece of wood which keeps the traces from chafing the side of the horse'. (h) 'to keep, maintain (in a certain state or position)'; *kadu ə du:r əŋ gənnas*, 'to keep the water warm'; *kadu ə kəvruy n sad*, 'to keep the saddle firm'; *kadu ta:n*, 'to keep a fire (alight)'; *kadu meun tr̥evn*, 'to keep in order'. (i) 'to keep (waiting)': *ma na i ovn mod i n əχ kadu əmma*, 'I am afraid I am keeping you waiting here'. (j) 'to keep, hold fast to': *kadu aδewid*, 'to keep a promise'. (k) 'to go to, keep up one's attendance': *may hi ŋ kadu i həsgol*, 'she goes to school'. (l) 'to keep a secret': *nëiθ o δim kadu dim by:d,* 'he can't keep a secret, he won't keep anything to himself'. (m) 'to put away' (Anglo-Welsh 'keep') : *neuχï gadu ə ḷyvr ma ?,* 'will you put away this book ?'; *mynd i ɣhadu,* 'to go to bed'. (n) Phrases : *kadu i ben,* 'to keep quiet about something. not to say a word'; *kadu ri:at, su:n, turu,* 'to make a noise'. (2) Intransitive : (a) 'to keep, remain in a certain position': *kadu dra:u,* 'to keep off'. (b) 'to keep' (of provisions, etc.), 'not to go bad'.

·*kadumï·gëï,* s.m., 'money-box'. Also *boks* ·*kadumï·gëï.*

kaf, s.m., caff, S.E., 'a grasp', esp. in the expression *kaf gwa:g.* i. e. 'a reaching out of the hand to catch hold of something and failing', e.g. in the dark, or 'to catch hold of something which gives way', e. g. in rock-climbing.

Kaf, s., caff, S.E., Eng. (Dial.) caff [a hoe, instrument for hoeing and earthing up potatoes], Wor., Shr., 'a three-pronged iron rake used e.g. for unloading manure from carts'.

kafjo, v.. caphio, D., s.v. 'abripere'. (1) 'to snatch': *kafjo arjan ən ·anə·vrëiθlon.* (2) 'to grope': *kafjo ən ə tuḷuχ.* (3) 'to guess': *daχi wedi kafjo n o lc:u, ond daχi ðim ən jaun.*

Kafjo, v., 'to use a *Kaf'.*

kaib, s.f., pl. *Keibja,* caib, D., 'mattock': *kaib gro:ys,* 'road-side pick'; *ṭro:yd kaib,* 'handle of a mattock'.

kaiŋk, s.f., pl. *Keiŋkja,* caingc, D. (1) 'main branch of a tree'. (2) 'knot' (in wood). (3) 'one of the strands of a thread or rope': *eda dair kaiŋk.* (4) with *kany : kany kaiŋk ru:in = kany klyl ru:in,* 'to decry some one'.

kais, s.m., pl. *Keifada,* cais, D., 'thing sought after, aim': *əna vy: i gais o, ag ə may wedi ga:yl o.*

kakka, s., caca, S.E., 'dung' (childish word).

kakkan, s.f., pl. *kaKenna, Kenna,* caccen, D., 'cake': *kakkan brjodas,* 'wedding-cake'; *kakkan dattus,* 'potato cake'; *kakkan berfro,* 'a kind of small scalloped cake, made of an equal weight of flour, sugar, and butter', cf. *krogan berfro; kakkan go:χ,* a kind of gingerbread.

·*kakKï·mukKi,* s.m., cacamwcci, D.; caccymwcci, G.O. ii. 49. 20, 'burdock' (Arctium Lappa and kindred species) = *Kedor ər wra:χ.*

kakkun, s.pl. and s.m.; sing. also *kakman,* f., caccwn, D., 'bumble-bee', but also used indiscriminately for any insect which buzzes : *mi vy:ð o ar ny:θ kakkun,* 'he will be on a hornets' nest'; *sunjan vel kakkun meun by::s ko:χ,* 'to buzz like a bumble-bee in a foxglove', said of some one who is always grumbling ; *kakkun mëirχ = gwenyn mëirχ,* 'wasps'; *kakkun kut,* a facetious name for a pig.

kakənas, s.f., cacynes, S.E., fem. of *kakkun,* a term of reproach for a woman : *ta:u ər he:n gakənas gəθral !*

kaχgi, s.m., cachgi, O.P., 'a submissive, cowardly fellow'—*gwel gəno vo gəmmyd kam na gnĕyd kam i aral;—jaχa krŏ:yn krŏ:yn kaχgi* (prov.), O.H.

kaχy, v., cachu, D., 'cacare'.

kal, s.f., caly, D., 'penis'.

kalad, adj., pl. *kledjon,* comp. *klettaχ,* caled, D.; sup. clettaf, G.R. 52. 6. (1) 'hard': * Kin glettad a χraig, a χarag;—vel hĕyarn sba:yn o galad,* 'as hard as Spanish steel'; *berwi wy:a ŋ galad,* 'to boil eggs hard'. (2) 'hardy': *ma: r gwarθag dy:on əŋ glettaχ i δal ə dəwyδ,* 'black cattle stand the weather better'. (3) 'hard, harsh' (of persons) = *to:st : kalad uθ ə tlaud.* (4) 'determined' = *pendervənol.* (5) 'fast, quick': *mynd əŋ glettaχ.*

kalan, s., calan, D., 'calends': *no:s galan,* 'New Year's Eve'; calan Mai (May 13) becomes *klamma;* calan gaeaf (Nov. 13) becomes *klaŋgĕya.*

kalan, s.f., pl. *kleni,* agalen, D. (1) 'whetstone' = *kalan hogi.* (2) 'bar' of salt or soap: *kalan o halan, kalan o sebon.*

kalap, s., 'gallop': *mynd ar galap,*—esp. in fig. sense: 'to go with zest, to go swimmingly': *may hi n mynd ar galap əmma heno* = *mynd ən huiljog, gləvar* (O.H.).

kalkjo, v., kalkio, W.S. [Calke], 'to caulk': *kalkjo loŋ.*

kalχ, s.m., calch, D., 'lime': *odyn galχ,* 'lime-kiln'; *karag galχ,* 'limestone'; *kalχ po:yθ,* 'quicklime'.

kalχan, s.f., calchen, "a stone or lump of unslaked lime", S.E.: *kin luyttad (wynnad) a χalχan,* 'as pale as a sheet'.

kalon, s.f., pl. *klonna, klanna,* callon, W.B. col. 416. 1. 2, etc.; Yny lhyvyr hwnn [25] 3; G.R. (4) 14; calon, D., 'heart'; also 'heart' of timber, etc.: *pul kalon,* 'the pit of the stomach'; *tori (i) galon,* 'to break one's heart', also, in much milder sense: 'to be down-hearted'; *may o wedi tori galon ən la:n löyu,* 'he has utterly broken his heart'; also, 'he has entirely lost heart'; *kodi χ kalon,* 'to cheer you up'; *o δivri kalon,* 'really, seriously, deeply': *daχi n mynd o δivri kalon ?,* 'are you really going ?'; *kary o δivri kalon,* 'to love deeply';—*o wĕylod kalon, o wĕylod ə ŋhalon,* 'from the bottom of my heart'; *mi δau o pen glu:iθ o ar i galon,* 'he will come when he feels inclined'; *vel bəδa i n tëimlo ar ə ŋhalon,* 'as I happen to be minded'; *dim əŋ kany o χ kalon ond əŋ kany i la:δ ər əsbryd,* 'not singing out of the fullness of one's heart, but singing to hide one's emotion'; *may o n la:n i galon,* 'he is a straightforward man', 'there is no deceit in him'; *eli ŋhalon, plesar ŋhalon,* 'the delight of my heart'; *ma n δa: gin əŋ klonna bo:d . . .,* 'we are delighted that . . .' As endearing expression: *ŋhalon ba:χ i !, ŋhalon annuyl i !, ŋhalon ayr i !*

kalpjo, v., 'to gallop'.

kalyn, v., calyn, D., corruptè pro canlyn; D.G. cxlvi. 12; clxxi. 24. 51; W.Ll. ix. 28; lviL 38; G.R. 52. 13; D.F. [vi] 12; [xii] 21, etc.; B.C. 48. 7; callyn, G.R. [132]. 15; [136]. 8. Imperative *klənuχ*. (1) 'to follow': *ma: r k̇i: ŋ kalyn ar əχ o:l χi*, 'the dog is following·you'; *tr̥oi i galyn po:b awal o wynt*, 'to trim one's sails to every breeze'; *kalyn k̇efyl a θrol*, 'to follow the occupation of a carter'. (2) sometimes used where in English 'to come off with, go with', etc., would be more usually employed: *may r plum əŋ kalyn ə pr̥okkar*, 'the lead comes off with the (red-hot) poker'; *may r y:d ən mynd i fur i galyn ə gwynt*, 'the chaff goes off with the wind' (in winnowing). (3) the expression *i galyn* (*i u galyn*) has sometimes the sense of 'also', 'with him', etc.: *basun ən lëikjo ᵭo vo ᵭu:ad əmma a r lyvr i galyn*, 'I should like him to come here and bring the book with him'; *may vənta ŋ gnëyd r y:n pe:θ i u galyn*, 'he does the same thing too'. (4) "to follow", "to keep company with": *du i ŋ kalyn hunna*.

kal, adj., call, D., 'sensible, wise, intelligent': *may hi ŋ gal jaun*, 'she is very sensible' (e. g. of a baby); *k̇iŋ galad a sarf*, 'as wise as a serpent'; *hannar gair i gal* (prov.), 'a word to the wise'; *pen gyl ə kal ve gyl ə m̩hel* (prov.), 'corruptio optimi pessima'; *t ədi v ᵭim əŋ gal* = (a) 'he is not in his right senses, not right in his head'; (b) 'he is lacking in practical common sense'.

kalinab, s., callineb, D., s.v. 'prudentia'; 'sense, intelligence': *kalinab k̇i:, k̇efyl*, etc.

kalino, v., 'to become sensible, wise': *may n hu:yr gla:s i ti galino*, 'it is high time for you to become wise'.

kam, s.m., pl. *kamma*, cam, D., 'step': *o gam i gam*, 'step by step'; *lo:n bo:st bo:b kam*, 'a high road all the way'; *hub, kam a nëid*, 'hop, skip and jump'; *kamma brëif̑on*, 'large steps' (cf. *brasgammy*); *ə kam kənta ədi r kam gora*, 'the beginning is half the battle'.

kam, s.m., cam, D., 'wrong': *gnëyd kam a ru:in*, 'to do some one a wrong'; *t o:ᵭ ə ŋhly:st ᵭim wedi gnëyd kam a vi:*, 'my ears did not deceive me'; *may o wedi ka:l kam*, 'he has been unjustly treated', e.g. in not being awarded the prize; *ar gam*, 'unjustly'; *aχyb i gam*, 'to defend oneself'; *gwëyθa kam kam lëidar* (prov.), 'the worst wrong is the wrong of a thief', i. e. 'a known delinquent is always exposed to suspicion'.

kam, adj., pl. *k̇ëimjon*, cam, D., 'crooked, bent': *k̇iŋ gammad a χr̥mman*, 'as bent as a sickle' (referring to a bent back);—*əŋ gam vel piso moχyn;—may o ŋ gam*, 'his back is bent'; *kloᵭja k̇ëimjon*, 'crooked walls'.

kambran, s.m., pl. *kambrenna*, cambren, S.E., 'a piece of wood placed between the sinews of the hind-feet of a slaughtered animal to hang it up and expand the legs'. Cf. Eng. (Dial.) cambrel, camerel, etc. [*kammaᵭ*].

kamdra, s.m., camdra, S.E., ' crookedness '.

·*kam·drëiljad*, s.m., camdreuliad, S.E., ' indigestion ' = *difig*
treiljad.

·*kam·drinjaθ*, s.m., camdriniaeth, S.E., ' bad or wrong treatment ';
' abuse '.

·*kam·dro:*, s., camdro, S.E., ' crookedness in dealing ': *welis i ðim*
·*kam·dro: arno vo ri o:yd*, ' he is perfectly straight in his dealings '.

kamða, s.f., pl. *kam·ða:y*, camfa, D., ' stile '.

·*kam·ðëyd*, v., cam-ddywedyd, Psalm cvi. 33, ' to say wrong '.

·*kamgə·merjad*, s.m., pl. ·*kamgəmer·jada*, camgymmeriad, D., s.v.
' error '; ' mistake ': *dəna vu:y o ·gamgə·merjad na ·nëysoni əri·o:yd*,
' this is the biggest mistake we ever made '; *ə məmryn lëia o*
·*gamgə·merjad*, ' the slightest mistake '.

·*kamgə·meryd*, v., camgymmeryd, D., s.v. ' allucinor ', ' oblucinor ';
' to mistake, make a mistake ': *may hi wedi ·kamgə·meryd χi hevo*
ru:in aral, ' she mistook you for some one else '.

kammað, s., cammedd, D., s.v. ' poples '; in the expression
kammað ə gar, cammedd garr, D., in human beings ' the ham or
inner angle of the joint which unites the thigh and the leg '—in
animals ' the hough '; and when slaughtered the angle above the
hoof on the hind-legs, by which carcasses are hung up in butchers'
shops, called in some parts ' camerel-houghs '.   I have heard the
following variations : *kamma gar* (O.H.); *kəmmaŋ gar, kəmman*
ə gar (J.J.); *kəmma gar* (Bangor).—*mi drawoð rubaθ ə ŋhəmman*
i ar (J.J.), ' something struck him on the bend of the knee '; *linin*
kamma gar, ' hamstring '.

kammog, s., pl. *kamoga*, cammeg, 1 Kings vii. 33 ; cammog,
G.O. i. 223. 3 ; ' felloe of a wheel '.

kammol, v., canmol, D., s.v. ' laudo '; camol, W.Ll. xcii. 59, ' to
speak well of ', ' commend '.

kammur, s.m., camwr, S.E., ' one who takes long strides ': *os*
by:ð gavl dy:n ən hi:r may o ŋ gammur maur.

kammy, v., kamy, W.S., ' to step ': *kammy dros garag*.

kammy, v., cammu, D., ' to bend ': *kammy i ben*, ' to bend his
head '; *kammy sgidja*, ' to tread down shoes on one side '; *mi*
gammoð honna ən le mynd i veun, ' that (nail) bent instead of
going in '.

kamoljaθ, s.m., canmoliaeth, D., s.v. ' laus '; ' praise '.

kamp, s.f., pl. *kampja*, camp, D.   (1) ' pre-eminence, excellence ':
le: by:ð kamp by:ð ɣhemp (prov.), ' where there is excellence there
will be defect '; *kamp ar ðy:n ədi bo:d ən ëirwir*, ' it is a fine thing
for a man to be truthful '; *dan gamp*, ' splendid ', e.g. *pa:r o sgidja*

dan gamp. (2) ' feat, achievement': *t ədi hunna ðim əɲ gamp garu,*
' that is not much of an achievement'; *t o:ys dim kamp ɪði hi vod
ən weḷ,* ' it is nothing for her to be proud of that she is superior';
daɲos i gampja, 'to show off'; *kamp i ti ðëyd be s ǵin i!,* 'you
can't guess what I have here!'; *du i wedi gnëyd kamp i χi
heno,* 'I have done something for you to-night which you could
not have done yourself'. (3) 'boisterousness, high spirits shown
by bodily action': *bo:d əɲ glonnog, gnëyd kampja.* (4) 'tricks,
mischief': *y:n da: jaun ədi o i nëyd kampja,* 'he is up to all kinds
of tricks'; *ən ḷaun kampja dru:g,* 'full of mischief'; *i lol a i gampja,*
' his humbug and mischievous tricks'.

kampjo, v., campio. T.N. 134. 15, ' to cut capers, to frisk about':
*ən nëidjo ag əɲ kampjo ;—ḱefyl əɲ kampjo a golug maureðog arno vo,
ond ən mynd ðim gwerθ,* 'a frisky horse of imposing appearance
but a slow goer' (O.H.).

kampys, adj., campus, I.G. 169 [47], ' splendid': *may r dɑwyð
ma ɲ gampys.*

·*kam·wëiθjo,* v., camweithio, S.E., ' to work awry'.

·*kam·əstyn,* ·*kam·estyn,* s.m., camystum, S.E., ' a cramped
posiiion': *riu orvað meun ·kam·estyn ðary mi.*

kan, adj., cann, D., ' white' in *bara kan,* ' white bread'.

kan, adj., can, W.B. col. 2. 38, 'a hundred': *kan ḷa:θ,* 'a
hundred yards'; *kan durnod (nurnod, njurnod),* 'a hundred days';
kan waiθ, 'a hundred times'; *de:ɲ mlu:yð kan mlu:yð ḱi:* (prov.),
'ten years are as a hundred years for a dog'; *kan kҫöyso,* 'a
hundred welcomes'. Cf. *kant.*

ḱan, s.m., pl. *ḱans, ḱanja,* ' can' = *pisar.*

ka:n, s.f., pl. *kanëyon,* cân, D., 'song': *ma: nu wedi gnëyd ka:n
arno vo,* 'they have made a song about him'; *piḷ o ga:n etto,* 'a bit
of song more'; *r y:n ga:n gron o hy:d,* said when some one
continually harps on the same string; *r o:n i ɲ gubod be vasa
dɪwað ə ga:n—digjo a fry:o,* 'I knew what would be the end of
it—anger and quarrelling'; *əvo: o:ð ər yuχa i ga:n,* 'he was the
loudest'.

kanan, s.f., canon, B.C. 107. 10; canan, B., ' cannon'.

kanjad, s.m., caniad, D.G. c. 2, 'the sounding of a horn or the
ringing of a bell as a signal to cease work': *hyd ganjad,* 'till the
bell goes'.

kanja·ta:d, s.m., caniattâd, D., ' permission'.

kanja·ta:y, v., caniattâu, D. Imp. *kanja·leuχ.* Pret. Pass.
kanja·taud, 'to permit', followed by the prep. *i :—a χanja·ta:y
bo:d . . . ,* 'granting that . . .'.

kanḷaθ, s., canllath, ' a hundred yards'.

kanḷau, s.m., pl. *kanḷauja,* canllaw, D., *kanḷau ə griſa,* 'banisters'; *kanḷau pont,* 'the parapet of a bridge'.

kannuyl̦, s.f., pl. *knuḷa,* canwyll, D.; cannwyll, W.Ll. vi. 60; cannwll, R.B. 198. 9, 'candle': *gola r gannuyl̦,* 'to light the candle'; *hevo kannuyl̦,* 'by candle light'; *kannuyl̦ wen,* 'tallow candle'; *kannuyl̦ vruːyn (vruynan),* 'rush-light'; *kannuyl̦ k̦erpyn (l̦ip̦rin),* 'a candle made with a piece of calico, etc., and tallow' (J.J.); *hëyarn knuḷa,* 'snuffers'; *kannuyl̦ korf,* 'a light supposed to be seen in the direction of a churchyard, prognosticating death'; also 'glow-worm' (J.J.) = *kannuyl̦ baχ laːs* (O.H.); *kannuyl̦ ə ḷəgad,* 'pupil of the eye'; *may kannuyl̦ i ḷəgad o wedi diſod,* 'he has become blind'.

kanny, v., cannu, D., 'to bleach': *r̦hoi diḷad aḷan i r hayl i ganny.*

kanol, s.m., canol, D., 'middle': *əŋ ŋhanol ər avol,* 'in the middle of the apple'; *kanol jonaur,* 'the middle of January'; *o ganol f̦iːr voːn,* 'from the middle of Anglesey'; *ma poŋkan ən i ganol,* 'there is a hump in the middle of it (the field)'; *ar ganol bytta,* 'in the middle of eating'; *ar ganol i bregaθ,* 'in the middle of his sermon';—also adjectively : *ə göydan ganol.*—The pronunciation *kənol* is also said to be heard at Bangor.

kansan, s.f. (1) 'a cane'. (2) 'a fine, well-set-up young woman': *kansan dal.*

kant, s., cant, D., 'the hoop of a wheel': *kant olwyn, kant tr̦oːyl̦.*

kant, s.m., pl. *kantoð, kannoð,* cant, D. (For pl. cf. cantoedd, B.C. 14. 6; 89. 5.) (1) 'a hundred': *kant o lεχi* (in quarries), '128 slates'; *kant o benwaig* (among fishermen), '126 herrings'; *may o drost i hannar kant,* 'he is over fifty'; *riu gant a hannar ən oːl,* 'about a hundred and fifty years ago'; *yːn kant ar bəmθag,* '1600'; *day gant,* '200'; *kantoð o vlənəðoð ən oːl,* 'hundreds of years ago'; *kannoð ar gannoð,* 'hundreds and hundreds'; *r̦hiu gant a miːl o beθa,* 'no end of things'. (2) 'a hundredweight': *kant o loː.*—Cf. *kan.*

kantal, s.f., kantel, W.S. [A cantell]. (1) 'border, brim': *kantal het,* 'the brim of a hat'. (2) 'ledge' (of rock, etc.), O.H.

kantoras, s.f., cantores, Eccles. ii. 8, 'singer'.

kantr̦ag, s.f., cantwraig, S.E., 'singer'.

kantur, s.m., pl. *kantorjon,* s.m. cantwr, S.E., 'singer : *pen kantur,* 'leader of the singing' (in a chapel).

kanθrig, s., canthrig, 'wheat-flour and oatmeal mixed': only in *bara kanθrig = bara kəmmysg.*

kanur, s.m., canwr, T.N. 129. 31, 'singer': *kanur smala,* 'comic singer'.

kanwaθ, s. and adv., canwaith, D., s.v. 'centies'; 'a hundred times'.

kanwyn, adj., 'white, bleached by being exposed to the sun' (O.H.).

kany, v., canu, D. Fut. S. 3. *kaniθ* [*ka:n*]. Pl. 2. *kanuχ*. Imperative *ka:n, kana*. (1) 'to sing': *tan gany a gwe·δi:o*, 'singing and praying'; *ka:n di: benniḷ mu:yn i θ nain, mi ga:n də nain i tiθa* (prov.), 'one good turn deserves another'; *mi gnaun i ạ tan gany*. 'I could do it easily'; *mynd adra tan gany*, 'to go home full of jollity'; *kany n i χorn*, 'to grumble';—metaph. "to sing out": *dəmma vi a de:r iδo vo nes o:δ o ŋ kany*, 'I gave him a blow which made him sing out'. (2) of various animals, such as 'to crow' (of a cock), 'to chirp' (of a cricket), 'to purr' (of a cat). (3) 'to ring' (of a bell): *t ədi r glo:χ ma δim əŋ kany*, 'this bell doesn't ring'; *daχi wedi kany ?*, 'did you ring?' (4) 'to sound' (of a horn). (5) 'to play' (an instrument): *kany r pjano, kany r organ*.

kaŋan, s.f., pl. *kaŋhenna*, cangen, D. (1) 'a small branch growing out of a main branch' (*kaiŋk*). (2) 'a strip of a girl': *kaŋan o hogan hëini*. Cf. D.G. lxxxvi. 5; G.O. i. 7. 1; T.N. 265. 32. (3) in bad sense: 'jade' (I.W.).

kaŋkar, s., cangcr, D., s.v. 'carcinoma', 'gangræna'; cancar, C.C.M. 103. 16; cancr, B.C. 31. 11. (1) 'canker: a disease peculiar to trees, and especially common in apple-trees, which causes the bark to rot and drop off'. (2) 'canker: a kind of ulcer in the mouth': *kaŋkar ar davod*. (3) expletive: *məŋ kaŋkar !, məŋ kaŋkar ko:χ !, be: gaŋkar sy ·arnaχi ?*; similarly *kaŋkar o be:θ !*, 'wretched thing!'

kaŋkṛo, v., cancro, S.E. (1) 'to have the canker'. Cf. *kaŋkar* (1). (2) 'to be eaten away by rust': *may o wedi kaŋkṛo*.

kap, s.m., pl. *kapja*, cap, D.G. xcv. 38; G.R. 49. 8; D.; B.C. 66. 23, 'cap': *ṛhəuχ əχ kap am əχ pen*, 'put your cap on'; *ro: i m o ɣhap i laur i ne:b*, 'I am not inferior to any one'; *kap a fi:g*, 'a peaked cap'; *kap ḷedar*, '? stonechat' (Pratincola rubicula).

kapjo, v., capio, B.C. 29. 8, 'to take off the hat, to cap'. Also fig. 'to cringe': *pëidjuχ a kapjo iδo vo*, 'do not cringe to him'.

kappal, s.m., pl. *kapeli, kapelyδ*, cappel, D., 'chapel', i.e. a Nonconformist place of worship; *kappal ḱeṛig*, 'Capel Curig'.

kaptan, s.m., pl. *kaptëinjad*, capten, 2 Kings xviii. 24, 'captain': *kaptan ḷoŋ*, 'a ship captain'.

kar, s.m., pl. *ḱeir*, carr, D., 'car': *ḷoǵi kar*, 'to hire a car'; *kar po:st*, 'mail-car'; *dy:n a i gar ar i ǵevn*, 'a man who has lost his temper' (O.H.);—in slate quarries: 'a wagon used for carrying rubble to the *tomman*':—*y:n medrys o r agor i r kar* [*agor*]; *kar ḷysg*, carr llûsg, D., s.v. 'traha', 'a mountain sledge for carrying hay, etc.'; *kar ḷa:δ*, 'a wooden table, hollowed out in the middle,

for killing sheep upon ' (J.J.); *kar ar ə bladyr*, 'cradle', i.e.
'a light frame of wood put over a scythe to preserve the corn and
lay it more evenly in the swathe '.

ka:r, s.m., câr, D.   (1) 'relative' (seldom used): *may o n dippin
o ga:r i mi*.   (2) a mode of affectionate address : *he:n ga:r*, ' old
fellow '.—Not used at Llanfairfechan (= *he:n frind*), but common
at Bethesda (O.H.).

kara, s.f., pl. *krëia*, carrai, D., ' lace' (for boots. etc.); *kara wen,*
' a kind of cord made from the skin of pigs ' (J.J.); *kara* is also
used for the middle-band of a flail (O.H.) ; *kara c:n*, ' throat-strap '
(of harness); *kara mo:r*, a kind of sea-weed (Chorda filum);
mi tənna i o əɲ grëia, ' I'll pull him into shreds ' (O.H.).

kara, s., a sheep's ear-mark, so called : *kara y:n torjad*, a curved
cut made with one stroke of the knife; *kara day dorjad*, a rect-
angular cut made with two strokes of the knife [*no:d*].

karad, s.m., pl. *karëidja*, carraid, D., ' car-load '.

karag, s.f., pl. *kerig*, carreg, D.   (1) ' stone ': *lixjo kerig, pledy*
(*hevo* or *a*) *kerig*, ' to throw stones '; *kokkyn, sup, tomman, tumpaθ
kerig* (*o gerig*), ' heap of stones '; *gwal gerig*, ' stone wall '; *karag
attab*, ' echo '; *karag da:n*, ' flint '; *karag galx*, ' limestone '; *karag
la:s*, ' sulphate of iron ' used for curing proud flesh in sores (cf. also
below); *karag rubjo*, ' rubbing stone'; *karag varx*, ' mounting stone'
(O.H.); *ɣhøuɣ garag arno vo*, ' forget it ', ' let bygones be bygones ';
—in restricted sense, ' slate ', also *karag la:s*, pl. *kerig glëifon ;
karag dro:*, ' a slate laid in a different position to the rest, to mark
each *hannar kant* (= 64) of slates '; *kerig melin*, ' blocks which go
to the mill to be sawn, and which are used for making tombstones,
etc.'; *karag na:ð*, ' slate pencil '.   (2) ' stone ' (of fruit).   (3) in pl.
' testicles '.

karatf, karaitf, s.pl., sing. *kratfan* (from which a new plural
kratfis is sometimes formed), carets, T.N. 173. 12, ' carrots': *tori
ɲ gratfan*, ' to snap like a carrot '; *karatf gwilijon*, ' wild carrots '
(Daucus Carota).

karatf, karadg, s.f., pl. *karadgis*, ' carriage '.

karban, s., carbin, S.E., only in *karban o geluyð*, ' an evident lie ':
r u:yti n dëyd karban o geluyð.

karbul, adj., carbwl, S.E. ; cf. carnbyled, G.O. ii. 168. 20.   (1)
of things, ' clumsy, poor ': *adroðjad karbul* (= *ble:r, ·di:-ðim jaun*),
' a poor recitation '.   (2) of persons, ' doddering, fumbling ': *may
n xwi:θ gweld ər he:n ðy:n na, may o wedi mynd ən rëit garbul ;—
nt o:ð o ɲ garbul uθi hi ?*, ' wasn't it a wretched performance ?' (e.g.
of a speech).   (3) of persons ' clumsy ': *karbul !*, ' clumsy !'; as
subst. *ta:u ſ he:n garbul gwirjon !*

kardjo, v., ' to card ' (wool): *gwëy a xardjo a xodi maun* was
formerly regarded as women's work (O.H.).   Cf. *gardjo*.

kardotta, v., cardotta, D., 'to beg'.

kardottas, s.f., cardotes, S.E., 'beggar'.

kardottyn, s.m., cardottyn, D., s.v. 'mendicus'; 'beggar'.

kardyn, s.m., pl. *kardja*, kard, W.S.; cardieu (pl.), B.C. 23. 16, 'card' (of any description).

karedig, adj., caredig, D., 'kind': *·vɔðuχi mor garedig a . . . ?*, 'will you be so kind as to . . . ?'; *gëirja heb vo:d ɔŋ garedig*, 'unkind words'.

karedigruyð, s.m., caredigrwydd, D., s.v. 'beneficium', 'gratitudo'; 'kindness': *di:olχ ɔn vaur am ɔχ karedigruyð*, 'thank you very much for your kindness'; *gurθod karedigruyð*, 'to refuse a kindness'.

kariktor, s.m., 'character'; esp. of persons, e.g. a worthless 'character'.

karjad, s.m., pl. *krjada*, cariad, D., s.v. 'amor'. (1) 'love'. (2) 'darling': *ŋharjad ba:χ i*. (3) 'lover': *·r ɔdani n he:n grjada*.

karjadys, *krjadys*, adj., cariadus, 2 Sam. i. 23, 'loving'.

karjo, v., kario, W.S.; cario, Sion Tudur in G.R. 380. 5. Fut. S. 3. *kariθ*. Pret. S. 3. *karjoð*. Pl. 3. *karson*. Imperative *karja*, *karjuχ*, 'to carry': *forð garjo maun*, 'a road for carrying peat'; *karjo rubaθ ɔŋ gɵulad*, 'to carry something in the arms as a bundle'; *mi garson beθ ovnaduy o gerig ɔno*, 'they carried an immense amount of stones there'; *karjo gwair*, 'to carry hay'; *karjo stry:on*, 'to tell tales';—also expressed by *karjo* alone: *karjo po:b pe:θ i ru:in ;* —*os ɔdi hi ŋ karjo i vjaun, may hi ŋ karjo aḷan*, 'if she brings tales into the house she is sure to take them out'.

karjur, s.m., cariwr, T.N. 17. 29, 'carrier';—also applied to horses: *ɔdi r ḳefyl ɔŋ garjur da: ?*, 'is the horse a good carrier?'

karkas, s., 'carcass';—used opprobriously: *hel dɔ garkas a fur a ti: !*

karkud, s.m., cf. carcwd, M.F.: *ta:u ʄ he:n garkud bɔχan !*, said to a child who wants to be master over everybody (O.H.).

karχar, s.m., pl. *karχara*, carchar, D., 'impediment, fetter', esp. 'a cord of hay, etc., attaching the fore-leg of an animal to the neck': *may hi n dippin o garχar arna i*, 'it is rather a tie for me'; *karχar kry:ð*, said of tight boots.

karχary, *kɔrχary*, v., carcharu, Acts xxii. 19, 'to fetter with a *karχar*'.

karlam, s.m., pl. *karlamma*, carlam, Judges v. 22, 'gallop': *mynd ar garlam*, 'to gallop, to go full speed'.

karlammy, v., carlammu, C.C.M. 154. 13, 'to gallop'; 'to go full speed'.

karlum, s.m., carlwm, D., 'ermine': *k̯in wənñad a r karlum* ;— *mynd vel ə karlum*, 'to go like a flash';—as term of reproach: *ta:u ṛ he:n garlum gwirjon (garlum ḷum)*, O.H.

karḷuyd, adj., 'faded': *he:n frog, ʃo:l garḷuyd* (Bangor).

karḷyd, adj., carllyd, S.E., 'amorous'.

karn, s.m., pl. *karna*, carn, D. (1) 'hoof' (of a horse—not used of cattle = *ewin*): *mynd nerθ ə karna*, 'to go full speed'; *dail karn r ebol*, 'colt's foot' (Tussilago Farfara). (2) 'hilt, handle': *karn kəḷaθ, karn ebiḷ ;*—fig. *i r karn*, 'thorough, to the backbone': *·meθadis i r karn ;—sevyḷ ən i garn*, 'to adhere to what one has said'; *iṛoi n i garn*, 'to prevaricate'; *dy:n ən sound ən i garn*, 'a trustworthy man'.

karnaδ, s.f., pl. *karneδi*, carnedd, D., s.v. 'lithologema'; 'heap of stones' (in general sense), but only in phrases such as the following: *o:ys ·gənoχi ar* (garden) *δa: ? na:g o:ys, may hi ŋ garnaδ o ǵeṛig* (J.J.); *ə dre: wedi mynd i laur əŋ garnaδ ylu* (O.H.);—(in particular sense) 'prehistoric heaps of stones, old burial-places, etc.' (O.H. frequently) ;—*ə garnaδ*, old name for the mountain now called *ə drəsgol* (Y Drosgol), O.H. Cf. Carnedd y Ddelw (Ordnance map). O.H. has a story about a gold cross found in the cairn there ;—*karnaδ δavyδ*, 'Carnedd Ddafydd'.

karneujan, kneujan, v., cf. cyrnewian, M.F.; Eng. (Dial.) carny, carney ['to flatter, wheedle'], 'to whine' = *gnëyd riu he:n nada, gnëyd su:n kṛi:o : kneujan am vu:yd a dim iʃ'o vo* (O.H.) ;—*do:s o r van ma i garneujan !* (Llanfairfechan).

·karn·ḷ̈eidar, s.m., pl. *·karn·ḷadron*, carnlleidr, D., s.v. 'auto-lecythus'; 'an arrant thief'.

karp, s.m., pl. *karpja*, carp, D., 'panniculus, pittacium'; 'a ragamuffin': *ṛ he:n garp*. The original sense, 'rag', is transferred to the diminutive *k̯erpyn*, q.v.

k̯arpad, s.m., pl. *k̯arpedi*, karpet, W.S.; carbed, B.C. 34. 21, 'carpet': *k̯yro, knokjo k̯arpedi*, 'to beat carpets'.

karpan, s.f., term applied to a woman of a miserable, sickly appearance: *ṛ he:n garpan dlaud !*—also to sheep: *he:n garpan sa:l o δavod* (Ö.H.).

karpjog, adj., carpiog, D., s.v. 'pannosus'. (1) 'ragged'. (2) 'in a broken manner': *ʃarad əŋ garpjog ;—gwëiθjo ŋ garpjog*, 'to work in an untidy, slovenly, irregular manner'. (3) 'sickly, decrepid, all to pieces': *karpjog jaun ədi pobol wedi mynd ən he:n ; i hçeχid wedi mynd əŋ garpjog*.

karʃ'un, s.pl., garsiwn, W.S. [Garison]; karsiwn, W.Ll. lv. 70; cf. L.G.C. 64 [120], *he:n garʃ'un = hen havlig, he:n dakḷa*.

kartṛa, s.m., pl. *kartṛevi*, cartref, D., 'home': *oδi kartṛa*, 'away from home'; *breθyn kartṛa*, 'homespun'. [*adra, gartṛa*].

kar̦revol, adj., cartrefol, D., s.v. 'domesticus'. (1) 'home-like'.
(2) 'home-staying'. (3) 'warm-hearted': *y:n kar̦revol jaun ǝdi o.*
(4) 'on familiar terms, unconstrained': *mynd ǝn hol̦ol gar̦refol hevo vo; may o wedi mynd ǝy gar̦revol akku ru:an.*

kar̦revy, v., cartrefu, 2 Cor. v. 8, 'to make one's home': *l̦e: may o y kar̦revy?*, 'where is his home?'

karθ, s.m., carth, D. (1) 'tow, cotton waste, etc., such as is used for cleaning purposes': *r u:ti vel ta:n i r karθ (meun karθ)*, said of some one who is ready to take part in any disturbance (*ǝm barod i vynd at bo:b helynt*), O.H. (2) 'mist': *gla:u ma:n, karθ a niul,*—also *karθ niul.* Apparently a confusion with *tarθ*, but O.H. has both forms.

karθan, s.f., carthen, D. (1) 'winnowing-sheet', made usually of hemp (O.H.): *ǝn sy:χ vel ǝ garθan*, 'as dry as a bone'. (This phrase is the only instance in which the word now occurs in ordinary speech, and its meaning is generally forgotten.) (2) 'a sheet placed upon the ground by gleaners to thresh their corn': *l̦ẹ̈yny r garθan ar laur* (O.H.). (3) 'a quilt for a bed, made of wool or other substance' (O.H.). (4) 'a kind of cloak' (?): *kodi i χarθan a fur a hi:* (O.H.). Cf. C.C. 461. 7, Nawr gwae finne na bae Garthan, Neu hws Ceffyl am fy nghefen.

karθy, v., carthu, D., 'to cleanse, clean out': *karθy r bẹ̈ydy, karθy kut ǝ varlan;—kuttar karθy*, 'a drain behind cows in a cow-house';—(fig.) *mi dǝ garθa di al̦an*, 'I'll turn you out' (O.H.).

karu, s.m., pl. *k̦ẹ̈iru*, carw, D., 'stag': *korn karu*, 'stag-horned moss'.

·karudan, s.f., carwden, D. xc. 7, 'the chain which passes over the saddle of a draught-harness and supports the shafts, backband'.

karur, s.m., carwr, D.G. lxxxiii. 39, 'lover'.

karvan, s.f., pl. *karvanna*, carfan, D. (1) 'one of the sides which form the frame of a cart' (O.H.): *ar ǝ garvan may r hesban sy n dal ǝ k̦ẹ̈yad ǝn sǝund* (O.H.). (2) ['a strand of rope'—Anglesey, hence] *mynð ǝn ðu:y garvan*, 'to split into two parties'.

kary, v., caru, D. Fut. S. 1. *kara*, 2. *kari*, 3. *kariθ*. Pret. Pl. 3. *ðary nu gary* (not *karson*, cf. *karjo*). Imperative *ka:r; karuχ.* 'to love'.

ka:s, s.m., câs, D., 'hatred': *rubaθ daχi wedi r̦hoid ǝχ ka:s arno vo*, 'something you have taken a dislike to'.

ka:s, s.m., pl. *kasys.* (1) 'case': *ka:s pilo, gobennyð, rasal. sbektol, kl̦ok;*—also 'the cover of a book'. (2) 'frame' (of an animal): *may ka:ys gu:eðol arni hi.* (Cf. *kasol.*)

ka:s, adj., câs, D., 'hateful, disagreeable, nasty, tiresome, un-pleasant': *turu ka:s*, 'an unpleasant noise'; *ka:s ar gl̦y:sț*, 'unpleasant to the ear': *he:n waiθ ka:s ǝdi fevjo*, 'shaving is a disagreeable business'; *peːθ kaːs jaun ədi koḷi rubaθ vel na,* 'it is very tiresome losing a thing like that'; *pobol gaːs,* 'disagreeable people'; *may ŋ gaːs jaun ˑarnoχi,* 'it is very nasty for you'; *may ŋ gaːs ǵin i,* 'I hate'.

kasag, s.f., pl. *ꞓesig,* caseg, D., 'mare': *kasag ən drom o ǵiu,* 'a mare in foal', opp. to *kasag waːg ;—kasag vagy,* 'a brood mare'; *ꞓiu kasag,* 'a foal before being weaned'; *kasag ëira,* 'a (rolled) snowball', cf. B.C. 59. 5; *kasag ə ðrəkꞓin,* 'fieldfare' (Turdus pilaris).

kaˑsaːy, v., cassau, D., 'to hate'.

kasgal, s.m., casgl, D., 'gathering' (on a finger, etc.).

kasgan, s.f., pl. *kasgja,* casgen, T.N. 355. 34, 'cask'.

kasgjad, s., pl. *kasǵëidja,* 'caskful'.

kasgljad, s.m., pl. *kasgljada,* cascliad, Gen. i. 10. (1) 'a gathering' e. g. on the finger. (2) 'a collection' (at a place of worship). Cf. *hel, knokka, ofrum, ofrəmmy.*

kasgly, v., casglu, D. Imperative *kasgla ; kasgluχ,* 'to gather'.

kasol, adj., ˑ 'plump'; cf. Eng. 'in good case': *may o ŋ gasol— fil iˑr butʃar* (O.H.)—A somewhat stronger word than *ḷʊvndeu* (O.H.).

kast, s.m., pl. *kastja,* cast, C.C.M. 56. 13 ; G.O. i. 229. 4, 'trick, antic': *ən χwara poːb maːθ o gastja,* 'playing all sorts of tricks'; *riu heːn gastja druːg,* 'mischief'; *anoð tənny kast o heːn ǵefyl* (prov.), 'it is hard to cure an old horse of a trick'.

kast, s.m., Eng. cast, 'a piece of knowledge possessed by some one to the detriment of another': *may gəno vo gast arno,* 'he knows something to his detriment' (W.H.); *ma na ovn arno ꞧhag iðo vo ðëyd ə kast* (O.H.).

kastaḷ, s.m., pl. *ꞓestyḷ, kasteḷa, kasteḷi,* castell, D., 'castle'.

kastjog, adj., castiawg, O.P., 'tricky'.

kaʃˑo, v., Eng. case, 'to bind (a book)', 'to put a cover on (a book)'.

ꞓat, s., Eng. cat, in *χwara ꞓat [χwara]*; also the piece of wood used in the game so called.

katjad, s.f., cataid, S.E., 'a pipeful' (of tobacco). Cf. *ꞓetꞛyn.*

katꞧin, Kattrin, W.L. xxiii. 51, 'Catherine'.

katꞧis, s.f., 'cartridge'.

kaiʃ, s.m., pl. *katʃis,* kaits, W.S. (1) 'cage': *kaiʃ deryn ;—*fig. *r oːð pobol es talum meun kaiʃ—dim arjan, dim doktor na dim byːd* (O.H.), 'in old days people had no option—they had no money, no doctor nor anything'. (2) *katʃis dëvaid,* 'sheep-pens at a fair' (O.H). (3) facetiously for 'stomach': *oːs na ðigon ən də gaiʃ di ?*

kattal, s.pl., kattel, W.S. [Cattell]; catal, T.N. 327. 42, 'cattle' (seldom used = *gwarθag*): *peniɡa kattal*, old place-name at Llanfairfechan, where cattle were shod (O.H.).

ka:θ, s.f., pl. *kaθod*, cath, D., 'cat': *ka:θ vre:χ, ka:θ driḷiu*, 'tabby cat'; *na:u ḇvu ka:θ*, 'a cat has nine lives'; *may r kaθod ən djəuljo ag ən ɡhegi*, 'the cats are spitting and swearing' (cf. *herwa*); *ɡhegi vel ka:θ*, 'to curse like a trooper'; *ka:θ əɲ kodi χrɟ:χ* (= *gwrəχyn*), 'a cat arching her back'; cf. also *meujan, kany i χrəudi, kany i χru:θ*; —*mynd vel ka:θ i gəθral*, 'to go like mad'; *mynd vel ka:θ am levriθ*, 'to go (as eagerly) as a cat after milk'; *prəmny ka:θ meun ku:d (sa:χ)*, 'to buy a pig in a poke'; *kadu kaθod meun ku:d*, 'to let sleeping dogs lie'; *bliɲo r ga:θ d at i χumfon*, 'to spend to the utmost'; 'to fleece'; *χwipjo r ga:θ*, 'to go about tailoring from house to house'; *gweld vel ka:θ*, 'to have sharp eyes'; *ma na riu ga:θ əɲ ɲhuppur paub*, 'every one has a skeleton in his cupboard'; *may n ðigon o:yr i rewi kaθod*, 'it is intensely cold';—*ka:θ*=also a kind of 'boa' worn round the neck by women,—*ka:θ vo:r*, pl. *kaθod ə mo:r*, 'common blue skate' (Raia batis); *ka:θ vo:r stəds*, 'thornback' (Raia clavata); *ka:θ vo:r bigog*, 'starry ray' (Raia radiata). Cf. also *morgaθ*;—*u:y ka:θ vc:r*, 'skate's egg', "mermaid's purse".

kaug, s.m., pl. *kəugja*, cawg, D., 'milk-pail' (obsolete).

kaujo, v., bancawio, D, 'redimire; tenui filo effractum vincire'; W.Ll. (Voc.) gosod bach wrth: *kaujo ba:χ*, 'to fasten a fish-hook to the gut'.

kaun, s.pl., sing. *kəunan*, cawn, D., 'thin, straggling grass': *riu he:n gaun ən tvvy ar di:r sa:l;—t o:ys na ðim ond kaun ən ə ka:y, t ədi o ðim ən werθ i dori.*—Also applied to a kind of mistiness coming over the sun (O.H.). Cf. W.M.M. cwmwle cawn.

kaur, s.m., pl. *kəuri*, cawr, D., 'giant': *kaur o ðy:n*, 'a powerful, courageous man' (morally); *r o:ð o ɲ gaur ḷond i ðiḷad ond ru:an may i ðiḷad ən ḷak arno*, 'he was a big strapping fellow, but now his clothes hang loosely on him'. [For pl. cf. cawri, D., s.v. 'gigantomachia'; Gen. vi. 4; cowri, W.Ll. ix. 68; D.F. [7] 1; D.P.O. 263. 35.]

kaus, s.m., caws, D., 'cheese' (in the aggregate). Cf. *kosyn. bara χaus (kaus)*, 'bread and cheese'; *pe ba:y r wyðva ɲ gaus mi vəða n haus kayl kosyn* (prov.), 'if "ifs" and "an's" were pots and pans there'd be no trade for tinkers'; *kaus əsgau*, 'elder pith'; *kaus ḷfant*, 'toad-stools'.

kavaɲk, s.m., term of reproach: *he:n gavaɲk garu ədi o.*—I have heard this word more than once from O.H., but on closer inquiry he confuses it with *kravaɲk*, and it must therefore be regarded as doubtful. Cf. W.M.M. habanc, 'a monster of a fellow'.

kavn, s.m., pl. *kavna*, cafn, D., 'trough': *kavn moχyn*, 'pig's trough'; *kavn bu:yd*, 'trough for cattle where the food is placed in front of the stall'; *kavn ə pëiljur*, used in bolting flour; *kavn pobɪ*, 'kneading-trough'. Cf. *havn.*

kavndra, s., cafndra, 'a hollow or place hollowed out' (O.H.).

kavnjo, v., cafnio, S.E., 'to hollow out': *kavnjo mëipan*, 'to hollow out a turnip'; *kavnjo pᵣen*, 'to hollow out a log' (e.g. to make a boat); *kavnjo torθ.*

kavod, s.f., pl. *kavodyð*, cawad, cawod, cafod, D. (1) 'shower': *kavod o laːu*, 'a shower of rain'; *mi vasa kavod ən nobl i əstuɳ ə ḷuːχ*, 'a shower would be a splendid thing to lay the dust'; *ᵣhuɳ kavod a χavod*, 'between the showers'. (2) *ə gavod*, 'a chill, generally with cold shivers running through one'; *ə gavod wynt*, 'rash'; *wedi torɪ aḷan r yː vaːθ a gavod wynt ;—kaːl ə gavod i r ḷᵇgaid* (O.H.). Cf. D., s.v. 'carbunculo', 'fulguritassunt', 'robiginosus', 'sideror'.

kavodog, adj., cawodog, D., s.v. 'nimbosus', 'showery'.

kawaḷ, s.m., pl. *ǩewyḷ*, cawell, D. (1) 'a basket used by farmers for carrying small articles on their backs'. (2) 'fisherman's creel'. (3) 'pannier': *baχy ə ǩewyḷ ar gyrn ə strodyr hevo ëᵣru* (J.J.). (4) in the phrases: *mi ǵestɪ gawaḷ*, 'you were disappointed; you drew a blank';—esp. 'to be jilted': *mi ǵeːs i gawaḷ gəni hi* (O.H.); *r oːð kawaḷ gwaːg əno*, 'it was a mare's nest'.

kay, v., cau, D. Fut. S. 2. *ǩëyi*, 3. *ǩëyˑiθ*. Pret. S. 1. *ǩëyis*, 3. *ǩëyoð*. Imperative *kay; ǩëyuχ.* (1) 'to shut': *kay ə druːs, ə fenast, ə ḷyvr ;—os ëi di mi ǵëya i ə druːs ˑarnati*, 'if you go, I'll shut the door upon you'; *kay ə druːs əɳ glᵉp*, 'to bang the door'; *kay dɔ ǵeːg*, 'hold your tongue';—elliptically: *may nu n medry kay arni hi pen ˑlëikjanu*, 'they can keep their lips closed when they like'. (2) 'to enclose': *kay kay hevo kḷauð, hevo poljon ar i penna*, 'to enclose a field with a hedge, with palings'. (3) 'to fill up' (a gap): *kay kḷauð*, 'to mend a hedge'; *tuːyrχ glëif'on i gay ə kᵣiːb*, 'sods to close the apex of a roof' (in a thatched cottage). (4) 'to button up': *kay koːt*, etc. ; 'to lace up' (of boots, etc.): *kay sǵidja.*

kay, adj., cau, D., 'closed, shut, enclosed': *ḷeː kay*, 'an enclosed place',—seldom used = *ḷeː wedi gay.*

kay, v., naccau, D. Pret. S. 1. *kais*, 3. *kaːð*, *kaːs*, 'to refuse': *may r teǩaḷ əɳ kay berwi*, 'the kettle won't boil'; *may r ḷidjart əɳ kay kay*, 'the gate won't shut'; *mi gaːs ag attab*, 'he wouldn't answer'; *mi gaif inna a mynd*, 'I wouldn't go either'; *ðary nu gay*, 'they wouldn't'; *may o ɳ kay bod ḷonyð i mi*, 'he is teasing me'. Cf. *nakka.*

kaːy, s.m., pl. *ǩëya*, cae, D., 'field'. Fig. *r uːti meun kaːy araḷ, wedi mynd i gaːy araḷ*, 'you are entirely off the point'.

kayl, s., caul, D., Eng. chyle, 'rennet'.

ka:yl (often shortened in quick speech to *kayl, ka:l* and *kal*), v., cael,
D. Fut. S. 1. *ka:(v)*, 2. *k̈ei̇*, 3. *k̈ei̇θ, k̈ei̇f*. Pl. 1. *kaun, ka:n,* 2. *k̈euχ,*
3. *ka:n.* Imp. S. 1. *kaun,* 2. *ka:l,* 3. *kai, ka:, ka:y (o).* Pl. 1. *ka:n,*
2. *ka:χ,* 3. *ka:n.* Pret. S. 1. *k̈e:s, k̈ei̇s, k̈evis,* 2. *k̈e:sl, k̈ei̇sl,* 3. *ka:θ,*
kavoδ. Pl. 1. *k̈euson, ku:son, k̈ëyθon, k̈ëyson.* 2. *k̈eusoχ, ku:soχ, k̈ëyθoχ,*
k̈ëysoχ, 3. *k̈euson, ku:son, k̈eyθon, k̈ëyson.* Plup. S. 1. *k̈eusun, ku:son,*
k̈ëyθun, 2. *k̈eusal, ku:sal, k̈ëyθal,* etc. Fut. Pass. *k̈ei̇r.* Pret. Pass. *kaud.*

I. Transitive, with noun or infinitive as object, ' to get, obtain,
have '. 1. in simple sense (1) before nouns (followed generally by
o, oruθ of things, *g̈in* of persons): *ka:yl bu:yd, brekwasl, k̈injo,* ' to
get, have food, breakfast, dinner ' ; *ka:yl annuyd,* ' to catch cold ' ;
ka:yl vannoδ, ' to get toothache ' ; *ka:yl dᴈχryn,* ' to have a fright ' ;
ka:yl kodum, ' to have a fall ' ; *ka:yl kwëir,* ' to get a thrashing ' ;
ka:yl ᴈsgol, ' to get schooling ' ; *ka:yl kanjata:d,* ' to get permission ' ;
ka:yl gaval, kᴈdjad, ' to get hold ' ; *ka:yl madal a,* ' to get rid of ' ;
ka:yl gwa:yθ, ' to get (something) worse ' ; *ka:yl benθig,* ' to get as
a loan ' ; *ka:yl ar lab,* ' to get on credit ' ; *ka:yl möyθa,* ' to be spoilt ' ;
ka:yl trᴄvn ar, ' to keep in hand ' ; *ka:yl k̈ip,* ' to catch a glimpse ',
etc. ; *ar ga:yl,* ' to be got, to be had ' ; *na: i δarlan o peŋ ga: i
amsar,* ' I will read it when I have time ' ; *ta:u ne mi g̈ei di glyslan,*
' hold your tongue or I'll give you a box on the ears ' ; *i o:δ dim
gair i ga:yl gᴈno vo,* ' one could not get a word out of him ' ; *pe
ka:ti dᴈ forδ χaun i δim,* ' if you had your way, I should get
nothing ' ; *pe ka:y o i forδ χaun i δim,* ' if he had his way, I should get
nothing ' ; *morjo bo:b kᴈula ga:y o,* ' to go on the sea whenever
opportunity offered ' ; *pe ka:ni n forδ χa: vo δim,* ' if we had our way,
he would get nothing ' ; *ka:n, pe ka:χi χ forδ,* ' they would, if you
had your way ' ; *mi δëydis i na χa:χi δim k̈injo hëi̇δju,* ' I said you
would not have any dinner to-day ' ; *mi gostiθ r y: vainl i gᴈvrjo
vo a χa:χi y:n newyδ,* ' it will cost as much to cover it (the umbrella)
as if you got a new one ' ; *r·hi: ga:θ δᴈχryn !,* ' she got a
fright !' ; *mi g̈ëyθun lawar o beθa am bedwar su:lḷ,* ' I might have
(should have) got many things for four shillings ' ; *g̈in ᴈ gwirjon
k̈ei̇r ᴈ gwi:r,* ' from the innocent the truth is obtained '. (2) before
infinitives (a) ' to get an opportunity of, obtain the means of ' : *mi
gaun weld etto,* ' we shall see ' ; *mi g̈ëi̇θ o weld pen ëi̇θ o aḷan,* ' he
will see when he goes out ' ; *ᴄhaid i mi dri:o darvod ᴈn o vy:an
i ga:l du:ad hevo χi,* ' I must try and finish pretty soon so as to be
able to come with you ' ; *er mu:yn ka:yl gubod,* ' in order to get to
know ' ; *χe:s i δim ·ond ·mynd,* ' it was all I could do to go ' (and
nothing more). (b) ' to cause, to get . . . to ' : *may n anoδ ka:yl
·yδynu godi,* ' it is difficult to get them to get up ' ; cf. also *ga:yl for
i ga:yl* used in quasi-conjunctive sense ; see *i* xvi. 6. (c) as peri-
phrastic form of the passive : *du i wedi ka:yl ᴈ ᴣheulyd aḷan,* ' I have
been turned out ' ; *by:δ ᴈŋ ka:yl i saθry,* ' it will be trodden upon ' ;
ᴈdi r boks ma am ga:yl i dorᵢ ?, ' is this box to be broken up ? '
2. ' to get ' where permission is implied. In the future and im-

perfect tenses the verb *ka:yl* often represents the Eng. 'I may ', 'I might' (Anglo-Welsh 'I shall', 'I should'). (1) before substantives: *ðary mi ovyn gaun i rëi o r l̩ɔvra ond k̓e:s ə ɳurθod*, 'I asked whether I might have some of the books but I was refused '; *gweld o:ð na ðim gwaiθ gu:sa vo*, 'to see whether there was not some work which he might have '; *o:ys ·gənəχi stamp g̓ëyθun i tan vory?*, 'have you a stamp I might have till to-morrow?'; *ga: i gupanad o de:?*, 'may I have (Anglo-Welsh 'shall I have') a cup of tea?' Ans. *keuχ*, 'yes '. (2) before infinitives: *ga: i roit hun ar ə burð?*, 'may I put this on the table?'; *mi ðo: i os ka: i ðu:ad*, 'I will come if I can ' (i.e. 'if I have permission ');—the infinitive is often understood, e.g. *mi ða:u o os k̓ëïθ o g̓in i da:d*, 'he will come if his father will let him '. 3. 'to find ': *do:s a vo: l̩e k̓ëisti o*, 'take it back where you found it '; *g̓ëisti o:yn ba:χ i vəny?*, 'did you find a lamb up there?'; *kaud o wedi maru*, 'he was found dead '. Cf. II. 4. 'to get, to make' with adjective or adverb in apposition: *ka:yl po:b pe:θ ən wastad*, 'to get everything straight '; *meθy ka:yl ə ðay pen l̩inin at i g̓ilið*, 'to be unable to make both ends meet '. 5. 'to get, to succeed in getting into a certain position ', with a verb of motion implied: *kayl i vy:s meun bru:as paub*, 'to have a finger in every pie '; *syt k̓e:sti də bi:g i veun?*, 'how did you get your nose in?'; *ka:yl i va:yn i r wal*, 'to achieve one's object '.

II. Intransitive: 'to get' (to a place): *ka:yl i le: gwa:yl*, 'to get to an unsatisfactory place '. This appears to be an imitation of English usage, but cf. the common use of *ka:yl* with *hy:d i* to express 'to find ', e.g. *du i wedi ka:yl hy:d i r dru:g*, 'I have found out what is the matter '; *dim ʃauns i χi ga:l hy:d ıðo vo*, 'no chance for you to find him '. In the negative, however, we have: *χe:s i ðim mo r hy:d ıðo vo*, 'I have not found it '.

ka:yr, s.f., pl. *k̓ëyra*, caer, D. Generally used in the plural with the meaning 'fortifications, stronghold '. O.H. applies the term *k̓ëyra* to the prehistoric fortifications on Penmaenmawr;—used of the sunset: *ꝺ hayl ən mynd dan g̓ëyra*, 'the sun setting '; *may hi dgest ən hayl ə g̓ëyra* (O.H.), 'it is just sunset '. Cf. B.C. 5. 12;— *ka:yr droia (druya)*, 'a maze' (J.J.; O.H.). Cf. D.P.O. 24. 18 and Eng. (Dial.) 'Walls-of-Troy', Abd.; *nant ka:yr droia (druya)* was the old name for the house at Llanfairfechan now called Nant Dafydd or Nant Uchaf (O.H.)—As place-name *ka:yr* is 'Chester': *k̓in kodi ku:n ka:yr*, 'very early in the morning '; *ʃi:r ga:yr*, 'Cheshire '; *ka:yr gəbi*, 'Holyhead '.

ka:yθ, adj., caeth, D. (1) 'constrained, in a state of constraint ', e.g. when one is in the company of some one who does not speak a word: *tëimlo i hy:n əɳ ga:yθ*. (2) 'confined ': *l̩e: ka:yθ*. (3) 'uncomfortable ': *daχi n i χlu:at i ɳ ga:yθ əmma heno?* (= *dim əɳ gəsyrys*). (4) 'breathing with difficulty ', applied to the chest: *daχi n tëimlo χ brest əɳ ga:yθ?;—may gəno vo vrest ga:yθ*, 'he has asthma '.

(5) used of one who is an obstruction to himself, stands in his own light : *may o ŋ ga:yθ iðo i hy:n, əm pëidjo gwerθy i beθa əm mŗhi:s ə fair ag əŋ ka:l koḷad wedyn* (O.H.).

Kebyst, s.m., cebystr, D. (1) 'part of a plough holding the different parts together'; 'the sheet or stilt of a plough' (O.P.) : *tru:yn ə Kebyst.* (2) 'cap of a flail' (J.J.). (3) as expletive : *məŋ Kebyst!, məŋ Kebyst wy:ḷṭ!, məŋ Kebyst ylu! ; bc: ğebyst!, beθ ğebyst wy:ḷṭ!,* 'what on earth!'

Kedan, s.f., ceden, D., 'lachne, villus'; in phrase *ən təvy n y:n ğedan,* 'growing close together'.

Kedor, s., cedor, D., 'pubes': *Kedor ər wra:χ = 'kakKi·mukKi,* 'burdock' (Arctium Lappa and kindred species).

Kefyl, s.m., pl. *kəfəla,* ceffyl, D., 'horse': *Kefyl gla:s,* 'grey horse'; *Kefyl gwina,* 'bay horse'; *Kefyl ko:χ,* 'brown horse'; *Kefyl melyn,* 'chestnut horse'; *Kefyl liu ḷa:yθ a χuru = o ðay liu* (J.J.), 'piebald horse'; *Kefyl bakſog,* 'a horse with thick hair round the hoofs'.— Of three horses tandem the foremost is *Kefyl bla:yn,* the middle *Kefyl pen,* and the last *Kefyl bo:n.*—The two horses ploughing are called *Kefyl ən ə gu:ys* and *Kefyl ar ə Kcvn.*—*dal Kefyl, toṟi Kefyl (i veun), toṟi Kefyl i laur,* 'to break in a horse': *Kefyl guy:ḷṭ,* 'a horse which has not been broken in'; *gwc:ð o gəfəla,* 'a pair (team) of horses'; *ar ğcvn Kefyl* (pl. *ar ğevna kəfəla*), 'on horseback'; *may o ar ğcvn i ğefyl,* 'he is very pleased with himself'; *tṟi:n Kefyl,* 'to groom a horse'; *tṟi:n Kefyl pobol eriḷ,* 'to mind other people's business'; *ṟhoi ə drol o vla:yn ə Kefyl,* 'to put the cart before the horse'; *Kefyl da: ədi uḷys,* 'where there's a will there's a way'.

Ke:g, s.f., pl. *Kega,* cêg, D., 'mouth': *agor Ke:g,* 'to gape'; *kay də ğeg,* 'hold your tongue'; *may gəno vo davod lond i ge:g, may o ŋ ğe:g i ği:d,* 'he is very talkative'; *mi ðəljaχ na θoða menyn ən i χe:k i,* 'you would think that butter would not melt in her mouth'; *ṟhøuχ əχ by:s ən i ğeg o i edraχ o:ys gəno vo ðannað,* applied to some one wrongly supposed to be harmless and innocent; *gnëyd Ke:g hyḷ,* 'to pull a face by contorting the mouth'—fig. (1) of one who cannot keep a secret: *ṟ hc:n ğc:g !* (2) 'mouth, entrance of anything': *Ke:g ə bont, ə tuḷ, ə sa:χ,* etc.—*əŋ ŷhe:g ər hayl,* 'right in the sun' = *ən ḷəgad ər hayl.*

Kega, v., cega. (1) 'to come to words' (as the prelude of a quarrel): *pen vy:ð day ðy:n wedi mynd i ğega, tawad ə kaḷa* (O.H.), 'when two men have come to words, let the wiser keep silent'. (2) 'to talk glibly': *Kega am rubaθ.*—Cf. Pe gwelsech chwi'r gwaeddi "Beef Nefyn" (i.e. herrings), Roedd Robyn, a'r hen fules frech, Wrth ochr y castell yn cega "Dowch yma cewch ugain am chwech". C.—'Marchnad Ca'rnarfon'. (3) 'to tell tales, gossip': *paid a mynd i ğega am dana i o r naiḷ dy: i r ḷaḷ* (O.H.); *ə vəruyn ən mynd aðra a χega po:b pe:θ vy:ð ən ə ty:* (O.H.).

Ķegid, s.pl., cegid, D., 'hemlock' (Conium maculatum), called also for the sake of distinction *ķegid ti:r sy:χ; ķegid du:r,* 'water hemlock' (Œnanthe crocata).

Ķegin, s.f., pl. *ķegina,* cegin, D., 'kitchen': *ķegin gevn, ķegin ba:χ* 'back-kitchen'.

Ķegjad, s.f., cegaid, S.E. 'mouthful' (of a liquid): *mi ge:s i dammad o vara a χegjad o ðu:r.*

ķegog, adj., cegog, S.E. (1) 'loquacious, glib-tongued': *ə ţhëi muya ķegog sy n ķodi strëiks* (O.H.). (2) 'apt to tell tales': *dyn ķegog* (O.H.).

ķegor, adj., cegoer, G.O. ii. 145. 22, "cold-mouthed" [*ķelan*].

ķegum, s., cegwm, S.E. (1) 'an empty talker': *hc:n gegum gwirjon.* (2) 'one who cannot keep a secret'.

ķegus, s., cêg and gŵst, 'gaping' (Llanllechid, I.W.).

Ķëi, s.m., 'quay': *Įuyθo Įoɲ ən ə Ķëi.*

Ķëibjo, v., ceibio, D., 'to use a *kaib,* to hoe'.

Ķëiljog, s.m., pl. *ķljogod,* ceiliog, D. (1) 'cock': *kɲi:b, ţagaĮ, sbardyn Ķëiljog,* 'the comb, wattle, spur of a cock'; *kuʃjo kljogod,* 'cock-fight'; *piĮ kljogod,* 'cock-pit'; *Ķëiljog χwiadan,* 'drake'; *Ķëiljog dandi,* 'bantam cock'. (2) transferred uses :— 'the top of the plough-beam' (I.W.); *Ķëiljog gwynt,* 'weather-cock'; *karjo ɲ gokkyn Ķëiljog,* 'to carry (some one) on the shoulders with one leg on each side of the neck' (J.J.; O.H.).

Ķëiljogas, s.f., 'a masterful woman' (I.W.).

Ķëilja, s.pl., ceilliau, D., s.v. 'scrotum'; 'scrotum'.

Ķëinjog. s.f., pl. *Ķëinjoga,* ceiniog, D., 'penny': *may n edraχ ən Įəgad ə gëinjog,* 'he weighs every penny carefully'; *wa:yθ i χi gëinjog ·sbarjuχi na Ķëinjog ·niĮuχi,* 'a penny saved is a penny gained'; *dim y:n gëinjog go:χ,* 'not a single penny' (*Ķëinjog* is frequently omitted after a numeral as *gwerθ du:y,* 'two pennyworth'); *pisin χwe:χ,* 'sixpenny piece'; *su:Įt a θair,* 'one (shilling) and three(pence)'; *χwëigjan,* 'ten shillings';—'fourpence' is always *gro:t.*

Ķëirχ; Ķëiχ (E.J.); *Ķerχ* (J.J.), s.m., ceirch, D., 'oats': *bara Ķëirχ,* 'oat-cake'; *blaud Ķëirχ,* 'oatmeal'; *bru:as Ķëirχ [bru:as].*

Ķëirχan, s.f., ceirchen, S.E., 'a grain of oats': *ən ja:χ vel ə gëirχan.*

Ķëiʃo, v., ceisio, D. Pret. s. 1. *Ķëiʃis,* 3. *Ķëiʃoð.* Imperative *kais, Ķëiʃa; Ķëiʃuχ.* (1) 'to fetch, seek': *kais də vagla a fur a ti i r lan,* O.H. (said facetiously to a man on board ship). (2) 'to try': *mi gëiʃis i gəno vo nëyd,* 'I tried to get him to (do something)'; *mi gëiʃiʃ i ə ɲora gəno vo bëidjo gnëyd dru:g,* 'I tried my best to get him not to do wrong'. (3) 'to mean, to do on purpose': * δarɥ o δim Ķeiſo*, 'he didn't mean to do it', i. e. 'it was by accident'.

Ķeiθiwad, s.m., caethiwed, D., 'captivitas, servitus'; cf. keithiwet, L.A. 121. 27; G.C. 130. 11, 'asthma' = *Ķeyθdra* (*ar ? guɥnt*).

Ķeiθiwis, adj., caethiwus, M.Ll. ii. 37, 29, 'causing constraint or discomfort': *may ɥ ǵeiθiwis i χi* (O.H.).

Ķeiθiwo, v., caethiwo, D., 'to keep in confinement, to keep a strict hand over': *dy:n ?ɥ Ķeiθiwo i wëiθjurs, i wraig, i blant*, i.e. not letting them go out, etc. (O.H.).

Ķekrɥ, Ķekran, v., ceccru, D., 'to wrangle, brawl': *may r δu:ɥ ?mma ?ɥ Ķekran fry:o o hy:d* (O.H.).

Ķekrɥn, s.m., cecryn, B.C. 70. 29, 'a contentious fellow, a brawler': *he:n ǵekrɥn ka:s*.

Ķekrɥs, adj., ceccrus, D., s.v. 'contentiosus', 'controuersus', 'emissarius'; 'contentious'.

Ķe:l, Ķe:lsan, s., 'keel'.

Ķelaiſ, ǵelaiſ, s.pl., gellhesg, D., 'flags' (Iris Pseudacorus). O.H. has *dgelaiſ*. This plant is called *delasg* at Red Wharf Bay, Anglesea; I have also heard *delaks* at Bangor. [Some of these forms suggest some connexion or confusion with 'delysc', W.B. col. 96. 1.]

Ķelan, s.f., celain, D., 'corpse', only in the expressions *Ķelan varu* and *Ķelan ǵegor*: *mi laδoδ o ɥ ǵelan varu*, equivalent to 'he killed him on the spot';—*mi welis i ? Ķi: pen o:δ o n ? bysnas o la:δ devaid ag mi sëiθis o tan o:δ o ɥ ǵelan ǵegor* (O.H.).

Ķelbrɥn, s.m., 'a worthless, good-for-nothing fellow': *r he:n ǵelbrɥn gwirjon I, he:n ǵelbrɥn bydyr !* (O.H.).

Ķelfɥn, s.m., a term of reproach: *he:n ǵelfɥn brunt I, he:n ǵelfɥn gwirjon I* (O.H.).

Ķelk, s.m., celc, D., 'a hidden store of money': *may g?no vo ǵelk ?n rula*;—also *pĝe:s Ķelk*.

Ķelkjo, Ķelkjan, v., cf. celcu, D. (1) 'to keep a secret store of money', e. g. a wife from her husband. (2) 'to embezzle'.

Ķelog, s.f., celog, 'coal-fish' (Gadus virens) = *χwitlin gla:s*.

Ķelpan, s.f., celpan, 'a slap on the face'.

Ķelpjo, v., celpio, 'to slap on the face'.

Ķelpjo, v., 'to gallop' = *kalpjo*.

Ķeluyδ, Ķelwyδ, s.m., pl. *kluyδa*, celwydd, D., 'lie': *dëyd kluyδa*, 'to tell lies'; also *kabatſo, klatſo, linjo kluyδa*;—*paly Ķeluyδ*, 'to concoct a lie'; *Ķeluyδ no:yθ*, 'a bare-faced lie'; *Ķeluyδ ?n d? δannaδ*, 'I give you the lie direct'.

Ķelvi, s.pl., celfi, R., 'tools'; 'odds and ends'.

Ꝁelyn, s.pl., sing. *Ꝁelənan*, f., celyn, D., 'holly-tree'; 'holly': *Ꝁelyn ə moːr*, 'sea-holly' (Eryngium maritimum).

Ꝁel̬, s.f., pl. *Ꝁel̬oð*, cell, D., 'cell' (in a prison).

Ꝁel̬war, v., cellwair, D., 'to scoff', 'to jest' (in a bad sense, e. g. of religious matters): *·ðəlaχi ðim Ꝁel̬war vel na.*

Ꝁel̬werys, adj., cellweirus, D., s.v. 'iocularis'; 'jocular, jesting' (see above).

Ꝁemfro, s.f., 'beach, edge of the sea-shore' (very often used by O.H., and heard also from another inhabitant of Llanfairfechan): *morlo* (seal) *əŋ gorvað ar ə ǵemfro* ;—*ar ə ǵemfro, glan ə moːr* ;— *i ben ə ǵemfro ; r oːð ə ǵemfro, glan ə moːr əŋ goːyd i ǵiːd* (after a wreck) ;—*Ꝁemfro graval a tuːod* ;—*ǵatja n nyŋd i r ǵemfro, glan ə moːr* ;—*gnëyd tyː ar ə ǵemfro.* (All O.H.). Apparently not used at Bangor.

Ꝁen, Ꝁem, s.m., cenn, D. (1) 'film': *magy Ꝁen*, 'to grow a film, to become mouldy'; *may barig əŋ ǵen gwyn ar ə ðëyar*, 'hoar-frost is a white film on the ground'; *ən yːn ǵen gwyrð drosto*, 'a green film all over it' (speaking of a pond); *dil̬ad ən yːn ǵen o vaːu.* (2) 'scales' (of fish). (3) 'lichen': *Ꝁen Ꝁerig.*

Ꝁena, s.m., pl. *knavon*, cenaw & cenau, pl. cenawon & imperitè cenafon, D., 'rascal': *heːn ǵena !; Ꝁena diːog ; Ꝁena glaːs*, 'arrant rascal'; *pëidjuχ kadu riːat, knavon baːχ !*, 'don't make a noise, you young rascals';—also fem.: *knavon ovnaduy ədi mamma əŋ ŋhxːraθ* (O.H.), 'stepmothers are terrible creatures'.

Ꝁenaduri, s.f., cennadwri, D., 'commission, instructions': *du i ŋ gnëyd ən oːl i ǵenaduri*, 'I am acting according to the instructions I received from him'; *dəna r ǵenaduri du i wedi χaːyl*, 'those are the instructions I received'.

Ꝁenedl, s.f., pl. *Ꝁenhedloð*, cenedl, D., 'nation'.

Ꝁenl̬ysg, Ꝁenslys, s.pl., cenllysg, D., 'hail': *buru Ꝁenslys (Ꝁenl̬ysg)*, 'to hail'.

Ꝁennad, cennad, D. (1) s.m.f. 'messenger'. (2) s.f. 'permission': *du i wedi kayl Ꝁennad i vynd* ;—*ǵida χ Ꝁennad*, 'by your leave'.

Ꝁenviǵenl̬yd, adj., cenfigenllyd, S.E., 'envious' (O.H.). Cf. *kənvigan.*

Ꝁeŋal, s.f., pl. *Ꝁeŋla*, cengl, D. (1) 'girth' of a saddle. (2) in pl. 'the girth of a yarn-winder' [*kogurn*]. (3) 'skein': *Ꝁeŋal o ðavað ; dal Ꝁeŋal*, 'to hold a skein while it is being wound'. (4) m. or f. applied to a thin person or animal: *rhiu ǵeŋal main ədi o ; heːn ǵeŋal o ludun* (= *hiːr, main, kyːl*).

Ꝁeŋlog, adj., cenglog, S.E. (1) 'thin, lean, skinny': *dyːn Ꝁeŋlog.* (2) *byuχ ǵeŋlog*, 'a cow with a white band round it', 'belted cow'.

Keŋly̆, v., cenglu, D. (1) 'to girth' (a horse). (2) 'to make wool into skeins'.

Ke:r, s.f., ker, W.S. [Gere], cêr, B.C. 57. 18; cf. D.G. lxiv. 26, ' gear, tools'; *ke:r mëïnar, ke:r go:.* Cf. *ġc:r, keryn.*

Kerad, Kerðad, v., cerdded, D. Imperative *ker ; kerux.* (1) 'to walk (as opposed to riding): *Kerðad ə ðu:y forð*, 'to walk both ways'. (2) 'to walk' (in general): *du i ðim əŋ gubod pa: mor vy:an daxi ŋ Kerðad*, 'I don't know how fast you walk'; *Kerðad uθ i vagla*, ' to walk on crutches'; *plentyn ba:x ðim ən medry Kerðad*, 'a small child unable to walk'; *kerad vesyl day*, 'to walk two and two'. (3) ' to go': *kerux fur*, 'go away' (*kerux* is much commoner than *eux* in this sense); *kerux ən əx bla:yn*, 'go on'; *kerux i no:l glo: i mi*, 'go and fetch me some coal'; *kerux a glo: i vəny r grifa*, 'take some coal upstairs'. (4) of the motion of ships: *ma na ġerðad da: arni hi.* (5) in quasi-transitive sense: *mi ġerðiθ ə ka:y i ġi:d os Këiθ o lonyð*, 'it (*marxwaļt*) will spread all over the field if it is left alone' (O.H.); *Kerðad ə dre:*, 'to pace up and down the town'. (6) used of a creeping sensation: *may rubaθ ən ə ŋherðad i*, ' I shudder', 'something makes me creep';—in reflexive sense: *Kerðad gwa:yd ə ŋhalon*, 'to be filled with awe'.

Kerbyd, s.m., pl. *Kerbəda*, cerbyd, D., 'carriage'.

Kerdod, s.. cardod, D., but cf. pl. cerdodau, s.v. 'eleemosynarius'; cerdodeu, S.G. 167. 25; cerdawd, M.A. 1. 196 a. 24; W.Ll. xlv. 57; cerdod, C.C.M. 29. 5; T.N. 298. 12, 'alms'.

·Ker-dəms, s.pl., 'ragamuffins' (I.W.). The Bangor equivalent is *·karidrəms.*

Kerðedjad, s.m., cerddediad, D., s.v. 'incessus'; 'walk, gait': *may na herk ən i ġerðedjad*, 'he walks with a limp'.

Kerður, s.m., cerddwr, O.P., 'walker': *flatfur o ġerður*, 'one who splashes as he walks'.

Kerjax, s.pl., ceriach, D., s.v. 'gerræ'. (1) 'rubbish': *rhiu he:n ġerjax;—hel də ġerjax o: na !*, said e.g. to a dismissed servant. (2) 'wretches'.

Kerlyn, s.m., cerlyn, B.C. 140. 25, 'a miserly, cross-grained fellow': *r he:n ġerlyn kəbəðlyd.*

Kern, s., pl. *Kerna*, cern, D., 'mala, maxilla'—only in *ble:u ə Kerna*, ' whiskers'.

Kernan, s., 'a blow on the side of the head'.

Kerpyn, s., pl. *karpja*, cirpyn (sic), D., s.v. 'pittacium', cerpyn, R.; G.O. ii. 247. 11. (1) 'rag': *tənny po:b Kerpyn o:b am dano vo*, 'to take off every shred of clothing'. (2) applied to a man of a miserable, sickly appearance: *r he:n ġerpyn tļaud.* Cf. *karpan.*

Kert, s.f., pl. *Kertja*, kert, W.S. [A carte]. (1) 'cart' (rare = *trol*). (2) ? *mi ro: i slap ən 'də ġert* (O.H.).

Kerlar; Kerijur (J.J.), s.m., certiwr, S.E., ' carter '.

Kerlmon, s.m., pl. *Kerlmyn*, ' carter '.

Kervjo, Kevrjo, v., cerfio, D., s.v. ' cælo, sculpo ', Eng. kerve (15–17 cent.), ' to carve ' (e.g. a name on a tree).

Keryδ, s.m., pl. *Kerəδon*. cerydd, D., ' reproof ' : *rhoi Keryδ ar ruːin ; derbyn ə Keryδ a sərθjo ar i vai*, ' to receive the reproof and acknow-ledge one's fault '.

Keryn, s.m., ceryn, D., s.v. ' instrumentum ' ; dim. of *Keːr, ɠeːr*. (1) ' tool, implement '. (2) ' any portion of a horse's harness '. (3) ' shred ' ; in phr. *tənny poːb Keryn oːδ am dano vo*, ' to take off every shred of clothing '. (4) (perhaps from *kaːr*), ' a tough customer ' : *heːn ɠeryn bliːn, heːn ɠeryn druːg*. Cf. G.O. ii. 178. 21 ; T.N. 182. 9.

Keryn, s., ' a kind of wild duck '. Mentioned in the ' Clorianvdd ' for Feb. 22, 1912, among the birds of Anglesey, where it is described as the largest of the wild ducks.—Used at Bangor. Perhaps ' sheldrake '.

Kesal, s.f., pl. *kəsëilja*, cessail, D. (1) ' arm-pit ' : *o dan i ɠesal, ' under his arm* '; *rhaid i r vrayχ wëiθjo o r ɠesal*, ' we must work hard '; *Kesal vorδuyd*, ' hollow of the thigh '. (2) ' a small inlet ' : *Kesal ən mynd i veun o r fanal* (O.H.).

Ketlan, s.f., dim. of *Kettal*; *bara dan ɠetlan* (W.H.) = *bara dan badal*, ' pan bread '.

Kettal, s.f., ' hanging kettle, pot, or pan '—differs from *kroχon* in the sides being straight : *torθ o dan ə ɠettal* (O.H.), ' pan-loaf '; *Kettal breːs*, etc. Cf. *tekKal*.

Kettog, s.f., pl. *Ketoga*, cettog, D., s.v. ' corbis '. (1) ' box ' in *Kettog halan*, ' salt-box '; *kettog luya* (J.J.) ' box for keeping spoons '. (2) ' belly ' : *ɠesti lond də ɠettog ?* (3) = *dyːn boljog* : *heːn ɠettog o heːn δyːn* (O.H.).

Kettyn, s.m., pl. *katja*, cettyn, R. [a piece of something] ; G.O. ii. 237. 32, ' tobacco-pipe ' = *pibal* : *gola, tanjo Kettyn*, ' to light a pipe '; *luyθo, lenwi Kettyn*, ' to fill a pipe '; *pen Kettyn*, ' bowl of a pipe '; *koːys Kettyn*, ' pipe-stem ' : *oːδ ə duːr ən duːad i laur vel köysa katja* (O.H., speaking of heavy rain).

Keθin, adj., cethin, D., ' hard '; ' unyielding ' : *dyːn, Kerig, koːyd Keθin* ; —*ɠelig Keθin*, ' a worthless kind of pear ' (O.H.) ;—*rhewi ŋ ɠeθin, ən oːyr ɠeθin* (O.H.) ;—*gaːll ɠeθin*, ' a steep hill ', i.e. hard to ascend : *may hi ŋ ɠeθin jaun driŋo i vəny hon ;—maː ŋ ɠeθin jaun arna i* ' it is very hard upon me '.

Kevn, s.m., pl. *Kevna*, cefn. D., ' back ' : *r oːδ ə gwynt ən ə ýhevn*, ' the wind was behind me '; *ar ɠevn Kefyl*, ' on horseback ', pl. *ar ɠevna kəfəla ; gorvaδ ar wastad i ɠevn*, ' to lie on one's back '; *ən u:ysg i ǵevn*, 'backwards'; *sərθjo dros i ǵevn*, 'to fall over backwards', e.g. in "catching a crab"; *ʃarad ən ðru:g əŋ ỹhevn ru:in*, 'to speak evil of some one behind his back'; *ka:yl i ǵevn atio vo*, 'to get over it, recover himself'; *ə ǵẽya n du:ad ar əχ k̆evn χi*, 'the winter descending upon you before you are aware of it'.—In various transferred senses: *k̆evn la:u*, 'back of the hand'; *k̆evn iro:yd*, 'instep'; *k̆evn esǵid*, 'uppers', cf. D. s.v. 'semiplotia'; *k̆evn ə ty:*. 'back of the house'; *dru:s ə k̆evn*, 'back door'; *k̆eǵin ǵevn*, 'back kitchen' (= *k̆eǵin ba:χ*); *may ə parad əŋ ǵevn iðo vo*, 'the wall forms a back for it', e.g. a book-case; *rhoi rubaθ ar i ǵevn*, 'to put something on its back'; (of slates) 'to put them on their sides = *ar i hoχra*; *k̆evn o di:r = drym*, a 'ridge'; also *k̆evn ə ti:r ;—ar ə k̆evn ti:r ;*—hence in farming, a "land", i.e. 'one of the strips into which a ploughed field is divided by water-furrows (*r̆həχa*)'—also the first furrow turned in ploughing: *agor k̆evn*, 'to open the furrow';—*kanol k̆evn = drym*, 'the top or centre of the "land"' (cf. D. s.v. 'lira');—in slate quarries, *k̆evn* = 'a joint', i.e. 'a kind of more or less vertical crack or fissure intersecting the rock' (cf. *iro:yd*);—*ǵevn no:s, ǵevn trəmbað no:s*, 'in the middle of the night': *mi godoð o ǵevn no:s ;—ǵevn dy:ð gola, ǵevn kanol dy:ð gola*, 'in the middle of the day';—*k̆evn* is also used in the sense of 'protection', cf. *·di:ǵevn*, 'defenceless'.—also 'surety': *mi a:θ əŋ ǵevn iðo vo*.

k̆evnan, s.f., cefnen, D., s.v. 'dorsum'; 'brow of a hill, ridge' (= *drym*).

k̆evndar, s.m., pl. *k̆evndryd*, cefnderw, D., 'first cousin': *may o ŋ ǵevndar a mi:*, 'he is my first cousin'; *k̆evndar a χniθar o:ð ə ŋhaid a nain*, 'my grandfather and grandmother were first cousins'.

k̆evndras, s., 'the chain which passes over the cart-saddle of a horse, backband'.

k̆evngor, s.m., cefngor, 'the head of the stall in a cow-house' (cf. *ko:r*, Llanuwchllyn = *bẽydy*): *rhoid bu:yd i r gwarθag dros ə ǵevngor i r fotrum* (O.H.).

k̆evnog, adj., cefnog, D., s.v. 'animosus'; 'well off': *dy:n k̆evnog*, 'a man in easy circumstances'. Cf. G.O ii. 19. 12.

k̆evny, v., cefnu, D., 'vincere, superare'. (1) 'to get over' (i.e. so as to have at one's back, behind one): *du i wedi χevny hi n o søund*, 'I have got over it pretty well'. (2) 'to turn one's back': *k̆evny ar ru:in*.

k̆evrjo [*k̆ervjo*].

k̆ẽyad, s.m., caead, D., 'lid' (of a kettle, can, etc.): *mi ro: i ǵẽyad ar i bisar o*, 'I will make him hold his tongue'.—Also 'the tail board of a cart'.

k̆ẽyad, adj., caead, cauad, D. (1) 'closed': *i χe:k i n dyn əŋ g̯ëyad*, 'her mouth tightly closed'. (2) 'fenced': *ədi r van əŋ g̯ëyedig ? ədi, may hi ·əŋ ·g̯ëyad, vy:ð na ðim ḷawar o waið i ti.*

k̯eyedig, adj., cauedic, Cant. iv. 12, 'closed'; 'fenced'. See above.

k̯ëylan, s.f., pl. *k̯ëylanna*, ceulan, D., 'fibra, ripa'; 'bank of a river': *may r avon wedi ḷizo dros i χëylanna*, 'the river has over-flowed its banks';—*ḷuyḅyr ar hv:d ə g̯ëylan i vəny ;—gwyni ən χuθy dros ə g̯ëylan ;—ar ə g̯ëylan əmmyl*, 'on the very edge'.

k̯ëylo, v., ceulo, D., 'to curdle'.

k̯ëylys, s.pl. Cf. ceilỵs M.F.; Eng. (Dial.) kails; 'ninepins': χwara k̯ëylys.

k̯ëynan, s.f., caenen, D., 'a thin layer': *k̯ëynan o ëira.* Also used of a poor crop: *ədi r haið wedi g̯ino n ða: ? na:g ədi, wi:r. riu g̯ëynan go dena ədi o* (O.H.).

k̯ëyθára, s.m., caethdra, S.E. (1) 'confinement' (cf. *k̯ëiθiwo*). (2) 'asthma' (W.H.; O.H.) = *k̯ëiθiwad (ar ə gwyni).*

k̯i:, s.m., pl. *ku:n*, ci, D., 'dog': *k̯i: devaid*, 'sheep-dog'; *k̯i: ·hela*, 'hound'; *k̯i: gwa:yd*, 'bloodhound'; *kun ·ba:χ*, 'puppies'; ·*ga:si a χun*, 'bitch and puppies'; *k̯i: a i gumfon ən i avl, k̯i: swai*, 'a dog with his tail between his legs'; *edraχ vel k̯i: wedi tori gumfon*, 'to look cowed'; *kadu k̯i: a χɀvarθ və hynan*, 'to keep a servant and do my own work'; *k̯i: hc:n ədi k̯i: morgan* (prov.), 'old birds cannot be caught with chaff'; *boljad k̯i: beriθ dridja* (prov.), 'a dog's fill lasts three days'; *ə k̯i: g̯erðo (g̯erðiθ) g̯ëiθ* (prov.), 'he who goes far will prosper'; *gormod o budin dagiθ g̯i:* (prov.), 'one can have too much of a good thing'; *byu vel ku:n a mo:χ*, 'to lead a cat and dog life'; *dəðja r ku:n*, 'dog-days', cf. D., s.v. 'etesiae'; —*k̯i: mo:r*, 'dog-fish' (Scyllium canicula); *k̯i: drəkk̯in*, 'a partial rainbow' = *riu aruiðjon o la:u ən ər awyr* (J.J.). Cf. Peacock, 'The Glossary of the Hundred of Lonsdale': "Dog, 'a partial rainbow'."

k̯i:að, adj., ciaidd, D., s.v. 'cynicus'; D.P.O. 77. 12; 80. 5; 99. 2, 'cruel, brutal'.

k̯iba, s.pl., cibau, D., 'husks': *syi g̯erχ ·gu:soχi ? dru:g jaun, may o n ḷaun o g̯iba* (J.J.). [Not known to O.H. except as scriptural word. Cf. St. Luke xv. 16.]

k̯iðdaḷ, adj., cibddall, B.C. 58. 14, 'dull of comprehension' (W.H.; O.H.).

k̯ibin, s.m., pl. *k̯ibənna*, cibyn, D., s.v. 'testa'; 'a round wooden vessel with two handles, used especially for measuring corn'. Also the amount contained in a *k̯ibin* = 30½ lbs. (of corn); *pedwar χwari (maur)* = *y:n k̯ibin ; pedwar k̯ibin* = *y:n storad [kəbənnad] ;—may i benno vel k̯ibin,—wedi χwyðo vel k̯ibin*, said of a swollen face (W.H.).

kibog, adj., cibog, D., s.v. 'silus'; 'frowning, disagreeable-looking'.

kidil̯, s.f., cidyll, cidyll coch, D., 'tinnunculus';—*kidil̯ goːχ*, 'a kind of hawk' (O.H.), 'kestrel', Forrest (Falco tinnunculus), cf. *ǵenl̯i goːχ*. Only in current use in the expression *wedi gwil̯tjo ŋ ǵidil̯* (O.H.).

kiðjo, kiðjad, v., cuddio, D.; cf. ciddio C.C.M. 167. 14. Imperf. *kiðjun*. Pret. S. 1. *kiðis*, 3. *kiðjoð*, 'to hide'.

kiːg, s.m., cig, D. (1) 'meat': *kiːg moːχ*, 'bacon' = *bakkun*, *bekn*; *kiːg kiu*, 'chicken'; *baːχ kiːg*, 'meat-hook'. (2) in certain locutions, 'flesh': *kiːg a gwaːyd*, 'flesh and blood'; *kiːg maru*, 'proud flesh'; *kiːg noːyθ*, 'raw flesh', i.e. with the outer skin rubbed off: *əŋ kerðad nes oːyð o ŋ ǵiːg noːyθ*.

kiǵëiðdra, s., cieieddtra (sic), W.S. [Doggedness]; cieidd-dra, S.E., 'an act of cruelty': *wedi gnëyd kiǵëiðdra ən i wirjondab (i wil̯tinab)*, i.e. in a moment of passion (O.H.).

kiǵëyðlyd, kigəðlyd, adj., 'cruel, harsh, savage'; *may hi n ɽhyː ǵiǵëyðlyd o lawar hevo r plant na ; heːn ǵena kiǵëyðlyd bruni !*—(O.H.).

kiglid, adj., ciglyd, D.G. xix. 10, 'cruel, harsh, savage': *ɽ heːn ǵena kiglid !* (O.H.)

kignoθ, adj., cignoeth, T.N. 237. 14. (1) 'raw' of flesh with the outer skin rubbed off: *əŋ kerðad nes oːyð o ŋ ǵignoθ (= ǵiːg noːyθ)*. (2) 'of biting speech', said of one who does not mince matters: *ʃadur kignoθ*.

kigog, adj., cigog, D., 'fleshy'.

kigvran, s.f., pl. *kigvranod*, cigfran, D., 'raven' (Corvus corax): *mi aːθ i ëiðo ɽhuŋ ə ǵigvran a r kuːn*, 'his property went to the dogs', e. g. through a disputed will (J.J.).

kigwan, s., cigwen and cigwain, D., 'a sort of fork, like a toasting-fork, used for lifting puddings boiled in cloths out of saucepans, or for turning meat in a saucepan ; flesh-hook'.

kik, s.f., pl. *kikja*, 'kick'.

kikjo, v., cicio, T.N. 13. 24, 'to kick': *kikjo peːl droːyd*, 'football'.

kiks, s., in playing marbles, 'another go': *bara kiks*, 'another go is forbidden' (I.W.).

kixja, s.pl., cuchiau, pl. of cuwch, D., 'sulky looks': *drəχuχ ar i ǵixja vo !*, 'look at his sulky looks'; *gul̯un i ǵixja*, 'to let one's face fall'; *daŋos i ǵixja n erbyn peːθ*, 'to show one's displeasure at something'.

kixjo, v., cuchio, D.; cf. cichio, C.C.M. 194. 21, 'to frown': *pëidjuχ a kixjo χ ëilja arna i*, 'don't frown at me'.

kiχjog, adj., cuchiog, D., 'frowning, sulky': *may o n edraχ əŋ ǵiχjog jaun.*

Ki:l, s.m., cîl, D. (1) 'corner, recess, narrow opening': *Ki:l ə ləgad*, 'corner of the eye'; *dgo:y o vakko əŋ ǵhi:l i vo:χ*, 'a plug of tobacco in his cheek'; *Ki:l ə pentan*, 'the corner of the hearth'; *djaul Ki:l pentan ag aŋal pen forð [djaul]* ; *Ki:l ə durn*, 'half-closed hollow of the hand'; *ɼhoi Ki:l durn*, 'to bribe' (= *hiro*) ; *degum Ki:l durn*, 'the pay of a preacher'; *Ki:l durn =* also 'one who receives bribes'; *gaduχ ə dru:s əŋ ǵi:l gorad*, 'leave the door ajar' ; *agor Ki:l dru:s*, 'to open a door slightly'; *edraχ tɼu:y ǵi:l ə dru:s.* 'to peep through a door when ajar'. (2) 'a receding, retiring' (of the sun and moon): *may n ḻe: Ki:l hayl*, 'the place does not get the sun, is sheltered from the sun'; *o:s na ǵi:l hayl. ən nant ə velin ? o:ys, am bedwar mi:s*, 'is Nant y Felin without sun any part of the year?' 'Yes, for four months'; *Ki:l ə ḻëyad*, 'the waning of the moon': *o:ys na ḻëyad ? o:ys, riu ǵi:l ḻëyad.* (3) in phr. *knoi Ki:l*, 'to chew the cud'.

Kilbost, s., cilbost, S.E., 'the post⁻on which a gate hangs'. Also *Kilbost ə dru:s.*

Kildənny, v., kildynnu, W.S. [Draw a syde], 'not to pull together' (in fig. sense), said e. g. of two persons in partnership or of a man and wife.

Kildənnys, adj., 'refractory' (W.H.; O.H.).

Kilðant, s., pl. *Kilðannað, Ki:l ðannað*, cilddant, D., 'back tooth, molar': *gweld i ǵi:l ðannað, gweld Ki:l i ðannað*, 'to see the ugly side of him'.

Kiljo, v., cilio, D. (1) 'to retreat, retire'. (2) 'to take one's departure': *ma na lawar o dai gwëigjon əmma ; may r bobol wedi Kiljo.* (3) 'to go down', e. g. of a swelling. (4) 'to stand back, make room': *kilja* (= *kloſ'a*) is said to a horse or cow to make it stand close to the wall in a stable or cow-house (O.H.);—trans. 'to draw back, to take out of the way': *Kilja də dra:yd*, 'take your feet out of the way'; *Kilja də dra:yd o:ð ar ə mɼhəmmis i, ɼ he:n sort !* (O.H.), 'clear out of my premises, you old vagabond!'

Kilkin, s.m., cilcyn, D., s.v. 'ramentum'; 'a small piece left': *Kilkin torθ, ta:s (wair), Kilkin o vara ;—may hi wedi darvod, t o:ys na ðim ond Kilkin ba:χ o honi hi ;—may r kosyn wedi mynd əŋ ǵilkin.* Also 'a small piece cut off a corner': *tor ǵilkin o r garag vel hyn, mi vy:ð ən haus i θori*, 'cut a corner off the stone like this, it will be easier to cut it' = *ḻa:ð sglodyn, tori riu goŋol* (O.H.).

Kilvaχ, s.f., pl. *Kilvaχa*, cilfach, D., 'a sheltered place behind a knoll or rock; nook' = *ḻe: ba:χ koŋlog.*

Kimmint, Kimmin, s., adj., and adv., cymmaint and cymmain, D., cf. cimain, I.G. 540. 15; cimmaint, M.Ll. ii, 11. 25; cimin,

C.C.M. 130. 10; 'as much, as great, as many': *ǩimmin(t) ðuɣwaθ, dair gwaiθ, bedar gwaiθ,* 'twice, three times, four times as much, as many, as great'; *ǩimmin(t) araḷ, hannar ǩimmint araḷ,* 'as much again, etc.; half as much again, etc.'; *riu ǵimmint o arjan,* 'a certain amount of money'; *pëidjuχ a ṟhoid ǩimmint o vuːyd iðo vo,* 'do not give him so much food'; *oːn i wedi kaːl ǩimmint o hono vo ag oːð ənta wedi gaːl,* 'I had had as much of it as he had'; *ǩimmint vedar dyːn gəmmyd o wair,* 'as much hay as a man can take'; *syt na ·vasaχi n dëyd rubaθ ən ə kwarvod a χiθa ŋ gubod ǩimmint am ə peːθ ?,* 'how was it you did not say something at the meeting when you know so much about the matter?'; *dəna ǵimmint a syː,* 'that's all there is'; *t ədi o ðim ǩimmint a r ḷaḷ,* 'it is not so big as the other'; *ǵimmint vedra vo,* 'to his utmost'; *byːð ǵimmint a hənny n sgavnaχ,* 'it will be so much the lighter'.

ǩimmuχ, s.m., pl. *ǩimɔχod,* cimmwch, D., 'lobster': *ǵimmuχ gammuχ,* 'zigzag'; also *ǩimmaχ gammaχ.*

ǩin, adv., cyn, 'so, as', followed by the equative: *ǩin valχad a tasun i wedi kaːyl byuχ a ḷoː,* 'as glad as if I had got a cow with a calf'; *ǩin ðyːad a r vraːn ; ǩiŋ gəntad a r gwynt ; ǩin varwad a sglodyn,* etc., etc.; *ǩiŋ gəstal (gəstlad),* 'as good'; *hannar ǩiŋ grəvad a hiː,* 'half as strong as she'. Cf. *mor.*

ǩin, cyn, D.; cf. cin, C.C.M. 66. 5; 'before'. (1) prep.: *ǩin ə bora,* 'before the morning'; *ǩim pɛn r usnos,* 'in less than a week'; *daχi ifⁱo ǩinjo ǩin yːn ?,* 'do you want dinner before one?'; *mi ðaːu hi n oːl ǩin hənny,* 'she will come back before that';— prep. = conj.: *ǩin i mi gəχuyn,* 'before I start'; *ǩin iði duḷy,* 'before it gets dark'; *ǩin ə vo (= iðo vo) öiri,* 'before it gets cold'. (2) conj. *mi vyːð dolig ən ṟ haː ǩin ǩëi di o,* 'you will not get it till the Greek calends'; *ǩin r aː i,* 'before I go'; *ǩin daːu o,* 'before he comes'; *ǩin doifⁱ i əmma,* 'before I came here'.

ǩinhinin, s., cf. cynhinin, M.F.; D. has cinyn, 'segmentum', cinynio, 'concerpere, segmentare'; (pl.) cinhynion, G.O. ii. 156. 20. (1) 'something narrow': *riu ǵinhinin o bappyr i ola ǩetlyn.* (2) *hen beːθ main, saːl, dim gwerθ ;—* also a term of reproach: *taːu ṟ heːn ǵinhinin !* (All O.H.)

ǩinjo, s.m., pl. *ǩinjawa,* ciniaw, D., 'dinner'.

ǩinnis, s.pl., cennin, D.: *ǩinnis pedar* (O.H.), 'daffodils' (Narcissus Pseudo-narcissus); also called *dginnis pedar.* As the equivalent of 'leeks' the word is unknown here.

ǩiŋ, s.f., Eng. king, 'heads' (in tossing coins): *p ṟ yn ta duːy ǵiŋ ta duːy brits ?* (O.H.)

ǩiŋgron (J.J.), *ǵiŋgron* (LW.; O.H.), *ǵiŋrom* (W.H.), s., y Gin-groen fechan, D., 'stinkhorn' (Phallus impudicus): *drewi vel ǵiŋgron,* etc.

ǩip, s.m., cip, D., s.v. 'raptio'; 'glimpse': *ǵeːs i ǵip arno vo,*

' I caught a glimpse of him '; *ar ǵip,* 'at a glance': *ar ǝ ƙip kǝnía,* ' at the first glance'.

ƙipjo, v., cipio, D. (1) 'to snatch': *ƙipjo ar vry:s ; ƙipjo hel, fon,* etc. (2) 'to catch'. (3) 'to pick up' (words), e. g. of children : *ƙipjo ǵëirja i vǝny.* (4) 'to be slightly burnt, to be "caught"': *may r dorθ wedi ƙipjo.*

·*ƙip·olug,* s., cipolwg, S.E., 'glimpse': *mi ǵe:s i ·ǵip·olug arno vo,* ' I caught a glimpse of him'.

ƙippar, s.m., pl. *ƙippars ; ƙiperjad,* O.H., kiper, C.C.M. 97. 14, ' keeper', esp. a game or river keeper.

ƙirjad, s.m., pl. *ƙirjada,* curiad, D., s.v. 'palpitatio'; 'a beat' (of the heart, or in music).

ƙirjo, v., curio, D., s.v. 'emacio'; 'to pine, waste away'.

ƙis, call to pigs [*ǵis*].

ƙi:s, s., cîs, D., 'a blow': only in χwara *ƙi:s,* 'to play touch'.

ƙi:st, s.f., pl. *ƙistja,* cîst, D., 'chest': *ƙi:st blaud ƙëirχ,* 'bin for oatmeal'; *ƙi:st ve:ð,* 'tombstone in the shape of a shallow, oblong box'.

ƙiu, s.m., pl. *ƙǝujon,* cyw, D., ciw, C.M.M. 45. 14. (1) 'chicken', also *ƙiu ja:r :—may o n vray vel ƙi:g ƙiu,* ' it is as tender as chicken'; *kɔvri ǝ ƙǝujon ƙin ·yðynu ðy:or,* 'to count the chickens before they are hatched'. (2) 'the young of any animal': *ƙǝujon ḷuynog, gwniɲan, sammon ;—may o n disgul ƙiu ba:χ o r gasag na,* 'he is expecting a foal from that mare';—*ƙiu (kasag)* is the term applied to a foal until it is weaned. (Cf. *ebol*);—*ƙiu ·malifut [·malifuʔ]— ǝ ɲhiu annuyl i !* endearing term used to a baby;—*ƙǝujon gwyða,* ' catkins'.

ƙiuar, s., Eng. cure. (1) 'cure, remedy'. (2) 'means': *dǝna r inig ǵiuar i dal nu.*

·*ƙiu·pi:,* s., i. e. Q.P., 'a lock of hair brushed back from the forehead and standing up'.

ƙiurad, s.m., *ƙiuradjad* (W.H.); *ƙiuratjaid* (O.H.), kurat, W.S.; curad, D., s.v. 'curio', 'curate'.

ƙiurjo, v., 'to cure'.

ƙiwad, s.f., ciwed, D. (1) 'brood, troop, set'—always in derogative sense : *he:n ǵiwad ovnaduy ·ǝdynu ;—kaduχ ɲ gli:r oruθ ǝ ǵiwad ovnaduy na.*—This word is often treated as a plural, e. g. *ƙiwad bydron.* (2) ? *ma: nu n ṃhöini vel ǝ ǵiwad, ma: nu vel ǝ ǵiwad* (O.H.).

ƙḷaðy, v., claddu, D. (1) 'to bury' (in all senses). (2) 'to devour': *ƙḷaðy i vu:yd,* 'to eat heartily'. (3) 'to spawn' (of fish). (4) also intr. e. g. of seeds becoming covered with earth: *ma nu ɲ ƙḷaðy n weḷ ar dǝwyð sy:χ.*

k̦laguyð, s.m., pl. *k̦lagwïbi*, ceiliagŵydd, D., s.v. 'anser' : *seví θ o ði·n· mu·y na du·r ar ben k̦laguð*, cf. 'like water off a duck's back'.

k̦lai, s.m., clai, D.G. cxciv. 19 ; Gen. xi. 3 ; D., 'clay'.

k̦lais, s.m., pl. *k̦lëïʃa*, clais, D., 'bruise' : *dan i glëïʃa*, 'bruised, black and blue'.

k̦lamma, s.m., calan Mai ; calanmei, W.B. col. 31. 2, 'May 13' (hiring-time for farm servants).

k̦lamp, s.m., clamp, D., 'massa'. (1) 'lump' : *k̦lamp o do·ys*, 'a lump of dough'. (2) 'anything big' : *may o ŋ glamp o ðy·n maur*, 'he is a great big man' ; *mi roiʃ i glamp o glystan iðo vo*, 'I gave him a great box on the ears'.

k̦lampan, s.f. = *k̦lamp* :—*k̦lampan o ga·θ vaur*.

k̦landro, *k̦londro*, *k̦randro*, v., clandro, S.E. ; Eng. calendar. (1) 'to count' (money). (2) 'to calculate, reckon up' : *k̦landrux o ən əx meðul*.

k̦laŋ́ḗya, s.m., calan gaeaf ; cf. D.G. cxcii. 8, ' the winter calends ', i.e. November 13 (hiring-time for farm servants) ; *no·s k̦laŋ́ḗya*, the eve of that day ; *no·s ər he·n glanǵëya*, ' All-hallows Eve '.

k̦lap, s.m., pl. *k̦lapja*, clap, S.E.*, 'lump' : *k̦lap o lo·*, 'a lump of coal' (= *knap*) ; *tra·yd k̦lapja*, ' club-feet '. Cf. *knap*.

k̦lap, s.m., cf. clappian, R. [to tattle, to tell tales], 'a sneak' ;— *karjo k̦laps*, 'to carry tales'. Cf. Eng. (Dial.) claps, ' tales, gossip '.

k̦lapjan, v. [*knapjan*].

k̦lapjog, adj., clapiog, S.E., 'lumpy'.

k̦lark, s.m., pl. *k̦larkod*, clarc, B.C. 74. 15 ; pl. clarcod, 62. 19, ' clerk '.

k̦larkjc, v., ' to act as clerk '.

k̦latʃ, adj., cf. Eng. (Dial.) clatch [any piece of mechanical work done in a careless way ; a clumsy article], Sc., in the exp. *bara k̦latʃ*, ' badly risen, sad, doughy, unwholesome bread '.

k̦latʃ, s., ? Eng. (Dial.) clash [the sound made by a heavy clanking or a crushing blow, etc.], Sc., Nhb., Yks., *gun k̦latʃ*, ' pop-gun ' ; *wedi tori ŋ glatʃ*, ' broken clean in two '. (Cf. *k̦raiʃ*.)

k̦latʃ [*k̦raiʃ*].

k̦latʃo, v., Eng. (Dial.) clatch [to tell tales of a person], Chs., 'to tell lies' : *k̦latʃo* (= *kabatʃo*) *k̦luyða*.

k̦latʃur, s.m., ' liar ' : *he·n glatʃur ədi o*.

k̦laud, adj., tlawd, D., ' poor ' (rarely used = *țlaud*).

k̦lauð, s.m., pl. *k̦loðja*, clawdd, D. (1) properly ' a mound made by piling up the earth dug out of two parallel trenches, and placed between them'—the earth thus piled up forming the base of a hedge : *may kḷauð o dan ə gwryːχ.* (2) ' a boundary to a field or enclosure, or to a road, whether it be a wall or a hedge ' : *kḷauð drain*, 'a hedge' as distinguished from a wall ; *foːs ə kḷauð*, ' ditch by the side of a hedge '; *kḷauð tervyn*, ' boundary wall'; *toṛi pen kḷauð*, ' to trim the top of a hedge'; *toṛi gwymmad kḷauð*, 'to trim the side of a hedge '; cf. also *sgutʃo, tokjo ;—kay kḷauð*, 'to mend a hedge '; *pḷəgy kḷauð*, 'to bend a hedge '; *toṛi kḷauð a i stufjo*, 'to cut a hedge and fill the gaps with thorns '; *r oːð o n mynd o glauð i glauð*, ' he was staggering along from one side to another ', e. g. of a drunken man.

kḷaːv, adj., pl. *kḷëivjon*, claf, D., ' sick, ill ' : *kḷub kḷëivjon*, ' sick club ' (except in this expression rarely used) = *saːl, gwaːyl.*

kḷavr, s., clafr, D., ' scab' (in sheep) ;—also applied to persons : *may meðdod wedi nëyd o ŋ glavr i ǵiːd.*

kḷebar, s., clebar, T.N. 444. 7, ' chatter, idle conversation ' : *dëyd kḷebar.*

kḷebar, v., ' to jabber, chatter ' : *paid a χlebar ən wirjon.*

kḷebran, s.m., clebran, S.E. (1) ' chatter, idle conversation '. (2) ' tell-tale ' : *hɛːn glebran ədi o.*

kḷebsyn, corr. of *kḷesbyn.*

kḷedar, s.f., pl. *kḷedra*, cledr, D., ' palm of the hand '.

kḷedi, s.m., caledi, Prov. i. 27 ; cledi, B.C. 73. 1, ' hardship, affliction ' : *meun riu gledi maur.*

kḷeduχ, s., caledwch, D., s.v. ' duritas ' ; ' hardness ' (in all senses) : *kḷeduχ myːl*, ' stupidity '.

kḷedy, v., caledu, D. ; cledu, M.Ll. i. 170. 21. (1) Trans. ' to make hard, firm ' : *kḷedy o dan ə reːls ar ə cɔmman*, ' to harden the ground beneath the rails on the refuse heap .˙ a slate-quarry '; *kḷedy o gumpas poːst, ǵaːt*, etc. (2) Intr. ' to harden ' : *nuɔ;. ːuenyn wedi kḷedy* (= *feṛy*).—Also applied e.g. to the settling down of hay in a hay-stack = *gustun* ;—with *ən*, ' to set to in earnest ' : *mynd ən ara deːg ə durnod kɔnta ag əŋ kḷedy əni hi ər ail dyːð* (O.H. in speaking of setting out to walk for a long distance).

kḷeða, s.m., pl. *kḷəðva*, cleddyf, D. ; cleddau, Rev. i. 16, ' sword ' : *ma na i ovn o vel guːr a χleða*, ' I am terribly frightened of him ' (i.e. as of a man with a sword); *i oːs na i ovn na dyːn na χleða* (O.H.); *kḷeða bleðyn*, cleddyf Bleddyn, D., s.v. ' splen '; ' spleen '.

kḷegar, v., clegr, D., s.v. ' glacito '; clegar, T.N. 322. 2. (1) ' to quack ' (of ducks). (2) ' to talk loudly, shout ' : *day ðyːn əŋ kḷegar hevo i ǵilið ; dyːn əŋ kḷegar penwaig.*

kḷëidir, s.m., clei-dir, 1 Kings vii. 46, ' clayey land '.

kḷëimjo, v., kleimio, W.S.; cleimio, B.C. 46. 23; cf. L.G.C., 265. 7, 'to claim': *mi kḷëimja i o.*

kḷëinſo, v., kleinsio pen hoel, W.S. [Clenche], 'to clinch': *kḷëinſo höylan—y:n ən dal murθul ar i ſen hi a r laị ən i χḷëinſo hi.*

kḷëiog, adj., cleiog, S.E., 'clayey'.

kḷëirjaχ, s.m., cleiriach, D., 'an old decrepid person' (LW.)

kḷëiſo, v., cleisio, D., 'to bruise': *mạy r knaud wedi glëiſo ; may r avol wedi glëiſo.*

kḷëivis, s. Eng. (Dial.) clivvis, clevis; see also N.E.D., s.v. 'clevis', 'a piece of iron used for fastening a truck to a rope when going up or down the incline of a quarry'. Cf. *koịral.*

kḷek, s.f., clecc, D.; Eng. (Dial.) clack, 'snap': *ṛhoi kḷek ar ə maud*, 'to snap my fingers'; *a χḷek ar ə maud a fur a vi:*, 'off I went, snapping my fingers';—*may r plant ən tənny bəsaδ koχjon ag əŋ gnëyd kḷek hevo nu ;—toṛi karag əŋ glek*, 'to break a stone with a snap'; *darvod əŋ glek*, 'to finish all of a sudden'. Cf. *kḷep.*

kḷekjan, v., cleccian, D.G. clviii. 48; B.C. 94. 20; Eng. (Dial.) clack; M.E. clacken, 'to rattle, clatter, etc.': *may r ſenasị əŋ kḷekjan*, 'the window is rattling'; 'to crackle' (of a fire); 'to crack' (of a whip); 'to clatter' (of stones); 'to chatter' (of teeth);—*pṛen əŋ kḷekjan uθ i doṛi ;—δary o ſarad nes o:δ ə kubul əŋ kḷekjan*, 'he spoke till the whole place rang';—of things which crunch beneath the teeth, e. g. something burnt : *kḷekjan dan δannaδ ; —kḷekjan i vaud*, 'to snap the fingers'.—Cf. *kḷepjan.*

kḷeχor, s.m., cf. clechor, M.F. = *dy:n siȥvnig, peŋgalad, ḷaun o stimja druːg* (J.J.); *dy:n fǝrnig, k̃in vrəntad a vedar o voːd* (O.H.).— *ṛ heːn gleχor gwirjon !* (O.H.)

kḷem, s.f., pl. *kḷemja*, clem, R. [a slice, a piece], 'a patch on the sole of a shoe'.

kḷem, s.f., Eng. (Dial.) clam, clem [a slow starvation], 'state of starvation, destitution': *may hi wedi mynd əŋ glem arno vo*, 'things are in a bad state with him'; *may o wedi gnëyd i hy:n əŋ glem*, said of one who has done for himself, e. g. by being turned off from his work through his own fault—(O.H.); *may o m byu ar leịty r glem*, 'he lives from hand to mouth' (W.H.).

kḷemjo, v., clemio, C.F. 1890, 332. 33, 'to patch the soles of boots'.

kḷemjo, v., clemio, C.F. 1889, 677. 22; Eng. (Dial.) clem [to starve for want of food], 'to starve, to be destitute'; *dy:n əŋ kḷemjo i hy:n (a digon o breːs gəno vo)* O.H. ;—*dy:n wedi ka:l i glemjo am i waiθ i hy:n*, 'a man who has brought himself to destitution through his own fault' (O.H.).

klemman, s., 'a large piece' (I.W.); *klemman o vreχtan* (= *tavaḷ, kḷɷutan, kluf*).

klemp, s.m., Eng. clamp, 'a piece of iron placed under the toe of a shoe'.

klempan, s., 'a blow with the back of the hand' (O.H.).

kleːn, adj., sup. *klenja*, clên, T.N. 183. 5; Eng. clean; 'pleasant, nice, agreeable': *dyːn kleːn*, 'a nice fellow'; *dyːn kleːn jaun i ſarad*, 'a pleasant-spoken man'.

klennig, s.m., calennig, C.C.M, 52. 17; cylenig, I.G. 541. 4; celennig, D., s.v. 'strena'; 'a New Year's gift'.

kleŋk, s.; ? Eng. (Dial.) clenk, form of clank [a sounding blow], w.Yks. For the sense development cf. *kleut* and *kleutan*. (1) 'anything flat' (I.W.): *kleŋk o vara* = *pisin maur go ða:* (O.H.). (2) 'a fall' (I.W.). (3) 'a shock to the body caused e. g. by making a false step': *dyːn ɔŋ kaːl kleŋk uθ gam gwaːg* (O.H.); cf. *klerk*. (4) fig. 'a loss' = *koḷad*: *mi gavoð o dippin o gleŋk*, e. g. through being deceived in a bargain, by the death of a horse (O.H.); *mynd o r naiḷ gleŋk i r ḷaḷ.*

kleŋkjog [*kloŋkjog*].

klep, s.m.f., clep, D.G. ccxvi. 37; C.C.M. 417. 1; B.C. 96. 17; clap, D.G. cxlvi. 20; C.C.M. 251. 4; Eng. clap; cleppe (13th cent.). (1) 'bang, clap': *ɣhoi klep ar ɔ druːs, kay ɔ druːs ɔŋ glep*, 'to bang the door'; *klep ar ɔ maud! be du i n hidjo arno vo ?*, 'I don't care *that* for him', i. e. a snap of the fingers. (Perhaps a confusion with *klek*.) (2) 'clapper of a mill': *ſarad vel klep melin.* (3) 'chatter': *ɣhoi i glep i vjaun; riu heːn glep o hyːd; du i wedi lary ar i heːn glep o.*—in pl. *karjo kleps*, 'to tell tales' (cf. *klap*). (4) 'mouth': *kay dɔ glep!* (5) 'chatterer, tell-tale': *ɣ heːn glep!*

klepgi, s.m., clepgi, T.N. 345, 36, 'a chatterer' = *dyːn ɔn ſarad o hyːd ag ar draus paub:—taːu ɔr heːn glepgi gɔθral!*

klepjan, v., clepian, S.E.; Eng. (Dial.) clap [talking, prating]; clep [to chatter, gossip, tattle, tell tales]. (1) 'to rattle, bang' (cf. *klekjan*): *may r druːs ɔŋ klepjan*, e. g. through being left open in a draught; *klepjan am wyːa*, 'to go round at Easter rattling stones together to beg for eggs'. (2) 'to jabber, chatter'. (3) 'to ask persistently': *paid a χlepjan arna i vel na (ɔŋ govyn am beːθ na ꞏvedruχi m o i roid o)*; *klepjan ſarad; klepjan o hyːd am vreχtan.* (4) 'to gossip': *klepjan stryːon, klepjan am ruːin o hyːd.* (5) 'to clap' (the hands).

kleppaχ [*kreppaχ*].

kleppyn, s.m., dim. of *klap*, 'a small lump'. Cf. *kneppyn*.

klerk, s., 'a sudden sharp knock', e. g. of the foot against a stone;

also with the hand, etc.: *mi ro:θ o glerk arna i ;*—fig. *may o a i glerk ar baub,* ' he finds fault with every one ' = *hel bëia.*—(J.J.; unknown to O.H.).

klerkjan, v., ' to give a sudden sharp knock ';—fig. ' to find fault ' (J.J.; unknown to O.H.).

klerl, s., ' a lounging ' (J.J.; unknown to O.H.).

klertjan, v. (I.W.; E.J.; J.J.).; O.H. has *klertjan* and *klertjo*; cf. Eng. (Dial.) clart [to do anything in a sloppy, slatternly way; to trifle, bungle over work; to idle, waste time], Bnff., Nhb., Cum., e.Yks., Not., n.Lin., ' to lounge ': *klertjan ən le: gwëiθjo ; əɲ klertjo gwëiθjo ; əɲ klertjan hevo i waiθ ; klertjo hyd ə walja, ar ə bonl, ar ə burδ* (i. e. with one's elbows), *ar ə ɽha:u* (i. e. with one's hands resting on the handle).

klerlog (J.J.); *klertjog* (O.H.), adj. corresponding to above : *dy:n klertjog.*

klesbyn ; klebsyn (E.J.), s.m., pl. *klesöja.* (1) ' clasp ': *klesbyn klogsan,* ' the clasp of a clog '. (2) in slate quarries ' clasp ', i. e. one of two pieces of iron of different lengths inserted into a split made by a chisel. Between them is placed a larger chisel (*ky:n kɽaig*) which is then driven in with a mallet.

kleut, s., clewt, S.E.; Eng. clout [a blow]. Cf. the dialectical form cleaut, Lan.; also clut, Corn. [' to fall with a clut ' = ' to fall in a heap '; and ' to fa' clout ', Sc. ' to fall to the ground with force ']—in phrase : *disǵin i laur əɲ gleul,* ' to fall in a heap '.

kleutan (I.W.; J.J.; O.H.); *kləutan* (E.J.). s.f., pl. *kleutja,* clewtan, S.E.; Eng. clout. (1) ' anything flat ' (I.W.)—of a stone in a wall : *əɲ gorvaδ i ǵi:d əɲ gleutan ar ə mortar—may ǵini hi wely da:* (O.H.); —*kleutan o vrexlan, durx* (dywarch), *dorθ*—of bread that has not risen properly : *may r bara n y:n gleutan.* (2) ' a blow ': *sərθjo ɲ gləutan ar laur,* ' to fall in a heap, to fall with force '. (3) ' a fine, strapping woman ': *dəna gleutan de:u nobl.*

klëyar, adj., clauar, D., ' lukewarm '; ' warm ' (of wintry weather).

klikjad, s.m., pl. *klikjada,* klickiet, W.S.; cliccied, D.; Eng. clicket (still in Dialects), ' latch of a door '; *klikjad ǵe:n,* ' jawbone '.

klino, v. = *tlino,* tylino, D., ' to knead '.

kliŋkum, s., clincwm, S.E., ' importunate harping on the same string ': *kliŋkum o hy:d am ər y:n pe:θ ; dəna gliŋkum o hy:d iʃo i xa:l hi; kadu kliŋkum* (O.H.).

klip, s.m., pl. *klipja,* clip, R. [a precipice], ' a steep hill ': *may hun əɲ glip go drum ;—dros glip penman·maur,* alluding to the road between Llanfairfechan and Penmaenmawr.

klip, s.m., pl. *klipja,* clips, M.Ll. ii. 115, 19, ' eclipse ': *klip ar ər hayl.*

klipjo, v., 'to clip': *klipjo kзfзla hevo sisurn.*

klippan, s.f., 'hill' = *klip*:—*klippan vaur* (O.H.).

klippan, s.f., clipen, S.E., 'a slap on the face with the palm or back of the hand' (not so violent as *Kelpan*).

klippus, s., cnippws, D., 'talitrum'; 'a slap' (O.H.).

kli:r, adj., clîr, B.C. 26. 24. (1·) 'clear' (of the weather). (2) 'clear', i.e. at a safe distance: *r зdu i n sevyl зη gli:r oruθ ŗhei ni*, 'I keep clear of those people'. (3) 'cleared': *le: kli:r*, 'a place which has been cleared'. (4) 'entirely': *meθy η gli:r*, 'to fail entirely' = *meθy n la:n.*

klirjo, v., clirio, B.C. 116. 31. (1) 'to clear up' (of the weather): *ma: r dзwyδ wedi klirjo.* (2) 'to clear, clear away' (of tables, food, etc.): *klirjo r burδ, klirjo r suppar.*

klistjog, adj., klustioc, W.S. [Ered], pryf klustioc [An erwygge]—*pŗy: klistjog*, 'earwig'.

kljaran; klaran (O.H.), s., term of reproach used of dull, slow, stupid persons; *kljaran з ko:yd*, a kind of bird (sp.?).

klo:, s.m., pl. *klöia*, clo, D., 'lock': *ŗhoi klo: ar з dru:s*, 'to lock the door'; *kadu dan glo:*, 'to keep under lock and key'; *tul з klo:*, 'key-hole' = *tul gorjad; klo: klut*, 'padlock'; *ma:yn klo:* [*ma:yn*]; —fig. *klo: ovnaduy зdi ëira*, 'snow is a terrible impediment'.

klob, s.m., pl. *klobjon*, cf. klobos, W.S. [Cloddes]; Eng. (Dial.) clob [A lump or clod of earth or clay], Devon, 'a hard clod of earth': *pŗen i gyro klobjon ar з ti:r* (J.J.—not known to O.H.).

kloban, s.f., cloben, B.C. 33. 1. (1) applied to something big: *kloban o fon.* (2) 'a virago': *kloban o δnas, kloban δru:g*,—also used in a much weaker sense: *may hi n he:n globan δru:g*, 'she is a naughty girl' (applied e.g. by a mother to her daughter); *tyd зmma ŗ he:n globan!* (to a dog).

klobar, s., 'a wooden mallet formerly used for breaking clods' (O.H.).

klobjo, v. (1) 'to break' (clods): *muθul pŗen i globjo klai.* (2) 'to beat, knock': *mi klobjoδ o; klobjo nu зn i ģiliδ.*

klobor, klobar, s., pl. *klobors, klobars*, cf. Eng. (Dial.) clobber [mud, clay, dirt], Ayr, 'a hard clod of earth': *gorδ bren i valy klobors.*

klobyn, s.m., pl. *klobja*, clobyn, S.E., 'a large lump': *klobyn maur o budin, o lo:, o ëira, o glai;*—also applied to persons: *klobyn o δy:n*, 'a fine strapping fellow';—as term of reproach: *ta:u ŗ he:n globyn gwirjon.*

klo:d, s.m. (?), clod, D., 'praise, fame'.

kloðjo, v., cloddio, D. (1) 'to dig a ditch' = *ɪoɾi fo:s*. (2) 'to dig out', e.g. people from under fallen earth.

kloðjur, s.m., cloddiwr, D., s.v. 'fossor'; 'one who digs ditches'.

klo:f, adj., cloff, D., 'lame'.

klofi, v., cloffi, D., 'to be lame, to limp'.

klofni, s., cloffni, D., s.v. 'claudicatio'; 'lameness'.

klofrum, s., cloffrwym, D., s.v. 'pedica'; 'a rope for tying round one of the fore-legs of a refractory cow at milking-time to prevent it from kicking, and fastened with a piece of wood behind the knee' (O.H.).—fig. 'hindrance': *mi vy:ð ɔɲ gloɪrum garu ·arnoχi*, 'it will be a great hindrance to you' (I.W.).

klogi, *kɔvlogi*, v., cyflogi, D., 'to hire'; 'to go into service' (*hevo*): *fair gɔvlogi*, 'hiring-fair'.

kloguyn, s.m., pl. *kloguini*, clogwyn, D., 'a steep piece of rock';— in slate quarries, 'the face of the rock'; *kloguyn dru:g*, 'a piece of rock which cannot be used for slates';—fig. *mynd ɔn erbyn ɔ kloguyn*, 'to run one's head against a stone wall' (O.H.).

klogɔrnað, adj., clogyrnaidd, S.E., 'uncouth, rugged': *kɔm·ra:ig klogɔrnað*, 'clumsy, uncouth Welsh'; *byuχ, köydan, kraig glogɔrnað*.

kloi, v., cloi, D. Fut. S. 3. *kloið*. Pret. S. 1. *klois*, 3. *kloioð*. Pl. 3. *kloison*. Imperative *klo:; klo:uχ*. Pret. Pass. *klo:ud*, 'to lock': *daχi wedi kloi arno vo ?*, 'have you locked it up?'; *·r öyðanu wedi χloi hi*, 'they had locked her up'.

klöior, s.f., cloer, D., 'foruli'; 'a small receptacle in a chest' (I.W.).

klok, s.m., pl. *klokja*, clocc, D.; cf. D.G. ccxvi. 35, 'clock': *may r klok ɔn tipjan, ɔn taro*, 'the clock is ticking, is striking'; *wëindjo r klok*, 'to wind the clock'; *may r klok igjan mynyd ɔn vy:an, ɔn slo:*, 'the clock is twenty minutes fast, slow'; *bɔsað ɔ klok*, 'hands of the clock'; *klok pen davad*, 'an old-fashioned clock with weights'.

klokjur, s.m., clociwr, T.N. 17. 43, 'clock-maker'.

kloksan, s.f., pl. *klokſa*, cf. kloc, W.S. [A clogge]. (1) 'clog': *klokſa a bakſa*, 'clogs and footless stockings'. (2) 'shoe' (to put under the wheel of a cart).

klokſur, s.m., clocsiwr, T.N. 17. 31, 'clog-maker'.

klo:χ, s.f., pl. *kloχa*. (1) 'bell': *kany r glo:χ*, 'to ring the bell';— applied to singing in the ear: *may gin i glo:χ ba:χ ɔn ɔ ɲlhy:st;— may gini hi glo:χ uθ bo:b daint*, said of a loud-voiced talkative person (cf. below); *kloχa babis*, 'hare-bells' (Campanula rotundifolia), but Mr. J. E. Griffith informs me that in Anglesey this name is applied to the daffodil. (2) 'clock', in speaking of the time of day: *vaint (ɔd)i o r glo:χ ar ɔr amsar jaun ?*, 'what is the correct time?'; *am vaint o r glo:χ ?*, 'at what time?'; *tri: o r glo:χ*, 'three o'clock'. (3)

used of the voice: *kodi i glo:χ*, 'to speak in high tones'; *a i glo:χ ən yuχ na ne:ʊ*, said of a loud-talking, self-assertive person. (4) in pl. 'bubbles': *ə du:r əy kodi y gloχa*, e. g. on the surface of a lake during heavy rain (J.J.; O.H.). Cf. D., s.v. 'bulla'.

kloχderan; kloχǵeran (O.H.), v., cf. clochdarddain, clochdran, S.E., 'to talk loudly, shout'.

kloχjan, v., clochian. (1) 'to ring bells': *ə kloχyð ən kloχjan* (more commonly *kany r glo:χ*). (2) 'to talk, make a noise': *paid a χloχjan; kloχjan ſarad ən ḷe: mynd; be u:ti y kloχjan ən ḷe: mynd?*

kloχyð, s.m., pl. *kloχəðjon*, clochydd, D., 'sexton, parish clerk'.

klomman, s.f., pl. *klomennod*, colommen, D.; clomen, M.Ll. ii. 114, 12, 'pigeon': *vel klomman ən i θy:*, said of a woman who dresses well but has a dirty house.

klompan, s.f., cf. clompan, M.F., 'anything big' (I.W.):—*he:n glompan*, a term of reproach for a woman, whether big or small (O.H.).

klompyn, s.m., term of reproach, the masc. equivalent of above (O.H.).

klondid, s., calondid, D., 'magnanimitas'; 'anything tending to raise the spirits, such as good news, etc'; esp. in the expression *gair o glondid*, 'a cheering word'.

klondro [*klandro*].

klonnog, adj., calonnog, D., s.v. 'animosus'; 'hearty, in good spirits': *χwerθin muya klonnog*, 'to laugh as heartily as can be'; *kefyl klonnog*, 'a spirited horse'.

kloŋk, adj., cf. Eng. (Dial.) clunk [to emit a hollow, interrupted sound as of a liquid issuing from a bottle or narrow opening], Sc. 'addled': *may r u:y y gloŋk*.

kloŋk, s., clonc, S.E. [a hollow sound like that made by striking a metal vessel], Eng. clank, 'the sound of the nave of a cart-wheel working regularly on its axle'.

kloŋk, s., pl. *kloŋkja*, 'a slant, inclination one way or another', *ən iavlyd aḷan ne i veun: may kloŋk əno vo;*—in pl. 'bumps, protuberances': *ma na he:n dolkja a kloŋkja ar hy:d ə forð.*

kloŋkjan, v., clonkan, clonco, S.E. [to make a hollow sound]; Eng. clank, and (Dial.) clonk, Cum. (1) said of the sound of the nave of a cart-wheel working regularly on its axle. (2) 'to talk noisily': *be u:ti y kloŋkjan ən wirjon?*

kloŋkjo, v., said of a cart swaying from side to side owing to un-evenness in the road: *ə drol əy ka:l i χloŋkjo;*—used also of persons walking in a similar fashion.

kloŋkjog, kleŋkjog, adj., clonciog, S.E., 'full of protuberances', "bumpy": *ḷe: kloŋkjog; may r forð ən dolkjog ag əy gleŋkjog.*

kloŋkuy, *klɔŋkuy*, s.m., pl. *kloŋkuy:a*, cloncwy, S.E., 'an addled egg'; also as adjective: *ma: r wy:a ŋ gloŋkuy i ģi:d*, 'the eggs are all addled' (O.H.).

kloran, s.f., cloren, D., 'tail of a horse': *toṛi i gloran*; *klu:y r gloran.*

klorjanny, v., clorianu, S.E., 'to weigh in scales';—fig. 'to weigh in the mind, to think out': *erbyn i klorjanny nu.*

klorjon, s.f., pl. *klorjanna*, clorian, D., 'scales'.

klos, adj., klos ne gayad, W.S., [Close]; cf. L.G.C. 306 [18]; clos, T.N. 238. 9. (1) 'close' (of the weather) = *mul, gwiģil, trɔmmaδ.* (2) 'friendly, unassuming' (opp. to "standoffish"). (3) 'close, miserly'.

klo:s, s.pl., clôs, W.LL (Voc) s.v. 'llawdr'; R.; B.C. 75. 3; 117. 19; Eng. (small) clothes; 'knee-breeches': *gwisgo r bais a r klo:s*, 'to wear the breeches' (of a wife); *tṛoi klo:s*, euph. for 'ventrem exonerare'.

klofo, v., closio, T.N. 106. 36; S.E., 'to close up to, to come close'; 'to be friendly, unassuming': *may o ŋ klofo ·atloχi.*

kləudjo, v., 'to cloud, thicken': *ḷa:yθ wedi hel at i ģiliδ, wedi deχra tṛoi, deχra syro, deχra kləudjo.*

kləus, s., Eng. (Dial.) clow [hurry, bustle, confusion], Yks., 'a row, disturbance': *kodi kləus = kodi rəu.*

kləufo, *kləunfo*, v., 'to keep harping petulantly' (about the same thing); *kləufo am ər y:n pe:θ o hy:d; paid a χləufo, t ədi o m ģin i*, 'don't keep on asking, I haven't got it'.

kləut, s.f., in the phrase *ar ə gləut*, 'destitute' (Bangor). Cf. *klut.*

kləutan [*kleutan*].

klɔvar, s.pl., 'clover'.

kloverog, adj., 'full of clover': *gwair kloverog.*

klu:ad, v., clywed, D. Fut. S. 1. *klu:a*, 2. *klu:i*, 3. *klu:iθ* [*klyu*]. Pl. 1. *klyun*, 2. *klyuχ, klu:χ*, 3. *klu:an.* Imperf. (frequently used with pret. meaning), 1. *klyun, klu:n*, 2. *klu:at*, 3. *klu:a.* Pl. 1. *klu:an*, 2. *klu:aχ*, 3. *klu:an.* Pret. S. 1. *klu:is*, 2. *klu:ist*, 3. *klu:oδ.* Pl. 1. *klu:son*, 2. *klu:soχ*, 3. *klu:son.* Plup. S. 1. *klusun*, 2. *klu:sat*, 3. *klu:sa.* Pl. 1. *klu:san*, 2. *klu:saχ*, 3. *klu:san.* Imperative *klyu; klyuχ.* Imperf. Pass. with pret. meaning *klu:id.* (1) 'to hear': *ma: nu ŋ klu:ad mor vain*, 'their sense of hearing is so acute'; *klu:ad vel ka:θ*, 'to have sharp ears'; *klu:ad po:b smik*, 'to hear the slightest sound'; *ma:y o ŋ klu:ad ɱ drum*, 'he is hard of hearing'; *·glu:soχi ru:in əŋ gwëiδi?*, 'did you hear any one shouting?'; *r öyδun i n sa:l peŋ glu:n i lais o*, 'the sound of his voice made me ill'; *taro r po:st ga:yl i r parad glu:ad*, 'to strike the post so that the wall may hear', i.e. 'to give a hint to some one by speaking to some one else'; *klu:ad ar ə galon*, 'to feel inclined': *mi δa:u o peŋ glu:iθ o ar ι galon ;—χlu:if i δim gair am le: iδi hi*, 'I heard nothing about a situation for her'; *ˑgluːsoχi soːn am dano vo?*, 'have you heard of him?'; *χluːis i ðim am i saluχ o*, 'I did not hear a word of his illness'; *χluːis i riˑoːyd a m klistja m ono vo*, 'I never heard of it'; *os klyuχi, neuχi anvon i mi?*, 'if you hear, will you let me know?'; *muya vyːð dyːn byu, muya weːl a muya glyu* (prov.), 'we live and learn'. (2) 'to listen', only in the imperative: *klyuχ = gwranduχ*. (3) 'to taste': *daχi ŋ kluːad ə buːyd ən ðaː?*, 'does the food taste nice?'; *ə ķiːg gora gluːis i eriˑoːyd*, 'the best meat I ever tasted'; *klyuχ hun*, 'taste this'. (4) 'to smell': *daχi ŋ kluːad hogla bakko?*, 'do you smell tobacco?'; *klyuχ ə gwahanjaθ hogla*, 'smell the difference'. (5) 'to feel': *kluːad iʃo buːyd*, 'to feel hungry'; *daχi n i χluːat i n oːyr?*, 'do you feel cold?'; *klyuχ ə puysa sy no*, 'feel how much it weighs'; *daχi ŋ kluːad ļe maː: nu m pigo?*, 'do you feel where they prick?', e. g. nails in a boot; *may hun ən veðal, klyuχ*, 'this is soft, feel'.

klub, s., 'club': *klub ə bara syːχ*, 'a destitute state', used especially with reference to marriage: *aros di ŋenaθ i nes ёi di i glub ə bara syːχ*.

klubjo, v. (1) 'to put into a club': *klubjo arjan*. (2) 'to put away, save up': *uːti ðim əŋ klubjo dim?* (3) 'to keep possession of', "to stick to": *may o wedi klubjo nu i ǵiːd*—(O.H.). Cf. T.N. 409. 5. Fe glybiodd y cwbwl yn fanwl i'w fol.

kluf, s.m., pl. *kləfja*, 'a large piece, lump, chunk': *kluf o vreχtan*.

klufyn, s.m. (1) 'a large piece, lump': *klufyn o gaus, o varą*. (2) applied to a big boy or girl (J.J.; O.H.): *may ŋ glufyn o hogyn ǵin ti* (O.H.).

klukjan, v., clwccian, R. (1) 'to cluck' (of fowls). (2) 'to complain of some bodily infirmity': *syt may wil? klukjan dippin mav o ə dəwyð oːyr ma* (O.H.).

kluːs, adj., comp. *kləsaχ*, pl. *kləʃon*, tlws, D., pretty: *hogan gluːs;—dyn baːχ kluːs ədi o*, 'he is a nice little man'.

klustur, s.m., 'cluster'; also used of things in a mass together; *təvy ŋ glustur*, 'to grow close together'; *ˑvəðanu ˑarnoχi n yːn klustur*, 'they are on you in swarms' (of flying insects).

klut, s.m., pl. *klətja*, klwt, W.S. [A clout]; clwtt, B.C. 24. 13; Eng. (Dial.) clout, clute [rag, patch]; O.E. clūt; cf. *kleut, kleutan*. (1) 'rag, piece of linen', etc.; 'baby's napkin': *klut ar ben gliːn*, 'knee-rag used by workmen'; *gorvað vel klut*, 'to lie like a log'; *sərθjo vel klut*, 'to fall like a log'. (2) in slate quarries, when a block (*plyːg*) has been split with a chisel (*kyːn brasoļt*) and the pieces so obtained have been cut longitudinally and transversely, and again split into the thickness of about sixteen slates, each of these pieces is called a *klut*, 'a reduced block'. (3) 'patch': *gosod klut*, 'to put on a patch'; *ˑgəmmanu glut?*, 'will they bear patching?'; *kloː klut*, 'padlock'. (4) 'patch of ground': *klut o diːr;—klut gla:s,* ' a lawn, patch of grass '; *kḷut kʌʋri,* in slate quarries, ' the place where slates are counted ', ' stacking-ground ';—*bo:d ar ə kḷut,* ' to be left stranded, to be turned out of hearth and home '; *dəna ṇhu: ar ə kḷut,* i. e. *heb ðim gwaiθ, heb gartṛa, wedi ka:yl i tavlyd aḷan* (O.H.).

kḷutlyn, s.m., clyttyn, C.L.C. ii. 20. 28, 'a small rag ': *kḷutlyn ar ben gli:n,* ' knee-rag '.

kḷu:y, s.m., clwyf, D., ' disease ', but only used in specific cases as ə *kḷu:y* (of sheep), ' the rot '; *kḷu:y du:r* (of sheep), ' red water '; *kḷu:y penna,* ' mumps '; *kḷu:y melyn,* ' jaundice '; *kḷu:y r brenin,* ' scrofula '.

kḷu:yd, s.f., clwyd, D., s.v. ' sedile '. (1) ' hen-roost '. (2) said of things growing or clustering close together : *ma: nu ŋ glu:yd əmma,* ' they grow close together here '; *may ambaḷ y:n əŋ glu:yd o lay.*

kḷuydan, s.f., clwyden, D., said of things growing so close together as to form, as it were, a covering : *may r ba:u* (weeds) *ən y:n gluydan dros ə tattus i ɟi:d* (O.H.).

kḷuydo, v., clwydo, S.E., ' to roost '.

kḷuyðog, adj., celwyddog, D., ' lying, mendacious ': *stry:on kḷuyðog,* ' lying tales ' ;— *kəθral kḷuyðog !*

kḷuyður, s., celwydd-wŷr (pl.), 1 Tim. i. 10, ' liar '.

kḷuyvo, v., clwyfo, D., ' to become afflicted with disease ': *ma: r devaid wedi kḷuyvo* (O.H.).

kḷuyvys, adj., clwyfus, D., s.v. ' morbosus '; ' diseased ': *may i ləgaid o ŋ gluyvys,* ' his eyes are heavy with sickness ' (LW.).

kly:d, adj., sup. *kletla,* clŷd, D., ' sheltered, cosy ': *may n edraχ əŋ gly:d jaun,* ' it looks very cosy '; ə *ty: kletla i r kḷauð,* ' the sheltered side of the wall '.

kḷydo, v., cludo, D., ' to carry ' (occasionally heard, but *karjo* is the usual word).

klyl, s.m., clul, D. (1) ' knell ';—in fig. sense : *kany klyl ru:in,* ' to give a very bad account of some one ': *may hun a hun əŋ kany də glyl ən aru, ən dëyd bo ti wedi mynd ən o:l ḷa:u, wədi sərθjo i riu drəbini ;—ma na he:n glyl garu 'gənoχi,* ' you are always harping on the same string '. (2) ' a lanky fellow ': *he:n glyl main* (W.H.; O.H.). Cf. *kyl.*

klylbo, s.m., ' a lanky fellow ': *riu he:n glylbo* (O.H.).

klymmaχ, s.m., climmach, D., s.v. ' longurio '; D.P.O. 249. 24, ' a tall ungainly fellow ': *he:n glymmaχ da: i ðim ədi o,—hogyn ne ðy:n heb i orfan.*

kly:n, s.f., pl. *klinja,* clûn, D., ' the leg from the knee upwards, thigh '; *pen ə gly:n,* ' hip '; *asgurn pen ə gly:n,* ' hip-bone '; *o gly:n i gly:n,* ' from side to side '; *brëixja vel ə ŋlhinja,* said of thick arms.

klyro, s.m., term of reproach : *ta:u ɣ he:n glyro gwirjon!* (O.H.).

kly:st, s.f., pl. *kli̯istja*, clûst, D., ' ear ' : *may də gly:st ən dena jaun.* ' you have sharp ears ' ;—opp. *te:u* ;—*may ǵin i glo:χ ba:χ ən ə ŋlhy:st,* ' I have a singing in my ear ' ; *may ǵin i biǵin ən ə ŋlhy:st i,* ' I have earache ' ; *may hi wedi χuθy n i χly:st,* " she has got round her " ; *dəna ðu:r ən i glistja vo!,* ' there 's unpleasant tidings for him ! ' ; *r o:ð ə ðay ən ə gly:st,* ' they were quarrelling ' ; *may o ən ə gly:st hevo vo,* ' he is at him, tackling him ' ; *wedi mynd o gly:st i gly:st,* ' to have become a matter of common talk ' = *wedi mynd ən ɣhigum ǵin baub ;—may o ŋ gly:st i ǵi:d,* ' he is all ears ' ; ' he knows every bit of gossip ' ; *ʃarad ar draus pen a kli̯istja,* ' to talk thirteen to the dozen ' ; *gwasgy r gly:st,* ' to keep one 's counsel ; not to say anything ' ; *r o:ð ə ðay gly:st ə ŋlhy:st,* ' they were whispering together ' ; *may ǵin vo:χ ba:χ glistja* (prov.), ' little pitchers have long ears ' ; *may kli̯istja ǵin gloðja* (prov.), ' walls have ears '. Transferred uses : *kly:st ə dgug, ə guppan, ə kibin, ə radal̡, ə teḵal̡,* ' handle ' ; *kly:st piḵḵin,* sheep's ear-mark so called [*no:d*] ; *klyst gam* (of a plough), ' ratchet ' ; *kli̯istja ə dro:yl̡* (?) ; *kly:st ə ga:θ,* any shell of the genus Pecten ; *kly:st ·elifant,* name of a shell, Mya truncata ; *klyst l̡əgodan,* ' mouse-ear chickweed ' (Cerastium).

klystan, s.f., clusten, S.E. (1) ' a box on the ear ' : *mi rois i glamp o glystan iðo vo.* (2) in slate quarries : when, in pillaring (*pl̡ery*), the line, instead of continuing straight, turns off sharply to the right or left either through a flaw in the slate or through clumsy workmanship, the place where this occurs is called *klystan*.

klystog, s.f., pl. *klystoga*, clustog, D., ' cushion ' ; ' pillow ' (for the latter O.H. has *pilo* only).

klystog, adj., ' obstinate, stubborn ' (J.J.; O.H.). Also as substantive : *ɣ he:n glystog stiupid!* (O.H.).

klystogað, adj., ' obstinate, stubborn ' (W.H.; J.J.; O.H.).

klystogyn, s.m., ' an obstinate, stubborn fellow ' (J.J.).

klystoχi, v., ' to become obstinate or stubborn ' (J.J.; O.H.).

klystvëinjo, v., clustfeinio, S.E., ' to prick up one 's ears, to listen attentively ' : *əŋ klystvëinjo am ə məwyd i klu:ad nu.*—Frequently used.

klyu, s.m., clyw, D., ' sense of hearing ' : *kol̡i i glyu ;—mi m̦haroð ə vre:χ go:χ ar i χl̡yu hi,* ' the measles injured her hearing ' ; *mi ëiʃ i lerpul hevo ŋlhyu,* ' I went to Liverpool about my hearing ' ; *əŋ ŋlhyu plant,* ' in the hearing of children '.

kləmmog, adj., clymmog, D., s.v. ' nodosus ' ; ' knotty ' : *kortyn kləmmog.*

kləmmy, v., clymmu, D., s.v. ' ligo ', ' vincio ' ; ' to tie, bind ' : *kləmmy kulum,* ' to tie a knot '. Intr. *kləmmy am rubaθ,* ' to twist round something ', e. g. of a creeper. Also *klummo.*

kl̥ᵊnrag, s.f., canlynwraig, 'mistress' = *kᵊmanas*.

kl̥ᵊijo, v., clyttio, D., s.v. 'consarcino', 'resarcio'; 'to patch'.

kl̥ᵊtjog, adj., 'patchy': *gwa:l̥t kl̥ᵊtjog*, 'hair coming off in patches'.

kl̥ᵊtʃur, *sgoᵈᵧn kl̥ᵊtʃur*, s.m., (?) 'lump-sucker' (Cyclopterus lumpus) = *ja:r vo:r*.

kl̥ᵊvar, adj., clyfar, T.N. 98. 35. (1) 'clever'. (2) 'good-looking; of good appearance': *hogan glᵊvar, l̥avn o ᵈᵧ:n kl̥ᵊvar. kefyl ivaᵑk kl̥ᵊvar ; farm go glᵊvar.* (3) 'pleasant, agreeable' (of persons) = *kl̥ɛ:n ;* (of things) *may hi n mynd ar galap ᵊmma heno = huíljog, glᵊvar* (O.H.). (4) 'well off': *pobol glᵊvar.*

kna:, s.m., knaf, W.S. [A knaue]; cnâ, B.C. 21. 7; cnaf, T.N. 15. 35. (1) 'knave'. (2) 'a stingy, niggardly fellow': *he:n gna: = he:n gravur.* In the following examples from O.H. the meaning is not clear: *may o vel kna:, ·vedruχi ẟim ka:l gwarad o hono vo ;— may o vel kna: ar ᵊ ŋhevn o hy:d ;—may o ᵊmma vel kna: am arjan, dim posib gnëyd i fur a vo:.*

knady, v. = *kᵊrnady* (I.W.).

knap, s.m., pl. *knapja*, knap, W.S. [A knoppe]; cnap, D.; cf. Eng. (Dial.) knap, 'a lump': *knap o lo:, do:ys, ᵬren*, etc.; also 'a small loaf made from a piece of dough left over when baking': *du:y dorθ a χnap* (O.H.)—of persons 'a stunted, dumpy individual as broad as he is long': *r he:n gnap ; knapja merχaid* ;—in pl. 'sweets'.

knapjan, knapjo, v., cnapian, S.E. (1) 'to make into a lump, to huddle up': *paid a χnapjo dᵊ dra:yd*, 'don't screw up your feet' (said e. g. to a child who is trying to prevent a pair of boots being put on); *paid a χnapjo dᵊ göysa*, e. g. in bed. (2) 'to become lumpy' (of the sea). (3) 'to set' (of apples): *may r vala ŋ knapjo*, 'the apples are setting', i. e. becoming round (O.H.).

knapjog, adj., cnappog, R.; cnapiog, S.E., 'lumpy': *glo: knapjog.*

knappan, s.f., cnapen, S.E., 'a small stunted person': *he:n gnappan veχan.*

knappyn, s.m., 'a small stunted person'.

knarvon, Caernarfon, 'Carnarvon': *ᵊŋ ŋharvon*, 'in Carnarvon'.

knaud, s.m., cnawd, D., 'flesh'.

knaur, s.m., cnowr, D.G. clxxxii, 37, 'chewer': *knaur ᵬakko öyẟun i pᵊyt hᵊnny.*

knava, v., cynhauafu, D.; cynhauafa, S.E. (1) 'to dry', expressing the action of the sun and air on a standing crop: *may r gwynt a r hayl ᵊn i knava nu.* (2) 'to expose a crop to the sun and air for the purpose of drying it', esp. hay. (3) Intr. 'to dry in the sun and air' (of a crop).

knavaẟ, adj., cnafaidd, S.E., 'knavish'.

knawas (I.W.); *knavas* (O.H.), s.f., cenawes, G.O. ii. 70. 17 ; T.N. 102. 38, 'vixen' (said of a woman).

knay, s.pl., sing. *knĕyan*, f. cnau, D. (1) 'nuts; hazel-nuts' = (for sake of distinction) *knay kyl̦; knay frëinig*, cnau ffrengig, and cneuen ffrangeg, s.v. 'nauci', D., 'walnuts'; *knay bi:t/,* 'beech-nuts'; *knay ə ðĕyar*, 'earth-nuts' (Conopodium denudatum); *eval gnay*, 'nut crackers'; *y:n go:yg o:ð ə gnĕyan*, 'I was clean sold in the business' (I.W.); 'she turned out an empty nut' (of a rejected girl), J.J. ; *toṛi knay gwëïgjon*, 'to be on a useless quest'.

knebrun, s.m., pl. *knebrəna*, cynhebrwng, D., s.v. 'exequiæ'; 'funeral': *knebrun maur*, 'a public funeral'; *knebrun ba:χ*, 'a private funeral'.

knegwaθ, s.f., ceinhiagwerth, I.G. 610 [38]; ceiniogwerth, M.Ll. i. 138. 18; ceinhiogwerth, B.C. 140. 2, 'pennyworth'.

knëïtjo, v., ? yskipio (=) krychneitio [Skyppe], W.S.; crychneitio, D., s.v. 'persulto'; cf. cneitio, M.F., '(?) to twinkle' (of stars): *be daχi n veðul nëïθ i vory? may tu:yð gwy:l̦t ən əmmyl, ma: r se:r əŋ knëïtjo* (O.H.), 'what kind of weather do you think we shall have to-morrow? There is stormy weather coming, the stars are twinkling (?)'.

knëïvjo, v., cneifio, D., 'to shear': *knëïvjo devaid.*

knëïvjur, s.m., cneifiwr, D., 'shearer'.

kneks, s.pl., cnecs, T.N. 308. 27, 'quarrel, strife'; *kodi kneks,* 'to rake up old scores, to stir up strife'; *—rubaθ i nëyd kneks.*

kneppyn, s.m., cnepyn, S.E., dim. of *knap.* (1) 'a small lump'. (2) 'anything small and round': *kneppyn ə dru:s*, 'handle of the door' = *durn; kneppyn ə tebot*, 'the knob on the lid of a tea-pot' = *knoltyn; kneppyn o dorθ*, 'a small round loaf'. Cf. also *knappyn.*

knesol, adj., cynhesol, S.E. (1) 'acceptable, to one's liking; taking'. (2) 'warm-hearted, amiable'.

knesruyð, s.m., cynnhesrwydd, D., 'warmth'.

knesy, v., cynnhesu, D.; cynnessu, s.v. 'calefacio'; 'to become warm': *ma: ŋ knesy*, 'it is getting warmer' (of the weather); *nëif i gnesy ar o:l ïði vuru*, 'it will get warmer after the snow'; *vedra i ðim knesy hëïðju*, 'I can't get warm to-day'; *ar o:l i mi gnesy ən ə gwely*, 'when I am warm in bed'. Cf. *tummo.*

kneujan [*karneujan*].

knevin, *kənevin*, adj., cynnefin, D., 'accustomed'.

knevin, *kənevin*, s.m., cynnefin, Ezek. xxi. 30, 'sheep-run, a tract of land where there are rights of sheep pasture';—also of persons: *may o wedi du:ad ən o:l i u he:n gənevin.*

knĕya, s.m., cynhauaf, D., 'harvest': *knĕya gwair*, 'hay-harvest'; *amsar knĕya, ən ə knĕya*, 'at harvest time'; *ṛhuŋ ə ðay gnĕya*, 'between hay and corn harvest'.

knidu (I.W.); *kniɔ́ju* (O.H.), s.m., 'an insignificant person' (I.W.); *ꞅ heːn gniɔ́ju bɔꭓan* (O.H.).

knigjad, s.m., cynnygiad, S.E., 'offer'.

kniːꭓ, s., cnûch, D., 'carnal desire'.

knilo, v., cynnilo, D., 'to economize': *ɔŋ ŋ́ena r saːꭓ may knilo* (prov.), 'one should economize from the beginning and not only when the article is nearly finished'.

kniθar, s.f., pl. *kniθerod*, cyfnither, D., 'first cousin': *may hi ŋ gniθar a mi.*

kniu, s.m., pl. *kniuja*, cniw, S.E., 'knee', i.e. 'a stanchion on the gunwale of a boat to hold fast the seat' (Bangor);—in a more extended sense: *ꭓhummo loŋ ɔdi ꭓhoi ɔ kniuja* (O.H.).

knjalun (I.W.); *kɔrjalun, kɔrnjalun, kꭓɔnjalun* (O.H.), s., carnialwn, cernialwn, crialwn, S.E., 'a restless person'.

knoi, v., cnoi, D. Fut. S. 1. *knoːa*, 3. *knoiθ*. Pl. 3. *knoːn*. Pret. S. 1. *knois*, 2. *knoːð*. Imperative *knoː; knɐuꭓ*. (1) 'to chew, gnaw': *maː ꞅ heːn aːsı wedi gnoi o*, 'the old bitch has gnawed it'; *knoi bakko*, 'to chew tobacco'; *knoi ꞣiːl*, 'to chew the cud'; *brifa vytta, mi ǵ̈ei gnoi etto*, 'make haste and eat: you can digest afterwards'. (2) 'to ache';—substantively: *may knoi arna i*, 'I have a stomach-ache'.

knok, s.f., pl. *knokja*, cnocc, D.; M.Ll. i. 222. 10, 'knock, slap, stroke': *ammal i gnok dyr garag* (prov.), 'dropping water wears away the stone'; *heb wëiθjo knok*, 'without working a stroke'; *byða gnok*, 'plunging churn'.

knokjo, v., knockio, W.S.; cnoccio, D.; cf. D.G. cxxxv. 33, 'to knock, beat, strike': *knokjo uθ ɔ druːs*, 'to knock at the door'; *mi knokja i di nes bɔði di n ðaɬ (bosı)*, 'I'll strike you blind'; *knokjo ruːin ar i ǵevn*, 'to clap some one on the back'; *knokjo ꞣarpedi*, 'to beat carpets'; *maː r dɔwyð wedi knokjo nu*, 'the weather has caught them' (e. g. blackberries).

knokka, v., keiniocka, W.S. [no meaning]; ceiniocca, D.P.O. 26. 19; T.N. 228. 38, 'to collect' (in a place of worship).

knokkur, s.m., keiniockwr, W.S. [no meaning], 'one who collects in a place of worship'.

knornyn, knonyn [kɔnron].

knotłyn, s.m., cnotyn, T.N. 280. 35. (1) 'the small knob on the top of the lid of a tea-pot, kettle, cap, etc.': *knotłyn tebot* (O.H.) = *kneptyn*. (2) of persons, an epithet implying diminutiveness: *knotłyn o hogyn;—ɔ ŋnhotłyn baːꭓ!*, endearing term to a baby (O.H.).

knova, s., pl. *knoˑvëyð*, cnofa, D., 'an aching'—especially used of the stomach: *may knova ɔn vɔ moli.*

knu:d, s.m., pl. *knǝda*, cnŵd, D. (1) 'crop': *ail gnu:d*, 'second crop'. (2) 'mass' in such expressions as *may o n y:n knu:d o lay* (*χwain*), O.H. (3) *knu:d o ëira*, 'fall of snow'. Cf. F.N. 34 (18).

knuḷbran, s.m., pl. *knuḷbrenni*, canhwyllbren, D., 'candlestick'.

knuḷyn, knuyḷyn ; knunḷyn (J.J.; O.H.), *kuninḷin* (O.H.), s.m., pl. *knunḷǝna* (J.J.), cnewyll and cnywyll, sing. cnewyllyn, D., cynhwyllin, M.Ll. i. 247. 23, 'the kernel of stone-fruit' ; 'the seed itself as opposed to the husk' ; 'the core of an apple' (O.H.); 'the pith of elder' (O.H.); 'the centre of a tree which has been cut down' (O.H).

knuyad, knöyad, s., cf. canwyr, D., 'a sheep's ear-mark so called: a V-shaped slit at the tip of the ear, the tip being thus removed' [*no:d*].

kny:, s.m., pl. *knǝvja*, cnu, D., 'fleece',

knǝrvy [*kǝnhǝrvy*].

knǝsvuyd, s., cynhesfwyd, 'a meal taken formerly during harvesttime at about four o'clock in the afternoon, consisting of bread and butter and buttermilk'.

knǝvjo, v., 'to wrap up wool after shearing'.

ko:, s.m., côf, D. (1) pl. *köya*, cf. couau, T.N. 85. 24, 'memory': *may gǝno vo go: arðerχog*, 'he has a splendid memory' ; *may o n weḷ i go: na vo:*, 'he has a better memory than he' ; *ko: da: ġin i !* (ironically), 'what a memory I have !'; *pe:θ garu ǝdi ko: plentyn*, prov. implying that the events of one's childhood are vividly remembered. (2) 'remembrance, recollection': *ma: ġin i go: da: am ǝχ ta:d*, 'I remember your father very well' ; *may ŋ go: ġin i i mi vynd*, 'I remember going' ; *s ġin i ðim ma:θ o go:*, *s ġin i va:θ o go:*, 'I have not the slightest recollection'; *goḷun pe:θ dros go:*, 'to forget a thing'. (3) 'mind' in phrase: *mynd o i go:*, 'to go mad'; *mynd o i go: la:s*, 'to go raving mad'; *dy:n o i go:*, 'a madman'; *daχi o χ ko: ?*, 'have you lost your senses?' (4) in pl. *kovjon*, 'remembrances': *kovjon gora at . . .*, 'my kind remembrances to . . .'.

kob, s.m., pl. *kobja*, Eng. cob, 'embankment', e. g. with floodgates where a river enters the sea: *may r avon wedi ḷivo dros ǝ kobja*, 'the river has overflowed the embankments'.

kob, s., 'cob' (horse).

koban, s.f., pl. *kobana*, coban, S.E., 'night-gown'.

kobjo, v., 'to make an embankment' (O.H.).

koblar, s.m., cobler, D.G. ccxvi. 34, 'cobbler'.

kobljo, v. (1) 'to cobble': *ma na i iſᶜo kobljo ar ǝ sġidja*. (2) 'to do a thing clumsily, anyhow' = *gnëyd ǝm ·bum·batſ* (*·butſi·batſ*), *·strim·stram·sireḷaχ*. (3) 'to play "conquers" or "cobblers" with chestnuts' ;—hazel-nuts were also employed, a hole·being drilled at each end and the interior filled with cobbler's wax ; *knay kobljo,* 'nuts used in the above game'.

koblyn, s.m., koblyn, W.S. [A goblyn]; coblyn, W.Ll. (Voc.), s.v. 'llewyrn', 'tremyniad'; cf. coblynnod, D., s.v. 'lemures'. (1) in such phrases as the following : *mynd vel ə koblyn,* 'to go like mad'; *ar ǵevn i goblyn,* 'in a rage'; *mi aːθ hiː ŋ goblyn ylu arni hiː,* 'she flew into a temper with her'; *məŋ koblyn ylu !,* asseveration ; *beː goblyn uːħ n nëyd ?,* 'what on earth are you doing?' (2) 'rogue': *ə koblyn baːχ !,* used esp. of children.

koblyn, s.m., Eng. (Dial.) cobbler [the fruit of the horse-chestnut tree ; the nuts used in the game of cobbler], Stf., War., n.e.Wor., 'the conquering nut in the game of "conquers" or "cobbler"': *ə ɟhoblyn i valiθ əχ knay χi i ǵiːd.*

kod, s.pl., sing. *kodyn,* 'cod': *kodyn krëigja,* 'cod, rock-cod' (Gadus morrhua) ; *kodyn ĺuːyd,* 'bib, pout' (Gadus luscus) according to Forrest, but this species is certainly called here *bodyn ə mlinyδ,* and my informants distinguish between the two ; *kodyn ĺëyog,* 'cod after spawning'.

koːd, s.f., pl. *koda,* côd, D. (1) 'bag for keeping money': *oːys na arjan ən ə goːd ?* formerly said when the cuckoo was heard for the first time (J.J.). (2) 'stomach' (of a cow, etc.): *ə goːd vaur,* 'rumen' ; *ə goːd baːχ,* 'omasum' ; *pĺisgan ə goːd,* 'the membrane of a cow's stomach' ; *koːd moχyn,* 'stomach of a pig' ; *goːd wen,* 'a kind of cake made of oatmeal (*rhənjon*), suet, and currants, baked like a loaf, and eaten formerly at Christmas time' (J.J.). Cf. D. s.v. 'faliscus venter'.

kodan, s.f., pl. *koda,* coden, D., 'pod, shell' (of beans and peas): *tənny pyːs o r koda = dyːo pyːs ;—kodan ëyraχ, kodan ëira,* 'puff-ball' (Lycaperdon). D. has côd eurych and côd euraid without meaning ; O.P. has coden hyred. Also called *sniʃin bugan.*

kodi, v., codi, D. Fut. S. 3. *kodiθ, kuːyd, kəvyd.* Pret. Pl. 3. *kodson.* Imperative *koːd ; koduχ.* Pret. Pass. *koduyd,* 'to raise, rise'. I. Transitive: (1) 'to raise, lift up': *kodi i ben,* 'to raise his head'; *koːd də hyːn,* 'get up'; *kodi ĺuːχ,* 'to raise dust'; *may hi ŋ kodi ĺuːχ,* 'dust is flying'; *kodi* (sc. *pṛiːδ*) *at ə taĺtus,* 'to earth up potatoes'; *may hi ŋ kodi n wynt,* 'the wind is rising'; *kodi saχad ar ben kĺauδ,* 'to lift a sack on to a wall';—esp. of bread : *may byrym əŋ kodi bara,* 'barm makes bread rise';—*kodi korf,* 'the initial ceremony at a funeral: a service held at the home of the deceased before carrying the body to the grave';—fig. *kodi ə lais,* 'to raise the voice'; *nëiθ hənny godi χ kalon,* 'that will cheer you up'; *kodi r byːd ə mhen i ǵiliδ,* 'to set the world at loggerheads'. (2) 'to pick up'; *may r adar wedi kodi r hada,* 'the birds have picked up the seeds'; *kodi bawad o hono vo,* 'to pick up a handful of it';

gwelux̱ be nëif i godi ar ə loːn nëiθjur, 'look what I picked up on
the road last night'. (3) 'to dig up, pull up' (of plants): *kodi
iatius,* 'to dig potatoes'; *mqv hi ꞑ kodi r̥hëi o ˙honynu ag ən i
hay nu aḷan,* 'she is taking up some of them and planting them
out'. (4) 'to dig up' (earth, etc.): *tiːr glaːs ˀədaχi ꞑ kodi i vəny,*
'land covered with grass which you dig up'; *may r glaːu wedi kodi
r loːn nes may hi n rëyan,* 'the rain has churned up the road into
gravel'. (5) 'to get out, obtain from out of': *ḷe maː nu ꞑ kodi ə
k̑erig,* 'where they get the stone' (from out of the quarry); similarly,
kodi tikkad, 'to buy a ticket'; *kodi pappyr newyð,* 'to take
in a newspaper regularly'. (6) 'to tear out', *kodi dolan,* 'to
tear a page out of a book'. (7) 'to pull out': *kodi höiljon,* 'to
pull out nails'. (8) 'to copy': *kodi pɛːθ o ḷyvr,* 'to copy something out of a book'. (9) 'to remove': *kodi r druːg i fur,* 'to
remove the matter'. (10) 'to grow': *kodi yːd.* (11) 'to build':
kodud ə velin. (12) 'to charge': *be daχi ꞑ godi am ə r̥hëi nʔ,* 'how
much do you charge for those?'; *maː nu ꞑ kodi r yː vaint n injon,*
'they charge exactly the same'. (13) 'to impose' (of taxes): *kodi
ir̥eθi,* 'to tax'. (14) 'to set going': *kodi diwigjad,* 'to set going
a revival'; *kodi kany,* 'to lead the singing'. (15) 'to cause, bring
on': *kodi k̑wilið ˙arnynu,* 'to make them ashamed of themselves';
kodi blyːs, 'to excite a desire'; *hənny kodoð o,* 'that brought it on',
i.e. the headache; *kodi ovn ar,* 'to frighten'; *kodi əsva,* 'to
tickle'; *kəsgy meun tyː sy ꞑ kodi r dr̥eːθ,* 'sleeping in a house is
what makes it subject to rates' (cf. 13). (16) 'to hunt up, rake
up, trump up': *kodi kneks,* 'to rake up old scores'; *pëidjux̱ kodi heːn
beθa,* 'let bygones be bygones'. (17) 'to cause to get up': *kodi
mer̥χaid ə noːs.* (18) in knitting stockings, 'to increase the stitches'.

    II. Intransitive: (1) 'to get up': *kodi ar i draːyd,* 'to
stand up'; *kodi ar i isla,* 'to sit up'; *koːd i vəny,* 'get up':—
esp. 'to get up•out of bed'; *kodi o dani hi,* 'to agitate (against
something)'. (2) 'to rise': *r̥ hayl, ə lëyad əꞑ kodi;—ə mənəðoð
sy ꞑ kodi o gonuy,* 'the mountains which rise from Conway';
may r̥hiu ðruːg wedi kodi ˙r̥hənθynu, 'there is bad blood
between them';—*kodi n vaur,* 'to swell up': *ə boχa ꞑ kodi
n vaur,* i.e. when puffing out the cheeks. (3) 'to come up'
(of plants): *welis i rëi wedi kodi n i dail,* 'I saw some which
had come up into leaf'. (4) 'to come out' (of a stain): *ədi
o ꞑ kodi ruːan ʔ,* 'is it coming out now?' (e.g. ink out of a coat).
(5) 'to clear up' (of the weather): *may hi ꞑ kodi m braːv etto,* 'it
is clearing up again'; *may hi ꞑ kodi n hayl,* 'the sun is coming
out'; *huraχ mi ðaːu i godi at ə pnaun,* 'perhaps it will clear up by
the afternoon'. (6) *kodi n laːn,* 'to come to nothing, to break
down': *mi godoð ən laːn mynd ə mlaːyn hevo farad sëysnag,* 'I
didn't keep up speaking English'; *mi godoð ən laːn arno vo ar
ganol i bregaθ,* 'he broke down in the middle of his sermon'.

    kodjad, s.m., codiad, D., s.v. 'ortus'; 'rising': *bara heb ðim kodjad əno vo*, 'bread which has not risen'; *kodjad ər hayl*, 'sunrise'; *ar godjad ər hayl*, 'at sunrise'; *ar i godjad*, 'just after getting up'; 'the first thing in the morning'; *paid a mynd ar də godjad vel hyn; mi aː i əno vory ar ə ɲhodjad*;—also 'a rise' in wages, etc. ;—*kodjad tiːr*, 'rising ground'.

kodl, s.f., 'nonsense': *heːn godl wirjon ədi o i ǵiːd*, 'it is a pack of nonsense from beginning to end'.

kodlan, s.f., 'a woman who talks in a nonsensical manner'.

kodlas, kodljas, s.f. = *kodlan* : *ŗ heːn godlas ðjaul!*

kodljan, kodljo, kodlo, v., codlo, T.N. 16. 17. (1) 'to mess about with': *paid a kodljo r duːr na, vaχgan*. (2) 'to talk nonsense': *taːu a χodlo;*—trans. 'to talk in a nonsensical manner about': *kodljo peθ*. (3) 'to trump up': *kodljo riu heːn strëyon druːg*.

kodljur, kodlur, s.m., 'a nonsensical talker' = *dyːn əɲ kodljo pɔθ*,—*dim pen na θiːn ar i sgurs*.

kodlyn, s.m. = *kodljur*.

kodog, adj., codawg, M.A. 111. 160 a, 39, 'having bags': *gumman kodog [gumman];*—fig., implying wealth: *edraχ əɲ godog*, 'to look well-fed and well-clothed' (I.W.).

kodum, s.f., pl. *kodəmma*, codwm, D., 'fall': *kayl kodum*, "to come a cropper"; *ma na bəmθag ļaːθ o godum i r duːr*, 'the water has a fall of fifteen yards'; *hyn a hyn o godum*, 'so much fall' (speaking of hanging a criminal); *meļyd, gaval kodum*, 'to wrestle'; *kodum ʄevn*, 'wrestling by placing the arms round the waist': *χwara kodum ʄevn;*—*kodum kļoːs*, 'wrestling by placing the arms round the waist and catching hold of the band of the breeches'; *kodum brëiχja*, 'wrestling by catching hold of the collar of one's adversary's coat with each hand'.

kodur, s.m., codwr, D.G. cviii. 10, 'the man who puts the hay into a cart';—also *kodur kany*, 'the leader of the singing'; *kodur bora*, 'an early riser'.

kodəmmur, s.m., codymwr, S.E., 'wrestler' (O.H.).

kodəmmy, v., codymu, *S.E., 'to give some one a fall' (O.H.).

kofa, s.m., coffa, D., 'remembrance', only in the phrase *kofa daː am dano*, 'blessed be his memory'.

kofi, s.m., coffi, C.C.M. 210. 10, 'coffee': *kofi kristin*, 'toasted barley-bread ground with a rolling-pin, on which boiling water is poured and a little brown sugar added' (O.H.).

koftjo, v., Eng. quaff, 'to gulp down, drink greedily': *ˑmaːy o n i goftjo vo!*

kogal, s.m., cogail, D., 'distaff';—as term of reproach, *heːn gogal gwirjon!*

kogjo; kokjo (O.H.), v., coggio, R. [to cheat]; cogio, C.L.C. ii. 24. 26; Eng. cog [to cheat, deceive]. (1) 'to pretend': *may hi ŋ kogjo bot i n medry garðjo, ond vedar hi ðim,* ' she pretends she can garden, but she can't '; *dim ən ə gwëylod—əŋ kogjo bo:d ar ə ŋwynab,* ' not really, but looking as if I was '. (2) ' to cheat ' = *tuylo* (O.H.).

kogjur; kokjur (O.H.), s.m., cogiwr, B.C. 21. 28, ' swindler '.

kogor, v., cogor, D., ' to cackle ' (I.W.).

kogurn, s., cogwrn, D., s.v. ' trochus ', ' articulus ', ' cochlea ', ' gradus '; ' a winder for winding wool '. It consisted of an upright piece placed in a stand (*sto:l*) with a hole in the middle; attached to the upright were two cross-pieces which met at right angles in the middle (*stəlenod dirwin,* cf. D., s.v. ' girgillus ';—' winding-blades ', O.P., s.v. 'estyll'; ystyllod dirwyn, W.S., ' blades '). Round the ends of these and attached to them were *keŋla,* and upon them the wool was wound (O.H.); *ţroi ən i gogurn,* ' to try and tone down, get out of what one has said '.

köïdjo, v., coedio, S.E. (1) ' to timber, floor, etc. ': *köïdjo ţy:.* (2) ' to thrash ': *mi köïdja i di* (O.H.).

köïdjog, adj., coedog, D., ' woody, well-wooded ': *ļe: köïdjog jaun ədi baŋgor.*

köïġi, v., coegi, G.O. ii. 50. 27, ' to speak sarcastically ' (I.W.).

köïgni, s., coegni, D., ' fatuitas, vilitas '; ' sarcasm '.

köïθi, v., coethi, T.N. 305. 36; cydgoethi, G.O. ii. 251. 29, ' to bark ' = *kəvarθ.* Sometimes used transitively instead of *annos,—do:s i göïθi r devaid i vəny.*

kokjan, v., kokian val iar, W.S. [Cacle], ' to cackle ' (of hens): *ţŗesi ķin dɛχra doduy ag əŋ kokjan wedyn.*

kokjo, v., ' to cock ': *kokjo gwair.*

kokkos, s.pl., sing. *kokəsan,* f.; O.E. coccas, ' cockles ' (Cardium edule); *kokkos gwlanod* (Scrobicularia piperata); *kokkos ə vra:n* (Tellina solidula); *kŗeġin kokkos,* ' cockle-shells '; *olwyn gokkos,* ' cog-wheel ', cf. T.N. 16. 10; *kokkos biumaras,* epithet applied to the inhabitants of Beaumaris.

kokkyn, s.m., pl. *kokja,* Eng. cock, ' heap ': *kokkyn o ġerig wedi hel o r ka:y;—po:b pc:θ ən y:n kokkyn ar ə ļaur;—kokkyn gwair,* ' small haycock ' (cf. *mudul*); *kokkyn gwynt,* a number of sheaves of corn placed standing against one another in such a manner that the rain will run off them; they are only so placed when bad weather is expected.—Peat is first piled in threes, then made into *kokja,* and finally into *ţëisi : gnëyd nu ŋ gokja ar i penna i ġi:d;—kokkyn ķëïljog [ķëïljog];—kokkyn ŗhustyr,* ' obstacle '; ' contentious person ' = *dy:n ən erbyn po:b pc:θ—ən erbyn paub—may gəno vo bin i roid ən nhi:n paub—ən tənny pobol eriļ i botʃo* (O.H.);—*kokkyn hiţjo,* ' a mark set up for throwing at '.

ko:χ, adj., pl. *koχjon,* côch, D., ' red ': *ķiŋ goχad· a gwa:yd,* ' as red as blood'; *ḳiŋ goχad a ḷuynog*, 'as red as a fox' (said e. g. of parched ground); *boχa ḳoχjon*, 'red cheeks'; *bəsað ḳoχjon*, 'foxgloves'; *mavon ḳoχjon*, 'raspberries'; *gwa:ḷt ḳo:χ*, 'red hair;— ðay go:χ nēiθ gəθral*, prov. referring to persons with red hair; *byuχ go:χ*, 'red cow'; also 'lady-bird'; *ḳefyl ḳo:χ*, 'sorrel horse'; *ʃugur ḳo:χ*, 'brown sugar'; *pennog ḳo:χ*, 'red herring'; *ə vrc:χ go:χ*, 'measles';—as subst. *ḳo:χ ḷerpul*, 'magenta'.

ḳoχðy, adj., cochddu, S.E., 'brown': *gwla:n ḳoχðy, davad goχðy*.

ḳoχi, v., cochi, D. (1) 'to turn red, to blush': *ḳoχi d at ə ḳḷistja*, 'to blush to the roots of the hair'. (2) 'to be smoked' (of herrings, etc.): *veḷ pennog ḳo:χ əŋ ḳoχi*. (3) 'to be scorched' (of land): *may r ðēyar əŋ ḳoχi* (J.J.). (4) 'to plough' = *tṛoi ti:r:— may hun a hun wedi ḳoχi ḷawar* (J.J.; O.H.). (5) 'to turn soil': *ṛhipjo paḷy = dim ond i goχi o* (i.e. the soil). (6) of hay: 'to become " burnt".' Cf. *gwair, ḳədyn*.

ḳoχḷuyd, adj., cochlwyd, 'reddish brown'.

ḳoχni, s.m., cochni, D., s.v. 'rubedo'; 'redness'.

ḳol, s.pl., sing. *ḳoḷyn*, còl, D., 'awns' (of barley): *gweniθ ḳol* (J.J.; O.H.), 'bearded wheat'.

ḳolar, s.f., pl. *ḳḷeri*, coler, D.; D.G. xlix. 28, 'collar'.

ḳolbjo, v., cf. colbio, M.F. (1) 'to talk nonsense': *paid a ḳolbjo n wirjon = boðro* (J.J.); *ḳolbjo ʃarad* (O.H.). (2) 'to beat, strike': *mi ḳolbja i di l* (O.H.).

ḳolbjur, s.m., 'one who talks nonsense': *hc:n golbjur gwirjon* (O.H.).

ḳolbran, s.m., ? cwlbren, O.P. [bludgeon]; D.G. cxcvi. 49, 'beetle' (formerly used in washing clothes). J.J.

ḳolera, ḳḷera, s., 'cholera'.

ḳoljog, adj., coliog, D., 'having long awns': *haið ḳoljog*.

ḳolkaθ, s.f., pl. *ḳolḳerθi*, coelcerth, D.; colcerth, I.D. xiii. 19; coelceth, B.C. 48. 5, 'bonfire';—formerly lit on *no:s glaŋgëya* (O.H.); *r o:ð o ŋ golkaθ*, 'it was all in a blaze'.

ḳolma, ḳolman, ḳolmjo [*holma*].

ḳolsyn, s.m., pl. *ḳolsys*, colsyn, T.N. 184. 27; Eng. coals; 'hot cinder': *glo: wedi ḳa:l i losgi ŋ golsyn*. (Cinders = *sindars*.)

ḳoḷyn, s.m., pl. *ḳoləna*, colyn, D., 'sting'. Cf. *ḳol*.

ḳoləðjon, s.pl., c.f. coludd, D., 'intestines' (O.H.).

ḳoḷ, s.m., còll, D. (1) 'loss', in the phrase *mynd ar goḷ*, e.g. *may r ḷyvr wedi mynd ar goḷ*, 'the book is lost'. (2) 'defect': *ma na riu goḷ əno vo*, 'he has a screw loose somewhere'. Cf. D., s.v. 'mancus'.

ḳoḷad, s.f., pl. *ḳoḷedjon*, colled, D., 'loss': *ma na lawar o goḷedjon*

akku əm maŋgor, 'great losses have been suffered over in Bangor';
i koḷad n̦huː ədi o, 'it is *their* loss'; *vəða i ðim blewyn ar ə ŋhoḷad,*
'I shall not lose anything by it'; *byːð koḷad aru ar d oːl di,* 'we
shall miss you very much'.

koḷan [*kyḷ*].

koḷedur, s.m., colledwr, D., s.v. 'perditor'; 'loser': *mynd əŋ
goḷedur hevo r tyːː.*

koḷi, v., colli, D. Fut. *koḷiθ* (*kyḷ*). Pret. Pl. 3. *koḷson.* Imperative *koḷ,
koḷa.* I. Transitive: (1) 'to lose': *r oːð o wedi koḷi poːb peːθ ar oːl
koḷi i wraig a i blant,* 'he had lost everything after losing (by death)
his wife and children'; *du i wedi koḷi bottum,* 'I have lost a button';
'a button of mine has come off'; *koḷi amsar,* 'to lose time'; *koḷi
r aval,* 'to let go one's hold'; *koḷi r forð,* 'to lose the way'; *koḷi
i olug,* 'to lose one's sight'; *koḷi i gəmˑraːig,* 'to lose, forget his
Welsh'; *koḷi tiːr,* 'to lose ground'. (2) 'to miss by being too late
or through some other cause': *may o wedi koḷi r treːn,* 'he has
missed the train'; *mi goḷif i r əsgol ðoːy,* 'I was too late for school
yesterday'; *mi goḷis ðurnod i nëyd o,* 'I had a day off (from work)
to do it'; *gaː i goḷi dy lyːn ʔ,* 'may I have Monday off?' (3) 'to
lose' as opposed to 'to win': *koḷi r raːs,* 'to lose the race'.
(4) 'to shed': *may r gaːθ əŋ koḷi i bleːu,* 'the cat's fur is coming
off';—used also of corn which has become over-ripe and is
shedding its grain = *buru, droni.* (5) 'to spill, to drop; to be
spilt': *koḷi duːr, ḷevriθ,* etc.;—*may r priːð wedi koḷi,* 'the earth is
spilt' (e.g. out of a flower-pot). (6) 'to let in' (of liquids): *maː r
sǵidja ma n koḷi duːr,* 'these boots let in water' (opp. *daḷ*).

 II. Intransitive: (1) 'to fall back, fall away, decline, go out of
use', etc.: *du i ŋ koḷi o hyːd,* 'my health is steadily growing worse';
may ə ŋlhyu ŋ koḷi, 'I am losing my hearing'. (2) 'to go to
perdition': *os kyḷ ə kaḷ ve gyḷ ə n̦heḷ* (prov.), 'corruptio optimi
pessima'; *wedi i vuru i u goḷi,* 'gone to perdition', i.e. 'hanged'.
(3) 'to fail': *os kyḷ ə glaːu | o r duyran ə daːu, | os kyḷ ər himða | o r
duyran daːu hiθa,* 'if the rain fails it comes from the east, if the
fine weather fails it comes from the east too'. (4) 'to run' (of
colours). (5) in phrase *koḷi arno i hyːn,* 'to go crazy': *deχra koḷi
tippin arna iː və hyːn öyðun i,* 'I was wool-gathering a bit'.

koːm, adj., Eng. calm, 'calm, unruffled': *duːad əŋ goːm; may o
n yːn koːm* (I.W.).

kommɨs, s., komins, komyns, W.S. [Cōmones], 'common', i.e.
'common land'.

kono, s.m., cono, C.C.M. 83. 32; 94. 6; 98. 25; 101. 6; T.N.
456. 22. (1) according to J.J. 'a small dog', but I am unable to
obtain confirmation. (2) of persons—as applied to a child, *kono
baχ* = 'a plucky little fellow' (J.J.), but *heːn gonᵊ* = 'a little old
man with a sharp temper' (*fᵊrnig*), J.J.—O.H., however, gives

he:n gono = *he:n voi rëit gal*;—*may o n ormod o he:n gono i ti, nëi di ðim by:d hevo hunna;—dy:n kalad ən i vargan a fo:b pe:θ*, i. e. ' a knowing old fellow '.

konstant, adj., Eng. constant ; ' permanent ': *daχi wedi ka:l le: go gonstant ru:an*, ' you have a fairly permanent position now ' (O.H.).

konstro, v., konstrio, W.S. [Constrewe] ; constro, T.N. 179. 39 ; Eng. (Dial.) conster [to understand, fathom, put a construction upon a person's behaviour], Yks., Dev., I. of W., ' to fuss ' ; ' to pry into ' ; ' to puzzle oneself over ' = *ən troi ag ən trosi ; χwiljo i meun po:b pe:θ*, etc.

konstrur, s.m., ' one who pries into others' affairs and knows all the gossip about them ' = *χwiljur da: jaun i ubod am beθa* (O.H.) :— *ḱeruχ atto vo: os taχi i∫o gubod, may o n he:n gonstrur garu* (O.H.).

konuy, Conwy, ' Conway ': *avon gonuy*, ' the River Conway '.

konyn, s.m., pl. *konjon*, properly speaking the sing. of cawn. Cf. conin, B.B.C. 89. 2 ; konyn, W.B., col. 462. 30 ; conyn, R. (1) ' a stalk which a cow has left in grazing.'; cf. *ḱeunan*. (2) 'stump': *konjon ëiθin, gry:g*. (3) 'stump of a thing nearly worn away, and only fit for burning ': *riu he:n gonyn o vrus ; may o wedi mynd ən he:n gonyn*.

koŋgran, s., pl. *kəŋgrod*, ' conger-eel ' (Conger vulgaris).

koŋḱro, v., kwnkwerio, W.S. [Conquere], concwero, C.C. 95. 20, ' to conquer ': *may i nuyda wedi goŋḱro vo*, ' his passions have got the better of him '.

koŋkwerur, s.m., cwncwerwr, Sion Tudur in G.R. [369]. 21 ; (pl.) cwncwer-wyr, Rom. viii. 37, ' conqueror ': *may o n ðigon o goŋkwerur arno vo*.

koŋlog, adj., conglog, cf. B.C. 66. 23, ' full of corners or angles ', said e. g. of a house or field of irregular shape.

koŋol, s.f., pl. *koŋla*, congl, D., ' corner ': *koŋol ə ty:, ə barklod*, etc. ;—*ma: r van ma ŋ goŋol gənnas jaun*, ' this is a very warm corner ' ; *rhøuχ o ar ə goŋol*, ' hang it on the corner (i. e. top angle) of the door '.

kop, koptyn, s., coppyn and pryf coppyn, D., only in *pry: kop, pry: koptyn*,—pl. *prəvaid koppi*, ' spider ' ; *gwe: pry: kop*, ' spider's web '.

kop, a call to a horse to make it come to the speaker.

kopjo, v., copîo, D.P.O. 179. 26, ' to copy '.

koppa, s.f., coppa, D. (1) ' crown of the head', only in *koppa waḷtog* as *gəry po:b koppa waḷtog o ·honynu i furð*, ' to drive away every man-jack of them '—used of animals as well as persons, and sometimes corrupted into *koppa walgo*. (Perhaps scriptural: cf. Psalm lxviii. 21.) (2) ' tuft of feathers on the heads of certain fowls : *koppa o bly: ar i fen* (O.H.).

koppar, s., kopyr, W.S.; coppr, D., s.v. 'ærarius', etc.; coppor, W.Ll. (Voc.), s.v. 'alcan'; copr, B.C. 67. 5, 'copper'.

koppi, s.m., pl. *ko·pi:a*, copi, Josh. viii. 32; coppi, 1 Macc. xi. 37, 'copy'.

koppis, s.pl., 'coping-stones' (O.H.).

koppog. adj., coppog, D., s.v. 'cristatus'; 'crested', 'having a tuft of hair on the head': *ja:r goppog* (O.H.).

koppyn [*kop*].

ko:r, s.m., pl. *kora*, côr, D., 'choir'.

koraχ, s.m., pl. *koraχod*, corrach, D. [Cymmwythach corrach a simmach, Prov.], 'dwarf'; also as term of reproach: *he:n goraχ !* Applied also to trees, etc.: *ɩ ədi hɩ ðim gwerθ i ti gadu ɾ he:n goraχ na* (O.H.). Cf. *kuraχ*.

korði, v., corddi, D. (1) 'to churn'. (2) 'to work up and down as in churning', e. g. with a jumper in a hole which has been bored in slate. Cf. also *may r djaul ən i gorði o*, 'the devil is in him'. Cf. C.C. 12. 15.

korðjad, s.m., corddiad, S.E., 'the amount of butter made at one churning'.

korður, s.m., corddwr, S.E. [one who churns], 'churn': *asgal ə korður*, 'the beater of a churn'. Cf. *ɩyða*.

korf, s.m., pl. *kyrf*, corph, D. (1) 'body': *uθi nerθ enaid a χorf*, 'at it like niggers'; *ɾ he:n gorf*, term applied to the Calvinistic Methodists. (2) 'dead body': *kodi korf* [*kodi*]; *kannuyl korf* [*kannuyl*]; *deryn korf*, 'owl'= *dəly:an*. (3) applied to the main part of things: *korf pren*, 'stem of a tree'; *korf ə drol*, 'body of the cart'; —similarly *əŋ ɣhorf ə durnod, ə no:s*, 'during the day, the night'.

korfolaθ, s.m., corpholaeth, D., s.v. 'corporatio'; 'whole, entirety': *ɾ ho:l wla:d ən i χorfolaθ*.

korforol, adj., corphorawl, D., s.v. 'corporalis'. (1) 'bodily'. (2) 'large-bodied'.

korfyn, s.m., corfyn, L.G.C. 80. 7, dim. of *korf*, 'body, dead body': *mu:y na hənny ðeïl ər he:n gorfyn*, 'more than the body can endure'.

korgi, s.m., pl. *korguns*, corgi, W.S. [A curre dogge], 'a kind of sheep-dog in use sixty or seventy years ago, rather long in body, black in colour, and of little use' (O.H.);—also as term of reproach: *he:n gorgi ba:χ !*

korkas, s.f., 'a piece of cork about eight inches square, to indicate the position of a net in the sea' (O.H.).

korkyn, s.m., pl. *kyrks*, kork, W.S. [Corke]; corc, D., s.v. 'suber'. (1) 'cork' (in general): *ko:ys gorkyn*, 'a cork leg'. (2) 'a cork', e. g. for a bottle or for floating a net.

korχwiglan, kornχwiglan, s.f., pl. *korχwiglod, kornχwiglod,* corn-chwigl, D., ' peewit ' (Vanellus vulgaris).

korlan, s.f., pl. *korlanna,* corlan, D., ' sheep-fold '.

korn, s.m., pl. *kyrn, kornja,* corn, D. (1) ' horn ' : *korn ɔyuχ, maɪwan,* etc., ' the horn of a cow, a snail, etc.'; *may o a i gorn dano,* ' he has his knife in him '; *i χa:l hi ar i gorn,* ' to get a stunning blow ' = *ka:l ḷond i vol, tegan jaun, slap jaun* (O.H.); *mi g̈ëif i laſad ar i gorn o,* ' I got a glass on account of him ' or ' because of the occasion '; *mən ə korn ḍy: !,* asseveration. (2) in various transferred senses : (a) *kyrn ər arad,* ' handles of the plough ' (O.H., but not J.J., who had *dərna r arad*); (b) *korn ə vyuχ,* any shell of the genus Dentalium ; (c) *korn ə guδu,* ' throat, neck ' : *tori korn i uδu,* ' to break one's neck ':—also *korn : r̥hoi tr̥o: n i gorn o,* ' to wring its neck ; (d) *korn gwynt,* ' wind-pipe '; (e) ' chimney (outer) ', ' chimney-pot ' : *may r gwynt wedi χuθy r korn i laur ;—iy: ba:χ y:n korn, mu:g main,* ' a cottage with one chimney and small smoke ';—*ə mu:g ən du:ad o r korn* ; (f) ' horn, hooter ' : *may r korn ən mynd* ; (g) *korn bu:yd,* ' horn used at farms for calling the hands to meals, etc. ',—sometimes formed of a shell [*kr̥ogan*] ; (h) ' an instrument for administering medicine to animals, a drenching horn '; (i) from Eng. corn (?), ' a corn on the foot or hand ' ; cf. D., s.v. ' callus ', ' morticini '. (3) adjectively of things made of horn : *bottum korn,* ' a horn button ' : *roisun i δim bottum korn am dano vo,* ' I wouldn't give a button for it '.

kornal, s.f., pl. *kornela,* cornel, D., ' corner ',—more commonly *koŋol.*

kornas, s.f., epithet applied to a strong woman (O.H.) : *r̥hiu he:n gornas o δənas.*

·*korn·briδo,* v., cf. corn briddo, C.F. 1890, p. 314, ' to turn up the ground with the horns ' (of cattle), O.H. ;—also of persons, im-plying violent temper : *be u:ti y ·korn·briδo ?* (O.H.).

kornelog, kərnelog, adj., cornelog, C.C.M. 140. 27, ' full of corners or angles '. Cf. *koŋlog.*

·*korn·gənnaδ,* v., cf. corn gynnal, C.F. 1890, p. 314, ' to talk loudly ' (O.H.).

kornjo, v., cornio, D., s.v. ' arieto ', ' petulcus '. (1) ' to horn ' (of cattle). (2) ' to speak evil of ' : *kornjo dyn ən i ǵevn.* (3) ' to wrangle, brawl ' : *day δy:n əy gornjo i ǵiliδ.* (4) ' to grumble ' = *grugnaχ ən erbyn pe:θ.*

kornjog, adj., corniog, D., s.v. ' cornutus ' ; ' horned ' : *da: kornjog* is sometimes used to express ' cattle ' in contradistinction to *da: ply:og,* ' poultry '.

kornjur, s.m. (1) ' one who has faults to find in every one ' (*i gyrn o dan baub*). (2) ' grumbler '—(O.H.).

kornχwiglan [*korχwiglan*].

kornuyd, s., pl. *kornuydyð*, cornwyd, D., 'boil' = *navad*.

koron, s.f., pl. *krana*, coron, D. (1) 'crown'. (2) 'crown-piece, five shillings': *du:y bynt a χoron*, 'two pounds five'; *hannar koron*, 'half-crown', pl. *hannar krana*.

korpus, s.m., corpws, D.G. cvi. 43; B.C. 6. 9, 'body', generally 'dead body': *ðary mi olχi i he:n gorpus tlaud ;—r he:n gorpus tlaud !* = also 'poor old fellow !'

kors, s.f., pl. *korsyð*, cors, D., 'bog' = *wëyn*.

korsan, s.f., pl. *korsenna*, corsen, D., 'reed'; also 'the stalk of growing corn'.

korfog, adj., corsog, D., 'marshy'.

kortyn, s.m., pl. *kortna*, cordyn, cort, D.; cortyn, B.C. 68. 5. 'cord', applied e. g. to the rope of the gallows; also to the rope foundation underneath the mattress of an old-fashioned bed: *rhoi matja niuburχ ar ə kortyn* (O.H.);—*rhoid ə kortyn am i uðu i hy:n*, 'to cut one's own throat' (metaphorically); *nëidjo tru:y r kortyn*, 'to skip with a skipping-rope'.

korwynt, s.m., corwynt, D., 'whirlwind'.

koryn, s.m., coryn, D., 'crown of the head': *ma na χwilan ən i χoryn hi*, 'she has a bee in her bonnet'; *r o:ð rubaθ ən i goryn*, 'he had something in his head', i. e. 'he had brains'; *may o wedi mynd əŋ goryn mo:yl*, 'he has become bald on his crown'; *hi:r i goryn*, 'long-headed'; *koryn het*, 'crown of a hat'.

ko:sb, s.f., cosp, D., 'punishment': *rhoi ko:sb ar*, 'to punish'.

kosbi, v., cospi, D., 'to punish': *kosbi a dgeljo*, 'to punish and imprison'.

kosi, v., cosi, D. (1) 'to itch, tickle': *kosi ḷəgad de:, ḷawenyð o bo:b ḷe:, kosi ḷəgad χwi:θ, dagra vel ə gwli:θ*. (2) 'to thrash': *mi kosa i di os na θewi di*.

koslyd, adj., 'itching; itch-producing'.

ko:st, s.f., pl. *kostja*, côst, D.; cf. also W.B., col. 428. 15; D.G. iii. 31, 'cost, expense': *may o n vu:y o go:st na niḷiθ o byθ*, 'he will never pay for his keep'; *ar i go:st o*, 'at his expense'; *gwëiθjo ar i go:st o*, 'to work in his pay'; *du i ŋ gwëiθjo ar və ŋho:st və hy:n*, 'I work on my own account'; *rhoid arjan ar go:st i ru:in*, 'to put some one into court for debt'.

kostjo, v., costio, D.; M.Ll. ii. 61. 25; B.C. 93. 21, 'to cost'.

kostog, s.m., costog, D., 'molossus'; cf. B.C. 38. 18; 136. 5; P.G.G. 249. 2; G.O. i. 229. 4. (1) 'a burly man': *dy:n trum a ḷaun bol i gi:d* (O.H.). (2) 'quick of tongue' = *pert, parod i air* (J.J.). (3) 'a conceited, self-satisfied fellow' (O.H.). Cf. also *sløuki*.

kostys, adj., kostus, W.S. [Costyouse]; costus, D., 'expensive': *mi̇̈ ëiθ ɔŋ gostys jaun arna i*, 'it will be very expensive for me'.

kosva, s.f., cosfa, S.E. (1) 'an itch'. (2) 'a thrashing'.

kosyn, s.m., cosyn, D., 'a cheese': *kosyn o gaus*.

ko:t, s.f., pl. *kotja*, 'coat': *ko:t wëy*, 'jersey'.

kotjo, v., Eng. cut, 'to spay'.

kotral, s.f., pl. *kotrela*, Eng. (Dial.) cotterel [a pin, screw, wedge, or bolt which fastens something in its place], 'an iron pin, the upper part of which is divided into two parts, which is placed through a hole in the *klëivis* to fasten a truck to a rope' (J.J.).

ko:tʃ, s.f., pl. *kotʃys*, coits, C.C. 120. 23, 'coach': *pobol ɔ go:tʃ vaur*, 'mail-coach passengers' (the chief purveyors of news in the old days), hence: *pu:y sy n dëyd? pobol ɔ go:tʃ vaur*, 'Who says so?' 'Some one I can't name' (I.W.);—*ko:tʃ ba:χ*, 'perambulator'.

kottas, s.f., pl. *kotesod*, cotes, S.E., 'a spayed cow'.

kotton, s., 'cotton': *eda gotton*.

kottum, s.m., cottwm, D., 'cotton'; only in the phrase *wedi̇̈ gwisgo at ɔ kottum*, 'threadbare' (Bangor).

kœudal, s., Eng. (Dial.) caudle [a mess, muddle, entanglement: also a miner's term for·a thick and muddy fluid], Cornwall, 'anything of the consistency of porridge' (I.W.); *pe:θ sy wedi̇̈ kɔmɔsgy hevo du:r ne rubaθ* (J.J.);—*ɤhiu gœudal = kɔmɔsgva* (J.J.). Cf. *krœudal*.

kœudgan, s.f., Eng. gouge (in slate quarries), 'an iron chisel with a concave blade for cutting grooves across blocks of slate with a view to dividing them'; (in making clogs) a similar instrument for hollowing out the wooden sole.

kœugan; kœukan (J.J.), s.f., cf. cawg, D., 'a small vessel formerly used for milk—in shape either tapering upwards or bulging out in the middle': *kœugan bri:δ, kœugan bren*.

kœugjad, s., kawgeit, W.B., col. 230. 20; cawgaid, S.E., 'as much as a *kœugan* will hold'.

kœuk, s.pl., *kœukja*, cf. cowciau, Medd. An. 176. 36; Eng. (Dial.) cogs, Shr., 'one of the turned down ends of a horse-shoe'.

kœulad, s.f., pl. *kœulëidja*, coflaid, D.; cowlaid, C.C.M. 140. 28; cywled, P.G.G. 19. 14; 39. 10. (1) 'an armful': *kœulad gwair, kœulad o redyn*:—*may o wedi̇̈ garjo vo n i gœulad*, 'he carried it as a bundle in his arms'; *kœulad ba:χ a i gwasgy n dyn* (= *den*), 'a small armful tightly pressed together', a proverbial expression corresponding to 'grasp all, lose all', Fr. "qui trop embrasse mal étreint"; so also *may o wedi̇̈ kɔmmyd gormod o gœulad; basa n wel i̇̈δo vo lai o gœulad*. (2) used of persons of great size: *kœulad o dɔnas*, 'a very big woman'. (3) 'unborn child': *may nu ŋ kɔmmyd riu* (rue) *i la:δ ɔ gœulad*.

kɐulẽïdjo, klöidjo, v., cofleidio, D.; cywleidio, P.G.G. 287. 11; cowleidio, P.G.G. 300. 6; 324. 6, 'to embrace'.

kɐuləðjo, kluəðjo, v., cywilyddio, D., 'to shame'; 'be ashamed'.

kɐuləðys, kluəðys, adj., cywilyddus, D., 'shameful': *hc:n dro: kɐuləðys.*

kɐunslar, s., Eng. counsellor, "a woman who always insists on having her rights and uses language to that effect", T.G.G. 1902, 30. 32:—*hc:n gounslar ovnaduy ədi hi* (O.H.).

kɐunʃo, kɐunʃur [*kɐuntjo, kɐuntjur*].

kɐunt, s., 'count': *kadu gɐunt vaint vy:ð o bo:b y:n,* 'keep count how many there are of each'.

kɐunt, s., cownt, C.C. 13. 11; 173. 19; 435. 9, Eng. account. (1) 'account': *ļyvr kɐunt,* 'account book'. (2) *ar gɐunt,* 'on account of, with regard to': *ar i gɐunt o,* 'with regard to him'; *po:yn ar i gɐunt o,* 'sorry on his account';—*pẽïdjuχ a mynd i ðim trafarθ ar ə ŋhɐunt i.* (3) 'reckoning': *ar bo:b kɐunt sy ǵin i,* 'as far as I can reckon'. (4) 'esteem': *may gəno vo gɐunt ən ə ǵəmra:ig,* 'he has esteem for, makes account of Welsh'.

kɐuntjo, v. (1) 'to account, consider'. (2) 'to reckon, add figures up'.

kɐuntjur; also *kɐunʃur* (I.W.), s.m., 'reckoner': *may o ŋ gɐuntjur rẽït ða:,* 'he is very good at reckoning'.

kɐupar, s.m., cowper, C.L.C. ii. 22. 17, 'cooper'.

kɐupog, s.f., Eng. cow-pox, 'vaccination'.

kɐuran, adj., cywraint, D., 'skilful'; "'cute": *dy:n kɐuran, gwaiθ kɐuran.*

kɐuras, s.f., cowres, D., s.v. 'gigas'; 'giantess'. (Cf. the place-name *fedogad ə gɐuras* in Bwlch y Ddeufaen);—used of an imperious woman: *may hi ŋ gɐuras ar baub.*

kɐurt, s.m., pl. *kɐurtja,* kwrt, B.H. 143. 1; W.S. [A courte]; cowrt, C.L.C. iv. 40. 1. (1) 'yard'. (2) 'court of law' (W.H.). Cf. *kɐut.*

kɐurtjo, v., 'to put into court, to summons'.

kɐuʃo, v., cawsio, S.E., 'to curdle', said of milk when the butter is beginning to show in it; *may o n deχra kɐuʃo* (= *toṛi*). This is the next stage to *briθo.*

kɐut, s.m., pl. *kɐutja,* 'yard' (E.J.; W.H.). Cf. *kɐurt.*

kovjo, v., cofio, D. Fut. S. 1. *kovja,* 2. *kovi,* 3. *koviθ.* Pl. 1. *kovjun,* etc. Pret. S. 3. *kovjoð.* No plural. Imperative *kovja; kovjuχ.* (1) 'to remember': *du i n meθy kovjo i enu vo,* 'I don't remember his name'; *mi go·vja i am ðano vo,* 'I will remember about him'; *kovja am də vɐuyd !,* 'mind you remember!' (2) 'to mind in phrases like *kovja ðẽyd ə gwi:r !,* 'mind you speak the truth !' (3) in the imperative, a kind of expletive 'mind !', 'my word!': *ma:y hi n o:yr, kovjuχ!*, 'my word! it is cold!' (4) in complimentary messages, 'remember': *kovjuχ vi at ɔχ mam*, 'remember me to your mother'. (5) 'to remind': *kovjuχ i mi ɔynd vory*, 'remind me to go to-morrow'.

kovjur, s., 'one who has a good memory': *may o ŋ govjur jaun.*

kovys, adj., cofus, D., s.v. 'memor'; 'having a good memory'.

kɒwan, s.f., cywen, D., 'pullet';—also 'child'; cf. Eng. 'chick'.

kɒwar, ku:ar, s.m., cywair, D.; cywer, P.G.G. 16. 10; 83. 19, etc., 'state': *ɔm ṃha gu:ar daχi hëïðju?*, 'how are you to-day?'; *meun kɒwar pṛiodol*, 'in a proper state';—in music *ku:ar ḷeðv, ku:ar ḷon*, 'minor, major key'; also used figuratively.

kɒwarχ, ku:arχ, s.m., cywarch, D., s.v. 'cannabis'; 'hemp': *puḷ ku:arχ*, 'pool where hemp was watered or rated'; *ku:arχ du:r* (O.H. and Bangor), probably 'hemp agrimony' (Eupatorium cannabinum).

kɒwir, adj., cywir, D. (1) 'correct'. (2) 'true, faithful': *may o ŋ gɔwaiḷ kɒwir i χi*, 'he is a true friend of yours'.

ko:yd, coed, D. (1) s.pl., 'wood, timber': *wedi nëyd o go:yd kḷedjon, kṛɔvjon*, 'made of hard, strong wood' (J.J.); *maly ko:yd*, 'to chop wood'; *toṛi ko:yd*, 'to cut wood'; *palis ko:yd (o go:yd)*. 'a wooden partition'; *nid po:b ko:yd nëïθ drol*, 'not every kind of wood will make a cart'; *du:ad at i go:yd*, 'to come to oneself', said e.g. of one who has gone beyond his powers and come to understand his position, his proper level. (2) s.m., pl. *kŏydyð*, 'a wood': *meθy gweld ɔ ko:yd ġin brenja*, 'not to see the wood for the trees'. (3) s.pl., sing. *kŏydan*, f., 'trees': *kŏydan vedwan*, 'a birch'; *kŏydan vala*, 'an apple-tree'; *kŏydan eḷig*, 'a pear-tree'; *kŏydan drops*, 'fuchsia'; *toṛi ko:yd ar ɔ ġeḷḷyð*, 'to cut down trees on the slopes' (cf. also under 1); *dan ɔ gŏydan i moχal ɔ gla:u*, 'under the tree to shelter from the rain';—also frequently 'plant', e.g. growing in a pot: *koy:d mevys*, 'strawberry plants'; *ko:yd ḷy:s*, 'bilberry plants'.

ko:yð, s., cyhoedd, D.; c'oedd, D.G. App. xiv. 38, 53, in the phrases *ar go:yð, ar go:yð gwla:d, ar go:yð by:d*, 'in public'.

ko:yg, adj., coeg, D., 'empty': *knëyan go:yg*, 'an empty nut',— only used in the phrase *y:n go:yg o:yð ɔ gnëyan [kna:y]*.

kŏyglyd, adj., coeglyd, T.N. 152. 34, 'sarcastic'.

ko:yl, s.m., pl. *kŏiljon*, coel, D. (1) 'omen, inference': *gnëyd kŏiljon*, 'to draw inferences'; *asgurn ko:yl [asgurn]*; *ɔ drɔdyð waïθ by:ð ko:yl*, 'the third time is lucky'; *t o:ys na ðim ko:yl ·arnynu n ɔ ġëya*, 'you cannot draw inferences from them in the winter' (referring to cows which, by feeding on the top of a hill, are supposed to indicate fine weather); *ko:yl gwra:χ ar o:l byḷḷa yud*, 'an old wives' fable '. (2) 'credibility, reliability' : *ɩ o:ys na ðim ko:yl ar ə pe:θ r u:ti n i ðëyd;—ɩ o:ys dim ko:yl arno vo,* ' he is not reliable '. (3) ' credit ' : *ar go:yl,* ' on credit ' = *ar lab.*

ko:ys, s.f., pl. *köysa,* coes, D., 'leg' : *ko:ys bren, ko:ys gorkyn,* ' a wooden leg' : *ko:ys la:s,* ' shin bone of beef' ; *köysa n ɩavlyd alan,* ' bandy legs ' ; *kəmmyd ə go:ys,* ' to run away'. In various transferred senses : (a) ' leg ', e. g. of a table : *ko:ys bur ;* (b) 'leg' of a pair of tongs ; (c) ' handle ' : *koy:s brus, sospan ;* (d) ' stalk ' (of a plant or flower); (e) ' stem ' (of a pipe).—Masc. in these senses (I.W. ; but not at Bangor).

köysgoχ, kösgoχ, ·ko:ys·go:χ, s.f., pl. *koysgoχjad,* coesgoch, D. (1) ' redshank ' (Totanus calidris). (2) ' red-leg robin, herb Robert ' (Geranium Robertianum).

köysnöyθ, köysnoθ, kösnoθ, adj., coesnoeth, O.P., ' bare-legged ' : *mvnd əŋ göysnoθ dröydnoθ,* ' to walk with one's shoes and stockings off '.

ko:yθ, adj., coeth, D., ' polished, skilled in utterance ' : *gnëyd χi n vu:y ko:yθ ən ər jaiθ ; jaiθ go:yθ.* (Seldom used.)

kɹa:, s.pl., cra, craf, D., ' ramsons ' (Allium ursinum).

kɹab, s.m., ' a kind of receptacle in a cart, beneath the seat of the driver, for putting any small article, e. g. when going a distance '.

kɹab, s., ' the smallest pig of a litter ' ; hence *rìu he:n grab o hogyn,* applied to a small boy (O.H.).

kɹabjo, v., ' to shrink, waste away ' (J.J.; O.H.).

kɹablyd, adj., ' shrunk, wasted ' : *dylo kɹablyd.*

kɹa:f, s., craff, R., ' a grasping, laying hold of ' : *ma: nu n ɣhoid ə drain a i blëyna i vəny a i bona i laur, am vod ə guynɩ əŋ kəmmyd ḷai o gra:f ən ə bona* (O.H.) ;—*ɩ o:ys na ðim kɹa:f ar i storì = ɩ o:ys na ðim pen na θi:n arni hi* (O.H.).

kɹa:f, adj., crâff, D., ' keen ' (of sight) : *golug kɹa:f ;—edraχ əŋ gra:f,* ' to look intently ' ;—also, in general ' quick, intelligent, observant '.

kɹafy, v., craffu, D., 'fixis oculis intueri'; ' to look intently ' : *kɹafy hənny ·vedruχi,* e. g. in semi-darkness.

kɹafys, adj., craffus, D.P.O. 11. 9, ' quick, intelligent, observant '.

kɹai, s.m., crau, D. ; crai, W.Ll. (Voc.) s.v. ' mŵn ' ; ' eye ' of a needle : *kɹai nəduð ðy:r ;* also of axes and hammers *kɹai wy:aḷɩ, murθul, gorð : may r iɹo:yd* (handle) *ən du:ad o r kɹai.*

kɹai, s., in the phrase *kany n i grai* (cf. M.F. canu ei grai, p. 8): 'to spread unfavourable reports as to the misfortunes or delinquencies of some one ' (the opp. of ' to sing the praises of some one ') : *dy:n wedi peχy, dy:n ən mynd ən o:l ḷa:u, a pobol eriḷ əŋ kany n i grai* (O.H.).

ḳrai, crai, D., in the phrase *newyð sbon danḷi grai*, 'bran-new'. Cf. 'bran-span-new'.

ḳraig, s.f., pl. *ḳrëigja*, craig, D., 'rock'.

ḳraiθ, s.f., pl. *ḳrëiθja*, craith, D., 'scar': *dan i grëiθja* (O.H.), 'scarred'.

ḳrak, s.m., pl. *ḳrakja*, 'crack': *may ḳrak ɘno vo*, 'he is nearly a bankrupt'.

ḳrakjo, v., craccio, C.C. 357. 14, 'to crack'.

ḳra:χ, s.pl., sing. *ḳraχan* (*ḳraχod* is also used for the plural), crach, D., 'scabs, sores': *ḳraχan ar ɘ wymmad*, 'a scab on the face'; *mynd ɘŋ gra:χ i ḳru:yn nu*, 'to become covered with scabs';—*riu he:n gra:χ wedi kodi tɾuyðo vo i ġi:d*;—*ma: ḳega devaid ɘŋ gra:χ i ġi:d ar o:l bytta ëiθin*;—also of excrescences on trees;—*ḳreġin ḳraχod*, 'barnacles';—*dail ḳra:χ*, 'fox-glove plant' (Digitalis purpurea);—as depreciatory epithet: *he:n graχan sa:l o dɘðyn*, 'a wretched tenement';—used adjectively: *ḳra:χ voneðig*, 'snob'; cf. T.N. 4. 8; *ḳra:χ böiri*, 'to spit after clearing the throat'; cf. G.O. ii. 113. 10.

ḳraχgoyd, *ḳraχgod*, s.pl., crachgoed, 'the shoots which grow out of the stump of a tree which has been sawn off' (O.H.): *briga ḳraχgoyd, ko:yd ḳraχgoyd*.

ḳramman, s., crammen, Lev. xiii. 2, 'a scab such as forms over a wound' (O.H.).

ḳrand, adj., sup. *ḳrandja*, Eng. grand (T.N. 4. 12), 'smart, stylishly dressed': *ru:m grand*, 'a fine room'; *po:b pe:θ wedi wisgo ɲ grand*, 'everything draped magnificently'; *daχi n edraχ ɘŋ grand*, 'you look smart'.

ḳrandruyð, *ḳranḷruyð*, s.m., grandrwydd, T.N. 9. 24, 'smartness, showiness in dress, etc.'

ḳraŋk, s.m., pl. *ḳraŋkod*, crangc, D., 'crab'. Fishermen distinguish between *ḳraŋkod koχjon*, which are edible, and *ḳraŋkod glëiʃon*, which are not: *bodja ḳraŋkod*, 'crabs' claws'; *ḳraŋk wisgjur*, "peeler", i.e. a crab which has cast its shell.

ḳraŋḱi, s.m., cf. Eng. cranky; term of reproach: *ɼ he:n granḱi gwirjon*.

ḳrap, s., crap, D., 'raptio, præhensio'; crab, B.C. 30. 26; cràp, 148. 22, 'smattering, inkling, idea': *ḳrap o sëysnag*, 'a smattering of English'; *may gɘno vo grap ar gɘmra:ig*, 'he has a smattering of Welsh'; *riu grap ar ɘ forð*;—*riu grap am waiθ*;—*ɼ o:ð ġin baub riu grap i nëyd klokʃa r amsar honno*, 'every one had some idea how to make clogs at that time'.—Cf. T.N. 209. 24.

ḳrapjo, v., crapio, S.E. (1) 'to pick up': *ḳrapjo ġëirja*, 'to pick up words'. (2) used of an action done in an imperfect way: *riu grapjo darḷan, gweld, dy:aḷ.*

ḱra:s, adj., crâs, D. (1) 'dry, parched': ər hayl əŋ gnēyd ər haið əŋ gra:s. (2) 'rough, acrid, saucy': kəmma bu:yļ a mənað ; paid a ſarad mor gra:s. (3) 'harsh, discordant': ļais ḱra:s ; he:n duru ḱra:s ;—often used of thunder when heard directly overhead: may n̥ iŗany ŋ gra:s jaun. (4) 'rough to the touch'.

ḱrasog, adj., 'rough, acrid, saucy in speech': dy:n ḱrasog = dy:n ən ſarad ən egar.

ḱrasy, v., crasu, D., 'to bake' (as distinguished from pobi, it implies the act of baking the dough in the oven, whereas pobi means the whole process): ən ə ty: daχi ŋ ḱrasy ? na:ḱ i, mynd aļan a vo: (sc. ə to:ys) ;—avol wedi grasy, 'baked apple'; ḱrasy bara = also 'to toast bread'.

ḱraɪʃ (I.W.) ; kļaɪʃ (E.J.), s., Eng. (Dial.) cratch [stomach], Yks., 'stomach': be sy n̥ də glaɪʃ di ? Cf. kaɪʃ.

ḱraɪʃ, s., Eng. crash (?), in the phrase toŗi n̥ graɪʃ, 'to break clean in two'. Cf. also toŗi ŋ glaɪʃ, toŗi ŋ glaɪʃan.

ḱraujo, v., 'to place pieces of slate (ḱrauja) round the sides of a waggon when carrying away rubble' (J.J.) [ḱrawan].

ḱravaglaχ (O.H.) ; kravagljaχ (J.J.), s., cf. cryfaglach, cyfraglach, Rhys, Celtic Folklore, p. 450. (1) 'a tree whose leader has been cut and which throws out small branches in all directions' (J.J.). (2) dy:n ·di:·nerθ, ble:r, dim səmmyd, dim mynd əno vo (J.J.).

ḱravaŋk, s.m., pl. ḱravaŋa, crafangc, D., 'claw': myndo i gravaŋa vo, 'to get out of his clutches'; ḱravaŋk ə vra:n, 'crow's foot' (Ranunculus bulbosus); bloda ḱravaŋk ə vra:n, 'buttercups'.

ḱravaŋy, v., crafangu, S.E. (1) 'to grasp, clutch': ḱravaŋy ə kubul iðo vo i hy:n. (2) 'to climb by catching hold of small protuberances': ḱravaŋy i vəny r graig.

ḱravaɪ, s.m., pl. ḱravaɪja, 'scarf'.

ḱravjad, s.m., crafiad, D., s.v. 'scalptura'. (1) 'a scraping'. (2) 'a slight grasp, a touching': rois i gravjad arni hi (= gaval, tuɪʃad əni hi), O.H.

ḱravur, s.m., crafwr, S.E. (1) 'one who scrapes together'—of a niggardly man: he:n gravur am arjan,—in good sense, he:n gravur go səund am i dammad ədi o. (2) 'a sarcastic man'.

ḱravy, v., crafu, D. (1) 'to scratch (where one itches), to scrape, to chafe': ḱravy r ḱro:yn, 'to scrape the skin'; ḱravy asgurn, 'to pick a bone'; ḱravy guðu, 'to clear the throat'; ḱravy fur, 'to scrape away' (e.g. a piece of paper stuck on to something); kadu ə tŗëiʃja ŗhag ḱravy oχor ə ḱefyl, 'to keep the traces from chafing the sides of the horse'; may hunna ŋ ḱravy i linja n̥ aru uθ ĝerðad, 'that man is knock-kneed'.—Substantively, ə ḱravy, "the itch". (2) 'to scrape together': ḱravy r ŗhent a r iŗeθi, 'to scrape together

the rent and taxes'. (3) 'to paw the ground' (of bulls, etc.).
(4) fig. 'to annoy, be sarcastic to': *kravy ruːin*; also abs.: *r oːð o
ŋ kravy n ovnaduy*, 'he was terribly sarcastic'.

krawan, krawon, krewyn, s., pl. *krawenna* and *krauja*, crawen,
D., 'crusta'. (1) 'a covering': *mi dʒviθ ɔŋ grewyn dros ɔ lyn i
ɡiːd*, 'it grows till it forms a coating over the whole lake' (O.H.);
briu a krawan ar i oːl o (O.H.), alluding to the hard flesh which
appears after a scar has healed (cf. *kramman*); *ɔ kroːyn wedi kodi ŋ
grawan* (J.J.);—also the 'crackling' of pork: *krawan kiːg moːχ*
(J.J.); *mi ɡcːs i riu grawan dena baːχ o ɡiːg moχyn* (O.H.). (2) in
slate quarries, 'a piece of slate which has been rejected, no matter
what the size may be'. They are often used to place round the
sides of a waggon when carrying rubble.—In former times it was
the custom to start a strike by sending a *krewyn* round, passed from
hand to hand, with instructions written on it, so as to bring about
concerted action.

krcːd, s.f., crêd, D., 'belief, faith, trust': *r oːð faʃun grcːd gɔno
vo ɔn i daːd*, 'he had such trust in his father'.

kredo, s., kredo, W.S., 'creed': *daχi wedi newid ɔχ kredo*, 'you
have changed your creed', i.e. 'you are going to be married'.

kredy, v., credu, D. (1) 'to believe': *d ɔdu i ðim ɔŋ kredy i vod
o wedi boːd rusyt*, 'I don't believe he ever existed, somehow'; *dim
ɔŋ kredy bod dyu meun boːd, dim ɔŋ kredy ɔn i vëïbil*, 'not believing in
the existence of God, not believing in his Bible'; *r ɔdu i ŋ kredy
meun lawar o beθa ovargöylys vel na*, 'I believe in a number of
superstitions like that'; *·χredanu ·m onaχi*, 'they would not believe
you'. (2) 'to think': *ty: a for na du i ŋ kredy maːy hi*, 'I think it
is somewhere near there'.

kreft, s.f., pl. *kreftja*, crefft, D.; cf. W.B., col. 65. 25; D.G.
xliii. 5; cv. 65; B.C. 75. 14; M.E. creft (11th–14th cent.), 'craft,
trade, calling'.

kreftur, s.m., krefftwr, W.S. [A craftesman], 'craftsman': *may o
ŋ greftur daː*.

kreglëïʃo, v., crugleisio, B.C. 114. 11; cregleisio, T.N. 330. 1, 'to
shout', especially in connexion with singing: *kreglëïʃo kany; kana
a faid a χreglëïʃo*.

kregog, adj., carregog, D., s.v. 'saxeus', 'saxosus'; 'stony'.

kregyr, s., crŷr, cryhyr, crehyr, D., 'heron' (J.J.) = *kryː glaːs*.—
Not known to my other informants.

krëïʃo (O.H.); *krɐuʃo* (J.J.), v., 'to go round selling herrings,
potatoes, fruit, etc.'

krëïʃon, s.pl., cf. creision, Isaiah lxiv. 2, used to intensify: *may
m boːyθ grëïʃon, ʳhewi ŋ grëïʃon*.

krĕiſʿur, krŏiſʿur, s.m., 'one who goes round selling herrings, etc.' Cf. *krĕiſʿo.*

krĕiθan, s.f., creithen, S.E., dim. of *kraiθ,* 'scar'.

krĕivjon, s.pl., creifion, D., s.v. 'ramentum', 'strigmentum'; 'scrapings', e.g. 'the remains of food, after cooking, in a pan, etc.'; 'the remains of tallow which has melted on a candlestick'.

krempog, s.f., pl. *krempoga,* crempog, D., 'lightcake, pancake'.

krentſ, s., Eng. (Dial.) cranch (*kranſ*), [to grind, gnash the teeth, to set the teeth on edge], Nhb., West., Yks., in the exp. *krentſ ə ku:n,* 'sorrel' (Rumex Acetosa, etc.).—Also called *ķerıks ku:n, dılıs ku:n, syrans ə ku:n, daıl sirjon.* (*Ķerıg sgo:l* is the usual form at Carnarvon.)

kreppaχ, kleppaχ, s.f., crebach and creppach, D., 'ariditate et marcore contractus'; 'numbness of the hands through cold': *öırni maur ar ə dylo,* (J.J.); *gwa:yd ɪn feɪy ɪn ə bɪsað = winθraw* (O.H.).

kreuſjo, v., Eng. recruit, 'to recover from an illness'.

krevy, v., crefu, D., 'to beg, entreat': *may o ɲ krevy ·arnoχi vriſʿo,* 'he begs you to make haste'.

krevyð, s.f., crefydd, D., 'religion'.

krewyn, s.m., ? crewyn, D., dim. of craw, 'hara': *krewyn o y:d, o datıus,* 'a store of corn, potatoes' (I.W.).—J.J. looked upon this as an Anglesey word.

krewyn [*krawan*].

krĕy, v., créu, D., 'to create'.

krĕylon, adj., creulawn, D.; G.R. [106]. 19, 'cruel'.

kri:, adj., cri, D., only in *bara kri:, kakkan gri:,* 'bread without barm in it baked in a pan or on a griddle'.

kri:b, s.m., pl. *kriba,* crib, D. (1) 'comb': *daint kri:b,* 'tooth of a comb'; *kri:b ma:n,* 'small-toothed comb'; *daıl kriba sant fraid* (O.H.), 'wood betony' (Stachys Betonica). (2) 'comb' (of a cock): *kri:b ķeiljog.* (3) 'apex' (of a roof, etc.): *kri:b ty:, kri:b ta:s, kri:b ə to:.* (4) fig. *tori i gri:b,* 'to lose one's character' = *tori i vri:.*

·*kri:b·ðeiljo,* v., cribddeilio, R., 'to do business dishonestly, e.g. by representing goods to be of a quality which they are not'.

kribin, s.f., pl. *kribinja,* cribyn, D., 'rake';—as term of reproach, 'a niggardly, grasping individual' = *kravur.*

kribinjo, kribənjo, krəbinjo, v., cribinio, D., 'to rake': *heb i gribinjo n la:n,* 'not well raked'.

kribinjon, krəbinjon, kərbinjon, s.pl., cribinion, S.E., 'rakings', e.g. corn left on the fields and raked together.

kṛiblin, s., ' something shrunk ' : *rubaθ wedi kṛibəχy, wedi mynd i
ğiliδ nes may r kṛoːyn ən ḷak, a ṛhəχa a kuisi arno vo* (J.J.—not
known to O.H.).

kṛibo, v., cribo, D. Imperative *kṛiba*, ' to comb '.

kṛibog, adj., cribog, D., ' cristatus, cacuminatus ' ; ' rising to its
apex steeply on both sides ' : *mənyδ kṛibog ;—may r ṭyː n ṛhyː gribog
i χi vynd i vəny heb əstol*, ' the slope of the roof is too great for you
to go up without a ladder ' ;—of persons, applied to one who has a
high opinion of himself. (All O.H.)

kṛibəχy [kṛəbəχy].

kṛiglin, s., pl. *kṛiglod, kṛiglis*, cruglyn, G.O. ii. 240. 10 ; cf. Eng.
(Dial.) griggles [small apples left on the tree after picking ; small
worthless fruit, vegetables, etc. left after gathering], w.Cy., Wil.,
Cor. ; also griglens, w.Cor., and derivative griggling, ' scrap ' =
məmryn :—poːb kṛiglin o hono vo ; may o wedi darvod boːb kṛiglin.

kṛiglis, s.pl., cruglys, S.E. ; cf. cryglus, D.G. ccxvii. 5 ; creiglys,
H.D., ' crakeberry, crowberry ' (Empetrum nigrum).

kṛik, s.m., pl. *kṛikja*, Eng. crick, ' a rheumatic pain ' ; *kṛik ən ə
guδu*, ' stiff-neck ' ; *du i ŋ grikja i ğiːd*, ' I am aching all over '.

kṛikjad, s.m., krickiad, W.S. ; criccied, D. ; criccad, C.C. 476. 21,
' cricket ' (insect) : *may r kṛikjad əŋ kany.*

kṛikmala [kryːd].

kṛimmog, s.f., pl. *kṛƶmoga*, crimmog, D. (1) ' shin '. (2) ' spur
of a mountain '.

kṛimp, s., Eng. crimp [to crumple ; also (dial.) ' to be niggardly ',
Devon]. (1) applied to things which have been burnt to a cinder :
ḷosği ŋ grimp ; wedi nēyd əŋ grimp. (2) of persons : ' a stingy
fellow, a screw ' : *heːn grimp !*

kṛimpan, s.f., ' a stingy woman '.

kṛimpin, s., ' something dry and burnt up ' : *maː ṛ hayl wedi ḷosği
poːb man əŋ grimpin ;—may o ŋ grimpin grəminstin*, ' it is dried up ' ;
so also *kṛimpin grampan* in the popular rime : *gwraig ə ṭyː a tēyly
daː | os 'gweluχi n δaː, gaː i grempog ? | may ŷheːg əŋ grimpin
grampan ; | may mam ən ṛhyː dlaud i brənny blaud, | may ṇhaːd ən
ṛhyː δiːog i brənny ṭṛiːog ;*—as applied to persons, ' a stingy fellow,
a screw ' : *ṛ heːn grimpin !*

kṛimpjo, v., crimpiaw, O.P. [to pinch, or crimp], ' to be burnt,
scorched, " caught " by the fire '.

kṛimpjo, v., ' to ask ' : *paid a i grimpjo vo etto* (O.H.).

kṛiːn, adj., crîn, D., ' dry and brittle '.

kṛino, v., crino, D., ' to become dry and brittle '.

krinſan, v., Eng. (Dial.) crinch, Sc., 'to grind' (of the teeth): *paid a χrinſan də ðannað arna i* (O.H.).

krini, adj., 'stingy': *he:n ðy:n krini* (O.H.).

kriniaχ, adj., crintach, D., 'stingy';—as subst. *r he:n griniaχ !*, 'the old screw!'

kriniaχlyd, adj., crintachlyd, *S.E. 'stingy'.

kriniaχruyð, s.m., crintachrwydd, D., 'stinginess'.

kri:o, v., krio, W.S.; crio, D. Fut. S. 3. *kri:θ*. Pret. *kri:s*, 'to cry', e.g. of a child; *bëiχjo kri:o = gnëyd nada*, 'to bellow, to howl'; *hornjo kri:o*, 'to cry out of temper'.

kripjad, s., cripiad, S.E., 'a scratch'.

kripjo, v., cripio, D., 'to scratch': *du i wedi ka:l ə rrhipjo gin ə ga:θ*.

kripjo, v., crippian, C.C. 37. 28, 'to creep' = *kripjan, kropjan*:— *mi gripjoð i vəny hy:d ðannað ə graig*, 'he crept up the jagged edges of the rock'.

krippil, s.m., krupul, S.G. 167. 23; krypyl, W.S.; crypl, W.Ll. xcix. 6; crupul, C.L.C. i. 17. 25; crippil, C.C. 334. 12; 351. 2, 'cripple': *wedi mynd əη grippil gla:n*.

kri:st, Crist, 'Christ': *jesy gri:st*, 'Jesus Christ'.

kristin [krəstyn].

kristjon, s.m., pl. *kristnogjon*, Cristion, Acts xxvi. 8 ;. Cristianogion, Acts xi. 26 (the latter is a 'learned' development of Cristionogion), 'Christian'.

kristnogol, adj., Cristionogol; crystnogawl, M.A. ii. 195. 23; Cristnogol, P.G.G. 201. 28, 'Christian'.

kriu, s.m., pl. *kriuja*, Eng. crew, 'a number, band, mass, crew': *kriu o verχaid a beχgin ivaηk ;—kriu o blant ;—hel nu η griu al i gilið ;—kriu o hogja al v o:yd i ;—kriu bargan* (in slate quarries), 'the partners in a bargain'—generally consisting of three, who hire a young man to work for them by the day.

kri:ur, s.m., criwr, B.C. 75. 10, 'town crier'.

krius, s.m., Eng. cruise: *may hi wedi mynd ar ə krius i rula* (O.H.), 'she has gone gadding about somewhere'.

krjadyr, kradyr, s.m., pl. *krədirjaid*, creadur, D., s.v. 'creatura'; 'creature': *kradyr ka:s, kradyr bli:n*, 'a tiresome creature'; *krjadyr divir* (*—kle:n, —nëis*), 'a nice, pleasant individual': *krjadyr ba:χ !*, 'poor fellow!'; *he:n grjadyr !*, 'poor old thing!'; *he:n grjadyr digri*, 'a funny old character'.

krjavol, kravol, kravons, s.pl., criafol, D., 'mountain-ash berries': *köydan grjavol*, 'mountain ash'.

kṛo:g, s.f., crog, D., 'cross' in *gu:yl ə gro:g*, 'Holy Cross Day' (Sept. 14), which occurs in the expression *may hi m buru sgrəmpja gu:yl ə gro:g*, 'it is pouring great drops of rain', alluding properly to the heavy rains of late summer.

kṛogan, s.f., pl. *kṛegin*, cragen, crogen; D. (1) 'shell': *pəsgod kṛegin*, 'shell fish'; *kṛegin kokkos*, 'cockle-shells'; *kṛegin westras*, 'oyster-shells'; *kṛogan la:s* (pl. *kṛegin glëiſon*), 'mussel' (Mytilus edulis); *kṛegin mo:χ*, 'the shells of the whelk' (= *gwiχjad mo:χ*); *kṛogan blakkan* (Mya arenaria); *kṛogan berfro* (i.e. Aberffraw), 'big clam'; *kṛogan dgo:b*, Cardium echinatum and other species of the same genus; *kṛogan jago*, Cypræa europæa or any shell of similar shape, e.g. the cowrie; *kṛogan nëidar*, 'a small shell, something like a periwinkle, of a greyish colour, with white spots' (? Neritina fluviatilis); *kṛogan vu:yd*, 'a large foreign shell of spiral shape with the apex removed, used in farms for calling the hands to dinner, etc.' [*korn*]; *kṛogan agor*, a small shell of similar shape to the latter (app. Turritella), sometimes worn as an ornament on a watch-chain; *kṛogan gasgljad*, 'a kind of foreign shell of a silvery colour (Haliotis), used formerly for collecting in chapels'; *kṛegin heðuχ*, 'money'; *mynd i u grogan*, 'to sulk, to retire to one's tent'. (2) 'gill of a fish' = *drogan, tagaḷ*. Cf. D. crogen pysgodyn, 'branchiæ'.

kṛogi, v., crogi, D., 'to hang, be hanged' (on the gallows); cf. *hoɲjan*:—*θa:l meðul ðim i grogi dy:n*(prov.), 'suspicion is not sufficient to hang a man'; *gnëyd ṛha:f i grogi i hy:n* (prov.), 'to make a rope to hang oneself with'; *ma: hunna wedi mynd i grogi, d o:s na ðim dal arno vo*, 'that fellow has gone to be hanged: there is no stopping him'; *gaduχ iðo vynd i grogi*, 'let him go and be hanged to him'; *i ëiθ o ðim dros i grogi !*, 'he'll be hanged if he'll go !'; *mi dəsgoð o i grogi*, 'he learnt it perfectly'; *·tṛi:uχi i grogi !*, 'try your very best !'; *du i wedi gnëyt i ru:an i χrogi !*, 'I've done it now!'

kṛogliθ, s.f., croglith: *dy gwenar ə grogliθ*, 'Good Friday'. W.S. has 'dyw gwener y croglith'. So in all Books of Common Prayer.

kṛogur, s.m., crogwr, S.E., 'hangman'.

kṛöini, *kṛöinjo*, v., croeni, D., also croenio, S.E., 'to form skin': *peθ wedi kṛuinjo ar i wynab o*, e.g. of a milk pudding;—(of a wound) *briu ən deχra kṛöinjo*, 'a wound beginning to heal by the formation of new skin'; *eli kṛöini*.

kṛöinjog, adj., croenog, S.E., 'with a thick skin or crust', said of ground which has not been ploughed for a long time; (of persons) 'thick-skinned', so also of horses, potatoes, etc.; (of stone) 'having an unworkable exterior'.

kṛöiŋgi, s.m., croengi, 'a crusty fellow' = *dy:n kṛo:ys, ka:s, ·an·huylys a i gəmdogjon* (J.J.).

kṛöisi, v., croesi, D. (1) 'to cross': *kṛöisi r avon,—ə stry:d*. (2) 'to cross out, erase'.

kŗokbran, s.m., crogpren, D., ' gallows '.

kŗokbris, s., crogbris, S.E., ' extortionate price ' : *ṛhoi kŗokbris am dano vo*.

kŗokkaḷ (I.W. ; J.J.) ; *kŗogaḷ* (O.H.), s.m., cnoccell, D., ' talitrum ' ; ' woodpecker ' : *kŗokkaḷ ko:yd* (J.J.).

kŗoksan : *do:s i də groksan !*, ' go and be hanged to you ! '

kŗo:χ, adj., croch, D., ' acer, vehemens, violentus ' : *dy:n kŗo:χ = dy:n maur, audyrdodol, dy:n a tempar yχal* (O.H.).

kŗoχon, s.f., pl. *kŗoχana*, crochan, D. ; crochon, T.N. 67. 28, ' an iron pot suspended by a hook above the fire ' ;—applied to persons : *pen kŗoχon*, ' numskull, idiot '.

kŗombil, s.f., crombil, D. (1) ' gizzard '. (2) ' stomach of any animal ',—of human beings : *ṛhəuχ lond əχ kŗombil o vu:yd ;—mi rois i lond i grombil o vu:yd iðo vo*. (3) ' heart ' (of a mountain, etc.) : *əy ŗŗhombil ə mənyð*.

kŗonni, v., cronni, D., ' to collect ' : *du:r əy kŗonni ;—kŗonni du:r ha:ḷi ;—wedi kŗonni ḷawar jaun o ləvra ;—kŗonni du:r ṛhag iðo redag i fur* (e.g. with a dam) ;—*du:r wedi gronni a θolpja a χeŗig*, ' water dammed up with sods and stones '.

kŗonva, s.f., cronfa, S.E., ' collection ', e.g. of water stopped up by a dam : *kŗonva o ðu:r ;*—also of money collected for some object : *ṛhoi rubaθ ai ə gronva*.

kŗoŋgast, s.f., cingroengast, *dənas ga:s vydyr* (O.H.).

kŗoŋgi, s.m., cingroengi, *dy:n ka:s bydyr* (O.H.) : *ta:u ə kŗoŋgi kḷuyðog ! ; ta:u ər he:n groŋgi gwirjon !*

kŗop, s.m., pl. *kŗopja*, ' crop ' = *knu:d*.

kŗop, s.m., ' crop ' (of a bird).

kŗopjan, v., croppian, D. [The O.E. past participle ' cropen ' (from ' créopan ') gave rise to a past tense ' crope ' which still survives as ' crop ' in dialects], ' to creep ' (of children).

kŗopjo, v., croppio, C.C. 357. 12, ' to crop ' : *pu:y he:n vyuχ vy:o y kŗopjo də wa:ḷi?*, said to some one whose hair has been cut badly.

kŗoppa, s.f., pl. *kro·pa:yð*, (in slate quarries) ' a kind of fault in the strata which, instead of being level, are tilted at an angle '. It is somewhat similar in appearance to a *sglont* (q.v.), but it differs from a *sglont* in two ways : a *kŗoppa* slopes, whereas a *sglont* is perpendicular, a *kŗoppa* is a sort of cleavage, a *sglont* a sort of joint. Hence, when it is worked the result is often a fall (*rub*), and it is thus frequently the cause of accidents ;—*kŗoppa χwiθig* slopes in an opposite direction to the ordinary *kŗoppa*, and is not so dangerous.

kŗo:θ, s.f., pl. *kŗoθa, kŗəuθa*, croth, D. (1) ' womb '. (2) ' calf of the leg ' : *kŗo:θ ə go:ys ;—kŗo:θ ər hosan*, ' the thick part of the leg of a stocking'. (3) anything protuberant : *i ǵeːg ∂n ḷai na i groːθ o* (O.H.), describing a vessel which increases in bulk below the mouth, e. g. a *ḳroχon.*

ḳroθal, s., pl. *ḳriθiḷ*, crothell, D.; G.O. ii. 60. 28. ?'gudgeon' (Gobio fluviatilis), but this fish, according to Forrest, is not found in Carnarvonshire.

ḳroθog, adj., crothog, D., 'bulging'.

ḳr∂udal, s.f. = *k∂udal.* Cf. Eng. (Dial.) crowdy [a kind of porridge ; and various mixed foods] : *nes may o n yːn gr∂udal*, 'till it is all mixed up '.

ḳr∂udi, gr∂udi, s., Eng. (Dial.) crowdy [a small fiddle], Som., Dev., Cor. (1) in phrase *kany i χr∂udi, kany gr∂udi* (of cats), 'to purr '. (Cf. also crowd, 'to purr', Som., Cor.) (2) in such phrases as *be uːti ŋ kany n d∂ gr∂udi?*, 'what are you whining about ?', i. e. *kuyno heb aχos.* (3) in phrase *kany ḳr∂udi (gr∂udi) ruːin*, 'to cry down somebody' = *dēyd vod o n mynd ∂n oːl ḷaːu*; also *kany ḳr∂udi ∂ŋ ŷhevn dyːn.*

ḳr∂uk, s.m. [*ḳr∂ukwaḷi*].

ḳr∂uk, s.m. (1) 'croak of a raven'. (2) 'the noise heard in the belly of a horse when running' : *ḳr∂uk ∂m mol ḳefyl.*

ḳr∂ukjan, v., crowccian, M.Ll. i. 163. 31 ; Eng. (Dial.) crowk [to croak ; also of the bowels, to rumble, make a noise], Cum. (1) 'to cackle' (of hens). (2) 'to grumble': *ḳr∂ukjan ∂n erbyn poːb peːθ.* (3) 'to make a noise in the belly when running' (of horses).

ḳr∂ukjo, v., 'to croak' (of ravens).

ḳr∂ukwaḷi, s.m., cf. Eng. (Dial.) croke [refuse of any kind], Der., Linc., 'coarse grass which grows on mountains and other rough places, and which the cattle will not eat '.

ḳr∂upar, s., crwper, D.G. ccviii. 60. (1) 'crupper: a strap extending from the backband of a horse to the tail'. (2) 'crupper: part of a horse '. Cf. *ḳrump.*

ḳr∂uʃa, s.pl., 'idle tales' = *χwedla ·diːrsail: kodi ḳr∂uʃa*, 'to rake up old scores'.

ḳr∂uʃo, v. (1) 'to talk unintelligibly': *paid a ḳr∂uʃo n wirjon, du i δim ∂n dyːaḷ be uːti n i δēyd.* (2) 'to gossip, talk about other people's business': *be uːti n i gr∂uʃo ʃarad?*

ḳr∂uʃo [*ḳrēiʃo*].

ḳroːyn, s.m., pl. *ḳruːyn*, croen, D., 'skin': *dim ond ḳroːyn ar ∂r asgurn*, 'nothing but skin and bone'; *may r gavod ∂n taro at ∂ ḳroːyn*, 'the shower stings the skin'; *mi l∂χiθ ∂ d∂uyδ ma at ∂χ ḳroːyn*, 'this weather wets you to the skin'; *t oːys na δim djogi ∂n i groːyn*, 'there is no laziness in him'; *may o n ḷond i groːyn*, 'he is plump, sleek'; (fig.) 'he is a pompous man'; *dyːn a χroːyn*

lena, 'a thin-skinned, "touchy" man'; *kuppurð kṛo:yn*, facetious
expression for 'stomach'; *vedrun i ðim byu ən ə ŋṛho:yn tan . . . .*
'I could not rest until . . .'; *un i ðim syt ə may o n esmuyθ ən i
gro:yn*, 'I do not see how he can be easy in his mind'.—In various
transferred senses:—(a) 'plausibility' applied to a story: *t o:yð
gəno vo ðim kṛo:yn ar ə stori* (E.J.), 'his story was not plausible',
'his story did not hang together' (cf. Irish, croiceann do chur ar
sgéal); (b) 'skin, peel of fruit, etc.': *tənny kṛo:yn avol*, 'to peel an
apple' = *plikjo avol*; (c) 'skin', e.g. of a rice pudding; (d) 'a
layer of vegetation (e.g. lichen) covering something': *kṛo:yn gla:s*,
'a layer of grass', e.g. *kṛo:yn gla:s ən təvy ar bri:ð ə wa:ð*, 'a
layer of grass growing on the molehill'; also 'a green surface
covering mud';—*he:n gro:yn*, said of a field which has not been
ploughed for many years (cf. D.G. clix. 43); fig. of persons: *he:n
gro:yn o be:θ ədi o*, 'he is a crusty old fellow'; (e) 'a hard surface
caused by exposure to the sun, etc.': *magy kṛo:yn*, said of peat
which has been exposed to the weather to dry: *əŋ kodi nu n dair
məunan i vagy kṛo:yn ;—·savanu ðim ar i penna heb gro:yn*; (f) 'the
exterior, unworkable coating of stone in quarries'; (g) of the sea:
ə mo:r əŋ gro:yn ar i wymmad o, i.e. 'like glass'.

kṛöynan, s.f., croenen, D., 'cuticula'; *may də gröynan di n dena
jaun*, 'you are very thin-skinned, "touchy"'.

·*kṛöyn·dena*, ·*kṛön·dena*, adj., croendeneu, 'thin-skinned, "touchy"',
quick at taking offence'.

kṛöyndeu, adj., croendew, D., s.v. 'callosus'; 'thick-skinned'
(lit. and fig.).

kṛo:ys, s.f., pl. *kṛöysa ;* *kṛuisi* (O.H), croes, D. (1) 'cross'. (2)
'a place where several roads meet, a cross-road': *pedar forð ən
du:ad i r y:n gro:ys*. (3) 'a burden, weariness': *he:n aḷt drom ədi
hon, t e:? i:a wi:r, ma:y hi ŋ gro:ys*, 'this is a nasty hill, isn't it?
Yes, indeed, it is hard work'; *may n mynd əŋ gro:ys drom ·yðynu*
(e. g. of a misfortune). (4) 'impediment': *ela by:ð na riu gro:ys i
attal i χi vynd*, 'perhaps there will be some impediment to prevent
you going'.

kṛo:ys,· adj., croes, R. (1) 'in the shape of a cross': *kadaχ
gro:ys*, 'a handkerchief bound on the head crosswise, used formerly
as a remedy for headache'; *pu:yθ kṛo:ys*, 'cross-stitch'; *ḷəgad
kṛo:ys*, 'a squint'. (2) 'in the wrong direction': *ḷŋky ŋ gro:ys*,
'to swallow (something) the wrong way'. (3) 'at cross purposes':
kṛo:ys wëiθjo n erbyn i ǵilið. (4) 'contrary': *əŋ gro:ys i r gəvraθ*,
'contrary to the law'; *əŋ gro:ys i wastraf*, 'the contrary of wastefulness'; *tənny ŋ gro:ys*, 'to oppose, demur, express an opposite
opinion, kick against': *tənny ŋ gro:ys ə naiḷ i r ḷaḷ*, 'to provoke one
another, to nag at one another'. (5) 'cross, bad-tempered'.

kṛöysawy, v., croesawu, D., 'to welcome'.

·ǩro꞉ys·dənny, v., croesdynnu, T.N. 114, 23, 'to be at loggerheads': ma꞉ r gu꞉r a r wraig əŋ ·ǩro꞉ys·dənny ; ma na rɐu o hy꞉d.

ǩröyslon, s.f., croeslon, 'a cross-road, a road which crosses another': tɾoi i r gröyslon ;—pedar ǩröyslon.

ǩröyso, s.m., croesaw, D., 'welcome': ǩröyso !, 'welcome !'; i o꞉ys vaur o gröyso i nc꞉b vynd əno ru꞉an, 'there is not much welcome, inducement, for any one to go there now'.

ǩröysɐugar, adj., croesawgar, S.E., 'affable, cordial'.

ǩröyu, ǩrëyu, adj., croyw, D., 'clear': dëyd rubaθ əŋ gröyu, 'to say something clearly'; toɾi r ġëirja ŋ gröyu ;—du꞉r ǩc̦yu, 'fresh water' (as compared with du꞉r ha꞉lt).

ǩrub, s.m., crwb, S.E.; Eng. (Dial.) crub [a crust, crumb of bread], Ken., Sus., Dor., Som., Dev. (1) 'lump, chunk', esp. ǩrub o vara, 'a lump torn from a loaf fresh from the oven'. (2) applied to persons: ǩrub o hogyn, 'a boy of 13 or 14, old enough to begin to earn something'. (3) in slate quarries: 'a defective foot-joint where the slate, instead of being level, rises in concave shape'.

ǩrub, s., Eng. (Dial.) crub [manger], Sc., Cum., Som., Dev., 'stomach' (facetiously): ġe꞉sti lond də grub ? = lond də ġettog (O.H.).

ǩrub, s.m., 'croup'.

ǩrubi, s., crwbi, S.E.; cf. D., s.v. 'gibber', crwban, cefn-grwba, 'hump': dy꞉n a ǩrubi ar i ġevn, 'hunchback' (O.H.); kodi ŋ grubi, 'to rise like a hump' (O.H. in speaking of the water in a great flood) ; ɾhag iðo (i. e. ə ti꞉r) godi n ormod o grubi (J.J., speaking of ploughing).

ǩrubjo, v. (1) 'to stoop', e. g. of old people = ə ǩevn əŋ guɫun (O.H.). (2) 'to thrash': mi ǩrubis i o, 'I thrashed him.' (O.H.).

ǩrubyn, s.m., crwbyn, S.E., dim. of ǩrub:—riu he꞉n grubyn o hogyn, 'a little scrub of a boy'; ə ŋrhubyn ba꞉χ annuyl!, said e. g. by a mother to her baby; dy꞉n wedi mynd əŋ grubyn, 'a man with a stoop'. (All O.H.)

ǩruk, s.m., pl. ǩrukja, krwck, W.S. [A payle], 'tub' for washing, mixing food for horses or pigs, baking, salting, etc.: r o꞉yð hi m buru vel tasa hi n du꞉ad o gruk, 'it was raining bucketfuls';—the phrase may o n du꞉ad vel o gruk is also used in speaking of a person's eloquence.

ǩrukkud, s., crwcwd, D.G. xc. 17 ; the same word as kurkud q.v. As term of reproach : ta꞉u r he꞉n grukkud ! (O.H.).

ǩrumfast, ǩrəmfast, s.m., pl. ǩrumfasija, crwmffast: ǩrumfast o hogyn, 'a big strapping lad', alluding to a boy of about fifteen (cf. ǩrub, hoglaŋk).

krump, s., 'rump': the part of a horse immediately above the tail; also of persons: *may o ŋ karjo i vayχ ar grump i di:n* (O.H.).

krun, adj., fem. *kron*, pl. *krɔnjon*, crwn, D., 'round': *ŋ grun vel avol*, 'as fat as a dumpling'.

krunar, s.m., 'coroner'.

kru:st, s.f., crŵst, D., s.v. 'crusta', 'crustum': O.F. crouste. (1) 'crust', e. g. of a pie (not of bread = *krɔstyn*); applied also e. g. to the skin of a burnt rice pudding. (2) 'growth upon stones, trees, etc.' (3) 'blow' (J.J.—not known to O.H.).

krutlyn, s.m., pl. *krɔtja*, crwtyn, O.P., 'a small boy of seven or eight years of age'.

kru:θ, s.m., pl. *krɔθja*, crwth, D. (1) 'hump, bunch on the back'. (2) 'basket' in *kru:θ sgotta*, 'a fisherman's basket'. (3) 'fiddle', only in the phrase *kany i χru:θ*, 'to purr' (cf. *krɵudi*). (4) 'salt-box': *kru:θ halan = kettog* (which is the usual word).

kruθi, adj., 'hunch-backed' (I.W).

kruydredig, adj., crwydredig, D.P.O. 73. 17, 'wandering': *dy:n, devaid kruydredig.*

kruydro, v., crwydro, D., 'to wander'.

kruydryn, s.m., crwydryn, G.O. i. 233. 3, 'wanderer, tramp': *wedi mynd ɔŋ gruydryn maur* (O.H.), 'having become a regular tramp'.

kruydyr, s., crwydr, D., 'wandering': *may r δavod wedi mynd ar gruydyr.*

kry:, adj., fem. *kre:*, comp. *krɔvaχ*, pl. *krɔvjon*, crŷf, D., 'strong': *dy:n kry:*, 'a strong man', either as regards strength of muscle, etc., or as regards health.—applied to tea, etc.: *may r te: ŋ gry:*,—of a blow, 'heavy': *ɣhoi slap gre:*, 'to deal a heavy blow';—of soil, 'rich': *ti:r kry:*. Cf. *bra:s.*

kry:d, s.m., crûd, D., 'cradle'.

kry:d, s.m., crŷd, D., 'ague'; *krikmala = cryd y cymalau*, 'rheumatism'.

kry:δ, s.m., pl. *krɔδjon*, crydd, D., 'shoemaker'.

kry:g, adj., crŷg, D., 'hoarse'.

·*kry:* ·*gla:s*, ·*kry:r* ·*gla:s*, ·*kry:δ* ·*gla:s*; *kryglas* (J.J.); s.m., crŷr, cryhyr, crehyr, D., 'heron', i.e. crŷr glas. Cf. *kregyr.*

kry:χ, adj., crŷch, D., 'curling': *pen kry:χ, gwa:ltɪ kry:χ.*

kry:χ, s.m., crŷch, cf. D.G. App. iii. 12. (1) 'rough water in a river'. (2) name applied to certain flaws in slate: *kry:χ hy:d*, 'a defective stripe about one inch wide running more or less in the same direction as the grain, but obliquely and irregularly; *kry:χ traus*, 'a similar stripe, one or two inches wide, running across the grain. Both these defects make that part of the rock utterly worthless; *kry:χ dy:* is a flaw of a different nature, like a splash of ink on the slate. Slate with this defect can be worked, but it is of brittle, inferior quality.

kryn, adj., cryn, D., ' fair, good' (before nouns of quantity or numerals): *may na gryn dippin o:ð akku i r knebrun*, 'it is a good long way to the funeral from my home'; *may na gryn dippin o buysa ɔno vo*, ' it weighs a good deal'; *kryn lawar*, 'a good deal'; *er s kryn bɔmθag mlɔnað*, ' a good fifteen years ago'; *am gryn ðe:ŋ mynyd*, 'for fully ten minutes'.

kry:s, s.m., pl. *krɔsa*, crŷs, D., ' shirt'.

krɔban, s., ' a thrashing': *mi rois i grɔban iðo vo.* (Not the same as *kurban*, which is a stronger term.)

krɔbibjon, kɔrbibjon, s.pl., cyrbibion, S.E., 'smithereens, shreds': *may r dilad wedi tori n raks grɔbibjon, tori n gɔrbibjon ylu*, ' the clothes are torn to shreds'. Also *wedi malirjo, wedi maly n raks grɔbibjon* (*n va:n grɔbibjon*);—*hel ɔ krɔbibjon, tavl ɔ krɔbibjon*, ' collect the bits, throw away the bits';—fig. *may o wedi mynd ɔn raks grɔbibjon*, implying ' he has become a bankrupt'.

krɔbinjo [*kribinjo*].

krɔbinjon [*kribinjon*].

krɔbjad, s., ' a good quantity': *bytta krɔbjad ; krɔbjad o yud*, etc. Cf. *krub*.

krɔbjo, v., ' to pull a piece with the hand from a loaf fresh from the oven': *paid a krɔbjo r dorθ.* Cf. *krub*.

krɔbuyl, v., crybwyll, D., ' to mention'.

krɔbɔχlyd, adj., cf. crebach, D., 'ariditate et marcore contractus'; ' in wrinkles, creases': *wedi smuðjo ŋ grɔbɔχlyd*, ' badly ironed' (of clothes), ' creased in the ironing'; *gwynab krɔbɔχlyd*, ' wizened, lined face'. [For variations in pronunciation see below.]

krɔbɔχy, krebɔχy, kribɔχy (O.H.); *krebɔχy, krɔbaχy* (W.H.), v., krybychu, W.S. [Shrynke]; cyrbychu, crepachu, crebychu, D., s.v. ' contraho'; cf. *kreppaχ* and L.A. 54· 7; 153· 29, ' to shrink, crease by shrinking'.

krɔdeðy, v., cyfrodeddu, D.; crydeddu, M.Ll. ii. 148. 19, ' to twist two threads together' (O.H.). Cf. *kɔvrodað*.

krɔdyras, s.f., creadures, S.E., 'creature': *ɔ grɔdyras /*, 'poor thing!'

krɔf·hay, v., cryfhau, D., ' to strengthen'.

krɔgni, s., crygni, D., ' hoarseness'.

krɔgy, v., crygu, D., ' to become hoarse'.

krɔkjad, s., as much as will fill a *kruk*, q.v.

krɔχjad, s.m., crychiad, D., s.v. ' ruga', ' patagium'; ' gathering (in a dress), pleating; crease'.